INTERNATIONAL INTELLECTUAL PROPERTY ANTHOLOGY

ANDERSON'S

Law School Publications

ADMINISTRATIVE LAW ANTHOLOGY
by Thomas O. Sargentich

ADMINISTRATIVE LAW: CASES AND MATERIALS
by Daniel J. Gifford

ALTERNATIVE DISPUTE RESOLUTON: STRATEGIES FOR LAW AND BUSINESS
by E. Wendy Trachte-Huber and Stephen K. Huber

AN ADMIRALTY LAW ANTHOLOGY
by Robert M. Jarvis

ANALYTIC JURISPRUDENCE ANTHOLOGY
by Anthony D'Amato

AN ANTITRUST ANTHOLOGY
by Andrew I. Gavil

APPELLATE ADVOCACY: PRINCIPLES AND PRACTICE (Second Edition)
Cases and Materials
by Ursula Bentele and Eve Cary

A CAPITAL PUNISHMENT ANTHOLOGY (and Electronic Caselaw Appendix)
by Victor L. Streib

CASES AND PROBLEMS IN CRIMINAL LAW (Third Edition)
by Myron Moskovitz

THE CITATION WORKBOOK
by Maria L. Ciampi, Rivka Widerman, and Vicki Lutz

CIVIL PROCEDURE: CASES, MATERIALS, AND QUESTIONS
by Richard D. Freer and Wendy C. Perdue

COMMERCIAL TRANSACTIONS: PROBLEMS AND MATERIALS
Vol. 1: Secured Transactions Under the UCC
Vol. 2: Sales Under the UCC and the CISG
Vol. 3: Negotiable Instruments Under the UCC and the CIBN
by Louis F. Del Duca, Egon Guttman, and Alphonse M. Squillante

COMMUNICATIONS LAW: MEDIA, ENTERTAINMENT, AND REGULATION
by Donald E. Lively, Allen S. Hammond, Blake D. Morant, and Russell L. Weaver

A CONSTITUTIONAL LAW ANTHOLOGY
by Michael J. Glennon

CONSTITUTIONAL LAW: CASES, HISTORY, AND DIALOGUES
by Donald E. Lively, Phoebe A. Haddon, Dorothy E. Roberts, and Russell L. Weaver

THE CONSTITUTIONAL LAW OF THE EUROPEAN UNION
by James D. Dinnage and John F. Murphy

CONSTITUTIONAL TORTS
by Sheldon H. Nahmod, Michael L. Wells, and Thomas A. Eaton

CONTRACTS
Contemporary Cases, Comments, and Problems
by Michael L. Closen, Richard M. Perlmutter, and Jeffrey D. Wittenberg

A CONTRACTS ANTHOLOGY (Second Edition)
by Peter Linzer

CORPORATE AND WHITE COLLAR CRIME: AN ANTHOLOGY
by Leonard Orland

A CRIMINAL LAW ANTHOLOGY
by Arnold H. Loewy

CRIMINAL LAW: CASES AND MATERIALS
by Arnold H. Loewy

A CRIMINAL PROCEDURE ANTHOLOGY
by Silas J. Wasserstrom and Christie L. Snyder

CRIMINAL PROCEDURE: ARREST AND INVESTIGATION
by Arnold H. Loewy and Arthur B. LaFrance

CRIMINAL PROCEDURE: TRIAL AND SENTENCING
by Arthur B. LaFrance and Arnold H. Loewy

ECONOMIC REGULATION: CASES AND MATERIALS
by Richard J. Pierce, Jr.

ELEMENTS OF LAW
by Eva H. Hanks, Michael E. Herz, and Steven S. Nemerson

ENDING IT: DISPUTE RESOLUTION IN AMERICA
Descriptions, Examples, Cases and Questions
by Susan M. Leeson and Bryan M. Johnston

ENVIRONMENTAL LAW (Second Edition)
Vol. 1: Environmental Decisionmaking: NEPA and the Endangered Species Act
Vol. 2: Water Pollution
Vol. 3: Air Pollution
Vol. 4: Hazardous Wastes
by Jackson B. Battle, Robert L. Fischman, Maxine I. Lipeles, and Mark S. Squillace

AN ENVIRONMENTAL LAW ANTHOLOGY
by Robert L. Fischman, Maxine I. Lipeles, and Mark S. Squillace

ENVIRONMENTAL PROTECTION AND JUSTICE
Readings and Commentary on Environmental Law and Practice
by Kenneth A. Manaster

AN EVIDENCE ANTHOLOGY
by Edward J. Imwinkelried and Glen Weissenberger

FEDERAL EVIDENCE COURTROOM MANUAL
by Glen Weissenberger

FEDERAL RULES OF EVIDENCE (Second Edition)
Rules, Legislative History, Commentary and Authority
by Glen Weissenberger

FEDERAL RULES OF EVIDENCE FOR UNITED STATES COURTS AND MAGISTRATES
by Publisher's Staff

FIRST AMENDMENT ANTHOLOGY
by Donald E. Lively, Dorothy E. Roberts, and Russell L. Weaver

INTERNATIONAL ENVIRONMENTAL LAW ANTHOLOGY
by Anthony D'Amato and Kirsten Engel

INTERNATIONAL HUMAN RIGHTS: LAW, POLICY AND PROCESS
Problems and Materials
by Frank C. Newman and David Weissbrodt

INTERNATIONAL INTELLECTUAL PROPERTY ANTHOLOGY
by Anthony D'Amato and Doris Estelle Long

INTERNATIONAL LAW ANTHOLOGY
by Anthony D'Amato

INTERNATIONAL LAW COURSEBOOK
by Anthony D'Amato

INTRODUCTION TO THE STUDY OF LAW: CASES AND MATERIALS
by John Makdisi

JUDICIAL EXTERNSHIPS: THE CLINIC INSIDE THE COURTHOUSE
by Rebecca A. Cochran

JUSTICE AND THE LEGAL SYSTEM
A Coursebook
by Anthony D'Amato and Arthur J. Jacobson

THE LAW OF DISABILITY DISCRIMINATION
by Ruth Colker

Continued

THE LAW OF MODERN PAYMENT SYSTEMS AND NOTES
by Fred H. Miller and Alvin C. Harrell

LAWYERS AND FUNDAMENTAL MORAL RESPONSIBILITY
by Daniel R. Coquillette

MICROECONOMIC PREDICATES TO LAW AND ECONOMICS
by Mark Seidenfeld

PATIENTS, PSYCHIATRISTS AND LAWYERS
Law and the Mental Health System
by Raymond L. Spring, Roy B. Lacoursiere, M.D., and Glen Weissenberger

PROBLEMS AND SIMULATIONS IN EVIDENCE (Second Edition)
by Thomas F. Guernsey

A PRODUCTS LIABILITY ANTHOLOGY
by Anita Bernstein

PROFESSIONAL RESPONSIBILITY ANTHOLOGY
by Thomas B. Metzloff

A PROPERTY ANTHOLOGY
by Richard H. Chused

THE REGULATION OF BANKING
Cases and Materials on Depository Institutions and Their Regulators
by Michael P. Malloy

A SECTION 1983 CIVIL RIGHTS ANTHOLOGY
by Sheldon H. Nahmod

SPORTS LAW: CASES AND MATERIALS (Second Edition)
by Raymond L. Yasser, James R. McCurdy, and C. Peter Goplerud

A TORTS ANTHOLOGY
by Lawrence C. Levine, Julie A. Davies, and Edward J. Kionka

TRIAL PRACTICE
by Lawrence A. Dubin and Thomas F. Guernsey

TRIAL PRACTICE AND CASE FILES
by Edward R. Stein and Lawrence A. Dubin

TRIAL PRACTICE AND CASE FILES with *Video* Presentation
by Edward R. Stein and Lawrence A. Dubin

FORTHCOMING PUBLICATIONS

BASIC ACCOUNTING PRINCIPLES FOR LAWYERS:
With Present Value and Expected Value
by C. Steven Bradford and Gary A. Ames

CONSTITUTIONAL CONFLICTS
by Derrick A. Bell, Jr.

EUROPEAN COMMUNITY LAW ANTHOLOGY
by Anthony D'Amato and Karen V. Kole

INTERNATIONAL HUMAN RIGHTS: LAW POLICY, AND PROCESS (Second Edition)
by Frank C. Newman and David Weissbrodt

PRINCIPLES OF EVIDENCE (Third Edition)
by Irving Younger, Michael Goldsmith, and David A. Sonenshein

UNINCORPORATED BUSINESS ENTITIES
by Larry E. Ribstein

INTERNATIONAL INTELLECTUAL PROPERTY ANTHOLOGY

EDITED BY

ANTHONY D'AMATO

Leighton Professor of Law
Northwestern University School of Law

and

DORIS ESTELLE LONG

Professor of Law
The John Marshall Law School

ANDERSON PUBLISHING CO.
CINCINNATI

INTERNATIONAL INTELLECTUAL PROPERTY

2035 Reading Road / Cincinnati, Ohio 45202
800 582-7295 / E-mail: andpubco@aol.com / FAX: 513 562-8110

Library of Congress Cataloging in Publication Data

International intellectual property anthology / edited by Anthony D'Amato and Doris Estelle Long.
p. cm.
Includes bibliographical references and index.
ISBN 0-87084-373-7 (alk. paper)
1. Intellectual property (International law) 2. Intellectual property. I. D'Amato, Anthony A. II. Long, Doris E.
K1401.I585 1996
341.7'58—dc20 96-7025
CIP

Contents

EDITOR'S PREFACE *xvii*

ACKNOWLEDGMENTS *xix*

CONTRIBUTING AUTHORS *xxi*

PART I

FOUNDATIONS

CHAPTER 1 INTRODUCTION *3*

A. Overview *3*
  1. The Dynamics of Protecting International Intellectual Property *3*
  2. Forms of Intellectual Property *5*
    a. Copyrights *5*
    b. Patents *5*
    c. Trade Secrets *6*
    d. Trademarks *7*
    e. Industrial Designs *7*
    f. "Neighboring Rights" *7*
  3. What is the Concept of "Property"? *7*
  4. Dynamics of the Global Market *8*
  5. A Short History of Treaty Protection of Intellectual Property *8*
  6. Efforts Toward Harmonization *9*
  7. Remedies *10*

B. Defining the Issues *10*

C. The "Problem" of Intellectual Property Protection *11*

D. The Current System for the International Protection of Intellectual Property *13*
  1. Treaty Regimes *13*
  2. National Systems *14*
  3. Treaty Definitions of Copyright *15*
  4. The Problem of Patentability *15*
    a. The Inventor's Reward *15*
    b. Novelty and Non-Obviousness *16*
  5. Trademarks, Goodwill and the "Use" Problem *20*
  6. Varying National Approaches to Trade Secrets *20*
  7. The Uncertain Value of Industrial Designs *22*

E. A "Problem" Sampler *22*

CHAPTER 2 UNDERLYING THEORIES OF INTERNATIONAL INTELLECTUAL PROPERTY PROTECTION *25*

A. Defining Intellectual Property *25*

1. The Philosophical Debate over the "Nature" of Intellectual Property *25*
   a. Utility or a Natural Right? *25*
   b. The Theory of Property *26*
      1. Locke and Intellectual Property *27*
      2. Hegel, Individual Will and Non-Western Cultures *32*
2. Defining Protected Values *36*
   a. Appellations of Origin *36*
   b. Technology and Wealth *36*

B. Economic Considerations *39*
1. International Trade *39*
   a. Intellectual Property and International Trade *39*
   b. The Economics of Intellectual Property Rights Protection *41*
      1. The Economic Impact of Intangibility *41*
      2. Conflicting Theories of Economic Value *42*
   c. The Case Against Intellectual Property Rights Protection *45*
   d. The Case for Intellectual Property Protection *46*
   e. The "Economics" of Database Protection: A Case Study *47*
2. The Common Heritage of Mankind *53*
   a. Traditional Perspective of the Developing World *54*
   b. The Economic Liberalization View *55*
   c. Perspective of the Developed World *57*
   d. Case Studies in Conflict *57*
      1. The Caribbean Basin and Copyright Protection *57*
      2. Thailand and Pharmaceutical Patents *59*
      3. US Pressure on Thailand *59*

C. Transplantation *61*
1. Transplanting Intellectual Property Values *61*
2. Legal Transplants *62*
   a. Realist Arguments for Transplants *62*
   b. Normativist Arguments about Transplants *63*
   c. Relativist Challenges to Transplant Analysis *63*
3. Historical Problems *65*
   a. Printing Privileges and Copyright Monopolies *65*
   b. The Suppressive Role of Historical Copyright *66*
   c. The Harmonizing Role of Historical Accuracy *69*
4. Cultural Problems *70*

D. Harmonization *71*

PART II

ISSUE AREAS

CHAPTER 3 THE CULTURAL IMPACT OF INTELLECTUAL PROPERTY FORMS *75*

A. Copyright *75*
1. The Protection of Art and Literature *75*

2. The Protection of Folklore as Culture 76
3. The Role of Cultural Exclusions 79
B. Patent 79
1. Biodiversity 79
2. Protocol for Products Made with Biota from Pristine Ecosystems 82
C. Trademarks 83
D. Trade Secrets 84

CHAPTER 4 NEIGHBORING RIGHTS 85

A. "Rights Neighboring to Copyright" 85
1. Scope 85
2. Historical Development 86
3. Relationship to Copyright 87
4. Relationship to the Paris Convention 89
5. Relationship to TRIPS 89
B. The Protection of Performance Rights 90
C. The Protection of Broadcast Rights 90
D. The Protection of Sound Recordings 92
1. The Rome Convention 92
2. Protection for Aural Performances 93
3. The Problem of US Adherence 93

CHAPTER 5 THE PROTECTION OF CULTURAL PATRIMONY 95

A. Intellectual Property as Culture 95
B. The Protection of Cultural Property 96
1. Art as Cultural Heritage 96
2. The Definition of Cultural Patrimony 96
3. A Second View 96
4. The Dual Nature of Cultural Property 97
5. The Debate over Cultural Nationalism 100
6. The Property Aspects of Cultural Artifacts 103
7. Protection Regimes 103
8. The Retention of Cultural Property 104
9. The Problems of the Colonial Era 106
10. Authorship, Cultural Patrimony and Intellectual Property 107

CHAPTER 6 BEYOND ECONOMICS: THE PROTECTION OF AUTHORSHIP AS A CULTURAL VALUE 111

A. Authorship and the Protection of Personality 112
1. The Evolving View of Authorship 112
2. The Author as Romantic Genius 114
3. The Protection of Author Personality 115
4. The US View of Authorship 118
5. The EC View of Authorship 118

B. The Moral Rights Debate *120*
1. Included Rights *121*
a. The Right of Disclosure *121*
b. The Right of Paternity *121*
c. The Right of Integrity *121*
d. The Right of Withdrawal *121*
2. The Berne Definition *121*
3. Historical and Philosophical Development *123*
a. Monist v. Dualist *123*
b. Natural Rights, Economic Rights and Personality *123*
c. Alienability and the Marketplace *125*
4. Moral Rights and Censorship *128*
a. Editorial Control *128*
b. The Aesthetic Veto *129*
5. The Treatment of Moral Rights in Selected Countries *130*
a. The United Kingdom *130*
b. Australia *131*
6. The Debate over Adoption of Moral Rights in the United States *134*
a. Historical Background *134*
b. The Visual Artists Act *135*
c. The Problem of Transplantation *137*
d. Market Impact *138*
C. *Droit de Suite* and Resale Royalties *141*
1. The Role of Natural Law *141*
2. Diverging Views of "The Starving Artist" *145*
3. Compensation for Personality *145*
4. Equality Among the Arts *147*
5. Economic Impact *149*
6. The Foreign Experience with *Droit de Suite* *152*
7. The *Droit de Suite* Debate in the US *153*
a. The View of the Copyright Office *153*
b. A Reply *155*
D. Applications *157*
1. Performance Art *157*
2. Motion Pictures *161*
3. Parodies *165*
4. Musical Works *167*
5. Works-for-Hire *171*
6. Patents *177*
7. Multinational Treaties and the Protection of Culture *179*
a. Culture as Commodity *179*
b. The Canadian Free Trade Agreement *180*
c. "Television Without Frontiers" *181*
1. The Directive *181*
2. Cultural Diversity *182*
3. The "Americanization" of Culture *184*

PART III

PROCEDURES AND REMEDIES

CHAPTER 7 TREATY REGIMES *189*

A. Multinational or Bilateral Solutions to Intellectual Property Protection? *190*
1. Bilateral Agreements *190*
a. Special 301 *190*
2. Multinational Treaties: An Overview *192*
a. WIPO and UNESCO *192*
b. WTO *193*
B. The Enforcement of Treaty Obligations *193*
1. Treaty Interpretation *193*
2. Reservations *195*
a. Definitions *195*
b. The Vienna Convention *196*
c. Desirability of Reservations *197*
3. The Absence of Harmonization Standards *198*
4. The Choice of National Treatment, Reciprocity or Minimum Rights *199*
a. Territoriality and the Need for National Treatment *199*
b. Territoriality and the Problem of Reciprocity *199*
c. The Continuing Viability of National Treatment *200*
5. The Establishment of Minimum Standards *203*
a. The Impact of National Treatment on Minimum Standards *205*
b. The Failings of National Treatment *205*
c. Minimum Standards for What? *206*
d. Minimum Standards and Enforcement Procedures *207*
C. The Retroactivity Principle *207*
D. GATT v. WIPO *209*
1. The Jurisdictional Dilemma *209*
2. The Enforcement Paradigm *210*
E. Major International Intellectual Property Treaties *212*
1. The Bi-Polar Structure *212*
2. The Paris Convention *213*
a. An Historical Overview *213*
b. Major Provisions *219*
c. Exceptions to Protection *219*
3. Copyright Under International Copyright Conventions *220*
a. An Historical Overview Of The Origins Of Copyright *221*
1. Reciprocity Treaties and Bilateral Agreements *222*
b. The Universal Copyright Convention *222*
1. Major Provisions *222*
2. Conflict with Berne *223*
c. The Berne Convention *224*
1. An Historical Overview *224*
2. Major Provisions *227*

3. Minimum Rights 228
4. Minimum Rights (Continued) 229
5. Future Issues 229
4. TRIPS 230
a. An Historical Overview 230
1. The Effort at Harmonization 230
2. Intellectual Property Protection as a Trade Issue 232
3. The Uruguay Round Negotiations 235
b. Major Provisions 236
c. Major Provisions (Another View) 238
d. A Step Forward? 239
e. Future Issues 242
5. NAFTA 242
a. An Historical Overview 242
b. Major Provisions 243
c. Major Provisions (Another View) 246
F. Case Studies 248
1. The Former Soviet Union and Intellectual Property Protection 248
a. Patents 248
b. Copyright 248
2. Asia and the Protection of Intellectual Property 251
a. Japan 251
b. China 252
c. India 253

CHAPTER 8 REGISTRATION, USE AND THE PROCESS FOR FORMAL PROTECTION OF RIGHTS 255

A. Formal Requirements for Obtaining Copyright Protection 255
1. US Formalities 255
2. The Berne Convention and the Elimination of Copyright Formalities for Foreign Authors 256
B. Formal Requirements for Obtaining Patent Protection 257
1. The Patent Cooperation Treaty 257
2. Patent Protection and the First to File Debate 258
C. Formal Requirements for Obtaining Trademark Rights 259
1. The Madrid Agreement 261
a. Brief Overview 261
b. Application 261
c. US Problems with the Original Madrid Agreement 261
d. The Madrid Protocol 265
1. Purpose 265
2. Brief Overview 265
3. US Concerns and the Madrid Protocol 266
2. The Community Trademark 269
a. Application 270
D. Formal Requirements for Obtaining Trade Secret Protection 274

CHAPTER 9 REMEDIES 275

A. Civil Remedies 275
1. EEC and Supranational Protection 275
a. The Treaty of Rome and the Free Movement of Goods 275
b. Supranational Rights and Remedies 279
2. The Establishment of Minimum Enforcement Standards 282
a. NAFTA and Regional Enforcement Standards 282
1. Comparison with Prior Multinational Treaty Regimes 282
2. An Overview of Enforcement Provisions 282
3. Applications 284
b. TRIPS and Multinational Enforcement Standards 284
3. The Protection of Well-Known Marks 286
a. Article 6bis 286
b. Relief for the Unauthorized Use of Internationally Well-Known Marks 287
c. The Role of Domestic Law in Fashioning Relief 287
d. Application 288
4. The Definition of Infringement 290
5. Selected Civil Protection Regimes 290
a. Self-help 290
1. Education 290
2. Special 301 291
a. Procedures and Application 291
b. 301 and Bilateral Relief 293
3. Anti-Counterfeiting Programs 296
b. Civil Law Suits 297
c. Treble Damages 298
B. Criminal Penalties 299

CHAPTER 10 GOVERNMENT "TAKINGS" OF INTELLECTUAL PROPERTY 301

A. Takings 301
1. State Responsibility for Economic Injury to Foreign Nationals 301
2. Types of Injury 302
B. Compulsory Licensing, "Fair Use" and Copyrights 305
1. Compulsory Licenses 305
2. "Fair Use" Exceptions 305
3. Collection Levies 308
4. Practical Applications 309
C. Compulsory Licensing and Patents 310
1. Compulsory Working, Abuse and Revocation 314
2. Theory and Practice 315
D. Compulsory Licensing and Trademarks 317

CHAPTER 11 EXTRATERRITORIALITY AND THE "BORDER" PROBLEM 319

A. The Territorial Nature of Intellectual Property Rights 319
B. Universality versus Territoriality 320
C. Comity 320
D. Extraterritorial Application of National Laws 321
1. The Rise of the Multinationals 322
2. US Applications 322
3. Balancing Competing Concerns 328

CHAPTER 12 HARMONIZATION 333

A. Harmonization and the EEC 333
1. Copyright Harmonization 334
a. Rental Rights 337
b. Proposed Harmonization Directives 338
2. Trademark Harmonization 340
B. Patent Harmonization 342
1. Should the US Adopt First-to-File? 343
a. Some Additional Thoughts 345
b. US Testimony 346
2. Should the US Adopt Prior User Rights? 347
a. US Testimony 348
3. Should the US Adopt Early Disclosure of Patent Applications? 348
4. Should the US Adopt a Twenty-Year Patent Term? 349
C. Case Studies 350
1. The Japanese "Patent Wars" 350
2. China and the Protection of Intellectual Property Rights 353

PART IV

EMERGING BATTLEFIELDS

CHAPTER 13 TECHNOLOGICAL INNOVATIONS 357

A. Protecting Computer Software 357
1. Harmonizing Conflicting Laws and Policies 358
2. The EC Software Directive 365
3. The Problem of Application 367
B. Technology Transfers 369
C. Cyberspace and the Border Problem 370
D. The Problem of Satellite Broadcasts 375
E. The Protection of Foreign Broadcasts 379

CHAPTER 14 UNDERDEVELOPED COUNTRIES 381

A. Intellectual Property Protection in Developing Countries 381
1. Economic Views of Underdeveloped Countries 383

2. The Benefit of Free-Riding 385
3. Copyrights 386
a. The Role of Copyright in Economic Development 386
b. The Problem of Inadequate Enforcement 386
4. Patents 386
a. The Problem of Patent Protection in Underdeveloped Countries 386
b. General Relationship Between Patent Benefits and Level of Economic Development 387
5. Trademarks 389
a. The Protection of Trademarks in Underdeveloped Countries 389
b. The Conflict Between Consumer Savings and Goodwill 389
B. The Conflict Between the "Haves" and the "Have Nots" 392

CHAPTER 15 EMERGING MARKET ECONOMIES 393

A. Copyrights 393
1. The Commonwealth States: A Case Study 394
a. The Needs of Emerging Market Economies 394
b. The Choices Faced by the CIS 394
B. Trademarks 396

APPENDIX

I Paris Convention for the Protection of Industrial Property 399
II Berne Convention for the Protection of Literary and Artistic Works 413
III Treaty Establishing the European Community 431
IV International Convention for the Protection of Performers, Producers of Phonograms and Broadcasting Organizations 439
V Universal Copyright Convention 449
VI Patent Cooperation Treaty 461
VII European Communities Trademark Harmonization Directive 487
VIII North American Free Trade Agreement 497
IX Agreement on Trade Related Aspects of Intellectual Property Rights 515
X Protocol Relating to the Madrid Agreement Concerning the International Registration of Marks 541
XI Trademark Registration Treaty 551

INDEX 565

Editors' Preface

The most rapidly growing subject in the law school curriculum today is Intellectual Property. The increasing student demand for this subject reflects a perception that as we approach the beginning of the new century, the creation, protection, and exploitation of artistic and scientific property will be the United States' most important business asset. There seems to be a "critical mass" of artists and inventors in the U.S. who are able to produce books, motion pictures, television shows, and computer software, that generate an increasing percentage of gross national product and are in great demand in the global marketplace. It is already acknowledged that the single most important goal in US trade policy is the protection of American intellectual property against piracy abroad.

This Anthology is devoted to the international side of Intellectual Property. International Intellectual Property Law is largely a matter of treaty regimes, but also of reciprocal national legislation for the protection of literary and artistic works and scientific invention. On the world stage there are analogues to domestic intellectual property rights that, in varying degrees, establish copyrights and patents, protect trade secrets, trade marks and industrial designs, and protect "neighboring rights" to these forms. In addition, international intellectual property law deals with a subject that has no domestic-law analogue, namely, the protection of cultural patrimony.

This Anthology collects and excerpts some of the best and most thoughtful essays on International Intellectual Property Law. The controlling provisions of the major treaties in the field are included in a comprehensive Appendix. The Anthology can serve as a supplement to courses in International Private Law, International Business Transactions, and International Trade Law. In addition, it may serve as a reader or a supplement to a course devoted solely to International Intellectual Property Law. Since Questions and Comments are included, it could also serve as a coursebook for International Intellectual Property Law.

We have organized the book according to the theories underlying the protection of International Intellectual Property rights. As illustrations of these theories, we have selected for specific treatment those topics that lend themselves most readily to the underlying theories. Thus we have considered the historic and philosophical foundation of copyright protection in the context of the protection of culture and personality. By contrast, issues regarding compulsory licensing to ensure public use of certain forms of intellectual property are most clearly delineated in the context of patents. We leave it to the good judgment of the professors and students to extrapolate theories from one topic and apply them to related topics.

The international norms that protect intellectual property are found primarily in developing treaty regimes such as the Paris Convention for the Protection of Literary and Artistic Works, the North American Free Trade Agreement, and Agreement on the Trade Related Impact of Intellectual Property Rights. But the norms also develop through the more subtle legal process of "harmonization"—the conscious alignment of national legislation through bilateral and multilateral understandings among nations.

There are no easy solutions to the issues posed by the excerpts collected in this Anthology. Differences in culture and economic development do not miraculously disappear as technology and communications shrink the world. We anticipate that the issues highlighted in this Anthology will remain a source of contested legal accommodation as nations continue to struggle with the question of what norms, if any, should be established and secured for the protection of intellectual property rights.

Acknowledgments

We deeply appreciate the help of the administration, staff and students of the Northwestern University School of Law and The John Marshall Law School. In particular, we would like to thank Dean David Van Zandt and Dean R. Gilbert Johnston, Yolanda Aparicio, Gwen Konigsfeld, Vanessa Saffold, Pat Welsh, Dorothy Wesson, Mary Ruth Coffey, Adrian Gough, Matt Houchens, Dawn Johnston and Michael Reddy and our respective family, friends and colleagues for their support during this project.

And thanks to our editor at Anderson Publishing Company, Sean Caldwell.

Contributing Authors

Frederick M. Abbott
Christopher Aide
Dean C. Alexander
Jay Alexander
Elliot C. Alderman
M. Jean Anderson
Robert A. Arena

Jeff Berg
Cathryn A. Berry
G.M.C. Bodenhausen
Lisa J. Borodkin
Margaret A. Boulware
Carlos Alberto Primo Braga
Bartram S. Brown
Peter Burger

Stephen L. Carter
Adrienne Catanese
Robert A. Cinque
Jack A. Cline
Jan Corbet
Monique L. Cordray

Anthony D'Amato
Russell J. DaSilva
Theodore H. Davis
A. David Demiray
Katharine S. Deters
Jeffrey M. Dine
Michael L. Doane
Paul Durdik

Amy R. Edge
Angela J. Paolini Ellard
Cole M. Fauver

Kent S. Foster
Jonathan Franklin
Mario Franzosi

John King Gamble, Jr.
Paul Edward Geller
Jane C. Ginsburg
Tara Kalagher Giunta
David S. Glass
Bal Gopal Das
Wendy J. Gordon
Robert A. Gorman
Mark Grady

David M. Haug
Valerie L. Hummel
David Hurlbutt
Robert A. Jacobs
Peter Jaszi
Herman Cohen Jehoram
Ian Johnstone
Gianna Julian-Arnold

Lawrence G.C. Kaplan
Stefan Kirchanski
Edmund Kitch
Stephen A. Konigsberg
Otto Konrad

David Lange
Marshall A. Leaffer
John C. Lindgren
Doris Estelle Long
Gary S. Lutzker

Charles R.B. Macedo
Stanely S. Madeja
Harold G. Maier
Roger W. Mastalik
Ted L. McDorman
Shilpa Mehta
John Henry Merryman
R. Carl Moy

Halina Niec

Kirsten Peterson
Catherine Logan Piper
Laura A. Pitta
Robert W. Pritchard
Robert Purcell
Jeffrey A. Pyle

Michael B. Reddy
J.H. Reichman

Arthur B. Sackler
Guistino Sanctis
Michael D. Scott
Roger E. Schechter
Geert Wolfgang Seelig
Roberta L. Shaffer
Nina Shafran
Lily H. Shang
Chris Shore
Neil F. Siegel
Laurie E. Simon
Carol Sky
Leslie Steele Smith
John E. Somorjai
John P. Spitals
Willaard Alonzo Stanback
Stacie I. Strong
Mark C. Suchman
Brad Swenson

Bonnie Teller
Frank C. Turner

Russ Var Steeg
Jean-Francois Verstryrge
Victoria J. Vitrano
Charles Von Simon

Karen Waller
Moana Weir

Shira R. Yashor
Craig J. Yudell

Patrick G. Zabatta
Xiao-Lin Zhou

PART I
FOUNDATIONS

1

Introduction

Organized multinational attempts to establish international norms for intellectual property protection have existed for well over 100 years. Given the intangible nature of the rights sought to be protected, the nature and scope of these rights have been hotly debated, making the process of international consensus slow and uncertain. This Chapter provides a brief overview of some of the issues arising from efforts to develop international protection norms. It contains excerpts that briefly discuss the present national law and treaty regimes for the protection of intellectual property. Other excerpts outline the problems posed by the absence of an international consensus, including the economic trade impact the present lack of consensus has on the global marketplace.

Since a systematic study of international intellectual property law cannot begin without an understanding of what the term "intellectual property" entails, the Chapter also contains a brief overview of the five "traditional" forms of intellectual property protection—copyrights, patents, trade secrets, trademarks (including service marks and other source designators) and industrial designs (including utility models). While there exists some generalized consensus regarding the types of works to be included as "intellectual property," the precise nature of these works remains the subject of contested debate. Consequently the excerpts in this Chapter use the generally accepted definitions from various international treaty regimes.

A. Overview[1]

1. The Dynamics of Protecting International Intellectual Property

The common law did not develop property rights in products of the mind. Thus, while an author would own the physical manuscript upon which she wrote her novel and a musician would own the sheets upon which his score was written, there was no common law concept of ownership over the intellectual content of the novel or music. Others could reproduce and reprint the words or music without paying anything to the author or composer. The need for copyright protection was a legislative innovation. The United States Constitution, in a rare example of providing a textual reason for one of its provisions, gives Congress the power

> To promote the progress of science and useful arts, by securing for limited times to authors and inventors the exclusive right to their respective writings and discoveries. [Art. I, Sec. 8].

Most countries have done the same thing. National legislation providing for copyright, patent, and trade mark protection exist with variations throughout the world.

If we consider just the *incentives* of authors, artists, and inventors, we probably would conclude that national protection is all that is needed. It is hard to imagine an author in the United States saying, for example, that she will not proceed to write her novel unless she is able to copyright the work in foreign countries.

Yet in the past hundred years there has

---

[1] Written for this Anthology by Doris Estelle Long and Anthony D'Amato. Copyright 1996 Doris E. Long and Anthony D'Amato.

arisen a growing and accelerating drive for international protection of the creative works of authors, artists, and inventors. If this drive cannot be explained by the need to provide original production incentives, what accounts for it? Clearly as international trade expands throughout the world, nations believe that they should capture the value of the intellectual property of their own creative personnel. Again, to take an example from the United States, a Hollywood film today typically generates a large portion of its revenues from foreign distribution. Although the film company would probably make the film even if it could only capture revenues from domestic exhibition, the United States itself benefits from copyright protection in foreign countries that allows the film to be licensed for exhibition abroad. These revenues flow to the United States, helping the nation's balance of trade. They are also a substantial source of income to the government when it taxes the film company's profits. Moreover, a thriving film industry provides jobs and raises the nation's economic level.

Another aspect of international intellectual property is an increasing awareness of a purely national right to intellectual property, known as "national patrimony." In the nineteenth century, nations allowed many of their cultural artifacts (the Elgin Marbles, to take a prominent example) to be removed (for pay) to museums in other countries. Today there is legislation in many countries prohibiting even privately owned cultural artifacts to be sold to foreigners.

Every country in the world today has its domestic artists and inventors who stand to increase their income if there is world-wide protection of intellectual property rights. Yet it is quite clear that there is an imbalance among nations regarding the total worth of their exportable intellectual properties. To stay with the motion picture example, it is a fact that although nearly every country has a domestic motion-picture industry, the world-wide licensing income of just one country's movie industry (the United States) today exceeds the world-wide licensing income of all the other countries combined. Thus, as a matter of elementary economics, we might expect at least some countries to tolerate the domestic "pirating" of American motion pictures in order to avoid paying substantial licensing fees to the United States. Today, China is an actual example of a country that apparently tolerates widescale pirating of American films.

In short, the situation exists today where some countries generate substantial, commercially desirable artistic works and inventions (call them the "haves") and other countries do not generate equivalent domestic value in intellectual property (the "have-nots"). What reasons would motivate the have-nots to pay substantial licensing fees to the haves instead of simply pirating (stealing, appropriating) the intellectual property?

An exploration of these reasons opens up a window to the present Anthology. We are concerned, in the pages that follow, not only to provide a description of international intellectual property law, but to look at its underlying dynamics in order to understand why it is where it is today and to predict where it is going. We will find, for example, that one basket of reasons the have-nots are motivated to join the trend toward international intellectual property protection is that inequalities in one field (*e.g.*, motion pictures) may be counterbalanced by inequalities in other fields (novels, music, scientific inventions, and so forth). Another basket of reasons is the sense that inequalities can shift over time. (For example, the domestic Hong Kong film industry is particularly explosive today and is finding that its products are increasingly sought after in many other countries. No one can claim with assurance that Hollywood will remain in first place forever.) Third, retaliation for pirating can take the form of boycotts of conventional trade. Thus, if nation A's intellectual property is pirated by nation B, nation A may retaliate by imposing trade barriers against B's exports of conventional goods and merchandise. Fourth, it may be unclear (and desirably unclear!) where to draw the boundary between intellectual property rights and conventional property rights. For example, we may ask to what extent trade secrets, industrial designs, secret formulas, etc., are really part of the final exported product or whether they can be abstracted from that product—the Aristotelian puzzle between form and substance. Fifth, the definition of "intellectual property" will be seen to involve a combination of procedure and substance. We must know not only what kinds of intellectual properties can be secured under existing treaties and legislation, but also the procedures involved in securing them, their duration, and the scope of rights granted to the owner. Interacting complexities of this nature may lead to a "path of least resistance" in international markets: that securing intellectual property throughout the world coheres with the nature of the world capital market, whereas trying to transform it into a "free good" would lead to complexities that could undermine other kinds of trade. Sixth, there may be a normative claim in favor of the protection of intellectual property: that it is indeed the creator's own property, and to expropriate it without pay is contrary to morality or to natural law.

You will find additional reasons for the trend toward globalized protection of intellectual property that will emerge from the readings that follow. Yet the trend is by no means secure or inexorable. Study of this fascinating field will reveal spotty areas of resistance as well as fertile areas of rapid growth, depending on the kinds of intellectual properties involved and the never-ending trade negotiations among nations. But the most important justification for examining the reasons for protecting intellectual property internationally is that such a study is the best way to understand the dynamics of international intellectual property protection. Mere acquaintance with the provisions of international treaties and national legislation relating to copyrights, patents, trademarks, trade secrets, and industrial designs, will not suffice. Accordingly, we have collated the writings of leading international experts in this field, each of whom goes below the surface to explore the underlying dynamics of his or her particular contribution.

2. Forms of Intellectual Property

a. Copyrights

> "A copyright is a form of protection provided by a national government to authors of original works of authorship including literary, dramatic, musical, artistic and certain other intellectual works." —*U.S. International Trade Commission.*

"Copyrights" generally includes within its scope of protected subject matter works of artistic and literary expression, including books, poems, pamphlets and other writings, musical compositions, cinematographic works, drawings, paintings, sculpture, photographic works, illustrations, maps and dramatic works. Differences among nations arise regarding the precise categories of works to be protected, the need for fixation of such works in a tangible medium and the degree of creativity or originality required for protection to attach. Copyright usually attaches upon the creation of a protected work. Among the rights granted the copyright owner are the exclusive right to reproduce the work, to disseminate it to the public, and to adapt and/or translate it. Restrictions on these rights may exist in the form of compulsory licenses and "fair use" exceptions to an owner's exclusive rights. Such exceptions are generally granted for the purposes of criticism, news reporting and education.[2]

There is no consensus on the duration of copyright protection although the Berne Convention establishes a copyright term, for most protectable works, of the life of the author plus fifty years.

b. Patents

> "A patent is a grant issued by a national government conferring the right to exclude others from making, using, or selling the invention within the national territory."—*U.S. International Trade Commission.*

"Patents" are generally defined to include scientific inventions concerning products and processes in all fields of technology, including machines, manufacturing products, chemical and electrical structures and compositions, and processes, so long as such inventions are new, useful and non-obvious. Differences among countries arise regarding the category of scientific inventions to be pro-

[2] For a detailed discussion on the role of compulsory licensing and other governmental sponsored "takings" of intellectual property, *see* Chapter Ten.

tected (for example, some countries do not protect inventions concerning pharmaceutical or agricultural products, or products or processes arising from bio-genetic engineering), the degree of novelty and/or non-obviousness required for protection to attach, and the obligation to "work" or use the patented product or process in the country granting the patent. Generally, patent protection arises only upon government grant after review of an application filed by the inventor containing specific claims describing the invention. Differences exist regarding the degree of disclosure in a patent application, the effect of filing upon a patent applicant's own rights as against prior inventors of substantially similar inventions, the nature of the review (including what acts constitute prior art sufficient to bar patent protection) and whether the application may be published prior to the patent grant to permit challenges to the patentability of the claimed invention.[3] Among the rights usually granted a patent owner are the right to exclude others from making, using or selling in the granting country the product or process claimed by the patent. Restrictions on these rights may exist in the form of compulsory licenses requiring the "working" or use of the patent in the granting country or allowing others to use those patents deemed to be of "national significance" to the public health or welfare of the granting country.[4] The term of patent protection varies; however, the Agreement on Trade Related Aspects of Intellectual Property Rights[5] establishes a patent term of at least twenty years from the date of filing.

c. Trade Secrets

> "A trade secret is information, including a formula, pattern, compilation, program, device, method, technique, or process that derives independent economic value, actual or potential, from not being generally known, and not being readily ascertained by proper means, by other persons who can obtain economic value from its disclosure or use, and is the subject of efforts that are reasonable under the circumstances to maintain its secrecy."—*U.S. International Trade Commission.*

"Trade secrets" (which until the North American Free Trade Agreement[6] had not been the express subject of a multinational treaty) generally includes secret information that has commercial value due to its secret nature and that has been subject to reasonable steps under the circumstances by the person lawfully in control of the information to keep it secret. Among the types of secret information which are generally considered to constitute trade secrets are know-how and show-how relating to confidential formulas, programs, processes, devices and the like. Differences exist regarding the precise category of information to be included, the degree of commercial or economic value which the secret nature of such information must have and the steps which must be taken to maintain the secrecy of such information. Trade secrets do not have to be registered in order to be protected. The owner is granted the exclusive right to use and disseminate the trade secret under circumstances designed to protect its continued secrecy. These rights may be restricted through compulsory licensing under situations similar to those arising under the patent laws.[7] Trade secret protection generally lasts only so long as the information remains secret.

---

[3] For a detailed discussion of recent efforts to harmonize patent filing requirements, *see* Chapter Twelve.

[4] For a detailed discussion on the role of compulsory licensing and other governmental sponsored "takings" of intellectual property, *see* Chapter Ten.

[5] For a detailed discussion of the TRIPS Agreement, *see* Chapter Seven. For the text of the Agreement, *see Appendix IX.*

[6] For a detailed discussion of the North American Free Trade Agreement, *see* Chapter Seven. For the text of pertinent provisions of this Agreement, *see Appendix IX.*

[7] For a detailed discussion on the role of compulsory licensing and other governmental sponsored "takings" of intellectual property, *see* Chapter Ten.

d. Trademarks

> "A trademark is any word, name, symbol, or device, or any combination thereof, adopted and used by a manufacturer or merchant to identify his goods and distinguish them from those manufactured or sold by others."—*U.S. International Trade Commission.*

"Trademarks" generally includes within its scope of protectable subject matter any sign or combination of signs which is capable of distinguishing the goods or services of one undertaking from those of another. Among the "signs" protected are words, figures, symbols, drawings and, in certain instances, numbers and letters. Differences exist among nations regarding the degree of distinctiveness required before a particular category of signs is granted protection, the categories of signs which may be protected (for example, whether sounds, scents, package and container designs and shapes or geographic marks may be subject to trademark protection), the degree and type of use of the mark required in the country before protection attaches, the degree and type of evidence required to prove a mark has achieved inherent distinctiveness and whether such marks may be owned by non-juridical entities. In most countries, rights to a mark attach upon registration so long as such mark is used in the granting country within a specified period of time.[8] In others rights generally attach upon use. Among the rights granted to the trademark owner is the exclusive right to use the mark in connection with those goods or services for which the mark has been registered (if registration is a substantive requirement for protection) or on which the mark is used (if use is the substantive requirement). Some countries expand these rights to preclude the unauthorized use of the mark on associated or related goods. Trademark protection generally lasts as long as either the registration or use of the mark on the goods or services in question.

[8] For a detailed discussion of trademark registration requirements, *see* Chapter Eight. For a detailed discussion of various multinational treaties treating the problem of trademark registration practices, including the Madrid Union and the Protocol, *see* Chapter Eight and *Appendix X.*

e. Industrial Designs

Many countries also include the term "industrial designs" as a form of protected intellectual property. "Industrial designs" generally includes those design elements which are not subject to patent protection but have some degree of novelty and/or originality that warrants protection against unauthorized use. Some countries distinguish between functional aspects of a design (which are protected as a "model") and aesthetic or ornamental aspects of a design (which are referred to in such countries as "industrial designs"). Differences exist among nations regarding the degree of novelty or originality required and whether such design must also be non-obvious or distinctive in some fashion before protection attaches. Whether protection arises as a result of use or registration depends on national laws. Similarly, the scope of rights afforded owners of such designs and the duration of those rights differs based on whether protection is considered analogous to patents, trademarks, copyrights or some combination of the three.

f. "Neighboring Rights"

In addition to these five basic types of intellectual property, many nations include so-called "neighboring rights" among the bundle of rights whose protection is of concern to intellectual property owners. "Neighboring rights" may be loosely defined as rights which do not arise directly from the five major types of intellectual property (patents, copyrights, trade secrets, trademarks and industrial designs) but which are "neighboring" to such rights. The most prevalent example of "neighboring rights," at least among European nations, is the protection granted to performers and broadcast organizations.[9]

3. What is the Concept of "Property"?

The simple fact that no uniform definitions exist for the five basic forms of intellec-

[9] For a detailed examination of the question of "neighboring rights," *see* Chapter Four.

tual property amply demonstrates the scope of the problem facing nations attempting to establish uniform norms of protection. The use of the term "property" itself in describing the bundle of rights represented by these basic forms incorporates an array of philosophical and cultural assumptions about the nature of those rights (*i.e.,* that such rights qualify as intangible "property" over which any one entity has the right of control) that are themselves subject to intense debate. The definitional efforts are further complicated by problems of translation.

Since the issues are "international in nature," the impact of language cannot be minimized. For example, among the issues which has been the subject of heated debate in the international community is the scope of rights granted an author for the act of creation. These rights, premised on the value added to the work by the unique personality of the human creator, differ from the rights granted under a nation's copyright laws. They generally include the rights of patrimony (or attribution), integrity, withdrawal and disclosure. In France the concept is referred to as "droit moral," in Germany, "urheberpersonlichkeitsrecht," in the United States "moral rights or inherent rights." Similarly, while the US uses the term "copyright," France uses the phrase "droit d'auteur" (or "droits de l'auteur") and Germany uses the term "urheberrecht" to refer to a creator's right to control the reproduction and dissemination of her works. Although these phrases are rough equivalents of one another, such equivalency does not fully reflect the differing philosophical and legal precepts represented by the original, untranslated phrases.

4. Dynamics of the Global Market

The history of the development of international standards for intellectual property protection largely reflects the history of the growth of trade and technology. As technology advanced in the fields affecting the creation of literary and artistic works, the potential subject matter for copyright protection similarly advanced. Early national copyright laws granted rights to authors of written literary works, charts and music. The invention of photography, sound recordings, motion pictures and computer software required further refinements and expansion in the types of works protected under copyright law. Similarly, the development of patent law largely reflects technological advances in the areas of science and the useful arts.

Concurrently with the advance of technology in the areas of art and science, transportation and communication media similarly evolved from the oxcart to supersonic transports and from smoke signals to digital and satellite communications. These developments helped create a global marketplace for intellectual property based products. The increasingly international nature of this marketplace in turn gave rise to growing concerns over the differing levels of protection afforded such products. As a result, countries which granted little or no protection to intellectual property became havens for pirated and counterfeit products. Such piracy inevitably had an adverse economic impact on the intellectual property owner, affecting both local sales in the country where the pirated goods were manufactured and, as such products were increasingly exported abroad, foreign sales as well. The problem of worldwide counterfeiting has led developed countries to renew their efforts to increase international levels of intellectual property protection. Differing views regarding the economic desirability of such increased protection, however, continues to frustrate such efforts.[10]

5. A Short History of Treaty Protection of Intellectual Property

The desire to establish international protection norms for intellectual property is not new. In the area of copyright, the Berne Convention for the Protection of Artistic and Literary Works was first established in 1889. In the areas of patent, trademark and industrial designs, the Paris Convention was first established in 1883. Just as national laws concerning intellectual property have been

---

[10] For additional articles regarding the economic impact of the failure to protect intellectual property rights, *see* Chapter Two.

continuously revised to reflect changes in technology, these multinational treaties, and their progeny, have undergone numerous revisions, reflecting increasingly sophisticated minimum standards of protection.[11]

Given the territorial nature of intellectual property rights,[12] early bilateral and multinational treaties generally directed their efforts to requiring that adherents grant the identical level of protection to foreign and domestic owners ("national treatment").[13] Subsequent treaties focused on establishing minimum substantive levels of protection. Most recently, with the adoption of the Agreement on Trade-Related Aspects of Intellectual Property ("TRIPS"), international treaties have begun to focus on establishing minimum procedural levels of enforcement, including minimum remedies available against infringers.[14] Each treaty poses unique problems regarding the interpretation of its requirements, the transplantation of such requirements into each adherent's national laws and the enforcement of treaty obligations against non-complying nations.

From the early days of the Berne and Paris Conventions until the present day, efforts to reach an international accord regarding intellectual property protection norms, have generally been accompanied by divisive debates regarding the scope of protection to be granted such property. The positions taken by various nations reflect their differing (and often unreconcilable) philosophical, cultural, historical, economic and political points of view regarding the need for strong IP protection.

Although disputes regarding the scope and nature of protection to be afforded intellectual property generally arise between developed (or industrialized) and less developed (less industrialized) nations, negotiations during the Uruguay Round demonstrated a lack of accord between developed nations as well.[15] In reality, any country's position regarding the desired scope of protection will depend on the philosophical foundations supporting the protection of such property (*i.e.,* is the source of protection the desire to protect the creative spark or the unique contribution of the human personality to literary, artistic or scientific works?; is it to encourage the costly investment in time and research required to create new works?; is it to protect the public from confusion or harm?). It will also be based on the role in the nation's culture and history that the protection of expression, ideas and invention has attained. Those countries which historically and culturally have perceived the unrestricted dissemination of ideas and written works as a desirable goal will generally provide less protection than countries which place an economic value on the dissemination of such works. The degree of protection afforded "works of the mind" (whether ideas, inventions or literary or artistic expressions) will also be based on considerations of existing international norms, the perceived economic impact that protection might have on the technological and industrial development of the country in question, and the political pressures (both domestic and international) that are brought to bear on the issue.[16]

6. Efforts Toward Harmonization

Despite the absence of complete international agreement, countries are demonstrating an increased interest in harmonizing their national laws with those of leading developed countries. Such efforts at harmo-

---

[11] For a discussion of the history of the Berne and Paris Conventions, *see* Chapter Seven. For the text of these Conventions, *see Appendices I and II.*

[12] For a detailed discussion regarding the territorial nature of intellectual property rights and its impact on international protection norms, *see* Chapter Eleven.

[13] For a detailed discussion regarding the conflict between national treatment, reciprocity and minimum substantive norms for intellectual property protection, *see* Chapter Seven.

[14] For a discussion of various intellectual property treaties, *see* Chapters Seven and Eight. For the text of the major treaties, *see Appendix.*

[15] For a discussion of the negotiations resulting in the TRIPS Agreement, *see* Chapter Seven.

[16] For a detailed discussion of the philosophical foundations for intellectual property protection, *see* Chapter Two. For a detailed discussion of the cultural and economic issues underlying the question of intellectual property protection, *see* Chapters Two and Three.

nization are apparent in the recent spate of harmonization directives issued by the EEC, renewed attempts to establish trademark registration treaties, the negotiation of TRIPS and its establishment of minimum substantive *and* enforcement norms for intellectual property protection, and recent efforts under the auspices of the World Intellectual Property Organization to reach a consensus regarding patent registration.[17]

7. Remedies

Many "traditional" forms of intellectual property may include products that impact on the health, welfare or safety of the public, including medical and agricultural products and processes. The "public interest" nature of these products raises serious issues over conditions which the intellectual property owner should be allowed to impose on the use of such products. The right to compulsory licenses, the scope of "fair use" exceptions to an intellectual property owner's exclusive rights and other forms of government sanctioned "takings" are hotly debated.[18]

Where protection is deemed inadequate in a particular country, either through a lack of substantive laws or a failure to enforce existing laws, some intellectual property owners have sought to use their own national laws and courts to protect their rights through the extraterritorial application of such laws.[19] Given the admittedly territorial nature of most intellectual property rights, these efforts have led to increasing conflicts regarding the perceived violation of a nation's sovereign rights over the acts of its citizens. Such border conflicts have not been limited solely to efforts to enforce laws extraterritorially. New technologies such as satellite broadcasts and the global information superhighway have seriously undermined the viability of standard border enforcement measures in prohibiting the dissemination of pirated products and raised the nightmare scenario of multiple infringing sites arising from a single unauthorized broadcast of a copyrighted work.[20] Without agreed-upon international standards, remedies in such cases will depend increasingly upon the vagaries of national laws and the fortuity of the infringer's location.

Given the breadth of issues surrounding the question of international intellectual property protection, the establishment of international protection norms will continue to be a slow process. As each country begins to understand the rationale behind other countries' different treatment, some basis for an accommodation between admittedly conflicting interests becomes possible. This accommodation occurred in the 1880s when the Berne and Paris Conventions were established and continues today with the signing of the TRIPS Agreement and continuing efforts to establish harmonized standards for registration and enforcement procedures, and for substantive protection requirements. None of these multinational treaties contains the ultimate solution. They do, however, represent a steady evolution from national treatment to substantive standards,[21] and from substantive standards to procedural norms.[22] Such progress bodes well for future accommodations.

B. Defining the Issues[23]

Safeguarding intellectual property rights from foreign infringers has emerged as one

---

[17] For a detailed discussion of recent attempts at harmonization, *see* Chapter Twelve. For a detailed discussion of the corollary issue of the need for harmonized standards for emerging technologies, *see* Chapter Thirteen.

[18] For a detailed discussion of issues underlying government "takings" of intellectual property, *see* Chapter Ten.

[19] For a detailed discussion of the territorial nature of intellectual property and the problems posed by the extraterritorial application of national laws, *see* Chapter Eleven.

[20] For a detailed discussion of the border enforcement problems posed by emerging communication technologies, *see* Chapter Thirteen.

[21] For a detailed discussion of national treatment issues, *see* Chapter Seven.

[22] For a detailed discussion of procedural protection norms, *see* Chapter Nine.

[23] David I. Wilson, *A Trade Policy Goal For The 1990s: Improving The Adequacy And Effectiveness Of Intellectual Property Protection In Foreign Countries*, 1 TRANSNAT'L LAW 421. Copyright 1988 University of the Pacific, McGeorge School of Law, David I. Wilson. Excerpt reprinted with permission.

of the most important trade policy goals of the United States during the 1980s. Previously, the US government viewed the inadequacy of intellectual property protection in overseas markets as a technical matter. In recent years, however, it has become apparent that extensive intellectual property protection is indispensable for rewarding innovation—perhaps the most significant advantage United States companies have over their foreign competitors. Absent worldwide respect for the protection of intellectual property rights, American companies are unable not only to obtain the rewards for their inventions—which translate into sales, profits, and employment—but also to finance research and development for the next generations of their products.

American companies feel the sting of infringement worldwide. Losses from inadequate intellectual property protection occur in the country where the infringing products are made, in third countries to which the products are exported, and in the United States where infringing products are imported. The US International Trade Commission (ITC) estimated that 6 to 8 billion American dollars in annual sales were lost in 1984 by United States industry due to foreign product counterfeiting, passing off, and copyright and patent infringement. More recently, the ITC reported that losses for 1986 have increased to 23.8 billion dollars.

United States trade policy has focused on two concerns regarding intellectual property rights: one, protecting American intellectual property rights in the United States from foreign infringements, and two, ensuring protection of United States intellectual property rights in foreign countries.[24]

C. The "Problem" of Intellectual Property Protection[25]

The intellectual property problem involves the unintended transfer of wealth from the industrialized country economies to the developing and newly industrialized country economies. In this case, wealth takes the form of technology protected in the industrialized countries by patent and trade secret, goodwill protected by trademark and other indication of origin, expression protected by copyright, and design protected by design patent and semiconductor layout protection legislation. Intellectual property is tangible wealth, often easily appropriated and reproduced. Unlike tangible wealth, which must be mined, grown, or manufactured and is therefore subject to finite limitations of ownership or use, intellectual property wealth can be reproduced and used without depriving its creator/owner of possession or use and almost without practical limit. Once created, the marginal cost of reproduction is often near zero. The intellectual property problem therefore concerns devising a mechanism for protecting industrialized country intangible wealth, distinctly requiring the cooperation of developing countries and newly industrialized countries, which by providing such protection forego a potential economic windfall.

Demands for protection of intellectual property are often based (implicitly or explicitly) on a theory of natural law or moral right—the idea that intellectual property is naturally owned by the person who creates it and that appropriation from that person without compensation is wrongful (whether such appropriation is purely domestic or international). However, national policies on the scope of legitimized intellectual property rights vary widely depending on the results of a cost/benefit analysis balancing the immediate public welfare against long-term interests in private capital formation.

---

[24] An important procedure for preventing infringement by foreign entities in the US is litigation of intellectual property cases before the US International Trade Commission (ITC) pursuant to Section 337 of the Tariff Act of 1930, 19 U.S.C. § 1337 (1983). Section 337 litigation has a number of advantages over litigation in the Federal courts, including: (1) a statutory deadline of one year in most cases and 18 months in more complicated cases (as compared to typically lengthy Federal District Court proceedings.) [19 U.S.C. § 1337 (b)(1) (1983)]; (2) a lack of jurisdictional problems over foreign entities because Section 337 confers in rem jurisdiction, *i.e.*, jurisdiction over the imported goods; and (3) a more effective remedy in most ITC cases than federal district courts—a general exclusion order which directs the Customs Service to exclude from the US infringing products made by any entity, not just the entities that were parties in the ITC Proceedings.

[25] Frederick M. Abbott, *Protecting First World Assets in the Third World: Intellectual Property Negotiations in the GATT Multilateral Framework,* 22 VAND. J. TRANSNAT'L L. 689. Copyright 1989 Frederick M. Abbott. Excerpt reprinted with permission.

National policy, as opposed to natural law, has shaped the grant of the intellectual property right. While a combination of self-interest and equity have given rise to a system in which states grant to foreign nationals intellectual property rights protection equivalent to that accorded to local entities, the scope of local protection has not been intuitively derived from natural law.

The intellectual property problem is not a failure by the developing countries to recognize the social or economic utility of granting and protecting rights in intellectual property. In the industrialized countries themselves, the most well-reasoned studies of patent systems have been inconclusive with respect to the social or economic utility of those systems. No significant empirical study as yet has demonstrated the beneficial impact of the patent grant on economic growth or social development. A study yielding such results might indeed be possible, but it is in the realm of the future. Attempting to persuade developing countries that the industrialized countries are promoting enhanced intellectual property protection to accelerate the former's economic growth is neither necessary nor appropriate at this point. The intellectual property debate stands on firmer ground if premised on recognition that the industrialized countries are attempting to protect an increasingly important component of their national wealth.

Quantifying the intellectual property problem in terms of financial losses to industrialized country business enterprises due to unintended (or unauthorized) appropriation of intellectual property by developing country enterprises is difficult because it involves several highly uncertain factors. First, losses to industrialized country enterprises take the form of lost revenue opportunities, and calculation of such losses requires the hypothesis of unaffected revenues. Second, because intellectual property is often easy to reproduce and difficult to trace, the extent of unauthorized appropriation and use involves speculation. Data collected from industrialized country enterprises by government agencies or trade organizations are not likely to be subject to the kind of rigorous examination required for a least-biased estimate of losses.

QUESTIONS AND COMMENTS FOR YOUR CONSIDERATION

1. Is it possible for the losses from the unauthorized reproduction and sale of pirated products to be quantified in some reasonably acceptable manner? What factors would you consider? What obstacles would you face?

2. Do the countries which do not prohibit the unauthorized reproduction of and sale of products containing intellectual property suffer economic harm? If intellectual property rights are primarily territorial in nature (*see* Chapter Eleven), why should one country care whether the intellectual property rights of a foreign citizen are infringed? For a further discussion of those issues, *see* Chapters Two, Three and Six.

3. Which is better for protecting international intellectual property: a treaty or "harmonization"? Do they amount to the same result in practice? Which approach seems to offer more protection to the artist or inventor?

D. The Current System for the International Protection of Intellectual Property

1. Treaty Regimes[26]

The current international system for the protection of intellectual property consists of a variety of treaties administered by international organizations (primarily the World Intellectual Property Organization, or WIPO), which essentially coordinate nation-state legal regimes that are relied upon to provide both substantive norms and enforcement procedures. The principal international treaty for the protection of patents, trademarks, and industrial designs is the Paris Convention for the Protection of Industrial Property (Paris Convention), which was concluded in 1883, was last revised in 1967, and has approximately ninety-eight Member States. WIPO administers the Paris Convention. The principal features of the Paris Convention are the obligation of states to extend national treatment to residents of other states and a right of priority to applicants of foreign Member States for their patent, trademark, and design filings. The Paris Convention permits Member States to take legislative measures providing for the grant of compulsory licenses for patents in, for example, cases of non-work.[27]

Proponents of enhanced intellectual property protection criticize the Paris Convention with respect to patents because: (1) it does not adequately address the subject matter of technologies; (2) it does not set a minimum patent term; (3) it does not expressly provide for payment of full compensation for compulsory licenses; (4) it is too permissive with respect to the granting of compulsory licenses; and (5) though providing for recourse to the International Court of Justice in disputes between Member States, the Convention does not establish standards for national enforcement and cannot, in any event, be considered to provide a meaningful dispute settlement mechanism. Critics express similar concerns over the lack of substantive standards and enforcement mechanisms for trademarks.

The most important international treaty for protecting copyright is the Berne Convention for the Protection of Literary and Artistic Works (Berne Convention). The Berne Convention is administered by WIPO. Major features of the Berne Convention, to which over seventy-five states are parties, are the extension of national treatment to foreign authors; the recognition of a minimum copyright term (generally the life of the author plus fifty years); the establishment of "moral rights" of authors (*e.g.*, granting the right to authors to protect the integrity of artistic works after transfer of their economic interests); and the requirement of a lack of formalities for obtaining copyright protection. Like the Paris Convention, the Berne Convention provides for the submission of disputes over its interpretation or application to the International Court of Justice. On October 20, 1988, the United States Senate approved accession to the Berne Convention, partly in an effort to allay international doubt as to the United States commitment to protect intellectual property.

The Berne Convention is primarily criticized for its lack of an effective dispute settlement mechanism. The attitude of the United States copyright industries toward this treaty has been summarized as follows:

> The protection offered by these rules, however, cannot cure many of the intellectual property problems faced today by America's creative industries. First, national treatment becomes meaningless when the national laws of developing countries are inadequate, or not enforced. Second, the limited number of signatories and the Universal Copyright Convention's lack of application to nonmember countries also diminish

---

[26] Frederick M. Abbott, *Protecting First World Assets in the Third World: Intellectual Property Negotiations in the GATT Multilateral Framework*, 22 VAND. J. TRANSNAT'L L. 689. Copyright 1989 Frederick M. Abbott. Excerpt reprinted with permission.

[27] *Editors' Note:* The non-working of a patent occurs when the inventor does not use or manufacture the patented invention in the country where the patent has issued. Thus, for example, if an inventor owns a patent for the identical invention in countries A and B, but only manufactures the product or licenses others to use the product in country A, the patent would be worked in country A and would *not* be worked in country B. As discussed more fully in Chapter Ten, failure to work a patent in a particular country may lead to the imposition of a compulsory license or in involuntary abandonment of the patent in that country.

their effectiveness. Finally, the lack of mechanisms for consultations, for dispute settlement or for remedying violations limits their usefulness.[28]

In addition to its failure to provide adequate substantive norms and dispute settlement procedures, the current treaty system is criticized for its lack of attention to certain important subject matter areas. No international treaty exists regarding the protection of trade secrets (although most countries would appear to grant some form of local protection). There is sufficient doubt as to the protection afforded to semiconductor layout under existing copyright law that a significant number of countries, including the United States and Japan, have adopted *sui generis* legislation covering the protection of such designs. The Council of the European Communities adopted a 1986 directive obliging all European Communities Member States to adopt such laws.

2. National Systems[29]

The international treaty system, while providing minimum substantive standards in a few intellectual property rights areas, does not presently operate as an effective substantive rule-making system, nor does it meaningfully address domestic enforcement procedures. These matters are presently reserved to the internal legal systems of individual states, and as a result substantial disparities prevail in substantive rules, enforcement procedures, and enforcement practices. The scope of the basic substantive differences is apparent from a review of the WIPO Report to the GATT working group on trade-related aspects of intellectual property (TRIPS), which provides a comprehensive, although general, current survey of the intellectual property laws in force throughout the world (both in GATT and non-GATT countries).

In a 1989 Foreign Trade Barriers Report, the US Trade Representative's office identified the most serious existing defects (from the standpoint of United States Government) in important foreign intellectual property legal regimes. The findings in the Report were set out in terms of substantive law and enforcement deficiencies rather than as quantifications of losses. The Report highlights in a significant number of developing countries and newly idustrialized countries a lack of patent subject matter coverage for chemicals and pharmaceuticals, short patent terms and overly permissive compulsory patent licensing, and inadequate copyright legislation and enforcement with respect to the audio, video, and software sectors.

---

28 Basic Framework of GATT Provisions on Intellectual Property: Statement of the Views of the European, Japanese and United States Business Communities 88-89 (1988).

29 Frederick M. Abbott, *Protecting First World Assets in the Third World: Intellectual Property Negotiations in the GATT Multilateral Framework,* 22 VAND. J. TRANSNAT'L. 689. Copyright 1989 Frederick M. Abbott. Excerpt reprinted with permission.

QUESTIONS AND COMMENTS FOR YOUR CONSIDERATION

1. In 1994, as part of the Uruguay Round of negotiations under the General Agreement on Trade and Tariffs ("GATT"), an Agreement on Trade Related Aspects of Intellectual Property Rights (TRIPS) was adopted. This Agreement establishes minimum enforcement standards for protecting intellectual property rights. *See* Appendix IX for text of TRIPS. To what extent does this Agreement respond to the protection concerns raised in the article you have just read?

2. For further discussion of international treaty regimes' handling of the protection of intellectual property rights, *see* Chapter Seven. For the texts of the major intellectual property treaties, *see* Appendix.

3. Treaty Definitions of Copyright[30]

A copyright is a collection of discrete rights for controlling disposition of the content of the original work. Most rights are determined under the domestic laws of various countries rather than by treaty. However, there are several significant exceptions: (1) the rights of attribution and integrity, which are inalienable even upon assignment of the copyright, and survive the death of the author for the term of the copyright; (2) the exclusive right to make and authorize translations; (3) the exclusive right to make or authorize reproductions, including sound and visual recordings of writings; (4) the exclusive rights to publicly perform or translate dramatic, dramatico-musical, and musical works. In addition, authors of literary and artistic works hold the exclusive right to: (1) broadcast and rebroadcast the work, and to authorize the same; (2) publicly recite or authorize public recitation; (3) translate or authorize translation; (4) adapt, arrange, or alter the work, and authorize the same; and (5) adapt for cinematography and broadcast as a cinematographic work.

Some countries, although not the United States, may also grant "droit de suite," an inalienable right of the author that may include financial interest in any transfer in ownership of the copyright. This follows the general tenet of the Berne Convention which sets forth minimum protections and provides that member nations may grant stronger protections than the treaty requires. The rights in most major, developed countries, however, are reasonably consonant with those available in the United States due to the US adherence to the Universal Copyright Convention and the Berne Convention.

The minimum duration of copyright protection is also determined by treaty. Terms for copyright under the Berne Convention are as a general rule, at least fifty years from the time the work is published or made; but for cinematographic works, at least fifty years from completion of the work. Terms for copyright under the Universal Copyright Convention are slightly different: (1) as a general rule, protection lasts at least the life of the author plus twenty-five years; and (2) for photographs and works of applied art, at least ten years. Where there is joint authorship and terms are measured relative to the author's death, the duration is determined on the life of the last surviving author.

[30] Margaret A. Boulware, Jeffrey A. Pyle, Frank C. Turner, "Symposium: *Intellectual Property: An Overview Of Intellectual Property Rights Abroad;" 16* Hous. J. Int'l L 441. Copyright 1994 Margaret A. Boulware, Jeffrey A. Pyle, Frank C. Turner. Excerpt reprinted with permission.

QUESTIONS AND COMMENTS FOR YOUR CONSIDERATION

1. For further definitions of copyrightable works, *see* 17 U.S.C. § 101. *See also* Article 2 of the Berne Convention in *Appendix II.*

2. Any original expressive composition can be copyrighted. But not every original invention can be patented. As you read the next section, keep in mind this basic difference between copyrights and patents.

4. The Problem of Patentability

a. The Inventor's Reward[31]

The European Court of Justice defines the specific subject matter of patents as the guarantee that the patentee has the exclusive right to use an invention and place it into circulation for the first time. This may be done either directly or through the grant of licenses to third parties. Under this defini-

[31] John E. Somorjai, *The Evolution of a Common Market: Limits Imposed on the Protection of National Intellectual Property Rights in the European Economic Community,* 9 Int'l Tax & Bus. Law. 431. Copyright 1992 International Tax & Business Lawyer. Excerpt reprinted with permission.

tion, a patent rewards the creativity of the inventor by allowing the patent owner to exploit his patent commercially, but only to the point where the invention is placed into circulation. Once the invention has been sold and is in the market, the patent owner no longer has control over its use and can no longer earn profits.[32]

b. Novelty and Non-Obviousness[33]

Patents generally protect the novel and unobvious functional aspects of useful articles or processes. The Paris Convention does not actually define "patent," but merely provides that the term includes the various types of patents recognized under the laws of each member country. A patent is a statutory right granted to an inventor or the inventor's assignee by a national government to exclude other people from practicing the invention disclosed and claimed in the patent specification. In most countries, the right to exclude typically extends to making, using, and selling the patented invention. The patent grant is limited in duration to a set number of years typically measured from the filing date of the application for patent. Although some countries have grants that are renewable or extendable under specific conditions, a patent is generally not renewable once the patent has expired or has been forfeited.

The patent, which is the intangible right to exclude, is sometimes confused with the patent specification, which is the written disclosure of the invention. The written disclosure describes a particular embodiment of the invention and includes several numbered sentences called "claims." The right to exclude extends only to what is claimed, which can be and usually is distinct from what is disclosed in the patent. For instance, the written disclosure may describe a machine of which all but a small part is well-known technology. The claims need only include that part which is not well-known and, if patentable, can otherwise omit the well-known technology. In this manner, insignificant departures from the particular embodiment described in the patent specification will not prevent infringement if an accused device embodies that which is described in the claims.

The claims define the invention and are generally located at the end of a patent or patent application. Often the claims are more narrow in scope than the description of the invention contained in the body of the patent or application. However, some countries, notably the United Kingdom, permit what are called "omnibus claims." Omnibus claims usually read as "the invention substantially as shown and described," and are unpatentable in the United States. The claims, however broad or narrow they may be, define the scope of protection the patent provides. Without patent protection, anyone, including the inventor and the inventor's competitors, can use the invention for any purpose.

There are many variations on the standard patent described above. The term "patent," as used in the Paris Convention, specifically includes patents of importation, patents of improvement, certificates of addition, inventor's certificates, petty patents, utility models, and utility certificates. Other patent forms include revalidation patents and the European patent. The Paris Convention does not require a member country to implement each different type of patent but does require that some form of patent protection exist.

There are three basic requirements for patentability. The first requirement is "novelty"; the second requirement is "nonobviousness" (or "inventive step"); and the third requirement is "intrinsic usefulness." Most countries require absolute novelty throughout the world at the time the patent application is filed. Absolute novelty means there must be no public disclosure or commercial exploitation of the invention before a patent application is filed. The United States is one of the few jurisdictions with a one year grace

---

[32] *Editors' Note:* The author is discussing the question of exhaustion of patent rights in the European Community. Under the doctrine of exhaustion of rights, once a patented article is sold the patentee cannot exercise control over its subsequent use. The loss of the ability to control the subsequent resale of an item containing a patented object, however, does not eliminate the patentee's right to control the future license or the use of the patented invention. For a further discussion of the principle of exhaustion of rights, *see* Chapter Nine.

[33] Margaret A. Boulware, Jeffrey A. Pyle, Frank C. Turner, Symposium: *Intellectual Property: An Overview Of Intellectual Property Rights Abroad;* 16 HOUS. J. INT'L L 441. Copyright 1994 Margaret A. Boulware, Jeffrey A. Pyle, Frank C. Turner. Excerpt reprinted with permission.

period to file a patent after public sale or disclosure of an invention. Even a single public disclosure or a single offer for sale anywhere in the world before the application is filed can prohibit a patent from issuing on the application in most of the world.

The European definition of novelty is fairly typical: "An invention shall be considered to be new if it does not form part of the state of the art" which "shall be held to comprise everything made available to the public by means of a written or oral description, by use, or in any other way." The only exceptions to this are regularly scheduled exhibits and officially sanctioned trade shows, but these provisions are rarely applicable.

The significant exception to the application of the novelty requirement arises under the Paris Convention. The Paris Convention provides that a "right of priority" exists upon the first filing of an application in a member country and the right subsists for one year, during which time acts by the applicant will not forfeit patent protection in other member countries. This is sometimes referred to as "convention priority," and the application date of the first filed application in a member country is sometimes called the "priority date."

Therefore, US nationals need only maintain absolute novelty until an application is filed in the United States, provided that all countries of interest are members of the Paris Convention and counterpart applications are filed in the national offices of those countries within the one year priority period. However, convention priority is a right that can be waived or lost, most notably by failing to formally claim priority or by failing to file an application within the one year priority period.

The general rule is that any public disclosure or any sale anywhere in the world prior to filing the US patent application will forfeit potential patent rights in every country except the United States. Rare exceptions in the international community do exist. For instance, Canada provides limited grace periods in some circumstances. However, there is no uniform exception to the general rule, and the prophylactic practice of assuming all countries require absolute novelty is strongly recommended wherever possible.

To be patentable, an invention must not be obvious to a person of ordinary skill in the technical field of the invention. Europeans call this requirement the "inventive step." Although the analysis is much more complicated, the test is essentially whether an average person who works in the particular field would deduce, realize, or discover the invention from information in the public domain. However, the test is applied more subjectively in Europe and elsewhere than in the United States. Convention priority discussed above does not significantly affect the application of this requirement except to the extent that it prevents acts occurring within the convention period from rendering the claimed invention "obvious."

"Utility" can be defined as "intrinsically useful," that is, not solely for decoration, ornamentation, or other aesthetic purposes. Some foreign countries call this "industrial application" or "industrial applicability." Regardless of the term used, the definition is always circular. Most inventions have no difficulty meeting this requirement, particularly electrical and mechanical cases. Compositions of matter, however, are sometimes challenged on this basis. Convention priority does not affect the application of this requirement in any way.

Included among the types of inventions which may be subject to protection are agricultural products, including plant varieties. The United States protects new varieties of plants in three ways. First, the Patent Act protects asexually reproduced plant varieties; that is, plants, like fruit trees, reproduced by cuttings. Second, the Plant Variety Protection Act protects sexually reproduced varieties; that is, plants, like crops, reproduced by pollination. Finally, the Patent Statute may protect some plant varieties through its protection of manufactures and compositions, which are not products of nature.

Internationally, protection may be found in member countries of the International Union for the Protection of New Varieties of Plants (UPOV) or through similar plant breeder's rights legislation as enacted by individual countries. However, UPOV applies only to sexually reproduced plants and vegetation as opposed to asexually reproduced plants. UPOV requires that protected plants be distinct, uniform, and stable. To be considered distinct, the variety must be clearly distinguishable by one or more important characteristics from any other variety whose existence is a matter of common knowledge. To be considered uniform, "the variety must be sufficiently homogeneous, having regard to the particular features of its sexual reproduction or vegetative propagation." To be considered stable, the variety must be stable in its essential characteristics; it must remain true in its description after repeated reproduction or propagation. If the three conditions are met, the period of protection ranges from fifteen to eighteen years. The grant of protection allows the breeder to control the commercial marketing and selling of the reproductive or propagating material of the plant variety.

Outside the UPOV, many countries provide alternative or additional protections. For example, in Canada, new legislation granting a "plants breeder's right" was recently enacted, but will not become effective until implementation regulations are finalized. Canada grants the exclusive right to sell or commercially produce propagating material of plant varieties and to authorize the same. The right is limited to the extent that the plant variety must be distinguishable, stable, and homogeneous, but experimental uses are excluded. The right does not include a prohibition on importing propagating material, farmers' rights to noninfringing uses of seeds (such as milling) and replanting of such seeds, or use of propagating material as a source of genetic variation for new strains.

QUESTIONS AND COMMENTS FOR YOUR CONSIDERATION

1. For further definitions of patentable works, *see* 35 U.S.C. § 101. *See also* Article 1 of the Paris Convention, in *Appendix I*.

2. In dealing with a patent case, a court anywhere in the world will want to examine the policy reasons for protecting patents. These policy reasons can be grouped under at least four theories. These theories are primarily economic—that is, they seek to examine the risks and rewards to society that are attendant upon rewarding a limited-time monopoly to the inventor.

3. The first and simplest theory of patent protection is the reward theory. The reward theory begins with the assumption that some inventions, once they become known, are easily copied and imitated. Presumably no one would want to invent such an invention and put in the years of research and expenses that would be required. Thus the patent system exists to prevent free riding—*i.e.*, subsequent copying by others. By granting the inventor a limited-time monopoly, the patent system makes it possible for the inventor to recapture her investment in inventing and developing the invention. Naturally, this theory could be construed in such a broad way as to apply to every invention. But if it did, then it would not be a useful theory. Instead, the "reward theory" operates to exclude certain kinds of inventions. The inventions that are excluded are those that would exist even if there were not a patent system. For example, suppose that it wouldn't take much effort or expense to invent a wholly new product, the Self-Effacing Gizmo. Under the reward theory, the first person to invent the Self-Effacing Gizmo would be denied a patent. What do you think of this theory? Is it fair? Is it administrable?

4. A second theory of patent protection, associated primarily with Professor Edmund Kitch, is called the "prospect theory," to signify its connection to gold and silver prospectors.[34] An inventor would stake out the intellectual territory defined by his invention, the way a gold miner might stake out a claim regardless of its immediately knowable commercial value. This theory would not require a patent applicant to spell out the future commercial benefits of his invention, because, like a gold mine, that fact may not be initially knowable. Does this theory strike you as realistic? It may be realistic in some cases: the inventor of LASER

light, for example, probably had no way of foreseeing its use in optical surgery. On the other hand, if people could patent any new invention, such as a Self-Effacing Gizmo, that had no knowable commercial value when patented, wouldn't the Patent Office be clogged with thousands of "useless" inventions? Then, when something useful is invented, a prior patent owner of a useless invention might file a lawsuit claiming infringement and stating that the new "useful" invention is simply an application of his own invention.

5. A third theory of patent protection can be called the "trade secret avoidance theory." Under this theory, if patent protection did not exist, firms would have a huge incentive to protect their inventions through trade secrets. They would overinvest in "hiding" their inventions by building elaborate complex, impenetrable housings for their inventions, or else overinvesting in useless "decoys." In order to avoid the social waste that would come from overinvesting in trade secrets, this theory says that patent protection is an economically efficient alternative. Do you agree? Would this theory require that patent protection be *denied* to an invention that was so easily imitated that it could not be protected by an elaborate trade secret cover?

6. Finally, a fourth theory of patent protection is the "rent dissipation" theory associated with Professors Mark Grady and Jay Alexander.[35] Certain inventions "signal" ways in which they may be improved (the telephone is a conspicuous example). If people rushed to make improvements on an invention, there would be two adverse consequences. First, society would lose money because of all the redundancy of effort that goes into making improvements. (This redundancy of effort gives rise to the term "rent dissipation.") Second, if the improvements were patentable, then the original inventor might be left with little or nothing. For example, Alexander Graham Bell's telephone was a rudimentary product; it could easily have been improved. Any improvement would immediately take over the market if it were in competition with Bell's own model telephone. Thus, the "rent dissipation" theory says that an invention is patentable IF it itself signals ways in which it may be improved and made more commercially useful. What would not be patentable under this theory? An invention that is so basic—like a law of nature that somebody discovers and gets a Nobel Prize for—that it can't be improved! As Professors Grady and Alexander say, "Under our theory a 'principle of nature' is unpatentable—not because it is comparatively worthless, but because a subsequent race among improvers is unlikely. Note that the reward theory suggests exactly the opposite result: because the discovery of a principle of nature is typically more valuable and costly to discover than, say, a new way of bleaching animal furs, reward theory predicts that Nobel prize-winning ideas will receive broad protection." What do you think of the "rent dissipation" theory? Would it surprise you to learn that, under American patent law at least, the theory accords fairly well with the results courts have reached in patentability cases (even though the courts did not make explicit use of the theory)?

---

[34] *See* Edmund W. Kitch, "The Nature and Function of the Patent System," 20 J.L. & Econ. 265 (1977).

[35] *See* Mark F. Grady and Jay I. Alexander, "Patent Law and Rent Dissipation," 78 Virginia L. Rev. 305 (1992).

5. Trademarks, Goodwill and the "Use" Problem[36]

A trademark represents a guarantee that the owner has the exclusive right to use that mark for the purpose of placing products containing the mark into circulation for the first time. The economic value of a trademark often depends on the mark's reputation among the consuming public for quality (its "goodwill" value). Theoretically any word, name, or symbol (including alphanumeric marks and word and design combinations) can qualify as a protectible mark. If the commercial symbol at issue is used to identify or distinguish goods, it is referred to as a "trademark"; if the symbol is used to identify or distinguish services, it is referred to as a "service mark." Not all commercial symbols qualify for protection. To the contrary, only commercial symbols that function as true source designators can be protected. Thus, a mark must not only be used to designate the source of the goods or services, but it must also be distinctive. Although many countries restrict the protection of a mark to prohibiting the unauthorized use of similar marks on those products on which the mark is used or registered, in the United States, the more distinctive the mark, the greater the degree of protection afforded.

In addition to "traditional" categories of trademarks, such as word and symbols, the United States also protects such diverse categories as color, smell, and sound, so long as such categories are used as distinctive source designators. One of the fastest categories of protectable source designators is "trade dress." The term has been defined to include "the total image of the product and may include features such as size, shape, color or color combinations, texture, graphics or even particular sales techniques." Because of its broad scope, trade dress has been used to protect such diverse items as book covers, the design elements on greeting cards, exercise bike designs, restaurant decor, cheerleader uniforms and the use of adoption papers with toy dolls. Such trade dress elements must be both distinctive and non-functional before they can be protected as source designators.

The United States is one of the few countries to require actual use of a mark. Most countries protect marks upon registration. This can lead to inconsistent treatment of famous or well-known marks which have been used or advertised in a country but which have not been registered. One of the most pressing issues facing the global market today is the scope and enforcement of foreign trademark rights. International treaties concerning trademark rights currently include the Paris Convention, the TRIPS Agreement, the Madrid Protocol and the Trademark Registration Treaty.[37]

6. Varying National Approaches to Trade Secrets[38]

There is no single, universally applied definition for "trade secret," even within the United States. Exactly what constitutes a trade secret has been the subject of continuing debate and is closely tied with topics such as unfair competition and covenants not to compete. The only constant in the law of trade secrets is that the subject matter of a trade secret must retain some degree of secrecy. As a general rule, a trade secret can be any information not commonly known in the relevant industry that is used in connection with a business to obtain a competitive advantage and the information is secret, is identifiable, and is not readily ascertainable.

The most common definition for a trade secret in the United States is:

> Any formula, pattern, device or compilation of information which is used in one's business, and which gives him an opportunity to obtain an advantage

---

[36] Doris E. Long, *Unfair Competition and the Lanham Act.* Copyright 1993 The Bureau of National Affairs, Inc. Excerpt reprinted with permission.

[37] *Editors' Note:* For further definitions of trademarks, *see* 15 U.S.C. § 1145. *See also* Article 6 of the Paris Convention and Article 15 of the Agreement on Trade Related Aspects of Intellectual Property in *Appendices I and IX,* respectively.

[38] Margaret A. Boulware, Jeffrey A. Pyle, Frank C. Turner, Symposium: *Intellectual Property: An Overview Of Intellectual Property Rights Abroad;* 16 Hous. J. Int'l L 441. Copyright 1994 Margaret A. Boulware, Jeffrey A. Pyle, Frank C. Turner. Excerpt reprinted with permission.

> over competitors who do not know or use it. It may be a formula for a chemical compound, a process of manufacturing, treating or preserving materials, a pattern for a machine or other device, or a list of customers.... A trade secret is a process or device for continuous use in the operation of the business. Generally it relates to the production of goods, as, for example, a machine or formula for the production of an article.[39]

This definition is extremely broad, but not all subject matter within the definition is necessarily protectable because it must also (1) be unavailable to the public and (2) not be readily ascertainable by independent investigation.

The European Economic Community (EC) refers to trade secrets as "know-how" and defines the term as "a body of technical information that is secret, substantial, and identified in any appropriate form."[40] This definition includes information important in whole or significant part to a manufacturing process, or a product or service, or the development of either and excludes information that is "trivial" and "which can reasonably be expected . . . to be capable of improving the competitive position" of one who has access to the know-how.[41]

Mexico recently defined "trade secret" as "any information having industrial utility that is kept in confidential fashion, regarding which sufficient means or systems have been undertaken to preserve its confidential nature and limit access thereto" and "relates ... the nature, characteristics or purposes of products, production methods or processes, the means and forms of distribution or trade, or the rendering of services."[42]

As in Europe, the secret must be fixed in a tangible medium of expression to be identified[43] and protected. In contrast, South Korea's newly enacted trade secret law, modeled after Japanese and German statutes, defines a trade secret as technical or business information useful for "production, sales, and other commercial activities" that (1) is not generally known; (2) has independent economic value; and (3) has been kept secret by reasonable efforts.[44]

Commentators identify three instances when trade secret protection is particularly useful: (1) to protect a patentable invention during a patent pendency; (2) to protect information related to a patented invention but not covered by that patent; and (3) to protect information or subject matter that is (a) not patentable or which is only partially patentable (only narrow protection available); or (b) where the party wants to continue to have rights in the subject matter beyond the term available through patenting. For instance, because many countries have yet to approve the patentability of lifeforms, trade secret protection may be the only viable alternative to protect the invention.

When the invention is the end product, trade secret offers only limited protection. Once the product is sold, there is no protection to prevent the reverse engineering of the product and subsequent production and marketing by third parties. Thus, trade secret protection can be valuable when the invention is a formula or production process. Within the arena of biotechnology, this might include expression vectors, a production organism, or some other manufacturing method.

The main advantage to trade secret protection is the cost. To establish and maintain trade secret protection, only the costs of research, development, and security measures are incurred. The primary disadvantage is that a trade secret must remain

---

[39] Kewanee Oil Co. v. Bicron Corp., 416 US 470, 474-75 (1974).

[40] Commission Regulation 556/89 (on the Application of Article 85(3) of the Treaty to Certain Categories of Know-How Licensing Agreements), art 1., I(7), 1989 O.J. (L61) 7.

[41] *Ibid.*

[42] Manuel A. Gomez-Maqueo, *Analysis of Mexico's New Industrial Property Law,* 42 PAT. TRADEMARK & COPYRIGHT J. (BNA) 383 (1991).

[43] *Editors' Note:* The requirement of identification has the potential for eliminating trade secret protection. As noted in the article and in the Overview in this Chapter, one of the key elements for trade secret protection is that the information in question be kept confidential. Registration and other requirements of written disclosure increase the risk that the trade secret will be disclosed and its value as a trade secret will be destroyed.

[44] *Trademark Assignment & Trademark Licensing in Korea,* 8 LEE & KO REPORT 1, 4 (1992).

secret. The consequence of imposed secrecy is that it cuts off the supply of new information to a field which thrives on the open exchange of information through publication and presentation. The absence of information on new discoveries and progress can only work to inhibit development. Additional disadvantages of trade secret protection include the limitation that there is no right given to the holder of a trade secret to prohibit the independent development and commercialization by third parties and that trade secrets are not recognized in many countries.

Trade secrets do not have formal protection procedures. Because of their secret nature, national governments do not require submission of applications or any other form of official sanction. The larger issue relating to trade secrets is their maintenance, since affirmative action must be taken to maintain the trade secret as a "secret." Therefore, to protect a trade secret, the inventor should immediately take reasonable steps to prevent disclosure.[45]

7. The Uncertain Value of Industrial Designs[46]

Utility model and industrial design protection are sometimes considered lesser forms of protection but can be commercially significant. Utility models are typically directed to the functional aspects of a design, whereas industrial designs usually protect the aesthetic aspects of a design. For example, in Germany, a utility model can be a tool, implement, or other article with a novel, unobvious configuration having industrial application. Japan and other countries have similar protection. The level of inventiveness, as well as the scope and duration of protection, is less than that for a standard patent.

Utility model protection, for all its similarity to a standard patent, is not necessarily an exclusive alternative to a patent. For example, Germany grants utility model protection as a supplement to patent protection. German utility model protection also has several distinct advantages over a German patent, including: (1) lower standards for invention and novelty; (2) quicker processing and granting of rights; and (3) lower cost. Thus, utility model protection can be highly valuable regardless of the prospects for patent protection.

There is no direct counterpart to utility model protection in the United States. In the United States, industrial designs correspond more closely to design patents, which protect the appearance of a product rather than its functional aspects. The functional aspects of a product or invention are the exclusive realm of the utility patent. The primary difference from protection in the United States is that utility models and industrial designs in most foreign countries need only be novel, whereas in the United States, patented designs must be novel and unobvious. The end result is that protection for certain intellectual property can be obtained overseas but not in the United States. Similarly, utility model protection may be available where patent protection is not, as where absolute novelty required for patentability in a country may not exist but may not be required for a utility model.[47]

E. A "Problem" Sampler[48]

The Foreign Trade Barriers Report of the US Trade Representative's Office contained a useful catalogue of then pending intellectual property trade barriers on a country-by-country basis. This catalogue continues to provide a useful overview of the types of

---

[45] *Editors' Note:* For further definitions of trade secrets, *see* the US Model Trade Secret Act. *See also* Article 39 of the Agreement on Trade Related Aspects of Intellectual Property in *Appendix IX.*

[46] Margaret A. Boulware, Jeffrey A. Pyle, Frank C. Turner, Symposium: *Intellectual Property: An Overview Of Intellectual Property Rights Abroad;* 16 HOUS. J. INT'L L 441. Copyright 1994 Margaret A. Boulware, Jeffrey A. Pyle, Frank C. Turner. Excerpt reprinted with permission.

[47] *Editors' Note:* For further definitions of utility designs, *see* Article 25 of the Paris Convention in *Appendix I.*

[48] Frederick M. Abbott, *Protecting First World Assets in the Third World: Intellectual Property Negotiations in the GATT Multilateral Framework,* 22 VAND. J. TRANSNAT'L L. 689. Copyright 1989 Frederick M. Abbott. Excerpt reprinted with permission.

problems the US and other developed countries face in protecting their intellectual property rights among newly industrialized and emerging market economies.

In 1989 The Foreign Trade Barriers Report of the US Trade Representative's office catalogued the following intellectual property trade barriers on a country-by-country basis:

1. Argentina's lack of pharmaceutical product coverage, weak computer software protection, and permissive compulsory licensing;
2. Brazil's lack of pharmaceutical process and product patent coverage, permissive compulsory licensing, short effective patent duration, and weak copyright enforcement;
3. Canada's permissive broadcast retransmission policies and compulsory licensing, and price controls for patented pharmaceuticals;
4. Chile's lack of patent coverage for chemicals, pharmaceuticals, and foodstuffs;
5. China's lack of copyright protection for software and lack of patent protection for pharmaceutical products and substances obtained by means of chemical processes;
6. Columbia's lack of patent coverage in various areas, short patent duration, permissive compulsory licensing, trademark restrictions, and gaps in copyright coverage (no explicit mention of software) and enforcement (virtually 100 percent video cassette appropriation);
7. Egypt's lack of copyright coverage and enforcement in a variety of areas (including audio/video and software), lack of pharmaceutical and foodstuff patent coverage, inadequate patent term, and permissive compulsory licensing;
8. Inadequate audio/video copyright enforcement in Belgium and the Netherlands (European Communities intellectual property concerns are addressed with respect to specific countries);
9. Finland's lack of pharmaceutical product patent coverage;
10. Greece's lack of service mark protection, copyright enforcement regarding video cassettes, and software coverage;
11. The Gulf Cooperation Council's (Saudi Arabia, Kuwait, Bahrain, Qatar, the UAE and Oman) lack of copyright legislation and extensive audio/video and software appropriation, lack of adequate patent protection, and lack of trademark law enforcement;
12. India's lack of patent coverage for chemicals, pharmaceuticals and foodstuffs, short patent terms, permissive compulsory licensing and royalty restrictions, inadequate copyright enforcement (primarily software and books), obstacles to registering and protecting trademarks, and limited trade secret protection;
13. Indonesia's lack of patent legislation and copyright and trademark enforcement;
14. Italy's lack of copyright enforcement with respect to audio, video, television broadcasts, and computer software;
15. Japan's inefficient patent and trademark system and relatively short copyright term;
16. Korea's inadequate enforcement of new copyright legislation (audio, video and software), counterfeiting of sporting goods, and discriminatory patent procedures;
17. Malaysia's permissive copyright compulsory licensing and video appropriation;
18. Mexico's lack of biotechnology and foodstuff patent coverage and permissive trademark compulsory licensing, limited trade secret protection, disclosure of pharmaceutical and agricultural chemical testing information, restrictions on technology transfers (including royalties), and uncompensated television retransmission;
19. Nigeria's inadequate copyright (audio and video) enforcement;
20. Norway's lack of pharmaceutical product patent coverage;
21. Pakistan's lack of pharmaceutical product patent coverage, inadequate pharmaceutical process patent enforcement, permissive compulsory patent licensing, ineffective copyright enforcement (books and video), and inadequate trade and service mark protection;
22. The Philippines' permissive compulsory licensing and royalty restrictions regarding patents, inadequate trademark enforcement, and permissive cancellation, significant copyright limitations and audio/video appropriation, and royalty limitations on unpatented technology transfers;
23. Portugal's weak copyright (audio, video, and television) enforcement;
24. Spain's inadequate copyright (soft-

ware and video) enforcement and transitionally inadequate pharmaceutical and chemical product patent protection;

25. Taiwan's inadequate copyright (books, software, and video) and trademark enforcement, and lack of biotechnology and foodstuff coverage;

26. Thailand's lack of patent coverage for pharmaceuticals, foodstuffs, and agricultural machinery, short patent term, permissive compulsory licensing, inadequate trade and service mark protection, and inadequate copyright coverage (computer software) and enforcement;

27. Turkey's lack of pharmaceutical and biotechnology patent coverage and inadequate copyright (books, audio/video, and software) enforcement;

28. Venezuela's lack of patent subject matter coverage (unspecified), short patent term and patent licensing restrictions, inadequate trademark registration system and enforcement, and inadequate copyright (video) enforcement;

29. Yugoslavia's lack of pharmaceutical, alloy, and chemical product patent coverage and short patent term.

A SUGGESTED CLASSROOM PROJECT

Select a country identified in the problem sampler and prepare a brief report regarding (1) what changes, if any, have occurred in the country's intellectual property laws since 1989 (2) and whether such changes have responded to the concerns identified in the report.

2

Underlying Theories of International Intellectual Property Protection

The success of efforts to establish agreed-upon international intellectual property protection norms depends largely on the perceived impact which the adoption of such norms may have upon a country's economic and political development. Where restrictions on the use of intellectual property are seen as adversely impacting the ability of less-developed nations to establish an industrial base or to become sufficiently technologically advanced to compete in the global marketplace, such restrictions are often hotly contested. Terms such as "common heritage of mankind" are often used to defend the refusal or failure to provide strong intellectual property protection. By contrast, industrialized countries, which are generally perceived as exporters of intellectual property, rely upon the economic rights which inhere in "property" to defend strong protection standards. This Chapter focuses upon the underlying theories of intellectual property protection which inform the present debate. It begins with an analysis of the conflicting philosophical and economic theories underlying the intellectual property protection debate. It then examines the impact which the transplantation of non-domestic legal concepts may have on developing countries. The Chapter then concludes with a review of the theoretical basis for current efforts to harmonize domestic intellectual property laws.

A. Defining Intellectual Property

1. The Philosophical Debate Over the "Nature" of Intellectual Property

a. Utility or a Natural Right?[1]

The notion of rewarding the discoverer or creator for giving society a useful thing is ancient. Perhaps the earliest known recording of this idea is found in Aristotle's Politics, which dates back to the fourth century B.C. In a discussion of relative merits of different constitutional systems, Aristotle sharply criticizes a proposal by Hippodamus of Miletus, who called for a system of rewards to those who discover useful things. Hippodamus' proposal evinces the basic utilitarian philosophy that if you reward the creators of useful things, you get more useful things. Equally relevant is Aristotle's counterargument that such a system of individual reward may otherwise reduce social welfare. Aristotle's concern was that a reward for revealing information to the state would give rise to fraudulent claims of discovery of malfeasance on the part of public officials. The modern social welfare concern is that intellectual property rights, being legal monopolies, may place too heavy a burden on commerce and free trade.

---

[1] Paul Durdik, *Ancient Debate, New Technology: The European Community Moves to Protect Computer Databases,* 12 B.U. INT'L L.J. 153. Copyright 1994 Boston University International Law Journal. Excerpt reprinted with permission.

The schools of thought which have emerged have segregated themselves into two main camps, and tension arises between their conflicting philosophical underpinnings. On the one hand, the Utilitarians are closely allied with the labor theory of intellectual property, which teaches that property rights are rewards for the effort expended in creating the thing to be protected. This paradigm is known for its contributions to the various methodologies for calculating infringement damages. In contrast, the Natural Rights school teaches that a creator always has a moral right to her creative work. This paradigm is most often credited with the requirements of creativity or originality in works in order for them to be protected by copyright. Contrary to favoring either paradigm, copyright jurisprudence borrows heavily from both these schools, switching whenever convenient, often in mid-sentence.

b. The Theory of Property[2]

Every now and then, the rather discrete and insular world of scholars who care about intellectual property rules turns its collective attention to whether intellectual property is really property at all—or, to put the matter consistently with the vagaries of the field, whether intellectual property (whatever that is) is property (whatever that is) in the same sense that other things are property (whatever that is).

There are two different senses in which one might use the term property. The legal theorist will refer to property and mean the relevant set of legal relations. In ordinary language we will refer to property and have in mind a thing, a res, which implies an owner. Rarely do the two senses come into conflict.

Yet the conflict—or, more properly, the tension—is real. True, even Lockean property theory is not a pure natural law theory; Locke's vision was that property rights should inhere in the act of creation because that was how one would provide incentives to create. Yet it is useful to contrast the vision of property rights as adhering in creation from the vision of property rights as existing for other instrumental purposes. The contrast matters because if creation implies a property right in it, then the identity of the thing is less important; the more instrumental one's conception, the more the range of rights will vary with the perceived societal benefit of the production of the particular thing.

Intellectual property rules are deeply bound up in incentive structures—a point, perhaps, less teleological than communicative in nature. In other words, it may be that intellectual property rules do not reflect the ownership presumption because there is something unique about intellectual property itself that dictates a different set of considerations, but it is also possible that intellectual property rules tend to be different because we lack the guidance (and discipline) of coping with ordinary conversation about intellectual property. There isn't any ordinary conversation about intellectual property. Those who have no professional reason to be involved with it rarely think about it. (We tend to covet fancy homes, not valuable patents.)

And because there is no conversational discipline to force us to think of intellectual property in terms of commonsense everyday categories, we tend to think of it in ridiculous categories instead. This explains, for example, why courts and commentators constantly refer to intellectual property rights as monopolies—all right, limited monopolies—even though the typical proprietor of intellectual property lacks the market power (and often, as Edmund Kitch has noted, the incentive) to extract monopoly rents. But fooled by the inadequacy of the language used to describe intellectual property rights, the courts have treated them as presumptively dangerous, to be limited and hemmed in at every turn, lest the proprietors of these "monopolies" wreak havoc in the markets.

For the most part, beginning an analysis of intellectual property rules with a presumption of property instead of a presumption of dangerous monopoly would affect the law only at the margins.

There are some obvious patent law changes. Patent terms might be different—

---

[2] Stephen L. Carter; *Does It Matter Whether Intellectual Property Is Property?* 68 CHI.-KENT L. REV. 715. Copyright 1993 Chicago-Kent College of Law. Excerpt reprinted with permission.

indeed, there would be no reason to limit them. The consistent view that mathematical algorithms are not patentable, no matter how much investment might have been required to produce them, would be overturned. The patent misuse defense would be relegated to where it should be anyway: the field of antitrust, where it would be studied, correctly, as a barrier-to-entry problem.

Copyright law would probably show greater differences, for we would surely continue our march toward a recognition of the creator's moral rights, with all the difficulty and complexity that recognition entails. We might also be less finicky about whether creativity implies something other than "sweat of the brow," adopting something more akin to the patent standard under which creativity is not negatived by the way in which the invention is made. (Whether A owns the oil discovered on her land does not depend on whether she was looking for it or stumbled across it.)

The fair use field would continue to move toward a greater sensitivity to the market effects of a particular use that the creator says is infringement and the copier says is privileged. The Supreme Court, despite much criticism, has recently, and sensibly, treated the effect on the market for the copyrighted work as the most important of the four statutory factors. Although commentators have excoriated the Supreme Court for purportedly failing to take into account other societal interests—such as the interest in the dissemination of information—a conversational habit that begins with the property presumption might be too much for even so admittedly significant an interest to overcome. After all, our great societal interest in allowing everyone to enjoy the great outdoors allows the government to buy private land and turn it into parkland, or to allocate land it already owns for that purpose, but does not allow A to trespass on private land in order to enjoy the view.

Finally, consider the area of trademarks. Certainly, one may conceptualize trademarks as property in the Lockean sense, in the same way that one may conceptualize copyrights and patents in that way: they protect the creator's right to the intellectual products of the mind. Put otherwise, the bare fact that the creator has brought the res into existence is the reason for its protection.

In American law, of course, it is axiomatic that trademarks are not property in this sense. At common law, and, for the most part, in federal statutory trademark law as well, rights in a mark are said to flow from its use, not from its existence.

But if trademarks were entitled to the property presumption, much of this settled law would be swept away. If A's ownership rights in a mark come because she has thought it up and not because she has used it to distinguish her goods in commerce, there is certainly no reason to make her use it before she has any rights.

Were property rights in trademarks based on the act of intellectual creation, the law would still forbid the appropriation of a generic word from the market language: no intellectual activity would have gone into its creation. But the matter of genericide might be treated differently—although one wants to give the matter more thought. The public's effort to appropriate the mark would not change its status as the intellectual creation of a particular individual.

One might argue, of course, that the public should be able to take the mark by a process not unlike adverse possession or perhaps eminent domain. Adverse possession, however, seems the wrong analogy, at least in the case of a mark whose owner is actively promoting and protecting it. Eminent domain—taking the mark from its owner for the perceived needs of the public market language—is a far stronger analogy. But if genericide is like eminent domain, then the rest of the takings equation must follow as well: the owner should be compensated for the value of the property lost!

In short, if trademarks were property, the public would have to pay for its linguistic sloppiness—literally pay, in cash, to compensate the owner.

1. Locke and Intellectual Property[3]

Locke tells us that in the state of nature there is no positive law parceling out owner-

---

[3] Wendy J. Gordon, *A Property Right in Self-Expression: Equality and Individualism in the Natural Law of Intellectual Property*, 102 YALE L.J. 1533. Copyright 1993. Excerpt reprinted with permission.

ship or giving any particular person the right to command anyone else. There are, however, moral duties that constrain persons' behavior toward each other.

Locke argues that these duties are imposed by God and are discernable by reason. The state of nature differs from civil society primarily because the former lacks judges who can give binding interpretations of the law of nature to resolve individuals' conflicting claims. People form civil society precisely because its authorities will provide a security for natural rights which is unavailable in the state of nature.

Since all humanity is equal in the state of nature, the duties we owe others are also the duties they owe us, and the rights I have against others they have against me. One can discern in Locke's theory two general classes of rights: liberty rights (areas free of duty) and claim rights (areas where the rightholder is owed a duty by others). Using these two classes, one can identify four general sets of natural rights and duties particularly relevant to our discussion.

First and foremost, all persons have a duty not to harm others, except in some cases of extreme need. This right not to be harmed is lexically prior to the other natural rights; thus, except in cases of extreme need, the no-harm duty would prevail in any conflict arising between the no-harm duty and the other natural laws mentioned below. Second, there are two key liberty rights: 1) all persons have a liberty right to dispose of their efforts as they see fit, and 2) all persons have a liberty right to use the common—"the earth and all its fruits"—which God gave to humankind. These two liberty rights mean that, at least in the absence of extreme need, the law of nature gives no one a claim right over any other person's nonharmful use of her own efforts, or her nonharmful use of the common. Third, all persons have two central duties in regard to their resources. Each person has a duty to let others share in her resources (other than her body) in times of great need, so long as the sharer's own survival is not imperiled by such charity, and each has a duty to share any of her nonbodily resources which would otherwise spoil or go to waste. Fourth, all persons have a duty not to interfere with the resources others have appropriated or produced by laboring on the common. This duty is conditional, and is a keystone in the moral justification for property rights.

Taken together, these duties and liberties generate moral claims and entitlements. Of these, some we possess by virtue of what we do, and some we posses by virtue of our humanity. Of the humanity-based entitlements, three are most important: our claim right to be free from harm, our claim right to have a share of others' plenty in times of our great need, and our liberty right to use the common. We might call these three unearned rights "fundamental human entitlements."

As individuals we can take actions that cause us to deserve more or less than these fundamental human entitlements would dictate. Most notably, if we work productively, our labor may entitle us to own more goods than less industrious people are entitled to have. But by our own actions we cannot give ourselves a right to impair others' fundamental human entitlements. We cannot "earn" a right to harm others, or a right to impair their access to the common.

Locke's property theory has many strands, some of which are overtly utilitarian and others of which draw on varying notions of desert. To the extent that his theory purports to state a nonconsequentialist natural right in property, it is most firmly based on the most fundamental law of nature, the "no-harm principle." The essential logic is simple: Labor is mine and when I appropriate objects from the common I join my labor to them. If you take the objects I have gathered you have also taken my labor, since I have attached my labor to the objects in question. This harms me, and you should not harm me. You therefore have a duty to leave these objects alone. Therefore I have property in the objects.

Similarly, if I use the public domain to create a new intangible work of authorship or invention, you should not harm me by copying it and interfering with my plans for it. I therefore have property in the intangible as well.

Labor is not property. Property has at least two meanings in the law. We can say that "property" is any vested entitlement, or alternatively "property" can mean that particular complex of entitlements—such as the right to exclude and the power of transfer—usually associated with ownership. It is a mistake to think that only property in the latter sense is protected against harm. The positive law protects a wide variety of nonowned interests from malicious harm, even to the extent of invalidating a malicious property owner's ordinary entitlements. The interests that courts have protected range widely beyond property: examples range from mental tranquility to prospective advantages such as wild ducks not yet caught or barbers' customers. One need not approve these particular cases or doctrines to recognize that an interest is not disqualified from all protection simply because it is not ownable in the usual sense. These cases and doctrines seek to protect something from harm in which the claimant has an interest or stake. Does Lockean labor invested in a tangible or intangible item constitute such a stake?

Locke himself offered no precise definition of the kind of appropriative labor that could give rise to a property claim, and his notion of labor has been much debated. The ambiguities of his text are multiplied when one tries to extrapolate from its physical examples, such as picking up acorns, drawing water from the river, or putting land under cultivation, to the intangible realm. Some things, however, are fairly clear. Aimless effort is not labor. Appropriative labor involves altering what was in the common in a way that makes it usable and thus more valuable to humanity. It may also involve a kind of psychological identification, an "infusion of personality." Most important from the perspective of the laborer's claim, however, is the laborer's purposiveness. A stranger's taking of another's labored-on objects is likely to merit legal intervention only if the taking interferes with a goal or project to which the laborer has purposely directed her effort. If the taking does interfere, the actor needs some special justification for doing it. The scope of the laborer's purpose will help to define the scope of the rights she can assert.

The idea that copying intellectual products cannot be harmful because intellectual products are physically inexhaustible "public goods," would appear to lack merit. Copying can harm important interests even if the copying does not deprive the creator of physical use of her creation. For example, if someone creates music not only for the sake of listening to it herself, but also for the purpose of feeding herself by selling the royalties to it, she can be harmed by a bootleg copyist as severely as if he took the physical sheet music out of her den or stole the food she had bought. The intellectual laborer requires some kind of anti-copying protection if her property in her creations is to be meaningful.

There are, however, some differences between tangible and intangible property that may be relevant from a normative standpoint. When a stranger takes the apples another has labored to pick, he steps into the laborer's shoes; by the terms of the hypothesized situation, the laborer and the stranger are the same except insofar as one has labored and one has not, so the stranger is no better situated than the laborer was to eat, sell, or make pies from the fruit. From an economic perspective, therefore, the transfer of apples to the stranger's possession has no predictable allocative significance except insofar as it may alter laborers' future incentives in negative ways—discouraging labor and encouraging laborers to make wasteful expenditures on defensive measures to protect their harvests. By contrast, if a stranger copies an intangible product, he is not stepping into the laborer's shoes. Since the copyist does not divest the laborer of possession, the copying adds another source of the intellectual product to the world. If the copyist distributes many copies to the public, it will decrease the "deadweight loss" to which an author's right against copying almost always gives rise. Unlike physical takings, then, copying produces a positive short-term allocative effect which could outweigh its long-term negative incentive effects on future creators. Does this difference in potential economic effect justify the harm caused by the copyist stranger in a way that the harm caused by apple-taking stranger cannot be justified? From a Lockean perspective, it does not.

For the public's needs to justify harming the laborer they must have some particular moral weight, such as claims based on exigency ("charity"), or the public's own right to have unharmed access to the common. Nothing in a natural-rights framework gives the public the *per se* entitlement to cheap access to what the laborer has produced. As I have argued elsewhere, the public has no prima facie right to the price and quantity of intellectual products that would be available in a world devoid of intellectual property law. The public has no more right to the "benefit of another's pains" than the apple-taking stranger had.

"Deadweight loss" merely measures the difference between what society gains from an intellectual product distributed subject to anticopying restraints, and what society would gain from a freely-copied intellectual product. Avoiding "deadweight loss" is a natural right only if the public has a right to free copying. As just discussed, it has no such right. Granting laborers anticopying rights that may make some works more expensive or less accessible thus does not deny the public anything to which it is entitled, with the result that the unconsented copyist who harms the laborer is not justified by the benefit his act may give the public. The claims of the laborer who produces intangibles and the claims of the laborer who works with physical objects are therefore of equal strength.

In a civilized society, human beings create the reality around them. Our direct surroundings are buildings and landscape architecture rather than woods and natural water. To be a creative maker of new meanings, a rational being needs access to her heritage. Just as land is necessary for farmers to bring forth fruit (in Locke's imagery), a common of previously-created intangibles is necessary for creators to bring forth new works of the imagination. Too broad a set of intellectual property rights gives one set of persons potential control over how that "created" reality can be interpreted. In other words, it can give them control over what the world means. Such control would deny others the understanding, or "naming," that is one crucial way humans interact with the world.

New creators inevitably and usefully build on predecessors. In her invention of techniques, discoveries, ideas, or themes, the new creator speaks out of a history, and the very value of her contribution will depend upon her advancing upon what has come before. The inventor of the automobile builds on one predecessor's invention of metal-smelting processes, another predecessor's invention of gears, another predecessor's invention of the wheel, and ultimately on the efforts of some Promethean cave-dweller who, in discovering how to make fire, laid the groundwork for the internal combustion engine. The pattern is not limited to the technological culture. Artists learn from predecessors the laws of perspective, the uses of oils, acrylics, and watercolors, and the very traditions that give meaning to their productions. As for music, it is often argued that there is a limited vocabulary available for musical composition, and that composers will inevitably and necessarily work in a received tradition, as well as re-use prior themes. Communication depends on a common language and common experience. Labor itself is guided and organized by anterior ideas.

One cannot assume that early creators or their heirs would consent to the use of property by others to create new intellectual products if the first creators had control of these necessary prior resources. Some owners might consent to others' use without demanding compensation. Some might agree to compensated use. But others might refuse to sell altogether or charge more than the new creators can afford. More significantly, the cost of tracing ownership and effecting transactions could itself be prohibitive, particularly for fundamental ideas of fairly ancient origin, such as the discovery of perspective. For example, basic story ideas are fundamental building blocks in this way. From Romeo and Juliet to West Side Story and beyond, the plot in which children from warring factions fall in love has provided fruitful ground for a host of authors. Yet it took a twentieth-century decision of the Second Circuit Court of Appeals to make clear this story idea could not be owned. Had the decision been otherwise, who knows how many potential claimants could demand a toll from the next film producer to come along.

Thus, if perpetual property existed in all intangibles, many creators would have to choose between using someone else's property without permission, or forgoing creation of their own. Because of transaction costs, the possibility of transferring rights through the market would not help substantially. For new creators to flourish, they must be able to draw on an array of prior creations that are not privately owned.

Many commentators have indeed suggested that intellectual property rights cost no one anything. For example, Steven N.S. Cheung recently traced the "something-for-nothing" thesis from Jeremy Bentham, through J.B. Say and John Stuart Mill, to J.B. Clark, and applied it to patents: "If the patented article is something which society without a patent system would not have secured at all—the inventor's monopoly hurts nobody. His gains consist in something which no one loses, even while he enjoys them." That is, if A makes something that did not exist before, excluding B from using it will arguably leave B unharmed. In Lockean terms, the claim is that because B still has free access to the same public domain elements that A had, her ability to use the common is unimpaired.

If indeed a creative person creates something, and denying others access to it imposes no costs on the latter, then giving the creator rights of exclusivity would seem justified. But there is no reason to suppose that rights to intangibles invariably conform to this pattern. Mill was wrong to suggest that no one ever "loses" by being prohibited from "sharing in what otherwise would not have existed at all." That an intellectual product is new, would not have otherwise existed, and may initially bring benefit to the public, does not guarantee that later exclusions from it will be harmless.

Consent does not eliminate the problem. In a pervasive media culture there will always be "seepage"—some ideas and some images will impinge on one's consciousness whether or not one has sought them out. If there is only one culture (and whether technological or literary culture is at issue, the point is the same), a person who wishes to contribute to it usually is required to use the tools of that culture. Giving first creators ownership over any aspect of the culture, even if that aspect is newly created, may make a later creator less well off than he or she would have been without the new creation. Intellectual products, once they are made public in an interdependent world, change that world. To deal with those changes, users may have need of a freedom inconsistent with first creators' property rights. If they are forbidden to use the creation that was the agent of the change, all they will have to work from will be the now devalued common. The proviso eliminates this danger. It guarantees an equality between earlier and later creators. The proviso would thus ensure later comers a right to the broad freedom of expression, interpretation, and reaction which earlier creators had, a right which cannot be outweighed by other sorts of benefits.

Current intellectual property systems give rights in excess of what a Lockean model would justify. For example, American patent law gives a patentee exclusive rights enabling her to prohibit persons who independently invent the same thing from using the product of their own labors. Such an expansive set of rights, clearly not justified by a Lockean system, can only be justified by reference to norms other than natural rights. Similarly, copyright law gives authors rights over the "derivative works" that others make by building on their creations. To be justified under a Lockean notion of labor, the derivative work right would have to be quite narrow, giving an initial creator control over only those new works by others that significantly interfere with her own plans for the work. Yet current copyright law is not so limited; authors are entitled to control derivative works that they did not anticipate and that do not interfere with their own plans. If such legal rights, not justified by natural law, impose a net harm on the public, the natural law right against unjustified harm might well condemn them. For such legal rights to be justified, therefore, a cost-benefit analysis would have to show that they represent a net benefit to society. To the extent these doctrines produce net positive economic results for the public, they can be justified, at least to the extent that they do not infringe any of the public's nonfungible interests.

Even more clearly, the public is owed compensation if courts or legislatures violate the proviso by creating private rights that impair the public's access to the common. As discussed above, the common is a species of property. And as the Takings Clause of the [US] Constitution's Fifth Amendment indicates, when government takes property, it should pay. What is true for private property should be true for public property as well. When the government infringes the public's natural rights, it should pay compensation. Intellectual property law can be crafted to do precisely this. The legislature and the judiciary can ensure that they grant rights that infringe some fungible interest safeguarded by the proviso only when the law also gives the public compensatory benefits, particularly in terms of providing incentives. Thus, although the natural-rights approach is usually thought to be inconsistent with a public-benefits approach to intellectual property, it in fact supports a demand that significant components of intellectual property law be crafted to serve the public benefit.

2. Hegel, Individual Will and Non-Western Cultures[4]

Patents and other types of intellectual property rights are intended to prevent people from commercially exploiting ideas or inventions without fair compensation to the originators. The concept comprises two competing social objectives: the need to encourage technical innovation and the need to disperse the benefits of that innovation throughout society. These objectives compete because the market forces that encourage one discourage the other. Decreasing a good's price tends to increase its dispersion. But if the price of acquiring the innovation includes only the cost of raw material (that is, if the idea itself costs nothing), then the inventor gets no market compensation for his or her effort. If inventors have no economic incentive to invent, those who are motivated by profit will come up with fewer innovations to be dispersed. Conversely, as inventors are able to obtain more monopoly rent through their patents, their ideas will cost society more. As the monopoly rent increases, the innovations will be less widely dispersed and the social benefits will diminish.

As in many other political cultures, the way Europeans dealt with intellectual property in particular was shaped by the way they thought of property in general. Hegel, Locke, and other European political philosophers wrote that property was one of the rights defining individual liberty. Hegel's conception of property is perhaps most directly applicable to the narrower notion of intellectual property: he wrote that property is, among other things, the means by which an individual could objectively express a personal, singular will. "In property," he noted, "a person exists for the first time as reason."[5] Hegel's civil society is an environment in which an individual aspires to establish a unique place, and property is the vehicle by which one's self-identity is acknowledged by others who are similarly striving for self-identity.

Locke wrote that in a primitive society where all resources are initially held in common, objects become property through an individual's labor: gathering the acorns, killing the deer, tilling the land.[6] As society matures, money becomes an expedient surrogate for the value of an individual's labor. Still, the essence of property rests not with an object's material characteristics, but in the thought and effort exerted by the individual upon that object to make it useful.

Two aspects of Hegel and Locke are pertinent to understanding the European traditions behind intellectual property. First is the importance given to individual human will in justifying and defining property. The "quiddity" of property is an intellectual phenomenon that arises from the way individuals conceive of themselves in their material environment. Property may therefore be the exertion of will over the transformation of material things, or it may be the exertion of intellect to create new ideas. Either would contribute to the Hegelian sense of self-identity, so a society that values individual liberty would seek to protect both.

Secondly, the European tradition places the individual and society in a relationship that is at least partially adversarial. Both Hegel and Locke envision civil society as a constraining environment for individuals aspiring to establish unique moral meaning. The marketplace is the arbiter through which an individual tries to establish and protect self-identity through voluntary exchange of property representing the individual's will. Society is thus very limited in its right to prevent an individual's fair accumulation, holding, and dispensation of prop-

---

4 David Hurlbut, *Fixing the Biodiversity Convention: Toward a Special Protocol for Related Intellectual Property,* 34 NAT. RESOURCES. J. 379. Copyright 1994, David Hurlbut. Excerpt reprinted with permission.

5 G. HEGEL, PHILOSOPHY OF RIGHT 235-6.

6 J. LOCKE, SECOND TREATISE OF GOVERNMENT 303-320.

erty. The needs of society per se would not justify taking an individual's property—including property in the form of ideas—without fair compensation.

European lawmakers recognized early the social utility of intellectual property rights; the evolution of intellectual property rights lagged only slightly behind the evolution of tangible property rights in European legal traditions. During the Renaissance, patent rights were bestowed by royalty or, as in the case of Italian city-states, by the ruling aristocracy. In the 18th and 19th centuries, the European trading powers entered into compacts providing for the mutual recognition of each others' patents. This culminated in 1883 with the International Convention for the Protection of Industrial Property, which included not only the major European trading powers but their colonies as well.

The European tradition of honoring patents was internationalized through the institutions of colonialism. That is, intellectual property rights were honored in Europe and by the Europeans who were governing Africa, Asia, and the Americas. But what about the post-colonial era, from 1945 to the present? It does not necessarily follow that the now-empowered indigenous political cultures of the developing world regard the ownership of ideas in the same way as their former colonial rulers. Indeed, some have attitudes toward tangible property that are squarely at odds with the views of Hegel, Locke, and other European political thinkers.

Many non-European political cultures do not assume an adversarial relationship between individual and society. Islamic and some African cultures go so far as to define self-identity not according to individual liberty but according to the individual's relationship with and contribution to society. What exists in many parts of the world is a non-utilitarian social paradigm in which "right" is not a function of individual good. Concepts of property are therefore different; if individual liberty is not the basis for self-identity, then the moral foundations of property must rest somewhere else.

In Ghana and other African countries, many indigenous societies considered tribal land and other economic resources the property of the tribe's ancestors. The symbol of this communal ownership was the stool on which the tribal chief sat; the chief was the personification of the living generation who had a fiduciary trust for future generations. Extended families and sometimes individuals could obtain a right of usufruct for tribal property such as land. A tribe member could then engage in agriculture and other economic activities that would benefit the user's extended family in particular and the tribe in general. Returning benefits to the tribe was the moral rationale behind the right of usufruct.

Intellectual property was not a particularly relevant concept for the Africans themselves because their traditions had no need for it. European patent law was introduced in Ghana and the rest of west Africa at the end of the 19th century largely in the interests of European gold mining companies. After independence in the 1960s and 1970s, Nigeria and other African countries discarded their inherited British-style patent laws and adopted new ones based on principles more consistent with their traditional values and more expedient to development. Nigeria's patent law, adopted in the 1970s, specifically excludes biological products and processes from patent protection and further says that other specific kinds of products can be deemed not patentable by decree in the interest of society as a whole.

In India, the cultural underpinnings of property have been chaotically shaped by conquest, feudalism, and colonialism. The moghul invasion of northern India brought with it a wholesale rearrangement of land ownership. The Muslim conquerors parceled out land to a system of feudal military lords who were to provide troops to the emperor if needed. As the Muslim conquerors were absorbed into the fabric of Hindu society, the institutions of feudalism were continued by the zamindars—the privileged landowners' class. When the British came in the 17th century, they found it expedient to allow the feudal system to remain largely intact. They consolidated their colonial domination in 1793 by recognizing the legal validity of the zamindars' holdings. Zamindars were responsible for paying taxes on their land, which was usually being cultivated and made productive by tenant farmers. At the same time, the zamindars were able to call on British forces to enforce their claims against challenges from outside their class.

With its traditions of land ownership so

broken throughout its history, India has had to rely on political dialogue to shape its philosophy of property. Throughout the first half of the twentieth century and up through independence in 1947, three distinct ideologies struggled against one another to define the economic relationship between the individual and the state in India: Western-style market liberalism, advocated by Sardar Vallabhbhai Patel; Soviet-style centrally planned socialism, advocated by Pandit Jawaharlal Nehru; and Mahatma Gandhi's vision of decentralized village-based social reform. Both Gandhi and Nehru believed that social reform leading to economic self-sufficiency and the alleviation of poverty was more important than the individual right of property, although Gandhi's political methods attempted to co-opt the propertied classes so that they would voluntarily participate in social reform.

Patel's political strength after Gandhi's death in 1948 enabled him to make economic liberalism the guiding philosophy behind the constitution that was drafted in 1949. When Patel died in 1950, Nehru attempted to institute both Gandhian social reforms and socialist economic planning but found himself constrained by the constitution and the propertied interests that dominated party politics and the civil service in many states.

Independent India has never offered strong protection for many kinds of patents, trademarks, and copyrights. Its rationale has been that alleviating the country's poverty is more important than any individual's right to derive monopoly rent from an idea. Pharmaceuticals in particular are freely copied in India with the result that medicines are available for as little as 7 to 20 percent of the cost of comparable drugs in the United States. Considering that its gross domestic product per capita in 1991 was $340 compared to $21,000 in the United States, India's economic incentive to maintain this price difference is substantial.

Because many of the world's political cultures differ so widely from European norms, and because concepts of property are shaped by the political cultures out of which they arise, one cannot assume that intellectual property laws will or should be the same from one country to another. Which social goal is to take precedence: rewarding pharmaceutical firms that come up with new medications or distributing the medications as widely as possible by keeping the prices low? Is it more important to reward biotechnology firms for developing high-yield varieties of crops and hardy livestock or to maximize the nation's agricultural productivity by enabling farmers to obtain the new seed and animal varieties as cheaply as possible? The way a country chooses to balance these conflicting goals is reflected in its domestic patent regime. Different political cultures make different choices, and sometimes there is no unanimity even among industrially advanced countries. Table 1 lists the countries that exclude pharmaceuticals, pharmaceutical processes, and plant and animal varieties (for the most part, new strains of livestock and crops) from patent protection.

The relevant point is not that the European philosophy of intellectual property is correct and everyone else in the world is wrong—or vice versa. What the foregoing discussion shows is more basic: that there are many different historic and cultural assumptions about the ownership of ideas. Were it not for trade, international law would be unconcerned with so many different national regimes for intellectual property because each would be strictly a matter of domestic policy. But the fact is that nations do trade, so the differences matter.

Fair participation in the global market depends on rules that bind each nation equally, otherwise market distortions will place some nations at a disadvantage. If the European individual-rights philosophy were to be the international norm for intellectual property rights, many pharmaceuticals and other new products would not be widely dispersed in the world's poorest countries where a great need for those products exists. On the other hand, if the socially oriented philosophy of many non-European cultures were the norm, then inventors (primarily European and American firms) would be deprived of some amount of compensation for their research and development. The choice may be distilled to an even more basic level: should individual rights or social well-being be the basic principle behind an international regime of intellectual property?

When sanctioned or encouraged by a government, the piracy of intellectual property obtained through trade with other countries is analogous to nationalization of foreign assets. The difference is that instead of tangible property such as oil field equipment or copper mines, the value being taken is monopoly rent created by a patent or copyright. The rent that would have been repatriated to the foreign inventor had the patent or copyright been protected is instead kept in the economy of the pirating country. Domestic patent royalties are similarly affected.

The factors that make intellectual property nationalization possible are virtually the same as those that make other kinds of nationalization possible. Only a sovereign government can create the administrative infrastructure necessary to enforce an intellectual property regime. If the government deliberately chooses not to do so, there is little any outside government can do. Even trade sanctions might cost the industrially advanced countries more than their affected industries would lose in patent rent.

Nationalizing tangible foreign property such as oil rigs has the immediate effect of adding to a country's domestic capital stock without any national savings having been invested. The net capital stock increases by government fiat, thus freeing a certain portion of national savings for investment in other productive processes elsewhere in the domestic economy. Like capital equipment, a patented idea is an input to a productive process, and the rent created by a patent constitutes a specific bundle of value that is normally part of the final price. By not protecting a foreign patent, however, the bundle of value that constituted the patent's monopoly rent does not show up in the final price; it stays in the pockets of consumers and thereby adds to the net wealth in the domestic economy. Nationalized monopoly rents, by taking the form of lower consumer prices, thus result in a net increase in social benefit in the economy without any domestic savings having been used. The increased social benefit is essentially the same as what results from nationalizing foreign-owned capital equipment: an increase in productive capacity—or similarly, a reduction in production costs—that otherwise would have been stimulated only by the investment of domestic savings.

The real policy question, therefore, is whether a developing country can get away with pirating intellectual property—or, to turn the question around, whether rich industrial countries can force poor countries to pay monopoly prices for goods protected by patent and copyright laws that exist in the rich countries but not in the poor ones. Moral arguments are inconclusive, so policy will largely be determined by who has the strongest economic leverage: the pirating country, or the country seeking to extract the monopoly rent offered by intellectual property protection.

QUESTIONS AND COMMENTS FOR YOUR CONSIDERATION

1. Fritz Machlup described the natural law theory with respect to the protection of patents as follows:

> The "natural-law" thesis assumes that man has a natural property right in his own ideas. Appropriation of his ideas by others, that is, their unauthorized use, must be condemned as stealing. Society is morally obligated to recognize and protect this property right. Property is, in essence, exclusive. Hence, enforcement of exclusivity in the use of a patented invention is the only appropriate way for society to recognize this property right.

Compare this view of "natural law" with Locke's labor view espoused in prior articles. What limitations does this view fail to consider? Machlup rejected this reasoning as a basis for granting patents. Are there non "natural law" bases for patent grants? What are they?

2. Given the differing philosophical foundations for various countries' treatment of intellectual property, can uniform international standards for the protection of intellectual property realistically be established? Do differing philosophical

foundations necessarily preclude international consensus? What reply would you make to those who espouse the differing theories set forth in these excerpts?

3. Do these articles suggest any way to balance an author or inventor's "property" interests with society's interest in relatively unrestricted access to such property?

4. For an examination of the conflicting philosophical foundations of copyright and the impact these conflicts have upon reaching international agreement regarding the protection of so-called "moral" or "non-economic" rights, *see* Chapter Six.

2. Defining Protected Values

a. Appellations of Origin[7]

Appellations of origin (*appellations d'origine*) are geographical denominations that indicate a product's origin, as well as particularly distinctive and renowned qualities associated with the location.

Within the broad classification of geographical terms, laws in some countries distinguish between indications of source and appellations of origin. An indication of source (indication de provenance) is merely a name designating a product by its source. Unlike an appellation of origin, an indication of source does not represent particularly distinctive or renowned qualities associated with the product's origin , although both designations refer to geographic locations.

France has been particularly adamant and outspoken in favor of stricter protection of appellations of origin for a variety of reasons. Foremost among them is that appellations of origin are common particularly in the wine and cheese industries.

In general, French laws are much more protective of domestic and foreign trade names and producers' rights. Further, France's long history of deference to geographic appellations establishes these laws firmly in practice and tradition. In contrast to the French system, United States law is less protective and primarily directed toward consumer protection. International conflicts develop because United States law permits domestic producers to use freely many foreign appellations of origin that would be legally protected in their countries of origin. For example, "champagne" is an appellation of origin in France and Britain, but not in the United States.

[7] Lrie E. Simon, *Appellations of Origin: The Continuing Controversy,* 5 J. INTL. L. BUS. 132. Copyright 1983 Northwestern School of Law. Excerpt reprinted with permission.

A QUESTION FOR YOUR CONSIDERATION

Both NAFTA and TRIPS (*see Appendices VIII and IX,* respectively) provide stricter protection for appellations of origin. How do these treaties resolve the problems of previously conflicting treatment for such appellations?

b. Technology and Wealth[8]

There is no general agreement on exactly what constitutes technology or how technology should be defined. The United Nations, in a document designed to help countries plan their technological development, has adopted a very broad view of technology,

[8] David M. Haug, *The International Transfer of Technology: Lessons That East Europe Can Learn From the Failed Third World Experience,* 5 HARV. J.L. & TECH. 209. Copyright 1992 The President and Fellows of Harvard College. Excerpt reprinted with permission.

referring to it as "a combination of equipment and knowledge." Other commentators, after acknowledging the ambiguity of technology and the fruitlessness of trying to define it with specificity, have settled on a more functional description. For example, some refer to technology as the systematic application of scientific or other organized knowledge into practical tasks. The developed countries appear to have adopted this functional definition. The Organization for Economic Co-Operation and Development ("OECD"), which includes many of the developed nations of the world, proposed that "technology means the systematic knowledge for the manufacture of a product, for the application of a process or for the rendering of a service, including any integrally associated managerial and marketing techniques."

Defining technology functionally adds an element of subjectivity. If "technology is, in fact, the use of scientific knowledge by a given society at a given moment to resolve concrete problems facing its development." then what constitutes technology will vary with the culture and with the level of development.

Authorities have had similar difficulties defining "technology transfer." There has been a general consensus that any workable definition of technology transfer must be functional rather than formal; however the specific definitions have varied. One scholar defined it as "the process by which science and technology are diffused throughout human activity." Another labeled it "the transmission of know-how to suit local conditions." Nevertheless, both authors were careful to point out that the transfer of technology requires a functional component—in order for there to be a true transfer of technology, there must be effective absorption of the transferred technology by the recipient country. Another commentator elaborated, "the important factor in defining technology transfer is that the recipient acquires the capability to manufacture itself a product whose quality is comparable to that manufactured by the technology supplier."

The traditional method of transferring technology has been through investment in wholly owned and controlled subsidiaries. Not surprisingly, this is the form of transfer that transnational corporations favor. They invest in developing markets in order "to protect the existing market, to create new markets, to bypass prohibitive barriers and import restrictions, to take advantage of cheap labor and skills, and to discover or protect raw materials." These interests can best be fulfilled by retaining ownership and control of the technology transferred to a foreign market incident to an investment in that market. Actually transferring the production technology to the foreign country would simply create unnecessary and unwanted competition and diminish profitability.

Joint ventures are long-term relationships involving the pooling of assets, joint management, profit and risk sharing, joint marketing, servicing, and production. In a typical agreement, technology is transferred primarily through technical liaisons, training, and continuing operational support. Perhaps most valuable, the transferring firm generally provides the recipient with on-going technical changes as they are developed during the life of the agreement. Foreign investors have recently become increasingly willing to participate in joint ventures and partnerships with firms in developing countries, so long as the majority of the equitable ownership remains in the hands of the transnational corporation.

Developing countries often lack a strong technological infrastructure, *i.e.*, the "support systems" that are necessary for the specific technology to function effectively. These support systems include hardware, technological education, the level of process technologies in the receiving firms, the capability to perform R & D work, and the ability to maintain technology and organizational infrastructure.

One of the consistent problems that third world nations have faced in successfully importing technology is that the technology acquired from developed nations is ill-suited to the third world's needs: "Technology is not usually produced directly for sale." It is therefore not normally developed for use in the third world. The small technology markets in developing countries and the limited profit-making opportunities they offer discourages technology exporters from adapting their technology to meet the particular circumstances of developing countries. Instead, corporations will offer the same technology that they sell in developed countries.

Developing nations are also often unable to discern their technology needs. Recipients normally choose technology based on imperfect information. The breadth of choices is often so overwhelming that the recipient is unaware of the full range of alternatives. This problem has become known as the "information paradox." The idea is that when someone is looking to acquire technology, he is ignorant of exactly what he is getting, otherwise there would be no need to acquire it. This paradox reveals that in transfer agreements there is always an element of suboptimality of information, which often leads to inappropriate technology being transferred.

By pursuing a "technology at any cost" strategy, developing countries failed to import technology at a rate that would allow them to study the imported information so as to develop internal sources of its production. The attempt by developing countries to leap stages of development by the importation of technology significantly in advance of the technological skills of the recipient economy will mean both that the technology is inexpertly utilized, and that the relevant expertise is not given an opportunity to develop. This failure has contributed to the underlying problem—the technological dependence of many third world nations. The dependence is likely to continue until those nations are able to increase their ability to deal with and develop technology.

The final reason cited for the difficulties that third world nations have had in developing technologically is that most of them lack a coherent, strategic plan for development: "The immediate post-war or post-independence period in the developing countries was marked by a total absence of any policy specifically dealing with technology." Although the last decade has seen the developing countries enact laws and regulations dealing with imports of technology, the legislative policies have been largely ad hoc and uncoordinated in nature and have had a short term perspective.

QUESTIONS AND COMMENTS FOR YOUR CONSIDERATION

1. To what extent does the problem of the scope of protection afforded a particular form of intellectual property result from a failure to achieve agreement on the definition of the bundle of rights to be protected?

2. Can the problems discussed above regarding developing nations' efforts to obtain effective technology transfers be corrected through treaties establishing intellectual property protection norms?

3. What is the effect on investment resulting from the absence of intellectual property laws or the lack of enforcement of such laws?

4. Do intellectual property laws help meet some or even the most important challenges facing developing countries?

5. If protecting intellectual property rights increases the cost of use of the property in question, why should developing countries grant such protection to needed technology?

6. For a further discussion of the problems posed by the emergence of new technologies, *see* Chapter Thirteen.

B. Economic Considerations

1. International Trade

a. Intellectual Property and International Trade[9]

From one angle, intellectual property rights derogate from the norms of free competition in order to overcome the "public goods" problem inherent in the commercial exploitation of intangible creations and to elevate routine technical skills to progressively higher levels.

The changing nature of innovation under modern conditions, and the corresponding pressure such changes exert on conventional assumptions about the nature of competition itself, have exacerbated this unsatisfactory state of affairs. Almost without realizing it, let alone questioning it, traditional legal lore has assumed that manufacturers of most unpatented goods sold on the general products market can fend for themselves without governmental intervention to restrain the exercise of their competitors' legal rights to imitate. To this end, the patent system functions negatively by driving all unpatented innovation onto the general products market where free competition prevails.

The mixture of legal norms applicable to intellectual creations, including trade regulation laws, is evolving in two opposing directions. One trend favors the reduction of market-distorting practices that affect both domestic and international trade in the traditional objects of protection; the other tends to increase legal restraints on trade, including barriers to entry, affecting new objects of protection that would otherwise have to endure the rigors of free competition.

By providing exclusive property rights in return for the production of scarce intellectual goods, statutory intellectual property law seeks to overcome the risk of market failure that inheres in public goods generally and to ensure that free-riders do not appropriate the benefits that would otherwise accrue to investors in research and development. The positive role of these disciplines is widely acknowledged despite a lack of empirical support. Nevertheless, policymakers concerned to promote investment in important new technologies often overstate the supposed benefits of specific intellectual property regimes while ignoring the negative economic functions of these regimes in relation to the complementary operations of competition law generally. If it was true that intellectual property laws balanced incentives to create against opportunities to compete in the specialized markets for qualifying intellectual goods, a healthy by-product of these laws was that courts and legislators traditionally drove nonqualifying intellectual goods onto the general products market where free competition prevailed. The negative economic functions of a mature patent system, for example, have been summarized in the following terms:

1. Nonpatented innovations remain subject to price competition and are free to imitate if disclosed;
2. Undisclosed, unpatentable innovations are free to reverse engineer but not to steal;
3. Patented inventions are not infringed by nonequivalent innovation;
4. Unfair competition law may not repress product imitation in the absence of confusion.

While providing temporary monopolies to stimulate the production of high-risk, intangible creations, intellectual property law supplies statutory periods of artificial lead time to compensate, at least in part, for the loss of natural lead time that occurs when intellectual goods are subject to rapid imitation. When no statutory exclusive rights apply, the availability of natural lead time largely depends on unfair competition norms operating through laws protecting trade secrets and confidential information. What seems insufficiently understood is that these laws determine the pace and direction of competition based on ordinary or routine skills by requiring second comers to reverse-engineer undisclosed, unpatented innovation by proper means.

In practice, the mesh between intellectual property law and the laws governing confidentiality and trade secrets was imperfect even during the nineteenth century, when

---

[9] J.H. Reichman, *Beyond The Historical Lines of Demarcation: Competition Law, Intellectual Property Rights, And International Trade After The Gatt's Uruguay Round,* 20 BROOK. J. INT'L L. 75. Copyright 1993 by the Brooklyn Law School. Excerpt reprinted with permission.

traditional forms of engineering occupied the forefront of attention and clear lines still separated theoretical from applied science as well as industrial from artistic property laws. Of particular concern in this period were commercial designs, both aesthetic and functional in nature, whose creative contribution is usually embodied in products sold on the general products market. Because neither classical intellectual property law nor classical trade secret law guaranteed industrial designers sufficient lead time against slavish duplication, free-riding second comers could appropriate the benefits accruing from investment in innovative design without contributing to the costs of research and development. As a result, both statutory intellectual property laws and the general laws of unfair competition are still struggling to fill this gap in most industrialized countries.

By now it has become evident that today's information technologies, together with other important new technologies, such as integrated circuit designs and biogenetic engineering, slip through the cracks between intellectual property law and trade secret law into that same netherworld of chronically insufficient lead time that previously engulfed industrial art. Stated simply, today's most valuable technologies often fail to meet the nonobvious standard of patent law because they partake of merely incremental advances beyond the prior art, while their functional character remains alien to both the spirit and economic assumptions of copyright law, which implements cultural rather than industrial policies. Yet, such technologies obtain little or no natural lead time in classical trade secret law because they consist essentially of intangible scientific or technical know-how that becomes embodied in products sold on the open market. Any third parties who obtain the tangible products can quickly duplicate the valuable information they contain and thereby appropriate the fruits of the innovator's investment in research and development, with no corresponding investment of their own. Under modern conditions, in other words, a major problem with the kinds of innovative know-how underlying important new technologies is that they do not lend themselves to secrecy even when they represent the fruit of enormous investment in research and development. Because third parties can rapidly duplicate the embodied information and offer virtually the same products at lower prices than those of the originators, there is no secure interval of lead time in which to recuperate the originators' initial investment or their losses from unsuccessful essays, not to mention the goal of turning a profit.

Responding to the lack of protection for applied scientific know-how as such, governments have tended either to deform the patent and copyright laws in an effort to accommodate subject matter for which the classical regimes are inherently unsuited or to multiply hybrid legal regimes granting exclusive property rights to unpatentable innovation that has nowhere else to go. Both tendencies generate cumulative protectionist effects that offset the long-term competitive gains expected from major harmonization exercises.

Under the rubric of recent developments, one may note a revived interest in the patenting of computer programs (despite a successful campaign to bring software within the Berne Convention on the excuse that patents were unavailable); a legislative proposal to lower the nonobviousness standard for biogenetic processes affecting recombinant DNA in the United States; and a proposal to protect noncopyrightable databases under *sui generis* regimes in the European Union. The protection of plant varieties internationally has shifted from a modified copyright approach to a modified patent approach without elevating the prerequisites of eligibility, just when most developing countries will find themselves obliged to protect plant varieties under the TRIPS Agreement.

To complete the picture, one should recall that the protection of innovative functional designs under patent-like standards in the utility model laws some countries enacted a long time ago has given way to mandatory protection of virtually all integrated circuit designs on modified copyright principles in countries adhering to the GATT. This, in turn, has led the United Kingdom to protect virtually all functional designs in an unregistered design right, operating on modified copyright principles, that requires no appreciable creative contribution to qualify. A variant of the United Kingdom's unregistered design right has been endorsed by the Commission of the European Union, and wholesale protection of functional designs in the European Union would increase the pressure on the United States to follow suit. Meanwhile, the United States federal courts already protect product configurations for an indefinite period of time under a spurious theory of "appearance trade dress;" the Swiss unfair competition law of 1986 permits innovators to interdict slavish imitation of technologically novel products until the costs of research and development have been recuperated; and the Japanese unfair competition law of 1993 prohibits slavish imitation of most product configurations for a period of three years.

These developments compromise the competitive ethos from within. Traditionally, trade secrets laws invest competitors with an absolute right to imitate every unpatented, noncopyrightable product provided they reverse-engineer its innovative features by proper means. Notwithstanding the competitive mandate handed down from the nineteenth century, the overall trend today is to override classical free-market premises and to organize in their stead a system in which virtually every product sold on the products market comes freighted with the exclusive rights of intellectual property laws.

QUESTIONS AND COMMENTS FOR YOUR CONSIDERATION

1. What balance should be struck between unrestricted competition and protection of intellectual property rights?
2. Are there instances when intellectual property rights should not be enforced to permit "unrestricted competition"? When? What factors would you consider in making this decision.
3. For a further discussion of the impact of intellectual property protection on foreign trade, *see* Chapter Nine.

b. The Economics of Intellectual Property Rights Protection

1. The Economic Impact of Intangibility[10]

At the core of all intellectual property theory lies the basic observation that information has economic value—both to individuals who possess it and to society as a whole.

It is hard (perhaps even impossible) to imagine an economic system in which ideas do not play a central role; in this sense, at least, intellectual goods are as fundamental as any other class of commodities. The economic characteristics of ideas, however, set them apart from the material goods that form the focus of most economic thinking. To illustrate this, consider a "pure" intellectual good—an idea that can be both transmitted and stored without cost or degradation. Although a substantial initial investment may go into the development of such a good, once it exists the marginal cost of providing it to consumers is zero: the "supply" of any existing idea is effectively unlimited. In this respect, pure intellectual goods present problems similar to those posed by more conventional "public" goods such as highways, wells and lighthouses. Inventors are unlikely to invest more in the fixed costs of innovation than they can recoup from the sale of new ideas to consumers; but at zero marginal cost, optimal allocation occurs only when producers provide their ideas to the public free of charge.

Two additional, distinctive attributes of

---

[10] Mark C. Suchman, *Invention And Ritual: Notes On The Interrelation Of Magic And Intellectual Property In Preliterate Societies,* 89 COLUM. L. REV. 1264. Copyright 1989 Directors of The Columbia Law Review Association, Inc. Excerpt reprinted with permission.

intellectual goods—attributes shared with neither private goods nor public goods—aggravate this market failure. The first of these is the possibility of "secondary production": the purchasers of an intellectual good can resell it to third parties with little or no diminution in value, and they can do so while leaving their own holdings intact. In this regard, intellectual goods occupy a precarious middle ground between public goods, which usually flow from a single source and cannot be resold, and private goods, which can be resold but, once resold, are no longer available to the original purchaser. As a result, any release of a pure intellectual good on the open market eliminates the inventor's monopoly, producing a competitive environment in which price rapidly falls to zero.

The second distinctive attribute of intellectual goods, discontinuous marginal utility, complicates the situation still further. Unlike both private and public goods, an idea is only valuable to a given consumer the first time she receives it: "When an individual consumes the intellectual good '2 + 2 = 4' for the first time, something new has been learned and personal welfare is enhanced. When the consumer receives the same message a second time, however, its value is reduced to zero." This state of affairs dramatically hinders marketing, since buyers rarely know the value of information until they have sampled it, but once they have done so, their incentive to purchase vanishes.

The upshot of all this is an inherent instability in markets for ideas. Because inventions are costly to develop but inexpensive to imitate, society will systematically underinvest in the creation of knowledge. At the extreme, rational producers will refuse to invest in innovation at all, preferring to wait and appropriate new ideas from the few individuals for whom invention is its own reward. In short, without intervention, a free market in pure intellectual goods is impossible.

QUESTIONS AND COMMENTS FOR YOUR CONSIDERATION

1. To a large extent, the value placed on the protection of intellectual property rights depends upon whether the nation in question is an exporter or importer of intellectual property. Given the intangible nature of intellectual property, many developing nations have resisted efforts to treat intellectual property as a trade item. To what extent has intellectual property been commodified so that it can be properly treated as a matter for international trade negotiations?
2. What are the arguments against such treatment?

2. Conflicting Theories of Economic Value[11]

The debate on intellectual property rights at the GATT level has thus far been dominated by the following issues: the question of jurisdiction (the *WIPO v. GATT* debate), the interpretation of the negotiating mandate of the Punta del Este Declaration, and procedural questions (the precedence of the anti-counterfeiting code negotiation and the pace of negotiations on TRIPS *vis-à-vis* other negotiating groups in the Uruguay Round). Some believe that the debate has focused on form rather than substance, and hence has failed to generate results. If one tries, however, to identify substantive issues that are at the core of the debate, changing the focus would not help bring the negotiating parties any closer to consensus. There are major conflicts in the way different nations approach the issue of intellectual property rights protection lurking behind procedural discussions.

At the legal level, the conflict reflects a century old debate on the territoriality of intellectual property rights laws and its

---

[11] Carlos Alberto Primo Braga, *The Economics Of Intellectual Property Rights And The GATT: View From The South,* 22 VAND. J. TRANSNAT'L L. 243. Copyright 1989 Vanderbilt Journal of Transnational Law. Excerpt reprinted with permission.

implications for international trade. Another legal dimension of the debate is to what extent infringement of private property rights can be attributed to the state, justifying external reprisals. The Uruguay Round can be interpreted as a new attempt to promote universality in the protection of intellectual property rights. Previous attempts, beginning with the Paris Convention for the Protection of Industrial Property of 1883, have always encountered difficulty in imposing strict international law standards in the area of intellectual property rights. The continuing debate is even more complex because of its ambitious coverage and the widespread perception that the United States is trying to translate its domestic provisions into international standards.

The debate also carries clear political connotations. After all, a common definition of international leadership is based on the capacity of a country to maintain a relative primacy in the generation and commercialization of new technologies. Some analysts interpret the growing concern of industrialized nations with intellectual property rights as an attempt to control the diffusion of new technologies or "as a weapon in the struggle of 'haves' against 'have nots'." Accordingly, the ultimate goal of the industrialized countries would be to freeze the existing international division of labor by way of the control of technology transfers to the Third World. Another political dimension of the debate from the perspective of Least Developed Countries has to do with the role of foreign capital in these economies. The major beneficiaries of better intellectual property rights protection, at least in the short run, would be transnational corporations. In most Third World countries, a reform of intellectual property laws perceived to favor foreign capital would be highly controversial.

There are also significant philosophical differences along the North-South divide with respect to intellectual property rights. In the First World, intellectual property protection is usually presented "as a fundamental right comparable to rights to physical property." The criticism of countries with "defective" intellectual property systems is often designed to stress the high moral ground from which these attacks are made. The thesis that natural law provides a firm basis to the notion of inherent rights in products of the mind, however, is at best debatable. One can make an eloquent case for the importance "to conceive of ideas as property, and of property not solely as material but also as spiritual." Yet, the history of the evolution of national patent systems suggests that "economic expediency" has usually dominated legal and moral considerations. As a consequence, any attempt to present a country's intellectual property system as a model of "enlightened" virtues is bound to face a great deal of skepticism in the Third World. Moreover, in contrast with developed economies, Least Developed Countries tend to assign a higher weight to "social" interests (often loosely defined) than to private interests. Intellectual property systems always entail a compromise between private and social interests. Arguments against intellectual property rights protection for pharmaceutical and food products, for example, are often based on social considerations, such as the objective of avoiding price increases in health and nutrition.

At the core of the conflict between industrialized countries and Least Developed Countries, however, are some basic economic issues. A common belief was that lawyers took intellectual property rights protection too seriously while economists took the issue too lightly. Economists' attitudes towards intellectual property rights, however, have been changing significantly over the last decade. The growing share of knowledge-intensive products in international trade, the economic impact of new copying technologies, the possibilities of world-wide integration brought by communication networks, and the increase in international technological rivalry have magnified the economic significance of "piracy." At the same time new technologies (computer software, semiconductor chip design, etc.) are challenging existing patterns of intellectual property rights protection. Consequently, there is growing interest in the economics of intellectual property rights. Nevertheless, the analysis of the costs and benefits of more sound intellectual property systems for Least Developed Countries is still in its infancy.

The conventional reasons for intellectual property rights protection—to promote investments in research and development (R&D) and technological innovation, and to encourage the disclosure of new knowledge—

are not enough to make an economic case for the adoption of intellectual property laws. First, one can argue that there are other institutional arrangements which could in theory generate the same results of the concession of legal rights in new knowledge. As Dasgupta and Stoneman point out, the theory of public goods suggests at least two other solutions for the problem of efficient production and allocation of knowledge: (1) the direct production of knowledge by the government which would "allow free use of it, and finance the expenditure by the imposition of lump-sum taxes"; or (2) the encouragement of "private production of knowledge by the imposition of (differential) subsidies for their production and the levying of lump-sum taxes to finance these subsidies."

It is, however, important to recognize that the economic rationale for intellectual property rights protection goes beyond the issue of underproduction of knowledge in the absence of government intervention. It requires that the benefits associated with increased production of knowledge be greater than the costs due to its underutilization, a possible byproduct of monopolization. The literature tends to support the proposition that a net positive welfare effect results from intellectual property rights protection. This conclusion, nonetheless, becomes disputable when the focus of analysis changes from a closed economy (or from a global perspective) to an open economy. Berkowitz and Kotowitz, for example, point out that a national government "is bound to value the welfare of its own citizens or residents more heavily than that of foreigners." In this context, they were able to derive results showing that for a Least Developed Country a shorter period of patent protection (vis-a-vis an industrialized country) may be optimal in terms of national welfare. Lyons adopts a more provocative position based on these results, stating that "[t]here appears to be little reason for small countries to adopt a patent system."

The implications of these results for the North-South debate on intellectual property rights, however, have to be qualified. First, the model is developed for a small country "in which little invention takes place and/or in which invention markets are competitive." Some of the newly industrialized countries (NICs) of the Third World no longer fit this description. Second, the model assumes away the possibility of retaliation against defective intellectual property systems. As recent United States actions against Korea, Taiwan, and Brazil, as well as European Community measures against Indonesia suggest, the possibility of intellectual property-related trade retaliations has to be taken into account for an adequate evaluation of an intellectual property-system reform. Finally, the model does not capture some of the benefits that sound intellectual property systems may generate.

Despite these considerations it is important to recognize that for a Third World country a reform designed to increase intellectual property rights protection will tend to generate a welfare loss at its initial stages. Because Least Developed Countries are typically net importers of technology, a usual consequence of a more strict regime of intellectual property laws would be an increase in royalty payments to foreigners. A related cost would be the displacement of firms devoted to "piracy". From a social perspective, the costs of dislocation of "pirates" will only be relevant as long as foreigners benefit from the process (either by an increase in imports or by an increase in license fees paid by domestic firms to the foreign owners of intellectual property rights). As MacLaughlin, Richards, and Kenny point out the "transfer of sales or royalty payments to other nationals would represent merely a transfer of income from one member of society to another." In this context, this income transfer would not generate a social welfare loss.

Other social costs associated with the reform would be the opportunity cost of additional domestic R&D and the eventual loss of consumer surplus brought by higher prices that could result from the "monopolization" process. The issue of the opportunity cost of additional R&D has received little attention in the debate since most analysts seem to profess an unlimited admiration for the benefits of investments in R&D. Without disputing the importance of R&D for economic development, one should also take into account its related costs. In Least Developed Countries, human-capital tends to be the scarcest factor of production. As a consequence, an increase in domestic R&D will increase the demand for this scarce resource with potential implications for other productive activities and could even have a negative short term impact in terms of income distribution. Another source of potential costs, which were not considered in the model, are the local subsidiaries of transnational corporations. Local R&D by these companies can be translated into future royalty payments abroad if intellectual property rights "reside with the parent company, regardless of the location of the research." The model also does not take into account the costs of establishing an effective, intellectual property system (from the organization of a "cadre" of patent examiners to the costs of enforcing intellectual property rights). For a small Least Developed Country, these costs can be substantial.

Turning now to the social benefits that a Least Developed Country would achieve by enforcing more strict intellectual property rights, one could list the following impacts: (a) cost savings associated with new technologies developed by additional R&D and by the disclosure of new knowledge; (b) cost savings associated with technological transfers that could only occur under more strict intellectual property rights protection; and (c) additional investment fostered by the new regime of protection. Items (a) and (b) can be interpreted as the main channels through which the benefits of technological change are translated into economic growth. Other potential benefits could accrue in the form of higher quality products becoming available for consumption and through the contribution of better national intellectual property rights protection to world technological growth. The magnitude of this contribution is an open question, but it seems reasonable to assume that the impact of any individual intellectual property reform in the Third World would be marginal at best.

c. The Case Against Intellectual Property Rights Protection[12]

Those who oppose more strict intellectual property rights protection tend to dispute the benefits...partially based on the hypotheses that domestic R&D will not respond significantly to the reform, that the growth impact of any additional R&D will be marginal, or that capital formation and technological transfer are not very sensitive to intellectual property rights protection. Some alternative formulations...are: local incompetence; a very inelastic supply of human capital; the argument that intellectual property rights protection is only one of the relevant variables which explain R&D and that it can be ineffective in the absence of additional conditions (such as a larger stock of human capital); the belief that modern technology is carried forward by large enterprises (particularly transnational corporations); and doubts about the net contribution of foreign capital to economic development.

The criticism is also directed to the cost aspects of an intellectual property-system reform. First, it is argued that the weight of additional royalties would be disruptive given the foreign-exchange constraint faced by many Least Developed Countries. Second, a high value is assigned to the perceived benefits of having access to technology in the cheapest possible way. According to this approach, by "taxing" imported products of the mind, Least Developed Countries would be lowering the costs of important inputs in the productive process and they would increase consumption possibilities. The question of dislocation of "piracy," however, does not receive much attention from those who oppose more strict intellectual property laws in the Third World for tactical and legal reasons. For some countries, particularly those with problems of enforcement of intellectual property laws, it would not be wise to acknowledge the magnitude of the problem. For many Least Developed Countries the problem simply does not exist since from a legal standpoint their intellectual property systems comply with international agreements, such as the Paris Convention (which allows each country to choose its own patent conditions as long as there is no discrimination against non-nationals). As Barbosa notes, entrepreneurs in countries with "defective" intellectual property systems, from a United States perspective, could at best be called corsairs with all the legal licenses to operate.

---

[12] Carlos Alberto Primo Braga, *The Economics Of Intellectual Property Rights And The GATT: View From The South,* 22 VAND. J. TRANSNAT'L L. 243.

d. The Case for Intellectual Property Rights Protection[13]

The economic arguments for intellectual property rights protection in the Third World are built around the concept of self-interest. Emphasis is usually placed on the high social rate of return from investments in new technology and the tendency for under-investment in this area when intellectual property rights are not well-protected. The effectiveness of local R&D is heralded and the micro benefits of sound intellectual property regimes is suggested by case studies at the firm level. Some analysts, such as Sherwood, recognize that these benefits are difficult to quantify, but they tend to stress that small firms and universities will become much more active in the process of technological innovation under enhanced intellectual property rights protection.

An argument which is becoming quite influential is the thesis that presently "technology drives investment" and to the extent that technology "is reluctant to flow where it is not protected" the lack of an adequate level of protection could stunt technological transfer and foreign investment. The relationship between technology and investment can also be explored at the domestic level based on the proposition that enhanced intellectual property rights protection, particularly trade secret laws, would be an important stimulus for local capital formation.

Turning to the social costs of a reform, analysts tend to downplay the importance of the displacement of pirates. This attitude reflects strong assumptions about labor mobility in the Third World coupled with the belief that growth in sectors benefited by the reform would rapidly absorb displaced workers. The potential loss of consumer surplus is also downplayed because these benefits would be achieved at the high cost of fostering imitation and copying instead of invention and creativity.

A final comment worth making at this point concerns the role of bureaucracies in the intellectual property systems of the Third World. These bureaucracies are quite influential in the debate and tend to adopt a critical view of First World proposals for enhanced intellectual property rights protection. Their attitude is often influenced by ideological interpretations, such as the concept of technological imperialism. It is important to recognize, however, that their attitudes also reflect the predominance of a scientific ethos which has at its basis the norm of complete disclosure. This "culture," as Dasgupta poses it, is hostile to the view of knowledge as a private capital good that is the foundation of the so-called mature intellectual property systems of the industrialized economies. Consequently, the dialogue between technology-oriented interests and government bureaucracies, an important domestic facet of the intellectual property rights debate, tends to be a difficult one.

[13] Carlos Alberto Primo Braga, *The Economics Of Intellectual Property Rights And The GATT: View From The South,* 22 VAND. J. TRANSNAT'L L. 243. Copyright 1989 Vanderbilt Journal of Transnational Law. Excerpt reprinted with permission.

A QUESTION FOR YOUR CONSIDERATION

Discussions regarding the divergent underlying economic theories for intellectual property protection tend to divide the proponents of each theory into two camps—the developed ("have") countries and the developing ("have-not") countries. Are there instances when a developing country might reject the economic view that considers protection of intellectual property rights of greater economic value than lack of protection?

e. The "Economics" of Database Protection: A Case Study[14]

The copyright laws of the United States and the European Union have become key forces in the international competition for market share in one of the most dynamic sectors of the world economy. The United States and the European Union have embarked on divergent regimes for the copyright protection of computer databases. The aim of European Union law is to protect local database developers by granting them ownership of the data collected in their compilations. In contradistinction, the aim of United States law is to maximize market efficiency by protecting only creative selection and arrangement of data and leaving the underlying facts free for the taking.

At the center of the division between the two regimes is a basic provision of United States copyright law; the "thin" protection granted to the facts in a data compilation. The protection is "thin" because the compiler of a database can only gain copyright for the creative way in which he has organized the data he collected; he does not, however, gain any protection for the effort, or "sweat of the brow," he has invested in the collection. No matter how many thousands of hours or millions of dollars are spent gathering data, traditional copyright law grants only a "thin" copyright in the creative organization and always leaves the facts collected free to be used by someone else.

The United States copyright approach to data compilations adheres to the creative selection approach. The Copyright Act of 1976 was interpreted definitively in the context of data compilations by a unanimous decision of the Supreme Court in *Feist Publications, Inc. v. Rural Telephone Service Co.* In an opinion by Justice O'Connor, the Court held that alphabetical listings in a telephone book did not contain the minimum level of creativity required for copyright. The *Feist* Court explicitly rejected the "sweat of the brow" proposition that the creator of a data compilation such as a telephone book should be economically rewarded for his effort regardless of the creativity it exhibits.

In contrast, the European Union has abandoned the fact/expression distinction for data compilations. In order to spur domestic development of computer databases, the "sweat of the brow" doctrine is at the heart of the Commission of the European Communities' Proposal for a Council Directive on the Legal Protection of Databases (Proposed Directive). Unlike *Feist*, which covers all compilations, the Proposed Directive is specifically targeted to computer databases. The Proposed Directive contains a two-tiered approach to database copyright. The first tier grants a copyright in creative selection and arrangement, which is largely consistent with existing international copyright law as embodied in the Berne Convention, and consequently with United States law as articulated in *Feist*. The second tier, however, is a *sui generis* provision which prohibits unfair extraction or copying of the facts in an otherwise unprotected work. While the Commission asserts that such an approach does not extend a copyright to facts, in actuality it has the effect of granting to the original compiler a limited "ownership" of the facts.

The drafters of the Proposed Directive appear to be interested in increasing the European share of a market central to the economic development plans of most industrialized nations. Intellectual property from movies to microchips is the engine driving United States foreign trade at the expense of many of her staunchest competitors. In 1990, the United States enjoyed a $12.6 billion trade surplus in copyright and patent license transactions; it was the only G-7 nation to run a surplus. In the same year, worldwide revenue in online databases was just over $9 billion. Though just a small segment of the larger intellectual property market, the database industry is among the fastest growing. While European database developers produced almost half the world total of databases, they accounted for only one quarter of the total revenue. This is because nonprofit producers (governments) still produce the majority (fifty-four percent) of European databases, whereas American databases are produced largely by the private sector (seventy-two percent).

---

[14] Charles Von Simson, *Feist or Famine American Database Copyright as an Economic Model for the European Union* 20 BROOK. J. INT'L L. 729. Copyright 1995 Brooklyn Law School. Excerpt reprinted with permission.

In a desire to reward the author, and hence encourage production of new works, copyright essentially grants the author a monopoly over the reproduction and dissemination of his creative expression for a limited period of time. Thus, copyright is also a tax to society, because the author may set any price he chooses for the work, though the work faces potential substitution if the price is too high and buyers opt instead for other, similar works. Competitors are prohibited from copying expressions without the author's consent. To produce new works, competitors must pay to license, or they must start from scratch. Hence the public may be burdened by higher prices or limited access to the copyrighted work. Copyright thus establishes a tax on readers, publishers, and competitors for the purpose of rewarding writers. In order to protect the copyright holder while mitigating the burden of his monopoly on his competitors and customers, the protection is limited to creative expression for a specific period of time. In contrast, if the purpose of copyright were solely to reward the author, copyright would be absolute in duration and scope. The limit is important because the purpose of copyright is not solely to reward the author, but rather to induce production at the minimum possible cost to society. The law, by limiting the ownership of data, thus favors its free movement and therefore contributes to the general progress of society.

In contrast, the policy behind the *sui generis* protection in the European Union's Proposed Directive is intended to maximize profit in information services for European providers of information services. This policy choice is not rooted solely in economics; European law also recognizes a moral right to intellectual property which is absent in United States law. Fundamentally, however, the Proposed Directive is intended to favor European database publishers at the expense of their customers and non-EU competitors.

The European Community's Proposed Directive for the Legal Protection of Databases embodies the "sweat of the brow" doctrine. It lags behind the United States in database development because the Union took this position. The strength of the Directive's approach is that it grants a property interest to an author for the work he expended. Unlike the convolutions of *Feist*, the "sweat" doctrine is relatively straightforward as a legal principle.

The Proposed Directive was enacted with the provisions of the Berne Convention for the Protection of Literary and Artistic Works in mind.

Specifically, Article 2(5) of the Berne Convention provides:

> Collections of literary or artistic works such as encyclopaedias and anthologies which, by reason of the selection and arrangement of their contents, constitute intellectual creations shall be protected as such, without prejudice to the copyright in each of the works forming part of such collections.

Thus, Article 2(5) grants protection to collections of artistic and literary works where the selection and arrangement is sufficiently creative.

The Berne Convention did not, however, contemplate protection for electronic databases, and no specific protection is outlined. In the first tier of its two-tiered approach, the Proposed Directive seeks to fill this void by making explicit the protection of database compilations exhibiting sufficient creativity in selection and arrangement. Thus, the first tier simply consolidates the law of the European Union around a standard to which the great majority of member states and the United States already adhere, and explicitly extends this protection to computer databases.

In contrast to the harmonizing effect of the first tier of the directive, the second tier represents something of a departure from the approach of the vast majority of Berne Convention signatories by creating an ownership right in the underlying data. This ownership right allows the database developer to prevent the unauthorized extraction or re-use of the contents of a database for commercial purposes. The developer thus owns the data he has compiled, regardless of the eligibility of the database for protection under the first tier.

In order to mitigate the monopolistic effects of the ownership right, the Proposed Directive also requires that the original compiler issue licenses to secondary compilers. This compulsory license is imposed when the database has been made publicly available and is the only source of a work or material.

Copyright as an Economic Policy Lever. From cars to computers to guns, we now take it for granted that all manufactured goods are made from interchangeable parts. A single supplier will sell commodity nuts, bolts and brake shoes to automobile manufacturers. A host of personal computer makers build their machines from the same chip. British gunsmiths claimed 150 years ago that it was impossible to make something as precise as a gun from interchangeable parts; highly skilled craftsmen were required to file each component, at an enormous increase in cost. But Samuel Colt's small company ultimately dominated the world market for guns by eliminating the need for custom-developed parts.

The revolution took place in manufacturing because standard interchangeable parts could be produced by a number of companies operating in a competitive market. From the parts manufacturer's perspective, costs were reduced because a single part could be sold to any number of finished product producers. From the finished product producer's perspective, costs came down because competitive bids could be solicited from a range of parts manufacturers.

This environment was a sharp contrast from a market in which the makers of customized parts could charge higher prices based on their protected market position. Their protected positions resulted from the cost and time associated with producing specialized parts for a single potential buyer. Competitors were reluctant to enter a market where they would be forced to start from scratch in order to service a single buyer who already had an entrenched relationship with the original developer of the part.

The same evolution from proprietary (produced by a single producer to fit a single assembly) to interchangeable (produced by multiple producers to fit multiple assemblies) parts that revolutionized the production of goods must continue to work in the production of information. From legal databases to industrial specifications to names and addresses of telephone subscribers to lists of registered trademarks, the market for electronic information will grow most quickly if the underlying data is free to subsequent compilers. This will ensure a competitive market by eliminating the protected market positions of original database compilers. Competition flourishes when subsequent compilers are not forced to start their database by going out and rediscovering the same data. Buyers benefit as the price of databases lowers through competition. The database market benefits as more databases are sold at a lower price.

The kind of competitive market that will allow this evolution to continue is a market where the average long-term price of a database is as close as possible to the database's marginal cost. The marginal cost of a good is the cost to the manufacturer (or author/publisher) of producing one additional unit. In a perfectly competitive market, all firms are too small in relation to the overall market to affect price. Thus, equilibrium for a profit-maximizing firm occurs where marginal cost equals the price set by the market. In other words, where the cost of producing one additional unit is equal to the revenue earned from selling it. Market price does not rise above marginal cost in a competitive environment because no firm may charge more than another; any attempt by a single firm to raise prices results in a loss of sales as buyers opt for lower priced products. If the market price were to drop below a producer's marginal cost, he would not gain enough revenue from the sale of a unit to cover his expenses in producing it, and would ultimately be forced to drop out of the market.

In contrast to this competitive market scenario, a copyright in underlying data will lead to a market more analogous to a monopoly. A monopoly is a market in which a seller may dictate supply, and hence price, because no alternative seller is available. Buyers in these markets pay more than they would in a competitive market, and thereby inefficiently transfer resources to the monopolist. In the context of databases, this situation is analogous to the market for custom gun parts in that once a compiler owns the data copyright, subsequent compilers will be reluctant to incur the costs of starting from scratch and entering a market already dominated by the original player. This leaves the original compiler in a protected market position in which he can charge monopolistic prices until a subsequent compiler can generate the same data from scratch.

This is not to say that in a competitive market every producer's price must always be equal to marginal cost. On certain occasions, a producer may invent an innovative new product with features that make it unique in the market at a specific point in time. During this "monopoly window" where the producer's product is unique, he may charge a price higher than other competitors who are bound to the marginal cost price. This higher price is not inefficient for two reasons. First, the higher price reflects the greater value of the product; if the product is not worth more, customers may opt to buy from lower priced competitors. Second, the "monopoly" price charged will only last for the limited period of time it takes for competitors to match the innovation and for prices to return to a marginal cost level in expectation of the next innovation. The pioneer's position is not protected by the copyright system; it is protected by his own ingenuity and the speed with which he brings a new product to market.

Given the efficiencies of a competitive market where long-term average price approaches marginal cost, the question for copyright policy makers is what form of protection should be granted to ensure investment in innovation of information products while allowing the commodity raw material, data, to move quickly and at low cost among suppliers of databases and between suppliers and customers. Assuming that the evolution of the database industry is analogous to the evolution of manufacturing industries, the lower costs of innovative production will increase competition and eliminate some competitors, the market will grow exponentially as less expensive, better products continue to attract new populations of customers. In order to evaluate the copyright options in light of these economic assumptions, it is illustrative to trace a database through its competitive life cycle, and to compare the effects of United States and European law on the likely investment by the compiler and the resultant cost to the consumer at each juncture of the product life cycle. The resulting analysis demonstrates that while United States and European law would have similar effects on database protection, in most respects the two approaches differ in one critical area: the United States approach ensures that database developers are free to rely on an inexpensive and plentiful supply of data, while the European approach adds cost and promotes inefficiency.

Identification of New Markets. In a competitive environment, development of a copyrightable database usually begins with the identification of a market niche and potential customers.

United States and European Union law are identical in their protection at this early stage. Producers who successfully identify original categories of information that are useful to users in a new market would enjoy two protected positions. First, developers would enjoy a time-based monopoly for the period of time that their product was the only one on the market containing the new category. For example, a database developer offering information to retailers on food-buying trends of Latino customers in San Antonio could charge a premium price for the information as long as that developer was the only source. The amount of the premium would depend only on how well they had identified a market for the product. Second, both United States law after *Feist* and European Union law under the first tier of the Proposed Directive would recognize a copyright in that information product because it is based on the creative selection of data and creates an original category. Copyright in creative selection and arrangement spurs investment in new products, as producers enjoy limited protection for their innovative category selection and organization.

Investment in market identification and category selection, not the ownership of data, is the proper source of advantage for a database in a competitive market. In a competitive market, developers of a novel format would gain copyright protection for that format, and set prices according to demand for their ingenuity. They would be released temporarily from the pressures of marginal cost pricing; as long as their product is either the first one available in the market or more ingenious than other available products, they can charge a premium price. This typically brief monopoly window is not, however, detrimental to the market because competitors may take the data and compete based on another novel format. The welfare of the market increases as consumers get better products through competition and developers get more customers because of the better products they are forced to develop to stay in business. Resources are not simply being transferred from customers to monopolists who are not driven to innovate. Consumers are paying higher prices because they perceive greater value in the innovative product they are purchasing.

Assessments of Multiple Data Sources. After a market for the data has been identified and useful categories of data developed, database developers must find sources of data to deliver to their customers. Occasionally, the required data may come from a single source. However, more often than not the data will come from multiple sources whose contents must be sampled and selected for usefulness in the particular database. For example, a demographic database may draw upon public sources, such as census data, property tax records, and voter registration files, as well as a wide variety of proprietary sources that contain data on the target group, such as purchasing patterns, or subscriptions to catalogs and periodicals. Often, the effort of collecting the right data involves extracting a needle of fact from a haystack of irrelevant information.

The cost-benefit analysis applied to the selection of data will differ depending on the legal regime. Under United States law, the cost-benefit analysis is relatively simple. Regardless of the originality in the selection and arrangement of the sources, the underlying data in the work is free to anyone provided they do not take the format. Thus, an American compiler of a new database would simply take the best quality data and target it to his market, provided he was not infringing upon the original compiler's creative selection and arrangement. Thus, the absence of copyright protection for data under the United States regime maximizes the power of market forces on databases that are already developed. Data is free because its marginal cost is zero. Absent transmission costs, it simply does not cost any more to deliver a completely developed database to the tenth subscriber than it cost to deliver it to the ninth. Profit is properly stripped from the ownership of underlying data.

Of course, while the data is free from copyright protection, many other mechanisms are available to protect it from competitors. Access to electronic information is, to a great extent, governed by contract. Software algorithms can make it difficult to access information without agreeing on how the information will be disseminated and reused. However, new distribution methods, such as on-line information gateways (the much ballyhooed Internet is a prime example) and easily portable compact disks containing vast compilations of material, are expanding access to parties who may not be in contractual privity with the database proprietors. These trends weaken contractual controls but should not shake the basic logic behind copyright protection limited to creative selection and arrangement.

In contrast to the United States approach, the Proposed Directive's "neighboring rights" scheme grants certain protection to the basic data as well as providing for traditional copyright for the creativity of the compilation. The original compiler thus owns the facts he has compiled for a limited statutory period. This arrangement skews pricing because the artificial monopoly allows the original compiler to charge a price above what he would charge in a competitive scenario until another compiler develops the data from scratch.

The Proposed Directive purports to limit the inefficiencies of this artificial monopoly by compelling the original compiler to license his data to any developers of derivative compilations if his work was the only source of the data in question. Compulsory licensing exhibits many of the same "bad tax" characteristics as those exhibited in an absolute copyright monopoly. In addition, the potential for abuse of a compulsory licensing system by large compilers, such as telephone monopolies, is enormous. Because original compilers who enjoy protected status would be unlikely to easily grant licenses to secondary compilers, compelling such licensing would often be settled through long and costly civil litigation.

Finally, the second tier of protection under the Proposed Directive is anticompetitive because it is not reciprocal. Non-EU database developers (principally American) will not be allowed to use the data developed by European developers protected by the directive. Moreover, American developers will face competition from European competitors operating in the United States under the provisions of *Feist*, which provides that data is free to all subsequent compilers. It remains an open question whether a European developer would be allowed to take the data of a non-EU developer and then gain an ownership interest in the copied data. Such a development could be highly injurious to both the marketplace and worldwide database suppliers because regardless of where databases are developed, many will be competing for the same global customers. Unfortunately, these unequal conditions will endure until bilateral agreements are worked out between the United States and the EU member states.

Preparing the Database for Market. Once data has been secured, either through original collection, licensing or the simple taking of unprotected data, depending on the legal scheme, the contents must be edited and refined for use in the new database and then blended into a presentation format. The goal is to organize and deliver the information in a way that enables the intended user to access needed information efficiently. Furthermore, most commercially significant databases are to some degree dynamic, requiring updating and revision either consistently or periodically.

Here, the economic effects of the two regimes will be most apparent to end users. Under the United States system, the cost of the database, and its resulting competitive advantage will be concentrated in producing an innovative product. Because the only legally sustainable competitive advantage available under the United States system will be its creative selection and arrangement, this stage of the product cycle will be fertile ground for investment. Users will benefit as producers are forced to compete by creating more user-friendly systems, formatting databases more cogently, and by creating hardware and software tools that enhance the ability of users to gather and synthesize unrelated data.

The cost of a database under the European scheme, on the other hand, will be reflected in the cost of gaining access to proprietary data. Because the original compiler owns the underlying data, the price charged for it will be a premium based on the lack of alternative sellers. For the potentially long period of time it will take competitors to either negotiate a licensing agreement or develop the data from scratch, the original compiler will have limited incentive to invest in more effective and easier-to-use products.

Clearly, the collection and assembly of information as well as the selection, coordination or arrangement of data are often extremely time consuming and expensive. The successful development and distribution of a database often depends on the solution of complex marketing problems. The process also calls for sophisticated knowledge of information science, the study of information seeking behavior, and of the details of storage and retrieval systems and computer programs. If the resulting compilation seems simple to the user, it is precisely because of the complex web of authorial activity that went into its design and execution.

In short, United States law recognizes that these complex factors are at the root of the competitive advantage of a compilation. The United States system rewards these important investments through the copyright protection of creativity. The European Union's Proposed Directive, on the other hand, will draw investment away from these strategic competitive features as EU developers struggle to compete at the less demanding stage of the original compilation of data.

The best argument for the United States copyright regime is that it most closely approximates a free market for data compilations with commodity data as the central feature. The price of a database will be set by its development cost and how well it has been designed through the various stages of the product development lifecycle. In contrast, the European scheme allows and sustains monopolies based on the original compilation of data. This scheme will allow original compilers to set monopoly prices limited only by inefficient compulsory licensing schemes.

The European Union's effort to protect domestic competitors now will be harmful to the market for databases in the short term and to the Europeans themselves in the long term. In the short term, because data will be purchased or developed from scratch each time, the large number of works produced by EU developers will be expensive. In the long term, the Europeans will ultimately suffer as non-EU competitors accustomed to competing for global customers based on the quality of their product will become more and more difficult to beat in the marketplace. These competitors, hardened by the market and forced to innovate, will beat the Europeans on every price performance front. It would be far better for the Europeans to rely on their ingenuity and face the reality of the market now.

Ultimately, the division between the two regimes represents a dam over which information will not easily flow. More than perhaps any other commodity, data must be allowed to move without barriers in order to allow the world economy to grow in the most efficient manner possible. Consequently, rationalization of the two approaches to the copyright protection of computer databases should be an indispensable part of negotiations between the United States and the European Union, both in the multilateral GATT environment and in more focused bilateral talks.

QUESTIONS AND COMMENTS FOR YOUR CONSIDERATION

1. In bilateral negotiations between the US and the European Union regarding the scope of protection for computer databases, is there a compromise position that meets the economic concerns of both countries?
2. The ability to protect pharmaceutical products under patent law is hotly contested. While the United States grants patent protection to such products, many other countries do not. What is the economic impact of these divergent approaches in the market for such products? On the market for the manufacture of the products? On the market for research and development for such products?

2. The Common Heritage of Mankind[15]

Intellectual property has always played a unique role in the economic evolution of industrialized nations. The history of patent and trade secret protection is filled with technological advances which have driven the industrialization engine of development. From the early days of the printing press to the onset of CD-ROM production and distribution in China in the 1990's, developing countries have similarly utilized the ability to produce and market copyright protected works of foreign authors as the backbone for their economic advancement. Developing countries do not generally possess a large body of intellectual property created by their own authors and inventors which can be marketed internationally. In the absence of sufficient nationally-created works, such developing countries have often used the intellectual property of other nations to enhance their industrial capabilities. Even the United States, in its early days as a newly emerging industrial nation, used its copyright laws to protect its nascent publishing industry. These laws did not grant other nations' authors the right to protect their works from the voracious requirements of the US domestic publishing industry.

The need for access by developing countries to intellectual property protected works has arguably grown more severe in the present technologically driven global economy. Much technology includes intellectual property elements. Thus, attempts to restrict a country's internal access and use of such technology through the enactment of international protection norms or procedures are seen by some developing countries as a direct challenge to their ability to play a significant role in the world economy.

Many scientific developments in the areas of medicine and agriculture also contain intellectual property elements. This unique role as an instrument of public health and safety further supports the desirability of providing unrestricted access to intellectual property.

Given intellectual property's undeniably historic role in the industrialization of a developed country and in improving the

---

[15] Doris Estelle Long, *The Role of Intellectual Property in Developing Nations.* Copyright 1995 Doris E. Long. Excerpt reprinted with permission.

health of its citizens, many developing countries assert that intellectual property should be considered the "common heritage of mankind." It should be freely available to all. Such free availability includes the right of transfer to developing countries without payment of compensation so that these countries can utilize this important heritage as instruments of public policy.

As a common heritage of mankind, instead of being protected by more stringent protection standards, they reason, such standards should be reduced, if not completely eliminated.

a. Traditional Perspective of the Developing World[16]

Formation of an international standard of protection for intellectual property sounds like a simple task. Problems arise, however, when one actually attempts to claim a property right to information in the global arena. The difficulty stems from divergent concepts of property and ownership, as well as the elusive character of the term "information." Different legal principles exist from country to country, stemming from the particular social, political and ideological experiences of each. Unsettled definitions of ownership and property with regard to information are most evident when one compares the developed and developing worlds.

Changing patterns of trade and technology revealed the schism between the developing and developed worlds in terms of intellectual property protection. The cost of creating intellectual property soared as research and development began requiring large-scale production, open international markets and protection against free-riding imitators. At the same time, the cost of pirating intellectual property plummeted as new technologies, such as photocopy machines, video cassette recorders and computer systems, lowered reproduction expenses. While these changes in trade and technology occurred, the developing world and the developed world adopted divergent attitudes toward the protection of intellectual property.

Because they are not major producers of intellectual property, developing countries have little incentive to vigorously protect it. Weak protection is justified on the grounds that the developing world needs maximum access to Western intellectual goods for its development and that stringent standards of protection are debilitating. Some developing countries maintain that knowledge and information are "the common heritage of mankind" and therefore should be made available at low cost. Most views are grounded in the premise that efficient use of knowledge is a fundamental requirement for economic growth. Therefore, the argument runs, technological information should be provided with minimal restriction because Third World development is in the interest of all nations.

Inadequate protection of intellectual property in developing countries occurs at both the substantive law and enforcement levels. On a substantive level, many developing countries fail even to recognize the three traditional areas of intellectual property protection: trademark, patent and copyright.

There are several reasons for nonrecognition. First, lax protection offers economic benefits to developing nations. Because pirates of intellectual property incur minimal production costs and no royalty payments, they are in a better position than legitimate producers to satisfy demands in developing countries. Moreover, by copying only successful products, pirates avoid the risk of market failure and, in the short run, enrich themselves and the country in which they operate.

Second, developing countries tend to have scarce government resources. As a result, they resist spending on the enforcement of foreign intellectual property rights. As with the importation of capital, developing countries often view the importation of intellectual property as a means of dominating and exploiting the economic potential of the importing country. Paying for imports or royalties is thus seen as an economic burden fostering a negative balance of trade.

At the enforcement level, many devel-

---

[16] Tara Kalagher Giunta, Lily H. Shang, *Ownership of Information in a Global Economy,* 27 GEO. WASH. J. INT'L L. & ECON. 327. Copyright 1994 George Washington University. Excerpt reprinted with permission.

oping countries provide weak or nonexistent protection of the intellectual property laws they have enacted. And unlike Western countries, developing countries have few strong lobbies of inventors, authors or companies that would benefit from strict intellectual property laws or the enforcement thereof.

From the developed world's perspective, information is a valuable commodity upon which its livelihood depends. Indeed, for some developed nations, the transfer of technology represents the major component of their income. These countries demand strict protection of their ownership rights, for organized piracy undermines the very incentive structure that trademark, patent and copyright laws were designed to promote.

Moreover, inadequate protection also undermines the goal of free trade. Absent sufficient protection, creators cannot recover the cost of their research and development. The result is lower production, fewer trading opportunities and higher costs to the consumer. In other words, piracy cuts directly into the developed country's profits and undermines its competitive edge.

b. The Economic Liberalization View[17]

Recent efforts toward economic liberalization in developing countries have made them more willing to strengthen intellectual property protection in order to attract foreign investment for local development. Empirical data suggest that pharmaceutical research and development is conducted most commonly in countries that protect intellectual property, and that areas where protection is increasing have been receiving increasing shares of research and development expenditures from US pharmaceutical firms. In addition, the availability of intellectual property protection in a developing country may encourage foreign firms to invest in product development specific to that country's needs. Stronger intellectual property protection may also facilitate technology transfer, since patentholders are more willing to sell technology to countries that guarantee ownership rights. Stronger protection also encourages local inventors to keep their technology in the country. Inventors from developing countries with weaker protection currently patent more heavily in the United States than do inventors from other developing countries.

The parameters of the developing-country intellectual property debate have been determined thus far by the need to protect high technology, and not by intellectual property issues unique to the developing world. Recently, however, increased interest in the economic potential of developing countries' rain forests has expanded the context of the debate, suggesting that developing countries have economic needs which are left unmet by the intellectual property system as it now exists. The motivations behind developing countries' and their inhabitants' growing insistence on increased property rights to biological material used in technological enterprise both correspond with and diverge from their historical reasons for adopting traditional intellectual property law systems. Much of this tension is evident in the intellectual property implications of medicinal plant and crop variety research.

The developed world's pharmaceutical industry has been a prominent source of the heightened interest in the rain forest, as pharmaceutical companies have begun to explore the forest more intensively for medicinal plants and information on their possible uses.

The developed world's renewed search for new plant material has been accompanied by a growing interest in the traditional knowledge of indigenous peoples. Native healers and other members of indigenous groups can draw attention to specific plants, while explaining their physiological effects and describing the processes through which they convert raw plant material into purer compounds. Such information can provide valuable clues to the identity of active molecules, greatly expediting their isolation in the laboratory. In fact, traditional knowledge has long been an integral part of drug development. Approximately three quarters of the plant-derived compounds currently used as pharmaceuticals have been discov-

---

[17] Kirsten Peterson, *Recent Intellectual Property Trends In Developing Countries,* 33 HARV. INT'L L.J. 277. Copyright 1992 President and Fellows of Harvard College. Excerpt reprinted with permission.

ered through research based on plant use by indigenous peoples.

Like the pharmaceutical industry, the international seed industry depends on plant genetic materials derived from crop varieties selected and improved by farmers in developing countries.

Along with the rain forests in which many of them developed, the traditional cultures of indigenous peoples are disappearing rapidly, making it likely that their typically orally-preserved knowledge of medicinal plants and agricultural varieties will be permanently lost. Like the rain forest, cultural knowledge has been assigned little economic worth, although it too is valuable for biotechnological innovation. Proposals for intellectual property reform with respect to cultural knowledge consequently mirror those regarding ownership of valuable plants: in both cases, the compensation for and recognition of such ownership, as a legitimate form of intellectual property deserving protection, is advocated as a means of providing economic incentives currently absent from the system.

Extending protection to the knowledge of indigenous peoples challenges the conventional distinction created by the practice of protecting unique knowledge but not unique raw materials. Increasing the scope of intellectual property protection in this way also raises questions about the patentability of knowledge that belongs to a group rather than an individual. Although the findings of a research group affiliated with a university or corporation are patentable, the cultural knowledge of an indigenous group and even the secrets of healers within a group are not, since they are considered to be public, common knowledge.

The desire for increased foreign investment as a means of achieving internal economic development has been a major impetus for developing countries' recent efforts toward providing enhanced intellectual property protection. Although the intellectual property policy debate has focused in the past on protection for high-technology products, new concerns specific to the developing world pose a challenge to the traditional debate. Specifically, the rain forest's economic promise for both developing and developed countries has revealed economic needs of developing countries which are left unaddressed by the existing intellectual property system.

The three types of response to these concerns—political action, multilateral cooperation, and private business transactions—reveal the developing countries' new attitude toward intellectual property while demonstrating their willingness to take control of property rights relating to their unique natural resources. While the success of each solution will depend in part upon cooperation by private and public institutions in the developed world, the direction of change will be determined largely by the innovations through which developing countries respond to the complex tensions among state and individual property rights and ecological concerns regarding the rain forest.

QUESTIONS AND COMMENTS FOR YOUR CONSIDERATION

1. Given the arguably conflicting philosophical, historical, economic and cultural imperatives between developed and developing countries for protecting intellectual property, is there an enforceable middle ground for international agreement? What standards would you develop for the international protection of patents? For copyrights? For trademarks? For trade secrets? To what extent, if any, does your answer depend on the economic value placed on a particular form of intellectual property?

2. One view of intellectual property protection sees such protection as a necessary corollary to encouraging the development of new works and inventions. Assuming that this view is correct, where should the balance be struck between encouraging the creation of new works and allowing developing countries to freely

use all works in their attempts at economic and industrial developments? What factors would you consider?

3. The TRIPS Agreement grants certain developing countries exemptions from its strictures for specified periods of time. (*See* Chapter Seven for a discussion of enforcement provisions under TRIPS.) Do these exemptions provide a sufficient balance between the conflicting interests of developed and developing countries? What dangers, if any, are posed by such exemptions? Is there any other method for balancing these conflicts?

c. Perspective of the Developed World[18]

Developed countries uniformly view intellectual property as embodying pure property rights, entitled to comprehensive international protection in order to assure a full economic return to creators and owners. Reducing the potential for uncompensated, infringing uses by enacting and enforcing international protection norms is perceived as beneficial for both developed and developing countries. By assuring a higher economic return to the authors of copyrighted works and inventors of patented inventions and trade secrets, such norms encourage such authors and inventors to expend the necessary research and development funds to develop such works. Thus, intellectual property, contrary to being a "common heritage of mankind" is, in fact, an individually developed property right whose use should be compensated as fully as any other property.

Developed countries further assert that viewing intellectual property as a common heritage of mankind is harmful to developing countries since it denies these countries the ability to develop their own intellectual property. By denying protection to intellectual property, developing countries, they reason, lose the economic incentive to their own authors and inventors to create native-developed technology which could then be exported to other countries.

[18] Doris Estelle Long, *The Role of Intellectual Property in Developing Nations.* Copyright 1995 Doris E. Long. Excerpt reprinted with permission.

d. Case Studies in Conflict

1. The Caribbean Basin and Copyright Protection[19]

Increasingly dependent upon the sale of information, the United States deems the international protection of intellectual property a vital trade issue involving its competitive advantage in the world market.

The United States argues that inadequate protection of copyrights has definable detrimental economic effects. At a time when it can hardly be afforded, the problem has resulted in the large-scale loss of jobs in the United States. Furthermore, the production of intellectual products has become extremely costly, requiring research, development, and large-scale production expenses. Increasingly, the United States needs an expansive international market to recover its investment costs. Unrecoverable costs, resulting from inadequate copyright laws and enforcement, discourage production of copyrightable material due to a loss of incentives and unavailability of funds.

The United States stresses that inadequate copyright protection causes other identifiable "trade distortions." For example, pirated products imported into the United States displace sales of legitimate items on the domestic market. In addition, if products are pirated in non-US markets, they decrease United States exports to those markets. Furthermore, pirated parts exported from those non-US markets to third countries again displace United States

[19] Valerie L. Hummel, *The Search For A Solution To The U.S.-Caribbean Copyright Enforcement Controversy,* 16 FORDHAM INT'L L.J. 721. Copyright 1993 Fordham University School of Law. Excerpt reprinted with permission.

exports. In contrast with the view of Caribbean countries, the United States argues that lack of enforcement is equivalent to a trade barrier because inadequate enforcement deters international trade.

Recent approaches to solve the problem have been trade-based, with the United States holding trade pacts hostage to its demands for better copyright protection.

By contrast, Caribbean countries have an unenthusiastic attitude toward their own laws as well as toward international copyright laws. Their attitude is due in part to their perception that copyright law limits free access to intellectual property, thus hindering economic development.

Despite their ambivalence regarding copyright law, a significant number of Caribbean countries are signatories to international copyright conventions. Therefore, the inadequate protection of intellectual property in the Caribbean is more closely attributable to nonexistent or ineffectual enforcement of the law than to a total lack of substantive copyright laws.

A major enforcement effort would be necessary to adequately protect foreign copyrighted material in the Caribbean. Achieving sufficient enforcement of copyright laws demands complex and very costly administrative and judicial systems. The infrastructure required to support such systems is severely lacking in Caribbean Basin countries. Basic services, as well as skilled workers, technicians, and administrative personnel, are either scarce or completely lacking. Further infrastructure problems include substandard communications facilities, airports, roads, and other means of transportation. The problem is compounded by the notoriously slow bureaucracies of many Caribbean countries.

The public, of course, would bear the cost of developing the judicial and administrative infrastructures necessary for copyright law enforcement. Developing countries in general are reluctant to allocate scant government capital to the enforcement of intellectual property laws. In the Caribbean, a severe shortage of foreign currency, coupled with the belief that available resources are better spent elsewhere, renders the enforcement of foreign copyright laws a secondary concern. Many view piracy as having the benefit of producing desperately needed intellectual property at little cost to the public and with less sacrifice of the funds demanded for the development of infrastructure.

The inability or mere unwillingness of government and judicial officials to enforce copyright laws may also stem from political instability and widespread corruption. Enforcement efforts are thwarted when enforcement officers can be bribed to allow incidents of infringement to escape the sanctions provided for by the law.

In addition, Caribbean countries simply have no tradition of protecting intellectual property. The lack of tradition contrasts with the United States, where copyright law is so ingrained in US jurisprudence as to be included in the Constitution. Unlike the United States, Caribbean countries have few authors, inventors, or companies that would lobby for, or benefit from, sound intellectual property laws. Therefore, US outrage as to "mere" copyright violations are sometimes met if not with bafflement, then at least without complete understanding.

QUESTIONS AND COMMENTS FOR YOUR CONSIDERATION

1. To what extent is a developed country justified in conditioning economic aid directed to fields such as industrial or educational advancement upon the protection of intellectual property rights?

2. Given the lack of a tradition of protection of certain forms of intellectual property, can the external imposition of protection norms affectively combat such lack of tradition?

2. Thailand and Pharmaceutical Patents[20]

A patent represents a government grant of a "monopoly" of limited duration on the use of an invention or discovery. Although patent laws vary from country to country, if an invention is novel, useful, and not obvious, and if the invention fits within the statutory categories of protectable inventions, it is generally patentable. Much of the controversy in international patent law surrounds variations, from country to country, in patentable categories. Because the owner of a patent can charge a royalty for the use of the patented invention, if a country refuses to recognize a patentable category, such a refusal will necessarily affect the cost of using a given technology in that country.

Western countries generally believe that a patent system provides the best overall incentive to encourage invention. Although this assertion is difficult to prove, it forms the basis for the extensive patent systems in Western industrialized countries, including the United States. This implicitly assumes that all economies necessarily benefit from an increased number of inventions. When an invention is granted patent protection, investors are more willing to invest because profits are higher if competition is reduced. Western Industrialized Countries also believe that patents encourage the development or transfer of the technology necessary to utilize the patent. Thus, according to the Western view, a system of patent laws can lead to economic development despite the cost of the royalties.

While the US Government and businesses subscribe to the views of the majority of other Western Industrialized Countries and contend that all countries would benefit from granting and enforcing patents on pharmaceuticals, many countries, including most Third World nations, do not grant patents for inventions in agriculture and medicine. These countries may fear drastic price increases that would result from paying royalties on patented pharmaceutical and agricultural technology as well as a loss of control over technology that is vital to national development. The Thai Patent Act, before its recent revisions, served as a typical example of the limitations developing countries place on their patent laws.

The Thai Patent Act ("Act"), originally passed in 1979, is the primary source of patent protection in Thailand. On February 27, 1992, the Thai Legislative Assembly passed a revision of the Act. The revision was intended to satisfy US objections to the 1979 Act.

The United States objected to several provisions of the Act as originally ratified. The strongest complaint of US patent owners was that the 1979 Act excluded pharmaceutical, agricultural, and biological products from patent protection, thereby causing a significant loss of revenue. US owners also complained that fifteen years was an insufficient term for patent protection. Finally, the 1979 Act provided that a patent must be worked in Thailand; otherwise, the patent would be subject to either a compulsory license or revocation.

3. US Pressure on Thailand[21]

In 1991, Thailand became one of three countries identified as a priority country under Special 301 for its failure to enforce copyrights and for deficient patent protection for pharmaceuticals.

The Thai government reaction was reserved. Then Prime Minister Chatichai Choonhavan was unconcerned about US threats, taking the view that what the United States did not buy, Japan would. Current Prime Minister Anand Panyarachun's more circumspect stance has been to recognize that the United States is now Thailand's largest export market and a world economic power, while at the same time indicating that the national interest must come first.

---

[20] Stefan Kirchanski, *Protection of US Patent Rights in Developing Countries: US Efforts to Enforce Pharmaceutical Patents in Thailand,* 16 Loy. L.A. Int'l & Comp. L.J. 569. Copyright 1993 Loyola of Los Angeles International and Comparative Law Journal. Excerpt reprinted with permission.

[21] Ted L. McDorman, *U.S.-Thailand Trade Disputes: Applying Section 301 to Cigarettes and Intellectual Property,* 14 Mich. J. Int'l L. 90. Copyright 1992 University of Michigan Law School. Excerpt reprinted with permission.

In 1987, the Thai government responded to US pressure to provide for stronger copyright enforcement and penalties by putting amendments to the Copyright Act before the legislature. However, significant opposition arose to the proposed legislation with a political intensity that resulted in an election, a new coalition government, and a reexamination of the entire copyright issue. The strongest opposition came from those arguing that change to Thailand's intellectual property laws amounted to capitulation to US bullying. Two years later Prime Minister Chatichai's defiance of the United States on the GSP issue was widely supported in Thailand. Thailand accepted cuts in GSP benefits from the United States rather than altering its intellectual property laws.

The prevailing view in Thailand is that the government should not yield to US pressure on intellectual property rights. For example, the government minister responsible for negotiating with the United States during 1991 was referred to as a "traitor" for allegedly yielding to US demands.

In the pharmaceutical area, those opposed to change in the Patent Act, such as the Thai Pharmaceutical Manufacturers Association, argue that foreign drug monopolies will take over the Thai market and this will lead to higher prices and a reduction in the availability of drugs to the poor. Other arguments against the Patent Act amendments can be raised, such as questioning the necessity of increasing intellectual property protection for US nationals when they already hold more patents, trademarks, and copyrights in Thailand than Thais, and bemoaning the increased outflow of royalties to be expected with enhanced intellectual property protection, but these are not significant positions taken by opponents to change in Thailand.

It is tempting to evaluate the Section 301 experience by determining whether its use has led to changes that benefit the United States. However, it is more appropriate to evaluate the Section 301 experience by looking from both the Thai and US point of view. Four specific criteria can be used: short term economics; long term economics; impact on the international regime (GATT); and short term political impact.

From the US point of view, the operation of Section 301 and its threat of embargoes has had an immediate positive economic effect. Thailand's intellectual property laws and practices are being altered to comply with the US demands. US companies can anticipate an immediate economic return. The immediate economic effect in Thailand of changes forced upon it by US use of Section 301 is one of expected increased cost for certain pharmaceutical drugs and increased government expenditures on enforcement of intellectual property law. There will also be an increase in royalty payments made to the United States because of increased intellectual property protection. The Thais will derive little short-term economic benefit from the changes made in response to Section 301 action.

Moreover, there exists resentment about the one-sided nature of the US Section 301 policy. The United States uses economic coercion to force change on Thailand, yet Thailand can expect no reciprocity from the United States when internal US policies are in question, such as subsidized rice exports that unfairly disadvantage Thai rice producers.

In the long-term, Thailand may be able to see some positive economic impacts from adopting the US recommendations. As an economic matter, some conclude that the protection of intellectual property rights, including patent protection for pharmaceuticals, should lead to substantial long-term benefits in the form of increased investment and developing technology. Moreover, it can be argued that if Thailand is to emerge as one of the newly industrialized countries, its intellectual property laws and practice must be brought into line with those of industrialized countries. The problem is that it is unclear whether industrialization precedes, or follows, intellectual property protection. The prevailing view appears to be that increased intellectual property protection leads to increased investment and economic development. However, it is difficult to reconcile this approach with the experiences of Japan, Taiwan, and Hong Kong. For example, Japan did not recognize certain types of patents until 1975, although today it is one of the strongest supporters of US efforts. As one author has commented:

> Though apparently it cost them international respect at the time, the Japanese policy of tolerating the copying of imports appears to have benefitted their economy in the early period of

development without producing long-term negative effects. Looking at the Japanese experience, a country presently in the early stages of development might choose a similar course.

It is worth noting that one study determined that the degree of intellectual property rights protection afforded by Thailand matches its current stage of economic development.

Where the international trading system is weak, as it allegedly is in intellectual property protection and trade dispute resolution, it can be argued that US unilateralism will lead the way in developing new and necessary responses to these issues. Section 301 results in pressure to agree in areas where a lack of international discipline is, in the long term, capable of undermining the entire international trading system.

While increased use of the GATT dispute settlement process is not inherently bad, the deadlines on GATT adjudication and compliance imposed under the US law are unrealistic.

More importantly, the United States itself does not comply with the standards, nor does it easily accept adverse GATT rulings. Regarding intellectual property, it is argued that a new approach is necessary to increase standards of protection.

US pressure on Thailand regarding intellectual property protection may have created significant short-term political costs in Thailand. As previously noted, there is significant opposition to Thailand's perceived capitulation to US pressure. The current unelected Thai government is in a position of not having to respond directly to such pressure. With elections coming, a politician's stance on standing up to US pressure could be important. Moreover, former military leader General Suchinda Kraprayoon expressed irritation with the US government's perceived meddling in Thai internal matters and has been quoted as saying that the United States was not the "world's big boss," and that "if I were the Thai Government, I would not allow the US to treat me this way." It has been speculated that the United States has softened its stand on Thai intellectual property issues because of the fear that resentment of any US action could lead to greater political instability.

From the US perspective, Section 301 has been successfully utilized to further its short and long term economic and international interests. However, it is clear that utilization of Section 301 against Thailand has not been without its costs. Resentment of US pressure tactics has created an anti-US political constituency in Thailand where none had existed and has created significant problems for the civilian government as Thailand seeks to regain democratic processes. The resentment is increased because of the one-sided nature of the US action—demanding changes from Thailand without rectifying US inadequacies and GATT inconsistencies that are detrimental to Thai interests. The unilateral nature of the US action does not create confidence in international rules upon which Thailand is dependent.

The perception in Thailand, regardless of how the dispute is portrayed by the United States, is of a stronger, more powerful friend publicly bullying its smaller, more vulnerable partner into complying with unwanted laws and practices. It is a perception that will not be readily forgotten in The Land of Smiles.[22]

C. Transplantation

1. Transplanting Intellectual Property Values[23]

Much of the early scholarship in the area of comparative law focused on the importation, reception and/or transplantation of one system's jurisprudence to another. For example, Roman legal concepts were "received" into much of Europe through their rediscovery in the Middle Ages and the "adoption" of these concepts into the emerging laws of countries such as France and Germany. Early differences between common law countries, such as England and the United States, and civil law countries, such as France and Germany, often arose as a result of the differing degrees to which Roman law concepts were adopted into each country's legal system. Efforts at developing

---

[22] Editor's Note: For a detailed discussion of Special 301, *see* Chapter 10.

[23] Written for this Anthology by Doris Estelle Long. Copyright 1996 Doris E. Long.

international standards of protection for intellectual property rights, whether through accession and compliance with substantive norms contained in bilateral or multinational treaties, or through the revision of present national laws as part of a country's efforts to "harmonize" its laws with other nations' treatment, necessarily require consideration of many of the same factors which affected earlier instances at reception and transplantation.

Regardless of the status of a country as a developed (industrialized) or developing (less industrialized or newly industrialized) country, its efforts to create or revise existing intellectual property law norms must begin with consideration of the effect the adoption of another country's norms will have—not merely on those laws affecting intellectual property—but on the country's historical and cultural treatment of such underlying issues as the ownership and use of intangible property, the protection of information and public access to ideas, information and expressions.

2. Legal Transplants[24]

A "legal transplant" may be defined as any legal notion or rule which, after being developed in a "source" body of law, is then introduced into another, "host" body of law. A classic example is found in the Corpus Juris Civilis, the compendium of Roman Law which the Emperor Justinian commissioned almost fifteen centuries ago. Law encapsulated in the Corpus Juris has found a host in Continental European law over the last thousand years. This process has been called the "reception" of Roman law into modern European law.

Copyright law governs how literary and artistic works may be exploited. The rise of copyright might have begun when paper and printing were first invented in China. Copyright statutes were in fact first instituted during the eighteenth century in Europe. With ever-accelerating technological advances, media exploitation has crossed national borders with increasing frequency and speed. As a result, there has been increasing pressure to extend and harmonize copyright law internationally. Legal transplants have served as a common device for achieving this end.

For example, in the middle of the nineteenth century, France threatened not to renew its commercial treaty with Belgium. As a condition of renewal, France required Belgium to adopt a copyright law, this at a time when French law provided a model for copyright on much of the European continent. The British Copyright Act of 1911 is another example: it was transplanted throughout the British Empire in the twentieth century, until such time as British colonies and dominions became independent and enacted their own copyright laws, more or less on the British model. Not all of these jurisdictions, however, fall squarely within Anglo-American legal culture: Quebec, India, and Israel, most notably, also draw upon different, pre-existing traditions.

How do transplants work? This question may take empirical and normative forms. Empirically, we may ask about the fate of transplanted law in passing from a source to a host body of law. This inquiry becomes problematic to the extent that linguistic, cultural, or historical perspectives change when moving from the source to the host body of law. Does the transplant nonetheless work much as it did in the source law, is it modified in form or substance in the different host law, or is it simply rejected by it? Normatively, to the extent the transplant takes place without significant change, we have to ask: is such slavish reception justified? And, if so, by reference to whose values?

a. Realist Arguments for Transplants[25]

A legal "realist" would treat the law, to quote Oliver Wendel Holmes, as a "body of systematized prediction" concerning the likely behavior of lawmakers and agents, from legislators through judges to the police. One could then make decisions in the light of such predictions or, where necessary, attempt to change the institutions of the law

[24] Paul Edward Geller, *Legal Transplants in International Copyright: Some Problems of Method,* 13 UCLA Pac. Basin L.J. 199. Copyright 1994 Regents of the University of California. Excerpt reprinted with permission.

[25] Paul Edward Geller, *Legal Transplants in International Copyright: Some Problems of Method,* 13 UCLA Pac. Basin L.J. 199. Copyright 1994 Regents of the University of California. Excerpt reprinted with permission.

resulting in predicted, but unfavorable behavior.

If, for example, a lawyer warned a business client that the law of another country was not adequate to protect creations in which the business had invested, the business could then seek to have copyright law thought to be effective at home transplanted into that country. The rationale seems simple enough: a country protects its nationals' property on its own soil with its laws, and comity generally leads other countries to protect foreigners' property on their soil, except for intellectual property which has not benefitted from this approach. One response to foreign failure to protect copyright would be proceedings, such as those in the United States, in which the business may petition its own government to use threats of trade retaliations against countries abroad serving as pirate havens.

b. Normativist Arguments About Transplants[26]

What might be called "normativist" positions pick up where realist arguments leave off. In this century, Hans Kelsen re-articulated the basic argument of such positions, namely that statements about facts, about what "is," cannot serve as adequate bases for statements about how the law "ought" to work. While realists might dwell on how a notion or rule "is" transplanted from one body of law into another, normativists would ask why the transplant "ought" to have effect as law. Normativism can be elaborated into different approaches to transplants.

The most ambitious of these approaches is "universalist" normativism. In a seminal analysis, Kant attempted to derive one overriding norm universally valid for any system of law. In copyright, arguments have been made for legal transplants on the basis of supposedly universal, "permanent cultural values." The title of the first copyright statute, the British Statute of Anne of 1710, already anticipates this sense of some common, higher aim of copyright law by setting out "the Encouragement of Learning" as the purpose of the statute. During the eighteenth century, in Enlightenment Europe, such notions as "learning" or "science" were broadly understood to include all products of mind, including literature, music, and the fine arts, that might advance human consciousness of the world.

Another approach might be called "systemic" normativism. Kelsen elaborated such a position, defining a system of law as including only such rules as may be generated consistently with its own underlying norms. This position may serve as the basis for arguing that transplants may not be understood as foreign notions or rules that a system of law passively takes on. If one system received law from another, as European civil law incorporated Roman notions, its own constitutive norms would at least have to validate them. From this point of view, universalist aims for copyright, such as "learning," "human consciousness," or "permanent cultural values," are at best window dressing, not justifications. Indeed, for systemic normativism, values as such, whether universal or local, cannot form the basis for adopting legal rules, since values themselves must derive from underlying norms for legal purposes. As a result, to understand the normative basis, for example, for the reception into China of the Berne model of copyright, some norm of Chinese law would have to be invoked. One could invoke the Chinese provision that, in the event of any difference "between the Civil Law of the People's Republic of China and its international treaties, the latter shall prevail." However, this principle itself seems to be borrowed from Continental European approaches to international treaties, raising the question of what underlying Chinese norm in turn validates it as a basis for further transplants.

c. Relativist Challenges to Transplant Analysis[27]

"Relativism" involves the suspicion that our own linguistic, cultural, or historical perspectives distort our knowledge of other such perspectives. Benjamin Lee Whorf encapsu-

[26] Paul Edward Geller, *Legal Transplants in International Copyright: Some Problems of Method*, 13 UCLA PAC. BASIN L.J. 199. Copyright 1994 Regents of the University of California. Excerpt reprinted with permission.

[27] Paul Edward Geller, *Legal Transplants in International Copyright: Some Problems of Method*, 13 UCLA PAC. BASIN L.J. 199. Copyright 1994 Regents of the University of California. Excerpt reprinted with permission.

lated this position in speaking of language as "a vast pattern-system" made up of "culturally ordained . . . forms and categories" that channel our "consciousness." This point of view does not lead to arguments against transplants as much as it makes them seem difficult, if not impossible, to analyze from our own, necessarily biased perspective.

The Italian maxim *traduttore, traditore*—translator, traitor—succinctly conveys the lesson of relativism. In the common and civil laws, whose languages share European roots, basic notions like "right" or "law" do not take on meaning consistently.

Starting at the linguistic dimension of relativism, we thus quickly encounter its cultural and historical dimensions. It is well and good to say that copyright law is to enhance "permanent cultural values" or to protect "the most sacred of properties." Nonetheless, such notions of "law" and "culture," not to mention "property" and "the sacred," if taken together, seem to refer to manifold processes not easily disentangled. As a result, we run the risk of encountering radically different types of entanglements of law and culture; indeed, the very concept of "law," not to mention "culture," may vary from place to place and period to period. Further, it cannot be assumed that the effect of law on culture will be as simple to see as that of a tool applied to raw material, say, the mark of a chisel used on a piece of marble. Generally, and certainly in copyright, we have to take account of intricate and subtle feed-back mechanisms between legal and other cultural processes, notably by way of the media.

Relativism, if carried far enough, leads to a kind of solipsism. It highlights epistemological obstacles that would make it difficult, if not impossible, to know just how transplants from a source law might operate in an exotic host law. The fact that languages are translated, however, gives us reason to believe that these obstacles are not insurmountable, even though "[t]ime, distance, disparities of outlook or assumed reference make this act [of translation] more or less difficult."

In transplants, we face the problem of translating terms from one language into another. Where transplants include open-ended notions, such translation becomes problematic.

In one of its dominant forms, linguistic relativism has focused on the tendency of differently structured languages to lead to different descriptions of reality. For example, the Hopi Indians, in the southwestern United States, have been observed to employ a verb system that enables them to make finer discriminations of the phases and unfolding of natural processes than one could easily do in any European language. It is nonetheless possible to learn to speak an exotic language with some competence, albeit imperfectly: if, hypothetically, we were dropped into the midst of a tribe with an unknown language, we could with increasing success translate as "rabbit" a word we heard the tribe repeatedly use while hunting, pointing to, or eating what appears to us to be rabbits. There would still remain the hard cases of all-too-frequent, open-ended notions: for example, the French word bois accurately translates into the English "wood" or "woods" often enough, but it is not clear whether *le Bois de Boulogne* is best translated as "Boulogne Park" or the "Boulogne Woods."

If we shift our attention to legal language, the problem of translation becomes much more complex. Legal discourse fulfills a large range of "performative" functions in implementing norms rather than merely making "true or false" statements about facts. However, some commentators still look to factual reference, not merely to test translations from different languages, but even interpretation within the same legal language. For example, realists suggest that, unless the law indicates the behavior it is to control by its very "words," it represents nothing but vague "paper rules." The fact of the matter is that legal discourse remains endemically riddled with value-laden, open-ended notions that resist factual clarification. Such discourse nonetheless allows legal practitioners to communicate, at least within relatively homogeneous legal cultures. Furthermore, conceptions of "fact" and "law," and of how facts relate to the law, vary from culture to culture. It often becomes necessary to understand these conceptions to disentangle meanings in other laws.

Of course, different legal notions differ in the extent that they are open-ended. For example, in the Berne Convention, the notion of "publication" is more precisely defined than the notion of a "work." Berne "publication" is defined by rather objective criteria, notably the requirement of making hard copies available to the public. The very fact that the case law has developed converging interpretations of Berne "publication" indicates that this notion is only marginally open-ended. By contrast, Article 2 of the Berne Convention only illustrates the notion of a protected "work" with an open-ended list of examples, and there is still debate on how to interpret this notion. Commentators offer conflicting answers to the questions: does the Berne Convention or national law determine the defining criteria of works, such as "originality" and "creativity"? and what legal effects, if any, follow from placing a work in the Berne list? Of course, if the language of the Berne Convention authoritatively defined "work," it would control how this notion was transplanted into the national laws of Berne countries; otherwise, domestic lawmakers would have discretion in defining it. The courts tend to ignore all these issues for the simple reason that there is a rough and ready consensus worldwide on the sense of "works." There are nonetheless, frequently enough, hard cases in which courts disagree on how to apply this notion. Cases of factual compilations, industrial designs, and computer programs are among the most notable.

Bear in mind that the notion of a "work" is understood against the background of aesthetic sensibilities that vary from culture to culture. For example, Brad Sherman describes the reluctance of the Anglo-Australians to dignify graphic creations by native Australians as "artistic works," much less find them to be "original" or "creative." The Anglo-Australians encountered obstacles to understanding how the term "work," as interpreted in cases involving European art, might apply in native Australian culture in which creative works take on different, but nonetheless rich significance. To take another example, the Peoples Republic of China, in its Copyright Act of 1990, introduced new categories of "works," for example, quyi works "based on traditional forms created mainly for performance through recitation, music, or both." As indicated above, some commentators might argue that works in this new category, if it is construed to fall outside the list in Article 2 of the Berne Convention, do not benefit from Berne minimum rights. Anglo-Australian incomprehension before Aboriginal art and Berne purism concerning unlisted works tend to have comparable effects with regard to transplanting relevant law. Either way, the "common core" meaning of the Berne notion of "work," historically the European meaning, is made the standard for non-European works.

In moving from language to culture, we have to widen our framework of analysis. Legislators or treaty drafters might blithely use a notion like "work" without contemplating the entire range of cases in which it might not always have clear meaning. It is in applying the notion in troublesome cases that difficulties might arise in interpreting the rules that it helps to articulate. These cases are likely to be entangled in complex cultural settings, in which a variety of factors come to bear on interpreting possibly applicable rules.

Such cultural inquiry might be broken down into the following questions: First, who, in the community of legal practitioners, has power to interpret a rule? Some systems tend to decentralize such powers in judges with discretion to refashion law case by case, while others tend to centralize them in legislators. Second, what values and theory direct the interpretation of rules? Some values are relevant to all law, such as equity and reliability, while others become relevant only in specific fields such as copyright. As well as encapsulating such values, legal theory may also entail premises about law itself that, depending on their tenor, differently guide the interpretation of legal language.

3. Historical Problems

a. Printing Privileges and Copyright Monopolies[28]

Since the late Renaissance the French Crown regulated the publishing industry;

---

[28] Jane C. Ginsburg, *A Tale of Two Copyrights: Literary Property in Revolutionary France and America,* 64 TUL. L. REV. 991. Copyright 1990 Tulane Law Review Association. Excerpt reprinted with permission.

publishing monopolies were an offshoot of royal censorship. The author, or more often, the publisher or bookseller, applied for permission to publish the work and sought the privilege of holding the exclusive right of its publication. Under the edicts of 1777-78, the Crown afforded printing privileges to both authors and printers. The author's privilege was perpetual, but once ceded to the publisher, or if initially acquired by the publisher, it lasted only during the life of the author. By the end of the ancien regime, much rhetoric proclaiming the sanctity and self-evidence of exclusive literary property rights had infiltrated the copyright debate, most of it propounded by publishers invoking authors' rights for the publishers' benefit, some of it by government advocates invoking authors' rights to curb publishers' assertions.

The system of printing privileges was conditioned upon compliance with formalities: deposit of copies in national libraries, inclusion of the text of the privilege in each printed copy, and registration of copies with the publishers' guild. Remedies afforded by the privilege included injunctions and damages, as well as seizure, confiscation, and destruction of infringing copies. In addition to controlling the right to publish the work, the Crown also regulated rights of public performance of dramatic works by vesting in the Comedie Francaise the exclusive right to perform such works.

b. The Suppressive Role of Historical Copyright[29]

When William Caxton brought the first press from Mainz to England in 1476, and installed it at Westminster at the Sign of the Red Pale, there is no reason to suppose that either he or his machine attracted much notice. The War of the Roses was still being fought on the plains of England; the attention of the Crown was fully engaged by this internecine strife. But in 1529, with the Tudor monarchy now more or less firmly on the Throne, and yet still in need of some means to suppress the steady stream of dissident speech that threatened the Establishment, Henry promulgated an Index Librorum Prohibitum, a formal edict against unlicensed manuscripts—an edict clearly meant to bring the press at last to heel. Other measures, including a formal system of licensing and censorship, followed almost immediately.

Copyright grew directly from these efforts at suppression. To be sure, formal licensing ended in 1694 when Parliament finally allowed the Printing Act to expire. But the Stationers Company, to whom Phillip and Mary had issued a Royal Charter as early as 1557, survived in the form of a guild. Lacking the protection of a license to print, however, and now confronting severe and unaccustomed competition in the form of what today we would no doubt call "pirate presses," the Stationers sought refuge in a petition to Parliament for an Act that would protect their "right of copy" in the books they themselves printed. Parliament responded, in 1709, with the first formal copyright act, the Statute of Anne. Anglo-American copyright, in all of its contemporary manifestations, can be traced directly to this Statute and to the history that led to its enactment.

Not only did the introduction of the press into English life lead directly to the development of copyright in Anglo-American law—the press led also, in somewhat less immediate but no less consequential ways, to our very ability even to think of creative expression as property. Indeed, were it not for the press, relentlessly propagating the linear text, intellectual property as we know it simply could not exist.

In theory, copyright can appear quite benign: what is protected under the law is merely the expression; the idea within the expression always remains available to all; eventually, when the term of copyright has run, even the expression itself is injected into the public domain, where others may make of it whatever use they please. In practice, however, the copyright system proves troublesome, for at least three reasons.

First, of course, the copyright system does lend itself, infrequently but recurringly, to efforts aimed at the direct suppression of speech. Copyright theories figured, for

[29] David Lange, *At Play in the Fields of the Word: Copyright and the Construction of Authorship in the Post-Literate Millennium*, 55-SPG Law & Contemp. Probs. 139. Copyright 1992 Law & Contemporary Problems. Excerpt reprinted with permission.

example, in the United States Government's efforts to prevent the Pentagon Papers from being published; in Howard Hughes's attempts to suppress unwelcome biographies; and in Time, Incorporated's efforts to prevent the publication of photographs of the assassination of President Kennedy. In these cases the efforts at suppression ultimately proved unsuccessful—though, significantly, they could not be dismissed out of hand. Other efforts, meanwhile, have succeeded: in the suit by Gerald Ford and his publisher against Nation magazine, for example, which had the effect of limiting and delaying the publication of Presidential memoirs; in J.D. Salinger's suit against a biographer who was prevented from publishing letters actually already on deposit in a library; and (in some ways more significant than either of these cases) in numerous suits by the proprietors of expression one might call "valuably bourgeois"—of which the first example that comes to mind is Walt Disney's action to suppress the satiric distortion of Mickey Mouse at the hands of the counterculture in "head comics," circa 1969-78.

Second, copyright is a major "player" in the establishment of institutions that, at a secondary level of engagement, also serve to validate some speech at the expense of other speech. I have in mind, of course, the institutional Press or Fourth Estate, which could not exist comfortably in its present form without some protection against copying. But the Press is small change compared to the rest of the media, including the entertainment industry, which are absolutely dependent upon intellectual property for the revenues that give the media their present character. And of course we prize that character for many reasons. Indeed, entertainment appears to be the last great field of productivity within which the United States enjoys undisputed hegemony throughout the world. In this connection, then, and others, intellectual property directly advances the economic and cultural interests of not merely the media, but the Nation at large.

Third, I would say that copyright is capricious. Sometimes, to be sure, it leads the creative individual to recognition and reward. Too often, though—or so I think—it threatens embarrassment and ruin. In this sense copyright seems to represent an assault upon creative expression or play, carried out in two rather specific ways. On the one hand, copyright imperils the essence of the creative process by penalizing the unconscious infringement. I suppose almost everyone knows how George Harrison's "My Sweet Lord" was found to be an infringement of the earlier "He's So Fine," despite the court's conviction that Harrison actually had no recollection of the earlier song when he composed his own. This is an outcome defensible, if at all, only if one sees the issues essentially in economic terms. The impact on creativity is altogether indefensible—at least I have never encountered a persuasive defense of it; and yet it is a mainstay of copyright jurisprudence that innocence is not a defense to a finding of infringement. Meanwhile, always, copyright inhibits (when, indeed, it does not suppress outright) the creation of what copyright lawyers call "derivative works": those works in which the invention lies in deliberate imitation and improvement—works which, historically, have been among the most sublimely creative human achievements.

These surely are troublesome aspects of the relationship between copyright and society. In each instance, copyright proves to be (or to have the capacity to be) suppressive. In each case the mechanism of suppression lies embedded in the concept of authorship. And here, surely, is a curious circumstance. We value authorship, or so we say insistently in the main theories of the field. And yet it appears, again and again, that we merely value some authors, and then at the expense of others. Eventually, it would seem, we must ask what it is, exactly, that we prize in authors.

Why do we "attach a certain importance" to authorship? Foucault tells us:

> The author allows a limitation of the cancerous and dangerous proliferation of significations within a world where one is thrifty not only with one's resources and riches, but also with one's discourses and their significations. The author is the principle of thrift in the proliferation of meaning. As a result, we must entirely reverse the traditional idea of the author. We are accustomed . . . to saying that the author is the genial creator of a work in which he deposits, with infinite wealth and generosity, an inexhaustible world

> of significations. We are used to thinking that the author is so different from all other men, and so transcendent with regard to all languages that, as soon as he speaks, meaning begins to proliferate, to proliferate indefinitely.
>
> The truth is quite the contrary: the author is not an indefinite source of significations which fill a work; the author does not precede the work; he is a certain functional principle by which, in our culture, one limits, excludes, and chooses; in short, by which one impedes the free circulation, the free manipulation, the free composition, decomposition, and recomposition of fiction. In fact, if we are accustomed to presenting the author as a genius, as a perpetual surging of invention, it is because, in reality, we make him function in exactly the opposite fashion. One can say that the author is an ideological product, since we represent him as the opposite of his historically real function. . . . The author is therefore the ideological figure by which one marks the manner in which we fear the proliferation of meaning.[30]

Rich in insight though this passage is, I think it still does not quite capture the subject. Foucault, himself a Marxist, says that "since the eighteenth century, the author has played the role of the regulator of the fictive, a role quite characteristic of our era of industrial and bourgeois society, of individualism and private property. . . . " And of course I think this is partly true. But his statement does not recognize—at least it does not acknowledge—the larger role of authorship in at least the three previous centuries as well—centuries in which, not bourgeois society, but rather the authority of the Crown, was implicated.

It is essential to intellectual property and authorship as we know them that there have been a press and a state. Plagiarism, attribution, distortion, truncation, mutilation, and the like—the so-called "moral rights"—are an obsession of the bourgeoisie. The fact remains that authorizing speech, historically, has been the work of the state—of any state, whether bourgeois or not. And it is for reasons implicit in that larger history that intellectual property and authorship cannot easily be defended in any society today which prizes freedom of expression.

The concept of personal and individual authorship, as we understand it today, was dependent upon the "invention" of the typographically fixed title page. Typographical fixity was also necessary to fix the identity of the text itself. Before the introduction of printing, works were copied and recopied, often introducing a multiplicity of minor errors, additions, or deletions by scribes. The proliferation of works attributed to classical authors (many now often cited with the prefix "Pseudo" before the name under which the work appeared) was a natural outcome of scribal culture.

As Elizabeth Eisenstein has demonstrated, "scribal culture could not sustain the patenting of inventions or the copyrighting of literary compositions. It worked against the concept of intellectual property rights." With the typographical fixity and attribution made possible by printing, authorship became a matter of personal responsibility, and respect for the "wisdom of the ages" correspondingly declined. Authorship and invention, the very acts to be rewarded by intellectual property law, may not be timeless concepts plucked from Heaven but may emerge in conjunction with—and be inextricably intertwined with—the technology that makes them possible. The relationship between intellectual property rights and technology poses a very important question: If laws are dependent for their emergence and validation upon technological innovations, might not succeeding innovations require that those very laws pass back out of existence?

One might have supposed that the end of copyright was at hand when photography entered the field in the nineteenth century. For the challenge to copyright offered by photography lay in the fact that the idea-expression dichotomy—which, as we have seen, was central to the concept of "property" in the linear text generated by the press—no longer made sense when the medium was one in which idea and expression could be perfectly merged—in which, indeed, idea and expression were meant to be merged.

---

[30] MICHAEL FOUCAULT, WHAT IS AN AUTHOR? 274 (1989).

And yet, as it happened, nothing happened. Copyright went right on trying to protect expression without appropriating ideas—which is to say, that copyright simply began to work even more imperfectly than before.

If intellectual property survives, it will be obliged to reckon with a reality foreign to its origins. No longer will it lend itself to the construction of authorship for the purpose of advancing and suppressing speech. Perhaps there will be room for encouragement of productivity and for appropriation of investment even so. But there will be no place for suppression; no balances to be struck against the interests of creativity; and no moral rights of authors to be served, save this one: that anyone who wishes will be free to play in the fields of the word.

c. The Harmonizing Role of Historical Accuracy[31]

The French and US copyright systems are well known as opposites. The product of the French Revolution, French copyright law is said to enshrine the author: exclusive rights flow from one's (preferred) status as a creator. For example, a leading French copyright scholar states that one of the " 'fundamental ideas' " of the revolutionary copyright laws is the principle that " 'an exclusive right is conferred on authors because their property is the most justified since it flows from their intellectual creation.' " By contrast, the US Constitution's copyright clause, echoing the English Statute of Anne, makes the public's interest equal, if not superior, to the author's. This clause authorizes the establishment of exclusive rights of authors as a means to maximize production of and access to intellectual creations.

Pursuing this comparison, one might observe that post-revolutionary French laws and theorists portray the existence of an intimate and almost sacred bond between authors and their works as the source of a strong literary and artistic property right. Thus, France's leading modern exponent of copyright theory, the late Henri Desbois, grandly proclaimed: "The author is protected as an author, in his status as a creator, because a bond unites him to the object of his creation. In the French tradition, Parliament has repudiated the utilitarian concept of protecting works of authorship in order to stimulate literary and artistic activity."

By contrast, Anglo-American exponents of copyright law and policy often have viewed the author's right grudgingly. One of copyright's reluctant advocates, Lord Macaulay, labeled the institution of copyright as "exceedingly bad," but was willing to tolerate it as the means to promote the dissemination of socially useful works. In this view, copyright should afford authors control no greater than strictly necessary to induce the author to perform his part of the social exchange.

Conceptions of French copyright law as author-oriented and of Anglo-American copyright law as society-oriented carry certain corollaries. In general, one may anticipate that the more author-centered the system, the more protective the copyright regime will be. And the extent of this author-centrism will promote some interests over others. For example, some argue that the different foci of the systems account for the active protection of authors' noneconomic moral rights to receive attribution for and preserve the artistic integrity of their creations in France, and for the traditional paucity of such safeguards in the US. Similarly, the French perspective will encompass most comfortably works of discernible literary or artistic content, while the US emphasis on social utility may explain its historically vigorous copyright coverage of works such as compilations conveying much information but little subjective authorial contribution, as well as its present receptivity to computer program protection.

Another consequence of different copyright conceptions pertains to the role of formalities. Formalities are state-imposed conditions on the existence or exercise of copyright. If copyright is essentially a governmental incentive program, many formal prerequisites may accompany the grant. For example, requiring the author to affix a notice of copyright, or to register and deposit copies of the work with a government agency, before the right will be recognized or enforced is fully consistent with a public-benefit view of copyright. But these requirements clash with a characterization of copy-

---

[31] Jane C. Ginsburg; *A Tale of Two Copyrights: Literary Property in Revolutionary France and America,* 64 TUL. L. REV. 991. Copyright 1990 Tulane Law Review Association. Excerpt reprinted with permission.

right as springing from the creative act. If copyright is born with the work, then no further state action should be necessary to confer the right; the sole relevant act is the work's creation.

Despite these paradigms, the differences between the US and French copyright systems are neither as extensive nor as venerable as typically described. In particular, despite the conventional portrayal, the French revolutionary laws did not articulate or implement a conception of copyright substantially different from that of the regimes across the Channel and across the Atlantic. The French revolutionary sources themselves cast doubt upon the assumed authorcentrism of the initial French copyright legislation. The speeches in the revolutionary assemblies, the texts of the laws, and the court decisions construing the laws, all indicate at least a strong instrumentalist undercurrent to the French decrees of 1791 and 1793. Similarly, while the law of US letters predominantly reflects and implements utilitarian policies, US law was not impervious to authors' claims of personal right. Indeed, some of the earliest US state copyright laws set forth author-oriented rationales of which any modern Frenchman would be proud—and from which some revolutionary legislators might have drawn considerable inspiration.

Historical accuracy may promote future legislative harmonization; now that increasing US participation in international copyright agreements and policy-making bodies calls key features of the US copyright system into discussion, one can properly argue that US copyright has not always been different from that of its Continental partners. The comparison of systems shows that their distinctions are neither original nor immutable. A copyright regime's initial instrumentalist formulation does not preclude later reception of more personalist notions of protection. By the same token, a modern author-oriented copyright system's reference to its utilitarian past may assist its absorption of newer productions perhaps remote from the core of the *beaux arts*.

QUESTIONS AND COMMENTS FOR YOUR CONSIDERATION

1. The history behind the recognition (or non-recognition) of protection afforded a particular form of intellectual property often reflects the philosophical and cultural role that form of intellectual property plays in a country's heritage. To what extent do the issues of historical censorship, free public access and exchange of ideas, and the grant of monopoly power to encourage the creation of new works influence current debates over the establishment of international intellectual property norms?
2. To what extent does the historical treatment of intellectual property preclude the effective enforcement of international protection norms? For example, can a history of piracy be overcome? If so, what is required?
3. For an historical overview of various attempts to establish multinational treaties governing the protection of intellectual property rights, *see* Chapter Seven.

4. Cultural Problems[32]

The artistic resource of a nation or a region has always been part of the fabric or glue of its culture. The significance of works of art as rallying points for a nation or a cause are well known. Picasso's "Guernica" is a good example of the symbolism and the power that an image by an artist can create, related to a political cause. This now world-famous work was a protest to the bombing of the city of Guernica, Spain, during the Spanish Civil War. The piece itself has become a symbol of the Spanish nation as it

---

[32] Stanley S. Madeja, *The Arts As A Cultural And Economic Factor In World Trade,* 14 N. Ill. U. L. Rev. 439. Copyright 1994 Northern Illinois University. Excerpt reprinted with permission.

now exists. The painting, which resided in the United States for a number of years, was recently returned to Spain, and now has a prominent place in a new museum, the Reina Sofia Museum of Contemporary Art in Madrid. "Guernica" is now owned by the Spanish people. It is but one example of the intrinsic, cultural, political importance of artifacts and art works to the national interest of a country.

Harry H. Chartrand defined the importance of intellectual property rights for the arts industry:

> Intellectual property rights provide the legal foundation for the industrial organization of the arts and sciences. But legal systems are products of specific cultures and different cultures recognize differing creative rights. In this regard, and in addition to problems about agriculture, GATT negotiations are floundering due to these differences. This trade dispute has implications not only for the global knowledge industry but for cultural sovereignty of the post-modern nation state.

The arts today pose a different problem than they did at the time of the creation of the United Nations Charter. They are now commodity-oriented rather than people oriented and thus are more accessible to a world audience. The potential for the art market of the next century is enormous if the communication giants of today create the proposed networks, bringing images, sound, and text into every home in the globe. The individuals who are able to create and orchestrate the images, write the texts, and create the sound or music are going to be extremely valuable human commodities in the future and will control the knowledge base. This will be an extremely valuable commodity in a sound/image society. Consequently, this is a factor in world trade that will be increasingly important to all nations in the next century, and the foundation for dissemination and ownership must be created in this century. The issue is critical to future development of arts in the world community as their role in the world economy continues to grow during the next decade.

For the first time in our history as a world of nations, the world community has the capability and the opportunity to communicate with the population in a multi-media format, *i.e.*, sound, imagery, language, and real time moving imagery. The capability exists to transmit and convey information, almost instantaneously, so that world cultures, world art forms, and world artists can interact in ways which transcend geographic barriers. The communication system provides a mechanism for every country to explain its own culture and its significant contributions to the arts. This capability has commercial and educational implications. It should assist us in arts appreciation and provide a balanced view of the arts and cultures of the world.

However, the arts have become an economic battleground in which the issues go beyond the economic concerns into the cultural domain. The French have been very adamant in current GATT talks about the necessity to preserve the French culture at any costs. A free media market in the European Union Nations would open up more markets and audiences for media products from the United States. This would threaten the guidelines set up in France and other European Union Nations which stipulate that 50 percent of the programming on television must originate in that country. This increases the necessity for communication and information exchange, but calls for a structure and process in which all can share the wealth without one part of the world exploiting the other.

D. Harmonization[33]

Intellectual property rights have been viewed classically as territorial in nature. As such, the recognition of any particular form of intellectual property, the scope of rights granted the owner of such property, if its existence was recognized, and the degree of protection afforded such rights were traditionally creatures of domestic laws. Since a nation's laws reflect the historical, cultural, economic and philosophic views of the country in question, standards for intellectual property protection necessarily diverge.

---

[33] Written for this Anthology by Doris Estelle Long. Copyright 1996 Doris E. Long.

So long as markets remained relatively isolated, the lack of uniform standards for the protection of intellectual property had little global impact. With the coming of the industrial age, and the increasing internationalization of the marketplace for intellectual property, the need for a uniform standard of protection became increasingly the subject of debate between nations. By the late 1880's two international treaty regimes had been established specifically to address the problem of international intellectual property law protection. Both the Berne Convention for the Protection of Literary and Artistic Works and the Paris Convention for the Protection of Industrial Works recognized the supremacy of domestic law in the area of intellectual property protection by basing their primary emphasis on the provision of national treatment. Yet each sought to develop some degree of uniformity among the laws of the member countries by establishing minimum standards which signatory nations agreed to incorporate in their domestic laws.

Treaty regimes such as the Berne and Paris Conventions serve a useful role in the development of a single international standard for intellectual property protection. Given the increasing complexity of multinational negotiations, however, the negotiation of such regimes can be a time consuming, and not wholly successful, process. Multilateral negotiations during the Uruguay Round for the General Agreement on Trade and Tariff that ultimately resulted in the Agreement on Trade Related Aspects of Intellectual Property Rights ("TRIPS") lasted nearly ten years and resulted in an agreement that largely adopted the minimum standards established by the Berne and Paris Conventions.

As a supplement to multinational treaty negotiations, many nations have sought to resolve the problem of conflicting domestic laws by seeking to harmonize their laws with those of like situated countries. Such efforts at harmonization are based upon the theory that, even if identity of domestic laws cannot be achieved, at least the most harmful differences can be minimized to afford a more uniform standard of protection. Transplantation of ideas and laws from other countries is a well established occurrence. Present day harmonization efforts are based upon the implicit view that common history, common philosophy, common economic goals, even common legal systems can be used as a basis for the successful transplantation of rules and norms from other countries.

PART II
ISSUE AREAS

3

The Cultural Impact of Intellectual Property Forms

Just as the decision to protect intellectual property is governed by the cultural, historical and philosophical background of a country, so too the forms of protection that are selected reflect the cultural imperatives of a country. This Chapter reviews the role that culture plays in the selection of which of the different forms of intellectual property to adopt. It begins with an examination of the role of copyright in the protection of a country's cultural heritage. The Chapter then explores the use of patent laws in protecting biodiversity and the problem of trademark protection and the Coca-Colanization of the world. It ends with a brief examination of the conflict between culture, trade secret protection and the encouragement of foreign investment opportunities.

A. COPYRIGHT

1. The Protection of Art and Literature[1]

Few would dispute that at least one segment of a country's cultural heritage is represented by its native-authored art and literature. Copyright has often been viewed as a source of encouragement for the development of home grown literary and artistic works since it promises economic recompense for the public use of such works. The early founders of the US republic recognized the critical role that copyright protection could play in the development of the arts by expressly providing for the enactment of appropriate copyright legislation "to promote the progress of . . . the useful Arts."

Since most domestic copyright laws are designed to protect artistic and literary expression, they have limited usefulness in protecting works of pre-literate societies, such as rituals, customs, folklore and other works which are not fixed in a tangible medium of expression. Such "unfixed" works, however, may be as important to a country's cultural heritage, and therefore, perceived to be as worthy of protection, as other classical forms of artistic or literary heritage. Thus, traditional, Euro-centric views of intellectual property protection, limited as they are to fixed literary and artistic works, do not include within their purview all artistic works which a country may desire to protect.

Traditional, Euro-centric views of intellectual property protection pose an added problem in providing an acceptable form of protection for all culturally desirable works of a particular culture or society. All creative endeavors to a certain extent build on what has come before. There is an old adage that there is no such thing as a truly new novel or genuinely original art. There are only advancements on what has come before. Copyright protection necessarily restricts subsequent authors' and artists' ability to use freely prior works so long as such works remain subject to protection. The necessary tension between protection and access motivates most decisions regarding the scope of protection afforded under a country's domestic copyright laws, including the existence

[1] Doris Estelle Long, *China, Russia and the United States: A Comparison of Cultural Choices.* Copyright 1996 Doris E. Long. Excerpt reprinted with permission.

and scope of any fair use or compulsory licensing exceptions. Consequently, even if a country chooses to enact domestic copyright laws, it may shorten the period of protection or narrow the category of protected works in order to protect culturally worthy works. Conversely, countries may protect aspects of works which have fallen into the public domain in order to protect the cultural integrity of such works. Thus, the form and scope of protection selected by an individual country will reflect the cultural imperatives sought to be served by that country's laws.

2. The Protection of Folklore as Culture[2]

Folklore is usually transmitted orally, by imitation or by other means. Its forms include language, literature, music, dance, games, mythology, rituals, customs, handicrafts and other arts. Folklore's basic traits are: (i) it is passed from generation to generation by unfixed forms; (ii) it is a community-oriented creation in that its expression is dictated by local standards and traditions; (iii) its creations generally are not attributable to individual authors; and (iv) it is being continually utilized and developed by the society in which it lives. Folklore perpetually identifies a nation's cultural history and is considered a fundamental element of a nation's cultural patrimony.

Because of its evolutionary and unfixed form, external sources subject folklore to substantial threats. Folklore, especially within developing countries, is being consumed by mass communication and importation of foreign cultural works. The risk of total dissolution of folkloric culture is prevalent if preservation actions are not taken. Economic exploitation of folkloric works has also been usurped by outside forces to the point that, even within a nation's own territory, nationals pay foreign publishers for reproductions of their own cultural works. Folkloric works also are victims of integrity violations in that they suffer mutilation, distortion, and misappropriation, particularly when recreated outside their natural habitat or without authorization. For example, an American production company could capture an African tribal ritual on film or tape and, upon return to America, incorporate the recording into a television documentary, movie, radio program, or advertisement without any obligation to remunerate the African performers for exploiting the ritual and without any obligation to accurately attribute the ritual to its creating tribe.

In general, the legal structure of copyright is ill-suited for adequately protecting folklore. Copyright laws recognize solely an individual author's creative expression as the authorship in a work and normally require fixation of the work in a tangible medium before limited duration rights will vest. Copyright entitlement does not retroactively extend to those works in existence prior to the enactment of copyright laws. Since folklore violates these generally established conditions, it is condemned to wallow in the unprotected marshes of the public domain unless special provisions are created to excuse its unqualifying nature.

A handful of states has extended legislative protection to works within the public domain. Public domain legislation is designed to "prevent or sanction use of public domain works in such a way as to prejudice their authenticity or identity."[3] Protection covers either works whose copyright protection has expired or works that would have been under copyright if such a system had existed at the time of their creation or had extended protection to their class of works. In some instances, protection extends beyond works of national origin to include foreign works.

To avoid stifling any creativity or distribution, public domain legislation strikes a balance between freedom of use and preservation of integrity. Sanctions are imposed only on those uses that violate the work's essence, cultural value, or reputation. Thus, modern adaptations, translations, or repub-

---

[2] Cathryn A. Berryman, *Toward More Universal Protection Of Intangible Cultural Property,* 1 J. INTELL. PROP. L. 293. Copyright 1994 Journal of Intellectual Property Law Association. Excerpt reprinted with permission.

[3] Working Group on Works in the Public Domain, Copyright Bull. vol.13, no. 4 at 33, 34 (1979).

lications are allowed as long as the work's character is maintained.

Authority to control public domain usage is vested in either the state or an agency designated by the state. In some instances, prior authorization is required before a national can exploit a public domain work. Other states preserve free use if the work's integrity is preserved.

One primary motive behind public domain statutes is the desire to retain safeguards on the author's personality through the moral rights of paternity and integrity. The state can act as the primary assertor of these moral rights if moral rights expire with economic rights or death, or as the secondary protector of moral rights if moral rights are perpetual and extend to the author's heirs.

A second motive for public domain legislation is the preservation of a state's cultural heritage. States adopt protective laws that will safeguard the cultural interests of the public, which implies that no confusion should exist between the original work and works resulting from any use made of it, and prevent abusive or prejudicial forms of the work from entering the public market. Noted public domain theorist Carlos Mouchet justifies this protection by stating:

> once a work has fallen into the public domain, it is in the public interest that its artistic integrity should be maintained, that the name of its creator should not be omitted, that the title by which it can be identified should not be removed or modified, that the work should not be reproduced in any imperfect or rough form, etc.

Mouchet goes on to say:

> when the State introduces administrative or penal measures with a view to the protection, safeguard and defence of a piece of cultural property, it is . . . acting . . . as the representative of the interests of the community.[4]

Thus, public domain legislation acts as a cultural consumer protection device by forestalling any intangible cultural product that misrepresents a pre-existing work. The state's interest in the author's contribution to its cultural heritage is preserved, and society is not misled by cultural impostors.

Additional requirements on the use of public domain works have been enforced by some states under the legal rubric of domaine public payant. Domaine public payant is a legislative scheme that imposes a fee for the use or economic exploitation of works in the public domain. Funds received are funnelled into societies that provide for the welfare of creative workers and their families or into state administrative agencies for the promotion of cultural activities and exchange.

Domaine public payant is characterized as a protector of cultural heritage because it can provide the financial means for nations to protect and preserve their cultural creations, particularly folklore. In practice, however, domaine public payant mainly functions as a promoter of intangible property by assisting authors to generate intellectual works, which benefit both the immediate society and its cultural heritage. In some ways, the system of domaine public payant effectuates a transfer of the author's economic rights at expiration of copyright to the state or to a delegated artists' association

Public domain legislation is the most prevalent method states choose to protect and exploit their folkloric creations. States can readily classify folklore as a segment of their public domain and thus can control folklore's usage.

The main drawback to relying on the public domain and domaine public payant is the lack of an international structure to enforce these protective measures extraterritorially. Because the bulk of abuse arises outside the borders of the country of origin, effective protection of a state's folkloric heritage is sometimes unachievable.

In countries that both extend moral rights in perpetuity and designate an authority to enforce those rights for folkloric works, folklore can secure relief from paternity and integrity violations. In most states, however, moral rights are codified within copyright law and satisfaction of

---

[4] Carlos Mouchet, *Problems of the "Domaine Public Report,"* 8 COLUM-VLA J.L. & ARTS 137, 146 (1983).

copyright prerequisites precedes any grant of moral rights.

The public has a legitimate interest in ensuring that its cultural works are preserved as their creators intended so that their inherent cultural value will not be lost or distorted. Some states recognize this interest by directly creating a public cause of action for integrity violations. This public interest justification also cohesively links moral rights with a state's rationalization for copyright. If the goal of copyright is the creation of works for society, it is counterproductive for works to be inaccurately disseminated, particularly if cultural works tell members of a society who they are.

One major criticism of state control over a public domain work's integrity is the potential for censorship by the state, *i.e.*, the state can control current creations by controlling access to their public domain inspiration. To avoid censorship possibilities, a state would need to implement guidelines as to what preserving the integrity of a work entails. A forum should be provided for consultation of public domain use issues. Experts suggest that designation of a publicly accessible, national depository, like the National Library of Congress, can act as a reference for satisfying the use guidelines and as a resource for accuracy in dissemination. One should note that these laws must balance preservation interests and public usage interests so that cultural development will continue to progress.

Intangible cultural property merits convention protection for several reasons. First, intellectual creations comprise a significant portion of a state's cultural patrimony and are actual reflections of culture. Second, intangible property facilitates societal development because each intellectual work expresses the dimensions of a society and each work tells the members of its creating society who and what they are. Third, intangible cultural property evokes the same response of cultural nationalism from a nation's people as tangible property. For example, "The Star Spangled Banner" instills the same sense of pride in Americans as the Washington Monument, yet only the Washington Monument is eligible for international convention protection. Lastly, intangible cultural property constitutes part of the "common heritage of mankind" and, as such, merits protection from destruction.

Intangible cultural property faces the same threats of destruction and inaccurate preservation that haunted tangible property prior to the Hague Convention. Mass media and piracy undermine intangible property, rather than armed conflict. Lastly, the "decontextualization" dilemma that plagued tangible property (i.e., if a work is taken out of context, a loss in value and information occurs) directly threatens forms of folklore and mirrors the loss suffered if works are not reproduced fully or accurately.

Multiple goals motivate the tangible property protection offered by conventions. Although preservation of physical works is the obvious objective, such action serves to achieve other goals, such as maintaining the work's integrity, facilitating distribution or access, ensuring truth and certainty, preserving the cultural identity of a particular people as well as the expression "embodied in the work," retrieving information, and preserving a cultural creation for the benefit of the "common heritage of mankind."

QUESTIONS AND COMMENTS FOR YOUR CONSIDERATION

1. What is the interplay, if any, between copyright and moral rights protection in connection with the protection of culturally significant works?

2. Does an author's moral rights necessarily end when the work enters the public domain? How do you balance an author's right to protect his personality interest and the public's "right" to use the work in question?

3. Are there other forms of intellectual property protection which could be used to achieve the same protection of cultural integrity as the public domaine payant?

3. The Role of Cultural Exclusions[5]

Although culture exists in forms that may not readily lend themselves to intellectual property protection (such as the Kenya Land Preserve, the Parthenon, the Great Wall of China or the Mayan Ruins at Chichen-Itza), those forms which lend themselves most readily to mass marketed commodification usually fit well within the confines of traditional copyright protection.

The increasing commodification of culture, in the form of mass marketed novels, sound recordings, motion pictures and television programs, has led to a growing demand to protect the culture of the importing nation from the deleterious effect that exposure to non-domestic culture may have on the development of native-grown, and more particularly, native-inspired works. One of the significant trends in international trade law in recent years has been the development of free trading zones between nations, such as the Treaty of Rome (establishing the European Community), the Canadian Free Trade Agreement and the North American Free Trade Agreement. Despite this focus on reducing trade barriers, thereby insuring a freer flow of intellectual property protected works, recently exclusions have been made to such free flow of goods based on the cultural content of such works. The EC, with its recent "Television Without Frontiers" Directive establishing quotas for the amount of non-domestic television programming broadcast through-out the EC,[6] the Canadian Free Trade Agreement and the North American Free Trade Agreement with their express exclusion of certain goods from the free-trading provisions of these treaty regimes based on the cultural content of such goods,[7] all represent recent efforts to narrow free trade objectives on the basis of cultural imperatives. Since the goods affected by such exclusions are most often subject to copyright protection, it appears that the use of copyright to protect culturally significant works has come full circle.

[5] Written for this Anthology by Doris Estelle Long. Copyright 1996 Doris E. Long.

[6] *Editors' Note:* For a more detailed discussion of the "Television Without Frontiers" Directive, *see* Chapter Six.

[7] *Editors' Note:* For a detailed discussion of these and other forms of cultural exclusions, *see* Chapter Six.

B. Patent

1. Biodiversity[8]

The trade dispute over intellectual property protection descended on the 1992 World Conference on Environment and Development in Brazil at an awkward time; like an unwanted house guest, no amount of ignoring it could make it go away. Persistent and intractable, the controversy confounded negotiations on the 1992 Convention on Biological Diversity to such an extent that it left the treaty little more than an impotent desideratum. The treaty attempts to promote diversity of species by encouraging developing countries to preserve their diminishing rain forests, wilderness areas, and wetlands. Yet it also calls for the "equitable sharing" of the economic benefits from patented processes using rare plant and animal species found in developing countries. These two goals are not necessarily irreconcilable, but the way diplomats attempted to combine them in the treaty set the bloc of less-developed countries at loggerheads with the United States, which refused to sign the agreement on the grounds that it did not go far enough in guaranteeing patent rights affected by the treaty.

Diplomats came to Rio de Janeiro in 1992 to negotiate environmental agreements, not trade issues, and the Biodiversity Convention was to be one of the crowning accomplishments of the Earth Summit. But patent protection is normally a trade issue—and a very contentious one. Thus it is not altogether surprising that the negotiators were able to address the issue of intellectual property rights in only a superficial way. The difficulty that arose underscores both the intrinsic links between environmental and trade issues, and how little the relationship

[8] David Hurlbut, *Fixing The Biodiversity Convention: Toward A Special Protocol For Related Intellectual Property,* 34 NAT. RESOURCES J. 379. Copyright 1994 National Resources Journal. Excerpt reprinted with permission.

is understood by advocates on either side. The longer this intellectual estrangement continues, the longer it will take to realize the goal of sustainable development, which was the theme of the Earth Summit.

Sustainable development means that current generations must leave future generations an environment and a stock of natural resources that is as good and as plentiful as those it received from past generations. The philosophy also says that technology and social organization affect the capacity of the biosphere to meet the economic demands placed on it. International trade is one of the most important forms of social organization by which natural resources are transformed into economic prosperity, but there has been little progress in clarifying the environment-related aspects of trade or the trade-related aspects of environmental protection. Intellectual property rights, already a contentious trade issue even without taking environmental arguments into account, is one piece of the sustainable development puzzle that needs deliberate and careful attention. Instead, the biodiversity convention deals with the issue in the worst possible manner: by equivocation in hopes that the controversy will simply go away.

What is needed to repair the Biodiversity Convention is a determined international effort to agree on core principles around which some consensus may be built. This article introduces one possible approach: the development of a new category of intellectual property rights that would be distinct from normal commercial patents and more relevant to the special circumstances and goals the Biodiversity Convention seeks to address.

The Biodiversity Convention raises two types of economic issues: the effect on the economy of a developing country of monopoly rent created by a patent, and the need to pay for environmental costs that are external to normal market forces.

Strictly speaking, rent is "payment for the use of a resource."[9] The rent for labor is wages; for capital, it is interest. For ideas and innovations, rent takes the form of royalties on patents or copyrights. When patents are protected, the royalties create monopoly rent that will last until the expiration of the patent or until the development of slightly modified imitations and alternatives.

The rationale for creating monopoly rent is that the firm may have necessary expenses that are in addition to the typical opportunity costs of capital and labor it has to pay to produce a certain level of output. Research and development, for example, often involve spending money on many research failures prior to the discovery of a marketable new product. The resources spent on the failures do not increase the firm's output nor do they add to productivity, yet they are an unavoidable part of the risk involved in research and development. The idea is that the monopoly rent created by a patent will compensate the firm for these nonproductive expenses.

On the other hand, monopoly rent also creates a net welfare loss to consumers. In deciding its intellectual property regime, the state has to decide whether the benefit of creating rents from royalties adequately offsets the loss to consumers.

The magnitude of the social loss may affect the diligence with which a country protects intellectual property through domestic policies. A government will have an incentive to encourage piracy of productive foreign technology if its people are too poor to pay the "legitimate" price and if it has no indigenous expertise to develop similar competing technologies of its own.

On the other side of the debate, patent holders often incur significant costs in bringing their new products to market. The United States pharmaceutical industry says it spent 16 percent of its total sales in 1991 on research and development—nearly $10 billion out of $60 billion in sales. Money for research and development comes from the higher prices made possible by product and process patents; this rent makes up a large part of the industry's total sales. The industry estimates that about 60 percent of the drugs on the market now never would have been developed had firms not been able to recoup their expenses through patent rent.

The incentive for pharmaceutical techno-piracy in a developing country is great because the patent accounts for a large portion of the price, and because including the patent rent in the price would prevent a large number of people from acquiring medi-

---

[9] THE NEW PALGRAVE: A DICTIONARY OF ECONOMICS, vol. 3 at 1014-1018 (J. Eatwell et al eds, 1987).

cations for which a demand exists. International trade adds another significant reason: little if any of the monopoly rent from the patent would be transferred to the economy of the pirating country if patents were protected. It would all be repatriated to the country of manufacture, depleting foreign exchange reserves and possibly adding to the country's debt burden.

In addition to the controversy over patents, the Biodiversity Convention also raises the issue of who pays for environmental protection.

Article 16 of the Biodiversity Convention says that

> The Contracting Parties, recognizing that patents and other intellectual property rights may have an influence on the implementation of this Convention, shall cooperate in this regard subject to national legislation and international law in order to ensure that such rights are supportive of and do not run counter to its objectives.[10]

The reference to "national legislation and international law" in regard to intellectual property rights raises a nettlesome question: which set of international laws? Currently a system of international principles is administered by the World Intellectual Property Organization (WIPO), a United Nations-affiliated body charged with facilitating compliance with a system of bilateral treaties and multilateral conventions on intellectual property rights. The principles that have been incorporated within the WIPO regime are generally consistent with the national patent laws of developing countries.

The WIPO treaties, which include the Paris Convention on patents, the Berne Convention on copyrights, and a number of other specialized instruments, gives member states significant latitude in excluding products and processes from patentability. Pharmaceutical products and processes, plant and animal varieties as well as biological processes for producing them, medical treatments for humans or animals, food products, chemical products, computer programs, fertilizers, agricultural machines, cosmetics, and nuclear inventions are among the items that various countries are entitled to exclude from patentability under the Paris Convention. The excluded items can thus be easily copied and widely distributed without regard to royalty payments to the inventor. The WIPO regime also recognizes the right of a country to impose compulsory licensing to ensure that patented products and processes are made available to the public. Developing countries often rely on patent exclusions and compulsory licensing to ensure the dissemination of new technologies in their domestic economies.

Another problem with the above provision in Article 16 is contained in the phrase that calls for the parties to ensure that principles of intellectual property rights (whichever system one may use to define them) "are supportive of and do not run counter to [the Biodiversity Convention's] objectives." In other words, if there is any conflict between protection of intellectual property rights and the objectives of the treaty, then intellectual property rights must give way. One may argue persuasively that the ecological objective of biological diversity should indeed take precedence over intellectual property rights. But the treaty also aims to achieve an economic goal: the "fair and equitable sharing of the benefits arising out of the utilization of genetic resources."[11] Even though the ecological and the economic goals both may be worthy, the two are different in nature and provide different contexts for weighing the social need to protect intellectual property rights.

The public trust doctrine provides a rationale and legal precedent for placing ecological protection above private property rights. But customary law does not support a similar canonical ordering between the redistribution of wealth and private property rights. If one is to infer such a link, it must be done on the basis of economic theory and not on the basis of customary law. And if one looks to neoclassical economics for a heuristic to determine how to achieve the "fair and equitable sharing" of benefits, the answer provided by theory is straightforward: let the concerned parties negotiate on the basis of their willingness to pay, and the market will

---

[10] United Nations Conf. Env't & Dev.; Convention on Biological Diversity, 1992, 31 I.L.M. 818 (1992) at art. 16.

[11] Biodiversity Convention, at art.1.

reach an outcome that will be fair and equitable. No legislative, administrative, or policy measures by a government would be necessary other than to minimize transaction costs.

Many economists outside the neoclassical school, however, have advanced equally cogent theories that explain how equity between trading nations can in fact diminish over time if market forces are left to themselves. Economists of the dependency school, a group largely identified with developing countries, argue that the path of successive market equilibria creates structural imbalances that leave developing countries at an unfair disadvantage in the international trading system. The structural disadvantage would necessarily increase over time if market forces were to continue unchecked by positive trade policies by both industrial and developing countries.

Biological diversity, the fair sharing of economic benefits, the fair protection of intellectual property rights, and free trade are not irreconcilable despite the complexity of the issues. The real tragedy in this story, however, is not the harm to intellectual property rights but rather the missed opportunity to further the ecological goal of biological diversity. The economic forces that make intellectual property so controversial a trade issue can be used as a potent tool to promote the diversity of species, but the treaty as it stands fails to do that. Had it followed the precedent of the ozone protection treaties, the Convention on Biological Diversity would have identified intellectual property rights as an issue to be researched by a special working group that would recommend a specific protocol at the next meeting of the parties. Such a protocol is still feasible; the next section sketches what it might look like.

2. Protocol for Products Made with Biota from Pristine Ecosystems[12]

The international community needs to develop and accept a special new category of intellectual property principles for products made with biota from pristine ecosystems. Such patents should be treated differently from normal patents on commercial products and processes, and should take account of the special situation and needs of developing countries.

Although other issues could be addressed, the four main points of the proposed protocol would be as follows.

1. All contracting parties—rich and poor—must agree to protect the patents of technologies for pharmaceuticals and other products made from the biota of pristine ecosystems in developing countries. The provisions of this article would apply only to those particular products that arise from national efforts to preserve biological diversity. Patents that use genetically engineered species or common species not protected by a conservation program would be excluded from this provision; protection of those patents would be left to WIPO and the GATT. The patents covered in this protocol would be protected according to the standards of national treatment and most-favored-nation treatment. In other words, all parties would be required to protect this class of product equally, regardless of whether the biota were taken from their own protected areas or those of another party.

2. A share of the revenues from the sale of pharmaceuticals and other products made from the biota of pristine ecosystems in developing countries must be returned to the countries from which the biota are taken. If developing countries are to be required to guarantee the monopoly rent included in the price of products made from their biota, then equity requires that they receive a share of that rent. Such a transfer would substantially support the objective of "fair and equitable sharing of the benefits arising out of the utilization of genetic resources."

3. The contracting parties must establish a multilateral fund to help developing countries acquire and distribute life-saving pharmaceuticals made from the biota of pristine ecosystems. An annex would list the kinds of drugs to be covered by the fund: heart medications, malaria medications, and inoculations against HIV, to name a few possibilities.

For the fund to work, the contributions

---

[12] David Hurlbut, *Fixing The Biodiversity Convention: Toward A Special Protocol For Related Intellectual Property*, 34 NAT. RESOURCES J. 379. Copyright 1994 National Resources Journal. Excerpt reprinted with permission.

of industrially advanced parties cannot be voluntary as is the case now.

4. The obligation of contracting parties to protect patent rights for technologies to make products from the biota of pristine ecosystems must be without prejudice to any kind of intellectual property not covered by the biodiversity technology protocol.

If these four points are incorporated in a biodiversity technology protocol, both developing and industrially advanced countries would stand to gain. Industrially advanced countries would get assurances that patents related to the Biodiversity Convention will be respected by all parties. In exchange, developing countries would be guaranteed a share of the rent created by the patents, compensating them for their efforts to maintain biological diversity in territories within their national jurisdiction. The special multilateral fund would ensure that higher prices would not put related life-saving pharmaceuticals out of the reach of people in developing countries who may need them. In short, a protocol based on these elements would strike a workable balance between the individual rights sought by industrially advanced countries and the social welfare sought by developing countries. Moreover, it would achieve this philosophical balance in a way that would not place the burden entirely on either side.

QUESTIONS AND COMMENTS FOR YOUR CONSIDERATION

1. Many domestic patent laws do not extend protection to naturally occuring plants, animals or other naturally occuring elements. *See* 35 U.S.C. § 101. What rationale, if any, would support a country's extending its patent laws to include protection of naturally occuring plants? Would extending patent protection to processes that use such plants be sufficient?

2. Could patent law be used to protect wild life preserves or other potential cultural areas of flora or fauna that do not qualify for copyright or trademark protection? Wouldn't such protection be directly contrary to the traditional purposes behind patent law protection, *i.e.*, the encouragement of the development of new inventions and discoveries?

C. Trademarks[13]

American movies play through-out the world; American songs are heard on radios in the far corners of the globe; McDonald's has opened fast food hamburger stands in countries as diverse as China, Russia and South Africa; and Coca-Cola and Pepsi-Cola are sold in almost every country. The "Americanization" of culture through the mass marketing of American films, songs, and computer programs has its corollary in what has been referred to as the "Coca-Colanization" of consumer goods.

In addition to serving as source designators, trademarks increasingly serve as signifiers of cachet in pop culture. Jeans may be roughly equivalent in style or quality, but it is the trademark on the pocket that often informs consumers choices, even when that trademark means that the identical product will cost more than its untrademarked domestically manufactured equivalent. Fears of a new wave of colonialization, in the form of brand loyalty to foreign owned marks, is premised in large part on the emerging global marketplace for trademark bearing consumer goods.

In the Eighteenth and Nineteenth centuries, European nations viewed their colonial counterparts as sources for raw materials and markets for finished products. In the Twentieth Century many former colonial dependents saw themselves placed in the identical situation except the finished products now were trademarked goods. Brand loyalty was encouraged through extensive advertising which made the imported goods

[13] Written for this Anthology by Doris Estelle Long. Copyright 1996 Doris E. Long.

more desirable in consumers' mind, even when such goods were roughly equivalent to goods bearing domestic trademarks. In the view of some nations, the protection of foreign marks represents the protection of cultural imperialism at its worst.

Trademark protection, however, is not limited to the protection of foreign source designators. Local brand loyalty is a well recognized fact of most regional markets. Moreover, ethnocentrism and cultural and national pride may all contribute to the development of strong domestic marks. Thus, the protection of trademarks may also serve to develop cultural and national pride.

QUESTIONS AND COMMENTS FOR YOUR CONSIDERATION

1. How could a local manufacturer develop sufficient brand loyalty to compete with multinational companies? Do the Paris Convention and the TRIPS Agreement allow for differential treatment between foreign and domestic marks?
2. What extent, if any, might culture play in the decision of the types of marks to be allowed registration?
3. Could trademark protection be used to protect certain native cultural symbols from appropriation as commercial symbols?

D. Trade Secrets[14]

The protection of secret, commercially valuable information is not so well established as other forms of intellectual property protection. While most nations offer some limited form of patent protection, few protect its sister form — trade secrets. In many instances this refusal to grant trade secret protection is based on historical and philosophical reluctance to limit the access and use of ideas and information absent some cultural reason for doing so. Trade secrets, by their nature, do not usually rise to the level of novelty or non-obviousness required for protection as a patent or utility model. They also rarely, if ever, qualify for the level of originality required for copyright protection. Yet trade secrets drive much of the industrialization of the developed countries.

Methods of manufacture, chemical formulas and plant construction techniques all yield readily to trade secret protection. They also often provide the commercial advantage that gives their owners the edge in the marketplace.

In order to develop the suprastructure and industrial base to permit continued industrialization, many newly emerging market economies and newly industrialized nations seek foreign investment. Such investment opportunities are often severely limited where countries deny trade secret protection. Multinational chemical, pharmaceutical and industrial companies who consider their trade secrets of vital significance to their economic success have little incentive to invest in manufacturing or research and development facilities when such would necessarily eliminate critical commercial assets. Thus, culture, which may preclude the protection of information *qua* information, collides directly with economic interest.

---

[14] Written for this Anthology by Doris Estelle Long. Copyright 1996 Doris E. Long.

4

Neighboring Rights

Throughout history, the emergence of new technologies including the printing press, photography, radio, and motion pictures, has strained the ability of intellectual property laws to protect the creative and economic interests of those who create or use these new technologies to embody or disseminate their works. With the globalization of the marketplace, the continual introduction of new and faster methods of reproducing, disseminating and communicating works has increased exponentially the need for international standards of protection. These new technologies have stretched the ability of traditional intellectual property forms to cover the needs posed by such new technologies. Instead of expanding copyright to cover these new technologies, many countries rely upon rights that are "neighboring" to copyright. This Chapter explores the phenomenon of "neighboring rights" and the impact of such rights on intellectual property protection issues.

A. "Rights Neighboring to Copyright"

1. Scope[1]

The term "neighboring rights" is an abbreviation of "rights neighboring to copyright." It was first used in 1948 at the Brussels Diplomatic Conference for the Revision of the Berne Convention. The expression appeared in a resolution with regard to a new subject, *not* to be dealt with in the old copyright convention itself: the protection of performing artists. The Brussels conference adopted two other resolutions, with regard to the protection of producers of recordings and the protection of broadcasts, respectively, without, however, using the term "neighboring right." The resolutions expressed the wish that the governments of the Berne Union countries consider the best means of assuring the protection of these three different interests, without prejudice to the rights of authors. This finally led to the International Convention for the Protection of Performers, Producers of Phonograms and Broadcasting Organizations, the Rome Convention of 1961. Here the three interests are bundled together, and although the Convention itself does not use the term "neighboring rights," it has been widely used since then in national legislation and in literature to designate the three rights conferred by the Rome Convention.

This should not obscure the fact, though, that several national copyright statutes also cover other "neighboring" or "related" rights. In Germany, for instance, we encounter rights not only of the three Rome beneficiaries but also of organizers of performances, a neighboring right of film producers, a right of photographers (where the photography is not a work), a right in editions of works or texts which are no longer protected, and a right concerning the publication of posthumous works.[2] The United Kingdom also confers a so-called "copyright" on cinematographic films, cable-transmissions and the typographical format of published editions.[3] Sweden has the so-called "catalogue rule," protecting a large number of informational

---

[1] Bonnie Teller, *Toward Better Protection Of Performance In The United States: A Comparative Look At Performer's Rights In The United States, Under The Rome Convention,* 28 COLUM. J. TRANSNAT'L L. 775. Copyright 1990 Columbia Journal of Transnational Law Association, Inc. Excerpt reprinted with permission.

[2] Dietz, Germany, Federal Republic in M. Nemer & P. Geller, International Copyright Law and Practice at FRG 122-130. 1 (1989).

[3] Cornish, United Kingdom, *id* at U.K.-62.

items in "catalogues, tables, and similar compilations." In the Netherlands there has long been protection for "non-personal writings" like telephone directories or broadcast listings, which are protected by what could be called a neighboring right, or pseudo-copyright.[4]

Rights neighboring to copyright, are, by definition, rights which are not genuine copyrights. They provide a strengthened protection against certain acts of unfair competition which can very loosely be associated with copyright infringements. Therefore they are situated "in the vicinity" of copyright. Only performers' rights constitute a special case.

2. Historical Development[5]

In this article, when talking about neighboring rights, I will restrict myself to the three "classical" neighboring rights of performers, producers of phonograms and broadcasting organizations.

As defined in Article 3 of the Rome Convention, performers are actors, singers, musicians, dancers and other persons who act, sing, deliver, declaim, play in or otherwise perform literary or artistic works. Their relation to authors and copyright protection has a truly curious history. Of course, before and during most of the nineteenth century, performers did not feel any need for protection along the lines of copyright; their performances could not be fixed on any recording or be reproduced, nor could they be broadcast or otherwise electronically transmitted to a wider public.

The picture changed radically with the inventions of professional sound recording, films, radio, television, cable-retransmission and all sorts of equipment for private recording. This technological revolution made performers as vulnerable as traditional authors to unauthorized exploitation by third parties Performers had to compete with records and films, and much live music in public places, for instance, was replaced by the increased use of records. The result was an unemployment problem for the whole musical profession. The individual performers needed protection against the unauthorized recording and reproduction of their performances and against unauthorized broadcasting or other communication to the public.

Judge Learned Hand wrote:

> [I]n the vast number of renditions, the performer has a wide choice, depending upon his gifts, and this makes his rendition pro tanto quite as original a 'composition' as an 'arrangement' or 'adaption' of the score itself, which Section 1(b) [of the 1909 Copyright Act] makes copyrightable. Now that it has become possible to capture these contributions of the individual performer upon a physical object that can be made to reproduce them, there should be no doubt that this is within the Copyright Clause of the Constitution.[6]

Also, in Europe, a number of scholars were and are of the opinion that performers should really enjoy full copyright protection and not just a nebulous and weaker "neighboring right." Nevertheless, the copyright protection of performers has not carried through on the international level of the Rome Convention.

Where the status of performers had been pushed down to that of beneficiaries of a "right neighboring to copyright," the protection of the organizational and technical achievements and financial investments of producers and broadcasters was now elevated to that same intermediate level of "rights neighboring to copyright." They both received full exclusive rights. The producers received the right to authorize or prohibit the reproduction of their phonograms and an optional right to remuneration in the case of broadcasting a record. The broadcasting organizations obtained rights with respect to rebroadcasting, fixation of broadcasts and certain reproductions.

In the literature there was and has been

---

[4] Herman Cohen Jehoram, Netherlands, *id* at NETH-20-22.

[5] Herman Cohen Jehoram, *The Nature of Neighboring Rights of Performing Artists, Phonogram Producers and Broadcasting Organizations,* 15 COLUMBIA-VLA J. OF LAW & THE ARTS 75. Copyright 1990 Columbia Journal of Transnational Law Association, Inc. Excerpt reprinted with permission.

[6] Capitol Records Inc. v. Mercury Record Corp., 221 F.2d 657 (2d Cir) (1955).

much opposition to this combination of totally different interests, but pragmatism and contentment combined with a certain degree of agreement between the three interdependent interest groups prevailed. Succinct criticism, however, pervades even the official WIPO Guide to the Rome Convention and to the Phonograms' Convention, where it is said:

> True, the purist may complain that, notwithstanding the skill and talent of a recording engineer or a broadcast producer, the making of a record or of a broadcast is, after all, an essentially industrial act, whereas the performances of artistes are of their nature acts of spiritual creation; and to mix them up together in one convention creates a hotch-potch. Nevertheless, the Rome Convention has done so, always with the guide-line of stopping the unfair appropriation of the labor of others.[7]

In many national statutes, however, the differences between the unfair competition protection of producers and broadcasters, on the one hand, and the protection of the artistic achievement of the performer, on the other hand, are generally recognized. One of the first symptoms is that moral rights are conferred on performers and not on the other two neighboring right owners. Also, the explanatory memorandum to, for instance, the German Copyright Act of 1965 stresses explicitly the difference between the respective artistic and technical-financial achievements involved. In a very recent Report on Copyright, the German government proposed to extend the uniform 25 year-term of protection of neighboring rights to 50 years only for performers, stressing anew the basic difference from the other beneficiaries of neighboring rights.[8] With an amending act of 1990 this has now indeed been realized. Perhaps this consequence goes a little far, but the message is clear. In England, Cornish speaks of "entrepreneurial copyright" in sound recordings and broadcasts.[9] Also in other international literature the fundamental differences are time and again stressed.

There was the fear that some countries might protect neighboring rights but not copyright proper. This objection was indeed addressed. According to Article 24 of the Rome Convention, it is only open for accession by States which are a signatory to either the Berne Convention or the Universal Copyright Convention.

In addition, Article 1 of the Rome Convention prescribes devoutly: "Protection granted under this Convention shall leave intact and shall in no way affect the protection of copyright in literary and artistic works."

The Rome Convention and the copyright conventions are completely equal and no pre-eminence of copyright has been established.

3. Relationship to Copyright[10]

In recent years an international ideological war has been raging over the relationship between copyright and neighboring rights. This war has been unleashed by the International Federation of Phonogram and Videogram Producers (IFPI), one of the most important international pillars of the development *and* practical implementation of copyright. On the topic of neighboring rights, IFPI now lashes out. Under the leadership of IFPI spokeswoman Gillian Davies, the thesis that neighboring rights are really copyrights is constantly advanced. It started with the following paragraph in the 1986 report of the WIPO/UNESCO Committee of Governmental Experts on audiovisual works and phonograms:

> Several participants expressed concern that the document (*i.e.*, the preparatory documents of WIPO/UNESCO) did not sufficiently emphasize the creative nature of phonogram producers on the basis of which the intellectual

[7] WIPO Guide to the Rome Convention and to the Phonogram Convention 12 (Geneva 1981).

[8] Bundestagdrucksache 7.7. 1989, nr. 11/4929.

[9] W.R. CORNISH, INTELLECTUAL PROPERTY 275 (1989).

[10] Herman Cohen Jehoram, *The Nature of Neighboring Rights of Performing Artists, Phonogram Producers and Broadcasting Organizations,* 15 COLUMBIA-VLA J. OF LAW & THE ARTS 75. Copyright 1990 Herman Cohen Jehoram. Excerpt reprinted with permission.

> property laws of several countries provided copyright protection rather than neighboring rights' protection, if any, to such producers. These participants requested that this point should be taken into account in any future work on the commentary.[11]

In 1961 producers had succeeded in elevating their purely entrepreneurial status to one of beneficiaries of "rights neighboring to copyright," by assimilation with the simultaneously degraded performers. Now, in 1986, they wanted further promotion to full copyright ownership.

It is true that common law countries already use the term copyright in relation to what on the European continent is still called "neighboring rights."

What then is the creative nature of phonogram producers on the basis of which copyright protection should be granted according to those participants in the WIPO/UNESCO Committee quoted above? Nimmer devotes a whole paragraph of his four-volume treatise on American copyright to this question. He quotes the House Report which indicates that "authorship" may be claimed by "the record producer responsible for setting up the recording session." Nimmer then says:

> If the act of 'setting up the recording session' were the record producer's only basis for claiming original contribution to the recording, and hence of 'authorship,' it would be ill based, indeed. This is no more an act of 'authorship' than is the act of one who makes available to a writer a room, a stenographer, a typewriter, and paper. The latter may be 'setting up' a writing session, but he is hardly the author of that which emerges from such a session. Nor may Congress simply create a legal fiction that a record producer is an 'author' if in fact he is not.[12]

Nimmer then goes on to find another basis in the House Report. It also refers to the acts of "capturing and electronically processing the sounds, and compiling and editing them to make the final sound recording." These are analogous to the acts of a photographer in capturing and photographically processing light images. "But," Nimmer continues, "if the author of such originality in photography is the photographer, the author of such originality in sound recording is the sound engineer who actually performs the task of capturing and electronically processing the sounds. It is true that the record producer may acquire the engineer's copyright by virtue of an employment for hire relationship, or possibly by direct assignment, but not merely by virtue of the fact that he 'set up' the recording session." There seems to be no basis for a record producer's independent copyright. He can only have a derivative copyright, derived through employment of a sound engineer or through assignment.

Aristotle once wrote: "It is not the deeds that move people, but the words about those deeds." Indeed the question of "copyright" or "neighboring rights" for producers seems a game of words and a confused game at that. There is, however, an idea in the background. Not only the idea of protecting producers of records and other carriers of information at the same level as authors, but of replacing authors by industry. The first symptoms of this are found in the new English Copyright Act and in the Green Paper on Copyright of the Commission of the European Communities.[13]

On the new English Act and its amalgamation of authors' rights and entrepreneurial rights Dworkin writes:

> Whether that portends a development which will permit entrepreneurial rights to overshadow authors' rights, the perennial fear of authors, remains to be seen. In that regard, the introduction of a rental right in favour of producers of sound recordings and films to the exclusion of authors with underlying copyright interests therein is unfortunate.[14]

---

[11] Audiovisual works and phonogram, preparatory document for and report of WIDO/UNESCO Committee of Governmental Experts, 22 Copyright 218, 2341 (1986).

[12] 1 Nimmer on Copyright §210 [A] [2] [6] (1990).

[13] Comm (88) 172 final, Brussels, 7 June 1988.

[14] Dworkin, United Kingdom in S. Stewart, International Copyright and Neighboring Rights 487 (1989).

In the European Communities' Green Paper on Copyright, it is, for instance, suddenly stated in the context of films and videorecordings that film composers should stop collecting independently their musical performing right royalties on the basis of cinema box office receipts. For economic expediency their rights should pass into the hands of the film producers. Another example from the Green Paper: "The Commission is proud it has concluded a bilateral agreement with Indonesia, which protects sound recordings for the record producers, without any simultaneous copyright protection for the composers of the recorded music."

This realization of a right neighboring to a copyright without a copyright proper is exactly the offending situation which the Rome Convention meant to prevent.

4. Relationship to the Paris Convention[15]

Neighboring rights typically "provide the legal mechanism through which countries adhering to the author's rights tradition protect sound recordings, performances and broadcasts without diluting the author's right regime." For example, the United States adopted a neighboring rights strategy when it enacted the Semiconductor Chip Protection Act of 1984 (codified at 17 U.S.C. §§ 901-914 (1988)).

The Paris Convention covers industrial property, such as patents, utility models, industrial designs, trademarks, trade names, and indications of source or appellations of origin, and the repression of unfair competition. It also imposes a general requirement of national treatment on all forms of industrial property as broadly defined in the treaty. The broad coverage of the Paris Convention arguably poses a serious obstacle to experimentation with a neighboring rights approach to new technologies, at least when the moving state seeks to condition its protection of foreigners on material reciprocity, as the United States did in the Semiconductor Chip Act. Although other countries have followed a similar strategy under pressure from the United States, this tactic has been criticized as a regrettable deviation from the national treatment clause of the Paris Convention that invites emulation by the developing countries. Efforts to stipulate an international convention covering semiconductor chip designs have broken down, owing mainly to the opposition of developing countries.

5. Relationship to TRIPS[16]

Neighboring rights under TRIPS receive fairly extensive protection. Performers have the right to prohibit the unauthorized fixation and broadcast "by wireless means" and "communication to the public" of their live performances. They also have the right to prevent the reproduction of bootleg recordings of such performances. These rights last "at least until the end of a period of fifty years computed from the end of the calendar year in which the unauthorized fixation was made or the performance took place." Producers of phonograms are expressly given the right to control the "direct or indirect reproduction of their phonograms." This right similarly lasts for 50 years, computed from the end of the calendar year in which the performance took place or the fixation occurred. In addition, broadcasting organizations have the right to prohibit the unauthorized fixation, reproduction, and/or rebroadcast "by wireless means" of their broadcasts. They also have the right to prohibit the unauthorized "communication to the public of such television broadcasts." These rights last for 20 years from the end of the calendar year in which the broadcast took place.

Any rights granted by member nations to performers, producers and broadcasting entities under TRIPS may provide for "conditions, limitations, exceptions and reserva-

---

[15] J.H. Reichman, *Goldstein On Copyright Law: A Realist's Approach To A Technological Age,* 43 STAN. L. REV. 943. Copyright 1991 Board of Trustees of the Leland Stanford Junior University. Excerpt reprinted with permission.

[16] Doris E. Long, *Copyright and the Uruguay Round Agreements: A New Era of Protection or an Illusory Promise?,* 22 AIPLA QJ 551. Copyright 1995 Doris E. Long. Excerpt reprinted with permission.

tions" to the extent permitted by the Rome Convention. Such "conditions, limitations, exceptions and reservations" arguably include the right to deny a public performance right to producers and performers of sound recordings, to impose reciprocity as opposed to national treatment for foreign phonogram producers, and to permit, without compensation to the right holder, private use and use for teaching or scientific research.

QUESTIONS AND COMMENTS FOR YOUR CONSIDERATION

1. Is it not clear, from the foregoing excerpts, that an attorney faced with protecting his client's rights, needs to elect between protecting performing rights under a "neighboring right" theory or under a copyright theory?
2. Should the attorney's decision turn on the scope of protection afforded by either alternative?

B. The Protection of Performance Right[17]

The Rome Convention is the only international treaty governing performers' rights. Like the major copyright conventions, the Rome Convention applies the principle of national treatment to qualified foreigners. That is, nations that are signatories must grant certain foreign performers (and broadcast organizations and producers) the protections afforded by the Convention minima. Foreign performers, though, are guaranteed national treatment only up to this minimum level because the Convention provides that national treatment "shall be subject to the protection specifically guaranteed, and the limitations specifically provided for in this Convention."

Article 7 of the Rome Convention grants performers "the possibility of preventing" the unauthorized "broadcasting and the communication to the public" of their unfixed or live work. Rather than conveying a property right, the drafters employed the "possibility of preventing" language to satisfy broadcasters' and authors' groups and to fit into national systems that address performers' rights through systems of law other than property, such as criminal law.

The Rome Convention requires a very low level of protection against the unauthorized broadcasting, use or reproduction of a fixed work. Article 7 specifies that performers shall have "the possibility of preventing . . . the reproduction, without their consent, of a fixation of their performance: (i) if the original fixation was made without their consent; (ii) if the reproduction is made for purposes different from those for which the performers gave their consent....; or (iii) if the original fixation was made under the Convention's equivalent of a fair use exception and the subsequent use does not conform with that exception." The many qualifications in this provision satisfy the public's need for widespread dissemination of entertainment, but deny performers full control over their works.

C. The Protection of Broadcast Rights[18]

In 1961, when the Rome Convention was adopted,
—FM radio hardly existed;
—transistor radios were still unknown;

[17] Bonnie Teller, *Toward Better Protection Of Performance In The United States: A Comparative Look At Performer's Rights In The United States, Under The Rome Convention,* 28 COLUM. J. TRANSNAT'L L. 775. Copyright 1990 Columbia Journal of Transnational Law Association, Inc. Excerpt reprinted with permission.

[18] Werner Rumphorst, *Neighbouring Rights Protection of Broadcasting Organisations.* 18 EUPR 339. Copyright 1992 Werner Rumphorst. Excerpt reprinted with permission.

—stereo transmissions belonged to the distant future;
—audio recording equipment was in its beginnings, and cassette recorders were still to be introduced;
—digital audio broadcasting (DAB) was hardly imaginable; and
—wide-spread commercial use of color television was still years away.

In economic terms, the importance of [the rebroadcasting] right lies today in private recording of radio and TV broadcasts. Article 15(1)(a) [of the Rome Convention] nonetheless permits contracting states to make an exception with regard to private use. As long as this is not supplemented by a levy on recording equipment and/or blank tape, to the benefit of broadcasting organizations, the right of fixation (combined with the generally admitted exception for private use) is rather useless. Theoretically, of course, this right could be helpful in combating deferred rebroadcasts. However, since the Rome Convention does not grant the right of distribution [to a rebroadcaster], a clever pirate will always pretend that he received the recording from a third party, rather than having carried out a fixation himself. As long as [the right of rebroadcast] is not accompanied by a right of distribution, its practical value is extremely limited.

Places where the public go to watch TV programmes against payment of an entrance fee have long ceased to exist. On the other hand, the public communication of radio and TV broadcasts on business premises (restaurants, hotels, department stores, hairdressers, and so on) is a widespread phenomenon. It serves the business interests in question. However, broadcasting organizations (unlike authors) have no rights in this regard.

In view of the technological development in the field of broadcasting since 1961 and the legislative purpose of, and justification for, the broadcasting organization's neighboring right, a modern version of a neighboring rights article for the protection of broadcasting organizations should include the following detailed rights:

(1) The right to authorize or prohibit
(a) the rebroadcasting of their broadcasts ('rebroadcasting' should include both simultaneous and deferred broadcasting, and 'broadcast' should be clearly understood to include satellite broadcasting);
(b) the cable distribution of their broadcasts, both simultaneous and deferred;
(c) the communication to the public of their broadcasts, whether or not the communication is to a paying audience or is made in places accessible to the public against payment of an entrance fee;
(d) any fixation of their broadcasts via sound or video recorder for other than private purposes, and any reproduction or distribution of such a fixation;
(e) any reproduction or distribution of legally made fixations, other than for private purposes;
(f) any still photograph of a television broadcast other than for private purposes, and any reproduction or distribution of such a photograph;
(g) distribution to the public, by any broadcaster, cable distributor or other distributor, of their programme-carrying signals transported by communications satellite when such distributor is not authorized by the broadcaster to do so.

(2) The right to receive equitable remuneration in respect of private recording of their broadcasts (levy on recording equipment and/or blank tape).

(3) Protection against importation and distribution of fixations or the reproduction of such fixations made without authorization in a country which grants no protection to broadcasting organizations.

An article drafted on the basis of the foregoing provisions could be introduced into any national Copyright Act, regardless of a future revision (if any) of the Rome Convention along the same or similar lines. By virtue of the principle of national treatment, broadcasting organizations from other contracting states would automatically enjoy the same protection.

QUESTIONS AND COMMENTS FOR YOUR CONSIDERATION

Given the rapid pace of technological change in the communication industry, which if any of the following ways should countries attempt to avoid the problem of obsolescence in their treaty provisions?

a. Require the participation of adherents in regularly scheduled conferences for reviewing the impact of technology on treaty obligations and for renegotiation of those provisions affected by technological developments?
b. Provide loosely worded or ambiguous treaty obligations that may be interpreted to apply to the new technologies.?
c. Engage in frequent bilateral negotiations to supplement multinational treaty obligations in order to establish a technological "gloss" on such obligations?

D. The Protection of Sound Recordings

1. The Rome Convention[19]

Two major international conventions affect the worldwide protection of sound recordings. The older convention, known as the Berne Convention for the Protection of Literary and Artistic Works, was joined by the United States in 1988. Although the Berne Convention does not mandate the protection of sound recordings, it does cover the international protection of musical compositions. The Berne Convention limits its subject matter to "literary and artistic works," and sound recordings are not included. Sound recordings are relegated to the lesser status of a "neighboring right" as covered by the Rome Convention on Neighboring Rights. The United States is not currently a signatory to the Rome Convention.

The Rome Convention is the only international convention that affects the decision to enact a performance right in sound recordings in the United States. The Rome Convention is significant because it ensures a right of remuneration to creators of works, such as sound recordings, that are unprotected by the Berne Convention. These protections are the so called "neighboring rights." Specifically, Article 12 of the Rome Convention provides:

> If a phonogram, published for commercial purposes, or a reproduction of such phonogram, is used directly for broadcasting or for any communication to the public, a single equitable remuneration shall be paid by the user to the performers, or to the producers of the phonograms, or to both. Domestic law may, in the absence of agreement by parties, lay down the conditions as to the sharing of this remuneration.[20]

The remuneration provision of the Rome Convention is based on reciprocity, meaning that a signatory can only withdraw the funds if the withdrawing country has a performance right in sound recordings for foreign nationals. Performers in countries that export royalty-producing creations in greater quantities than they import them are remunerated, thus providing incentive for their government to join the Rome Convention.

---

[19] Johnthan Franklin, *Pay to Play: Enacting A Performing Right In Sound Recordings In The Age of Digital Audio Brodacsting,* 10 U. Miami Ent. & Sports L. Rev. 83. Copyright 1993 Entertainment and Sports Law Review. Excerpt reprinted with permission.

[20] The International Convention for the Protection for Performers, Producers of Phonograms and Broadcasting Organizations, 496 U.N.T.S. at art. 12.

2. Protection for Aural Performances[21]

Article 12 of the Rome Convention governs the subsequent use of "phonograms." Phonograms are defined as "any exclusively aural fixation of sounds of a performance or of other sounds." Article 12 provides that "a single equitable remuneration shall be paid by the user to the performers, or to the producers of the phonograms, or to both. Domestic law may, in the absence of agreement between these parties, lay down the conditions as to the sharing of this remuneration."

The Convention, however, specifically allows countries to ratify the treaty with reservations regarding their adherence to Article 12. Reservations may take one of four specified forms.[22] The impact of the different reservations varies, but all serve to significantly dilute the effectiveness of the Rome Convention by reducing the amount of royalties paid transnationally.

The Rome Convention does not prohibit the imitation of a performance and does not address the problem of commercial sound-alikes. Although performers have the possibility of preventing some forms of unauthorized reproduction, "reproduction" is defined by the Convention as "the making of a copy or copies of affixation." As one commentator states, "the term reproduction cannot be stretched to cover so-called "sound-alikes."[23] The only concession to protecting moral rights in the Rome Convention is found in Article 11, which requires the use of the performers' names along with notice symbols.

3. The Problem of US Adherence[24]

Although the United States is the world leader in the export of sound recordings, it has not yet joined the Rome Convention, primarily because it does not grant performance rights in sound recordings. Therefore, the United States does not receive reciprocal performance royalties from other countries. In order to join the Rome Convention, the United States would have to either enact a performance right in sound recordings so that reciprocity would be a possibility under Article 12, or the United States would have to opt-out of Article 12.

There is little reason for the United States to join the Rome Convention while opting out of Article 12 because it would not gain the funds already set aside by other countries for the public performance of United States produced sound recordings.

---

[21] Bonnie Teller, *Toward Better Protection Of Performance In The United States: A Comparative Look At Performer's Rights In The United States, Under The Rome Convention,* 28 COLUM. J. TRANSNAT'L L. 775. Copyright 1990 Columbia Journal of Transnational Law Association, Inc. Excerpt reprinted with permission.

[22] A country can either: (1) make a total reservation, treating Article 12 as if it were not part of the treaty; (2) restrict payment for use in broadcasting only (as opposed to use in shopping centers, restaurants, etc.) or for use in certain kinds of broadcasts only (cultural or religious, for example); (3) limit its royalty payments only to those situations in which the producer is a national of another signatory nation; or (4) demand reciprocity and refuse payment where reciprocity does not exist. Rome Convention, Art. 16.

[23] S.M. STEWART, INTERNATIONAL COPYRIGHT AND NEIGHBORING RIGHTS 218 (1983).

[24] Johnthan Franklin, *Pay to Play: Enacting A Performing Right In Sound Recordings In The Age of Digital Audio Brodacsting,* 10 U. MIAMI ENT. & SPORTS L. REV. 83. Copyright 1993 Entertainment and Sports Law Review. Excerpt reprinted with permission.

QUESTIONS AND COMMENTS FOR YOUR CONSIDERATION

1. Are there reasons why performance rights should not be extended to sound recordings?
2. Should sound recordings be treated differently from motion pictures?
3. Many countries impose compulsory licenses for the right to perform sound recordings. (For a more detailed discussion of compulsory licenses, *see* Chapter Ten.) Develop a plan for administering such licenses, including a method for determining who should receive any funds collected for such purposes.

5

The Protection of Cultural Patrimony

There is an interesting interrelation between a nation's culture and the protection it gives to intellectual property. On the one hand, the form, scope and types of intellectual property that a nation chooses to protect are generally determined by that nation's own cultural heritage. On the other hand, the existence of intellectual property protection affects the nation's ability to protect its own cultural heritage.

This Chapter examines the interrelation between intellectual property and the protection of cultural patrimony. We start with a review of the traditional area of perceived intersection between intellectual property and cultural heritage. The traditional view, as we shall see, finds the closest analogue to cultural patrimony in the literary and artistic side of intellectual property, *i.e.*, copyright.

We then take up some of the unique problems posed by the protection of cultural patrimony that stem from its dichotomous nature—that it is an amalgam of property values and cultural values.

The Chapter ends with a consideration of the future role of intellectual property law in the protection of all forms of cultural patrimony. This role will undoubtedly be a function of an evolving view of authorship and the creative act. The evolving role of authorship in the protection of intellectual property will be discussed in greater detail in the next Chapter.

A. Intellectual Property as Culture[1]

It is accepted beyond peradventure that part of a country's cultural heritage is embodied in its art and literature. Such works fall within the traditional scope of protected intellectual property forms. "Culture," however, is not limited strictly to art and literature. To the contrary, monumental architectural works, geographical configurations, unique ecosystems, and religious ceremonies and artifacts are also included within the scope of the term "cultural heritage." Although much of the effort at establishing international intellectual property norms has been directed to the protection of traditional forms of culture, there is little reason why other forms of "culture" should not be considered when international intellectual property protection norms are being debated.

Like traditional forms of protected intellectual property, cultural patrimony has a dichotomous nature. Traditional intellectual property has a dual nature of intellect (intangibility) and property. Cultural patrimony is similarly divisible into separate components of tangible property and intangible cultural values. Given the strong role which the protection of culture plays in a country's decision regarding the scope of protection to be afforded intellectual property, an understanding of the issues and positions taken on the interrelated issue of the protection of cultural patrimony can serve to illuminate the debate.

---

[1] Written for this Anthology by Doris Estelle Long and Anthony D'Amato. Copyright 1996 by Doris E. Long and Anthony D'Amato.

B. The Protection of Cultural Property

1. Art as Cultural Heritage[2]

Artistic and cultural objects began to take on national identities during the Enlightenment, with the rise of nationalism and the creation of modern nations. We can observe during that period the "increase in importance of the monument—the main interest shifted away from the person of the artist to the work of art as such." After the French Revolution monuments were praised for their artistic, historical, and scientific features. People began to conceive of monuments as the "cultural heritage of a nation, an evidence of historical traditions, a historical identity card." This new function of works of art influenced a nation's attitude toward its heritage; the protection of cultural property became a goal shared by various societies. As art became closely associated with particular nations, government efforts to protect cultural property were directed primarily toward keeping monuments within the state boundaries. Legislative efforts of this nature were supported by the realization that "those objects of art constitute evidence of things other than themselves; they are documents informing us about a certain state of affairs, in particular about social relationships, being at the same time objects of price, exchange, value, property, goods which arose from the economic life of a given epoch."

[2] Halina Niec, *Legislative Models of Protection of Cultural Property,* 27 Hastings L.J. 1089. Copyright 1976 Halina Niec. Excerpt reprinted with permission.

2. The Definition of Cultural Patrimony[3]

Synonyms for cultural property include the terms "cultural patrimony" and "antiquities." Although these words are often used interchangeably, the choice of term often connotes a specific political stance. "Cultural patrimony" implies that an artifact is of such significance to a particular civilization as to be an inalienable birthright of its descendants. For example, Greek nationalists often claim that the Elgin Marbles in the British Museum are the cultural patrimony of Greece. Some cultural activists find even the term "Elgin" Marbles offensive, because the name refers to the British lord who removed the sculptures from the Parthenon in 1816. Accordingly, they generally prefer the term "Parthenon Marbles" for the sculptures now in the British Museum.

3. A Second View[4]

"Cultural objects" are also referred to as "cultural property," "cultural goods," "cultural patrimony," or "national treasures." Some definitions of cultural property are extremely broad, including any object that has both property attributes and cultural significance.

[3] Lisa J. Borodkin, *The Economics of Antiquities Looting and a Proposed Legal Alternative,* 95 Colum. L. Rev. 377. Copyright 1995 Lisa J. Borodkin. Excerpt reprinted with permission.

[4] Victoria J. Vitrano, *Protecting Cultural Objects in an Internal Border-Free EC: The EC Directive and Regulations for the Protection and Return of Cultural Objects,* 17 Fordham Int'l L.J. 1164. Copyright 1994 Victoria J. Vitrano. Excerpt reprinted with permission.

QUESTIONS AND COMMENTS FOR YOUR CONSIDERATION

1. Are traditional forms of intellectual property covered by the definitions of "cultural patrimony" provided above? Would novels be covered? Paintings? Computer software? Architectural works? Patented machines?
2. What forms of intellectual property seem to be best suited to protect those categories of works which might be included in a broad definition of "cultural patrimony"?

4. The Dual Nature of Cultural Property[5]

The protection of cultural property is developing as a fundamental concern of international law. A growing network of bilateral and multilateral treaties addresses the treatment of cultural property during armed conflict, regulates its import and export, and, most recently, governs its repatriation to source countries and peoples. Individual nations have taken measures to protect what they perceive to be their cultural patrimony via state ownership laws and domestic import and export regulations. Indigenous peoples, ethnic and religious groups and organizations, on their own account and through their national governments, are actively seeking repatriation of objects of significance to their respective cultural identities. Although these treaties, domestic laws, and efforts at repatriation have as their goal protection of objects of cultural significance, the legal regime these sources have produced treat such objects primarily as property.

Objects of cultural property cannot be stripped of their cultural significance. They are not merely items of property any more than children are the property of divorcing parents. Recognition of cultural significance is an integral part of determining the best means of protecting cultural property.

There are two schools of thought concerning cultural property. The first school of thought, usually identified as cultural internationalism, is primarily concerned with physical preservation of objects. This school articulates concerns in terms of property law principles. The arguments of acquisitive nations, museums, collectors, and archaeologists, all of whom seek to protect their holding of or access to cultural property for aesthetic, scholarly, educative, or merely possessory purposes, generally belong to this school of thought. The property law principles they espouse include rights of title, possession, conquest, repose, and bona fide purchase. The second school of thought, usually termed cultural nationalism, is primarily concerned with the cultural significance of cultural property. Its arguments are often framed in terms of principles of human rights law. The demand is for cultural dignity and cultural self-determination. Arguments for repatriation of objects of cultural significance to source nations or to peoples belong to this school of thought. This paper asserts that the disputes between these schools of thought are really disputes over which aspect of cultural property deserves greater legal protection. Although the common ground between these two camps is concern for preservation of objects of cultural significance, preservation means different things to different interests.

An item of cultural property is an object that is of cultural significance. It therefore has two aspects. The first aspect is the property aspect, which derives from the fact that cultural property consists of tangible, movable objects. The implication of calling something property suggests that it can be owned, or at least possessed and controlled. The second aspect is the cultural aspect, which derives from the cultural significance of the object. Perhaps the most effective way to demonstrate the two aspects of cultural property is to consider an example of a specific item of cultural property.

The war gods of the Zuni people, a Native American tribe of the southwestern United States, are carved wooden idols usually two or three feet tall. These Ahayu:da (ah-ha-YOO-dah), carved by the tribe's Bear clan, appear to be simple, rather abstract faces. The objects are rare because the clan only carves two per year. The commercial market for these sculptures sets their value between US $5,000 and US $10,000. These facts demonstrate the property aspect of cultural property. The objects, tangible and movable, are described in terms of shape, size, rarity, and commercial value. The property aspect may be starkly shown by the fact that documentation dating back to the early 1800s shows that anthropologists, archaeologists, geologists, explorers, and other visitors to the Zuni Pueblo near Santa Fe often took the war gods from the Zuni's tribal shrines. Not everything that can be stolen is necessarily property, but most likely these objects were taken because they were valued as property. Thieves foreign to the culture that produced

[5] Roger W. Mastalir, *A Proposal for Protecting the "Cultural" and "Property" Aspects of Cultural Property Under International Law,* 16 FORDHAM INT'L L.J. 1033. Copyright 1993 Fordham University School of Law. Excerpt reprinted with permission.

such objects could not understand, or at least did not respect, the cultural significance of the items.

Considering only the property aspect of the Ahayu:da, however, tells only part of the story. The cultural aspect of cultural property is demonstrated in the cultural significance of such items to the people who created them. The Ahayu:da were placed in a shrine where their powers were invoked to protect the tribe. Each Ahayu:da serves as guardian for the tribe until relieved by a new one. The older ones must remain in place, contributing their strength until they decay and return to the earth. The war gods are meant to be exposed to the weather so that they can do their work as religious objects. Disintegration under the force of the elements is necessary to their function. Although they can exist as objects, as property, when displayed in a museum, they cannot serve their cultural purpose. Another part of the cultural aspect of these objects is that they cannot be treated as property in the usual sense because no individual can own them. The Zuni began retrieving the war gods from institutions and collectors in 1978. The recent return of the carved figures has boosted tribal morale and a sense of cultural identity. This effect on the morale of the tribe flows from the cultural aspect of cultural property. Cultural property is integral to the esteem that people hold for themselves and their past. It is also integral to their identity.

Cultural significance gives particular objects value to a culture or to a collector. Cultural property stripped of cultural significance would be merely property, more or less beautiful or rare and more or less valuable on the basis of that beauty or rarity only. Defining cultural property without reference to its culture is not only foolish, but dishonest. It attempts to strengthen claims of ownership while denigrating the very thing that gives an object some of its value to the holder. Nonetheless, recognition of the cultural aspect of cultural property has rarely been apparent in efforts to define or protect it.

Perhaps the most widely accepted definition of cultural property is found in Article 1 of the UNESCO Convention on the Means of Prohibiting the Illicit Import, Export and Transfer of Ownership of Cultural Property (the "UNESCO 1970").[6] The first notable element of this definition is that it consists of a list of categories of property.

The most notable element of the definition of cultural property in UNESCO 1970, however, is that it leaves to the individual states designation of specific items from the various categories as cultural property. The states may restrict the definition. The United States, for example, has limited the definition of protected cultural property in the 1983 Convention on Cultural Property Implementation Act. Under the US definition, objects do not become cultural property

---

[6] United Nations Educational, Scientific and Cultural Organization Convention on the Means of Prohibiting and Preventing the Illicit Import, Export and Transfer of Ownership of Cultural Property, Nov. 4, 1970, 823 U.N.T.S. 231, reprinted in 10 ILM 289 (1971) [hereinafter UNESCO 1970]. Article 1 states:

> For the purposes of this Convention, the term "cultural property" means property which, on religious or secular grounds, is specifically designated by each State as being of importance for archaeology, prehistory, history, literature, art or science and which belongs to the following categories: (a) Rare collections and specimens of fauna, flora, minerals and anatomy, and objects of paleontological interest; (b) property relating to history, including the history of science and technology and military and social history, to the life of national leaders, thinkers, scientists and artists and to events of national importance; (c) products of archaeological excavations (including regular and clandestine) or of archaeological discoveries; (d) elements of artistic or historical monuments or archaeological sites which have been dismembered; (e) antiquities more than one hundred years old, such as inscriptions, coins and engraved seals; (f) objects of ethnological interest; (g) property of artistic interest, such as: (i) pictures, paintings and drawings produced entirely by hand on any support and in any material (excluding industrial designs and manufactured articles decorated by hand); (ii) original works of statuary art and sculpture in any material; (iii) original engravings, prints and lithographs; (iv) original artistic assemblages and montages in any material; (h) rare manuscripts and incunabula, old books, documents and publications of special interest (historical, artistic, scientific, literary, etc.) singly or in collections; (i) postage, revenue and similar stamps, singly or in collections; (j) archives, including sound, photographic and cinematographic archives; (k) articles of furniture more than one hundred years old and old musical instruments.

UNESCO 1970, Art. 1, 823 U.N.T.S. at 234-36.

until they have been removed from or are threatened with removal from their cultural context.

Although UNESCO 1970 emphasizes the property aspect of cultural property, its definition of cultural property is at least partly in terms of cultural significance and cultural context. Recognizing that cultural property can be defined only partially by its age, provenance, category, or threat of pillage, UNESCO 1970 defines cultural property as "property which, on religious or secular grounds, is . . . of importance for archaeology, prehistory, history, literature, art or science."

The definition does not contemplate the designation by indigenous peoples of objects sacred to them as cultural property. The state-centric element is also apparent in that the cultural significance of objects is determined by "importance for archaeology, prehistory, history, literature, art or science," not by importance to the cultural identity of a people or group. The values stated are largely external to the cultural identity of a people or group. Is the judgment that of a living people, defining for themselves their relationship to the world, or the judgment of external academics applying some sort of absolute criteria? The recognition of "religious or secular grounds" upon which to base the importance of cultural property is insufficient entry for the significance of objects to peoples or groups. The Preamble suggests recognition of the importance of cultural property to cultural identity, but even here the nation-state is the unit of identity, not the ethnic group or indigenous people to whom such objects may have the greatest cultural significance.

Setting aside the questions of what is to be protected, and who shall define it, concentration on the property aspect of cultural property inevitably raises the question, "Who Owns The Past?" If cultural property can be properly defined, who may own it? Is "ownership" of cultural property even possible? The problem of ownership has several facets.

A principal text on art law identifies the major problems in protection of cultural property as (1) illicit trade and (2) repatriation. Both problems involve questions regarding who may properly own, or possess, cultural property. Trade cannot be illicit if it does not dispossess someone of the right to licit trade. Similarly, no one may gain return of cultural property unless they can show "better title."

Reflecting the dichotomous nature of cultural property, the question of ownership might be reformulated in two parts. First, should cultural property be returned to source countries or peoples? This is the repatriation issue. Second, who is a legitimate claimant of and who can legitimately release cultural property to the possession of another? This is the replevin issue. A rough way of classifying these issues is that the first is a human rights/self-determination issue, and the second is a property issue. Repatriation is a moral issue concerned with right treatment of diverse cultures and objects significant to them. Accordingly, the focus of this moral inquiry is on the cultural significance, the cultural aspect of cultural property. Replevin is a title issue, based on who has a superior right to possess particular items of cultural property, defined by objective criteria. Its focus is the property aspect of cultural property.

In addition to the possessory interests suggested by the question of who owns the past, there are myriad interests based on use and enjoyment. These interests may be divided into those of the source nations and those of acquisitive nations, although there is some overlap between them. For source nations, the first interest is specific cultural value, or concern over wrenching cultural property away from the culture in which it is embedded. Second, there is an archaeological interest in preventing destruction of the records of civilization. A third interest is in the integrity of the work of art or object of cultural property, which means simply that it should not be dismembered. Fourth is an interest in physical safety of cultural property from deterioration. A fifth interest is an economic one, measured in terms of the price the object would bring on an open market (intrinsic value), and the tourist dollars generated by presence of the object in a nation (extrinsic value). Sixth, cultural property has artistic value independent of its cultural significance. Seventh, is the so-called distribution interest. Cultural property may demonstrate to the world the achievements of the culture of a nation if it is disseminated. Eighth, there is an interest in mere retention, or "hoarding," as the right of source nations and peoples. Finally, there is an interest in preserving the national patrimony as a matter of pride and identity, as well as intrinsic and extrinsic economic value.

The interests of acquisitive nations are equally diverse. First is again the interest in preservation, or the physical safety of the objects above. Second, there is an interest among colonial powers and victorious powers in times of conflict in the humiliation of a conquered people by dispossessing them of their cultural and artistic treasures. Third, there is the interest of "good faith purchasers" that their ownership or possession of objects not be unjustly disturbed, or disturbed without compensation. Fourth, acquisitive nations have an interest in enriching their own cultural patrimony by acquisition from external sources. Fifth, like source nations seeking appreciation of their culture abroad, acquisitive nations have an interest in the breakdown of parochialism in a global society. Finally, acquisitive nations have an interest in maintaining access to cultural property for archaeological purposes.

A QUESTION FOR YOUR CONSIDERATION

Copyright under US law is also treated as having a dual nature. Ownership of the object in which the copyrighted work is embodied is not the same as ownership of the copyright. *See* 17 U.S.C. § 202. Does this provide a useful analogy for the treatment of cultural patrimony?

5. The Debate over Cultural Nationalism[7]

> The British say they have saved the Marbles. Well, thank you very much. Now give them back. —Melina Mercouri[8]

[The Elgin Marbles were removed from the Parthenon in the Nineteenth Century and were eventually housed and are currently located in The British Museum in London. The removal and retention of these Greek antiquities has formed the basis for a bitter and divisive debate over the role of cultural nationalism in the retention, repatriation and protection of cultural patrimony.]

Any estimate of the morality of Elgin's actions has to take account both of his motives and of the results of what he did. His motives, though certainly mixed, included a large element of reverence for the Marbles and the intention of removing them to a safer place. He also wished to bring the Marbles to the attention of the world and to see them used to advance the arts. The passion for Greek antiquities was still in its early infancy even in England and France, where the works of the Romans were more highly valued. Elgin's removals focused Europe's attention on the magnificence of the Marbles and other works of Greek art of that period. One result was that Greek superseded Roman art as the ideal, both in high and in popular culture. Elgin was convinced of the superiority of Greek over Roman art, and through his actions and the resulting acquisition of the Marbles by the British Museum, the rest of the world came to share his opinion.

Elgin was also motivated by nationalism: he wanted the Marbles for England and feared that they would otherwise go to the French. It is clear that Elgin hoped to advance his own career and may at times have thought that the Marbles would help. In that hope he was disappointed, in part, because of Byron's influence. Financially, there is no evidence that Elgin ever expected the Marbles to be profitable, although he

---

[7] John H. Merryman, *Thinking about the Elgin Marbles*, 83 MICH. L. REV. 1881 (1985). Copyright 1985 by John H. Merryman. Reprinted by permission.

[8] Quoted in Sunday Times (London), May 22, 1983, at 15, col. 1.

probably hoped to recover his expenses. In any event, the Marbles were his financial ruin. He went deeply into debt, often at high interest, to finance the work of his artists and the removal and shipment of the Marbles. The pounds sterling 35,000 that Parliament eventually paid for the Marbles were far less than the costs Elgin incurred. Indeed, it is possible to make of Elgin a nobly tragic figure: a man so dedicated to the cause of classic Greek art and to the acquisition and preservation of the Marbles that he sacrificed his career and his fortune for them.

I conclude that the legality of the removal of the Marbles is clearly established and that its immorality has not been demonstrated. The Greeks do not have a strong legal or moral case against Elgin. Minister Mercouri's and Byron's eloquence and art to the contrary notwithstanding, the British own the Marbles and, on balance, did not wrongly acquire ownership. For those who agree, that settles the legal and moral questions about the removal. There remains, however, the most difficult and interesting question of all: Should the British now return the Marbles to Greece? Independent of questions about the legality and morality of the removal is the argument that the Marbles should, on other grounds, be returned. Adequate analysis of this aspect of the case brings a new set of considerations into play, requiring us to consider the relative merits of nationalism and internationalism as guiding principles in the allocation of cultural property.

The discussion up to this point has been retrospective. We have looked at the historical record in order to assess the legality and morality of the British acquisition of the Marbles. What happened in the past strongly affects the present and future, so that one who properly acquired something normally has the legal right to keep and enjoy it and, if he wishes, to dispose of it. Thus if the Trustees of the British Museum became the owners of the Marbles in 1816, they own them today. Still, in no legal system is the right of property absolute; it is possible to establish new rules of property or modify old ones, and although the right of property is respected, it is subject to regulation and even, in extreme cases, to expropriation. Even if Britain properly acquired the Marbles, it is still possible to argue for their return to Greece.

The most obvious argument is that the Marbles belong in Greece because they are Greek. They were created in Greece by Greek artists for the civic and religious purposes of the Athens of that time. The appealing implication is that, being in this sense Greek, they belong among Greeks, in the place (the Acropolis of Athens) for which they were made. This argument, which I will call the argument from cultural nationalism, requires careful examination, since it is basic to the Greek position and because arguments like it are frequently made by other governments calling for the return of cultural property (and is strongly implied in their use of the term "repatriation").

In its truest and best sense, cultural nationalism is based on the relation between cultural property and cultural definition. For a full life and a secure identity, people need exposure to their history, much of which is represented or illustrated by objects. Such artifacts are important to cultural definition and expression, to shared identity and community. They tell people who they are and where they come from. In helping to preserve the identity of specific cultures, they help the world preserve texture and diversity. Works of art civilize and enrich life. They generate art (it is a truism among art historians that art comes from art) and nourish artists. Cultural property stimulates learning and scholarship. A people deprived of its artifacts is culturally impoverished.

The difficulty comes in relating the notion of cultural deprivation to the physical location of the Marbles. If the British had attempted to appropriate the identity of the Marbles, disguising or misrepresenting their origin, then the Greeks, and all the rest of us, would rightly object to such falsification of the culture. If such misrepresentation were encouraged or justified by their location in England, then one could see the basis for an argument that the Marbles should be returned to Greece. But in fact the British have from the beginning presented the Marbles openly and candidly as the work of Greek artists of extraordinary genius and refinement. Presented as they are, spectacularly mounted in their own fine rooms in one of the world's great museums, the Marbles honor Greece and Greeks. No visitor to the British Museum could come away with any other impression. By their removal to London and exposure in the British Museum, they have brought admiration and respect for the Greek achievement. As we have seen, that was one of Lord Elgin's intentions. In the most important sense the Greek cultural heritage has been preserved, arguably enhanced, by the British acquisition and display of the Marbles.

It is not clear that enjoyment of cultural value (as distinguished from economic and political value, which are discussed below) requires possession of the Marbles. Greeks need access to their cultural heritage, and access would be easiest and most direct if the Marbles were in Athens, but writings about the Marbles are widely published and well illustrated, and excellent reproductions exist. In that sense the Marbles are, or could easily be made to be, as accessible to the Greeks through reproductions as through the originals. There must be some cultural magic inherent in the authentic object, and not in an accurate reproduction, that speaks only to Greeks, or the argument fails. Still, the argument for possession as an aspect of cultural nationalism has an instinctive appeal.

The cultural nationalist argument is distinct from, but related to, two other arguments, one economic and one political. Economically, whoever has the Marbles has something of value: they would command an enormous price if offered for sale, and their presence in a public collection nourishes the tourist industry. Possession is obviously necessary in order to enjoy the economic value, and Britain has the Marbles. We have already seen, however, that the law seems to support the British acquisition and thus to sanction British enjoyment of the economic value. Indeed, providing the basis for allocating things of value is one of the important functions of law, and it is one of the things law seems to do particularly well. If the Greeks were to base their argument on the economic value of the Marbles, they would merely be rearguing a question of property law, claiming that they own the Marbles. As we have already seen, they would probably lose that argument. The applicable law is clear and, on the facts as we have interpreted them, favors the British.

The final component of the nationalism argument is political: the belief that the presence of the Marbles in England, or in any place other than Greece, is an offense to Greeks and to the Greek nation. Here the demand for the return of the Marbles is based on national pride. That sort of sentiment is close to cultural deprivation of the sort just discussed, but it is worlds away from it in a very important sense.

Nationalism in its broader meaning refers to the attitude which ascribes to national individuality a high place in the hierarchy of values. In this sense it is a natural and indispensable condition and accompanying phenomenon of all national movements. . . . On the other hand, the term nationalism also connotes a tendency to place a particularly excessive, exaggerated and exclusive emphasis on the value of the nation at the expense of other values, which leads to a vain and importunate overestimation of one's own nation and thus to a detraction of others. The weight one gives to this kind of argument for the return of the Marbles depends to a large extent on one's attitude toward political nationalism itself. No candid observer can deny its power in world affairs.

A QUESTION FOR YOUR CONSIDERATION

The debate over the repatriation of the Elgin Marbles underscores the conflicting problems of nationalism, cultural patrimony and cultural protection concerns. Which of the arguments provided above do you think strikes the appropriate balance between these conflicting concerns?

6. The Property Aspects of Cultural Artifacts[9]

Thieves often take stolen cultural property directly from countries with rich cultural heritages to civil-law nations where the purchaser of stolen property can gain good title. In a civil-law nation, a purchaser of stolen art acquires good title provided that she does not know or learn about the object's illicit removal from its rightful owner. In a common-law country, by contrast, a seller cannot transfer better title than she has. A thief in a common-law country thus breaks the chain of good title and any subsequent purchasers can never acquire good title. The original owner can therefore reclaim the object regardless of whether the purchaser knew she had bought a stolen object. Because some EC countries follow the common-law tradition while others have civil-law traditions, art thieves merely need to take a stolen object out of a common-law country and into a civil-law nation to "launder" it.

[9] Victoria J. Vitrano, *Protecting Cultural Objects in an Internal Border-Free EC: The EC Directive and Regulations for the Protection and Return of Cultural Objects,* 17 FORDHAM INT'L L.J. 1164. Copyright 1994 Victoria J. Vitrano. Excerpt reprinted with permission.

A QUESTION FOR YOUR CONSIDERATION

Is resolution of the ownership of the cultural artifact under a rightful title/property law analysis relevant to the question whether retention of an artifact such as the Elgin Marbles has a harmful cultural effect on Greece? On Great Britain? On the rest of the world?

7. Protection Regimes[10]

Most countries restrict the export of antiquities through a licensing scheme. Great Britain, France, Austria, Canada, and Australia have application procedures for removing an artifact from the country. The licenses granted under such schemes are usually specific to each artifact since each application must be reviewed individually.

The second broad strategy, nationalization of cultural artifacts, operates from the same principle as the nationalization of any other natural resource. Many Central American countries, such as Ecuador and Costa Rica, have laws that make all archaeological materials discovered after the effective date of the laws the property of the state. As of 1984, state claims to undiscovered archaeological artifacts could be found in countries of every region and economic and political stratum.

Export restrictions and nationalization laws are sometimes called "blanket" or "umbrella" laws due to their all-inclusive nature. These umbrella laws have been widely criticized because their breadth renders enforcement virtually impossible. As a result, source nations must rely on cooperation at international borders to retain what they have legislated as theirs. However, even this strategy can backfire, since, for example, American courts have refused to return artifacts when the governing national ownership statutes were overly vague.

Enforcement of antiquities laws is a severe, pervasive problem. Most artifact-rich countries focus their enforcement measures on the looters of archaeological sites, but these areas are notoriously difficult to police. By definition, many fresh archaeology sites are unknown. The guards at the known sites are frequently underpaid. Corruption at all levels of enforcement adds to enforcement difficulties. In some countries, customs officials can easily be bribed. Corruption can even extend to the highest levels of govern-

[10] Lisa J. Borodkin, *The Economics of Antiquities Looting and a Proposed Legal Alternative,* 95 COLUM. L. REV. 377. Copyright 1995 Lisa J. Borodkin. Excerpt reprinted with permission.

ment. In Greece, for instance, former Prime Minister Constantine Mitsotakis and his deputy police chief were implicated in a scheme to cooperate with an international syndicate of antiquities smugglers.

8. The Retention of Cultural Property[11]

Most nations attempt to retain cultural property.[12] They declare that cultural objects are state property ("expropriation laws"), or prohibit the expert of cultural objects ("embargo laws"), or give the state or domestic institutions a preemptive right to buy objects offered for export ("preemption laws"). Some laws mix these categories: they may totally forbid the export of particularly important objects; permit the expert, subject to preemptive purchase, of other kinds; and allow the export, with or without a permit, of less important objects. Others indiscriminately retain everything. Elucidated by administrative regulations and administered by governmental officials and agencies, these laws express the intention to keep cultural objects within the national territory. They are a form of export control. We can refer to them generically as "retention schemes."

Many of the most extensive retention schemes are found in nations rich in cultural artifacts but short of foreign exchange. Their development policies normally encourage export trade to earn foreign exchange to pay for imports and to finance domestic growth. But cultural property is an exception: despite a substantial and well-funded market for such objects abroad, export trade in cultural objects is prohibited or restrained. The contrast is striking and seems to call for explanation. What is there about cultural property that produces such an apparently counter-developmental policy?

The practice of national retention of cultural property has a superficial appeal; it seems to many people to be natural and reasonable, a normal expression of the obvious relation between the object and the national culture: Olmec heads clearly belong in Mexico because they are Mexican; classical Greek sculptures are Greek and belong in Greece. The retention of cultural property needs no justification; on the contrary, permitting cultural objects to be exported is what seems anomalous. How can one permit

---

[11] John Henry Merryman, *The Retention of Cultural Property,* 21 UCLA DAVIS L. REV. 477. Copyright 1988 John Henry Merryman. Excerpt reprinted with permission.

[12] The principal varieties of cultural property for present purposes are works of art and objects of archaeological, ethnological, and historical interest. Any comprehensive definition of cultural property would have to include these objects and many more. Thus, the UNESCO Convention on the Means of Prohibiting and Preventing the Illicit Import, Expert and Transfer of Ownership of Cultural Property, Nov. 14, 1970, 823 U.N.T.S. 231 (1972), 10 Int'l Legal Materials 289 (1971) [hereafter UNESCO Convention], defines cultural property in Article 1 to include:

> (a) Rare collections and specimens of fauna, flora, minerals and anatomy, and objects of paleontological interest; (b) property relating to history, including the history of science and technology and military and social history . . . ; (c) products of archaeological excavations . . . ; (d) elements of artistic or historical monuments . . . which have been dismembered; (e) antiquities more than one hundred yeas old, such as inscriptions, coins and engraved seals; (f) objects of ethnological interest; (g) property of artistic interest . . . ; (h) rare manuscripts and incunabula, old books, documents and publications of special interest . . . ; (i) postage, revenue and similar stamps . . . ; (j) archives, including sound, photographic and cinematographic archives; (k) articles of furniture more than one hundred years old and old musical instruments.

In some nations cultural objects and environmental treasures (including natural and artificial landscapes and ecological areas plus, in cities, urban structures and panoramas) are treated as fundamentally related to each other.

For a discussion of folklore as cultural property, *see* GLASSIE, ARCHAEOLOGY AND FOLKLORE: COMMON ANXIETIES, COMMON HOPES, IN HISTORICAL ARCHAEOLOGY AND THE IMPORTANCE OF MATERIAL THINGS 23 (L. Ferguson ed. 1977).

The entire question of the proper definition of cultural property for legal and policy purposes is large and unruly, and fortunately need not be pursued here. Works of art and archaeological, ethnological, and historical objects certainly qualify under any definition; museums acquire and display them, scholars study them, collectors collect them, and dealers sell them. National laws and international conventions provide for their preservation and regulate their trade. A strong international consensus supports their inclusion in any definition of cultural property.

the nation's "cultural heritage," or "cultural patrimony," to be taken abroad? National cultural objects held (imprisoned?) in foreign museums and collections should be rescued—"repatriated"—returned to their homeland, their *patria*. This concept of a "national cultural patrimony" is frequently cited and treated as an established political and legal category.

This is the basic cultural nationalist position, which has become part of Western culture. Cultural nationalism transcends jurisdiction and sovereignty; even though many "Greek" sculptures are in the British Museum and the Louvre beyond the reach of Greek laws, they remain Greek. Where do these attitudes come from? The major premise is nationalism itself.

European in origin, nationalism is a modern addition to the history of ideas emerging clearly only at the time of the French Revolution as nations become the primary actors in world affairs with nationalism as the supporting ideology. In Enlightenment thought, nationalism had humanist roots; it embodied liberal republican ideas of the kind expressed in the American Declaration of Independence in 1776 and the French Declaration of the Rights of Man and of the Citizen in 1789. But with the rise of romanticism and the relative decline of faith in reason and in the humanist ideal, the content of nationalism changed. Led by German philosophers and poets, such as Fichte, Herer, and Heine, nationalism acquired new premises and a romantic, mystical overlay. Concepts like that of the *Volk* (with *Volksgenosse* and *Volksgeist*) became current.

Under the romantic influence, conceptual distinctions between nationalism, patriotism, and national consciousness blurred. The way was opened to nation-worship, the adoration of national character, national achievement, national culture, national ambitions, and national policies. As each nation preened itself, nationalism became invidious. Patriotism and xenophobia became natural correlates. Nationalism justified violence when employed in the national interest. Nationalism which "begins as Sleeping Beauty . . . [and] ends as Frankenstein's Monster." Romanticism succeeded the Enlightenment; faith in rationalism declined; reason slept. In nationalism, as elsewhere, the sleep of reason produced monsters.

Nationalism in itself is neither good nor bad; the difficulty lies in the tune it has taken and the uses to which it has been put under the influence of romanticism.

The application of these attitudes of nationalism to cultural objects owes much to the English romantic poet George Gordon, Lord Byron. In 1821 the Greeks began their war for independence from four centuries of Ottoman rule. Byron was a powerful publicist for the Greek cause though (sic) his poetry and correspondence (and through his actions, dying of fever at Missolonghi while actively supporting the Greeks). The cause of Greek nationalism captured the Western imagination, where it was seen through romantic spectacles. Byron passionately opposed Lord Elgin's removal of the Parthenon sculptures, the "Elgin Margles," and wrote about the episode in two poems: *The Curse of Minerva* and *Childe Harold's Pilgrimage*. Although these passages contain some of his least memorable poetry, they were enormously effective as propaganda. The key premise was that of cultural nationalism: the Marbles were Greek and belonged in Greece. Since Byron, that premise has been solidly built into Western thought.

We need a term. The epithet "elginisme," coined by the French to refer to the wrongful (*i.e.*, by persons who are not French) removal of cultural property from its site, became part of the common language of discourse on cultural property. In a similar spirit we could use the term "Byronism" to characterize the application of romantic nationalism to cultural objects. Byronism has dominated post-World War II discourse on cultural property. It is the unexamined premise of much contemporary national and international policy toward cultural property. Let's examine it.

Much of the justification for cultural retention schemes is straightforward Byronism: the romantic attribution of national character to cultural objects, with the corollary that they belong in the national territory. When viewed objectively, this looks more like a statement of faith than a reason. Its effect, however, is no less because of that; it may indeed be more powerful in its candidly emotional appeal than any local argument would be. Consider these statements by Melina Mercouri in her campaign for return of the Elgin Marbles to Athens:

> This is our history, this is our soul. . . . You must understand us. You must love us. We have fought with you in the second war. Give them back and we will be proud of you. Give them back and they will be in good hands.

and

> They are the symbol and the blood and the soul of the Greek people. . . . We have fought and died for the Parthenon and the Acropolis. . . . When we are born, they talk to us about all this great history that makes Greekness.

Such statements appeal primarily to the emotions. They divert attention from the facts and discourage reasoned discussion of the issues.

We turn now to a different group of possible explanations for the existence of cultural property retention schemes based on the familiar power of governments to promote the general welfare of their people. Does the presence of cultural property in private hands in the national territory promote the general welfare? Does export impair it?

There is no serious debate about the proposition that cultural property should be preserved. If the object is damaged or destroyed the opportunity to study and learn from it, to enjoy it, to be inspired by it, is impaired or lost. Public action to protect and preserve cultural property appears to be not only reasonable but laudable. Public action to preserve contextual values also makes sense. To the archaeologist, ethnographer, or historian, an object may derive much of its significance from its context and the context may derive meaning from the object. If a stela is taken from a Mayan temple without full documentation, the value of the stela and the temple are diminished. The act of removal destroys information, impedes learning, and impairs enjoyment. The stela rendered anonymous by the act of undocumented removal, becomes an orphan; the temple, an amputee. "Decontextualization" of this kind is a genuine problem for parts of architectural monuments. Even for unattached works, loss of context can be a serious problem. Consider the case of the removal of a pot from the Etruscan tomb. Unless removal is accompanied by elaborate documentation of the site and its contents and identification of the pots's origin in the site, it leads to the irreparable loss of cultural information. It is a form of destruction, a kind of vandalism.

Loss of integrity is a related problem that is particularly applicable to works of art. A complex work, such as an altarpiece composed of several panels, arguably is greater than the sum of its parts. If one of the panels is removed and sold, both the panel and the remaining part lose something essential. Fidelity to the artist's conception is only a part of the problem; there is also the concern for the object's preservation in its authentic form. The purpose is to preserve the integrity of the culture, to avoid its falsification and decontextualization.

The *troika* of preservation, context, and integrity constitutes a set of higher "public welfare" values that transcend national interests and boundaries. They are concerned with *protection* of cultural objects, of things that embody or express or evoke the human record. Such objects, in the words of The Hague Convention of 1954, are "the cultural heritage of all mankind."

We have seen three plausible explanations of why nations try to prevent the export of cultural property: Byronism (*i.e.*, nationalist sentiment), protection (*i.e.*, preservation, context and integrity), and opportunity preservation (*i.e.*, if it stays in the national territory the nation may eventually acquire it at a bargain price or may decide to protect it). Other reasons have been offered and considered, but they do not survive inspection.

9. The Problems of the Colonial Era[13]

Prior to 1800, the prevailing "mercantilist" view of international trade assumed that the prosperity of a country could be maximized by policies which ensured a surplus of exports over imports. Since precious metals were used to settle international accounts,

---

Bartram S. Brown, *Developing Countries in the International Trade Order,* 14 N. Ill. U. L. Rev. 347.

this balance would generate a net inflow of gold and silver from the rest of the world. The implicit assumption was that the world's economic pie was of constant size, and therefore any gains experienced by one nation from trade had to come at the expense of its trading partners. In short, international trade was viewed as a zero-sum game.

In 1776, Adam Smith published his now classic work, Wealth of Nations, which explained that nations could engage in mutually beneficial trade. This analysis was taken one step further with the formulation of the principle of comparative advantage in the 19th century by David Ricardo and John Stuart Mill. As this theory shows, a nation can benefit from international trade even if it cannot produce any one good more efficiently than its trading partners. If each nation specializes in the production of those products which it can produce with the greatest relative efficiency, and can then trade freely with other nations for the other products it needs; the greater overall efficiency which results from this process increases the size of the world's economic pie, providing a higher standard of living for all. In short, international trade can be a positive-sum interaction.

Although we are familiar today with the economic division between the industrialized countries of the North and the developing countries of the South, the situation was quite different in the immediate Post World War II era. Many countries we know as developing countries today, and most of those in Africa and Asia, had not yet achieved independence from colonial domination in the 1940s.

From the beginning, many in the developing world viewed proposals for a free trade system as a threat to their hopes of rapid industrialization as well as to their independence and sovereignty. They feared an open trading system would make it impossible for the non-industrialized countries of the South to achieve industrialization because any new "infant industries" they might try to create would be unable to compete with the established foreign competition.

The history of relations between North and South has left many in the developing areas of the world with some palpable resentment about international economic relations, and developing countries have tried, with varying degrees of success, to maintain "Third World" political unity within the United Nations system. The nineteenth century "colonial" pattern of trade relations had been typified by a division of labor which prevented the industrial development of the South. The largely industrialized colonial powers had no interest in developing competing industries in their colonial possessions, thus they tapped their colonies as a source of primary commodities. This, in effect, relegated these developing areas to a peripheral role in the economies of their colonizing powers. The economy of the colonial "periphery" was used as a subordinate appendage of the industrial economy of the colonial "center" or "metropolis," supplying commodities to the metropolitan power and also serving as a market for industrialized goods. Those developing areas that achieved political independence sought to sever the economic dependency by establishing their own industries, and they were suspicious that free trade would serve only to perpetuate their underdevelopment.

10. Authorship, Cultural Patrimony and Intellectual Property[14]

In March 1993, a diverse group of educators, scholars and industry experts convened in Bellagio to discuss the relationship between the concepts of authorship, cultural patrimony and intellectual property protection. The Declaration which resulted from the conference highlights some of the future issues to be faced if traditional forms of intellectual property are extended to include objects of cultural patrimony. It states the following:

> **We**, the participants at the Bellagio Conference on intellectual property, come from many nations, professions and disciplines. We lawyers and literary critics, computer scientists and publishers, teachers and writers, envi-

---

[14] The Bellagio Declaration, March 11, 1993. Reprinted with permission from International Journal of Cultural Property (1995).

ronmentalists and scholars of cultural heritage.

Sharing a common concern about the effects of the international regime of intellectual property law on our communities, on scientific progress and international development, on our environment, on the culture of indigenous peoples. In particular,

Applauding the increasing attention by the world community to such previously ignored issues as preservation of the environment, of cultural heritage, and biodiversity. But

Convinced that the role of intellectual property in these areas has been neglected for too long, we therefore convened a conference of academics, activists and practitioners diverse in geographical and cultural background as well as professional area of interest.

Discovering that many of the different concerns faced in each of these diverse areas could be traced back to the same oversights and injustices in the current intellectual property system, we hereby

Declare the following:

First, intellectual property laws have profound effects on issues as disparate as scientific and artistic progress, biodiversity, access to information, and the cultures of indigenous and tribal peoples. Yet all too often those laws are constructed without taking such effects into account, constructed around a paradigm that is selectively blind to the scientific and artistic contributions of many of the world's cultures and constructed in *fora* where those who will be most directly affected have no representation.

Second, many of these problems are built into the basic structure and assumptions of intellectual property. Contemporary intellectual property law is constructed around a notion of the author as an individual, solitary and original creator, and it is for this figure that its protections are reserved. Those who do not fit this model—custodians of trial culture and medical knowledge, collectives practicing traditional artistic and musical forms, or peasant cultivators of valuable seed varieties, for example—are denied intellectual property protection.

Third, a system based on such premises has real negative consequences. Increasingly, traditional knowledge, folklore, genetic material and native medical knowledge flow *out* of their countries of origin unprotected by intellectual property, while works from developed countries flow *in*, well protected by international intellectual property agreements, backed by the threat of trade sanctions.

Fourth, in general, systems built around the author paradigm tend to obscure or undervalue the importance of "the public domain," the intellectual and cultural commons from which future works will be constructed. Each intellectual property right, in effect fences off some portion of the public domain, making it unavailable to future creators. In striking respects, the current situation raises the same concerns raised twenty years ago by the impeding privatization of the deep sea bed. The aggressive expansion of intellectual property rights have the potential to inhibit development and future creation by fencing off "the commons," and yet—in striking contrast to the reaction over the deep sea bed—the international community seems unaware of the fact.

Fifth, we deplore these tendencies, deplore them as not merely unjust but unwise, and entreat the international community to reconsider the assumptions on which and the procedure by which the international intellectual property regime is shaped.

In general, we favor increased recognition and protection of the public domain. We call on the international community to expand the public domain through expansive application of concepts of "fair use," compulsory licensing, and narrower initial coverage of property rights in the first place. But since existing author-focused regimes are blind to the interests of non-authorial producers as well as to the importance of the commons, the main exception to this expansion of the public domain should be in favor of those who have been excluded by the authorial biases of current law.

Specifically, we advocate consideration of special regimes, possibly in the form of "neighboring" or "related" rights regimes, for the following areas:

Protection of folkloric works.

Protection of works of cultural heritage.

Protection of the biological and ecological "know-how" of traditional peoples.

In addition, we support systematic reconsideration of the basis on which new kinds of works related to digital technology, such as computer programs and electronic data bases, are protected under national and international intellectual property regimes. We recognize the economic importance of works falling into these categories, and the significant investments made in their production. Nevertheless, given the importance of the various concerns raised by any such a regime—concerns about public access, international development and technological innovation—we believe that choices about how and how much to protect databases should be made with a view to the specific policy objectives such protection is designed to achieve, rather than as a reflexive response to their categorization as "works of authorship."

On a systemic level, we call upon states and non-governmental organizations to move towards democratization of the fora in which the international intellectual property regime is debated and decided.

In conclusion, we declare that in an era in which information is among the most precious of all resources, intellectual property rights cannot be framed by the few to be applied to the many. They cannot be framed on assumptions that disproportionately exclude the contributions of important parts of the world community. They can no longer be constructed without reference to their ecological, cultural and scientific effects. We must reimagine the international regime of intellectual property. It is to that task this Declaration calls its readers.

QUESTIONS AND COMMENTS FOR YOUR CONSIDERATION

1. The definition of who qualifies as an author, and what role authorship should play in determining (1) whether works should be subject to protection and (2) who should control the use of such protected works has been hotly contested. (*See* Chapters Two and Six).

2. What view of authorship and its role in the protection of cultural works does the Declaration propose? How does this view compare with the "Romantic" view of authorship? Are the two views incompatible?

6

Beyond Economics: The Protection of Authorship As A Cultural Value

Regardless of the form, all intellectual property, as "products of the mind," must be created by human intervention (even if that intervention is the creation of a machine which then creates the intellectual property in question). The decision to protect intellectual property, and the nature and scope of such protection, reflects the value that a particular culture places upon the creative act. The role of the author/artist becomes imbued with a variety of historical, philosophical and cultural values that have a direct bearing on the amount of protection afforded the author's work. This Chapter begins with an examination of the evolving view of "authorship" in the pantheon of protection-worthy values. In order to highlight the cultural value issues behind the protection of authorship, we then turn to the philosophical, historical and economic underpinnings behind the debate over the protection of droit morale (moral rights). Droit morale are rights granted to authors in compensation and protection of the act of creation. These rights generally exist in addition to any copyright or neighboring rights granted. Droit morale consists of four basic rights—the right of publication, the right of paternity, the right of integrity, and the right of withdrawal. This Chapter explores the precise grant of rights provided under various moral rights regimes. It also includes discussions regarding the role which moral rights protection plays in the censorship of "undesirable" creations and the impact of moral rights on diverse categories of protectable works. Since a natural corollary to the issue of an author's "moral" rights is an artist's right to enjoy the economic benefits of resale royalties (droit de suite), the Chapter includes several excerpts discussing droit de suite and the Visual Artists Act. We end with a brief discussion of the role of intellectual property in protecting "cultural" values as underscored in debates regarding the use of cultural exclusions in various multinational treaties and the EC's "Television Without Frontiers" Directive. For a further discussion of the role intellectual property may play in promoting culture, including its use to protect folklore and the impact of cultural exclusions on the future economic development of indigenous cultural works, refer back to Chapter Two.

A. Authorship and the Protection of Personality

1. An Evolving View of Authorship[1]

The "author" has been the main character in a drama played out on the parallel stages of literary and legal culture. By the mid-seventeenth century, well before the English enacted the 1709 Statute of Anne, writers began to assert claims to special status by designating themselves as "authors." During the eighteenth century, "authorship" became intimately associated with the Romantic movement in literature and art, expressing "an extreme assertion of the self and the value of individual experience . . . together with the sense of the infinite and the transcendental."[2] Until very recently, the position of the "author" as a category in literary criticism was: central not only in theory but in practice: in the way single-figure studies dominate criticism; in the organization of texts in "complete editions"; in biographies; and above all, in the idea of style, of a marked writing characteristically the "expression" of a person's "mind" or "psyche" whose essential identity scrawls across a page and declares its imaginative "ownership" of these self-revealing and self-constituting lines.

Law's reception of "authorship" began well before the heyday of Romanticism in the late eighteenth and early nineteenth centuries. In fact, British and American copyright presents myriad reflections of the Romantic conception of "authorship"—even if they sometimes remind one of images in fun-house mirrors.

The connection between "moral rights" and the complex values associated with the Romantic conception of "authorship" is clear. In the words of one treatise:

> The primary justification for the protection of moral rights is the idea that the work of art is an extension of the artist's personality, an expression of his innermost being. To mistreat the work of art is to mistreat the artist, to invade his area of privacy, to impair his personality.[3]

Another commentator puts the proposition differently, arguing that behind moral rights is the belief that "authors" are "almighty creators who pour particular meanings into their creations and therefore inherently have undisputed authority over the uses and interpretations of those creations."[4]

Given this genealogy, moral rights (unlike other copyright interests) are not in the marketplace; they are inalienable, although subject to waiver in particular instances. Such a legal application of "authorship" can only impede the free commerce in intellectual and artistic productions that Anglo-American copyright traditionally has fostered.

In effect, moral rights represent a charter for private censorship. They put the force of legal sanction behind one of the cultural functions of the "authorship" construct identified by Michel Foucault in "What Is an 'Author'?":

> [I]f we are accustomed to present the author as a genius, as a perpetual surging of invention, it is because, in reality, we make him function in exactly the opposite fashion. The author is . . . the ideological figure by which one marks the manner in which we fear the proliferation of meaning.[5]

A discernable pattern emerged in which the law's embrace of Romantic "authorship" has led to both the commodification of creative products and the disempowerment of their creators and consumers. Whatever we may think of the cultural implications of this pattern, a movement toward "authors' "

---

[1] Peter Jaszi, *Toward a Theory of Copyright: the Metamorphoses of "Authorship,"* 1991 Duke L. J. 455. Copyright 1991 by Peter Jaszi. Excerpt reprinted with permission.

[2] The Oxford Companion to English Lit. 842 (in Drebble 5th ed. 1985).

[3] J. Merryman & A. Elsen, Law, Ethics and the Visual Arts 145 (2d ed. 1987).

[4] Beyer, "Intentionalism, Art and the Suppression of Innovation: Film Colorization and the Philosophy of Moral Rights," 82 Nw. U.L. Rev. 1011, 1027 (1988).

[5] M. Foucault, What is an Author? in Textual Strategies: Perspectives in Post-Structuralist Criticism 159 (J. Harari ed. 1979).

moral rights in the United States does not appear to fit that pattern. However, just such a movement is underway.

Moral rights were a considerable focus of interest in the discussions leading up to the adoption of the Berne Convention Implementation Act of 1988. The Act made it possible for the United States to adhere to the 1971 Paris Act of the Berne Convention for the Protection of Literary and Artistic Works by modifying certain aspects of American law to comply with the Convention "minima." Although Article 6 of the Convention appears to require member countries to recognize the attribution and the integrity rights, publishers and other commercial distributors vigorously opposed any incorporation of these rights into American law. As a result, Congress took no legislative action in 1988 to introduce such provisions into the scheme of copyright, pursuant to its minimalist approach to Berne adherence. Indeed, reflecting the political compromise that underlay American adherence to Berne, the legislative history was drafted to emphasize that "the implementing legislation is completely neutral on the issue of whether or how protection of the rights of paternity and integrity should develop in the future."

Legislative neutrality notwithstanding, ensuing years have seen real movement toward the reception of moral rights in the United States. Indeed, the first manifestations of the trend go back even further to a line of cases that involve journalists and biographers seeking to quote from unpublished manuscript materials under the fair use doctrine. In decisions which echo, without literally invoking, the "droit de divulgation" of French "moral rights" doctrine, American courts have conferred on copyright owners near-absolute power of control over unpublished works—no matter how newsworthy or germane to a would-be users' scholarly projects. In effect, the courts are endorsing the use of copyright as a device to enforce private censorship in the name of "authorship."

Evidence of the trend toward the recognition of moral rights no longer is restricted to judicial actions. In 1990, Congress passed the first moral rights legislation in the history of American copyright—the Visual Artists Rights Act of 1990. Contained as Title VI of the Justice Improvements Act of 1990, the Act provides protection for the paternity and integrity rights of certain graphic artists, sculptors, and photographers.

"Authorship" has been (and continues to be) strategically invoked, suppressed, or revised to mediate the inherent and repetitive manifestations of the tension between access and ownership. But the function that "authorship" has played in the evolution of copyright doctrine cannot be characterized as neutral. To a point, in the domain of intellectual property, "authorship" has remained what it was in eighteenth-century England—a stalking horse for economic interests that were (as a tactical matter) better concealed than revealed, and a convenient generative metaphor for legal structures that facilitated the emergence of new modes of production for literary and artistic works.

Seeing through the concept in this way suggests that it would hardly be surprising if "authorship" continued to oscillate. The prevailing view of "authorship" is often that which best serves the immediate interests of copyright proprietors who distribute the works as commodities. The collective interests of the ultimate consumers of works may be served as well. For although it is traditional to view copyright doctrine as a battle between the interests of copyright owners (who are only incidentally ("authors") and copyright users, in practice, those interests are remarkably congruent. Both sellers and buyers have a considerable stake in the maintenance of an orderly market with plentiful supplies of new works at reasonable prices.

Copyright doctrine's intermittent insistence on "authorship" for its own sake reflects the continuing, autonomous significance of the cluster of values associated with the term from its first appearances in English letters, including individual self-proprietorship, creative autonomy, and artistic originality—values which were supplemented and enriched as the specifically Romantic vision of "authorship" took form. Although the dissemination of these values, along with other aspects of possessive individualism, initially facilitated the development of a commodity market in intellectual productions, their survival had the potential to interfere with the further development and smooth functioning of that market. As such, "authorship" may not so much facilitate commodification as impede it. Thus, the overall incoherence of the law's account of "authorship" may be best understood as reflecting a continuing struggle between the economic forces that (at least in the abstract) would be best served by the further depersonalization of creative endeavor and the ideological persistence of an increasingly inefficient version of individualism.

In sum, "authorship" is simultaneously an artifact of the marketplace in commodity art and a throwback to early, pre-industrial ideas of the artist's relation to society. Thus regarded, "authorship" contains within itself the contradiction at the base of all copyright doctrine. The conflict is not the familiar opposition between ownership and access, but the more fundamental, generative tension between the collectivism of the marketplace and the prerogatives of the autonomous individual.

2. The Author as Romantic Genius[6]

An author stands apart from all humanity. This notion is one which is firmly embedded in the Western mind, and although it has its detractors, it remains the idea of authorship which one must address. Yet this conception of the author is relatively recent in the course of intellectual history, arising out of the Romantic preoccupation with the originality of the individual imagination.

What distinguishes Romantic conceptions of authorship from previous conceptions is their insistence upon the individuality and originality of the author. The notion that an author (particularly one of talent) is distinct within society is thousands of years old. That an author is somehow superior is, however, a relatively new idea. Classical thought as expressed by Plato and Aristotle grants authors separate status but it relegates them to the level of mere artisans.

In the discussion of the nature of art found in the tenth book of Plato's Republic, Socrates posits that there exist three tiers of existence for every object. Using the example of a bed, Socrates states that there is the idea of a bed, which is the essence of the bed as God would make it; there is a bed a carpenter makes; and there is the bed an artist paints. It follows that all artists, writers and painters alike, are imitators of imitations, and as the world of ideas is possessed of ultimate value and as art is twice-removed from that world, it is inferior both to the essence and appearance of an object. Further, the effect of art upon its audience is detrimental, for in representing appearance it nourishes feeling rather than reason. Ultimately, Plato denies poets admittance to his ideal Republic.

Aristotle is not as harsh in The Poetics. He views the poet as the indispensable efficient cause, an agent who extracts the form from natural things and imposes them upon an artificial medium. However, the poet's feelings or desires simply do not enter into the discussion as a means of explaining the subject matter or form of a poem.

On first glance, this mimetic theory of art held sway well into the eighteenth century. In *The Mirror and the Lamp* M.H. Abrams notes that a writer as reputedly radical as Edward Young in arguing for the Romantic notion of "original genius" a generation before Samuel Coleridge still adhered to the mimetic theory: "Imitations are of two kinds: One of nature, one of authors."[7] On closer inspection, however, a shift had occurred in the critical perception of the author and his work well before the eighteenth century. The author was still viewed as an imitator, but attention was now focussed upon the author's relationship with his audience rather than with the universe he was imitating.

In his Preface to Shakespeare Samuel Johnson articulated the new creed: "the end of writing is to instruct; the end of poetry is to instruct by pleasing."[8] The audience was the final arbiter of taste. If a work did not instruct it was trivial; if a work did not please it was a failure. Ultimately, Johnson held that Shakespeare's defect was that "he

---

[6] Christopher Aide, *A More Comprehensive Soul: Romantic Conceptions of Authorship and the Copyright Doctrine of Moral Right,* 48 U. Toronto Fac. L. Rev. 211. Copyright 1990 Christopher Aide. Excerpt reprinted by permission.

[7] M.H. Abrams, The Mirror and the Harp 12 (New York: Oxford University Press 1953).

[8] Samuel Johnson, Johnson on Shakespeare in W. Raleigh ed. 16 (Oxford University Press 1908).

seems to write without moral purpose . . . It is always a writer's duty to make the world better, and justice is a virtue independent on time or place."[9] Abrams terms this responsibility of the author to his audience the "pragmatic theory of writing."

Romanticism flew in the face of the mimetic and pragmatic theories of authorship by focusing squarely upon the relationship of the author to his work. It is this focus, coupled with the corollary notion that an audience has no claim upon an author, which it animates the doctrine of moral right. All artistic works result from the overflow, utterance or projection of the thoughts and feelings of the author. The author himself becomes the major element generating both the artistic product and the criteria by which it is to be judged. That, briefly put, is the central Romantic conception of the author.

Romanticism celebrates innate genius. Moral right, however, protects every author regardless of his work's merit. How, then, does Romanticism influence this doctrine, if at all?

The appeal of Romanticism is that it makes us all potential artists. Whether we are matters less than the fact that we believe we are. If that is so we all have a stake in the protection of creative works. Should we realize our artistic potential in some great or small way, moral right defends both the integrity of our work and, because of Romanticism's emphasis upon the unity of author and work, the integrity of our respective selves.

Another different answer rests in the metaphor of the author as creator. The metaphor implies divinity and this exalted state was fundamental to Romantic conceptions of authorship. In 1800 Wordsworth retained enough of the Neo-Classical about him to write in his preface to the Lyrical Ballads that a poet was "a man speaking to men"; however, he was a man "endowed with more lively sensibility, more enthusiasm and tenderness, who has a greater knowledge of human nature and a more comprehensive soul."[10] The totality of vision which a writer possessed placed him upon a higher plane of existence than the rest of humanity, maintained the Romantics.

It is my belief that moral right emerged in large part to protect genius. As genius is not always instantaneously or universally recognized, moral right casts its protective mantle over everything which has been granted copyright. Legal scholars argue in a similar vein. In "Doctrine of Moral Right: A Study in the Law of Artists, Authors and Creators" Martin Roeder declares:

> when an artist creates, he does more than bring into the world a unique object having only exploitive possibilities; he projects into the world a part of his personality and subjects it to the ravages of public use. An author needs protection from a savage public.[11]

In a more restrained manner than Roeder, Russell DaSilva comments with regards to moral right that the author has, in a sense, made a gift of that society with respect to his creative genius.[12]

Implicit within both Roeder's and DaSilva's comments is the idea that an author's "personality" or "creative genius" be somehow protected. Yet the so-called originality of any author's work is a subject of much literary controversy. If, in fact, an author's work is not original, then one of the fundamental supports for copyright laws comes crashing down, and with it any moral right to that work.

3. The Protection of Author Personality[13]

As a general matter, the owner of an object or the owner of the copyright, if he pleases, may refrain from vending or licens-

---

[9] *Id.* at 14.

[10] W. WORDSWORTH, PROSE WORKS OF WILLIAM WORDSWORTH, Vol. II, A, B. Grosart ed. (New York: AMS Press Inc. 1967) at 87-88.

[11] M. ROEDER, DOCTRINE OF MORAL RIGHT: A STUDY IN THE LAW OF ARTISTS, AUTHORS AND CREATORS 557 (1940).

[12] R. DaSilva, *Droit Moral and the Amoral Copyright*, 28 BULL. COPYRT SOCT'Y 1, 12 (1980).

[13] Carl Settlemyer III, *Between Thought and Possession: Artists' 'Moral Rights' and Public*, 81 GEO. L.J. 2291. Copyright 1993 Carl Settlemyer III. Excerpt reprinted with permission.

ing and content himself with simply exercising the right to exclude others from using his property."[14] The arbitrary exercise of this right could lead to suppression of creative works in a wide array of situations such that the work would never be seen by the public.

"The overarching object of copyright law in the United States is to encourage the widest possible production and dissemination of literary, musical, and artistic works."[15] This theme, sounded repeatedly by the modern Supreme Court, was also the basis for preconstitutional copyright statutes enacted by the original states. Those statutes were intended to "encourage persons of learning and genius to publish their writings, which may do honor to their country and service to mankind."[16] By conferring the privilege of a limited term monopoly on creators of literary and artistic works, copyright law seeks to afford them a fair return on their creative efforts. This should, in turn, increase the likelihood that they will produce and disseminate those works. Copyright is thus a mechanism for strengthening our society by encouraging the free flow of ideas. It is intended to guarantee, rather than thwart, public access to the thoughts and expressions of others. As noted by the late Professor Melville Nimmer, "implicit in this rationale is the assumption that in the absence of such public benefit the grant of a copyright monopoly to individuals would be unjustified."[17] After this "monopoly" has lapsed, creative works enter the public domain and are free for all to use or reproduce as they choose.

In furtherance of this dissemination-oriented policy, the law provides that almost all interests in copyright are fully alienable. Furthermore, the employers (or certain commissioning parties) of creative artists are deemed to own all copyright interests in works made for hire from the moment of their creation. This thorough system of alienability of copyright interests ensures that the progress of creative expression into the marketplace will be unimpeded when a willing buyer encounters a willing seller.

The rights of publication are multidimensional. They include the right to refuse to create, and the "absolute right to decide when (and whether) a work of art is complete, and when (and whether) to show it to the public."[18] With this "divulgation" right, "the author [has] complete authority over the decision to publish, sell, unveil, or by any other means make his work public."[19]

The sovereignty of the artist over a work until she chooses to disclose it under French law is best illustrated by *L'affaire Rouault*, a case in which an art dealer kept 806 canvasses of the painter Rouault locked in his room. From time to time, Rouault would visit to put finishing touches on the paintings. Upon the dealer's death, his heirs claimed ownership of the works, but because Rouault claimed the works to be unfinished, the court held that ownership had never passed to the dealer. Stating that "the painter remains master of his work, and may perfect it, modify it, or even leave it unfinished if he loses all hope of making it worthy of himself," the court ordered that the paintings be returned to Rouault provided he repay to the heirs advances the dealer had paid him.[20] The divulgation right has been expanded in recent decades in France, Germany, and Japan, for example, to encompass the positive right of an author to prevent others from suppressing her work against her will.

Opponents of "moral rights" argue that these European doctrines are, in general, "alien" ideas fundamentally inimical to the purposes and foundations of American copyright law. While "moral rights" doctrines are based on natural law principles and are designed to protect the personality interests of the creative artist, American copyright law is "not primarily designed to provide a special private benefit" to creative artists, but to encourage the dissemination of these works to the public.[21] Opponents claim that the adoption of moral rights doctrines would

---

[14] Fox Film Co. v. Doyal, 286 U.S. 123, 127 (1932).

[15] PAUL GOLDSTEIN, COPYRIGHT: PRINCIPLES, LAW AND PRACTICE § 1.1 (1991).

[16] Library of Congress, Copyright Enactments 1783-1900 (Copyright Office Bulletin No. 3) 10-11 (1900).

[17] NIMMER & NIMMER, Nimmer on Copyright § 1.03 [A] (1991) (citations omitted).

[18] John H. Merryman, *The Refrigerator of Bernard Buffet,* 27 HASTINGS L.J. 1023, 1028 (1976).

[19] Russell J. DaSilva, *Droit Moral and the Amoral Copyright*, 28 BULL. COPYRIGHT SOC'Y, 1, 17 (1980).

[20] Judgment of Mar. 19, 1947. Cour d'appel, Paris [1949] D.P. 20.

[21] Sony Corp. of Am. v. Universal City Studios, 464 U.S. 417, 429 (1984).

upset the intellectual property and tangible property interests of noncreator copyright owners and skew the natural balance of risk and reward between creative and financial contributors to creative works. They are particularly troubled by the right of withdrawal and the right to object to the context in which an artist's work is presented. Recognition of the latter, for instance, could permit artists to prohibit "improper interpretive borrowing and adaptation of their creations."[22] In short, opponents argue that recognition of the "moral rights" of artists in the United States would ultimately discourage the dissemination of creative works to the public.

The economic reasoning supporting this conclusion is straightforward. If authors retain inalienable personal rights in their creations, buyers will pay less for the works because they are restricted to purchasing a truncated bundle of property rights in those works. This reduced remuneration would not only injure artists, but would also, the reasoning goes, have the aggregate effect of reducing incentives for artists to create, thus reducing the availability of creative works to the public. The wholesale adoption of "moral rights" doctrines could therefore tremendously destabilize the country's very lucrative, yet very risky, entertainment industries.

Professor Robert Gorman sets forth the critics' position on this issue most persuasively:

> The principal entertainment and cultural industries of the United States are highly collaborative. They contemplate and depend upon a wide variety of derivative forms in their distribution to the public, and are historically regulated by individually and collectively negotiated agreements. The introduction into these industries of a right—exercisable by any one of a host of collaborative contributors—to protest the alleged distortion or modification of a particular literary or artistic contribution is extremely problematic. At best, it introduces an element of instability and uncertainty, as well as the frequent possibility, because of the increased threat of litigation, of delay in public access to and enjoyment of entertainment vehicles. At worst, it threatens to prevent altogether the dissemination to the United States and international public of a host of cultural and entertainment materials in forms that are varied, appealing and affordable. Any significant limit upon the ability of producers and publishers to disseminate works in these secondary markets—dissemination which commonly can mean the difference between a losing and a profitable business venture—runs a substantial risk of chilling investment in the arts and entertainment fields. This may in turn reduce the financial support of an innovative creative endeavor—a result that will obviously be harmful to the public interest. Introduction of moral rights into these industries (particularly if these rights are statutorily declared to be inalienable and non-waivable) will also unsettle the network of contractual agreements that have been developed over many years in the various industries and that appear on the whole to be working quite successfully and fairly.[23]

Other critics object to the expansion of moral rights in this country on noneconomic grounds. Many moral rights advocates wish to protect not only the physical integrity of artworks, but also the contextual "integrity" of literary, musical, and dramatic works by preventing "improper interpretive borrowing and adaptation of artists' intellectual creations."[24] Critics consequently charge that " 'moral rights' advocates are taking, if unwittingly, a position of cultural conservatism, inhibited expression, and unnecessary deference to creators' intentions."[25] Moral rights could be used as "a charter for private

---

[22] Lawrence A. Beyer, *Intentionalism, Art and the Suppression of Innovation: Film Colorization and the Philosophy of Moral Rights,* 82 NW. U.L. REV. 1011, 1016 (1988).

[23] Robert A. Gorman, *Federal Moral Rights Legislation: The Need for Caution,* 14 NOVA L. REV. 421, 423-24 (1990).

[24] Beyer, *supra* note 22 at 1016.

[25] *Id.*, at 1018.

censorship,"[26] in direct conflict with the purposes and functioning of the American copyright system.

4. The US View of Authorship[27]

There is precedent in American law for singling out artistic works for special treatment. Even though American law has generally viewed artistic works as property, it has treated them as a special kind of property. The United States Supreme Court made this point as early as 1834 in *Wheaton v. Peters*[28] when it held that an author's natural property right to the fruits of his labor was realized by the sale or transfer of the material object when it was first published, and that any property rights held by the author thereafter derived from federal statutory protection under the copyright clause of the United States Constitution. The Constitution provided for and Congress enacted legislation to confer property status on products that had no claim for such protection under the leading theory of the day. Not only were products of the mind treated specially, but distinctions were made within this category that resulted in separate branches of the law, such as copyright and patent law. Thus, "writings" were distinguished from "discoveries." Indeed, a legislative distinction was made between "works of authorship" and useful articles. These distinctions reflect the view that different principles are at work and that not all products of the human mind need be included in the right of personality.

The Copyright Act of 1976 manifests the unique nature of "original works of authorship" even when they are considered as having only property or economic aspects. Despite the fact that copyright is classified as personal property, it is a peculiar form of personal property indeed.

The reason for the special treatment accorded "original works of authorship" is traceable to the promotion of artistic creativity, and it has been traditionally recognized that personality protection has been an important factor in this regard. The right of disclosure is a case in point. As early as 1849, in *Prince Albert v. Strange*,[29] the personal aspect of the right of first publication in common law was noted. In the 1969 case of *Estate of Hemingway v. Random House*,[30] the New York Court of Appeals not only reaffirmed this principle but also noted the link between personal and economic interests. Despite the virtual abolition of common-law copyright by the 1976 Act, the United States Supreme Court recently reiterated in *Harper & Row v. Nation Enterprises*[31] the personal aspect of the right of first publication and pointed out the interrelationship between the economic and the personal aspects of the right and freedom of speech.

5. The EC View of Authorship[32]

On 29 October 1993, the Council of Ministers adopted a Directive harmonizing the term of protection of copyright and certain related rights. The directive fixes the duration of protection to the highest existing level in any Member State: life of the author plus 70 years for most copyright works, and 50 years from execution, fixation or publication for performers' and producers' rights. It contains special provisions regarding films in it Articles 2 and 3.

Article 2, headed "cinematographic or audiovisual works," specifies that the principal director of such work is to be regarded as its author or one of its authors, Member States being free to designate other coauthors (Article 2(1)).

---

[26] Peter Jazsi, *Toward a Theory of Copyright: The Metamorphoses of "Authorship,"* 1991 DUKE L.J. 455, 497.

[27] Edward J. Damich, *The Right of Personality: a Common-law Basis for the Protection of the Moral Rights of Authors,* 23 GA. L. REV. 1. Copyright 1988 Georgia Law Review Association, Inc. Excerpt reprinted with permission.

[28] Wheaton v. Peters, 33 U.S. (8 Pet.) 591 (1834).

[29] 2 DeG. § Sm. 652, 64 Eng. Rep. 293 (1849), *aff'd*, 1 Mac. & 6. 25, 41 Eng. Rep. 1171 (1849).

[30] 23 N.42d 341, 244 NE2d 250, 296 N.45. 2d. 771 (1968).

[31] 471 U.S. 539 (1985).

[32] Pascal Kamina, *Authorship of Films and Implementation of the Term Directive: The Dramatic Tale of Two Copyrights,* 8 E.I.P.R. 319. Copyright 1994 Pascal Kamina. Excerpts reprinted with permission.

The present assumption under UK copyright is that the producer is the sole author of a film.

Cinematographic and audiovisual works are not given protection as such, but through the copyright on their recording, that is, the "film" under Section 5(1) of the Copyright, Designs and Patents Act 1988. The producer is granted authorship of this film by Section 9(2) of the Act. Accordingly, since the author of the film is the "person by whom the arrangements necessary for the making of the film are undertaken," the question of joint authorship in the film can only arise among co-producers. In other words, the director and authors of the component elements (script, scenario, music, decor and so on) are deprived of any copyright interest in the final cinematographic or audiovisual work.

Creators of the contributory works are nevertheless given separate copyrights in their contributions, each measured by reference to the life of the individual author.

Who then should be considered the author of the dramatic audiovisual work embodied in the film? Under Section 9 of the CDPA, the author of the dramatic work is its creator. In this respect, UK law is back to its pre-1956 state. It seems clear that the director will qualify as author of the audiovisual work: "Since a director is almost always responsible for the manner in which a film is shot, it is he would supply the film with its original character and therefore be the author of the dramatic work."[33] The question of the other contributors is too complex to be fully answered here, but I would argue that being the creator of a component of a larger composite work is not sufficient under UK copyright to claim joint authorship in the whole, roughly, joint authorship implies that contributors work in collaboration and that the part contributed by each author is not distinct in the final work. Hence the script or scenario writer is probably the only contributor who will almost always meet these conditions. According to the same principle, it is unlikely that under UK copyright the musical composer or the creator of the decor would be considered as a co-author. The question of other contributors like the editor or the director of photography remains to a large extent open, their situation depending on their input in the final work and on the creative freedom they are given by the director.

---

[33] LADDIE PRESCOTT AND VITTORIA, THE MODERN LAW OF COPYRIGHT, Butterworth 1980 at 7.11.

QUESTIONS AND COMMENTS FOR YOUR CONSIDERATION

1. If you were deciding who should be given the right of authorship to a particular work, what factors would you consider?

2. Whom would you consider the author of the following works: A motion picture based upon a script based upon a best selling novel? A software program created by artificial intelligence? An interactive video game? A radio program created and marketed by an unincorporated joint venture?

3. What effect does the decision on ownership have upon the ability or right to protect a work on an international level?

4. What impact, if any, does the prior "romantic" view of authorship have on the question of control over the work in question?

5. Famous directors such as Alfred Hitchcock are frequently referred to as the "auteurs" of their motion pictures. Might it not be argued that, at least in some cases, their contribution to the film exceeds in creativity and importance the writer upon whose book or short story the film was based?

B. The Moral Rights Debate[34]

France is normally held up as the model for moral rights law, but many Western European civil law countries espouse the doctrine, with some variation. The doctrine's origin is entirely judicial, perhaps unusual in a legal system that stresses legislative over judicial lawmaking.

There are four basic rights that constitute the *droit moral*; not all systems recognize all of them. They are: the right of publication (*droit de divulgation*), the right of paternity (*droit de paternite or droit au respect du nom*), the right of integrity (*droit de respect de l'oeuvre*), and the right of withdrawal (*droit de repentir or de retrait*). Each of these rights is compound, each consisting itself of a small bundle of rights.

The right of publication is the right of the author to choose whether or not to present her work to the public. As one author notes, it protects the artist from having her "lack of inspiration considered to be a breach of contract."[35]

The right of paternity is the right to claim authorship of one's work, to prevent others from unjustly claiming authorship, and to prevent having one's name falsely associated with another's work. The right of paternity includes the right to publish pseudonymously.

The right of integrity includes the "right to authorize or prohibit any modification of [the author's] work,"[36] and to protect against distortion of the work. It also includes the right to prevent mutilation of or derogatory action toward the work. This was the right at issue in the Buffet case, where the buyer of a refrigerator painted by Bernard Buffet attempted to sell the individual painted panels of the refrigerator separately; the court enjoined the sale.

The right of withdrawal is the least exercised moral right. Its formal existence is rare outside France and countries that derive their law from France. There is wider recognition of a right to make corrections, particularly in later editions. The author may be required to pay damages when he withdraws a work from circulation, as is clearly the case in Spain. The right of withdrawal may exist in common law countries, but only under compelling circumstances and in very limited cases. Even French commentators question the efficacy of the right of withdrawal.

While there is universal recognition of the author's right "to affirm his paternity in a work, or to defend his integrity in it," there are two approaches to enforcement of these rights. The civil law countries of Latin America, Africa, and East Asia spell out the right with particularity in their copyright laws, while the common law countries generally leave moral rights to the protection of the courts. Statutory recognition of moral rights has grown, however, in common law countries. For example, India, Israel, and other nations have adopted moral rights legislation within their copyright law, while the United States has adopted the Visual Artists Rights Act, and Australia has undertaken consideration of moral rights.

The countries that protect the right of divulgation as part of copyright law are civil law counties and countries whose law derives from the civil law. The right is apparently widely respected, with variation as to extent and statutory wording. Common law countries provide such protection under the law of privacy or secrecy, and through the refusal to specifically enforce personal service contracts.

Fewer countries, as noted above, recognize the right of withdrawal. Only France and countries deriving their law from France protect it extensively. Some other countries, including Spain, which historically adopted the French model in many respects, adopt a more limited right to make changes or corrections. Moreover, some countries only require the publisher to make such changes on publication of a new edition.

The right of retraction, to fully cancel an assignment of rights to publish, is the least recognized of the four moral rights. The method of executing the right is seldom detailed in statutory law. In all countries recognizing the right, the author must pay

---

[34] Jeffrey M. Dine, *Authors' Moral Rights In Non-European Nations: International Agreements, Economics, Mannu Bhandari, and the Dead Sea Scrolls,* 16 MICH. J. INT'L L. 545. Copyright (c) 1995 University of Michigan Law School. Excerpt reprinted with permission.

[35] Raymond Sarraute, *Current Theory on the Moral Right of Authors and Artists under French Law,* 16 AM. J. COMP. L. 465, 468 (1968).

[36] STEPHEN STEWART, INT'L COPYRIGHT AND NEIGHBORING RIGHTS 73, 7374 (2d ed. 1989).

full compensation. Indeed, in Spain, for example, if the author later decides to publish the work, she must offer it to the original assignee on the original terms.

1. Included Rights

a. The Right of Disclosure[37]

The right of disclosure is based upon the notion that only the artist can possess any rights in an uncompleted work. This right therefore gives the artist control over his work from the time of creation. Furthermore this right encompasses the artist's right to decide whether a work corresponds to the artist's original conception, at what moment the work is completed, and whether the work is worthy of the artist. The American analog of this right is found in copyright law, which protects the "right of first sale" and the "right of first publication" as soon as the work is fixed in any tangible medium of expression.

b. The Right of Paternity[38]

The right of paternity safeguards a creator's right to have her name attached to her work. The derivation of this right is founded upon the injection of the artist's creative personality into her work, thus vesting her right to claim authorship. Generally this right is perpetual, unassignable, and is not barred by statutes of limitation. Moreover, the right of paternity protects against falsely attaching an artist's name to a work she did not create. American courts have not expressly recognized the right of paternity but have granted similar relief on other theories.[39]

c. The Right of Integrity[40]

The right of integrity is also known as the right to modify and to prevent deformation. This right prohibits the modification, alteration, or distortion of an artist's work without her permission. The right of integrity, just as the right of paternity, is generally perpetual, unassignable, and free from any statute of limitation. The laws of the United States do not expressly protect an artist's right to integrity. However, American legal protection has been found in the Lanham Act and specific state statutes.

d. The Right of Withdrawal[41]

The right of withdrawal permits the author to retrieve her work even though it has been sold or published. When this right is granted, an artist can recall her creation if she experiences a change of heart from that which originally provided her inspiration for the work. However, the artist will usually be required to compensate the individual in possession for any losses that the renunciation might cause. The right of withdrawal is founded on the assumption that the public will forget works to which it has previously been exposed. This assumption has caused many commentators to doubt the viability of this right. Where the right of withdrawal is recognized, however, it is generally limited to literary works. The United States does not recognize the right of withdrawal in any form.

2. The Berne Definition[42]

Article 6bis of the Berne Convention of 1886 provides *inter alia*:

---

[37] Jack A. Cline, *Moral Rights: The Long and Winding Road Toward Recognition,* 14 Nova L. Rev. 435. Copyright 1990 Jack A. Cline. Excerpt reprinted with permission.

[38] Jack A. Cline, "*Moral Rights: The Long and Winding Road Toward Recognition,*" 14 Nova Law Rev. 435. Copyright 1990 Jack A. Cline. Excerpt reprinted with permission.

[39] *See, e.g.*, Ellis v. Hurst, 66 Misc. 235, 121 N.Y. Supp. 438 (Sup. Ct. 1910) (utilizing the right to privacy); Clemens v. Press Publishing Co., 67 Misc. 183, 122 N.Y. Supp. 206 (Sup. Ct. 1910) (contract rights); Fischer v. Star Co., 231 N.Y. 414, 132 N.E. 133 (1921) (unfair competition).

[40] Jack A. Cline, *Moral Rights: The Long and Winding Road Toward Recognition,* 14 Nova Law Rev. 435. Copyright 1990 Jack A. Cline. Excerpt reprinted with permission.

[41] Jack A. Cline, *Moral Rights: The Long and Winding Road Toward Recognition,* 14 Nova Law Rev. 435. Copyright 1990 Jack A. Cline. Excerpt reprinted with permission.

[42] Jeffrey M. Dine, *Authors' Moral Rights In Non-European Nations: International Agreements, Eco-*

> Independently of the author's economic rights, and even after the transfer of the said rights, the author shall have the right to claim authorship of the work and to object to any distortion, mutilation or other modification of, or other derogatory action in relation to, the said work, which would be prejudicial to his honour or reputation.

Paragraph 1 of Article 6bis of the Berne Convention protects the rights of paternity and integrity. Moral rights protection was introduced into the Berne Convention in 1928, and was slightly amended in 1967. While the rights are separate from and not transferred with the copyright, they are not clearly inalienable. The rights of divulgation and withdrawal are not included in Berne.

Under the second paragraph of Article 6bis, moral rights must last at least as long as the economic rights, but countries that did not provide moral rights protection prior to acceding to the Convention are excepted from this requirement. In those countries, protection need only last until the author's death.

The third paragraph of the article provides that enforcement of the provision is to be through the national law "of the country where protection is claimed." Thus, an American being sued for violation in Israel of moral rights should be subject to Israeli law. An American being sued in Israel for a violation of American copyright law should be subject to American law.

One can envision a number of moral rights regimes, each allocating the costs and risks differently. A system that does not recognize moral rights imposes the cost by default on the author, who takes the risk that an unscrupulous user will damage her reputation by misattribution or by distortion of her work. This does not allow risk-averse authors to accept lower sums for a guarantee of no infringement of moral rights. A system that provides uncertain recognition (as in the United States) allows some degree of bargaining over risk; but in all probability, except for authors with substantial bargaining power, the risk will nonetheless be placed on the author, who will be insufficiently compensated for accepting it. A system that allows for full-recognition of moral rights but also for assignment or waiver by contract would similarly keep risks on authors who lack sufficient bargaining power to refuse waiver or those who seek increased payment for shouldering the risk. However, the costs to the user, both in compensation to the author and transaction costs, will be somewhat higher, since such waiver must be bargained for expressly. Finally, a system that provides inalienable and unwaivable moral rights places the cost of violation squarely and solely on the user, but does not allow the possibility of increased rents for the risk-accepting author.

Where moral rights are a default rule subject to negotiation and the parties have equal bargaining power, the author will demand a higher price for assuming the risk of violation, or accept a lower one for placing the risk on the user. The price will reflect the cost of the possible damage and the degree of risk.

Most authors, however, probably do not possess bargaining power equal to that of the user. In that case, as also where such rights are uncertain, the user can force the author to bear a disproportionate part of the risk and cost of violation. Thus, it would seem that, in the absence of equal bargaining power between authors and users, inalienable and unwaivable moral rights are the only ones that fully prevent users from externalizing the costs of infringement. However, while inalienable and unwaivable rights protect the weak or risk-averse author, they reduce the possible return to the risk-accepting author. It may be that allowing waiver or alienation of the moral right would result in the greatest net gain over all authors, risk-accepting and risk-averse.

Many non-European countries, developing or newly industrialized, joined the Berne Union shortly after gaining independence. Several commentators suggest, however, that the decision to accede to Berne was frequently the result of pressure to join from former colonial rulers. These countries only belatedly realized that the high level of protection that the Berne Convention required was ill-suited to their needs for, among others, inexpensive educational

---

nomics, Mannu Bhandari, and the Dead Sea Scrolls, 16 MICH. J. INT'L L. 545.

material. Their concerns led to the negotiations that culminated in the Appendix to the Berne Convention adopted at Paris in 1971. However, they apparently never objected to the moral rights provisions of the Berne Convention.

Moral rights laws serve to protect national authors against damage by other nationals, as in Mannu Bhandari, and by foreigners, as in Qimron. Moral rights require indigenous industries to operate at a higher level of sophistication than would otherwise be the case. Although the cost of producing works thereby increases, suggesting lower production, the lower risks to authors might induce more to publish for reduced payment demands. In addition, some externalities might also be viewed as justification, such as improved reputation of indigenous authors and publishers outside the country. It seems likely that the importance of the indigenous protection rationale increases in proportion to the growth of copyright industries.

3. Historical and Philosophical Development

a. Monist v. Dualist[43]

The history of moral right in copyright statutes does not much antedate the 1928 Rome Revision of the Berne Convention on copyright. Until that time moral right was judge-made law. Most legal scholars begin their discussion of moral right's genesis by referring to French judgments of the nineteenth century. Some scholars go further in their investigation of moral right, tracing the principle's history from pre-Christian times to the present day. Until the end of the Middle Ages, however, authors' rights generally were limited to a ban on plagiarism and it was not until the eighteenth century that the notion of moral right as it is now understood even began to be discussed.

In France, prior to the French Revolution, virtually all rights in intellectual property were conferred by the Sovereign. The revolution led to an abolishment of this royal privilege and the French copyright laws of 1791 and 1793 affirmed the existence of writers' pecuniary rights as "emanating from the creative activity of the author." An author's moral right, as distinct from an author's pecuniary right, did not receive statutory recognition; however, it arose from the spirit of these laws and from the philosophy of individualism which infused the French Revolution particularly, and Romanticism generally.

In German, during the nineteenth century, a debate arose between Joseph Kohler and Alfred Gierke as to the composition of moral right. Kohler argued that moral right was distinct from the exploitative rights an author had in his or her work, while Gierke argued that moral right was an aspect of the exploitive right. The former "dualist" view prevailed in France to be embodied in the law of 11 March 1957. The latter "monist" view triumphed in Germany and is now articulated in the West German law of 9 September 1965. Nevertheless, the thrust of both these laws is a comprehensive protection of both the author's rights are inalienable.

Neither England nor the United States accord express recognition of moral right in their respective copyright acts.

b. Natural Rights, Economic Rights and Personality[44]

One can hardly begin a study of *droit moral* without pausing to observe the inexhaustible reverence with which French jurists approach the subject of authors' rights. Pierre Recht accurately has observed, "When *droit moral* fanatics discuss moral rights, they take the attitude of a religious zealot talking of sacred things, or a Girondin reading the Declaration of the Rights of Man."[45] Perhaps one reason for this senti-

---

[43] Christopher Aide, *A More Comprehensive Soul: Romantic Conceptions of Authorship and the Copyright Doctrine of Moral Right,* 48 U. TORONTO FAC. L. REV. 211. Copyright 1990 Cristopher Aide. Excerpt reprinted with permission.

[44] Russell J. DaSilva, *Droit Moral and the Amoral Copyright: A Comparison of Artists' Rights in France and the United States,* 28 BULL. COPYRIGHT SOC'Y 1. Copyright 1980 Russell J. DaSilva. Excerpt reprinted by permission.

[45] P. RECHT, LE DROIT D'AUTEUR, UNE NOUELLE FORME DE PROPRIETE 281.

ment is that French scholars regard the *droit d'auteur* as a natural right, deeply rooted in the principles of the French Revolution from which modern French jurisprudence emerged. Indeed, scholars have sought the origins of *droit moral* in the earliest periods of recorded history. Until the end of the Middle Ages, however, recognition of authors' rights generally was limited to a ban on plagiarism, and it was not until the eighteenth century that the notion of *droit d'auteur*, as it is now known, came into being.

During the *Ancien Regime*, virtually all rights in an intellectual work were conferred by the sovereign, and generally were bestowed upon printers. Rights in books went scarcely beyond a monopoly on the reproduction of the work for a fixed term, and did not even include a right to sell the work. Voltaire, in 1769, grumbled that druggists, by comparison, at least could sell their own concoctions freely.

Yet, even before the French Revolution and its emergent "natural right" concept of *droit d'auteur*, important principles of modern civil law were debated in France. As early as 1725, it was argued that an author had a perpetual property interest in his unpublished manuscript. Consequently, in the two decades preceding the French Revolution, various ordinances and decrees were published, which defined more explicitly the prerogatives of editors and publishers, and affirmed the existence of perpetual interests of writers "emanating from the creative activity of the author."

During the French Revolution, jurists sought to abolish any notion that *droit d'auteur* was a royal privilege. Early legislation eased the freedom to perform plays in public, and confirmed the authors' exploitative rights, based on the notion that these rights were inherent in the artist. The *droits patrimoniaux* at last were enunciated in the law of 19-24 juillet 1793. Although they—like American copyright—were primarily pecuniary rights, they expressed the principle that *droit d'auteur* was not merely a privilege of the sovereign, as in the *Ancien Regime*, but it was, rather, a natural right, arising simply from the author's act of creation.

Droit moral, on the other hand, emerged not from statute, but from judicially created doctrines, which developed slowly in the nineteenth century, and more rapidly in the twentieth. But *droit moral*, too, arose from the spirit of these laws, and from the philosophy of individualism which accompanied the French Revolution.

Scholars divide the history of *droit moral* into three periods: the first from 1793 to 1878; the second from 1878 to 1902; and the third from 1902 to 1957. During the first period, French scholars began to debate the "property" nature of an author's rights. Gastambide and his followers in the 1830's held to the traditional notion that *droit d'auteur* was a property right, albeit a temporary one.[46] On the other hand, Renouard and his school, influenced by Kant, preferred to dislodge authors' rights from the notion of property, and considered them instead to derive from a more abstract "right of personality."[47] Recht observes that opposition to the "property" characterization of *droit d'auteur* grew even stronger with the early influence of Marx in the 1840's and 1850's, and by the 1860's, a generation of "personalist" writers emerged, who strongly discredited the idea that *droit d'auteur* was a form of property.[48]

It should come as no surprise, then, that during this first period, the notion that there may exist non-property "moral" rights could easily gain acceptance in French courts. By 1880, the foundations had been laid in French jurisprudence for *droit de divulgation, droit a la paternite,* and *droit au respect de l'oeuvre*.

The doctrine of *droit moral* received even greater development in the second period, from 1878 to 1902. In this period, the application of traditional notions of property to *droit d'auteur* was virtually abandoned, and scholars continued to search for a more precise characterization of *droit moral*, and of its place in the larger *droit d'auteur*. Some French scholars, led by Pouillet, tended to hold onto fragments of the property notion of *droit d'auteur*, and developed a theory of "intellectual property," by which *droit d'auteur* combined certain elements of property with elements of purely personal or intellectual rights.

However, the central debate over the

---

[46] *See* 1 S. Stromholm, 1 Droit Moral de L'Auteur 150-53 (1966).

[47] *Id.*, at 154-56.

[48] P. Recht [*supra* note 45] at 58-60.

nature of authors' rights arose in Germany. Joseph Kohler developed a theory of "*Doppelrecht*," which considered an intellectual work to be a "*bien immateriel*," from which various rights of personality arose.[49] These personal prerogatives could be separated into two distinct categories of either a patrimonial or a moral nature. The other principal view, advocated by Alfred Gierke, considered both personal and patrimonial rights to be inseparable parts of a single "*Personlichkeitsrecht*."[50]

It was in the third period, from 1902 to 1957, that the debate over these two views became resolved. Kohler's "dualist" view triumphed in France, where to this day, *droit d'auteur* is considered to be a right of "*propriete incorporelle*" separable into moral and patrimonial rights. In Germany, the monist school prevailed, and as a result, moral rights ("*Urheberpersonlichkeitsrecht*") and exploitative interests form a single right, which expires seventy years after the author's death.

We see, then, that *droit d'auteur* is part of a larger debate over the meaning of "property" and "personality" rights in the Civil Law system. The debate, in fact, engendered two systems of authors' rights with different characterizations of *droit moral*—each purporting to be as vigilant of the authors' well-being as the other.

On the whole, however, artists' rights receive less respect under the American system than they do in France. *Droit de retrait* and *droit de repentir*, although their value is at best questionable, barely exist at all in the United States. The first category of *droit a la paternite*—the right to claim authorship of one's own creation—is underdeveloped in this country, and *droit au respect*, which is considered by the French to be the very essence of an artist's prerogative, is only in its infancy.

Furthermore, whatever moral rights do exist in the United States receive far less weight than they do in France, and although this difference ultimately may reflect only a discrepancy in social status between French and American artists, it also is rooted in legal realities. In the United States, authors' rights may more readily be waived, and they generally cease to exist upon the author's death. This contrasts markedly with the "personal, perpetual, inalienable and unassignable" character of *droit moral*. And in the United States, a contract between the artist and the transferee of his rights is presumed to be the repository of all of the artist's remaining rights in his work; French law will more readily look beyond contractual obligations in order to assert the artist's moral rights.

Thus, the French concept of *droit moral*, indeed all of *droit d'auteur*, is far more idealistic than any American notion of authors's rights. It proceeds from a romantic idea of the artist and his work; it treats artists as a special class of laborers, and art works as a special category of property; and at least in theory, it defends artists' rights even against the contract or property interests of third parties.

Within the conception of *droit d'auteur*, *droit moral* takes on a transcendent, even spiritual quality, which even its own name reveals.

In the United States, on the other hand, the protection of artists' rights beyond copyright has developed on a more pragmatic and democratic basis. American law refuses to recognize artists as a special class, and insists on a more equitable balance between the interests of artists and the interests of others who are involved in the exploitation, publication, or adaptation of works of art. Furthermore, American law characterizes the artist's work more as an object of commerce than as a product of the spirit, and the artist's rights of personality in his work generally must be protected by the same legal language which would be applied to any commercial venture.

c. Alienability and the Marketplace[51]

The French Law provides for the author's right of divulgation or first disclosure and the right of withdrawal or modification of an already disclosed work in addition to the

[49] *Id.* at 78.

[50] *Id.* at 84.

[51] Jeff Berg, *Moral Rights: A Legal, Historical and Anthropological Reappraisal,* 6 I.P.J. 341. Copyright 1991 Jeff Berg. Excerpt reprinted with permission.

. . . rights of "paternity" (attribution and integrity).

"Only the author can decide whether his work corresponds to his original conception, at what moment it is completed, and whether it is worthy of him"[52] Under the French statute the right of first disclosure is included in the moral rights regime: because moral rights are inalienable and perpetual in French law, this obtains even where economic rights or the material object itself has been transferred and can be enforced by the author's successors.

French law provides that despite a work's completion and a full assignment of rights of reproduction, exhibition, and performance the author retains a "right of modification or withdrawal as against the assignee."[53] This right is subject to indemnification for authors to invoke the right, since it applies only to publishing contracts (*i.e.*, it is "incorporeal" and does not attach to a physical object transferred).

French law protects the right to be recognized as the creator of a work, or to have it discloses anonymously or under a pseudonym. The author has a right of action against false attribution of her work to another, and a right to prevent use of her name on work she did not create or on works she did create but which have been mutilated.

The right of integrity arises when the work is marketed, sold or is subject to a contract or publication or performance. "From that time on the author has the right to insist that its integrity must not be violated by measures which could alter or distort it."[54] Special problems arise in the case of adaption of a work, *e.g.*, for film or television, where the adaptor's original creation is itself protected. Outright destruction of a work has been found within the scope of the right in France. The French law succinctly requires "respect for [the author's] name, his authorship, and his work."[55]

The right of action under the moral rights regimes has traditionally been limited to the author or her successor, even though a public interest in maintaining the integrity of cultural works is often given as one rationale for protection. The French law is extremely "personalist," specifying that the right is attached to the person of the author. Italy's 1941 statute provides for enforcement by "competent State authority," while Germany eschewed such a provision in its post-war legislation apparently out of nervousness about state supervision of culture.[56]

California pioneered a public interest regime for moral rights protection with its art preservation enactments of 1979 and 1982.[57] The Preamble to California Art Preservation Act cites both protection of the author's reputation and preservation of the integrity of cultural and artistic property as objectives. It protects rights to claim or to disclaim authorship and prohibits alteration or destruction, limiting this protection to "fine art" of "recognized quality," as in the opinion of expert witnesses including "artists, art dealers, collectors of fine art, curators of art museums, and other persons involved with the creation or marketing of fine art." The 1982 enactment provides for litigation of the rights by public or private non-profit interest groups. The regime permits an express written waiver of the rights by the artist, and it does not extend to an injurious association of the work or other "derogatory action." New York's law is oriented primarily to the protection of the artist's reputation and is limited to public display. It does not contain the controversial "recognized quality" requirement.[58]

Different national legislatures have resolved the issues differently. France and the United States have formulated their copyright legislation on the property analogy, while moral rights are grounded in the theory of personality rights. This resulted in a "dualist" theory with both philosophical and practical ramifications. Germany, apparently for purely philosophical reasons, adopted personality rights as the single

---

[52] Raymond Sarraute, *Current Theory in the Moral Rights of Authors and Artists under the French Law*, 16 AM. J. COMP. L. 465 (1968).

[53] Article 32 of the French Law of March 11, 1957.

[54] Sarraute *supra* note [52] at 480.

[55] French Law of March 11, 1957.

[56] J. MERRYMAN & A. ELSEN, LAW, ETHICS AND THE VISUAL ARTS 147 (2d ed. 1987).

[57] California Art Preservation Act, Cal. Civ. Code §§ 987, 989.

[58] New York Arts and Cultural Affairs Law, 14.51-14.59 (1983).

basis for both its copyright law and creator's moral rights: a "monist" legal framework.

As a practical result, French dualism freed the judiciary to develop the *droit moral* in comparative isolation from contractual and public policy issues arising from the grant of exploitive rights. Thus moral rights in France are, in theory at least, "personal, perpetual, inalienable, and unassignable." The rights inhere in the natural person of the creator of the work, and not in the work itself. Inalienability is considered by some proponents to be the transcendent principle of moral right, so that any contract for transfer of them will be in principle unenforceable. Perpetuity is accompanied by providing that the moral rights which do not require the author's personal will and judgment, such as modification, may be passed by will to the author's heirs. The foundation of the moral rights in the creative personality

> is a profoundly romantic characterization of the artist, perhaps conjuring up visions of poets in garrets, burning their lyric masterpieces for heat in the icy Parisian winter, or of Walt Whitman, crying out to the corporeal world, "I celebrate myself, and sing myself." Yet it is because of this characterization of the author and his art that French law feels a need to protect the honor of the author's personality and the integrity of his work. The author has, in a sense, made a gift of his creative genius to the world; in return, he has a right—a moral right—to expect that society respect his creative genius.[59]

By contrast, German theory rejected the essential distinction between exploitation rights and moral rights, building its entire copyright regime on the Kantian theory of expressive work as an extension of the creative personality. Where the French law provides for unqualified transfer of copyright as a form of "property" and maintains *droit moral* as perpetual and inalienable rights of personality, German monism required tailoring both moral rights and contractual assignment of commercial rights to fit a unified legislative scheme. German law compromised perpetuity of the moral rights by limiting them to its "life plus seventy years" term of copyright protection, and it compromised the free alienation of pecuniary rights by restricting inter vivos transfer to specific editions or series of performances rather than outright assignment of a copyright.

To bring the idea of culture into the theory of moral rights requires reexamining its premise that the source of creative work is in the "inviolable personality." The right of personality describes creative activity in terms of an entirely private expression of the self in the material object. Creative activity is considered the physical embodiment or result of the exercise of the individual will, whether formulated in terms of Romantic enthusiasm or Kantian principle. The expressionist theory leaves the source, the motivation, and the structure of "creativity" in the realm of subjectivity, consistent with the abstract freedom of choice of the free subject in liberal social theory. What is missing in this characterization of creative activity—as purely private in its expressive aspect and purely commercial in public exchange—is the essence of the work as communication, as involving an exchange of communally accessible and valuable meaning, *i.e.*, as symbolic exchange.

The law posits the created artwork at a point of intersection between the inalienable right of the artist, for whom creation is a permanent and almost sacred self-expression, and the system of market exchange demanding that products be freely available for efficient allocation.

In effect, the theory of personal rights purports to give artists a special exemption from the exigencies of the market system. Yet, in so doing, these "legalized" moral rights seem to evoke and protect many important characteristics of the gift. The right of disclosure acknowledges the tactical significance of giving or withholding a gift at a particular time. The rights of attribution, anonymity and pseudonymity recognize the creator's perennial entitlement to the intangible cultural debt owed for the work. Rights of modification and retraction are also consistent with the continuing claim of the giver over the gift. Finally, legal protection of the work's integrity ensures that the "honour

---

[59] DaSilva, *Droit Moral and the Amoral Copyright: A Comparison of Artists' Rights in France and the U.S.*, 28 Bull. Copyright Soc'y 1, 12 (1980).

and reputation" of the giver will not be depreciated by mutilation of the work, maintaining the gift's "increase" over time as a phenomenon "simultaneously material, social, and spiritual."[60] Nonetheless, these non-pecuniary interests in creative work, which were rooted in a rich collective appreciation of artwork as a unique cultural gift, have been transplanted to the less nourishing soil of the general law. Now they take the form of a set of universal and abstract "moral rights," entitlements to which "everyone" is equally entitled in theory. The case law indicates they are highly problematic in practice. The difficulty of integrating moral rights with copyright within modern legal doctrine arises from the larger problem of defining the status of "art" and other creative work in our culture, and whether vesting moral rights exclusively in the author really address the ancient, prescriptive, public interests in authenticity and orthodoxy.

The theory of gift exchange defines the importance of the work in terms of the community's acknowledgment of a cultural contribution. As the law moves toward the recognition of public interest reflected in the California art preservation legislation, it inevitably moves away from the Kantian theory of moral rights as an aspect of the creator's freedom to define and pursue ends. In this view, moral rights reflect "economic" values which are embodied in cultural status entitlements rather than the paradigm of market relationships. Thus we can understand the intuition that some cultural products are "priceless," irreducible to the abstract equivalences of market valuation.

4. Moral Rights and Censorship

a. Editorial Control[61]

The principle of moral rights does not pertain to morality, instead, it defines a regime of legal rights that attach upon the creation of a copyrightable work by, among others, authors, photographers, illustrators, songwriters, directors, and screenwriters. The Berne Convention describes moral rights in Article 6bis as: 1) the right to claim or disclaim paternity (attribution) of a work; 2) the right to object to distortion or mutilation of a work; and 3) the right to the creator's honor or reputation. Moral rights supplement existing economic rights which permit creators to profit from the performance, reproduction, or distribution of their works.

Editorial control will be jeopardized by the ability of creators to object under Article 6bis to any editorial modifications. Newspaper and magazine editors must edit articles, crop photographs, and adapt illustrations extensively to conform with specified viewpoint, context, or space requirements. This process is undertaken within tight deadlines that demand instantaneous decisions. Thus, editors can afford neither the time to obtain consent for specific uses of works nor to hesitate on decisions out of concern that they may subsequently be second-guessed in litigation. Broadcasters face similar challenges in the preparation of news programming. Broadcast and video editors must edit for content, advertising, time, sizing, and colorization reasons. The moral rights prohibition of distortion without the author's consent would ruin these industries and their ability to remain economically viable.

The radio and textbook publishing industries face a comparable but different moral rights dilemma under Article 6bis, the right to attribution. This requirement would obligate radio stations to credit composers and lyricists in addition to performers. The enormous encroachment on available airtime would impede programming and, at a minimum, irritate listeners. Textbook publishers have the same problems. Textbooks are generally researched, developed, and written by a team of scholars, writers, and editors. Each individual has a potential claim under the moral rights proviso to attribution. Thus, the added acknowledgement requirement undermines a carefully developed scheme.

The permutations and combinations of potential moral rights claims that confront these businesses is staggering. While a host of claims may not arise, it will take very few to upset a complex and stable set of copyright

---

[60] L. Hyde, The Gift: Imagination and the Erotic Life of Property (Vintage 1979).

[61] Arthur B. Sackler, *The United States Should Not Adhere to the Berne Copyright Convention,* 3 J.L. & Tech. 207. Copyright 1987 Journal of Law & Technology. Excerpt reprinted with permission.

relationships developed over two centuries. This disruption and uncertainty will inevitably cause editors and copyright owners to slow or change their procedures to the industry and public's detriment. In addition, they will be forced to accommodate challenges, or face subsequent objections in court at great expense and time. The litigation threat cannot be underestimated. The litigiousness of the United States is well-known and far greater than any Berne member nation. Furthermore, the prospect of litigating the highly subjective and volatile issue of what constitutes a moral rights violation is daunting.

The nonexistence of legal standards for the moral rights question imposes an arduous burden on the courts and the media industry. The courts will have the unenviable task of determining whether an alteration to a film or manuscript is a mutilation or a judicious edit. The uncertainty and threat of inconsistent judicial outcomes, due to the lack of legal standards, will destroy the editing process. Additionally, as is the case with libel challenges, media attorneys will review editorial work for moral rights violations. Unlike libel law, however, with its clearly delineated, judicially mandated tests, practitioners will have no basis for determining moral rights violations and will rely on ad hoc subjective interpretations. The unpredictability of the outcome will chill editorial freedoms, and therefore presents an unacceptable proposition.

b. The Aesthetic "Veto"[62]

Though surely the exception rather than the rule, the suppression of creative works against an artist's will is not a purely hypothetical problem. The ongoing debate about the level of protection creative artists' "moral rights" (recognized under the laws of many European nations) do and should receive under American law has brought to light the accounts of writers, photographers, and filmmakers whose works have proven very susceptible to suppression by others. These stories indicate that not only are the "moral rights" of artists—specifically, the right to divulge or to choose to make a work public—ill-protected under our copyright system, but that the distributional goals upon which that system is predicated are being thwarted.

As a general matter, the owner of an object or "the owner of the copyright, if he pleases, may refrain from vending or licensing and content himself with simply exercising the right to exclude others from using his property."[63] The arbitrary exercise of this right could lead to suppression of creative works in a wide array of situations such that the work would never be seen by the public.

Legislatively mandating that such a broad "aesthetic veto" be placed in the hands of the artist, especially in the context of multiple artists engaged in collaborative works, would therefore mean that moral rights could be used as "a charter for private censorship."[64] Such results would conflict directly with the purposes and functioning of the American copyright system. Thus, these adverse consequences ought to be guarded against even if that entails the continued sacrifice of artists' noneconomic interests to the brutalities of the marketplace and the continued appearance, to other Berne nations, that the United States is less than enthusiastic about adherence to the Convention.

Carl H. Settlemyer III. Excerpt reprinted by permission.

[62] Carl H. Settlemyer III, *Between Thought and Possession: Artists "Moral Rights" and Public Access to Creative Works,* 81 Geo. L. J. 2291. Copyright 1993

[63] Fox Film Co. v. Doyal, 286 U.S. 123, 127 (1932).

[64] Peter Jazsi, *Toward a Theory of Copyright: The Metamorphosis of "Authorship,"* 1991 DUKE L.J.

QUESTIONS AND COMMENTS FOR YOUR CONSIDERATION

1. Should moral rights grant authors an absolute right to censor the use of their works? To destroy such works?

2. What impact do you think a stong moral rights policy would have on the ability to parody or satirize another's work?

5. The Treatment of Moral Rights in Selected Countries

a. The United Kingdom[65]

"Moral rights" were never expressly incorporated into UK law until the Copyright, Designs and Patents Act 1988 ("the 1988 Act") which, as far as "moral rights" are concerned, came into force on 1 August 1989. Until that time there were one or two provisions in UK law (such as § 43 Copyright Act 1956) concerning "false attribution of authorship" which touched upon the subject matter of "moral rights," but nothing comprehensive or too specific. It was argued that torts, such as defamation or passing off, as well as contractual rights, were sufficient to protect authors in these circumstances. It has now been accepted, however, that these generalized protections are not enough.

Chapter IV pt I of the 1988 Act identifies four kinds of "moral right":

> (1) the right to be identified as author of a copyright literary, dramatic, musical or artistic work, or, as the case may be, as the director of a copyright film (§ 77);
> (2) the right for such an author or director not to have his work "subjected to derogatory treatment" (§ 80);
> (3) the right in certain circumstances for a person not to have a literary, dramatic, musical or artistic work (whether or not a copyright work) falsely attributed to him as author or to have a film (whether or not a copyright film) falsely attributed to him as director (§ 84);
> (4) the right for a person in certain circumstances who for private and domestic purposes commissions the taking of a copyright photograph or the making of a copyright film not to have copies of those works issued to the public or exhibited or shown in public or broadcast or included in a cable programme service (§ 85).

The law has at last recognized that there may be many circumstances where the author or the director of the work no longer owns the copyright in that work but should still be entitled to public recognition for his or her creative association with the work.

There are a significant number of exceptions to what has been called this "right to paternity," and in particular the right does not apply to computer programs, designs of typefaces or to any computer-generated work. It also does not apply where the author or director in question is an employee and the copyright automatically vests in his employer by virtue of a 9(2)(a) ("Person to be treated as author of film") or § 11(2) ("Works produced in course of employment") of the 1988 Act, as the case may be.

For the purposes of § 80, "treatment" of work is defined to mean:

> any addition to, deletion from or alteration to or adaption of the work, other than—
> (a) a translation of a literary or dramatic work, or
> (b) an arrangement or transcription of a musical work involving no more than a change of key or register ...

The treatment of a work is stated to be "derogatory" if the treatment "amounts to distortion or mutilation of the work or is otherwise prejudicial to the honour or reputation of the author or director."

It is clear that the necessarily subjective nature of establishing what is "derogatory" in a particular instance may lead to much fervent argument; particularly from a civil rights standpoint where one might be concerned as to whether this so-called right of integrity would limit legitimate freedoms of expressions such as satire or parody. In this context, there are a number of exceptions to the right of integrity, and in particular § 81(3) states that the right is not to apply in relation to any work made for the purpose of "reporting current events."

Whilst the so-called "moral rights" are included within the part of the 1988 Act generally entitled "Copyright" these rights are

---

[65] Sam Ricketson, "Is Australia In Breach of Its International Obligations With Respect to the Protection of Moral Rights?" 17 MELBOURNE U.L. REV. 462. Copyright 1990 Sam Ricketson. Excerpt reprinted by permission.

not really rights of copyright in the pure sense.

Section 86 provides that the rights conferred by § 77 ("to be identified as author or director"), § 80 ("to object to derogatory treatment of work") and § 85 ("to privacy of certain photographs and films") last as long as the copyright lasts in the work in question. The § 84 right ("false attribution") on the other hand is expressed to last for a period of 20 years after a person's death—this is a necessary distinction since, as mentioned earlier, the right to be protected against false attribution of a work does not merely apply to copyright works.

Section 87 of the 1988 Act drives a veritable "coach and horses" through the defenses of the legislation by providing that a person may give up all his moral rights by consent or by waiver and it may be expected therefore that the force of bargaining power may cause authors and directors to give up their rights unless and until a suitable code of conduct can be agreed.

Section 94 makes it clear that moral rights are not assignable but § 95 of the 1988 Act does enable moral rights to be transmitted on death to the heirs of the person in question.

Section 103 of the 1983 Act provides that an infringement of these moral rights is actionable as a breach of statutory duty owned to the person entitled to the right and goes on to provide specifically that, in relation to the § 80 right (the right to object to derogatory treatment of a work), the court may grant an injunction. It is not clear from this provision whether the Act is intended to exclude rights of injunction in relation to other kinds of moral right and one cannot immediately see why such rights of injunction should be so excluded.

The writer cannot say that the existence of these new moral rights shows, as Dr. Pangloss would have it, that everything is for the best in the best of all possible worlds or that, as Mr. Gradgrind would have it, these moral rights can be justified on a factual utilitarian basis because "facts alone are wanted in life." The writer also cannot say whether the easing of the author's lot will in any way dilute the essence of pure artistry which flows from the tormented minds of a Balzac or a Mozart but what the author can say is that these new moral rights may well produce some interesting legal arguments in years to come. With that thought, the writer intends to "go and work in the garden" (with respect to Voltaire).

b. Australia[66]

Australia is bound by the Paris text of the Berne Convention, Article 6bis of which is the same as the text adopted at Stockholm in 1967. What is required under this article can be stated as follows:

1. *Independence of moral rights:* It is clear that moral rights are independent of the author's economic rights. That is, their exercise cannot be tied to, or made dependent upon, the ownership or exercise of economic rights. This notion of independence is, of course, basic to the whole conception of moral rights.
2. *The rights required to be protected:* Only two moral rights require protection: those of paternity and integrity. Proposals to protect rights of disclosure were made and rejected at the time of the Rome Conference in 1928 and, in any event, are largely covered by the rights of first publication and distribution which are recognized as part of authors' economic rights in many countries.
3. *Duration of protection:* The basic principle established under para. (2) of Article 6bis is that the period of protection should be at least for the duration of the author's economic rights. Accordingly, the Convention adopts a neutral stance on the juridical nature of moral rights, that is, the monist and dualist theories referred to above. It also gives member countries flexibility in the way in which they protect these rights after the death of

---

[66] David S. Glass, *Moral Rights and the New Copyright Law,* 134 SOLICITORS JOURNAL 6. Copyright 1990 David S. Glass. Excerpt reprinted with permission.

the author: national laws may stipulate the persons or institutions who are to exercise these rights in that country. This may well be the heirs of the author, but it would be equally open to a member country to entrust the exercise of these rights *post mortem auctoris* to a government or public agency charged with the promotion of national culture or to some other analogous body. The latter course of action would be particularly appropriate where moral rights were protected after the expiry of the economic rights as any heirs of the author would by then be far removed from him or her.

4. *Mode of protection of moral rights:* Although Article 6bis contains no specific reference to this, it has been accepted from the start that Unison countries are not obliged to protect moral rights as part of their copyright laws. This was the historic compromise which enabled the inclusion of moral rights in the first place at Rome in 1928, and was confirmed at the time of the Stockholm Conference in the general report of Main Committee I. Countries are therefore free to adopt other means of protection for the rights specified in para. (1). Para. (3) further makes it clear that the "means of redress for the safeguarding of these rights" is a matter for the laws of the country where protection is claimed. This is the same as for the economic rights protected by the Convention, and means that the remedies available in each Berne country may vary considerably.

It is important to reiterate the obligatory nature of Australia's obligation to protect the two moral rights mentioned in Article 6bis(1). As a matter of treaty interpretation, there can be little doubt about this. The first task in treaty interpretation is to do so "in accordance with the ordinary meaning to be given to the terms of the treaty in their context and in the light of its object and its purpose." In this regard, the language of Article 6bis(1) is clear and unambiguous: the rights mentioned in that paragraph must be protected by each member country of the Berne Union.

The obligations under Article 6bis only exist with respect to foreign authors and works claiming protection in Australia pursuant to the provisions of the Convention. There is nothing in the article which concerns the protection to be given to Australian authors and works. On the other hand, as a matter of practical politics, it is difficult to conceive of a situation where the Australian Parliament would wish to treat foreign authors more favourably than Australian authors.

Australia is not a country where treaty obligations are directly implemented into municipal law, so that they can be directly invoked in our courts by foreign claimants. Specific legislative measures must be taken in order to give effect to treaty obligations.

In the event that Australia fails to accord the protection required under Article 6bis, it stands in breach of its obligation under Article 36(1) of the Convention "to adopt, in accordance with its constitution, the measures necessary to ensure the application of this Convention." This then raises the question of what, if anything, can be done to ensure compliance with the Convention by an errant member state.

Protection under current Australian law for the rights of authorship and integrity is to be found across a wide range of statutory, common law and equitable provisions:

(1) *The right to claim authorship:* Under statute, this is dealt with partially by the false attribution of authorship provisions of Part IX of the Copyright Act 1968. These impose a number of duties on persons not to make false claims of authorship of works or of altered versions of works.

(2) *The right of integrity:* This is protected only in small measure under the Copyright Act, in two provisions that have limited application and have never been the subject of judicial consideration. The first is subsection 35(5), which gives the authors of certain commissioned artistic works a veto over uses for a purpose other than that originally contemplated

> at the time of the commissioning of the work. The second is subsection 55(2) which provides that the compulsory license under that section in respect of the recording of musical works does not apply in relation to an adaptation of a musical work that debases the work. Apart from these provisions, the protection of the right of integrity in Australia is left to contractual arrangements where possible or the common law action of defamation.

In the light of the above, it may be concluded that Australian law probably provides sufficient protection for the right of integrity referred to in Article 6bis(1), but only very partial protection for the right to claim authorship. In so far as these protections only survive the author in very limited circumstances, there is a clear breach of para (2). These matters point then to the need for specific legislative action in order to achieve compliance with Article 6bis.

Are there any defenses or justifications for non-compliance that can be advanced? It could be argued that the subsequent practice of Berne Union countries establishes that there is agreement between them that the protection presently accorded under Australian law complies with the requirements of Article 6bis. Under the rules of treaty interpretation, it is possible to take account of any subsequent practice "in the application of the treaty which establishes the agreement of the parties regarding its interpretation." In this instance, the argument would be that the practice of Berne Union countries clearly established that the present forms of protection available for moral rights in common law countries such as Australia suffices for the purposes of Article 6bis. However, to establish such a practice, it is necessary to point to some positive agreement or understanding between the parties to the treaty in question: it is not possible to infer such an agreement from the mere absence of complaint. In the case of Article 6bis, it is impossible to establish such a positive agreement.

If it is accepted that Australia stands in breach of its international obligations under Article 6bis of the Berne Convention, what flows from this in legal terms? The Convention contains no specific provision dealing with its enforcement and has no sanctions against non-compliance.

QUESTIONS AND COMMENTS FOR YOUR CONSIDERATION

1. The Visual Artists Rights Act ("VARA") is the first effort to incorporate moral rights concepts into US copyright law. It states in pertinent part:

> The act further grants the author of a visual art the right "to prevent any intentional distortion, mutilation or other modification of that work which would be prejudicial to his or her honor or reputation ... and to prevent any destruction of a work of recognized stature." [17 U.S.C. § 106A]

Does VARA represent an adoption of the monist or dualist view of moral rights? Which rights—integrity, patrimony, publication, withdrawal—have been adopted?

2. What changes, if any, would you make in this statute?

3. How does U.S. moral rights law compare with that of Australia and Great Britain (two other common law countries)?

6. The Debate over the Adoption of Moral Rights in the United States

a. Historical Background[67]

Although the US Copyright Act grants only the economic rights to the copyright owner of an audiovisual work, judicial bodies have interpreted legal principles to protect the creator's personal rights, particularly in motion pictures. The United States officially states that these common law principles when pieced together, fulfill its obligations under the Berne Convention, specifically with regard to moral rights.

Before the enactment of the Visual Artists Rights Act, moral rights protection in the US was generally provided under contract law, unfair competition law (including particularly Section 43(a) of the Lanham Act, 15 U.S.C. § 1125(a)) and various defamation and privacy law provisions.

If a creator authors a work that is deemed a work of the employer or commissioner under a work for hire contract or assigns the copyright in the work, one recourse for the creator to claim authorship in the work is through careful contract drafting.

The use of contracts can provide extensive protection; however, creators often do not have the bargaining power to negotiate these contractual provisions. Additionally, even when integrity rights are contractually retained by the creator, they are often limited to alterations, distortions or modifications contemplated at the time of transfer. In short, contracts may seem to be the most powerful tool for a creator to retain moral rights in a creative work. However, it may be the least practical of tools because of a creator's frequent lack of bargaining power, broad interpretation of transfer of rights in favor of the legal owner, and limitation of rights to those expressly contemplated by the parties.

State unfair competition laws and their federal cousin, the Lanham Act, provide another means of shoring up creator's moral rights. The Lanham Act requires a showing that the use of another's name in connection with the work tends to deceive the public, and thus deprives the creator of the advertising value and goodwill that would otherwise result from the creator's name associated with the work. A creator may prevent the association of another's name with the work. A false attribution of authorship is equivalent to a deceptive practice under unfair competition laws and violates the Lanham Act, which prohibits false designation. Where no name appears on the work, this, too, may be [a] violation of the Lanham Act. The claim of false designation under either state or federal law is especially desirable because an injunction to prevent another from claiming authorship is an available remedy.

Unfair competition laws and the Lanham Act also may be applied to prevent a creator's name from being used in connection with the work of another. A plaintiff must show that the use of the creator's name tends improperly to imply that the creator has a greater role in the production—to deceive the public as to the creator's actual contribution to the work—and that injury is likely to result. The use of these laws in this regard may go beyond the moral rights of paternity and integrity as required by the Berne Convention. The attribution (paternity) right extends only to works by the creator while the US law extends a right of false designation, as well as attribution.

The most important development in the evolution of these laws in the copyright context is their application to right of integrity issues. Some courts suggest that a creator may object to material changes in the work as a violation of unfair competition laws. The alterations to the work must be such that the attribution to the creator would deceive the public and put the creator at an unfair economic disadvantage.

The watershed case linking the Lanham Act and the right of integrity was *Gilliam v. American Broadcasting Cos.*[68] The court found that the edited version of the Monty Python Group films shown by the American Broadcasting Co. omitted essential elements of the story line and "impaired the integrity of appellant's work and represented to the public as the product of appellant's [Monty

---

[67] Laura A. Pitta, *Economic and Moral Rights under US Copyright Law: Protecting Authors and Producers in the Motion Picture Industry,* 12 ENT. & SPORTS LAWYER 3. Copyright 1995 Laura A. Pitta. Excerpt reprinted with permission.

[68] 583 F.2d 14 (2d Cir. 1976).

Python's] what was actually a mere caricature of their talents."

In the context of false attribution, the right of publicity (a variation on the right of privacy) provides recourse for the wrongful use of the creator's name. Courts will generally prohibit the unauthorized commercial use of a person's name as an illicit expropriation of the proprietary interest in one's identity. The action is, however, limited to those acts that result in economic harm effected by the usurper. This is grounded in the idea that creators have a right to exploit their own identities to their economic advantage. They are entitled to enjoin the use of their names not only to prevent others from profiting from the economic benefits in their identity, but, to prevent false attribution.

A defamation cause of action aims to protect an individual's honor and reputation. False attribution using a creator's name may damage reputation and result in defamation. This may be an especially successful cause of action in cases in which an author's name is attributed to a work of a different genre or an inferior quality work.

Defamation is strongest as a tool to enforce a creator's right of integrity. Breach of a work's integrity implies that the work has somehow been transformed into an inferior one. Publication or display of an inferior work may damage the creator's reputation or standing in the community at large, or a particular artistic community, such as the motion picture industry.

Similarly, the tort action of invasion of privacy based on the false light theory provides recourse for the creator's right to integrity. This cause of action does not require injury (or likelihood thereof) to the plaintiff's reputation, but rather highly offensive misleading accounts for which the plaintiff may recover emotional distress damages. A creator of a work may be able to show that the alteration of the work created, in essence, a false attribution of the creator's name and led to emotional distress.

b. The Visual Artists Act[69]

US federal law did not overtly grant any moral rights to artists in America until June 1, 1991.

The Act specifically defines what types of works are "work[s] of visual artists rights." This definition is critical to artists. Artists can only take advantage of the Section 106A rights if the work that they create falls within the scope of the Act's definition. The Act defines a "work of visual art" as follows:

> (1) a painting, drawing, print or sculpture, existing in a single copy, in a limited edition of 200 copies or fewer that are signed and consecutively numbered by the author, or, in the case of a sculpture, in multiple cast, carved or fabricated sculptures of 200 or fewer that are consecutively numbered by the author and bear the signature or other identifying mark of the author; or
>
> (2) a still photographic image produced for exhibition purposes only, existing in a single copy that is signed by the author, or in a limited edition of 200 copies or fewer that are signed and consecutively numbered by the author.[70]

The Act also explicitly excludes certain types of works. Any work that is executed as a "work made for hire" cannot be considered a "work of visual art" within the scope of the Act. Furthermore, the Act's definition of a "work of visual art" does not encompass

> (i) any poster, map, globe, chart, technical drawing, diagram, model, applied art, motion picture or other audiovisual work, book, magazine, newspaper, periodical, data base, electronic information service, electronic publication, or similar publication;
> (ii) any merchandising item or advertising, promotional, descriptive, covering, or packaging material or container; or
> (iii) any portion or part of any item described [above].[71]

---

[69] Russ VerSteeg, *Federal Moral Rights for Visual Artists: Contract Theory and Analysis,* 67 WASH. L. REV. 827. Copyright 1992 Washington Law Review Association. Excerpt reprinted with permission.

[70] 17 U.S.C.A. § 101 (West Supp. 1992).

[71] 17 U.S.C.A. § 101 (2) (A) (West Supp. 1992).

In addition, any "reproduction, depiction, portrayal or other use of a work" used in connection with posters, maps, globes, merchandising items, etc. and works made for hire is not considered a "work of visual art," although the original of such a reproduction, depiction, or portrayal could be considered a work of visual art on its own merits. Consequently, the way that someone (a purchaser, for example) uses an artist's work can affect whether the work will be considered a "work of visual art" within the Act. For example, if a corporation were to purchase a large outdoor sculpture, display it in front of its office building, and were to subsequently adopt it as the company's logo or trademark, then, arguably, the sculpture itself could no longer be considered "a work of visual art" since it would then be used for "advertising or promotional purposes."

This definition has important ramifications for artists. First, in order for the Act to apply, artists must make sure that the medium in which they are working is one of the media that the Act contemplates. The categories of "works of visual art" are exhaustive. The Act in no way suggests that the drafters intended to open the door to permit media other than paintings, drawings, prints, sculptures, and still photographs. Secondly, artists must pay close attention to and observe the formalities that the Act's definition of "work of visual art" demands.

In order for a painting, drawing, or print to be considered "a work of visual art," artists must be certain that the work either (1) be executed as a single copy (*i.e.*, the original work itself); or (2) in a case where an artist wishes to make limited edition copies, she must be certain to make no more than 200 copies.

The Act grants to an "author of a work of visual art" the following rights:

1) The Right of Attribution: "to claim authorship" of a work of visual art;
2) The Right of Disclaimer: "to prevent the use of his or her name as the author of any work of visual art which he or she did not create;"
3) Another Form of the Right of Disclaimer: "to prevent the use of his or her name as the author ... in the event of a distortion, mutilation, or other modification of the work which would be prejudicial to his or her honor or reputation;"
4) The Right of Integrity: "to prevent any intentional distortion, mutilation, or other modification of that work which would be prejudicial to his or her honor or reputation;"
5) A Higher Level of The Right of Integrity for Works of Recognized Stature: "to prevent any destruction of a work of recognized stature."

These five rights, the Section 106A rights, are functionally discrete forms of the right of 2 and the right of integrity.

The power to waive or to refuse to waive the Section 106A rights clearly has economic value that artists can choose to exploit. Prospective art purchasers, no doubt, perceive the Section 106A rights as analogous to easements, encumbrances, or other "clouds on title" in real estate. Purchasers pay more for real estate when the title is clear than not or when they obtain a warranty deed as opposed to a quit claim. Similarly, prospective art purchasers can be expected to pay higher prices for works of visual art when the artists have waived their Section 106A rights as part of the bargain. Thus, by granting Section 106A rights to artists, Congress has, in essence, given an added economic value to artists.

For works created on or after June 1, 1991 (the Act's effective date), the Section 106A rights expire with the artist. In the case of joint authorship, the rights expire upon the death of the last surviving joint author.

The Act creates two rights that hinge upon whether a work has been or is in danger of being distorted, mutilated, or modified in a manner that would be prejudicial to the artist's honor or reputation. First, the Act furnishes a hybrid right that is fundamentally a cross between integrity and disclaimer. As was noted, this provision secures for artists the right to prohibit their names from being associated with their own works in instances where the works have been prejudicially altered. In addition, the Act gives artists the right "to prevent any intentional" prejudicial alteration. Thus, in addition to the right to disclaim authorship of works that have been prejudicially altered, artists have the right to prevent these prejudicial alterations ex ante. Although the Act does not attempt to define "distortion, mutilation, or other modification" in a positive way, it does specify certain things that will not be considered a "distortion, mutilation, or other modification." First, "[t]he modification of a work of visual art which is the result of the passage of time or the inherent nature of the materials is not a distortion, mutilation, or other modification ...." Furthermore, the Act dictates that "[t]he modification of a work of visual art which is the result of conservation, or of the public presentation, including lighting and placement, of the work is not a ... distortion, mutilation, or other modification ... unless the modification is caused by gross negligence."

c. The Problem of Transplantation[72]

The argument that *droit moral*, as it is known in France, could be adopted intact in the United States overlooks the significant differences in the historical origins of the two systems, and in the issues which have been the fulcrum of each system's development. In particular, as American copyright has evolved, its principal issues have focused on such questions as whether or not publication has occurred; whether or not copyright formalities have been observed; whether or not statutory definitions can be expanded to include new art forms and technological advances; and whether or not infringement has taken place.

Although American law regards copyright as a right separate from the material object itself, the question of the property character of author's rights'—the question which absorbed the attention of continental scholars—has not been a significant issue in the United States. It goes without saying that British and American scholars have been able to ignore the controversy between the monist and dualist views of *droit d'auteur*.

In comparison to the Civil Law system, the American tradition seems mechanical and uncompassionate. But it is important to observe that federal copyright derives from the Constitution, which not only creates the federal power to grant copyright protection, but also recites the basic philosophy on which the American system is based:

> To promote the Progress of Science and the Useful Arts by securing for limited Times to Authors and Inventors the exclusive Right to their Respective Writings and Discoveries. (US Constitution, Article I, Section 8, Clause 8)

The constitutional mandate reveals that American copyright arises not from a perpetual, natural right of "propriete incorporelle," as in France, nor even from a "right of personality," as in Germany, but rather from the sovereign's interest in promoting a socially desirable end.

This may, in fact, illustrate the most significant difference between the European and American systems. Under the Civil Law, the source of an author's rights is the author himself, and positive law exists to clarify, codify, and guarantee a right which presumably already exists when the author has performed the creative act. In the United States, while copyright cannot be called a mere privilege of the sovereign, it does exist primarily to the extent that positive law creates it, and that law springs not from the author's act of creation, but from a constitutionally recognized social purpose. Then any further protection of the artist beyond copyright—the American "moral" rights—also must reflect social needs, for those rights may be asserted only by application of legal and equitable principles, which balance the prerogatives of the artist with competing public or private interests.

We see, then, that the "amoral" American copyright actually embodies a system which aims more at social balancing than at unilaterally vindicating the artist's personal interests. This "social balancing" policy is clearly reflected in the 1976 copyright statute, which codifies the doctrine of fair use, expands the use of compulsory licenses, and eliminates perpetual common law copyright, at the same time as it extends the scope and duration of federal copyright protection. The same policy resounds in the California Art Preservation Act, which balances the artist's rights of personality against the competing interests of the artist's employer, the trans-

---

72 Russell J. DaSilva, *Droit Moral and the Amoral Copyright: A Comparison of Artists' Rights in France and the United States.* 28 BULL. COPYRIGHT SOC'Y 1. Copyright 1980 Russell J. DaSilva. Excerpt reprinted by permission.

feree of the work, and the proprietor of the building to which the work has been attached.[73] In this sense, the Preservation Act is not at all a *droit moral* statute, but rather a uniquely American legislation.

Thus, even as American law begins to recognize artists' rights beyond copyright, it does so within a tradition that is concerned for the interests of many parties; the American artist may indeed "sing" his own personality, but his copyright celebrates more than just himself. To adopt *droit moral* in the United States might require us to abandon that notion, and to subscribe to a tradition which our country does not share.

A traditional dilemma of the art world has been the conflict between interests of publishers, producers, and exhibitors of intellectual works, and the freedom of the creator. *Droit moral*, as it now is formulated in France, poses formidable challenges to the force of contracts between the artist and the exploiters of his work, but has not yet found a way to protect adequately the interests of the exploiter. Indeed, even zealous proponents of *droit moral* have criticized the failure of the French system to reconcile the interests of the exploiter. Indeed, even zealous proponents of *droit moral* have criticized the failure of the French system to reconcile the interests of the business community with those of the artist under contract. Thus, while *droit moral* achieves certain rights for artists, in practice it also may serve to aggravate the tension between artistic and commercial interests.

The French system also poses theoretical difficulties. It has been criticized for being based on the troublesome assumption that "moral" and "economic" interests can even be separated. The separation does appear somewhat artificial when we consider that an artist's name, reputation, and personality—like the goodwill of a business—are economic assets, and their violation gives rise to injuries which are at least analogous to business losses. Moreover, the Civil Law doctrine has not yet resolved the question of whether *droit moral* exists primarily to protect the artist or to protect his work, and how far it legitimately may go to protect either.

Finally, *droit moral* seeks to broaden the rights of the artist, but it ignores the fact that society, too, has legitimate interests in a work of art. While the artist may wish to withhold his work from public view or to preserve his creations from alteration or even from criticism, society has an interest in promoting education, in facilitating the diffusion of culture, and in stimulating new ideas, new art forms, and even new methods of exploitation, especially after an author or artist has been deceased for many years. The Anglo-American system, it has been argued, more effectively accounts for these interests.

This author advocates the conscientious legislative and judicial evolution of artists' rights through the expansion of existing American legal doctrines. As California has demonstrated, American legislation can accommodate many of the legal and equitable prerogatives enjoyed by French artists, without unfurling the banner of *droit moral*. As for the courts, what is needed is not so much a unification of the carious doctrines into a single theory of "moral right," but simply a clarification of the special factors to be considered as tort, contract and trademark theories continue to be applied to cases involving authors and artists. Such factors may best be studied by giving careful attention to the time-honored experience of the Civil Law.

d. Market Impact[74]

Certain characteristics of the arts and entertainment industries—particularly motion picture films (both theatrical and television films) and book, newspaper and magazine publishing . . . are pertinent to moral rights legislation.

Most of the product of these industries is intensely collaborative. In film, for example, the producer brings together a director, screenwriter, designers of sets and costumes, cinematographer, composer, actors and all manner of technical and creative contributors. The producer takes the economic risks and exercises business and, commonly, creative control.

The second pertinent feature of the arts and entertainment industries is their utiliza-

[73] Cal. Civ. Code § 987 (West).

[74] Robert A. Gorman, *Federal Moral Rights Legislation: The Need for Caution,* 14 NOVA L. REV. 421. Copyright 1990 Robert A. Gorman. Excerpt reprinted with permission.

tion of their works in a variety of "subsidiary" uses. Motion picture films are shown not only in theaters, but also on broadcast and cable television, over satellites and on airplanes, and in foreign nations, and they are marketed in cassette and disc form through rentals and sales. These uses contemplate all varieties of editing in terms of time-frame and content, commercial interruptions, dubbing in foreign languages, and the like.

Published books are also commonly exploited through revised editions and in subsidiary markets, including updated versions, abridgments, foreign-language editions, television and theatrical film versions, and adaptations that take advantage of new technological advancements, such as audiotapes (for trade books) and computer materials (for educational books). Educational books also contemplate frequent revisions in order to update text and pictorial content.

A third pertinent feature of the entertainment and cultural industries in the United States is that they have historically been regulated through elaborate contractual arrangements, voluntarily negotiated, and often negotiated on behalf of the principal creative contributors by strong and sophisticated labor organizations. These arrangements establish employer-employee relationships among most of the contracting parties and are negotiated within the framework of the "work made for hire" provisions of Section 201(b) of the 1976 Copyright Act. They commonly deal with such matters as the creative participation of directors, authors and the like in the development of subsidiary and derivative uses, and the credit to be given in connection with the exhibition, sale and advertising of the work.

The introduction into these industries of a right—exercisable by any one of a host of collaborative contributors—to protest the alleged distortion or modification of a particular literary or artistic contribution is extremely problematic. At best, it introduces an element of instability and uncertainty, as well as the frequent possibility, because of the increased threat of litigation, of delay in public access to and enjoyment of entertainment vehicles. At worst, it threatens to prevent altogether the dissemination to the United States and international public of a host of cultural and entertainment materials in forms that are varied, appealing and affordable. Any significant limit upon the ability of producers and publishers to disseminate works in these secondary markets—dissemination which commonly can mean the difference between a losing and a profitable business venture—runs a substantial risk of chilling investment in the arts and entertainment fields. This may in turn reduce the financial support of innovative creative endeavor—a result that will obviously be harmful to the public interest. Introduction of moral rights into these industries (particularly if these rights are statutorily declared to be inalienable and non-waivable) will also unsettle the network of contractual agreements that have been developed over many years in the various industries and that appear on the whole to be working quite successfully and fairly.

It is natural to ask whether untoward consequences have flowed from the incorporation of moral rights doctrine into the legal systems of many European and Latin American nations. Many of these nations appear to have flourishing creative communities in the arts and entertainment fields. Whether that is to any major extent attributable to the greater legal and business flexibility accorded producers, publishers, and other copyright owners and licensees under our legal system is difficult to determine empirically—as it is to determine whether, say, the creative arts in France or Italy would flourish to a greater degree were moral rights abandoned or sharply limited. One can reasonably assume, however, attributing economic rationality to those who invest in the arts and entertainment industries, that such investment will be promoted under a legal system in which authors—many of them working in the context of collaborations or of employment relationships—will not be accorded the right to exercise an aesthetic veto over the initial and secondary marketing of films, magazines, books and the like.

Even apart from economic modeling, moral rights abroad have indeed resulted in some odd limitations upon the display and marketing of works by copyright owners and licensees. Owners of buildings have been limited in making structural changes or in tearing down walls with murals. In a noteworthy case decided under the Canadian moral rights statute, a sculptor who had conveyed to a shopping center his sculpture of geese in flight was afforded an injunction against the center's bedecking the geese with ribbons at Christmas time.[75] Creators of music in the public domain have successfully challenged the use that music in motion pictures deemed inconsistent with the political views of the composer,[76] and artists have been permitted to challenge the exhibition of their works in a physical or artistic context they believed unsuitable. A textwriter of a book successfully challenged the publisher's selection of an illustrator on the ground that the illustrations were inferior in quality.[77] A songwriter (apparently after having transferred the copyright to another) has secured redress against the performance of his song with parody lyrics.[78] Courts have been invited to sit in judgment upon the nature and number of commercial interruptions in films shown in television. Set designers have successfully challenged the deletion of a theatrical scene in which their set was to appear,[79] and stage directors have successfully challenged the modification or omission of their stage directions.[80]

To some extent, then, moral rights doctrine as developed abroad has indeed resulted in some disturbing inhibitions upon the rights of copyright owners and licensees, and property owners, seeking to disseminate or adapt creative works. It appears however that the arts and entertainment industries abroad have learned to live with moral rights by largely ignoring those rights or substantially watering them down. Rights of attribution and integrity have—by statute or judicial decision—not been enforced when a user is taking action that is consistent with "proper usage" or with the "accepted manner and extent" or that is "reasonable" or "de minimis." A most significant limitation upon the integrity rights, applied in most foreign nations, is the right given to licensees to make alterations and modifications that are appropriate in light of the nature of the work and the purpose of the use; these are deemed allowable "adaptations" and are distinguished from "distortions," after the court considers whether the modifications preserve the "spirit, character, and substance of the work."

It is commonplace to permit moral rights to be waived, either in written or oral agreements or pursuant to the industry's customs and usages. In almost every foreign jurisdiction that recognizes the right of integrity, the author is required to assert that right in a fair, reasonable and good faith manner; the right will not be enforced if it is asserted "arbitrarily" or "vexatiously" or is "misused." A number of national laws incorporate the doctrine of fair use as a defense against moral rights claims (as with copyright claims, or permit certain education uses or parodies. Frequent adjustments are made for moral rights asserted by employees, or by joint authors, or by creative collaborators in works such as motion picture films, encyclopedias and periodicals.

Moral rights will inevitably conflict with US copyright law by permitting an author to veto certain uses of a work contemplated by the current copyright owner.

Our legal system has a number of policies that support the cultural enrichment of our public domain. All of these concerns for the public domain—and for fair dissemination and comment—may be jeopardized through the adoption of comprehensive moral rights legislation—particularly if, as in a number of foreign nations, moral rights are deemed to last perpetually, or at least for a longer period than the copyright.

Moral rights legislation will also create conflicts with the variety of individually and collectively negotiated contracts that permeate the film, broadcasting, and magazine, newspaper and book publishing industries. Finally the comprehensive incorporation of moral rights into United States law will inevitably bring before judges and juries matters of aesthetics for which they are ill-suited.

---

[75] Snow v. The Eaton Center Ltd., 70 C.P.R.2d 105 (1982).

[76] Soc. Le Chant de Monde v. Soc. Fox Europe et Fox Americaine Twentieth Century, Judgment of Jan. 13, 1984 1 Gax Pal. 191 (1954) D.A. 16, 80 (Cour d'Appel Paris).

[77] Pres. Dist. Ct. Utrecht, 27 Nov. 1975, *discussed in* Nimmer & Geller, *supra* note 5, at 45.

[78] Pres. Dist. Ct. Amsterdam, 21 Dec. 1978, discussed in Merryman, *The Refrigerator of Bernard Buffet*, 27 HASTINGS L.J. 1023, 1030-31 (1976).

[79] Leger v. Reunion des Theatres Lyriques Nationaux (1955), 6 R.I.D. 146 (Tribunel Civil de la Seine).

[80] *See* Judgment of Aug. 14, 1975, LGE Frankfurt-on-Main, discussed in DaSilva, at 31.

QUESTIONS AND COMMENTS FOR YOUR CONSIDERATION

1. What balance would you strike between author's rights and society's interest in the dissemination of an author's work? Are these interests necessarily conflicting?

2. Do you believe the US had met its obligations under Article 6bis prior to enactment of the Visual Artists Rights Act? If not, has the Visual Artists Rights Act corrected this failure?

3. Is there a rational basis for limiting VARA's scope of protection to visual arts?

4. How can the economic basis of U.S. copyright law be reconciled by the personality emphasis of moral rights protection? Is such reconciliation necessary? Can a moral rights theory be adopted using currently existing economic-based U.S. law? What problems, if any, do you foresee in adopting a moral rights approach to author's rights in the United States?

C. *Droit De Suite* and Resale Royalties

1. The Role of Natural Law[81]

For copyright purposes, a work of fine art has been likened to Cinderella: appreciated for its unique beauty by those who look upon it, yet subject to continuing unfair exploitation by those who control it. While nominally granted copyright protection by Congress in 1870, the *sui generis* nature of the fine arts has never been fully recognized by the law. Consequently, artists are not allowed to profit from the increased value of their work to the same extent as writers and composers. Until Congress passes *droit de suite* legislation, or some equivalent, this inequity in the American copyright scheme will remain.

The subject matter of copyright has expanded steadily since the first federal copyright law was passed over two hundred years ago. Originally limited to books, maps, and charts, copyright protection was subsequently granted to etchings, musical compositions, dramatic compositions, and photographs. The Act of 1870 finally extended copyright for the first time to paintings, drawings, statues, and designs "intended to be perfected as works of the fine arts."

The existing copyright rights of reproduction and performance, however, have proven to be nearly valueless because works of fine art are inherently incapable of being reproduced or performed in the traditional sense. Furthermore, although the 1976 Act gave fine artists the potentially valuable right to display their work publicly, as a practical matter, the first sale doctrine terminates this right upon its sale. Thus, the purchaser has the right to show a painting or a sculpture in a gallery or museum without having to obtain permission from the artist and without having to pay any royalty for its display. In sum, "the golden eggs of copyright for works of art seldom materialize, and when they do, they appear to have been laid by a hummingbird, not a goose."[82]

While the *droit de suite* is not an exclusive right since it does not allow the artist to prevent the further sale of his work, it is quite similar in nature to a compulsory license, long-recognized in American copyright law, in that the holder of the right is entitled to a royalty every time his work is resold. By amending the Copyright Act to include a resale royalty, Congress will finally recognize that fine artists have been unfairly denied a right given to all other authors—the

---

[81] Michael B. Reddy, *The Droit De Suite: Why American Fine Artists Should Have the Right to a Resale Royalty,* 15 LOY. L.A. ENT. L.J. 509. Copyright 1995 Loyola of Los Angeles Entertainment Law Journal. Excerpt reprinted with permission.

[82] Daniel Brenner, *A Two-Phase Approach to Copyrighting the Fine Arts,* 24 BULL. COPYRIGHT SOC'Y 97 (1976).

right to share in the future economic success of their works.

The Constitution's Copyright Clause gives Congress the power "to promote the progress of useful arts, by securing for limited times to authors the exclusive right to their writings." The Clause was modeled after the Statute of Anne, England's first copyright law, which was passed in 1709. [O]ne of the primary purposes of both English copyright law and its American descendant has always been to reward the creation of "useful art" by providing economic incentives for its creators. Adding the *droit de suite* to the Copyright Act would further the original intent of the Copyright Clause by "promoting the progress" of the fine arts. It would give artists the potentially lucrative right to participate in the increased value of their work.

Charles C. Pinckney and James Madison are generally given credit for drafting the Copyright Clause. The Clause was adopted and signed by the delegates to the Constitutional Convention meeting in Philadelphia on September 17, 1787. It is important to note that its authors intentionally avoided using the term "copyright" in its text, which allowed the Congress to expand copyright's protection far beyond the subject matter of the late eighteenth century.

The provision was uncontroversial, generating no debate in the convention or during the ratification process. However, the most authoritative source of constitutional intent, The Federalist, contains a passage written by Madison that makes it clear that since American copyright was based on the English common law right, "the utility of this power will scarcely be questioned because the public good fully coincides . . . with the claims of individuals."[83]

The United States Supreme Court recently reaffirmed this basic copyright principle in *Fogerty v. Fantasy, Inc.*[84] Citing language from *Sony Corp. of America v. Universal City Studios, Inc.*,[85] the Court stated that the Copyright Clause was intended to motivate the creative activity of authors and inventors by the provision of a special reward which must ultimately serve the public good. In short, rewarding the artistic success of individual artists through a resale royalty fulfills the original intent of the Copyright Clause: it gives them an economic incentive to create additional works of art, thus further promoting "the Progress of . . . useful Arts."

Opponents of the *droit de suite* have argued that it is incompatible with Anglo-American copyright law because of its distinct origin in French law. Yet, a careful analysis of the historical development of both the English law of copyright and its civil law counterpart in France reveals a common root in natural law. It is generally acknowledged that the evolution of moral rights was heavily influenced by natural law jurisprudence, but copyright's common law beginning as a natural, perpetual right is almost completely forgotten. The early misreading of a leading British copyright case by the United States Supreme Court led to the erroneous conclusion that Anglo-American copyright was derived solely from a statutory grant. Proper recognition of English copyright's foundation in natural law helps reconcile the apparent differences between American and French copyright law and provides an additional argument for passing *droit de suite* legislation in the United States.

Natural law is one of the oldest known legal theories, with two of its earliest advocates being Plato and Aristotle. Plato thought it was natural for law to tend toward "the discovery of the ideal form of perfect law," while Aristotle noted the difference between natural justice and conventional justice. The primary emphasis of early natural law was determining what was ethical and just as abstract principles common to all of humanity.

Cicero, the Roman lawyer and orator, was a student of the Stoics who revived the study of natural law and introduced the concept of jus gentium, or universal law, into Roman law. It is probable that Cicero influenced Gaius, an early commentator on Roman law who argued that natural law was derived from the reason of man, and hence provided the civil law with a non-theistic, philosophical basis. The first known citation to natural law theory in the context of literary property appears in Gaius' treatise on Roman law.

---

[83] The Federalist No. 43 at 288 (James Madison) (Jacob E. Cooke ed. 1961).

[84] 114 S. Ct. 1023 (1994).

[85] 464 U.S. 417, 429 (1984).

The Greco-Roman theory of natural rights was reasserted by Thomas Aquinas and other Christian philosophers in the twelfth century as a result of the rediscovery of the Roman Law Digests. Since then, there has been a conflict between believers of natural law theories and those who support the concept of positive legal codes. The former relies on reason and conscience to recognize universal, fundamental truths; the latter binds men because of sanctions built into social relationships and enforced by the state. Modern parallels to this dichotomy can be seen in the philosophical differences between the French tradition of moral rights and the American history of positive copyright law.

Even though Anglo-American copyright is generally thought to be a purely positivist creation today, there is ample evidence that early English copyright was based on the same natural law jurisprudence as French copyright. Blackstone's restatements of the law of literary property relied upon the theories espoused by Gaius in his treatise on Roman law, and Blackstone affirmed the natural law origin of literary justice. The debates in the sixteenth and seventeenth centuries among authors, booksellers, the public, and the Crown, which ultimately led to the passage of the Statute of Anne, were filled with references to natural law and the "inalienable" rights of authors. The first case to examine closely the legal basis of English common law copyright, *Millar v. Taylor*, clearly reveals the influence of natural law:

> The common law, now so called, is founded on the law of nature and reason. Its grounds, maxims and principles are derived from many different fountains . . . from natural and moral philosophy, from the civil and canon law, from logic, from the use, custom and conversation among men, collected out of the general disposition, nature and condition of human kind.[86]

In *Millar*, England's highest court at the time, the Court of the King's Bench, was called upon to decide what effect the Statute of Anne had on an author's common law copyright. The suit arose when bookseller Robert Taylor sold several copies of a work without the permission of Andrew Millar, even though he had previously purchased all rights in the book from its deceased author. While the Crown had long recognized that English booksellers had a perpetual property right in the works they owned prior to the enactment of the Statute of Anne, these sales had occurred after the twenty-eight year term of protection provided for in that statute. Was copyright still property to be held in perpetuity by its owner?

Blackstone, arguing for Millar, claimed that:

> There is a real property remaining in authors, after publication of their works; and that they only, or those who claim under them, have a right to multiply the copies of such literary property, at their pleasure, for sale . . . and that this right is a common law right, which always has existed.[87]

The terms "property" and "common law right" were used interchangeably at that time, and most importantly, both concepts were accepted by all four judges to be natural rights derived from natural law and justice. Further, three of the four also agreed that common law copyright was perpetual in duration, despite the statute's imposition of a twenty-eight year limitation. Thus, *Millar* recognized that authors have a natural property right in the fruits of their labor that had always existed at common law and was now merely codified by the Statute of Anne.

Five years after the issues in *Millar* were decided, the House of Lords reexamined them in a case with substantially similar facts, *Donaldson v. Beckett*.[88] In what one proponent of the natural law of copyright characterizes as the pivotal mistake among the "five accidents in copyright law,"[89] the Donaldson court concluded, in a 6-5 vote, that common law copyright had been completely supplanted by the statute, despite its "frequent admission that the natural and common law were the sources for rights that

---

[86] 98 Eng. Rep. 201, 223 (1769).

[87] Millar, 98 Eng. Rep. At 202.

[88] 1 Eng. Rep. 837 (1774).

[89] Gary Kauffman, *Exposing the Suspicions Foundation of Society's Primacy in Copyright Law: Five Accidents*, 10 COLUM.-VLA J.L. & ARTS 381, 399 (1985).

had been incorporated into the Statute of Anne."[90] Thus, English copyright was erroneously transformed from an innate right of authors derived from natural law into "nothing but a statutory privilege, a mere gift from Parliament."[91]

The United States declared its independence from Great Britain two years after *Donaldson*, but the new nation was still influenced by the English common law, including its original view of copyright as a natural right of authors. Further, the two most far-reaching events of the eighteenth century's Age of Enlightenment, the American and French Revolutions, were both fundamentally based on natural law theories. It is clear that the Founders were influenced by the natural law theories of Locke, Montesquieu, and Rousseau when they were drafting the Constitution's provisions, including its guarantees that the government shall not violate the inalienable rights of American citizens.

The Copyright Clause was originally intended to promote the public good by rewarding those responsible for the creation of useful works. Its co-author, James Madison, must have been aware of the decisions in *Millar* and *Donaldson* since he cited their holdings in The Federalist: "The copyright of authors has been solemnly adjudged in Great Britain to be a right at common law." Despite this constitutional history, which was based on *Donaldson's* acknowledgment of a common law copyright now codified and limited by the Statute of Anne, the United States Supreme Court, in *Wheaton v. Peters*,[92] denied that such a common law right ever existed. In the American view, "statutory protection [of copyright] not only secured common law rights and superseded them, it essentially negated and replaced them."[93]

The existence of a common law copyright derived from natural law was reaffirmed, however, in the dissenting opinions of Justice Thompson and Justice Baldwin. In Justice Thompson's opinion, common law copyright was "established in sound reason and abstract morality," which was protected by the "principles of right and wrong, the fitness of things, convenience and policy." Nevertheless, by disregarding Madison's belief that the Copyright Clause merely gave Congress the power to secure the natural right of authors at common law, as Parliament did with the Statute of Anne, the *Wheaton* majority's misunderstanding of the true origins of Anglo-American copyright became precedent, and was later incorporated into the legislative history of the 1909 Act.

Despite this disavowal by the courts and Congress, early American commentators continued to recognize natural law's contributions to the development of common law and statutory copyright protections for authors. In addition, the natural law basis of all copyright laws provided a legal rationale for the first supporters of an international copyright treaty, who ultimately prevailed with the worldwide adoption of the Berne Convention.

Clearly, the legal basis of Anglo-American copyright can be found in natural law, since early Roman law theories of literary property were used by English judges to affirm the pre-existence of a common law copyright, which was later codified and then relied upon by American courts. The Founders of the United States, living in an age which exalted the concept of natural rights, clearly relied on these and other natural law principles when drafting the Declaration of Independence and the Constitution, including the Copyright Clause. Hence, while it is generally assumed that the French origins of the *droit moral* and the droit de suite are incompatible with United States copyright theory, a careful examination of the history of British and American copyright demonstrates their shared reliance on natural law. Thus, the enactment of a resale royalty by Congress, which is often characterized as both a moral right and an economic right, would be an appropriate recognition of the natural law foundations of both French and Anglo-American copyright law.

American fine artists should have the right to a resale royalty because: (1) United States copyright law unfairly limits their ability to participate in the economic exploitation of their work; (2) the *droit de suite* fulfills the original intent of the Copyright Clause by promoting the creation of addi-

---

[90] Robert C. Hauhart, *Natural Law Basis for the Copyright Doctrine Droit Moral,* 30 CATH. LAW 53, 66 (1985).

[91] Kaufman, *supra* note [98] at 401.

[92] 33 U.S. 591 (1834).

[93] Id. at 624.

tional works of fine art; (3) copyright is derived from natural law, which recognizes the inalienable right of all creators to a continuing relationship with their work; and (4) it is in the long term interest of the United States to become a leader in international copyright law by voluntarily adhering to the *droit de suite* provisions of Article 14ter of the Berne Convention.

It is said that the *droit de suite* is a French moral right incompatible with Anglo-American copyright. A closer examination of the historical origins of copyright law in France and England shows that the copyright traditions of both nations share a common foundation in natural law. The leaders of the French and American Revolutions were heavily influenced by natural law principles and believed that natural justice for all people could be achieved by relying on reason and conscience to recognize universal, fundamental truths.

Since natural law underlies both United States and French copyright law, it is reasonable to insist that American fine artists be given the same rights as their counterparts in France. Congress can achieve a fitting form of natural justice by enacting a resale royalty, which is a unique blend of moral and economic rights.

2. Diverging Views of "The Starving Artist"[94]

The concept of the *droit de suite* for the visual arts derives in part from the romantic notion of the starving, albeit famous, artist who sold his works while yet an undiscovered young talent and who must live a life of poverty as others grow wealthy at the artist's expense. It also comes from a realization about the character of visual art, as opposed to books or music for example, that its value is in great part determined by its uniqueness and singularity of use.

In France and some other countries, the *droit de suite* concept gives the artist an ongoing monetary connection to the work of art by providing a legislated societal incentive for artists to continue to produce. The manner in which the royalty is computed varies from country to country. In Germany, the artist receives a percentage of the profits realized by the seller. Italy has a similar percentage of profits computation. In Belgium, the artist is considered to have an ongoing "contract with the buyer" and when profits increase the artist must receive a share of them to prevent "unjust enrichment." In France, the artist receives a certain percentage of the resale price whether there has been a profit or not. A system of registration has been established and yet, artists have not taken advantage of their ability to collect royalty payments. It also should be noted that the Berne Convention recognizes the *droit de suite* for foreign artists whose home countries provide a reciprocal right.

In attempting to explain why *droit moral* and *droit de suite* seemed to have developed to great heights in Continental Europe, and not to such a great extent in Britain or the United States, one must consider the entire cultural fabric of a society which law will only be a reflection thereof. While Europe had a long tradition of art and artisans, especially through Church sponsorship, the Puritans in England had no such toleration for art nor expectation of it in their daily lives. The American experience, on yet another level, was concerned with industrialization and economic expansion. It is no wonder then that the granting of copyrights in the United States was viewed as a type of social bribe to induce the artist to continue production . . . [t]o promote the progress of science and the useful arts.

3. Compensation for Personality[95]

The rights of visual artists in Europe have evolved around the recognition that artistic creations deserve special protection. Unlike

---

[94] Roberta L. Shaffer, *The Artist's Case For* Droit Moral *and* Droit Moral *and* Droit De Suite *Continues*, 15 INT'L J. LEGAL INFO. 1. Copyright 1987 Roberta L. Shaffer. Excerpt reprinted by permission.

[95] Elliott C. Alderman; *Resale Royalties in the United States For Fine Visual Artists: An Alien Concept*, 40 J. COPYRIGHT SOC'Y U.S.A. 265. Copyright 1992 by the Copyright Society of the U.S.A. Excerpt reprinted with permission.

authors and composers, who are able to distribute identical copies of their works, each having the same value, artists create unique or a limited number of objects. Artists are also different from other authors in that they cannot generally rely on repeated use of copies of their works. Since it has been argued that works of fine art are exploited with each sale, whether or not there is a profit, resale royalties rest on the desire to encourage artistic production by guaranteeing creators compensation, as with other economic rights.

In France, the seller pays for the privilege of having enjoyed a work of art during the time he owned it. Much like the author who receives royalties, the artist participates in the continuing exploitation of his works. Under French law, the artist shares in the total sales price of his work at resale. This approach, however, focusing strictly on the personality rights of the artist, accounts for neither the low profit margin on art sales, nor the seller's costs and dealer commission. Nor does it contemplate the inequity of permitting an artist to benefit from increases, without also having to share in the risk of loss.

The artist's royalty in Germany is premised on the belief that the increased value of a creation was always latent in it, and that increases in individual works are also due to the artist's continuing body of work. Thus, the increase in value in a particular work over time is what the artist should have received originally. Artists are exploited, in this view, because a work's true value is not realized until many years after its original sale, and without resale royalties the creators do not share in any appreciation. Since good art is ahead of public whim, artists should not be punished for their prescience.

In a free-market, however, the value of an object is what a willing buyer will pay a willing seller at a given time. Thus, when a young artist without a recognized market sells a work to a collector—who assumes the considerable risk that the work may decline in value—market forces dictate the price and terms of the exchange. And consistent with free-market property rights, the collector receives the interests he negotiated in the work as a *quid pro quo* for his gamble.

The intrinsic value supposition is also marked with other flaws. First, there is nothing inherent in the concept of art which furnishes artists with particular privileges. The relationship between the artist and his work is largely driven by cultural interests, and whether a work is valued, in and of itself, is a matter that varies from time to time and society to society. Second, factors other than the continuing efforts of the artist raise the value of a work. These include the premature death of the artist, his failure to live up to earlier promise, and any reduction in supply of an artist's work or inclusion in a well-known collection, as well as inflation in the art market generally.

The price of art, like other commodities, varies with supply and demand, and the artist is only one of the many factors that impact on price. Third, it is an economic reality that most art depreciates in value, so a royalty based on profit will not benefit most artists. As a matter of fairness, as well, it is difficult to ignore devaluation of currencies and conservation costs. Fourth, the intrinsic value concept relies on the attenuated connection between artists and subsequent and unknown sellers: eventually purchasers buy a share of the artist's fame instead of a work. Finally, the complexity of calculations makes a royalty based on appreciation difficult to implement.

Some argue that the Copyright Act has failed to provide economic incentives for visual artists comparable with those granted to authors and composers. Unlike other creators who can produce and market endless copies of their works, the fine artist creates only one or a very limited number of works—the very value of which lies in their uniqueness.

Authors and composers receive royalties through reproduction and performance rights for all the copies of their works that are exploited. Visual artists, on the other hand, are paid only for the initial sale of their works and have commercially insignificant reproduction rights. And unfortunately, they lose their most remunerative right—that of public display—once they sell their creations.

However, the comparison of the relative protection and remuneration of artists and other creators is rife with subjective determinations. Although authors who do not create unique works are rewarded by royalties and can produce numerous copies and reap the benefits, the value of works of fine art is determined by scarcity and such works do not require the same level of demand to secure a living for an artist. Indeed, even though some fine artists cannot fully exploit their reproduction rights, it may be argued nevertheless that the marketplace favors these artists. Additionally, successful artists—and those are really the only ones that copyright and *droit de suite* reward—secure ever increasing prices as their reputations grow and they sell successive works. In this way, in fact, they continue to maintain a connection with their body of work, even after sale, undercutting another primary argument supporting the resale royalty.

Most importantly, the sale of works subject to continuing royalties and works of fine art are not analogous. First, the former are sold in thousands of copies to large groups of customers, and until the last copy is sold, the author, entitled to remuneration for all copies, does not know the total revenue from the work; works of fine arts, on the other hand, are sold to one or a limited number of customers and the creator can control the distribution of his works and has all, or virtually all, this information at the time of sale. Second, the triggering event for the resale royalty is the substitution of one owner for another, rather than the distribution of another example of the original work, as is the case with works created in many copies. A more apt point of comparison perhaps would be the resale of a first-edition book, for which authors typically are not paid a royalty.

The essence of the resale royalty is the disparity between the initial sales price and the price for which a work is later sold. This concept fits easily within the European natural law systems that recognize a continuing relationship between an artist and his work, even after sale. Consistent with this view, possession of art is not like owning a widget: even after a work is sold it remains under the influence of its creator. The United States, however, follows the more traditional view of property rights—that the purchaser of an item for a freely negotiated price is the absolute owner—and is less receptive generally to restraints on free alienability. Indeed, the lack of alienability in the *droit de suite* is the most substantial restriction of the owner's rights: the transferee may receive and assign any or all of the author's exclusive rights that he has acquired in a work, but he is barred from obtaining the resale royalty.

The royalty also raises significant privacy concerns because artists would need to obtain certain information about sales prices and ownership that sellers, purchasers and other owners may not want to disclose.

It is imperative to identify the wrong that resale royalties would right. As a matter of policy, does Congress want to help struggling artists or provide an economic right that, like copyright rewards only commercially successful creators and frequent resellers?

Moreover, are the benefits of the royalty worth the concomitant costs: for example, does Congress want to make inherent value judgments about why people should buy art—whether for consumption or investment—and reward the true connoisseur who does not contemplate reselling his work? The resale royalty also encourages the creation of particular types of art. To be truly effective the *droit de suite* must be an incentive to produce works that are resold frequently: easel paintings and traditional sculpture, for example, where conception is embodied in a single object. Finally, does Congress want to eliminate, or even qualify, the First Sale doctrine, and abandon well-settled principles of free alienability in Anglo-American property jurisprudence?

4. Equality Among the Arts[96]

Proponents of the resale royalty, who predominantly have been lawyers, politicians, and some artists, though not art historians or art dealers, share a view of the artist, of his or her work, and of the art world. Although rarely stated explicitly, advocates of a legislative royalty subscribe to a romantic view of the artist, a view which initially developed in the late eighteenth and early nineteenth centuries. According to romantic theory, the truth or value of an artwork

---

[96] Neil F. Siegel, *The Resale Royalty Provisions of the Visual Artists Rights Act: Their History and Theory*, 93 DICK. L. REV. 1. Copyright 1988 by the Dickinson School of Law. Excerpt reprinted by permission.

springs from the special qualities of the artist who impresses upon the work a measure of his or her genius. In recognition of this genius, or of the truths to which this genius points, lay people experience aesthetic enjoyment. The artist J.S.G. Boggs, who was recently acquitted of charges of "reproducing" British currency, nicely summarized the romantic conception and illustrated its contemporary viability. Upon his arrest, Boggs stated: "It is my job to allow my thoughts and feelings to be expressed and communicated through visual work of my hands. For art to be true and just and honest, I must allow my inner self out."[97] The idea that the artist's inner qualities are most important is also expressed in Massachusetts' moral right statute, which provides that "fine art . . . is an expression of the artist's personality."[98]

The romantic theorist would argue that society benefits from its artists because most people are conventional or dull and need the artist to point out elements of beauty and originality and to spur them out of their docile acceptance of social norms and values.

The romantic conception envisions the artist as someone who, unlike the ordinary person, can recognize truth or beauty and can create beautiful objects or aesthetic experiences. The forms which the artist creates, therefore, are as much an element of his or her art, as any social or political message.

An alternative view to the romantic conception envisions the artist as a craftsperson whose work functions as a conduit for truths originating from sources other than within the artist. For example, in a painting of the Crucifixion or in a portrait of a political leader, such as Rigaud's Louis XIV, the most important aspect of the work is not how beautifully it is painted or what the artist may think, but rather the "extra-aesthetic" meanings which the artist has been instructed to represent: fundamental tenets of Christianity or certain assertions about the quality of the French government. In these examples, the artist conveys the ideas of someone else, and those ideas, not the artist's inspiration, give the work its value. According to this view, a painting or sculpture is only slightly different from any other object which is made to order, such as a magazine advertisement, handcrafted bookshelves, or dining room furniture. The artist/craftsperson does not impart to the work a spiritual quality, but rather a degree of technical competence, the sort of thing expected from any well-trained and hardworking individual.

The romantic view of art has been predominant for the past several centuries, and the resale royalty logically follows from this view. The qualities which the artist impresses upon his or her work never leave it, and whenever the work changes hands, any enjoyment which the new owner derives is solely attributable to the artist. Since the artist is responsible for the enjoyment of subsequent owners, he or she should collect a fee or royalty when the work is resold.

Developing another aspect of romantic theory, that great artwork rarely is recognized until some time after its creation, proponents claim that artworks sell initially for less than their true value. Two explanations are offered to account for the low initial prices. First, young unknown artists have little bargaining power and must sell their work at any price in order to survive. Second, since popular vision and taste lags behind that of the avant garde, buyers necessarily undervalue new work. Although a collector may have offered a higher price if he or she had recognized the work's actual value, such recognition is rare, and due to their lack of bargaining power, artists must accept low prices for new work. Advocates of the resale royalty argue that artworks are more accurately valued at later sales, when community taste has progressed, and that the royalty redresses the loss suffered by the artist at the initial sale.

Proponents of the resale royalty also argue that due to the nature of the various media of the several arts, present American law favors writers and composers over visual artists.

Opponents' arguments, which are primarily of two types, either attack particular provisions of a royalty proposal as ill-conceived or poorly drafted, or claim that "the establishment of resale royalties, far from helping artists or having only a neutral

---

[97] Weschler, *Onward and Upward with the Arts: Value—Category Confusion,* THE NEW YORKER, Jan. 25, 1988 at 95.

[98] Mass. Gen. Laws Ann. ch 231 sec. 85S (West Supp. 1988).

effect, would in fact be positively harmful to their interests."[99]

Art collectors, opponents of the royalty claim, purchase art objects not only for aesthetic satisfaction, but also for investment purposes. Since a royalty diminishes the investor's profit when an art-work is resold, if a royalty were enacted, the investment-minded collector would buy a commodity free of the resale royalty, rather than purchase a painting or sculpture and support a needy young artist. If a collector purchased a work of art, the royalty would be considered at the time of the initial sale, and the investor's offer diminished by the present value of the anticipated royalty. Since the artist has no bargaining power, he or she would have to accept this low offer. The effect of the resale royalty then would be to decrease both the number and the price of initial purchases. Fewer artists would sell fewer works and our artistic heritage would suffer.

Opponents of the royalty also note that art dealers, whose galleries are the primary places where new talent is brought to public attention, incur high costs when they organize exhibitions. Rarely do exhibitions pay for themselves. Usually, the costs of a show, including promotion expenses and gallery overhead, far exceed the amount received from the sale of exhibited works. Dealers support themselves and underwrite the expenses of the exhibitions through "back room" sales, which are the resales of works by well-known, long-established artists. If the resale royalty is enacted, profits from back room sales would diminish and fewer unknown artists would receive front room exhibition space. In this way, too, the resale royalty would hinder the development of new artistic talent.

Opponents of the resale royalty make one final practical argument. Young artists, they contend, are the one who need financial support and the resale royalty would benefit only a few well-established individuals who have already achieved financial success. Rather than waste time and money in the pursuit of a resale royalty, why not lobby for some other sort of art support legislation? Only from time to time do congressmen attend to the art world; when their attention is so turned, why not advocate more meaningful support measures?

[99] Weil, *Resale Royalties: Nobody's Benefits*, 77 ARTNEWS 58, March 1978.

5. Economic Impact[100]

The main components of the art world, in addition to artists, are dealers and auctioneers, collectors, museums and their professional personnel, art historians, art critics and the art press. Within the art world, the art market is the principal medium for the distribution of art and the compensation of artists. The art world has an ecology, its own set of inner relationships and interdependencies. As in other ecologies, what affects one part resounds throughout the system and is felt by all the others. Responsible policy-making for the art world accordingly considers the effects of proposals like the *droit de suite* on all the players.

The art market has two major sectors: the primary (first sale) market and the secondary (resale) market. The artist's main source of income is the primary market. She participates in that market by selling her works directly, through friends and acquaintances, at art fairs, and to people who come to the studio, or indirectly, through a dealer. Most artists would rather spend their time making art than in promoting and selling their work and in the many distracting but essential housekeeping tasks (maintaining systematic records, arranging shows, handling sales, dealing with correspondence, photography, framing, insurance, packing and shipping, etc.) that dealers normally perform for them. Acquiring a knowledgeable and effective dealer who is genuinely interested in and capable of supporting and promoting the artist's work and who will take care of housekeeping matters in order to free the artist to make art is a crucial step toward recognition and market success for the artist.

The secondary, or resale, market differs in important ways from the primary market. Here the auction houses are central players. They acquire works on consignment from

[100] John Henry Merryman, *The Wrath of Robert Rauschenberg*, 41 AM. J. COMP. L. 103. Copyright 1993 John Henry Merryman. Excerpt reprinted with permission.

collectors, museums and dealers. Their transactions are documented by widely distributed catalogs published in advance of the sale and by price lists published after the sale, establishing a publicly available reference point for pricing art works. Most dealers who operate galleries and promote the work of their artists in the primary market are also active in the resale market, which provides the operating funds needed to support the normally unprofitable primary market activity. Many other dealers operate only in the secondary market and do not represent artists, and some of them —called "private" dealers—work from apartments or homes by telephone and by appointment and maintain no public space.

The great majority of artists, however, are effectively shut out of the secondary market by simple economics. Auction houses and secondary market dealers do not accept their works for resale because they know from experience that such works are unlikely to resell at any price, and the few that did sell would bring commissions too small to cover the expense of sale. In fact, the only realistic source of income from their art is, for most working artists, first sales.

We turn now to a persistent folklore that clouds discussions of the *droit de suite*. This folklore (others have referred to it as a mythology) is congenial is discontented artists and to people who sentimentalize about the artist's life, but it has little connection with reality. Though demonstrably false, it persists in popular culture and among artists for a variety of reasons that it is unnecessary to explore here. In this folklore the world is unfair to artists of genius, who live in poverty while their works are resold at high prices by avaricious dealers to wealthy collectors.

The folklore also asserts that the artist is the sole source of the work's market value. As Pierredon-Fawcett puts it: "in commercial transactions, the cleverness of the speculator had little to do with the price increase, which was essentially attributable to the artist's genius."[101] Leaving aside the implication that all resellers are speculators (Are the collectors and museums who resell works as a normal part of their activity in building and refining their collections "speculators"?) and ignoring the economic naivete in the suggestion that speculation is an unsavory activity (An artist who holds back one of her current works for sale at a future time, when she hopes that it will bring a higher price, is a "speculator"), is it true that the artist is the sole source of all that market value?

At one level the question assumes a profound form: is the value of an artifact intrinsic or attributed? Was the value always there, placed in the work by the then unrecognized genius, merely waiting for recognition, or is it a social construct, the product of forces operating independently of the artist?

One common and superficially plausible argument in support of the *droit de suite* supposes that much of the increase in the value of earlier works now in the hands of collectors and museums is a result of the artist's genius and increasing reputation, which is in turn due to her continuing production of highly regarded works. Since the artist is the principal source of the increase in value, so the reasoning goes, it seems only fair that the artist share in the proceeds when her works are resold at a profit:

> [I]f a painting, which was initially bought for a few francs, later commands high sales prices, it is not because the painting improved with age. It is only because the author, who was unknown or unappreciated when he sold it, became famous and because that fame affects each of his works to which each new success gives a new value.[102]

One difficulty with this argument is that, as we have already seen, it ignores the value added to the artist's works by other art world players, such as critics, museums, collectors, dealers and auction houses. Another difficulty is that this argument only works to the artist's benefit if the work of art resells at a profit. But suppose it declines in value, as is far more often the case with the works of contemporary artists? Even recognized, successful artists sometimes have periods in which they produce disappointing work that resells at a loss, if it resells at all.

---

[101] Liliane de Pierredon-Fawcett, *The Droit de Suite in Literary and Artistic Property* (New Center for the Arts 1991).

[102] *Id.* at 12.

What happens when the vogue for a currently "hot" artist dies? Are those who bought her works entitled to a refund? Why not?

Many supporters of the resale proceeds right prefer to refer to it as a "resale royalty." Authors and composers, the argument goes, participate through royalties in the market success of their works. It is true that authors and composers can sell their works outright for an agreed price and forego royalties, as many do, but they have the option of bargaining for a royalty agreement with a publisher. Artists seldom have any such opportunity; hence the need for that *droit de suite*.

Of course artists can claim a copyright in their works, as authors do, and that gives them control over reproductions. For recognized, successful artists there may indeed be an appreciable market for reproductions for which they could contract with a publisher for royalties in the same way as authors and composers do. But, although making and selling multiple copies of the same work is a productive way of exploiting cast sculptures and "fine prints," it is less valuable for unique works, for which the normal method of exploitation is by exhibition.

An artist has the power to insist on an exhibition royalty by making it a term of the first sale, but there is no practicable way to make such an agreement "run with" the painting or sculpture to bind those who subsequently acquire it. These impediments to an exhibition fee could of course be corrected by amending the copyright act to give the artist continuing copyright control over public exhibition, analogous to the playwright's or composer's control over public performance of her work for profit. Or the artist could be expressly given a separate statutory right to an exhibition fee.

Artists' political action groups and artists' rights collection societies in the United States and Europe have not, however, pursued the exhibition fee idea with anything like the energy and enthusiasm that they have given to the *droit de suite*.

The resale proceeds right is also opposed by collectors, museums and some artists. They resist it for several kinds of reasons: collectors and museums because they see it as a tax that they would prefer not to pay when they dispose of works in the market; the art trade for the same reason and because they believe that it shifts some secondary market transactions (which are crucially important to most dealers and to their success in promoting the work of artists in the primary market) to jurisdictions that do not impose it. They observe that works of art are easily transportable to other markets, and they believe that at present the *droit de suite* by diverting auction transactions from France, significantly weakens the French and strengthens the British and American markets in contemporary art.

Knowledgeable artists oppose the right because they believe that it works to their disadvantage. They know that they have little possibility of significant income from the *droit de suite* because their works are not traded in the resale market.

There, indeed, a persuasive argument that the *droit de suite* would make things worse for most artists. Since the primary market is the artist's principal source of income, it is in the artist's interest that the supply of money available to buy the work of living artists remain stable or increase. The enactment of a resale proceeds right, however, is likely to have the opposite effect. The prospect of having to pay part of any resale proceeds to the artist may tilt those at the margin toward collecting something else: cubists or post-impressionists or surrealists or old masters or antiquities or, for that matter, oriental rugs or manuscripts or first editions or perfume bottles or classic automobiles or other collectibles to whose eventual resale the *droit de suite* does not apply.

At bottom my differences with supporters of the *droit de suite* can be explained by two related considerations. The first, already discussed above, is that these advocates display inadequate sensitivity to the art world as a whole. Their vision is dominated by the artist. The idea that other participants in the art world have legitimate functions and vulnerable interests does not arise. Though they mean well, these advocates are unfamiliar with the art market, particularly with the secondary market. They show little understanding of how critics, historians, collectors, museums, dealers and auctioneers add value to works of art. They seem unaware that, for most artists, participation in the resale market is unlikely and the probability of returns from the *droit de suite* small. Such errors lead them to suppose that the *droit de suite* costlessly offers substantial benefits to artists, when the costs—to collectors, museums and the art trade, and to most artists—are significant and the prospect of benefits to all but a small minority of artists remote.

Most fundamentally, the minds of some advocates of the *droit de suite* are confused by another tenet of the folklore: a peculiarly unsophisticated variety of market aversion that takes form as an expression of regret that works of art or other cultural objects are bought and sold — "commodification" is the currently stylish epithet. Collectors and dealers are denigrated as investors and speculators who contribute to the impairment of artistic values. Even museums, when they sell off works from their collections, become soulless commodifiers. Contact with the market soils the work of art, and participation in the market (except by artists who sell their works and might, under the *droit de suite*, receive a portion of resale proceeds) soils the participant. The people who invest their talent, time and money in activities that make and maintain the market for works of contemporary art, a market from which many artists derive the income that frees them to make art, are demonized. The art market and the art trade are transformed into enemies of Art, their interests unworthy of consideration in the debate about the desirability of enacting the *droit de suite*.

QUESTIONS AND COMMENTS FOR YOUR CONSIDERATION

1. Under US law, the first sale of a lawful copy embodying a copyrighted work extinguishes the author's right of control over the future distribution of that particular copy. How might Congress reconcile the first sale doctrine with droit de suite?

2. How would you resolve the administrative problems posed by a resale royalty? Are there other ways to support the goals of droit de suite without imposing a resale royalty?

3. Do the purported economic benefits outweigh the purported economic harm of droit de suite?

4. Does droit de suite pose the same problems of transplantation as droit morale?

6. The Foreign Experience With *Droit De Suite*[103]

Like Puccini's *La Boheme*, which opened with an artist and a poet shivering in a Paris garret, the *droit de suite* grew from a European, particularly French, awareness of the state of affairs of struggling artists at the turn of the century. Today, the *droit de suite*—the right of an artist to collect a part of the price paid when a work is resold—is based on the premise that visual artists are entitled to participate in an increase in the value of their works in ways that are not otherwise adequately addressed by copyright law.

The copyright law's rights of reproduction and distribution are better suited to exploitation of literary or musical works. A visual artist's expression is usually embodied in an end product, sold to a single purchaser. The artist's current work and reputation continue to affect the value of that earlier work. Many European countries, in the event of resale, allow artists to benefit from any increase in value of their works.

In 1920, France became the first country to recognize the *droit de suite*. Today, some 36 countries have the resale royalty, and several other countries that now purport to have *droit de suite*, however, lack implementing legislation. The level of commitment and the

---

[103] Reprinted from Copyright Office Report Executive Summary: *Droit de Suite:* The Artist's Resale Royalty.

characteristics of the national laws vary widely.

Whether the *droit de suite* will make the transition from an idealistic notion to an international norm depends both on commitment to *droit de suite* and creation of practical means to implement the goal of allowing artists to share in the profit of their work once it has left their hands.

Those countries that have most successfully implemented the *droit de suite* share certain characteristics. In France, Germany, and Belgium, for instance, the royalty is collected on the total resale price of the work. Measuring the royalty by the resale price departs from the rationale of allowing artists to participate in an *increase* in value, but is considered simpler and more practical. The difficulty in administering a royalty based on the difference between the purchase price and resale price may explain the law's disuse in countries such as Italy and Czechoslovakia.

Auctions are the minimum field of application in all countries which have adopted the *droit de suite,* because auctions sales are easiest to monitor. Including dealer sales increases the administrative challenge and the risk of noncompliance.

Although the *droit de suite* is inalienable and non-waivable, in almost all effective systems it may be transferred for purposes of collection through an artists' collecting agency.

The collection of the *droit de suite* through authors' societies is considered essential to a successful resale royalty. Only those countries with active and efficient national authors' societies, such as SABAM in Belgium, Bild-Kunst in Germany, and SPADEM and ADAGP in France, have effectively implement the *droit de suite.*

7. The *Droit De Suite* Debate in the US

a. The View of the Copyright Office[104]

The Copyright Office is not persuaded that sufficient economic and copyright policy justification exists to establish *droit de suite* in the United States. Neither the administrative hearing process nor independent research supplied the Office with sufficient current empirical data. Therefore, the Office could not accurately compare the respective remuneration of authors who create in many, and artists who create in limited, or unique, copies. Any conclusions that we could make about the number of artists who would benefit from the resale royalty would be based on anecdotal evidence and limited sample size. Most significantly, there is no clear evidence indicating the frequency of resale of works of fine art. Thus, even if Congress determines that the Copyright Act does treat fine visual artists in a manner less favorable than authors or composers, it is not clear that the resale royalty right is the best means to offset this disadvantage, particularly if it is not triggered with any frequency within the copyright term.

Many countries currently offer alternative solutions to improve artists rights that the United States might want to consider. Although the Copyright Office does not necessarily endorse any alternative solution, Congress might want to consider these alternatives:

Assuming that fine visual artists cannot exploit their intellectual property rights adequately under the existing copyright law, some form of broadened public display right might be an alternative to the *droit de suite.* Rather than depending on frequent resales within the specified royalty term, a considerable problem of the *droit de suite*, the display right would be triggered by the typical manner of exploitation of works of fine art—public display. Museums and public art galleries might pay a fee to display works of art publicly.

In theory, Section 106(5) of the Copyright Act already provides creators of pictorial, graphic and sculptural works with a public display right. However, the right is cut off by the First Sale doctrine in Section 109(c), that permits the owner of a copy to display his or her work publicly to viewers present at the place where the copy is located. Thus, with the *sale* of a unique work, the copyright owner is left with nothing to display, and with works created in limited copies the creator and object owner may mount competing displays.

---

[104] Reprinted from Copyright Office Report Executive Summary: *Droit de Suite*: The Artist's Resale Royalty.

Under existing law, if a work of art is alienated solely by rental, the artist retains the exclusive distribution right. However, very few artists have the market power to structure the art transactions so that works are rented and ownership of the copy of the work does not pass to the purchaser.

Even with works that are sold, the Copyright Act could be amended to allow the distribution right to survive with respect to commercial rental. The owner of the copy would receive the object, while the artist would retain the right to exploit the work by commercial rental. Thus, the owner of the copy would pay the artist a royalty for any commercial rental of the purchased work.

Another way to balance the interests of artists and collectors would be through some form of compulsory licensing and modification of Section 109. Upon payment to an artist of the purchase price for a work and a licensing fee for public display, the owner of a copy would be free to display the work with having to negotiate terms with the artist. Congress could also encourage artists by increasing federal grants or by increasing funding for purchase of artworks for federal buildings.

Should Congress determine that federal *droit de suite* legislation is the best way to help artists, the Copyright Office suggests consideration for the following model system.

The *droit de suite* has been effectively implemented only in those countries with active and efficient national authors' societies, such as SPADEM, in France and Bild-Kunst in Germany. Therefore, the Copyright Office suggests that Congress consider collective management of the *droit de suite* through a private authors' rights collecting society. The collection of art resale royalties would be handled on a direct or contractual basis, similar to collection of musical performance royalties by ASCAP and BMI.

The Copyright Office suggests that, if a resale royalty is enacted in the United States, it should apply initially only to public auction sales. Auction sales are easiest to monitor. Including dealer sales—or private sales . . . increases the administrative and enforcement challenge.

Based on the California and European experiences, a flat royalty of between three and five percent on the total gross sales price of the work seems most appropriate. There would be no need initially to set a threshold price to trigger the royalty mechanism if the royalty were applied initially only to auction sales, because auction sales usually deal in works with a minimum floor price.

In those countries that have most successfully implemented the *droit de suite*, including France, Germany and Belgium, the resale royalty is measured on the total resale price. Measuring the royalty by the resale price departs from the rationale of allowing artists to participate in an *increase* in value, but is considered simpler and more practical. The difficulty in administering a royalty based on the difference between the purchase price and resale price may explain the law's disuse in countries such as Italy and Czechoslovakia.

Any resale royalty legislation could contain a rebuttable presumption that a work has increased in value between the time of purchase and resale. The purchaser/reseller would have the burden of proving to the collecting society that a work had not appreciated in value and that a royalty was not due.

A term for the *droit de suite* coextensive with copyright seems appropriate. Under the current copyright law, this life of the author plus 50 years.

The *droit de suite* would be descendible in a manner analogous to copyright.

The resale royalty would be applied to foreign artists on the basis of reciprocity. This is consistent with the Berne Convention and the general consensus.

The Berne Convention recognizes an inalienable right to the resale royalty. The Office concludes that if a resale royalty is enacted in the United States it should be inalienable, but transferrable for purposes of assigning collection rights. The Office also suggests that the *droit de suite* be non-waivable. However, this latter suggestion may be subject to the ultimate resolution of the waivability of moral rights in the United States.

The Copyright Office suggests that any *droit de suite* legislation apply to works of visual art as defined in 16 U.S.A. § 101 and in the Visual Artists Rights Act of 1990, with the following exception: For works in limited edition, the Copyright Office would suggest that the statute should fix the number of copies to which the resale royalty would apply at 10 or fewer.

The Office suggests that, if Congress adopts a *droit de suite*, it should make the law prospective only, *i.e.*, effective only as to the resale of eligible works created on or after the date the law becomes effective.

b. Reply[105]

We have a different understanding of two basic areas: the function of creative works in the world and the role of artists in the socio-economic system.

The first area is pertinent because most of the thinking and comment concerning resale loyalty compares the sale of dissimilar objects: copies of books, or copies of musical scores are compared to a painting or a sculpture. As the Copyright Office correctly notes, this analogy is not useful clearly to delineate a new exploitation of the creative work.

The most appropriate analogy is to compare the painting to the original manuscript and the original score. None of these creative works, these objects, are fully functional in the marketplace until they serve their intended USE, that of communication. The book must be read, the play must be seen and heard, the music must be heard, and the painting must be seen, in order to be exploitable in the economic system. It is clear to any creator that what is really being transacted in the marketplace, whether book, music, play or painting, is the communicative use of the creations. If they were simply self expression, their purpose would be complete without putting them into the marketplace. Therefore, when the writer or musician receives a royalty it is really for the use of their creations not the actual objects they created. When a song is played on the radio, the royalty is obviously for use, not for an object.

Since it is possible to make copies of manuscripts and scores in order to use them, it is possible and usual to have both parallel and serial use of the creator's original. However, by definition, unique works of art cannot be duplicated, so the intended communicative use can only be accomplished serially. When the painting is sold, the artist's portion of the price is for the intended use: the seeing of the painting, the artist communicating to the audience. And when it is sold again, it is being used again by a different audience, just as the play or the music is used by a different group of people, at a different time, with the author receiving a royalty for each new production. The communicative use of the originals, whether by parallel or by serial mode, is called for by the very foundation of the Copyright law, Article I, Section 8, clause 8, of the Constitution, which gives Congress the power to promote the "progress of science" by giving creators "exclusive rights" to their "respective writings." The Register's Report speaks to this very issue: "this constitutional framework serves as a logical matrix for balancing creator and user rights."[106] Therefore, contrary to the final conclusion in the Report, the resale is "actually a new exploitation of the work" and therefore a "legitimate economic interest of visual artists."

The role of the artists in the socio-economic world of the art marketplace is widely misunderstood or unknown, but is vital to the discussion of resale royalty.

When Mr. Weber [of Weber Gallery in New York] said that art is not considered a serious endeavor by people in our country, he pointed to the debilitating romantic myth about artists that permeates American society, the myth that the artist "must" and "will" create, no matter what hardships or poverty, like a mindless creature or a machine. This myth was voiced several times by the opposition to resale royalty to prove that resale royalty would not encourage creativity as the copyright law intends. It is clearly behind the attitude that everyone else should be making money from art and taking no risks, but artists should be happy to just make art: behind the complaints of opponents of resale royalty is the belief that the wealth artists should get more wealthy. As dealers and

---

[105] Carol Sky, *Report of the Register of Copyrights Concerning* Droit De Suite, *The Artist's Resale Royalty: A Response,* J. OF COPYRIGHT SOC'Y 315. Copyright 1992 Carol Sky. Excerpt reprinted by permission.

[106] Register's Report at 128.

collectors clearly find nothing wrong with greater return on their investment, it is difficult to see why it should bother them for artists to do the same. This is the myth that has allowed the art market to function with absolutely no oversight.

Art is a serious endeavor. Artists run serious business, with all the concomitant expenses and problems of any business. In addition to making the art, artists must do the promotion, distribution, bookkeeping, office work, transportation, and if they must hire help, s/he must also deal with the employee issues. They do not simply stand in front of an easel or a block of stone.

It is apparent, in the real-life action of the art market, that the collector is paying the gallery or auction very well for services, and is receiving exactly what was bought, the use of an aesthetic object. In addition, perhaps the collector will make a profit in the future. The dealer will make another profit on any further action. The expenses of the dealer or auction house are being partially underwritten by both the collector and the artist. This market could not exist without the artist producing art. The artist produces it on about 30% of the sales price, which may go up to 50% or 60% at most, if s/he can keep going long enough and is lucky enough to become very successful. And, as can be seen, the artist has no bargaining power, almost no laws or regulations protecting his or her interests in the art market and is clearly at risk throughout the market process. In opinion of National Artists Equity Association (NAEA) the information in the Register's Report confirms the fact that artists are economically disadvantaged because they do not have the leverage or the legal framework to allow them to profit from their work in the same way that authors of reproducible objects may profit.

Throughout the Report, there are two assumptions that are interesting when looked at together. The first is that all or most contemporary art declines in value. The Report also assumes that the major reason collectors buy contemporary art is for investment purposes. The reality of the art market is that almost all collectors buy art because they like a specific work.

The Report emphatically states that the "encumbrance" of resale royalty is "antithetical to our tradition of free alienability of property." However, there is a long tradition of real estate encumbrance, such as deed restrictions and zoning laws.

QUESTIONS AND COMMENTS FOR YOUR CONSIDERATION

1. If artists create works for non-monetary reasons, what impact does or should this fact have on the debate over *droit de suite*?

2. If *droit de suite* is not inalienable, how can an author avoid being forced to give up her rights by more powerful publishers?

3. What benefit, if any, is obtained by granting a transferable, waivable *droit de suite*?

4. If performers are given the right to control their performances, what impact would such right of control have on the compensation for the author of the underlying work? Won't such control reduce an author's compensation since it will force the author to "split the pie" with the performer?

5. How effective are the proposed alternatives to *droit de suite*?

6. How would you resolve the problems of administration and compliance posed by a resale royalty?

D. Applications

1. Performance Art[107]

A young playwright, enrolled in a college graduate program, writes a two act play and directs and produces the initial performance of his work for the annual college theater festival. Funny, energetic, and a bit weird, his play is the hit of the festival. Subsequently, the playwright agrees to a more elaborate and "fully realized" production of his script, directed and produced by a fellow graduate student. Halfway through the rehearsal period, the playwright visits a rehearsal. He is shocked to discover that his eccentric, funny work has been twisted into a turgid, overly serious "soap-opera." The playwright protests and demands that the director stage his play in accordance with the manifest intent contained in the playwright's script. The director refuses, claiming the right to interpret and stage the author's play as the director sees fit. On opening night, prior to the commencement of the play, the playwright disavows the production to the discomforted audience.

Another example of college art students taking themselves too seriously? Perhaps; however, the incident graphically illustrates a conflict between the authors and interpreters of performance art that extends well beyond the academic environment. Indeed, the conflict between authors and interpreters of performance art at one time or another has affected much of the professional performance art community.

One of the most dramatic manifestations of this conflict began in 1984 when the Boston American Repertory Theater (Boston ART) purchased the rights to produce Samuel Beckett's "Endgame." Pursuant to these rights, the Boston ART staged a production of "Endgame" that allegedly made significant departures from Mr. Beckett's script. Instead of setting the play in a bare, cell-like room, as specified in Mr. Beckett's script, the Boston ART set the play in an abandoned subway tunnel with a bombed out subway car extending halfway across the stage. The Boston ART also cast two black actors to perform characters specifically described as white in Mr. Beckett's script. At one point during the play these actors froze silently in place while their lines were spoken out over an amplified sound system emanating from the rear of the theater. Finally, instead of the specified silence preceding the play's beginning, the Boston ART added an overture that Phillip Glass composed. Beckett asserted that these changes violated his rights as the author of "Endgame."

Mr. Beckett is not the only notable professional playwright to object to novel interpretations of his works.

The above described incidents all involve a conflict that pits performance art authors—playwrights, composers and choreographers—against the interpretive artists—directors, conductors and choreographers—who stage the authors' works. The authors of performance art are asserting a right to control the use of their work to protect the artistic vision they have imbued in their work, while the interpretive artists are claiming the right to control the author's work to communicate their own artistic vision.

Because all artists have impressed their thoughts and feelings, their inner being, into their art, artists want to control the presentation of their work. Artists are not the only creators who materialize themselves in their creations, but because the artistic mediums are subject to relatively few constraints of economy, efficiency, and physical environment, artists can inject more of their personalities into their creations than can the creator of a drill press.

The artist's freedom to inject his personality into his art is a double-edged sword, however. Because an artist's art largely is free from the constraints of economy, efficiency and physical environment, individuals other than the artist can easily distort or change the art. If an individual distorts or changes the artist's art, then the individual changes the artist's manifestation of his personality, and thereby wounds the artist's feelings. Thus, the plethora of personality in art, in concert with the fragility of its manifestation explains why artists attempt to control the presentation of their art and justifies recognition of the unique right of artists to protect the manifestations of their personalities

[107] Otto W. Konrad, *A Federal Recognition of Performance Art Author Moral Rights,* 48 WASH. & LEE L. REV. 1579. Copyright 1991 Washington & Lee Law Review. Excerpt reprinted with permission.

from distortion by others: an artist's moral right.

Europe and a large part of the Third World long have incorporated into their respective common-law and legislative schemes some form of moral rights protection for artists, including the authors of performance art. Within America, however, legal recognition of the moral rights doctrine has been much more recent and limited in scope. State and federal courts never have recognized artists' moral rights. State legislatures have recognized the doctrine, but they have limited its reach to the creators of visual art. Congress has followed the lead of these state legislatures and limited its recognition of moral rights to the creators of visual art. Thus, within the United States, a performance art author finds no explicit, legal recognition of his moral rights.

Any federal moral rights legislation must contend with two provisions of the United States Constitution: the copyright clause and the First Amendment. Of the two, the copyright clause is the least problematic. The United States Constitution provides that "Congress shall have the power ... [t]o promote the Progress of Science and useful Arts, by securing for Limited Times to Authors and Inventors the exclusive Right to their respective Writings and Discoveries." The United States Supreme Court has interpreted this language to mandate that any statute Congress enacts pursuant to the copyright clause must have the end of promoting the useful arts. The copyright clause is unique among the Article I powers because it explicitly specifies the means that Congress may use to reach the end of promoting the useful arts. That is, Congress must promote the useful arts and sciences by granting "Authors ... the exclusive Right to their respective" creations. In the past the Court has limited the meaning of this language to giving artists economic monopolies in their works, in other words, copyrights. Because moral rights, particularly integrity rights, embody the author's personality interests rather than the author's economic interests, congressional enactment of a moral rights statute for performance art authors could conflict with the Court's reading of the copyright clause's specified means.

The apparent conflict between a performance art author's moral rights and the copyright clause's specified means is illusory in nature, however. While in the past the Court has interpreted the word "Right" to denote economic right, the Court's interpretation only may reflect the fact that, until recently, the only rights Congress has attempted to confer on artists have been economic rights. In any case, the copyright clause itself does not delineate what the term "Right" encompasses. Thus, pursuant to the necessary and proper clause of the Constitution, Congress could expand the term "Right" to encompass the personality interests of performance art authors, provided the expanded definition of "Right" furthered the copyright clause's end of promoting the useful arts. Because moral rights protection for performance art authors would afford a security to performance art authors that would encourage creative activity, expanding the term "Right" to encompass such protections would promote the useful arts.

The First Amendment presents the most serious challenge to any federal statute extending moral rights protection to the performance art authors. Commentators consistently have suggested that a recognition of performance art author moral rights, particularly performance art author integrity rights, would abridge the First Amendment rights of the interpretive artists who perform the works of performance art authors. Whether or not these commentators ultimately are correct, because of performance art's unique collaborative aspects, affording moral rights protection to performance art authors raises more First Amendment concerns than moral rights recognition in any other artistic context.

For instance, in comparing performance art to visual art, the creator of a work of visual art originates and realizes the work by fixing it in a permanent, finished form. From that point forward, the only interaction with the visual artist's work typically will involve passive spectator observation, observation entailing very little communicative activity. In contrast, once an author has created a work of performance art, typically individuals other than the author will have to contribute effort involving communicative activity to fully realize the author's work. For example, while the composer of a symphonic work creates a self-contained piece of art in the form of finished sheet music, a conductor and many different musicians must perform the author's work to fully realize it. Thus, because of performance art's collaborative aspects, performance art affords many more opportunities for communicative activity than does visual art. As a result, Congress implicates the First Amendment if it attempts to control this communicative activity through statutory recognition of the moral rights of performance art authors.

Any analysis of the First Amendment issues surrounding federal recognition of a performance art author's basic moral right must begin with the concession that such legislation, particularly its integrity right component, would abridge the range of expression that interpretive artists could exercise when performing an author's work. When an interpretive artist performs an author's work in such a manner as to diverge from the author's text or fails to give correct attribution to the author, to some extent the interpretive artist is engaging in communicative activities. Federal legislation that punishes interpretive artists for such communicative acts would appear to fly directly in the face of the First Amendment's command: "Congress shall make no law ... abridging the freedom of speech."

However, the courts never have held that every law abridging an individual's expressive conduct violates the First Amendment. Instead, the courts have engaged in what Professor Nimmer has called "definitional balancing" to determine whether the First Amendment's protection encompasses a particular type of speech.[108]

To withstand a First Amendment challenge any federal legislation according performance art author moral rights would have to encompass an appropriate definitional balance. In developing such a definitional balance, one might consider importing copyright law's recognized demarcation between protected and unprotected speech, the "idea/expression dichotomy."

At first consideration, the idea/expression dichotomy appears aptly suited to the context of moral rights for performance art authors. A performance art author's moral rights only would encompass the author's expression. An author's integrity and paternity rights never would extend to the theme, message, or idea that a work of performance art attempts to communicate. Thus, an interpretive artist, with impunity, could inject new ideas into the author's work, distort the original ideas contained in the author's work or refuse to give attribution to the author's original ideas.

Despite the facial suitability of the idea/expression dichotomy as a definitional balance for performance art author moral rights, the idea/expression dichotomy and performance art moral rights, particularly integrity rights, are incompatible. This incompatibility stems from the fact that, particularly within the context of the performing arts, the distinctions between idea and expression are meaningless. Idea and manifested expression often are inextricably intertwined in performance art. In other words, the elements compromising the expressive component of a work of performance art—be they words, musical notes, characters, or movement—define the author's underlying ideas. Therefore, any modification to the author's expression, in some subtle manner, will inject new ideas into the author's work—ideas with First Amendment protection.

In practice, interpretive artists would attempt to use the intertwined nature of idea and expression to circumvent liability for violations of an author's integrity rights. Specifically, whenever an interpretive artist distorted an author's work in a manner actionable under moral rights legislation, the interpretive artist would assert that he had engaged in a form of "idea" creation that the First Amendment protects. Indeed, to secure the protection of the idea/expression dichotomy, interpretive artists would ensure that all of their modifications to authors' works reflected new ideas.

These observations lead to the following proposed demarcation between protected and unprotected speech: (1) where an interpretive artist incorporates speech into a performance of an author's work that is consistent with the author's message or the author's expression of that message, the First Amendment protects the interpretive artist's speech and prevents the government

---

[108] Melville. Nimmer, *Does Copyright Abridge the First Amendment Guarantees of Free Speech and Press?,* 17 U.C.L.A. Rev. 1180, 1184-90 (1970).

from regulating it; (2) where the interpretive artist incorporates speech into a performance of an author's work that modifies the author's message or expression of that message, the First Amendment does not protect the interpretive artist's speech, and the government may regulate it. The terms "author's message" or "author's expression" encompass any statement the author inserts in his work, including any attribution of authorship to the author. The term "modify" encompasses the interpretive artist's failure to communicate any message the author has placed in his work, including statements of authorship. Thus, this demarcation encompasses both the performance art author's rights of paternity and integrity. [For ease of discussion this demarcation will be termed "the corrective view of moral rights" or "corrective view"].

Having established a tentative demarcation for a basic performance art author moral right, the next step in a definitional balance analysis is to consider whether this demarcation advances the interests underlying both federal moral rights recognition and the First Amendment. The corrective view advances the copyright clause purpose that must underlie any congressional conference of exclusive rights on authors, promotion of the useful arts. If performance art authors are assured that their undistorted messages will reach the public, authors are encouraged to create, and, accordingly, will do so more often. In addition, because the corrective view allows performance art authors to protect the personality interests in their works, the corrective view furthers the interests underlying moral rights recognition for performance art authors.

However, the corrective view of moral rights hampers the interpretive artist's ability to modify the performance art author's message. This hampering may curtail the interpretive artist's freedom of expression. However, expression that distorts or silences another's message harms the marketplace of ideas and thus, should be subject to legal regulation. Therefore, the corrective view of moral rights does not encroach upon the First Amendment simply because it abridges an interpretive artist's ability to modify an author's message.

The corrective view of moral rights conditions an interpretive artist's liability on whether or not the interpretive artist's expressive conduct modifies speech that the author placed in his work of performance art. If federal legislation limited the "author's speech" to the explicit expression contained in the author's actual work of performance art (including the author's statement of authorship), determining moral rights liability would be a fairly straightforward task for the courts. Essentially, the courts would compare the alleged modification with the pertinent portions of the author's work of performance art.

Any vagueness inherent in this analysis would be limited to situations where the author's message was particularly subtle. In such instances it might be difficult for the courts to ascertain whether an interpretive artist's performance has diverted from the author's message. Nonetheless, the analysis would remain a simple process of comparison. As a result, the corrective view of moral rights continues to be a simple and fairly clear demarcation between protected and unprotected speech, particularly when compared to other demarcations that the United States Supreme Court has accepted.

QUESTIONS AND COMMENTS FOR YOUR CONSIDERATION

1. Should moral rights protection be extended to performance art?
2. Where should you strike the balance between the rights of the underlying artist and the performer's rights?

2. Motion Pictures[109]

In the United States, creators and producers of motion pictures are protected by the Copyright Act of 1976. Some countries (especially those of the civil law tradition) distinguish rights in such works from rights in other works, based upon the nature of the right holder, creator or corporate financier. The difference is largely due to the philosophical underpinnings of the copyright and author's right laws.

When protection of works was first shifting in the seventeenth century from a sovereign privilege to a statutory right, two schools of thought emerged. One school, natural law, was absorbed into the civil law countries and promoted especially by France and Germany. Because the authors invested their creativity, the works belonged to them. This school advanced the notion that protection should extend to both the author's economic and personal interests. Statutes merely codified these naturally existing rights.

With the advent of modern cinematography, its corporate organization and other technological advances, laws based upon natural law principles proved inefficient and inadequate because such laws do not extend full protection to corporate entities. On the basis of these principles, ownership of rights in a motion picture always vests in an individual first—only then may those rights be transferred or licensed; however, the personal rights remain with the creators. Because the focus is on the individual, this school is often referred to as recognizing *droit d'auteur* or author's right. This system poses a difficult problem for modern marketing of motion pictures. All the rights of each of the individuals involved must be addressed. A shortcut developed, in the form of presumptions as to ownership of rights and neighboring rights, to allow effective exploitation of the work.

Meanwhile, the common law was developing in a different way. Common law countries, especially the United States and the United Kingdom, recognized a common law right of perpetual duration based upon natural property rights; however, when codified by the legislators, only limited economic protection was extended to authors. The statutes did not codify natural law, they replaced it and created economic rights initially in the form of an exclusive reproduction right for a limited time. The purpose of this exclusive right was to protect the economic rights held by creators or publishers who purchased the original creator's rights. Thus, creators relinquished all rights in a work (unless otherwise contractually agreed) in exchange for pecuniary recompense.

In contrast to the situation in author's right countries, the developing motion picture industry brought no need to change the basis of the copyright protection system in the common law countries. Full economic rights could be held by a corporate entity.

In the latter half of the twentieth century, international copyright protection has become of much greater concern, as the motion picture industry has become supranational. This has brought a clash of the two systems and their philosophies. Author's right countries (*e.g.*, France and Germany) focus almost exclusively on the individual creator, while the common law countries (*e.g.*, United States and the United Kingdom) focus on the owner of the copyright, whether that is the creator, publisher, broadcaster or corporation.

In the United States, freedom of contract is one of the most sacred principles. Yet with the growing international emphasis on natural law (at least in the copyright field) and its own deeply rooted principles of meritocracy and individual recognition, the United States is being forced to rethink its copyright laws to protect the creator's noneconomic rights.

The owner of a copyright in an audiovisual work, including motion pictures, holds all the economic rights secured by the 1976 US Copyright Act. Audiovisual works are expressly identified as a category of copyrightable material.

Copyright in an audiovisual work includes the exclusive right to reproduce the work, to prepare derivative works, to distribute, and to perform or display the work publicly. For an audiovisual work, these rights encompass the entire work; however, they

---

[109] Laura A. Pitta, *Economic and Moral Rights under US Copyright Law: Protecting Authors and Producers in the Motion Picture Industry,* 12 ENT. & SPORTS LAWYER 3. Copyright Laura A. Pitta. Excerpt reprinted with permission.

do not affect the rights of underlying works. Because the derivative work is distinct from the underlying work, the legal owner of a copyrighted audiovisual work (the derivative work) holds full economic rights in such work.

The initial owner of copyright is the individual creator of the work unless the work is a "work made for hire." If a work is one made for hire, the employer is regarded as the author and is the initial owner in the copyright. A work is deemed a "work made for hire" if it is (1) prepared by an employee within the scope of his or her employment; or (2) a specifically commissioned work falling within one of nine enumerated categories, including motion pictures.

This is the essence of US copyright protection of motion pictures. The protection primarily benefits those who financed the production.

Producers of commercial motion pictures under author's right systems may receive protection in two forms: a legal fiction of the transfer of certain rights to the producer (usually corporate entity) and a neighboring right, a separate independent right granted to the producer.

The legal fiction of the transfer of certain rights is a presumption at law of an assignment or license of the economic rights of the authors of a motion picture to the producer. The presumption is most often statutory and found in the author's right statutory code of a country. The most striking legal fiction in the laws of Germany and France is the presumption from a contract between an author and producer of a motion picture that the economic rights (fixation, reproduction and public display rights) are licensed or transferred exclusively to the producer. The moral rights, however, remain with the creators and are inalienable. In a commercial motion picture, this may include a large number of individuals who have made a creative contribution.

Both the French and German systems have stop-gap measures to indicate the identity of the authors of a motion picture or audiovisual work for legal purposes. In France, the authors are presumed, in the absence of contrary proof, to be the author of the script, the author of the adaptation, the author of the dialogue, the author of the music composed for the work, and the director. Germany does not define the motion picture authors in its statutory code; however, German jurisprudence looks first to the director, cameraman and cutter as the authors. The designation of such individuals as authors of a motion picture is perhaps most critical when issues of moral rights arise, as these rights cannot be alienated.

The recognition that effective exploitation of a motion picture is best achieved by the producer led to legal presumptions of transfer of the creators' economic rights.

In addition to the rights granted through legal presumptions, producers often receive a separate and distinct right, a neighboring right. The Rome Convention of 1961 is the primary international document that recognizes neighboring rights as a conception separate from author's rights, but does not cover rights of motion picture producers. The Rome Convention focuses on protection of the "rights of performers, producers of phonograms, and broadcasting organizations."

This protection is critical in countries that only recognize the creators of works under their author's right laws. Thus, phonogram producers, performers and broadcasters receive a distinct but related type of protection. The Convention was written at a time when a great need was perceived for the protection of performers and producers of phonograms. Under many author's right systems, the producers of phonograms held no statutory rights of their own, such as reproduction or performance. The Rome Convention was designed to remedy this situation.[110]

Several countries also extended neighboring rights to producers of motion pictures and other cinematographic works. In fact, the neighboring rights often duplicate the rights transferred from the author to the producer under the presumption of transfer laws. However, neighboring rights were thought to be a necessary addition to the producer's arsenal to control piracy and to strengthen the bargaining position with licensees, such as broadcasters.

Both Germany and France grant a neighboring right that covers reproduction and performance to the producer of a motion picture. This right has a duration of fifty years;

---

[110] *Editors' Note:* For a detailed discussion of The Rome Convention, *see* Chapter Four.

and the author's right has a duration of life plus seventy years. Because the producer holds both a neighboring right and the economic rights of the authors under the presumption of transfer, the producer may not only exercise the neighboring right for fifty years, but may also exercise the author's rights for the length of the life of the longest living specified contributor plus seventy years!

The Berne Convention does not address the issue of neighboring rights, but touches on areas directly affecting such rights. Article 9 guarantees the right of reproduction in general. Article 11 ensures the author's right of public performance and communication to the public for the full copyright term. Article 11 gives the author the right to control broadcast, rebroadcast and other public communications of the work. Under the Berne Convention, however, it is left to each signatory nation to define who is an author. Thus, author's right systems may exclude corporate entities from "authorship" without running afoul of their international obligations.

The philosophical schism between the common law and author's right countries is straining relations in the intellectual property field. Some argue that productions that are deemed protected under neighboring rights doctrines are not Berne-protected. Thus, the Berne Convention philosophy of national treatment may give way to the "tit-for-tat" philosophy of reciprocity. National treatment requires that a Berne-member state give the same protection to foreign nationals of other Berne-member states that it provides to its own nationals. The reciprocity standard, in contrast, gives a foreigner protection only if the foreigner's country provides the same rights to the citizens of the country where protection is claimed. The philosophy of unconditional national treatment envisions a world where protection is based upon the worthiness of the production rather than the nationality of the author. Thus, the national treatment provisions of the Berne Convention are critical to the evolution of international harmonization of copyright protection.

An example of this strain is the French 1985 home taping law. Under the law, a royalty is collected on the sale of blank audio and visual tape. Its goal was to recompense authors' right holders for violations of their rights directly as a result of home taping. Twenty-five percent goes to a cultural fund, and 75 percent is divided among authors, producers and performers. The majority of works for which royalties are collected are US works, yet the cultural fund generated by the royalty pool subsidizes only French artists. European blank video and audio tape royalty collections amounted to over $150 million in 1988, yet Americans received an insignificant amount of these funds. It is argued that the statutes are not copyright laws, but "cultural endowments or tax laws," and alternatively that the works concerned are not Berne-protected subject matter. Additionally, it is argued that the United States has no comparable legislation, and is not a signatory to the Rome Convention on Neighboring Rights. Hence, the conclusion from these arguments is that US authors, creators, and producers are not subject to national treatment provisions.

In fact, the United States does have comparable legislation within the federal Copyright Act. The Audio Home Recording Act first enacted in 1992 imposes a statutory obligation to pay royalties based upon the manufacture or distribution of blank digital cassette tapes and home recording equipment within the United States. Royalties are designed partially to compensate authors and performers of sound recordings for home taping. Because the legislation is within the federal Copyright Act, national treatment obligations are applicable and a share of the royalties is available to all authors who are Berne Convention nationals in respect to protected material. Register of Copyrights Marybeth Peters states that current claimants include composers, lyricists, music publishers, music companies and performing artists from the US and other nations.

Although many European nations give national treatment with respect to royalties, some counter this argument saying that the United States does not provide significant reciprocity. The US law covers only the digital audio sector at roughly a 3 percent levy; some European nations such as Denmark cover both digital and analog, audio and visual tapes at a higher levy. Although the levy is larger, not all of it is returned to the right-holders; it is in part set aside to subsidize national artists. Additionally, under the Berne Convention national treatment standard, such comparisons are not appropriate. A signatory nation is obliged to grant national treatment without comparing the standards of the other nation's protection.

Another strain on relations is the possibility of *sui generis* protection for certain works, such as computer programs, data bases, and audiovisual works. It may be claimed that the subject matter is not Berne-protected, and thus a nation can create its own standards, including reciprocity requirements.

Americans are up in arms at what is seen as a violation of the terms and spirit of the Berne Convention. Also, they dread the prospect of having to negotiate each subject matter area separately, and feel that these laws have been implemented in an effort to exclude US producers and creators from the higher standards of protection available under these ancillary systems. Former US Register of Copyrights Ralph Oman stated his concern regarding the growth of such systems that

> siphon off effective protection from the copyright realm (for example, so-called video producers' right that would displace the Berne Convention concept of the "film maker" and let the Europeans bilk American film companies out of millions of dollars).

The perception that some author's right countries set up ancillary systems in an effort to circumvent national treatment provisions and discriminate against US artists and industries continues to grow. This view may be justified given that although the United Sates has enacted comparable laws (especially with regard to home taping), US right-holders in such nations could continue to be denied their just due because of subsidies to nationals deemed outside of the Berne Convention and reciprocity standards imposed instead of national treatment.

The United States has taken an expansive view toward Berne-protected works as compared to those of some author's right countries. The controversial areas regarding ownership are directly covered by US copyright law; author's right nations protect these areas by ancillary systems and neighboring rights systems. The United States refuses to recognize such rights as outside the Berne Convention, thus applying national treatment standards. In contrast, some author's right countries refuse to recognize ownership as in the common law nations.

The author's right countries have had great influence over the course of the development of the Berne Convention. For example, they have expanded protection under the Convention to include moral rights. The common law nations could not resist the tide indefinitely and have recognized these principles in their own laws.

Author's-right systems have also reshaped their laws to accommodate the need for protecting the interests of corporate financiers, a growing presence especially in the motion picture industry. But an imbalance persists: New ancillary laws designed to provide rewards for creators, such as blank tape levies are deemed outside of the Berne Convention, and consequently national treatment provisions do not apply. The United States is pushing for a broad reading of the Berne Convention, which includes all systems: author's right, neighboring right and ancillary systems.

The Berne Convention is to remain the respected standard of international copyright in the world. It must come to terms with all related subject matter. Corporate funding of the arts is becoming more the norm than the exception. Remedies for violations of rights available in national laws must be extended to all right-holders, creators and corporate financiers. National treatment in all related areas of protection is critical to the evolution of copyright protection on the international level. To exclude such subject matter from the Berne Convention would portend its failure.

Under the United States laws, creators and producers of audiovisual works receive more legal protection now than at any other time in history. Economic and moral rights are deeply rooted in its philosophy and are gaining strength in US laws. The United States had not recognized moral rights as intrinsic to its copyright laws until recently. Author's-right countries have long emphasized creator's rights over the rights of corporate financiers. The systems are slowly being forced to come together: The United States has recognized moral rights as a part of its legal protection under the Berne Convention, albeit under a patchwork of common law principles; author's right countries have provided for protection of corporate financiers, recognizing the necessity for effective exploitation of motion pictures. All laws related to author's right should be considered with the Berne Convention national treatment standards, regardless of the corporate or personal status of the owner. They should give authors and producers of motion pictures the legal right to recompense for their contributions. Only then will the barriers of nationality fall and be replaced by a harmonized system of international copyright protection based upon recognition of constituent worth without discrimination as to national origin.

QUESTIONS AND COMMENTS FOR YOUR CONSIDERATION

1. What impact does the definition of the "author" of a film have on the question of moral rights? Can more than one person be an author of a film? If so, what impact, if any, would this have on the ability to market a film for broadcast? on cable? on home video?

2. For a further discussion of the role of authorship on intellectual property protection, *see* Chapter Two.

3. The US protects cinematographic works as copyrighted works and grants protection to producers, performers and broadcasters under copyright law. Other nations grant protection as a right neighboring or ancillary to copyright protection. For a more detailed discussion of neighboring rights, see Chapter Four. What practical difference does it make whether a producer's right to control the reproduction of her film is protected under copyright or a neighboring right?

3. Parodies[111]

What transforms parodies from merely derivative humorous works into special works having "social value beyond (their) entertainment function," is the critical comment every "true" parody makes on the original at the same time as it makes us laugh. This critical and comic design endows parody with independent social and literary merit as a manifestation of both free speech and creativity. Parodies deserve a special place in copyright law, which the economic rights approach in copyright law wrongfully denies them.

Economic rights in the context of copyright are essentially legal property rights in a work. A copyright owner is given exclusive rights to enable him or her to profit from the commercial exploitation of protected works. In Australia and other English speaking countries both copyright legislation and case law are predicated upon these economic rights and no exception is made for parodies. By contract Continental European countries, most notably France, are not only concerned with the protection of the copyright owner's economic rights; they also protect moral rights in his or her creation. The moral rights theory regards an author's work as a manifestation of his or her personality, and ascribes an inalienable legal bond between authors and their works.

Since parody is aimed at the author's modes of expression and characteristic turns of thought or phrase, it is principally an attack upon the author's personality manifested in his or her creation. It is not an attack on his or her ability (or that of any assignee of the author's economic rights) to profit from, or exploit commercially, the copyright.

Indeed, more often than not, a parody may actually enhance an author's economic rights through increased demand for the original work thus given additional exposure and treatment.

———

[111]Moana Weir, *Making Sense of Copyright Law Relating to Parody: A Moral Rights Perspective,* 18 MONASH US REV. 194. Copyright 1992 Moana Weir. Excerpt reprinted with permission.

It has been said that to place parody in the context of the author's "right to respect" is nonsensical since a parody by definition aims to distort the original author's work and to treat it irreverently and comically. But whether such irreverence teaches the author's honor and reputation is a question of degree which a Court can determine on the facts of a particular case. The law can and should ensure that the secondary work does not so distort or "disrespect" the original as to damage the author's honor and reputation. A moral rights approach, rather than stifling artistic endeavours would only restrain parodies which harm the honor and reputation of the original author; otherwise parodists would be given free reign to make the best parodies possible—something hitherto denied them by the economic rights approach which does not discriminate between different kinds of parody.

Courts in common law countries have not appreciated the essential character of questions raised by parody as moral questions. They have instead erroneously regarded parody as a wrongful threat to the original author's economic interests.

Because parodies are not a threat to economic rights, the economic rights approach is flawed in principle, productive of confusion, and a constant barrier to legitimate criticism and creativity.

After noting that a parody's critical impact should be ignored because copyright law "is not designed to stifle critics," the Court in *Fisher v. Dees* [794 F.2d 432] went on to say that it must regard instead whether the parody fulfils the demand for the original: "Biting criticism suppresses demand; copyright infringement usurps it."

It is this economic factor of usurpation which Courts, particularly in America, have consistently regarded as the most important test in determining whether parodies infringe copyright in the original.

Usurpation is also the most decisive factor for determining whether the secondary work, despite prima facie infringement, is nevertheless to be allowed as fair use.

It is submitted that in whatever form, this test of whether the parody usurps or damages the market of the original is really misconceived. As Younger, J. noted in *Glyn* at the beginning of this century, the reason why burlesque had never been found to be an infringement was that, far from reducing or replacing demand for the original, the secondary work will often increase demand for the primary work by its additional treatment and exposure. So he perceptively notes: "It is well known that a burlesque is usually the best possible advertisement of the original and has often made famous a work which would otherwise have remained in obscurity."[112]

The market usurpation test in both its present or prospective mode has another surprising result: not only would it deny the legitimate interests of true parodists on the ostensible ground of protecting authors of original works; it would also deny the original author's legitimate moral claims to integrity, honor and reputation where these are imperilled by reckless parodies that can be shown to enhance the market value of the original.

In any event, a parody will rarely compete in the same market as the original work. Parodies and burlesques usually use serious works to make their humorous criticism more effective and more biting. But since they perform a comical and critical design—of lampooning or sending up the original—they will necessarily distance themselves from the primary works and thus appeal to a different audience (although there may, of course, be those who enjoy both the original and the parody). Only exceptionally will a parody satisfy the same market as the original—unless it is a parody of a parody, in true postmodernist style!

The Courts' excessive concern with the copyright owner's economic interests has also produced another weapon against parodies in the principle that a parody infringes the original if it can be shown to have been produced for commercial purposes.

The "commercial nature" test has resulted in bad decisions because, like the market usurpation test, it starts from a wrong premise: that parodies have no comic worth, so that to be protected a parody must have only artistic and not economic value. Yet if they perform their critical or humorous design effectively, secondary works will, of course, attract commercial value because of, and in addition to, their artistic worth.

---

[112]Glyn v. Weston Feature Film, [1916] 1 ch. 261, 268.

A moral rights approach explicitly appreciates the value of parody to democracy and artistic progress by weighting the balance in favor of the secondary users. It casts the onus on the original author to prove infringement only where he or she can show that the secondary work so distorts the original creation as to harm his honor or reputation.

The economic rights approach to copyright law in Australia and other English speaking countries is wholly inappropriate to the protection of parody. It wrongly perceives parody as an attack on the copyright owner's economic interests whereas what this genre potentially undermines if anything is the original author's moral right to the integrity of his work, and to honor and reputation.

By contrast the moral rights approach is uniquely suited to parody because the peculiar problems posed to copyright law by parodies and burlesques are fundamentally ethical and not economic. There is inevitable tension between a law which professes to further humankind's creative endeavours by protecting the extent to which works may be copied, and the need to encourage derivative literary forms whose intrinsic value lies in their unique critical and humorous purpose but which rely on other works for inspiration. The dilemma is not an economic one; it is a moral one which necessitates adjudication between conflicting public interests—the freedom of expression, creativity and humor represented by parodies and burlesques on the one hand, as opposed to the protection of the personality or integrity of authors' original works.

Mark Twain once wrote that "Only one thing is impossible to God, to find any sense in any copyright law on this planet."[113] If "any sense" is to be made of the copyright law relating to parody, it will be through the belated adoption of Australia's Berne Convention obligations relating to moral rights; and to see the protection of the original work's integrity and its author's honor and reputation as the only legitimate trammeling of the creation of the best (true) parodies.

[113] M. TWAIN, NOTEBOOK 381 (1935 ed.).

QUESTIONS AND COMMENTS FOR YOUR CONSIDERATION

1. What test should be applied to determine if a particular parody is "harmful to the artist's reputation"?
2. Does the extent of such harm depend upon the artistic success of the parody? The commercial success?

4. Musical Works[114]

Since moral rights exist independently of "economic rights," the author retains a degree of control even if he commercially exploited the creation by transferring his economic interests in the work. For example, a song's composer could invoke his moral rights to ensure that he is named as the author, or even to prevent the performance of the song in a form which he perceives as a "distortion, mutilation or other modification" that could damage his "honor or reputation." With the advent of music videos, digital sampling techniques and increasing popularity of music that incorporates sampled sounds, recognition of moral rights in the United States would empower composers to assert some control over the post-release use of their works by music publishers or other musical artists.

The Berne Convention expressly provides that moral rights are independent of "economic rights" in the works created by an author. Thus, an author's moral rights are unaffected by the transfer of the underlying work. Moral rights under Berne can be broken down into two categories: attribution

[114] Patrick G. Zabatta, *Moral Rights and Musical Works: Are Composers Getting Berned?* 43 SYRACUSE L. REV. 1095. Copyright 1992 Syracuse Law Review. Excerpt reprinted with permission.

and integrity. Attribution refers to the creator's right to claim authorship of the work, securing the fame (or notoriety) of the work to his credit. Integrity is the power to prevent an unauthorized, derogatory alteration of the work, enabling the author to prevent an undesirable use of the work which could impair his "honor or reputation."

These rights have broad ramifications. The Berne Convention takes an expansive view of the literary and artistic works it protects, and encompasses "every production in the literary, scientific and artistic domain, whatever may be the mode or form of its expression."[115] Berne then lists examples of works, specifically including "dramatico-musical works," and a myriad of other works. Thus, the rights of attribution and integrity are intended to enure to composers of musical works under Berne.

France is considered the birthplace of the moral rights concept. The doctrine of "le droit moral" reflects the notion that an artist has a natural right to the fruits of her creativity which cannot be conveyed away through licensing or transfer of the economic interest. A recent decision involving the colorization of the film "Asphalt Jungle" illustrates the modern French view of the right to integrity. The Cour de Cassation, France's highest civil court, emphatically reinforced moral rights, holding that the integrity rights of the film's American director, the late John Huston, had been violated by the conversion of the film from black-and-white to color. This case also stands for the proposition that moral rights should be evaluated according to the law of the country in which a claim is heard, not the country in which the author actually acquired the rights by creating a work.

In upholding the plaintiffs' moral rights claim, the Cour de Cassation cited a French law which bars infringement of integrity and attribution in countries whose domestic law fails to provide sufficient or effective protection to works produced by French artists. It therefore appears that despite its accession to the Berne Convention and the implementation of Section 106A, the Cour de Cassation believes that the United States inadequately protects moral rights.

Users, those whose business entails the consumption of the artistic works produced by others, have two intertwined concerns. First, they fear that the recognition of moral rights in authors will disrupt existing contractual arrangements involving intellectual property. Users undoubtedly wish to avoid a situation like the "Asphalt Jungle" case, where no mention of moral rights was made in the contract that assigned the author's copyright interests, as no such right existed in the United States at the time, but the court retroactively superimposed moral rights on the contract, frustrating the user's expectations.

A second problem is users' reluctance to have their future transactions complicated by creators' interests in attribution and integrity, as moral rights in the artist by definition divest the copyright owner of some discretion to subsequently use the work. Essentially:

> Film producers didn't want interference from directors and writers, television wanted to be able to slice up programs any way it saw fit, owners of old movies wanted to "colorize" them, publishers and editors wanted to remain free to edit manuscripts before printing them, and owners of works of art wanted to retain the right to display them in their bathrooms, alter, or even destroy them if they so chose.[116]

These attitudes reflect the intrinsic conflict between moral rights and the economic interests in intellectual property in the United States. The American value structure accentuates economic rights rather than personal interests like attribution and integrity. This emphasis is perhaps a reflection of the United States' Anglo-Saxon antecedents. The notion that one who produces a good shares an interest in that good with the person to whom she has conveyed title is alien to our concept of property, as our culture tends to consider property in more absolute terms. As a result, copyright protection in the United States "continues this country's tradition of safeguarding the pecuniary rights of a copyright owner, . . . ensur[-ing] the copyright owner's receipt of all

---

[115] Berne Convention at art. 2(1).

[116] Glenn Groenewold, *Congress in Action: Copyright Legislation,* UNIX REVIEW, vol. 7, No. 8 at 28 (August 1989).

financial rewards to which he is entitled . . . by virtue of ownership."[117]

Two years after acceding to the Berne Convention, Congress codified limited moral rights in federal law with the Judicial Improvements Act of 1990. In enacting Section 106A, The Visual Rights Act, the United States did little to advance the interests of the intended beneficiaries of moral rights—creators of intellectual property. Because of its very narrow parameters, Section 106A fails to meet the moral rights mandate conferred by the Berne Convention.

First, Section 106A only applies to some creators of "work[s] of visual art." Second, while the Berne Convention extends moral rights beyond the life of the author, under Section 106A, the author's life and his moral rights are coterminous. Furthermore, Section 106A allows the author to waive his moral rights, in contrast to the French position, albeit extreme, that moral rights are inalienable interests in the author's creation.

Even visual artists may be adversely affected by this development because in enacting Section 106A, Congress probably decreased the moral rights protection available under state law to many visual artists. Section 301(f)(1) of the Copyright Act provides, "all . . . rights that are equivalent to any of the rights conferred by Section 106A . . . are governed exclusively by Section 106A," thereby preempting state statutes that confer moral rights to creators of visual art.

To assess the impact of inadequate moral rights protection on composers of musical works, it will be instructive to discuss several cases that deal with moral rights issues in practical terms rather than in the abstract.

Shostakovich v. Twentieth Century Fox Film Corp.[118] involved a moral rights claim brought by prominent Russian composers who objected to the use of their music in a film that had an anti-communist theme. The court collapsed the plaintiffs' moral rights and tort claims, and found that there was no "clear showing of the infliction of a wilful injury or of any invasion of a moral right."[119] Thus, while recognizing the theoretical existence of a moral rights claim, the court chose not to provide a remedy on the facts of the case, citing the conflict between the moral right and the societal interest in using works in the public domain, and the lack of standards by which to determine whether or not such rights were violated. In contrast, the same facts, litigated simultaneously by the plaintiffs in France, resulted in a verdict in their favor. The French court held that there was "undoubtedly a moral damage."[120]

Shostakovich raises the question of whether a composer's integrity can be impaired by a faithful rendition of his song in an objectionable context. A composer who conveys his economic interest in a work could find that their transferee has licensed the song for use in a manner which the composer deems derogatory, reflecting poorly on the composer and thus prejudicing her "honor or reputation." Hypothetically, a composer who enjoys the reputation of providing musical scores for serious dramatic works could find her song licensed for use in a pornographic movie. Would the composer have a cause of action based on violation of her integrity? What if instead of a pornographic movie, the song was performed as a music video pursuant to a license from the copyright owner: would this violate the composer's integrity, as it "distorts" the personality that the composer injected into her song? Under the French holding in Shostakovich, the answer would probably be yes (or oui) in either instance, but the composer's success in such an action in the United States is far more dubious.

A supermarket tabloid provides an even more extreme example: what if a composer's song is used as background music for a scene depicting the rape of a child? While the licensing of the song "Honey Don't" was beyond the control of composer Carl Perkins,[121] he would ordinarily consider its use in a film to be "great." However, says Per-

---

[117] Roberta Rosenthall Kwall, *Copyright and the Moral Right: Is an American Marriage Possible?*, 38 VAND. L. REV. 1, 2 (1985).

[118] 196 Misc. 67, 80 N.Y.S.2d 575 (Sup. Ct. 1948), *aff'd*, 275 A.D. 692, 87 N.Y.S.2d 430 (1949).

[119] *Id.* at 70-71, 80 N.Y.S.2d at 578-79.

[120] Judgement of January 13, 1953 (Soc. Le Chant du Monde v. Soc. Fox Europe), Cours d'appel [1953] D. Jur. 16 (Fr.).

[121] *Editors' Note:* Carl Perkins had assigned his copyright in the song to a publishing house. Consequently, he had no right to control the subsequent use of his work.

kins, in the context of Prince of Tides, "people are asking me, 'Carl, why would you have a song in such a filthy place in a movie?' They are shocked, especially since they all know I started [a] child-abuse center. I am very damaged by this and very hurt." If Perkins were to bring suit for infringement of his integrity rights because he feels the use of his song in this context harmed his reputation, the central issue would be whether the use of "Honey Don't" damaged his honor or reputation as a songwriter, not his reputation in the community as a children's advocate. It thus seems that Perkins could not prevail in the United States or in France.

Digital sampling is another practice unique to the music industry which has potential moral rights implications. For the first time, a district court recently ruled that sampling constituted copyright infringement, issued a preliminary injunction to cease the sale of the infringing work and referred the matter to the United States Attorney for possible criminal prosecution for copyright infringement.[122] The case concerned the unlicensed use of a sample from Raymond "Gilbert" O'Sullivan's 1972 hit Alone Again (Naturally) in rapper "Biz Markie's" 1991 song Alone Again. Though this case could foreshadow subsequent decisions favorable to composers, the holding seems limited to instances where the composer is also the copyright owner, as it focuses on the copyright owner's proprietary rights and not on the creator's moral rights. As such, it has no direct bearing on the composer's moral rights of attribution and integrity.

A possible defense to sampling that constitutes infringement is the Copyright Act's fair use doctrine. In *Acuff-Rose Music, Inc. v. Campbell*,[123] the rap group "2 Live Crew" successfully invoked the fair use defense to an infringement action based on the group's parody of the Roy Orbison song "Oh Pretty Woman". Recognizing the commercial nature of 2 Live Crew's parody, the court nonetheless found that the character of the use supported the defendants, members of "an anti-establishment rap group [that used the song to] demonstrate how bland and banal the Orbison song seems to them." The court also noted that even though parody usually only permits the infringer to copy the amount necessary to conjure up the original work, the nature of a musical composition means that a parodist should be afforded more leeway. Finally, the court found that there will be no diminution of the value of "Oh Pretty Woman", since the intended audience of the 2 Live Crew version is entirely different from the Roy Orbison original.

While this case was a victory for rap artists, it vitiates composers' rights of integrity. Orbison's original "pretty woman" was transformed from "a pleasing image of femininity to bald-headed, hairy and generally repugnant [,] . . . completely inconsistent with the tone and story of the romantic original." Furthermore, the "off-color" content and context of the 2 Live Crew version could be construed as objectionable. While finding that "2 Live Crew's version is neither obscene nor pornographic," the court noted that "[e]ven if the work included pornographic references, that does not necessarily preclude a finding of fair use."

It therefore appears that the moral rights protection available to composers in the United States is inadequate to meet the guaranteed level of protection contemplated by the Berne Convention.

The legal system has a valid interest in judicial economy. Congress should not "open the floodgates" to allow every disgruntled artist to assert a claim sounding in moral rights. To assuage fears of frivolous litigation in hopes of a large monetary reward, Congress could limit damages for moral rights violations to actual damages or unjust enrichment or, in the alternative, to statutory damages, and exclude punitive damages. This is consistent with the notion that moral rights are personal and not pecuniary in nature.

On the other hand, there should be enough substance to moral rights that users will be encouraged to respect authors' rights of attribution and integrity. As a disincentive to the violation of moral rights, Congress could provide for fines to be levied against

---

[122] Grand Upright Music Ltd. v. Warner Bros. Records, Inc., 780 F. Supp. 182 (S.D.N.Y. 1991).

[123] 754 F. Supp. 1150 (M.D. Tenn. 1991). *Editors' Note:* The case decision by the District Court was ultimately upheld by the U.S. Supreme Court in *Acuff-Rose Music, Inc. v. Campbell*, 114 S. Ct. 1164 (1994), *rev'g*, *Acuff-Rose Music, Inc. v. Campbell*, 972 F.2d 1429 (6th Cir. 1993), *rev'g*, *Acuff-Rose Music, Inc. v. Campbell*, 754 F. Supp. 1150 (M.D. Tenn. 1991).

wilful infringers. Also, artists could be awarded the costs of bringing suit to vindicate their moral rights. Finally, criminal liability could be imposed on infringers in extreme cases.

QUESTIONS AND COMMENTS FOR YOUR CONSIDERATION

1. How do you balance a composer's moral rights against subsequent uses?
2. Should an artist have an inalienable right to control all subsequent use of his work? Where should the right attach and be judged? In the country of origin? In the country of use?

5. Works-For-Hire[124]

The laws of several EC Member States create problems for Americans who wish to exploit works made for hire in the EC. Foremost among these problems if the disparate treatment that Member States accord to authors whose status as author does not stem from creating a copyrighted work, but from the legal fiction supplied by work-for-hire rules. This legal fiction posits that when a creator constructs a copyrightable work in the context of certain employment relationships, authorship vests in the person for whom the creator works.

The dilemma posed by these divergent approaches was played out most recently in the French Supreme Court decision, *Huston v. La Cinq.*[125] In Huston, John Huston's heirs sought and obtained an injunction barring the broadcast of the colorized version of the film "Asphalt Jungle." Despite the fact the Metro-Goldwyn-Mayer Studios owned the original copyright in the film, the French High Court ruled that under French copyright law the heirs possessed the separate moral rights of paternity and integrity that the colorized film violated. Even assuming Huston purported to transfer or waive his moral right by contract, French law, and the law of eight other EC Member States, would invalidate such contractual efforts. Despite the warm reception Huston's heirs received in France, the United Kingdom, Ireland, and the Netherlands would not recognize their claimed moral right subsequent to a contractual transfer or waiver.

The conflict Huston addressed illustrates a significant inconsistency in EC copyright law, which greatly impacts the US work-for-hire doctrine. Copyright laws in the EC and those of the United States represent two different copyright traditions—the civil law dualistic system and the common law monistic system. The dualistic system consists of "two essential components, each with a different nature: moral right and economic right."[126] On the one hand, "moral right is a right of personality that protects the person of the author."[127] The right enables an author "to maintain respect for his work and, thereby, for his reputation. This right is perpetual and inalienable."[128] On the other hand, "the economic component of copyright is the right to exploit a work and draw profits from it and is by nature transferable."[129]

Under the monistic system, copyright as a whole safeguards "both the financial and intellectual interests of the author."[130] The monistic structure, unlike the dualistic structure, views authors' financial and intellectual interests as complimentary and therefore permits authors to profit from both. Thus, the United Kingdom, Ireland, and the Netherlands—all of whom adhere to the monistic system—allow authors to

---

124 Robert A. Jacobs, *Work-For-Hire and The Moral Right Dilemma in the European Community: A U.S. Perspective,* 16 B.C. INT'L & COMP. L. REV. Copyright 1993 Robert A. Jacobs. Excerpt reprinted with permission.

125 Judgement of May 28, 1991 (Huston v. La Cinq) Cass. Civ. 1991 Bull. Civ. No. 89-19.522 (Fr.).

126 Robert Plaisant, "France" in International Copyright Law and Practice 81 (1991).

127 *Id.* at 18.

128 *Id.*

129 *Id.*

130 ADOLF DIETZ, COPYRIGHT LAW IN THE EUROPEAN COMMUNITY 47 (1978).

transfer or waive their moral right. The dualistic system of all other EC civil law countries affects US work-for-hire owners most severely.

Because the work-for-hire doctrine inverts the concept of "creator as author" to "employer or principal as author," the doctrine is averse to many signatories' notions of author's rights. Those countries who feel that author's rights are strictly personal are offended by the prospect that one who pays for a creator's work in the course of employment or pursuant to contract acquires the copyright in that work.

The Berne Convention does not define the term "author." Instead, the Berne Convention leaves the concept to the ordinary meaning it has in each signatory.

In general, countries that unconditionally adhere to the "creator as author" concept do so on the premise that authors can only be natural persons.

Just as the Berne Convention omits any definition of "author" it also does not explicitly address the work-for-hire doctrine.[131]

The Berne Convention's moral right provision however, places a significant stumbling block between an employee's work and an employer. In addition, because the Berne Convention never affirmatively recognizes contractual waiver or transfer of moral right, it creates the same morass the French Supreme Court addressed in *Huston v. La Cinq.*[132] Overall, the Berne Convention furthers the dual copyright notions of separate economic and moral rights, and forgoes committing to the monistic view that copyright should only protect authors' commercial interests "for limited times."

Like the Berne Convention, the UCC relies on a policy of reciprocal national treatment. But, unlike the Berne Convention, it focuses on protecting authors' economic rights and does not explicitly address moral right. It does, however, tacitly approve of Contracting States adopting moral right under certain conditions.[133] Undoubtedly, the UCC's most significant departure from the Berne Convention is in the copyright formalities it imposes.

Like the Berne Convention, the UCC does not define "author." Several passages in the Convention, however, demonstrate a less strict approach to the "creator as author" rule than appears in the Berne Convention. For example, Article IV prescribes the minimum term of protection as the life of the author plus twenty-five years after her death. Following this prescription, the Convention addresses those Contracting States that compute duration "from the first publication of the work," and authorizes those states that do not use such a durational method to adopt such a method. This broad recognition of a "date of publication" measure diverges from the Berne Convention, which only applied such a measure to anonymous and pseudonymous works. Because work-for-hire is the other primary class of works that uses a "date of publication" measure, and because of employers and principals who acquire authorship status in such works are frequently corporate entities, the UCC could be read to approve of granting author's rights to non-natural persons. The

---

[131] However, Article 15(2) implicitly recognizes the doctrine since it addresses corporate authorship of a cinematographic work: "The person or body corporate whose name appears on a cinematographic work in the usual manner shall, in the absence of proof to the contrary, be presumed to be the maker of said work." Berne Convention, *supra* note 30, at Article 15(2). Corporate authorship can only arise by treating the corporation as author. A corporation, in turn, can only be an author through its employees, and only by virtue of work-for-hire principles. Hence, Article 15(2) incorporates work-for-hire, albeit implicitly, only in the context of cinematographic works.

[132] Judgement of May 28, 1991 (Huston v. La Cinq) Cass. Civ. 1991 Bull. Civ. No. 89-19.522 (Fr.).

[133] After setting forth specific economic rights that the Convention protects in Article IVbis(1), Article IV bis(2) states the following:

> 2. However, any Contracting State, may, by its domestic legislation, make exceptions that do not conflict with the spirit and provisions of this Convention, to the rights mentioned in paragraph I of this Article. Any State whose legislation so provides, shall nevertheless accord a reasonable degree of effective protection to each of the rights to which exception has been made.

Universal Copyright Convention, *supra* note 69, at Art. IVbis(2). By juxtaposing the exceptions that paragraph (2) authorizes with the term "[H]owever," the UCC impliedly sanctions moral right so long as it does not hinder exploitation of economic right. In theory, and sometimes in practice (as in Huston), this hindrance is inevitable.

fact that the United States was the motivating force for the UCC further supports this suggestion; US copyright law does not distinguish between natural and non-natural persons for authorship purposes and uses the date of publication as the alternative measure for works-for-hire.

The "Berne Safeguard Clause prohibits a Berne Convention country from denouncing Berne and relying on the UCC in its copyright relations with members of the Berne Convention."[134] Because all EC Member States belong to the Berne Convention and the UCC, the Berne Convention's preeminence undercuts the protection that the UCC theoretically affords to work-for-hire copyright holders. As a result, persons asserting rights as work-for-hire copyright holders in the EC must turn either EC or national copyright law.

National copyright protection is almost divided evenly between a strict author's rights approach and a common law-oriented, economic rights approach. Member States utilizing a strict author's rights approach protect creators through a rigid moral right regime that, by definition, also restricts ownership rights in works made for hire. Member States employing an economics rights approach allow contractual relations to control the extent to which moral right may apply and, consequently, support ownership rights in the works-for-hire.

Belgium. Belgian employees who create works in the scope of their employment acquire the copyright in the work.[135] Belgian law regards employees as authors who may then transfer their copyright interest to their employers.

Employee-employer transfers, however, do not give employers unfettered discretion in exploiting the work. "Moral right remains vested in each author even after full conveyance of all copyright-based economic interests."[136] Furthermore, the law does not permit authors to transfer or waive the moral right of integrity contained in Article 8.

Denmark. A composite of two statutory provisions suggests that Denmark also adheres to the civil law custom of separating copyright economic and moral rights. First, Section 1 employs a strict "creator as author" rule: "The person producing a literary or artistic work shall have copyright therein."[137]

Second, Section 3 gives the author several moral right protections: [including the rights of paternity and integrity.] Because no EC Member State (except Germany) prevents copyright transfers, Danish law would presumably permit an author to transfer her copyright to an employer if she created the work in the scope of employment. Such a transfer would not, however, create any limit on the employee's moral right. Since Section 3 prohibits an author from waiving her moral rights of attribution, paternity, and integrity in most circumstances, it is unlikely that a contractual effort to transfer these rights would succeed.

France. France's copyright law specifically addresses the work-for-hire doctrine. The first article of France's copyright statute establishes rules governing works-for-hire. The first paragraph provides: "The author of an intellectual work, shall, by the mere fact of its creation, enjoy an exclusive incorporeal property right in the work, effective against all persons."[138] It also states in part: "The existence, or the conclusion by the author of an intellectual work, of a contract to make a work, or an employment contract, shall imply no exception to the enjoyment of the right recognized in the first paragraph."[139]

In the employer-employee context, French courts have interpreted these provisions to give employers the economic component of copyright and employee-authors the moral right component. The employer need not secure a separate transfer of copyright since she "acquires the economic component of copyright upon execution of the employment contract."[140] Because the economic

---

[134] Marshall Leaffer, Understanding Copyright Law 347 n.18 (1st ed. 1989).

[135] Jan Corbet, *Belgium,* in INTERNATIONAL COPYRIGHT LAW AND PRACTICE (1991).

[136] *Id.* at 27.

[137] Denmark Copyright Law, in INTERNATIONAL COPYRIGHT LAW AND PRACTICE (1991) at ch.1, sec. 1.

[138] French Copyright Law, in INTERNATIONAL COPYRIGHT LAW AND PRACTICE (1991) at art. 1, para.3.

[139] *Id.* at art. 1, para. 1.

[140] *Id.* at 44.

component vests in the employer by virtue of the employment relationship. French law partially follows US work-for-hire rules.

French copyright law diverges from US law in the principal-independent contractor context. This context usually involves commissioned works or works that will constitute part of a collective whole. In France, authors of commissioned works retain both the economic and moral right to the principal. The United States, in contrast, does not require any transfer between the creator and the principal, provided (1) the parties have an express writing describing the work as one for hire, and (2) work falls into one of nine categories. Once the principal satisfies both these requirements, she acquires the same rights that an employer has over works created in the scope of employment.

A significant exception to general French work-for-hire rules exists for computer software. For these works, French law is entirely consistent with US work-for-hire in that employers acquire both the economic and moral right component of the copyright. By amendment in 1985, French copyright law now provides: "Unless otherwise stipulated, software created by one or more employees in the exercise of their duties shall belong to the employer together with all the rights afforded to other authors."[141] This provision represents a radical departure from France's strict moral right regime.

Germany. The concept of work-for-hire is entirely absent from German copyright law. German law adheres to the basic principle that only the natural person who creates a work can be the work's author. In the employment context, "the initial owner . . . of a work made for hire or of a commissioned work is . . . always the author . . . who actually created the work."[142] By vesting ownership in the employee or the independent contractor, the law requires employers to acquire copyright interests by contract.

German moral right provisions imply that an author may waive her moral right. Article 39 of the German Copyright Act states that "in the absence of any contrary agreement, a licensee may not alter the work, its title or the designation of the author."[143] These alterations concern the moral rights of integrity and attribution. The fact that this article refers to a "contrary agreement" indicates the Copyright Act recognizes contractual waivers of moral right. As one commentator has suggested, however, even though an author can waive her moral right of integrity under Article 39, the beneficiary of such a waiver does not have unlimited freedom to alter the work. Alterations are limited to those which do not constitute a "gross distortion" of the work.

Greece. Work-for-hire rules do not exist under Greek copyright law. Like most civil law countries, Greek law vests initial copyright ownership in the human being who actually created the work. Employers cannot alter this principle by contract. Instead, employers must acquire copyright interests in works made in the scope of employment in the same manner as any person or entity would acquire a copyright interest—by transfer from the author.

Employers must also contend with potential moral right claims. The Greek Copyright Act expressly provides for the right of attribution or paternity and the right of integrity. Greek law also generally recognizes two other moral right provisions: the rights of divulgation and access to the author's work.

Greece, like Germany, France, Denmark, and Belgium, adheres to the civil law notion that moral right is personal to the author and therefore nontransferable. Yet, despite the nontransferability of moral right, Greek law recognizes a narrow moral right waiver. A waiver could arise in relation to the rights of divulgation and paternity where an author contractually renounces her power to decide when to publish her work and agrees to publish without mentioning her name. A waiver of the right of divulgation would provide some relief to publishing houses that hold copyrights in books and other media and wish to time publication themselves. Similarly, an employer who holds the copyright in a work an employee created and

---

[141] Law on Author's Rights and on the Rights of Performers, Producers of Phonograms and Videograms and Audiovisual Communication Enterprises, at 45 (1985).

[142] ADOLF DIETZ, COPYRIGHT LAW IN THE EUROPEAN COMMUNITY 46 (1978).

[143] *German Copyright Law* in INTERNATIONAL COPYRIGHT LAW AND PRACTICE (1991) at art. 39.

who seeks to label the work as her own may benefit from a right of attribution waiver. In sum, although Greece does not preclude employers from disarming their employees of their moral right, Greek copyright law places significant hurdles in the way of unlimited economic exploitation of works-for-hire.

Luxembourg. The fact that Luxembourg is a civil law country and civil law countries (except for the Netherlands) uniformly follow the "creator as author" rule would indicate that only creators can secure copyright interests under the statute. By implication, this position precludes employers from acquiring copyright interest upon creation as work-for-hire rules generally dictate.

Employers and principals must acquire copyright interests by contractual transfers from employees or independent contractors. The interest that either may acquire is limited to the economic right of exploitation.

The fact that moral right "attaches to the author personally," indicates an author cannot alienate the right through an *inter vivos* transfer. Moreover, in view of Luxembourg's overall scheme, the personal nature of moral right also precludes moral right waiver. These prohibitions are consistent with most civil law countries and embody the usual limitations on works-for-hire that can potentially impair the economic exploitation of these works.

The Netherlands. The Netherlands is the only civil law country that has incorporated the work-for-hire doctrine into its copyright law. Three separate provisions form the basis of the Dutch work-for-hire scheme. First, Article 6 provides: "If a work has been produced according to the plan and under the guidance and supervision of another person, that person shall be deemed to be the author of the work."[144] This article would apply if, for example, an artist employs several artists at his or her studio to execute works. Article 7 is the second Dutch work-for-hire provision. In the event another person employs the supervisor and the latter oversees the creation of a work in the course of his or her employment Article 7 indicates that the supervisor's employer is the work's author.

In the Netherlands, employers' work-for-hire rights only arise in instances in which an employer "factually" addresses an employee to produce certain works. Article 7 will "not apply where the employee produces (other) works on his own initiative, whether in the time of his employer or even with the mere consent of his employer."[145]

Therefore, if an employee creates a work on his or her own initiative, even while using her employer's facilities, receiving payment from her employer, following her employer's instructions, and even if the work is the type of work that the employer generally produces, the employee will be the work's author and will acquire all copyright interest in the work.

Article 8 is the third provision addressing the work-for-hire doctrine. It states: "Any public institution, association, foundation or partnership which makes a work public as its own, without naming any natural person as the author thereof, shall be regarded as the author of the work, unless it is shown that making the work public in such manner was unlawful." This article covers work created in the course of a principal-independent contractor relationship. It also applies to all other works not covered by Articles 6 and 7 where an entity has contracted for the right to publish the work as its own. In theory, this provision greatly exceeds the scope of US work-for-hire rules since it permits an entity to acquire authorship status and all appurtenant copyright interests by publishing a work in its own name pursuant to contract. Article 8, unlike US law, does not require an agency relationship nor limits itself to particular categories of works.

The United Kingdom. The United Kingdom fully recognizes work-for-hire principles. Section 11 sets forth the work-for-hire rules that apply to works created on or after August 1, 1989:

> (1) The author of work is the first owner of any copyright in it, subject to the following provisions.
> (2) Where a literary, dramatic, musical

[144] Herman Cohen Jehoram, *Netherlands Copyright Law*, in INTERNATIONAL COPYRIGHT LAW AND PRACTICE (1991) at art. 6.

[145] *Id.* at 31.

> or artistic work is made by an employee in the course of his employment, his employer is the first owner of any copyright in the work subject to any agreement to the contrary.[146]

This section gives employers the status of authors and vests initial copyright interests in them absent any contrary agreement. Because employers acquire their interests upon creation and the employment relationship alone determines this interest, the British rule closely resembles the US approach. Similar to the CCNV "scope of employment" analysis, British work-for-hire interests depend on whether an employment relationship exists.

To determine whether such a relationship exists, the British . . . focus on "whether the work forms an integral part of the business."[147] This analysis depends on:

> whether the typical attributes of employment are present: whether regular sums are paid as wage or salary; whether income tax deductions are made on the "pay-as-you-earn" basis used for employees; whether there is a joint contribution to a pension scheme; whether national insurance contributions are paid by both parties as for an employee.[148]

Assuming some or all of these attributes are present, an employer will acquire the copyright interest in the work. Even if the employment relationship does not satisfy this test, an employer could nonetheless acquire a copyright interest unimpaired by moral right. Unlike most EC countries, the United Kingdom permits moral rights waivers.

The above overview of EC Member States' national work-for-hire rules reveals three interrelated problems. The first problem is that the Member States differ over how copyright ownership in works-for-hire may arise. At one extreme, Belgium, Denmark, Germany, Greece, and Luxembourg only allow creators to have the initial ownership interest and require employers to contract for copyright licenses or transfers. Somewhere towards the center, France requires principals to contract with independent contractors, but employers need not contract with employees. Similarly, Italy and Spain permit copyright ownership to flow directly to the employer in some instances,[149] but not in others.[150] At the other extreme, Ireland, the Netherlands, and the United Kingdom nearly always vest copyright ownership in employers and principals upon creation. In essence, no single copyright ownership rule prevails in the EC for works-for-hire.

The second problem is that the Member States disagree over who may be the author of a work-for-hire. This issue is significant since only an author can claim moral right. As a general rule, all EC Member States consider the natural person who created a work as the work's author. In relation to authors of works made for hire, however, two distinct approaches emerge. These approaches break down according to the civil and common law traditions. On the one hand, the civil law countreis, except for the Netherlands, adhere to the general rule almost without exception. On the other hand, Ireland, the Netherlands, and the United Kingdom deviate from the general rule and recognize employers and principals as authors of works made for hire.

The third problem arises from the divergent moral right treatments existing within the EC. The discrepancies characterizing moral right proceed directly from the problem of determining authorship in works made for hire. That is, the same civil law countries that strictly follow the "creator as author" rule also forbid moral right transfer and waiver. The identical common law coun-

---

[146] United Kingdom Copyright Designs and Patent Act 1988, sec. 87(2).

[147] William R. Cornish, *United Kingdom* in INTERNATIONAL COPYRIGHT LAW AND PRACTICE (1991) at 31.

[148] *Id.*

[149] *See, e.g.*, Italian Copyright Law, *supra* note 14, at Arts. 38, 45, 88 (publishers of collective works, all obtain economic copyright interest); Spanish Copyright Law, *supra* note 14, at Arts. 8, 51 (publishers of collective works acquire both economic and moral right copyright interest, and employers acquire limited economic interest without contract).

[150] *See* Fabiani, *supra* note 156, at 38 (in most contexts employers and principals must contract for copyright interests); del Corral, *supra* note 182, at 25 ("[s]ince . . . only natural persons can be authors . . . legal entities normally acquire copyright from such persons by contract.").

tries (and the Netherlands) that part from the "creator as author" rule also permit moral right transfer or waiver. Because these latter countries' work-for-hire and moral right regimes most closely resemble the US system, US work-for-hire copyright holders can expect the same treatment under these countries' laws as they would receive in the United States.[151]

[151] Of course this parallel reverberates in contexts other than work-for-hire. Copyright holders in any kind of work would do well to secure a moral right waiver or transfer in a copyright assignment. Insofar as the EC common law countries and the Netherlands are concerned, contracting for a transfer or waiver would relieve doubts as to whether authors could legally object to the contemplated exploitation of their work. Because this article solely addresses works-for-hire, it does not fully explore all of the broader questions raised by moral right transfer and waiver in other kinds of works.

QUESTIONS AND COMMENTS FOR YOUR CONSIDERATION

1. What solutions would you propose for the current work-for-hire conflict in the EC?
2. To what extent is harmonization of work-for-hire a viable alternative for moral right rules ? If harmonization is attempted, whose model should be adopted?
3. For a further discussion of the role of harmonization in establishing international protection norms, see Chapter Twelve.

6. Patents[152]

The traditional view of the institutions grouped in the category of intellectual property adopts a distinction between works of creativity, where attention is focused on the personality of the author, and technical accomplishments, where attention falls on the discovery. The first category relates to the domain of art, the second gives importance to the utilitarian aspects of the work. Such a bipolar view, based on an idea of the work of intelligence and creativity, seems to have been called into question by the latest technological and social developments. The consequence of any decline in such a view would be to sweep away the distinction between artistic property and industrial property.

Moral rights probably embody the essence of the right of authorship, that is, that very strong bond which links the author to his or her work, since the author is the subject whose personality is impressed on the work in an indestructible way. This justifies the fact that moral rights are not transferable, not renounceable, autonomous from financial rights and accompanied by a right of action aimed at their defense which is absolutely without limitation. These peculiarities represent one of the most pronounced differences from the monopolies which derive from patent protection. The figure of the inventor, compared to that of the author, loses centrality, since the invention, even if it gives prestige and reputation to the inventor, does not have any moral or personal implications for him or her at the moment of its realization by third parties. In a society dominated by technology, the position of moral rights becomes uncertain. If they are left untouched, this leaves copyright basically unprejudiced. However, if moral rights are affected, then this classic division of intellectual property will begin to show its limitation.

The realisation of systems able to carry out intellectual activities formerly considered the exclusive domain of man has reached a very advanced phase. Often the creative activity is the result of the collaboration between one or more human workers

[152] Mario Franzosi and Guistino de Sanctis, *Moral Rights And New Technology: Are Copyright and Patents Converging?*, 2 E.I.P.R. 63. Copyright 1995 Mario Franzosi and Guistino de Sanctis. Excerpt reprinted with permission.

and an intelligence system and it is not always possible to distinguish the contribution of the man from that of the machine. In these cases, one wonders who should be regarded as the author of the work, and who as the owner of the moral rights, assuming that they exist. The more obvious problem is the fact that, in principle, the present laws on the right of authorship require human origin in order for a work to be protected. The first legislators to overcome this impasse were the British legislators of the 1988 Act who expressly provided for the protection of works made by computer, that is, in circumstances where it is not possible to trace a human author, treating the author as the person who undertook all the preparations necessary for the creation of the work. It is very interesting to note that, with regard to moral rights, the British legislators inserted the first moral rights of the author in copyright, but the options open to authors are limited to the right of paternity, the right of integrity and the right not to be falsely attributed as the author of a work, and in many cases such rights are not applied. Such partial acknowledgment shows the existence of some gaps, or at least of some differences within the system.

Where computers, even if simplifying the activity of the author, do not bring any creative assistance to the realisation of the work, we have a traditional situation, because the computer's contribution is not conceptually different from that made by more traditional instruments, like paper and pen. Very similar is the case where man teaches the computer his ideas and his methods, which the computer then applies to real situations which are supplied to it later. Actually the intelligence system carries out mediation activity only, and if one excludes the temporal indications which arise from the fact that the machine can postpone, for a potentially unlimited time, the expression of the creation, one can understand that the moral rights concerned in no way differ from those of traditional authors.

When an intelligence system is endowed with the capacity to learn and to synthesize, allowing it to have creative skills, it is no longer possible to trace an author in the classic sense of the word, since the umbilical cord which traditionally links man to his creation is irreparably cut.

It does not seem possible to attribute any rights, either moral or economic, to the computer, which, even if it is responsible for the creation, is still a machine without a personality (in the legal or in the psychological sense of the word). The problem of identifying an author arises principally in connection with economic rights; it is not possible to enlarge on this here, but whatever direction is followed, moral rights will probably take their own path. This is because moral rights form part of the more generic right to personality, and, as already mentioned, in creations realized by a machine the umbilical cord which traditionally joins man, and thus his personality, to the work is irreparably severed. Therefore, until such time as artificial intelligence systems come to be regarded as endowed with their own personality, it does not seem possible to find a place for moral rights.

New technology has not altered, at least for the moment, some of the traditional aspects of intellectual and industrial property. The different identities of these two categories are confirmed by the growing interest shown in common law countries in moral rights. However, these institutions are undergoing a profound transformation. New technology has led to enormous financial investment in a field traditionally not involved in entrepreneurial activity—that of the right of authorship. Until this revolution affects works created according to traditional criteria, such trends do not seem to undermine the traditional centrality of the author, who still has all moral rights. However, for technological works and classic works produced by technological means, the object of protection changes: this is no longer the personality of the author but economic investment. The personality element of the creation is seriously compromised, if not lost, either because of the manner of the creation, or because of the use of technology in the creation process. Every time that the work is realized by a team of experts who use the technology and the capital put at their disposal by an entrepreneur, the frame of reference changes appreciably. When one or more computers participate, sometimes exclusively, the frame changes completely. One will always be concerned with creations, but only because of an objective creative value, the meaning of which inevitably approaches the well-known concept of inventive originality. With this conceptual change, the first legal aspect to disappear would certainly be that of moral rights. That would be justified not only by the absence of an object to protect, that is, the personality element, but also by the increase of dominant economic interests, which are at the root of the creation. The English legislation on copyright recognises the new industrial face of the rights of authorship, because, even though introducing some moral rights, it provides that these are not applicable in cases in which either there is an insufficient personality factor, or this personality factor is dominated by the entrepreneurial factor. Therefore, the Anglo-Saxon system, showing that some cases exist in which the person of the author loses that absolutely pre-eminent position which, traditionally, they have always had. This reveals movement away from the subjective aspect, neglecting continental system, showing that some cases exist in which the person of the author loses that absolutely pre-eminent position which, traditionally, they have always had. This reveals movement away from the subjective aspect, neglecting continental theories which assess the possibility of protecting the work only because of the personal imprint which these works received, and leading the assessment to a more objective originality.

The second aspect which has declined, or will soon decline, concerns the direct acquisition of the right. The requirement of industrialization in copyright has been pointed out by the EEC Directive on Software, which provided clearly for the possibility of a legal person to have rights of authorship directly, and which left single Member States the option of implementing such provisions. Italy, for example, did not implement this possibility, and left the old regulations unchanged, regulations which provide that rights of authorship could only arise in favour of the intellectual creator, while the employer could only obtain the exploitation rights by way of a derivative title. It seems necessary to allow a legal person separate from the creator to have the original economic rights to a work, for at least two reasons. First, it seems justified by the transformation of the creative action which, becoming personalised, could easily refer to a subject which is not the creator. Secondly, it seems equally important to allow the protection of works created by computer, on its own or with the aid of one or more persons, because if the old personality concept is adhered to, such works would not obtain protection until the time that computers endowed with their own personalities were produced.

In conclusion, the difference between the right of authorship and the patent system is no longer so well-defined as it was at the time of its origin. New technology inevitably leads to the painful abandonment of the view of personality which was at the root of right of authorship. It therefore leads likewise to a partial abandonment both of moral rights, the greatest expression of the personalization of the work, and of that intimate author-work bond which forced the absolute denial of the possibility of allowing original rights of exploitation of a work in favour of a third person, with regard to the author, or to a legal person; and it leads finally towards the recognition and the protection of works realized not by people, but by machines.

7. Multinational Treaties and the Protection of "Culture"

a. Culture as Commodity[153]

What if one day you woke up, turned on the radio and could not find an American song? What if you went to the movies and the only films were foreign? What if you wanted to buy a book, and you found that the only American works were located in a small "Americana" section of the store? Furthermore, what if you came home to find your kids glued to the television for back-to-back reruns of a French soap opera and two German police dramas? It sounds foreign, even silly, to an American. Ask a Canadian, a German, or a Greek the same question, however, and you will get a different reaction. Europe faced an inversion of this hypothetical scenario. At one point in the late

[153] Laurence G. C. Kaplan, *The European Community's "Television Without Frontiers" Directive: Stimulating Europe to Regulate Culture,* 8 EMORY INT'L L. REV. 255. Copyright 1994 Emory University School of Law. Excerpt reprinted with permission.

1980s, The Cosby Show was the top rated sitcom in both France and Germany. Even today, evening television in France includes reruns of Hogan's Heroes and Dynasty.

The European Community (EC) reacted to this predicament by passing a Directive—a law—requiring that its members dedicate at least one-half of their television air time to European-made programs. The Directive was the European answer to the fear that European culture was being assimilated into the "Great American Melting Pot," a fear corroborated by numbers, statistics, and trends. The tentacular American intrusion seemed to undermine the cultural autonomy (and in so doing stifled the cultural creativity) of the European countries. The experience was especially galling to the "old world" precisely because it was old and took pride in its multi-secular capital of culture. It was one thing for the United States to purvey jeans and Coca-Cola; it was wholly another, and far more ominous, to commodify culture.

b. The Canadian Free Trade Agreement[154]

Both international copyright conventions and domestic copyright laws may conflict with the concept of free trade. Free trade among nations is a concept which has increased in importance over the last several decades, as has been shown by the proliferation of multinational trading organizations such as the European Community (EC) and by free trade areas created by agreements such as the Canadian Free Trade Agreement (CFTA) and the North American Free Trade Agreement (NAFTA). The increasing incidence of international trading areas and organizations indicates that trade protectionism is on the decline as the interdependence of nations increases.

The concept of free trade focuses on the reduction of trade barriers. Actions by a state which restrict the flow of goods or services infringe on free trade. One of the more transparent restrictions of trade is a cultural exclusion, also known as a cultural exemption. Cultural exclusions, which exist in virtually all trading agreements, allow a state to limit the trade of goods and services involving that state's culture. Cultural exclusions severely limit or even prohibit cultural industries from competing in a free trade area. Although no trade agreement refers to them as such, cultural industries are essentially synonymous with copyright industries, which are defined as industries that produce copyrighted goods or provide copyrighted services. Some trade agreements seem to encourage the free trade of copyrighted goods through provisions increasing copyright protections for creative works. The holders of the copyright will therefore be inclined to introduce their creative works into the market. Cultural exclusions, however, severely diminish the effect of these provisions by restricting the entry of many copyrighted works into the international marketplace.

The Canadian Free Trade Agreement, signed by Canada and the United States, specifically excludes cultural industries from application of the treaty provisions. That section of the CFTA agreement, Article 2005, has been called the "cultural exclusion" or "cultural exemption" provision. Cultural industries have been defined as those involving the publication, distribution, or sale of books, magazines, periodicals or newspapers, film or video recordings, audio or video music recordings, and music in print. Direct transmission of radio and all radio, television, and cable broadcasting services, as well as satellite programming and network broadcast services, are also included in the cultural industries exclusion. As in most trade agreements, the terms "cultural industry" and "copyright industry" are virtually synonymous.

Cultural exclusions are promoted by states as a means of protecting their cultural integrity. In the case of Canada, many Canadian citizens feel very strongly that their culture is distinct from the culture of the United States and thus deserves recognition on its own merits. To Canadians cultural exclusions prevent an amalgamation of American and Canadian culture. However, the fact that Canada is the largest single

---

[154] Stacie I. Strong, *The Cultural Exclusion: Free Trade And Copyrighted Goods,* 4 DUKE J. COMP. & INT'L L. 93. Copyright 1993 by the Duke Journal of Comparative & International Law. Excerpt reprinted with permission.

importer of American intellectual property reflects the potential blurring of American and Canadian cultural boundaries.

The Canadian government has made the protection of Canadian culture and cultural industries a priority, with the creation and maintenance of the Canadian Broadcasting Corporation (CBC) as the most visible sign of that social policy. Television has also been the battlefield for a number of conflicts between the United States and Canada regarding programming and satellite transmissions, and as such is a prime example of the cultural exclusion at work.

The Canadian government uses the CBC as a means to promote uniquely Canadian values through various production subsidies and programming restrictions. However, the Canadian viewing public has clamored for American television programs, threatening the viability of Canadian programs. As the popularity of television viewing in Canadian daily life has increased, there has been a corresponding increase in American influences in spite of government subsidies of Canadian television. Some observers believe that vital information about Canadian cultural and political issues may no longer be available to segments of the Canadian public due to the predominance of American television programming.

CFTA's cultural exclusion may seem attractive in the short run, but the long-term effects could harm the Canadian economy and cultural industries as well as the economy and industries of the United States. In the near future, the Canadian government could continue to subsidize what is seen as a struggling domestic industry, thus protecting Canadian culture. Eventually, however, Canadian cultural industries will become less competitive on the global market and will continue to lose their audience members to readily available American books, movies, and television shows. Government assistance, such as subsidies, will not make Canadian cultural industries more competitive, and will not result in the kind of cultural protection that is envisaged by the exclusion, namely the increased availability and production of culturally significant goods and services. Because the cultural exclusion cannot effectuate either of its goals, it appears to be disguised restraint of trade used to protect Canada's cultural industries for economic, not cultural, reasons.

NAFTA in essence has duplicated the cultural exclusion provision of CFTA. Unlike CFTA, however, trade between Mexico and the United States is free of cultural exclusions. [T]he absence of a cultural exclusion will allow Mexican copyright industries to target the Hispanic population which is often ignored by, or even currently closed to, mainstream United States industries, resulting in a potential tidal wave of cultural trade. In addition, once United States industries see the profit-making potential from this largely untapped market, they will begin to target more products to that market, products which will be exportable to Mexico and South and Central America. This type of trade expansion benefits both states and is the result that free trade agreements are intended to produce; it would not be possible, however, under a trade agreement containing a cultural exclusion provision.

c. "Television Without Frontiers"

1. The Directive[155]

Article 6 [of the EC "Television Without Frontiers Directive"] defines a European work as follows:

> (a) works originating from Member States of the Community . . .
>
> (b) works originating from European third States party to the European Convention on Transfrontier Television of the Council of Europe [Council of Europe, May 5, 1989, reprinted in 28 ILM 857 (1989)] and fulfilling the conditions of paragraph 2;
>
> (c) works from other European third countries . . .

---

[155] Stephan A. Konigsberg, *Think Globally, Act Locally: North American Free Trade, Canadian Cultural Industry Exemption, and the Liberalization of the Broadcast Ownership Laws,* 12 CORDOZO ARTS & ENT. L. J. 281. Copyright 1993 Stephan A. Konigsberg. Excerpt reprinted with permission. (Selected Footnotes)

It further provides that

> The works [must be] works mainly made with authors and workers residing in one or more States referred to in Paragraph 1(a) and 1(b) provided that they comply with one of the following three conditions:
>
> (a) they are made by one or more producers established in one or more of those States;
>
> (b) production of the works is supervised and actually controlled by one or more producers established in one or more of those States; or
>
> (c) the contribution of co-producers of those States to the total co-production is preponderant and the co-production is not controlled by one or more producers established outside those States.

If unable to attain a majority proportion of European Works it is stated that where the majority cannot be attained, "it must not be lower than the average for 1988 in the Member State concerned." *Id.* Art. 4(2).

In direct reference to the quota system, Community Vice President Martin Bangemann, in charge of internal markets, made it clear that the Commission did not regard it as a legally enforceable commitment, but a "political obligation."

The Commission is convinced that increased activity in the cultural sector is a political and socio-economic necessity given the twin goals of completing the internal market by 1992 and progressing from a people's Europe to European Union. . . . The essential aim of the general guidelines proposed is to facilitate complementary action by the Commission and the Member States within the Community system and coordination and cooperation between the Member States consistent with Treaty rules.

In relation to the US the other production communities around the world have had limited success distributing mass media products internationally. In 1991, US-based productions accounted for 81% of all EC screenings (rising to a level of 90% in states such as the UK, Greece, the Netherlands and Ireland), 70% of all European box-office receipts, and 54% of all comedies and dramas broadcast on television.

Witness, for example, the decision by the French film industry to exclude all non-French speaking films from the Cesars (the French Oscars). Intellectuals fear that the French language, long under siege by English, needs defending.... French film industry officials, supported by Jack Lang and his Ministry of Culture, worry that French films are being swamped at the box office by Hollywood products. The language issue has never arisen with the Oscar because Hollywood can rightly assume that its national products will also be international hits.

2. Cultural Diversity[156]

The controversy [regarding the "Television Without Frontiers" Directive] focuses on two issues: first, whether Europe can legislate its culture (legally and practically); and second, whether there is a need for Europe to do so. In its broadest sense, this problem is linked to the enormous political stakes—identity, sovereignty, and independence—and the secondary, but still important, economic stakes-survival of the national industry. In a narrower sense, the dynamics of this issue are played out in the arena of European audiovisual communication. The rapid and widespread demographic and technological changes in Europe in the 1970s and 1980s set the stage for a virtual invasion of American culture. The EC responded in the form of the "Television Without Frontiers" Directive. Simply put, it was an attempt to regulate culture in Europe. The Directive presents an opportune case study in which to explore the issue of whether in fact a state can legislate culture or whether cultural protectionism is nothing more than economic self-promotion cloaked in cultural language.

Two theories explain the attraction of the European state to its present system of audiovisual media. One theory is political, entitled *la television toute-puissante* (the all-powerful television). This theory embraces

---

[156] Lawrence G.C. Kaplan, *The European Community's "Television Without Frontiers" Directive: Stimulating Europe to Regulate Culture,* 8 EMORY INT'L L. REV. 255. Copyright 1994 Lawrence G.C Kaplan. Excerpt reprinted with permission.

the practical strengths of television as a means of communicating with vast numbers of people. The second theory, labeled cultural uniformity, emphasizes the cultural link between television and the masses. Although there are two separate approaches, both theories recognize the connection between the cultural domain and political sovereignty.

The European state has been an active participant in its audiovisual landscape since the inception of advanced technological communication. Governments commissioned studies, funded research, allocated Hertzian frequencies, set national standards, and generally kept a paternal hand on the media with their economic and political potential in mind. The end product of a state-subsidized and state-controlled audiovisual communication industry was a well-funded and highly successful television and radio system. Broadcasters successfully created quality programs with cultural and political influence. These broadcasters played important roles in strengthening democratic values and in encouraging the arts. Because of the successful relationship between state and artist, the state scaffolding that held the industry together earned a place in the public eye as the natural order of things.

Television, therefore, has taken on a particular role in European society. It is an institution charged with upholding the fundamentals of democracy. For television networks, information is the cardinal obligation, the core of their activity. Networks criticized for the mediocrity of their programming nonetheless will concentrate their financial means on broadcast news rather than on entertainment programs. This phenomenon expressed itself recently in France in the confrontation between the partially-privatized network TF1 and its private rival La Cinq.

It is fair to conclude that the non-English-speaking European countries always have been intent on protecting their national sovereignty and culture. In many western European nations, government ownership of the media evolved as a way of protecting national culture from a flood of programs from nations with more sophisticated production capabilities. Despite an initial flirtation with free enterprise, most of these states adopted government-run systems instead of allowing private ownership. States routinely adopted strict regulatory barriers against foreign ownership and investment, and against foreign-produced programming. Similar restrictions also exist presently in commercial advertising, ranging from total bans in Denmark to content and time limitations in Germany.

In recent years, European countries watched as their sovereignty became undermined by the globalization or Americanization phenomenon. This invasion was at once egregiously apparent (the presence of American shows) and insidiously subtle (the way in which American values, images, and assumptions infiltrated the minds of both old and especially young viewers). The American programming market slowly invaded the markets of each European nation. The closer Hollywood came to dominating the market in Europe, the more the economic aspect of television programming extended from the cultural domain into the realm of political sovereignty.

"Television without Frontiers" was the coined name for the European Council Directive adopted on October 3, 1989 "on the coordination of certain provisions laid down by law, regulation or administrative action in Member States concerning the pursuit of television broadcasting activities." This Directive was a secondary piece of legislation offered to the Member States whose task was to implement the Directive into their own legal systems to make them effective.

Grosso modo, the Directive, outlined standards, rules and regulations touching on such areas as transfrontier broadcasting, advertising, the intra-EC flow of programs and information, and program content. The most important and controversial standard was the last, a mandatory program content quota. The quota required members to implement rules obliging public and private networks to earmark at least fifty percent of their total airtime for "European works." From a practical standpoint, this quota translated into a trade restriction on the amount of foreign (American) films and shows that could be broadcast in EC Member States. The quota made international waves because due to its potential to dramatically affect American and Japanese imports into Europe.

At the center of the debate surrounding

the Directive was justification of the quota system. None of the parties involved in the debate (*i.e.*, the United States and the EC) denied the importance of culture, and none denied that culture was worth protecting. The focus of this debate was whether there was a genuine need for Europe to protect its culture in this particular situation.

The Preamble outlined the purposes, aims, and goals of the Directive:

> It is essential for the Member States to ensure the prevention of any acts which May prove detrimental to freedom of movement and trade in television programmes or which May promote the creation of dominant positions which would lead to restriction on pluralism and freedom of televised information and of the information sector as a whole.[157]

The acts which "may lead to restriction on pluralism," referred, of course, to the dominant position held by imported American television programs. The goal in preserving pluralism in television programming was to ensure "the independence of cultural development in the Member States and the preservation of cultural diversity in the Community." These two goals combined to provide a cultural foundation on which the Directive's justification was to stand. "Pluralism" and "diversity" were the key words. They stood in the face of the prime time slots in Europe that had been dominated by American shows like Dallas, The Cosby Show, Baywatch, and, most recently, Quantum Leap.

The Directive provided that these policies and goals were to be implemented in the form of a quota, or minimum broadcasting requirement. Article 6 contained the language of the controversial cultural quota itself.

In layman's terms, the quota required that European broadcasters earmark more than fifty percent of their entertainment, education, and documentary programming for "European works." The practical effect was to reduce the quantity of foreign imported programs that dominated prime-time slots in the European programming grids. More specifically, in practice, the quota would diminish the amount of American programs broadcast on networks of Member States.

3. The "Americanization" of Culture[158]

The Television Without Frontiers: Green Paper on the establishment of the Common Market for Broadcasting, recognized a need to protect European culture from invasion: "Frequent warnings are heard about the dangers of cultural domination of one country by another in the cinema, although this is not a problem between Member States."[159] The attack, however, was directed outwards, in particular at the United States dominance of the media. According to the Commission "[t]he creation of a common market for television production is ... one essential step if the dominance of the big American media corporations is to be counterbalanced."[160]

The general feeling among the Community members according to the Commission is that the "Americanization" of Europe—being Kentucky Fried and Coca-Colonized out of existence—must be reversed.

The controversy surrounding the Directive involves, in particular, the European quota and content provision in Member State programming. Member States shall ensure where practicable and by appropriate means, that broadcasters reserve for European works, within the meaning of Article 6, a majority proportion of their transmission time, excluding news, sports events, games, advertising and teletext services. This proportion, having regard to the broadcaster's informational, educational, cultural, and entertainment responsibilities to its viewing

157 Council Directive 89/552 on Television Without Frontiers, pmbl.

158 Stephen R. Konigsberg, *Think Globally, Act Locally: North American Free Trade, Canadian Cultural Industry Exemption, and the Liberalization of the Broadcast Ownership Laws*, 12 CORDOZO ARTS & ENT. L. J. 281. Copyright 1993 Stephen R. Konigsberg. Excerpt reprinted with permission.

159 Television Without Frontiers: Green Paper on the Establishment of the Common Market for Broadcasting, COM(84) 300 Final 1984.

160 Green Paper at 33.

public, should be achieved progressively, on the basis of suitable criteria.

The EC subsequently established incentive programs in an attempt to promote European-wide production and distribution networks. These incentive programs, collectively referred to as the MEDIA program, provide for a wide range of incentives, which include the promotion of business partnerships as well as providing for tax benefits for program producers.

In justifying protection, French President Francois Mitterand warned that all of Europe may soon be watching American programs on Japanese televisions. However, the motivation behind the Community adoption of the Directive is clear from the various debates on the subject in the European Parliament. Representative Schinzel, Socialist party member from the Federal Republic of Germany, stated in the European Parliament that television broadcasting, in particular, is a critical cultural asset of the EC and is "of major significance to our democratic way of life and our cultural and social coexistence within the EC." Representative Kuijpers, a Rainbow Party member from Belgium, noted that the Directive was to be implemented not only to protect Community and European broadcast markets, "but also and above all of protecting Europe's cultural heritage, which—far more than we realize—is the victim of increasing Americanization." Actively supporting the implementation of a Community-wide 60% quota of European works, Representative Roelants Du Vivier, Rainbow Party member from France caustically stated:

> We want—to guarantee the diversity of cultures and their identity, to guarantee pluralism of expression, to protect copyright and to avoid an influx of cheap productions primarily from the USA—and I have no hesitation in talking about American cast-offs here—we have to act and provide adequate protection for Community works. Protectionism? Who is being protectionist if it isn't the United States, where the market is protected from productions from elsewhere?

The Community further justifies its zealous position by identifying measures within the US legal system. US law forbids any foreign government or their representatives to own broadcast stations. This restriction is extended to any alien or representative, and any alien-affiliated foreign corporation. If an alien or foreign-controlled corporation chooses to buy into the US market, they must first comply with the restrictive provisions imposed by Section 310 of the Communications Act of 1934. These restrictions relate to stock ownership, management control and citizenship requirements for foreign individuals and corporations. The policy and underlying justification for this legislation dates back to the Radio Act of 1912, which contemplated that a foreign-controlled radio station could seriously threaten national security by potentially interfering with American communications. The Community stresses that these US laws, as well as the FTA Exemption Clause, explicitly recognize culture as a separate and distinct animal from other goods and services, thereby warranting the restrictions.

The American reaction to the inclusion of the Exemption clause was swift. Jack Valenti, President of the Motion Picture Association of America, noted that if NAFTA is left unchanged, it will cause the film, TV, and video industry severe injury, putting its $ 3.5 billion trade surplus at risk. Jay Berman, President of the Recording Industry Association of America, stated: "The Canadians have deliberately confused commerce and culture. For the Canadians, culture is used to mask a real commercial interest. Most often this type of commercial self-interest will result in discriminatory treatment for United States copyright industries." For these reasons, the US entertainment industry has repeatedly called for renegotiation of the NAFTA Exemption Clause.

The EC did not escape criticism. Mr. Valenti, in response to the Directive, wondered whether "the culture of any European is so flimsily anchored, so tenuously rooted, that European consumers and viewers must be caged and blinded else their links with their historic and distinguished past suddenly vanish?"

However, despite all the criticism, the US still does not seem to recognize that there is a genuine problem. The United States domination of global entertainment markets has caused visible resentment.

QUESTIONS AND COMMENTS FOR YOUR CONSIDERATION

1. Are there other less restrictive alternatives the EC could have used to protect its cultural integrity?

2. What impact, if any, does the commodification of culture have on the role of GATT as a method for establishing international intellectual protection norms? (See Chapter Seven.).

PART III

PROCEDURES AND REMEDIES

7

Treaty Regimes

When a distinct class of disputes arise and recur among a group of nations, sooner or later they entertain the idea of entering into a treaty that could make it possible to avoid further disputes. Treaties are broadly classified as bilateral or multilateral. Bilateral treaties often include a more disparate set of provisions than do multilateral treaties. This follows from the fact that two nations, A and B, may have a number of contentious issues between them, and the treaty conference is a handy vehicle for horse-trading among issues and resolving all of them. Thus, a bilateral treaty might have provisions favored by A on matters of copyright, and provisions favored by B on a distinct issue such as a most-favored-nation customs agreement. In the Nineteenth Century, such omnibus bilateral treaties were often called Treaties of Amity, Commerce and Navigation. Today, it is more likely that the treaty conference between A and B might result, in the example above given, in two separate bilateral treaties: one on copyright and the other on most-favored-nation status.

As soon as three or more states come to a treaty conference, the resulting treaty is likely to be a single-issue treaty. It could be a huge issue (like the law of the sea), but it is nevertheless single-minded. This again is a function of the kinds of issues that tend to be resolved when three or more states meet. State A might have a particular claim against State B, which in turn might have a different claim against state C; it would be difficult and frustrating to get these separate matters resolved in a single treaty because the unaffected party would not necessarily know where its future interest may lie. Thus, multilateral conferences tend to be called with respect to a single issue. Copyright has its own multilateral treaties; patents its own; and recently there have been off-shoot multilateral treaties (TRIPS is an off-shoot of GATT).

This Chapter begins by looking at the bilateral and multilateral approaches to dispute avoidance by treaty. It continues with a discussion of treaty interpretation and treaty reservations (reservations only apply to multilateral treaties; there is no such thing as a reservation to a bilateral treaty).

Often the treaty that emerges from a multilateral treaty conference is noticeably shaped by the organization that provided the forum for the conference. A treaty that results from a UNESCO initiative thus might be different from a treaty that comes out of a conference sponsored by GATT or WIPO, even if the state participants are the same and issues are the same. Much of the debate going into the initial choice of forum centers on the perceived status of the sponsoring organization: is it political or neutral, pro-developed nations or pro-developing nations? This Chapter examines some of these issues, with a particular focus on the debate during the Uruguay Round Negotiations of GATT over the appropriateness of utilizing GATT as a forum for intellectual property concerns.

We conclude with a closer look at the major intellectual property treaties: The Paris Convention for the Protection of Industrial Property, the Berne Convention, the Universal Copyright Convention, the Agreement on Trade Related Aspects of Intellectual Property (TRIPS), and the North American Free Trade Agreement (NAFTA). We have already looked at the Rome Convention of 1961 that concerns the protection of neighboring rights, in Chapter Four. In the next Chapter, we will take a closer look at trademark and patent registration treaties, including the Madrid Agreement and Protocol and the Patent Cooperation Treaty. All the treaties named in this paragraph can be found in the Appendix.

A. Multinational or Bilateral Solutions to Intellectual Property Protection?

1. Bilateral Agreements[1]

The existence of differing legal regimes complicates intellectual property protection. A reasonable standard for one country may not be similarly viewed by another. Whether a country follows case law, as opposed to a civil code, may be highly determinative of the type of legal standard that country is willing to embrace.[2]

Bilateral agreements provide the most workable vehicle for addressing the contentious issues surrounding intellectual property protection. Unlike multilateral agreements, bilateral agreements are country specific and thus may provide more protection for owners of foreign rights.

The United States has recently enacted a number of bilateral agreements that take a hard line against intellectual property piracy. These agreements are usually subsequent to a US threat of trade sanctions pursuant to "Super 301" of the 1988 Omnibus Trade and Competitiveness Act.[3] These bilateral agreements have generally encouraged speedier and more substantial changes in suspect nations, as failure to comply might result in immediate trade sanctions.

For example, the People's Republic of China amended its intellectual property laws pursuant to a Memorandum of Understanding it concluded with the United States in January 1992. This document was drafted in direct response to threatened retaliation by the United States.

A bilateral approach can recognize and incorporate into the agreement the developing country's stage of development and genuine efforts to improve the system of intellectual property protection. In addition, bilateral negotiations present a workable environment in which the developed country can introduce the developing country to the benefits of protecting intellectual property.

a. Special 301[4]

Strong international protection of copyright removes the incentive of states to employ unilateral measures to ensure protection of works produced by their nationals. US trade sanctions against China were proposed because there was no other effective remedy available to the United States. Specifically, there were no international mechanisms in place to compel China to enforce its copyright laws.

The criticisms leveled at the United States for its use of the Special 301 procedures focuses not on the ends, but the means. The protection of intellectual property is

---

[1] Tara Kalagher Giunta, Lily H. Shang, *Ownership of Information in a Global Economy*, 27 GEO. WASH. J. INT'L L. & ECON. 327. Copyright 1994 George Washington University. Excerpt reprinted with permission.

[2] The fact that the US legal system is case law driven may explain why there is more litigation in the United States than in any other country. The adversarial system flourishes in the United States because it allows constant interpretation and reinterpretation of case law. Consequently, very broad discovery rules have evolved to accommodate litigation. *See* Fed. R. Civ. P. 26(b).

[3] 19 U.S.C. sec. 2411(b).

[4] Robert A. Cinque, *Making Cyberspace Safe for Copyright: The Protection of Electronic Works in a Protocol to the Berne Convention,* 18 FORDHAM INT'L L.J. 1258. Copyright 1995 Fordham University School of Law. Excerpt reprinted with permission.

supported by the majority of nations, although many express displeasure with the unilateral nature of "Special 301" actions. If successful, US judicial extension of extra-territorial jurisdiction would likely elicit a similar reaction.

Uniform standards are indeed difficult to attain when nations pursue bilateral agreements, each with its own terms. The threat of trade sanctions, moreover, is always accompanied by risk. The United States-China trade impasse may have been triggered by copyright negotiations, but its resolution involved political issues that are far afield from intellectual property.

QUESTIONS AND COMMENTS FOR YOUR CONSIDERATION

1. Super (or Special) 301 (19 U.S.C. § 2411, et seq.) is often used by the United States to encourage nations to enter into bilateral agreements regarding intellectual property protection. For a detailed discussion of Special 301, *see* Chapter Nine.

2. But what if 3 out of the 10 countries add a reservation to the multilateral treaty, and each of their reservations is different from the two others? Suddenly we have a far more complex interrelationship of legal obligations among themselves, but their relation to the reserving states is different. This follows from the fact that a reservation is interpreted reciprocally—it applies both to the reserving state and to all the other states in their relation to the reserving state. Under the Vienna Convention on the Law of Treaties, which has become a standard document for treaty interpretation among nations, a reservation that is "incompatible with the object and purpose of the treaty" is invalid (Art. 19(c)). If it were not for this rule, a reservation could frustrate the idea of having a treaty in the first place. However, courts are sometimes faced with difficult tasks of interpretation when an objection is made that a reservation should be struck down on the basis of its incompatibility with the object and purpose of a treaty. Most modern treaties avoid getting into this morass of interpretive difficulty by specifying exactly which of its provisions may be subject to reservation, or even specifying the kinds of reservations that may be made. When a treaty is explicit in this fashion, then any state that attempts to make a reservation that is disallowed by the treaty itself simply cannot become a party to the treaty. For a further discussion of the incompatibility rule, *see* Sec. B(2) later in this Chapter.

4. If state A is troubled by state B's violation of certain of A's claimed intellectual property rights, should A attempt to work out a bilateral treaty with B or should A put its efforts into a multilateral treaty and invite B to the conference? Could a bilateral treaty between A and B operate to impede a subsequent multilateral treaty solution? If you were a lawyer in a country's Foreign Office or State Department, would you advise your government to pursue a bilateral or a multilateral treaty approach? What practical reasons would you give in support of your choice?

5. What impact, if any, do bilateral agreements have on the standards established under multinational agreements?

2. Multinational Treaties: An Overview[5]

Multinational treaty regimes include both regional agreements, such as The Treaty of Rome (establishing the European Union) and NAFTA, and broad based, multination agreements such as the Berne Convention and the General Agreement on Trade and Tariffs ("GATT"). In the area of intellectual property protection the major multinational treaty regimes are administered either by WIPO (the Berne and Paris Conventions, among others), the WTO (the TRIPS Agreement) or UNESCO (The Universal Copyright Convention). Differences in the methods for altering these agreements and in their enforcement mechanisms often dictate which forum is selected. Regardless of the forum selected, the goal of these agreements is similar—to achieve a multinational solution to the problems caused by inadequate international protection of intellectual property rights.

a. WIPO and UNESCO[6]

The World Intellectual Property Organization is a specialized agency of the United Nations, having its headquarters in Geneva. WIPO's General Assembly is a representative body having delegates from each of its 116 member states. The General Assembly appoints WIPO's Director General, currently Director General Bogsch, who is in charge of the International Bureau (Secretariat). The objectives of WIPO are to promote the protection of intellectual property throughout the world and to administer the international intellectual property unions, such as the Berne and Paris Conventions.

The four major multinational unions that WIPO administers are the Paris Convention, the Berne Convention, the Madrid Agreement and the Rome Convention. The Paris Convention, which is over 100 years old, contains provisions relating to inventions, trade names, trademarks, industrial designs, utility models, indications of source, appellations of origin, and the repression of unfair competition.

The Paris Convention grants the rights of priority and national treatment. National treatment requires that a country cannot provide less favorable intellectual property treatment to foreigners than to its citizens. National treatment of the Paris Convention is often criticized—if a country chooses to provide no intellectual property protection for its citizens, the Paris Convention does not require it to provide intellectual property protection for foreigners either.

The Patent Cooperation Treaty ("PCT") implements the Paris Convention's right of priority, by providing a one year grace period from the date of the filing of a patent application in the home country to the filing in another member country.

The Berne Convention [which contains provisions relating to copyrights] receives much less criticism than the Paris Convention. Berne requires minimum standards of protection in addition to national treatment. Perhaps the reason for the minimum standards in Berne, but not in the Paris Convention, is because Berne applies special rules to developing countries. The Berne Convention has 88 members.

The Universal Copyright Convention ("UCC"), which is administered by UNESCO, is an alternative copyright treaty for non-members of Berne at its inception such as the US, Soviet Union and China. The foundation of the UCC is also national treatment. While the UCC provides minimum standards of protection, the standards are lower than those of Berne. Since the US and the former Soviet Union acceded to Berne, Berne has taken the primary role in formulating international copyright policy.

The Madrid Agreement, another WIPO agreement over a hundred years old, simplifies the procedures for filing trademarks and service marks in different countries. The US is not a member of Madrid, but is actively seeking accession to the Madrid Protocol.

The Rome Convention requires international protection for performers, producers of phonograms and broadcasting organizations; *i.e.*, neighboring rights. The Rome Convention provides for national treatment

---

[5] Written for this Anthology by Doris Estelle Long. Copyright 1996 Doris E. Long.

[6] Monique L. Cordray, *GATT v. WIPO,* 76 J. PAT E. TRADEMARK OFF. SOC'Y. 121. Copyright 1994 Monique L. Cordray. Excerpt reprinted with permission.

and specifies minimum rights. As of January 1, 1990, the Rome Convention had 32 members. The US was not a member.

b. WTO[7]

The World Trade Organization ("WTO") is the successor organization to GATT and is charged with overseeing the TRIPS Agreement. TRIPS utilizes the Paris, Berne and Rome Conventions to establish minimum standards of protection in addition to national treatment. It also establishes multinational enforcement standards for intellectual property rights.

[7] Written for this Anthology by Doris Estelle Long. Copyright 1996 Doris E. Long.

QUESTIONS AND COMMENTS FOR YOUR CONSIDERATION

1. Are there disadvantages to pursuing multinational solutions through multinational treaty regimes?
2. Under which treaty regime—bilateral or multinational—would you expect to obtain more stringent mechanisms for protecting intellectual property rights?
3. The choice of forum for negotiating a multinational treaty depends on a variety of factors, including the mechanism available to enforce treaty obligations and the potentially politicized nature of the forum. For a discussion of these issues, *see* Section C of this Chapter.

B. The Enforcement of Treaty Obligations

1. Treaty Interpretation[8]

The defining issue in both legal and literary interpretation can be characterized as follows: to what extent does the text have a determinate meaning, and to what extent is the reader free to interpret it as he or she chooses? This question is especially relevant to treaty interpretation where, more often than not, the contracting parties themselves have the final say about the meaning of particular provisions of the agreement in question (a phenomenon that can be labeled "auto-interpretation"). Because many international instruments do not provide for the submission of disputes to impartial tribunals, interpretation is a responsibility of domestic officials who are institutionally predisposed to interpretations preferred by their State and government.

Skepticism about the determinacy of meaning combined with the absence of an impartial interpreter can lead to the discomforting conclusion that treaty auto-interpretation is an unconstrained activity determined entirely by short-term national interests and power politics. In this article, I seek to counter that perception by positing the existence of a structure of constraints embedded in the process of treaty interpretation despite the absence of a disinterested interpreter. Interpretive authority, it will be argued, resides in neither the text nor the reader individually, but with the community of professionals engaged in the enterprise of treaty interpretation and implementation. This "interpretive community" is defined and constituted by a set of conventions and institutional practices that structure the interpretive process.

Of primary importance is the notion that treaties, unlike works of literature, embody a commitment to a distinctive process of interpretation. This commitment is rooted in the fact that a treaty is the product of the

[8] Ian Johnstone, *Treaty Interpretation: The Authority of Interpretive Communities*, 12 MICH. J. INT. L. 371–72, 380–82, 385–91, 418–19 (1991). Reprinted by permission.

consensual activity of two or more States, and its terms embody the collective expectations and interests of the parties. Because the parties to the treaty comprise the collective norm-creating body, the competence of authoritative interpretation is vested in the composite organ they form rather than either of them individually. If the treaty does not provide for a dispute resolution procedure, then an authoritative interpretation can only result from a process that embodies this notion of the parties as a composite law-making entity in some other way. In entering into a treaty, a State binds itself not only to the terms of the instrument (however interpreted) but also a process of intersubjective interpretation: the interpretive task is to ascertain what the text means to the parties collectively rather than to each individually. The activities and perspectives of the interpretive communities associated with this enterprise render treaty auto-interpretation something other than the exercise of unilateral political will.

The interpretive process, then, must be understood as part of an ongoing relationship in which the parties generate, elaborate and refine shared understandings and expectations.

The parties can be viewed as having implicitly agreed to a process of intersubjective interpretation because, while they expect disagreement over the meaning of terms, they do not expect every disagreement to signify a desire on the part of one or the other to revoke the treaty or terminate the relationship embodied in it. States comply with treaties primarily because they have an interest in reciprocal compliance by the other party or parties.

In understanding how treaty auto-interpretation is constrained, two interpretive communities can be identified: the community interpreters directly responsible for the conclusion and implementation of a particular treaty, and a broader, international community consisting of all experts and officials engaged in the various professional activities associated with treaty practice. The conventions and institutional practices of both interpretive communities have constraining effect, although the contribution of the latter is derivative in that its authority can be traced to the implicit agreement between the parties to engage in intersubjective interpretation.

1. *The Narrow Interpretative Community.* The exercise of formulating, negotiating, ratifying, and implementing a treaty generates an interpretive community of individuals within each contracting party who share what Fish calls "assumed distinctions, categories of understanding, and stipulations of relevance and irrelevance."[9] That is, the process of producing and living under a treaty generates a community (not out of whole cloth but out of already existing communities with an elaborate web of relationships to the new community) of people and institutions associated with the treaty. These people are the officials within each State (from the leader down) who have or had responsibility for any of the various steps involved in producing the treaty.

The constraining effect of this narrow interpretive community is felt, in part, though the expectations and beliefs controlled by the agreement. In the period prior to the making of an agreement, some sort of relationship exists or the agreement would not have been possible) that generates a body of knowledge shared by the parties. Officials within each State learn about the others' interests, values and assumptions, as well as their perspectives on the various components of the relationship. An agreement "crystallizes the learning of a particular period"[10] and the contacts made help spread common understandings about the precise terms of the agreement as well as its significance to the broader relationship. The agreement becomes a focal point around which expectations converge. Furthermore, by communicating and exchanging information the governments come to know their partners in the agreement and not merely know about them. The participants in the enterprise come to inhabit a common world—a world that does not simply come out of the shared beliefs and attitudes of it inhabitants but in fact generates those beliefs and attitudes through common participation.

---

[9] STANLEY FISH, DOING WHAT COMES NATURALLY, 141 (1989).

[10] Nye, *Nuclear Learning and US-Soviet Security Regimes*, 41 INT'L ORG. 371, 398 (1987).

2. *The Broader Interpretive Community.* Beyond the immediate interpretive community centered around the treaty itself, interpretation is constrained by an amorphous community of all those regarded as possessing the knowledge of an expert or professional in the relevant field. As Oscar Schachter explains, governments cannot escape legal appraisals of their conduct by other governments (expressed either individually or in collective bodies), political parties, international lawyers, non-governmental organizations and other organs of public opinion.[11] In the realm of military security, this community judgment is influenced by the opinions of governmental and non-governmental experts on international law, world politics and strategic affairs. The competency or expertise comes from training and immersion in some feature of the enterprise in which the experts and immersion in some feature of the enterprise in which the experts are engaged. As participants in the field of practice, they have come to understand its purposes and conventions, learned not merely as a set of abstract rules but through the acquisition of know-how, a mastering of the discipline or technique. Having participated in the techniques and discourse of international law, treaty interpretation and/or the subject matter of the treaty, they have become competent in the field.

The outlying interpretive community represents the institutional mechanism closest to an impartial arbiter that the structure of treaty auto-interpretation provides. It constrains interpretation primarily because States have an interest in maintaining a reputation for good faith adherence to treaties. As Henkin states:

> Every nation's foreign policy depends substantially on its "credit"—on maintaining the expectation that it will live up to international mores and obligations. Considerations of "honor," "prestige," "leadership," "influence," "reputation," which figure prominently in governmental decisions, often weigh in favor of observing law. Nations generally desire a reputation for principled behavior, for propriety and respectability.[12]

This interest combined with the implicit agreement between the parties to engage in intersubjective interpretation means the outlying interpretive community effectively checks and structures the interpretive activities of the parties.

2. Reservations

a. Definitions[13]

The three major classifications of treaty-qualifying unilateral statements are reservations, understandings, and declarations. A reservation is a formal declaration made by a state when it joins a treaty, a declaration that acts to limit or modify the effect of the treaty in application to the reserving state. A reservation is external to the text of the treaty and is an attempt to alter the negotiated package. Because reservations are made outside of the treaty negotiations, their amendment to the multilateral treaty may conflict with the original text of the treaty. The ultimate effect of the reservation will depend on the practice or rule of reservations applied and the existence or nonexistence of special provisions within the treaty governing inclusion and effect of reservations.

The term "understanding" is used to designate a statement not intended to alter or limit the effect of the treaty, but rather to set forth a state's interpretation or explanation of a treaty provision. In practice, understandings are sometimes used to provide a memorandum of the nation's interpretation at the time of signing in case of future judicial or arbitral proceedings.

A declaration is a unilateral statement of policy or opinion that, like an understanding, is not intended to alter or limit any provision of the treaty. It is considered to have

---

[11] Oscar Schachter, *Self-Defense and the Rule of Law*, 83 A.J.I.L. 259, 264 (1989).

[12] LOUIS HENKIN, HOW NATIONS BEHAVE: LAW AND FOREIGN POLICY 52 (2d ed. 1979).

[13] By Catherine Logan Piper, excerpted from: *Reservations to Multilateral Treaties: The Goal of Universality*, 71 IOWA L. REV. 295, 298 (1985). Reprinted by permission.

the least effect on the original treaty text and is used primarily to articulate a signatory's purpose, position, or expectation, concerning the treaty in question.

b. The Vienna Convention[14]

The Vienna Convention on the Law of Treaties defines a "reservation" as "a unilateral statement, however, phrased or named, by a State, when signing, ratifying, accepting, approving or acceding to a treaty, whereby it purports to exclude or modify the legal effect of certain provisions of a treaty in their application to that State." Among the pertinent provisions of the Vienna Convention regarding the force and effectiveness of a reservation are the following:

Article 19.[15]

A State may, when signing, ratifying, accepting, approving or acceding to a treaty, formulate a reservation unless:

(a) the reservation is prohibited by the treaty;
(b) the treaty provides that only specified reservations, which do not include the reservation in question, may be made; or
(c) in cases not falling under subparagraphs (a) and (b), the reservation is incompatible with the object and purpose of the treaty.

Article 20.

1. A reservation expressly authorized by a treaty does not require any subsequent acceptance by the other contracting States unless the treaty so provides.
2. When it appears from the limited number of the negotiating States and the object and purpose of a treaty that the application of the treaty in its entirety between all the parties is an essential condition of the consent of each one to be bound by the treaty, a reservation requires acceptance by all the parties.
3. When a treaty is a constituent instrument of an international organization and unless it otherwise provides, a reservation requires the acceptance of the competent organ of that organization.
4. In cases not falling under the preceding paragraphs and unless the treaty otherwise provides:
   (a) acceptance by another contracting State of a reservation constitutes the reserving State a party to the treaty in relation to that other State if or when the treaty is in force for those States;
   (b) an objection by another contracting State to a reservation does not preclude the entry into force of the treaty as between the objecting and reserving States unless a contrary intention is definitely expressed by the objecting State;
   (c) an act expressing a State's consent to be bound by the treaty and containing a reservation is effective as soon as at least one other contracting State has accepted the reservation.
5. For the purposes of paragraphs 2 and 4 and unless the treaty otherwise provides, a reservation is considered to have been accepted by a State if it shall have raised no objection to the reservation by the end of a period of twelve months after it was notified of the reservation or by the date on which it expressed its consent to be bound by the treaty, whichever is later.

Article 23.

1. A reservation, an express acceptance of a reservation, and an objection to a reservation must be formulated in writing and communicated to the contracting States and other States entitled to become parties to the treaty.
2. If formulated when signing the treaty subject to ratification, acceptance or approval, a reservation must be formally confirmed by the reserving State when expressing its consent to be bound by the treaty. In such a case

---

[14] Written for this Anthology by Doris Estelle Long. Copyright 1996 Doris E. Long.

[15] This Article is informally known as the "compatibility rule."

the reservation shall be considered as having been made on the date of its confirmation.

3. An express acceptance of, or an objection to, a reservation made previously to confirmation of the reservation does not itself require confirmation.

4. The withdrawal of a reservation or of an objection to a reservation must be formulated in writing.

Article 21.

1. A reservation established with regard to another party in accordance with Articles 19, 20 and 23:
   (a) modifies for the reserving State in its relations with that other party the provisions of the treaty to which the reservation relates to the extent of the reservation; and
   (b) modifies those provisions to the same extent for that other party in its relations with the reserving State.
2. The reservation does not modify the provisions of the treaty for the other parties to the treaty inter se.
3. When a State objecting to a reservation has not opposed the entry into force of the treaty between itself and the reserving State, the provisions to which the reservation relates do not apply as between the two States to the extent of the reservation.

Although the United States has not acceded to the Vienna Convention, it has relied upon it as an authoritative text for treaty interpretations in State Department communiques and in cases before international tribunals.

c. Desirability of Reservations[16]

Conceptually, the issue of the desirability of reservations is straightforward. Most arguments in favor of the liberal use of reservations have as their cornerstone the belief that the liberal admissibility of reservations will encourage wider acceptance of treaties.

The other edge of the sword, as it were, is that reservations necessarily reduce the uniformity and consistency (if not the integrity) of a treaty.

The exact nature of the balance between uniformity/consistency and universality may be complex. For example, it is possible that a point exists in the liberal use of reservations beyond which participation will be reduced as those states satisfied with a treaty feel its integrity is being stretched to the breaking point by the permissibility of reservations. This problem may be both latent and practical, *i.e.*, perceived because the treaty does not restrict the use of reservations, and an actual reaction to reservations that have been made. The point is that a direct proportionality between the liberal admissibility of reservations and wider acceptance of a treaty cannot be assumed.

---

[16] By John King Gamble, Jr., excerpted from: *Reservations to Multilateral Treaties: A Macroscopic View of State Practice*, 74 AM. J. I'L. L. (1980). Reprinted by permission.

QUESTIONS AND COMMENTS FOR YOUR CONSIDERATION

1. Assume that your government wants to join the Berne Convention but does not want to protect moral rights. Can it properly reserve compliance with Article 10bis?

2. For further discussion of treaty interpretation and reservations, *see* INTERNATIONAL LAW ANTHOLOGY, pp. 121-145.

3. The Absence of Harmonization Standards[17]

Article 10bis includes a general obligation to member countries "to assure to nationals of the Paris Convention for the Protection of Industrial Property effective protection against unfair competition." However, this provision has not afforded a meaningful guarantee, for the treaty's definition of unfair competition leaves too much room for inconsistent and uncertain application.

The text prohibits "any act of competition contrary to honest practices in industrial or commercial matters." [Article 10bis(2)] The two key terms are "act of competition" and "contrary to honest practices." These terms, however, refer to different legal regimes. According to a leading commentary on the treaty, the national law of each member country will determine what acts constitute "acts of competition," while international trade norms will determine the meaning of "honest practices."[18]

The treaty's failure to give content to these terms seriously weakens Article 10 bis. Consider the unauthorized adaptation of a computer program to a "hardware platform" for which it was not originally designed. Reference to a given member country's law may yield different responses as to whether the unauthorized transporting of the program would constitute "competition." If it would not, then even if the conduct complained of were "contrary to honest practices," the treaty apparently would not apply. For example, assume that breaking into computer security codes or tapping into telephone connections violates international norms of "honest practices." Assume also that, in the applicable forum, using the information thus acquired to create a related, but not directly competing program is not an act of "competition." In that case, the Paris Convention may not require awarding relief.

Similarly, even if the forum would classify the challenged act as "competition," if the act does not also violate international norms of "honest practices," then 10bis will not apply. Thus, if defendant "clones" a user interface, but does so using publicly available information, it is not clear that (in the absence of copyright protection) this act would violate international standards of fair play. As a result, one must question the ability of the Paris Convention to supply an alternative norm of intellectual property protection for computer programs.

[17] Jane C. Ginsburg, *Four Reasons And A Paradox: The Manifest Superiority Of Copyright Over Sui Generis Protection Of Computer Software*, 94 COLUM. L. REV. 2559. Copyright 1994 Directors of The Columbia Law Review Association, Inc. Excerpt reprinted with permission.

[18] G.H.C. BODENHAUSEN, GUIDE TO THE APPLICATION OF THE PARIS CONVENTION FOR THE PROTECTION OF INDUSTRIAL PROPERTY 144 (1968). The Guide enjoys a high degree of authority, as it was written by the Director of the United International Bureau for the Protection of Intellectual Property (BIRPI), the predecessor organization to World Intellectual Property Organization (WIPO), the entity charged with administering the Paris and Berne Conventions.

As an example of international trade norms, the recent GATT/TRIPs accord incorporates Paris Convention Art.10bis with respect to protection of trade secrets, and defines "a manner contrary to honest commercial practices" as "at least practices such as breach of contract, breach of confidence and inducement to breach, and includes the acquisition of undisclosed information by third parties who knew, or were grossly negligent in failing to know, that such practices were involved in the acquisition." TRIPS at Art. 39.1, 39.2 n.10.

QUESTIONS AND COMMENTS FOR YOUR CONSIDERATION

1. Although multinational treaties are intended to establish agreed upon international norms, such agreement may be lacking due to inconsistent treatment of terms. Is there any textual authority for extending "unfair competition" under Article 10bis to include computer software? To include trade secret protection?

2. What sources would you consider in deciding whether an act qualifies as contrary to "honest commercial practices"?

3. For a discussion of recent efforts to harmonize national laws through non-treaty regimes, *see* Chapter Twelve.

4. The Choice of National Treatment, Reciprocity or Minimum Rights

a. Territoriality and the Need for National Treatment[19]

The "territorial" view of intellectual property,[20] which maintained that an owner's rights ended at the border, necessarily gave rise to multinational efforts to establish international protection norms, culminating in the Berne and Paris Conventions in the latter part of the Nineteenth Century. Because of the accepted territorial nature of intellectual property rights, both Conventions relied largely upon a "national treatment" standard to assure uniform protection. Subsequent bilateral and multinational intellectual property treaties have similarly adopted a "national treatment" standard.

Where a "national treatment" standard is adopted, no agreement on the substantive rights granted an intellectual property owner is achieved. Each nation is required simply to provide identical protection under its domestic laws to both domestic and foreign rightsholders. Similarly, where "reciprocal treatment" is adopted, no agreement on an owner's substantive rights is achieved. Instead, each nation is required to provide identical protection under its domestic laws but only to the extent that the country of the foreign owner provides reciprocal rights.

Twentieth Century advances have called into question both the continuing viability of a territorial theory for intellectual property protection as well as the usefulness of a national treatment standard.

b. Territoriality and the Problem of Reciprocity[21]

I must now attack a widely accepted theory: the territoriality of intellectual property. There are more and more cases in which it is difficult to localize the origin or the infringement of intellectual property territorially. Research teams increasingly develop inventions by collaborating in many countries at the same time within the framework of multinational corporations or consortiums. Authors increasingly collaborate within worldwide telecommunication networks, creating works that are in turn susceptible of instantaneous dissemination throughout such networks. The difficulty is illustrated by the case in which the Nike company wanted to have its trademark attached to the clothing worn by Olympic athletes in Barcelona in 1992. A Spanish claimant had previously registered the name "Nike" as a trademark in Spain and sued to prevent the Nike Company from using this name in Barcelona. National treatment results in subjecting Nike to prior registration in Spain, just as it would any Spanish national. But should this purely territorial priority preclude disseminating a trademark worldwide? That was, in any event, where Nike wanted its mark televised from the Olympics.[22]

The increasing difficulty of localizing such facts territory by territory has manifold consequences. Reciprocity, if it limits protection to the level established in a country of origin, requires localizing the fact of innovation, creation, or first use in that country. If that fact takes place across national borders, for example, because of coproduction in many countries, selecting any one country of origin will at least partially result in a legal fiction. Further, to determine in what country to claim national treatment relative to rights of intellectual property, it is necessary to ascertain in what national territory to localize infringement of such property. Suppose, for example, that a pirate inputs a literary or artistic work into a worldwide telecommunication network without consent: the copyright

---

[19] Written for this Anthology by Doris Estelle Long. Copyright 1996 Doris E. Long.

[20] *Editors' Note:* For a detailed discussion of the territorial theory of intellectual property rights, *see* Chapter Eleven.

[21] Paul Edward Geller, *Intellectual Property In The Global Marketplace: Impact Of TRIPS Dispute Settlements?* 29 INT'L LAWYER 99. Copyright 1995 American Bar Association. Excerpt reprinted with permission.

[22] Ultimately, the case was decided on other grounds, notably the cancellation of the prior Spanish registration of a "Nike" mark. Appeal 325/91, *America Nike v. Amigo*, Judgment of Dec. 10, 1993, Juzgado de Primera Instancia no. 9, Section 1 (Court of first instance), Barcelona, Spain.

owner might not be sure in which country or countries to assert infringement claims—at points of input or access in the network, or both. Finally, the judge might hesitate in deciding which country's or countries' laws to choose to determine rights enforceable at such points. All these Gordian knots may be cut by imposing much the same rights for any given property across many countries at once. This the Paris and Berne Conventions began to do in establishing minimum rights for intellectual properties.

Both material reciprocity and national treatment presuppose the old doctrine that intellectual property originates, and is enforced, territory by territory. Not only does the TRIPS Agreement incorporate such territorial premises as the Paris-Berne regime brings with it, but it still bears traces of comparable premises in the GATT, which above all concerned trade in tangible goods that can always be located territorially, at given spots on this earth. The TRIPS Agreement effectively devotes many provisions to the old problem of controlling the traffic in infringing goods moving from one national territory to another. This perspective, however, is not necessarily always appropriate to more volatile forms of trade in intangibles, such as commerce in intellectual property or in services.

A purely territorial approach will not help us to confront the reality of the twenty-first century. Already today, the Internet is where prior art, relevant for determining the novelty of inventions, might be aired worldwide. Similarly, the Nike example illustrates how telecommunication allows trade and service marks to be used in transborder marketing campaigns.

QUESTIONS AND COMMENTS FOR YOUR CONSIDERATION

1. Famous or "well known" marks are subject to special consideration under Article 6b of the Paris Convention. (*See* Chapter Nine.) This special treatment appears to be directly contrary to the territorial view of intellectual property rights.
2. Because the authority of a country granting copyright protection extends only to its borders, differences in national copyright laws tend to define markets of varying opportunities. Thus, authors prefer to market in jurisdictions where their rights are actively protected. By contrast, manufacturers may prefer to operate in countries which permit free-riding so that their acquisition costs for distributed products are lower. What additional concerns are raised by the territorial view of intellectual property?
3. Given the above-described issues, as well as the globalization of the market, is a territorial view of intellectual property rights still viable?

c. The Continuing Viability of National Treatment[23]

The building blocks of international copyright seem to be territorial. In the past, these building blocks have always been nation-states, which concluded copyright treaties, these states have had to protect foreign works against acts of infringement localized within their territories.

The classic dynamics of international copyright started to gather momentum some five hundred years ago. Three types of classic processes followed each other in time; first, the impetus given by the print media to copyright lawmaking; second, the decentralization of copyright interests; and, third, the emergence of international copyright.

---

[23] Paul Edward Geller, *New Dynamics in International Copyright*, 16 COLUMBIA—VLA JOURNAL OF LAW & THE ARTS 461. Copyright 1992. Paul Edward Geller. Excerpt reprinted with permission.

The first classic process commenced in the fifteenth century. The printing press was introduced into Europe, and the church and kings sought to control the rising book trade. They gave publishers, in capitals such as Paris and London, state-protected monopolies to print and sell books the censors had approved. These monopolies were territorial: royal authorities—or, publishers, by powers delegated from the sovereign—policed these monopolies on national territories. Tensions arose, however, as print shops opened throughout the provinces, books were increasingly smuggled across borders, and the growing reading public also sought better access to printed works.

The second classic process, the decentralization of copyright interests, hit its stride in the eighteenth century. Control of the dissemination of works was shifted from centers of royal power, outward to individual authors and publishers. These parties were granted copyright as a private right, exploitable throughout the national marketplace and enforceable by any court on civil suit. Ultimately, neither the state nor copyright owners but the public buying books or theater tickets in this marketplace decided which works were to gain the widest dissemination. Note also that the first copyright law, the Statute of Anne of 1709, was enacted at the very moment England and Scotland were being joined into a common market.

The third classic process, internationalization, began to take effect in the mid-nineteenth century. Books moved easily between the many countries of Europe sharing close borders. These countries began to cover Europe with a complicated web of bilateral treaties in order to protect the works of their respective nationals abroad. These treaties varied greatly, and authors, publishers and lawyers soon began to ask how to make more uniform law to govern the growing international market for works. Some proposed that all countries adopt the same copyright code at once, but a more modest proposal prevailed: simply conclude one copyright treaty, binding as many countries as possible, to compel the same choice of laws in cases of foreign works. This process culminated in 1886, when ten countries, seven of them European, established the Berne Convention.

The Berne Convention began what one commentator has called the "dissolution of the territoriality" of copyright.[24] Under the Berne principle of national treatment, the law of each Berne country applies when copyright in a Berne-protected work is infringed on its national territory. A court can easily localize the distribution of pirate copies or unauthorized theatrical performances in a given country. The court choosing law pursuant to the Berne Convention, however, need not sit within the territory of the country whose law it is to apply. For example, a court in the United States asserted jurisdiction to apply the Berne choice of law to infringement taking place in Latin America.[25]

In the twentieth century, the media have been changing radically, setting new and continuing dynamics into motion.

First, the dominance of the print media gave way to a proliferation of other media. Second, as if in a kaleidoscope, copyright interests have been regrouping. New media have led copyright interests into turbulent regroupings. Performing artists acquired new importance with the advent of sound recording and motion pictures. Thus, Enrico Caruso became the first singer heard by fans, not merely in local concert halls, but in recordings sold worldwide. Enterprises specialized in different, competing media have lobbied for legal provisions serving their respective, conflicting interests.

Third, internationally, copyright has begun to splinter into uncoordinated rights [u]nder the pressure of new media and interests, copyright itself has begun to splinter into diverse rights. In response to these pressures, each Berne revision has introduced new minimum rights, such as the rights to control broadcasting and cable retransmission in Article 11bis and reproduction in Article 9 of the Paris Act. The Rome Convention has instituted neighboring rights, not only to satisfy performing artists reaching worldwide audiences, but also sound-

---

[24] GYORGY BOYTHA, FRAGEN DER ENTSTEHUNG DES INTERNATIONALEN URHEBERRECHTS IN WOHR KOMMT DAS URHEBERRECHT UND WOHIN GEHTES? 181, 182 (Robert Dittrich ed. 1988).

[25] London Film Prods. Ltd. v. Intercontinental Communications, Inc., 580 F. Supp. 47 (S.D.N.Y. 1984).

recording producers and broadcasting organizations.

This splintering of copyright threatens to undermine the Berne principle of national treatment for coordinating rights. For example, the Austrian copyright law imposed a levy on blank-tape cassettes to fund a royalty for the home recording of works. Austro-Mechana, an Austrian collecting society administering the levy, however, drew out over half of all such levies to finance programs that benefitted only national authors, irrespective of foreign claims to share in all the levies. The German collecting society, GEMA, challenged that construction of the law, and the High Court of Austria reasoned that the "controlling principle of national treatment in the law of the international copyright conventions" precluded Austrian national law from allowing such a "one-sided discrimination against foreign citizens."[26] More subtle devices have been used to undercut national treatment elsewhere: for example, in France, the 1985 Act instituted so-called neighboring rights for audiovisual producers, while specifying that holders of these rights are entitled to receive their distinct portion of blank-tape royalties. Of course, since no convention provides for national treatment relative to such so-called neighboring rights for audiovisual producers, this portion of the blank-tape royalties may be withheld from foreign claimants. More subtly yet, the local procedures of collecting societies sometimes have unintended consequences on the flow of copyright monies due to foreign claimants. Compounding these problems, there is great uncertainty concerning who owns splintering rights from country to country.[27]

At the threshold of the twenty-first century, more recent dynamics have been putting radically new stresses on the Berne system.

The first of these recent processes is political and legal. European nation-states, with their respective colonial empires, formed the Berne Union in 1886. European countries also played important roles in revising the Berne Convention repeatedly in this century. At present, however, these countries no longer need the Berne Union to stabilize legal conditions in the European media market. The reason is simple: the European Community has begun to function as a supra-national lawmaking authority in the field of copyright in Europe. Indeed, the Court of First Instance of the European Communities has recently declared that Berne provisions need not apply as between E.C. member countries if they conflict with E.C. law on point.

The second recent process represents a revolution in media trends. The media, once proliferating, are now being reconsolidated into telecommunication networks.

Works will continue to be available, albeit with decreasing frequency, both as hard copies obtained on the marketplace and as performances seen and heard in theaters or concert halls. But there will be less and less need to clutter up our files and shelves with printed matter, tapes or discs, or to make photocopies or recordings from books or broadcasts. We will simply receive works on demand in digital form from more or less centralized data bases, through more or less centralized telecommunication networks. The works will then be played back on high-fidelity and high-definition multimedia monitors. There will accordingly be a decreasing need to buy, rent or make hard copies. We have to ask what the consequences will be for international copyright.

The third recent process involves a shift from private to public international law, as well as to supranational law. The Berne Convention is above all an instrument of private international law, assuring private parties of rights in literary and artistic works. To have effect, these rights must be vindicated in national courts, to which private parties may have recourse in copyright disputes with other private parties. The GATT, by contrast, is essentially an instrument of pub-

---

[26] Judgment of July 14, 1987 (Einbehaltungsuerpflichturg decision) Obersten Gerichtshof 1988 Gewerblicher Rechtsschutz und Urheberrecht Internationaler Teil (GRUR Int) 365, 368.

[27] Not all countries vest the same economic rights in the same parties worldwide, and many countries have developed their own rules concerning copyright transfers. No systematic international instrument guides the courts in tracing out chain of title from original owners to ultimate transferees of rights effective from country to country. Furthermore, while some countries have systems for putting copyright transfers on the public record, not all countries do, and no treaty instrument regulates the worldwide effect of such recordation.

lic international law: it governs disputes between public entities, notably nation-states, and has procedures to adjudicate such disputes and to sanction states for violating its rules. European Community law is supranational: E.C. directives and judicial rulings may bind private parties or E.C. member states, eventually preempting national laws.

Think, for example, of Article 11bis of the Berne Convention. It is at the heart of the debate on the issue which has stretched the notion of territoriality to the breaking point: what country's law localizes acts of satellite broadcasting? One proposed resolution of this issue, I believe, illustrates how more powerful media drive us beyond the classically territorial framework of the private international law of copyright. The European Community is considering a proposed directive which defines acts of satellite communication to be subject to the law of the place where a work-carrying broadcast is uplinked to a satellite. At the same time, it is argued, since the directive would harmonize the applicable laws throughout the Community, no significant choice-of-law issues would arise within any satellite footprint inside the Community. Thus the entire question of how to localize infringing acts territory by territory seems to be mooted by recourse to supranational law.

Consider this issue of territoriality more broadly. A book or a theatrical performance exists at a given point on this earth. By contrast, a work may arise and be virtually accessible at all points throughout a telecommunication network worldwide. Suppose that I collaborate by telephone, facsimile transmission or modem with a team of coauthors scattered over five continents in creating a work. Suppose, further, that our work is stored without our authorization in a data bank for release into a worldwide telecommunication network, accessible in all those continents at once. Suppose, finally, that the work is improperly indexed in the data bank and that authorship is not properly attributed to the members of the creative team. Would it make sense to localize this work in any one country of origin or to localize its infringing storage or misattribution in any one protecting country? Indeed, in this case, creation and infringement quite simply take place throughout the network, across territorial boundaries.

As the Berne principle of national treatment is undercut, there is the clear risk of increasing the "Balkanization" of international copyright. That is, an increasing variety of copyright claims could be differently handled as between different pairs of countries.

In truth, international copyright now has to deal with more comprehensive telecommunication networks that transcend national territories. Only the European Community is now elaborating non-territorial copyright regimes for such networks.

The difficulty, however, is deeper. The Berne Union was Eurocentric from the start, in part because of European colonial dominance in the nineteenth century. Europe, with its many borders confined in a small space, also provided a microcosm of the world, in which to try out a territorial organized system of international copyright. In uniting, Europe now provides a new laboratory in which to experiment with supranational copyright schemes. For a variety of reasons, however, its models may well diverge from those more appropriately adopted in other environments.

We will, I believe, soon find ourselves faced with the following three options: first, adopt the new European models, if only for lack of anything better; second, adopt divergent schemes, thereby fracturing international copyright; or, third, develop a more comprehensive regime for copyright in the world at large. Such a regime could further bolster, or even in some cases supplant, national treatment with an even more comprehensive set of minimum rights. In any event, the media are making any territorial regime, with all its accompanying habits of thought, increasingly obsolete.

5. The Establishment of Minimum Standards[28]

The absorption of classical intellectual property law into international economic

---

[28] J.H. Reichman, *Universal Minimum Standards of Intellectual Property Protection Under the TRIPS Component the WTO Agreement*, 29 INT'L LAW

law will gradually establish universal minimum standards governing the relations between innovators and second comers in an integrated world market.

Among the many causes of the drive to overcome preexisting territorial limitations on intellectual property rights, two merit attention here. First, the growing capacity of manufacturers in developing countries to penetrate distant markets for traditional industrial products has forced the developed countries to rely more heavily on their comparative advantages in the production of intellectual goods than in the past. Second, the rise of knowledge-based industries radically altered the nature of competition and disrupted the equilibrium that had resulted from more traditional comparative advantages. Not only is the cost of research and development often disproportionately higher than in the past, but the resulting innovation embodied in today's high-tech products has increasingly become more vulnerable to free-riding appropriators. Market access for developing countries thus constituted a bargaining chip to be exchanged for greater protection of intellectual goods within a restructured global marketplace.

In response to these challenges, the TRIPS Agreement mandates mostly time-tested, basic norms of international intellectual property law as enshrined in the Paris Convention for the Protection of Industrial Property, and the Berne Convention for the Protection of Literary and Artistic Works, or in certain domestic institutions, such as laws protecting confidential information, that all developed legal systems recognize in one form or another. It also leaves notable gaps and loopholes that will offset some of the gains accruing from the exercise, especially with respect to nontraditional objects of intellectual property protection. In this respect, both the strengths and weaknesses of the TRIPS Agreement stem from its essentially backwards-looking character. To the extent that the TRIPS Agreement significantly elevates the level of protection beyond that found in existing conventions, as certainly occurs with respect to patents, for example, the developing countries are usually afforded safeguards that few would have predicted at the outset of the negotiations. Nevertheless, both developed and developing countries guarantee that detailed "enforcement procedures as specified in this [Agreement] are available under their national laws,"[29] and they all become liable to dispute-settlement machinery for claims of nullification and impairment of benefits that can lead to cross-sectoral trade sanctions.

Perhaps the most important "basic principle" that applies virtually across the board is that of national treatment of (that is, non-discrimination against) foreign rights holders. This principle of equal treatment under the domestic laws is then carried over to relations between states in the most-favored-nation (MFN) provisions of Article 4. The latter article ostensibly prevents one member country from offering a better intellectual property deal than is required by international law to nationals of a second member country and then denying similar advantages to the nationals of other member countries.

Taken together, the national treatment and MFN provisions attempt to rectify the damage that some states recently inflicted on the international intellectual property system by unilaterally asserting claims of material reciprocity with respect to hybrid legal regimes falling in the penumbra between the Paris and Berne Conventions. While the national treatment and MFN clauses both apply "with regard to the protection of intellectual property," it turns out that, for purposes of the TRIPS Agreement, the term "intellectual property" refers only to seven of the eight subject-matter categories (1) copyrights and related rights; (2) trademarks and (3) geographical indications; (4) industrial designs; (5) patents; (6) integrated circuit designs; and (7) trade secrets or confidential information. As regards neighboring rights covered by the International Convention for the Protection of Performers, Producers of Phonograms and Broadcasting Organizations (Rome Convention), national treatment and the MFN clause apply only to those rights that the TRIPS Agreement selectively provides, but not to rights generally flowing from that Convention.

---

[29] TRIPS Agreement at arts. 41–50.

a. The Impact of National Treatment on Minimum Standards[30]

Although computer software appears to be protectable under both the Berne Convention and the Universal Copyright Convention, the protection is not explicit. Because the protection is not explicit, computer software developers cannot be sure that computer programs will be protected. Even if it is conclusively determined that the copyright conventions protect computer software, their substantive terms are subject to criticism.

Both the Berne Convention and the Universal Convention provide for national treatment. National treatment means that member nations must treat non-nationals the same as they treat nationals. National treatment creates uncertainty as to the extent of protection granted to computer software by a given country. For computer software to be protected, two conditions must be satisfied. First, the country where the computer software was developed and the country where enforcement is being sought must be parties to one of the international copyright conventions. Second, the law of the country where enforcement is sought must protect computer software. The country where enforcement is sought, although a member of one or both international copyright conventions, may not protect computer software. A computer software developer would receive no protection in such a country. Alternatively, the extent of the protection granted by the country where enforcement is sought may not be clear.

Even if both of the conditions are satisfied and the country where enforcement is sought clearly grants protection to computer software, national treatment is problematic because it results in inconsistent results. The rights of the computer software developer will depend on the country in which enforcement is sought.

The principle of national treatment is particularly problematic if a member nation grants authors moral rights in their works. Moral rights are incompatible with works that are predominantly utilitarian, such as computer software. They grant the author the power to control the use of the author's work, which limits the value of the work to owners of copies, particularly if the work is utilitarian. The right of an author to withdraw a work is particularly troubling because "allowing a programmer to withdraw his software could be devastating to those who have used, and become dependent on the program."

---

[30] Robert A. Arena, *A Proposal for the International Intellectual Property Protection of Computer Software*, 14 U. Pa. J. Int'l Bus. L. 213. Excerpt reprinted with permission.

b. The Failings of National Treatment[31]

The argument that improving municipal laws will help secure intellectual property rights is founded on the related notions of "National Treatment" (NT). NT, as implemented in the Paris Convention for Protection of Industrial Property, requires signatory countries to treat individuals from a foreign country as they treat their own nationals. Thus, a host country is obligated to give foreign visitors, and their property the same protection that its municipal laws give to its own citizens.

However, shortcomings of applying NT become obvious if the applicable municipal laws are themselves insufficient. For example, the Paris Convention grants each signatory country the right to determine what is patentable. This means that each country creates its own specific intellectual property regime. Thus, countries with the res communis ideology[32] have flexibility under the Paris Convention to enact very limited or even no laws recognizing patentability. Consequently, NT creates a disparate level of protection in different countries. It does not ensure substantive equivalence. Thus, according to NT principles, a country with

---

[31] Jean M. Dettmann, *Gatt: An Opportunity for an Intellectual Property Rights Solution*, 4 Transnat'l Law. 347. Copyright 1991 University of the Pacific, McGeorge School of Law. Excerpt reprinted with permission.

[32] *Editor's Note:* The theory of "res communis" refers to the view of some newly industrialized countries that knowledge and intellectual property are "the common heritage of mankind" and, therefore, should be freely available for use by everyone.

a high level of protection must grant this higher protection even to foreigners of countries with a lower level of protection. However, when citizens from the country with a higher level of protection visit the country with a lower level of protection, they must settle for the lower protection of that country. In many situations, NT only provides a foreigner with inadequate protection from the host country's municipal laws. Thus, municipal law coupled with NT does not offer an effective solution to the distortions of intellectual property trade.

QUESTIONS AND COMMENTS FOR YOUR CONSIDERATION

1. The pratice of using national treatment under the Berne and Paris Conventions as the standard for international protection of intellectual property arose originally during the Nineteenth Century. Is this approach still a viable alternative for establishing international substantive norms?
2. What are the problems posed by such approach?

c. Minimum Standards for What?[33]

We now come to the theoretical heart of the problem: Paris, Berne, and related treaty provisions need not always mean the same thing in the abstract Cartesian universe of intellectual property as in the concrete Hobbesian world of trade wars and truces. In practice, domestic courts have interpreted the Paris-Berne regime, but only in cases between private parties, while TRIPS panels will apply Paris and Berne provisions in the TRIPS Agreement to disputes between public entities, that is, W.T.O. members. Domestic courts could construe Paris-Berne obligations differently than do TRIPS panels, resulting in jurisprudential schizophrenia between the private and public international laws of intellectual property.

Where is the source of such schizophrenia? It is not necessarily the distinction between private and public international laws. In principle, private and public international laws can reinforce each other, much like laminated sheets in plywood. A liberal system of private international law assures private parties of property rights in which they may freely trade across national borders. A liberal system of public international law, like the GATT, precludes nation-states from taking measures to restrain that freedom to trade in tangible goods at their own borders. The TRIPS Agreement coordinates these aims a bit differently, since it obligates W.T.O. members to undertake measures to protect property interests in intangibles both within and at their own borders. Nor does the danger of schizophrenia lie in the minimal rationale for protecting intellectual property at these points: technological innovations and media creations must at least be protected against misappropriation to assure some stable marketplace for them. The TRIPS Agreement imposes measures that, at a minimum, are intended to prevent pirates from raiding intellectual property anywhere in the global marketplace. Our danger rather arises out of the difficulty of fashioning rights of intellectual property at optimum levels to encourage investment without obstructing competition. Such rights should, to quote Professor Lehmann, serve as "restrictions in competition in order to promote competition."[34]

We would do well to ask just what the TRIPS consensus fixed: Is it confined to categories of rights which the TRIPS Agreement enumerates, or does it systematically

---

[33] Paul Edward Geller, *Intellectual Property In The Global Marketplace: Impact Of TRIPS Dispute Settlements?* 29 INT'L LAWYER 99. Copyright 1995 American Bar Association. Excerpt reprinted with permission.

[34] Michael Lehmann, *The Theory of Property Rights and the Protection of Intellectual and Industrial Property*, 16 INT'L REV. INDUS. PROP. & COPYRIGHT L. 525 (1985).

embrace Paris-Berne principles for adjusting levels of protection in the future? This question is critical for knowing how far TRIPS panels may go in resolving disputes between W.T.O. members, as well as the principles that might guide them on the way. Confined to standards that represent intellectual property at present levels, TRIPS panels may have to acquiesce in many gaps left in the present state of the law. The Paris and Berne Conventions share the same choice-of-law principles for adjusting protection in the future: national treatment bolstered by minimum rights. The GATT offered the comparable, if not stronger principle of most-favored-nation treatment, which was devised for trade cases. The TRIPS Agreement applies all these principles, but neither clearly nor coherently across the field of intellectual property.[35]

Turning now to gaps endemic to the Paris-Berne regime which the TRIPS Agreement largely, if not altogether, incorporates, [t]he most obvious set of gaps arises because Paris and Berne provisions establishing minimum rights are subject to varying readings. Commentators have noted the open texture of such Paris and Berne rights: some are mandatory; some may be implemented with varying degrees of discretion; and some are altogether optional. However, to this point, only national courts have construed these rights, deciding which ones are mandatory and to what extent national legislators or courts themselves have discretion in formulating the other rights or fashioning remedies for them. For example, national courts have had to decide how to interpret the rather shadowy language which, in Article 10bis of the Paris Convention, assures relief against unfair competition in an open-ended range of cases. National courts may, of course, refer to the often-rich jurisprudence of their own constitutional and private international laws in applying international Paris and Berne provisions to diverse cases. The TRIPS Agreement in itself provides no such background against which TRIPS panels may understand the Paris and Berne minimum rights that it incorporates.

d. Minimum Standards and Enforcement Procedures[36]

Even in those countries which make genuine efforts to comply with the strictures of TRIPs, copyright protection remains uncertain. Like the Berne Convention, protection under TRIPs is premised on national treatment. Thus, such critical issues as the treatment of non-literal copying and the scope of protection to be afforded new rights not covered by the Berne Convention remain subject to the vagaries of national treatment. The only exception is the expressly stated inclusion under TRIPS of computer software as a covered "literary work" under Berne under Article 10. Although one of the most significant developments under TRIPs is the establishment of minimum procedural norms for the enforcement of copyright, such procedural norms are to be included within the structure of a member's existing judicial system. Thus, procedures for protecting copyright will remain inconsistent even after TRIPs.[37]

C. The Retroactivity Principle[38]

When one state concludes a copyright agreement with another state, it is clear that

---

[35] Compare Articles 1(2) of TRIPS (covers "categories of intellectual property that are the subject of Sections 1 to 7 of Part II"), 3(1), and 4(c) (national and most-favored-nation treatment excluded for neighboring rights not "provided under this Agreement") with Articles 1(3), 2(1) of the Paris Convention (national treatment for industrial property "understood in the broadest sense" with respect to "advantages" that laws "now grant, or may hereafter grant") and Article 5(1) of the Berne Convention (such treatment for author's rights that laws "do now or may hereafter grant").

[36] Doris Estelle Long, *Copyright and the Uruguay Round Agreements: A New Era of Protection or an Illusory Promise?*, 22 AIPLA Q.J. 531. Copyright 1995 Doris E. Long. Excerpt reprinted with permission.

[37] *Editors' Note:* For a further examination of the minimum procedural enforcement standards established under TRIPS, *see* Chapter Nine.

[38] Katherine S. Deters, *Retroactivity and Reliance Rights Under Article 18 of the Berne Copyright Convention*, 24 VAND. J. TRANSNAT'L L. 971. Copyright 1991 Vanderbilt University School of Law. Excerpt reprinted with permission.

the works created or published in either state after the effective date of the agreement will be protected in both states pursuant to the treaty. When, however, works created or published prior to the effective date of the agreement are afforded copyright protection in one state and not the other, problems may arise regarding the recapture of those pre-existing works out of the public domain of the other state. This is particularly true when individuals in one state have invested time, money, and effort into exploiting the works of another state's authors in the absence of any legal duty not to do so, or when the term of copyright protection afforded to the works of one state's authors has expired in the other state. Although the exploiting individuals arguably are benefiting from the creative efforts of the authors and should not be entitled to have their interests protected, some scholars emphasize that these persons "have nonetheless acted in good faith in reliance on a given state of affairs, namely that these works were in the public domain and could be used freely."[39]

The retroactivity doctrine seeks to achieve a balance between the newly acquired copyright protection accorded the authors of one state and the reliance interests of previous exploiters of those works in the other state. At a minimum, the doctrine creates a temporary time period during which prior exploiters may continue to use the work to recoup some or all of their investments, after which time the copyright owners are afforded full and exclusive protection under the terms of the Convention.

Today, Article 18 of the Berne Convention, which embodies the retroactivity principle, provides:

> (1) This Convention shall apply to all works which, at the moment of its coming into force, have not yet fallen into the public domain in the country of origin through the expiry of the term of protection.
> (2) If, however, through the expiry of the term of protection which was previously granted, a work has fallen into the public domain of the country where protection is claimed, that work shall not be protected anew.
> (3) The application of this principle shall be subject to any provisions contained in special conventions to that effect existing or to be concluded between countries of the Union. In the absence of such provisions, the respective countries shall determine, each in so far as it is concerned, the conditions of application of this principle.
> (4) The preceding provisions shall also apply in the case of new accessions to the Union and to cases in which protection is extended by the application of Article 7 or by the abandonment of reservations.[40]

[39] Sam Ricketson, The Berne Convention for the Protection of Literary and Artistic Works 665 (1987).

[40] Berne Convention for the Protection of Literary and Artistic Works at art. 18.

QUESTIONS AND COMMENTS FOR YOUR CONSIDERATION

1. Are newly adhering countries required to provide retroactive effect to the protection granted under the Berne Convention? If not, what incentives, if any, exist to encourage retroactive application?

2. For an example of retroactive application, *see* 17 U.S.C. § 104A (restoring US copyright protection to certain public domain works).

D. GATT v. WIPO

1. The Jurisdictional Dilemma[41]

From the initial preparatory work prior to the September 1986 Ministerial Declaration commencing the Uruguay Round, many developing countries, including Brazil and India, hotly contested the propriety of using GATT to establish international substantive norms in the area of intellectual property protection. The position of these countries, simply stated, was that if there was any need for the development of international norms, WIPO was the proper forum. Part of the reluctance to use GATT as a forum for addressing the desirability for new or additional international standards for intellectual property protection derived from the perception of many of these countries that GATT was primarily a forum for the "have" nations. Thus, many developing countries were concerned that their needs would not be given sufficient consideration in the GATT arena. Furthermore, to the extent that international norms for the protection of, for example, copyright might be required, these countries believed that the Berne Convention, with its emphasis on national treatment, had already resolved the issue and that any changes which might be required should be dealt with only through WIPO which had responsibility for overseeing the Convention. As the East German representative indicated in his support of a statement by Cuba on behalf of the "Group of 77"[42] challenging the use of GATT to address intellectual property protection issues:

> The strong international links between economy, science, technology and culture do not exclude other organizations or agreements in their activities to be concerned with the problems of implementing intellectual property rights. Moreover, for legal certainty and comprehensiveness, the competence of WIPO and its direct participation should be maintained since the solution of these problems belongs to the scope of its duties.[43]

By contrast, the developed nations, including the United States, were strongly dissatisfied with efforts to resolve existing copyright issues under WIPO auspices. While developing nations saw WIPO as a generally hospitable forum for their concerns, many developed countries considered WIPO to be, at best, indifferent to their needs and, at worst, hostile, in view of renewed efforts by some developing countries to use WIPO to seek a lessening in the level of protection currently established under the Berne Convention.[44] The developed countries also perceived GATT as providing a forum where an international consensus could be reached regarding the scope of protection for works not covered by the Berne Convention—including software and computer databases—outside the potentially politicized open meetings required by

---

[41] Doris Estelle Long, *Copyright and the Uruguay Round Agreements: A New Era of Protection or an Illusory Promise?*, 22 AIPLA Q. J. 531. Copyright 1995 Doris E. Long. Excerpt reprinted with permission.

[42] The "Group of 77" was organized during the first United Nations Conference on Trade and Development (UNCTAD) in Geneva in 1965 and is composed of less developed countries. The aim of the group was to organize developing countries so that they could speak with one voice, thereby gaining increased negotiating clout. Some commentators, however, viewed this development as representative of an ideological split between democracies who put their faith in economic growth and Third World countries who seek a redistribution of wealth to less technologically developed countries. This perceived ideological split led the US and other developed nations to distrust certain fora since developing countries often used discussions at the United Nations, and its specialized agencies such as WIPO, as vehicles for advancing political objectives, including mandatory transfer of technology from the "haves" to the "have nots."

[43] GATT Negotiating Group Sets Talk This Week on U.S. Proposal, WIPO Will Join Discussion, 4 INT'L TRADE REP. 1358, 1359 (1987).

[44] Some developing countries had already sought to reduce existing intellectual property protection under WIPO on the theory that such property is the "common heritage" of mankind and should be freely available to all. Such free availability, they believe, included the right of transfer to developing countries without payment of compensation.

WIPO.[45] Finally, developed nations sought to rectify a perceived lack of adequate enforcement mechanisms under the Berne Convention. Although Article 33 of the Berne Convention provided that disputes can be brought before the International Court of Justice, at the time of the Uruguay Round negotiations not one such dispute had been brought in over 45 years.[46] Since WIPO had no other enforcement procedures for assuring that a member's laws complied with Berne's agreed-upon minimums, the developed countries sought to establish an enforcement mechanism under GATT which would force full compliance by all member countries, thereby assuring a minimum level of copyright protection in such countries.

2. The Enforcement Paradigm[47]

For rules to evolve into behavior-influencing norms which ensure compliance with the rules by the players, particularly in the context of international law, the rules must be invested with a high degree of legitimacy by the players. Sanction or coercion is insufficient in itself to engender the legitimacy which ensures compliance with the law. The foundations, in international law, of the obligation to comply with a norm is difficult to explicate with reference to any one theory, however there is widespread agreement that the "acceptability" of a rule is critical to a nation's observance of a rule as law.

Acceptance of a rule is distinct from consent to enforcement of the rule. Acceptance, which endows the rule with norm-generative character usually precedes consent to the rule's enforcement; sometimes however, acceptance arises after consent to enforcement of a rule. In the event that acceptance precedes consent to the rule's enforcement, the shape of the rule begins to acquire a distinctly normative profile in its function—demarcating, with fair level of precision, the legal rights and obligations it creates.

The roots of the "GATT v. WIPO" thesis with its pronounced emphasis on sanction based enforcement as the basis of a rule's binding character, derive from Austinian legal positivism. Austinian affinity for laws imperative nature locates the legally binding character of rules in their sanction based enforcement. Rules not supported by an effective sanction are defective for they cannot create any duty or obligation. Such laws are imperfect laws or deficient laws as they are without sanction. In consonance with its reasoning, international law, devoid as it is of any centralized sanction based enforcement system, cannot engender any binding obligations by itself. Thus it follows that in order to endow the rules created under international law with legitimacy it must be backed up by an enforcement mechanism.

The neo-analytic tradition, pioneered by H.L.A. Hart among others has lucidly elucidated the basic defect innate in the process of reasoning which predicates the validity of a rule on its enforceability. Such a process confuses "matters of fact with matters of right."[48] That X can by force compel Y to behave in a particular manner does not mean either that X has a right to compel Y to perform the act in question, nor can it imply that Y is under a duty or obligation to comply. Y may be "obliged" to obey but he is not under any "obligation" to do so. Enforcement alone, cannot imbue the rule with validity. The validity of enforcement in terms of its capacity to normatively ensure compliance with the rule will depend upon the legitimacy of the rule independently of

---

[45] WIPO meetings were almost always open meetings, thereby offering developing countries the opportunity for "political grandstanding at the expense of substantive discussion." By contrast, most GATT negotiations were generally conducted "outside the public spotlight, and the rhetoric used by the participants was genteel by contrast."

[46] Part of the reason for the lack of enforcement is the requirement under the UN Charter that a judgment by the International Court of Justice can only be enforced by voluntary cooperation or by referral to the Security Council. Since it is doubtful the Security Council would act to enforce an intellectual property judgment, absent consent, any such judgment would have no impact on the challenged conduct.

[47] Bal Gopal Das, *Intellectual Property Dispute, GATT, WIPO: Of Playing By the Game Rules and Rules of the Game*, 35 IDEA J.L. & TECH. 149. Copyright 1994 PTC Research Foundation of the Franklin Pierce Law Center. Excerpt reprinted with permission.

[48] *See generally* TERRY NARDIN, LAW, MORALITY AND RELATIONS OF STATES (Princeton 1983).

the rule's enforceability. Enforcement presupposes the legitimacy of the rule being enforced. Legitimacy of the rule arises from its acceptance by the participant, who consents to its enforcement. "The law is not obligatory because it is enforced: it is enforced because it is obligatory; and enforcement would otherwise be illegal."[49]

If from the ineffective compliance with obligations created by a rule without sanctions we arrive at the conclusion that the validity or obligations of a rule originates in its capacity to be enforced, we are confusing the effectiveness of a rule with its legal validity. The legal validity of a rule is not contingent upon its effectiveness. Effectiveness of a rule may be an empirical condition however it cannot be the criterion of a rule's validity. Thus, if enforcement relates to the rule's effectiveness alone, then it cannot be the source of the rule's legitimacy. The normative legitimacy of a rule lies in its acceptance; a rule which is internalized by its acceptance may be effective in terms of compliance with its obligations, even in the absence of any enforcement mechanism.

Arguments which are either impervious or attribute secondary importance to the role of acceptance in the evolution of behavior forming norms, particularly in the context of international law, are not well founded in theory and practice. Sanction-based enforcement may impart transient existence to rules in the short run, but it cannot be the basis for the normative legitimacy of the rules in the long run. In the absence of the former, rules cannot ascend to the status of behavior forming obligations.

It is true that disenchantment with existing multilateral forums, enervated as they are both by the absence of minimum enforceable standards as well as by the non-existence of an effective enforcement mechanism, motivated strategic interest groups to successfully lobby for the inclusion of an intellectual property agenda in the Uruguay Round of multilateral trade negotiations. However the praxis which formed the backdrop for the debate attached, from its inception, importance to the need to promote complementarity between the work of GATT and that of WIPO and to avoid duplicating the work of WIPO. Indeed, beyond the rhetoric, the texts of the proceedings through the different stages of the negotiations, unequivocally resonate with the recognition by the dominant parties of the need for TRIP to complement WIPO's efforts.

The discourse on linking trade with intellectual property was animated by a limited agenda from its origin. The objective envisaged had four basic aspects: establish substantive standards for intellectual property protection; efficient enforcement measures; dispute settlement mechanism; and the application of certain GATT provisions to intellectual property. The spring board of the trade based approach was informed by the concept of trade sanction. To that extent its scope was circumscribed. With trade based sanctions forming the anchor, the primary objective was to concretize the intellectual property standards already obtained under the aegis of WIPO by weeding out ambiguities with respect to the form and content of these obligations. The objective was not to create an alternative regime under GATT as much as it was to build on WIPO's contributions.

[49] GERALD G. FITZMAURICE, GENERAL PRINCIPLES at 45.

QUESTIONS AND COMMENTS FOR YOUR CONSIDERATION

1. What sanctions would you consider effective for ensuring compliance with treaty obligations?

2. What sanctions would you consider effective for ensuring protection of intellectual property rights? What factors would you consider in determining the scope of such sanctions?

3. For a discussion of the enforcement remedies provided by various treaty regimes to protect intellectual property, *see* Chapter Nine.

E. Major International Intellectual Property Treaties

The major substantive international intellectual property rights treaties are the Paris Convention, the Universal Copyright Convention, and the Berne Convention. The Paris Convention protects patents and trademarks, while both the Universal Copyright Convention and the Berne Convention protect copyrights. In addition, the recently amended General Agreement on Tariffs and Trade ("GATT"), a trade treaty, includes provisions for protection of intellectual property entitled "Trade Related Aspects to Intellectual Property Rights" ("TRIPS"). Another important treaty, which in many ways served as a precursor to TRIPS is the North American Free Trade Agreement ("NAFTA"), a regional trade agreement between the United States, Canada and Mexico that included intellectual property protection provisions. All of these treaties provide integral international protection of intellectual property rights. Each, however, also contains its own defects that impedes its ability to provide comprehensive international protection.

1. The Bi-Polar Structure[50]

Governments adopt intellectual property laws in the belief that a privileged, monopolistic domain operating on the margins of the free-market economy promotes long-term cultural and technological progress better than a regime of unbridled competition. Ordinary tangible goods that acquire value by satisfying known human needs in more or less standardized ways cannot escape the price-setting function of the competitive market. In contrast, intellectual goods acquire value by deviating from standard solutions to known human needs in ways that yield more efficient outcomes or that capture the public's fancy. Because intellectual goods define relevant market segments in terms of the novelty or the originality they purvey, their creators invent their own markets by stimulating demand for goods that did not previously exist.

The term "intellectual property" was not coined until the late nineteenth century. Only when Josef Kohler and Edmond Picard perceived that copyright, patent, and trademark laws had more in common with each other than with the older forms of property known to Roman law was it recognized that a new class of rights in intangible creations had arisen. Their use of the term "intellectual property" thus coincided with the drive for international regulation of both artistic and industrial property, a movement destined to produce a fully articulated and universally recognized legal discourse in little more than a century.

Taken together, the Paris and Berne Conventions purport to subdivide the international intellectual property system into two hermetically sealed compartments separated by a common line of demarcation. Literary and artistic property rights occupy one of these compartments; so-called industrial property rights occupy the other.

The origins of the bipolar structure can be traced to cornerstone provisions of the Great Conventions extant since their inception and to corresponding state practices recognized by most developed intellectual property systems. On the one hand, Article 1 of the Berne Convention established "a Union for the protection of the rights of authors in their literary and artistic works." Such works, categorized at length in Article 2(1), should receive automatic and mandatory protection in the domestic copyright laws of the member states. To avoid censorship and to liberate authors from overt and covert forms of patronage, these laws entitle almost all independently created works falling within the designated subject matter categories to a generous but relatively soft form of protection against copying only that lasts a long period of time.

On the other hand, Articles 1(1) and 1(2) of the Paris Convention established "a Union for the protection of industrial property" and identified certain legal institutions as the "object" of industrial property protection, namely, "patents, utility models, industrial designs, trademarks, service marks, trade

---

[50] J.H. Reichman, *Charting the Collapse of the Patent-Copyright Dichotomy: Premises for a Restructured International Intellectual Property System*, 13 Cardozo Arts & Ent L.J. 475. Copyright 1993 Yeshiva University. Excerpt reprinted with permission.

names, indications of source . . . and the repression of unfair competition." While some international minimum standards and the rule of national treatment apply to all these institutions, the Paris Convention entrusted the protection of industrial creations primarily to "the various kinds of industrial patents recognized by the laws of the countries of the Union." The patent paradigm and variants thereof classically confer a tougher form of protection on strict formal and substantive conditions for a relatively short period of time.

Governments seeking to maintain high levels of investment in technological innovation face an increasingly difficult task as the twentieth century draws to a close. They must preserve or restore the bases for healthy competition at a time when information is increasingly becoming the medium from which the most socially valuable artifacts are likely to be constructed. This task will require the elaboration of a new intellectual property paradigm that looks "beyond art and inventions." Such a paradigm must deal directly with the pervasive threat of market failure facing investors in unpatentable, noncopyrightable innovation under present-day conditions, without multiplying ill-conceived, socially harmful regimes of exclusive property rights.

2. The Paris Convention

a. An Historical Overview[51]

The Paris Convention for the Protection of Industrial Property was first concluded in 1883. Since its inception, the Convention has been revised six times, the last revision occurring in 1967 at Stockholm. Concurrent with the latest revision was the establishment of WIPO, which assumed responsibility from the United International Bureau for the Protection of Intellectual Property (BIRPI) for the performance of the administrative tasks of the Paris Union.

The national patent systems that existed prior to the Paris Convention often contained widely varying legal rules. The United States, for example, examined patent applications substantively, while many European countries did not. Most countries published the technical disclosures of patent applications upon grant, some held the disclosures in secret until after the patent expired, while still others published the disclosure immediately upon filing. Generally speaking, the variation between national provisions at the time appears to have been substantially larger than exists today.

These variations in national patent practices created procedural obstacles to the international assertion of patent rights. In those countries that published patent disclosures immediately upon filing, for example, the mere act of applying for patent disclosed the invention publicly. At the same time, other countries conditioned patentability on absolute novelty worldwide. Applying for a patent in one country could thus create an absolute barrier to obtaining a valid patent in another.

These procedural obstacles to patenting generally appear to have arisen inadvertently. There also existed at this time, however, another category of obstacles that national governments had erected purposefully. The obstacles in this second category were essentially protectionist. By the late 1800s European and United States scholars had explored the economics of patenting extensively. As explained below, many granting sovereigns had begun to manipulate their national patent laws to enrich themselves in relation to their trading partners.

Patent systems are large-scale governmental intrusions into the free-market economy. They involve manipulating social costs and benefits to increase the national wealth. Perhaps the most significant cost of such systems is the higher prices imposed on consumers of the patented advance. If the patented technology has some economic value the patent owner is able to impose single-source pricing on it—a price that is higher than would exist in a truly competitive market.

Patent systems exist because this social cost of higher prices is presumed to result in an increased pace of invention. Higher

---

[51] R. Carl Moy, *The History of the Patent Harmonization Treaty: Economic Self-Interest As An Influence*, 26 J. Marshall L. Rev. 457. Copyright 1993 The John Marshall Law School. Excerpt reprinted with permission.

prices transfer increased amounts of money from consumers of the patented technology to producers. Knowing this, inventors will strive to invent patentable technology more vigorously. Some will succeed who otherwise would have failed. The sophistication of the country's industrial base thus increases, and new technology becomes available to consumers. According to the presumption, the social benefits of this increased rate of invention are large enough to more than offset the costs of patenting.

In a purely domestic economy the national effects of these costs and benefits are linked together relatively tightly. Each unit of increased cost imposed on domestic consumers provides a unit of increased revenue to domestic industry. Evaluating such a patent system therefore involves, in large part, estimating the amount of increased invention that will actually result from a given increase in expected revenue. In addition, the increased resources diverted to a domestic patent owner are not wholly lost to the domestic economy. Rather, the domestic patent owner generally will reinvest all or a part of those resources, thereby mitigating the cost of patenting to some degree.

International patenting, on the other hand, de-couples the national effects of patenting. Assume that an inventor exploits the advance through patenting, not in his or her own country, but in a foreign country. In that situation industry domestic to the inventor's own country receives increased profits from patenting, but domestic consumers do not pay the associated higher prices. Instead, the higher prices are imposed on consumers in the foreign country. International patent transactions therefore reallocate wealth away from the granting country and into the country of the patent owner.

Prior to the Paris Convention many countries had acted on this basic economic truth. Their national laws included numerous, varied provisions that curtailed the domestic patent rights of foreign nationals. Some countries, for example, had adopted compulsory-licensing provisions. By their very nature, compulsory licenses lower the cost of the patented advance closer to multiple-source pricing. In addition, if the compulsory license is given to a domestic entity a portion of the foreign trade is prevented outright. Both these mechanisms reduce the amount of wealth that flows out of the country into the hands of the foreign patent owner.

Another type of protectionist provision motivated by the same economic calculation was the widespread presence of national working requirements. Generally, these provisions required patent owners to supply domestic demand for the patented technology through domestic production. The failure to do so resulted in the patent becoming invalid or unenforceable. Facially neutral with regard to nationality, working requirements had an obviously greater, purposeful impact on patent owners who were foreign. In essence, foreign patentees were required to either abandon their patent rights or behave as if they were domestic entities.

In addition to increased prices, patents impose another social cost that is relevant to international patenting: they retard further research in the patented technology. Patents commonly dominate inventions that remain to be discovered and patented themselves. Once a patent issues, therefore, every person other than the patent owner has a reduced expectation of return from further research in the areas of technology that the patent dominates. Rationally, then, researchers will reduce their inventive efforts in technology that is dominated by another's patent. If competition spurs the speed of research, this reduction in competition will slow industrial development over time. The issue in a purely domestic economy is optimally balancing the initial incentive to the original patent owner with the detriment to future researchers.

With international patenting, however, the problem becomes more complex. The teachings of an issued patent can travel beyond the borders of the granting sovereign and into other countries. Corresponding patent rights in such other countries may, or may not, exist. In countries where they do not, the public learns of the advance and yet is free from the economic impediment of dominating patent rights. Technological development therefore continues unabated. In countries where dominant patent rights do exist, in contrast, only the holder of the dominant patent is fully motivated to continue researching. Over time, this risks reducing the industrial sophistication of the patenting country in comparison to that of the non-patenting country.

These economic considerations spurred a number of countries to act during the early period of international patenting. Primary among those actions were national provisions that caused domestic patents to expire as soon as any corresponding foreign patent expired. In operation, these provisions freed domestic industry from the constraining effects of patenting as soon as the industry in another country became free.

In total, these various protectionist provisions inflicted immense difficulties on patent owners. Often, one simply could not obtain patent rights in a foreign country. Even if a foreign patent could be obtained, many times its continued existence depended on the patent owner rapidly initiating manufacture in that foreign country. This could be disadvantageous for many different reasons.

Prior to the Paris Convention essentially no international agreements addressed the obstacles to international patenting set out in the preceding section. Instead, patent owners who wished to assert patent rights in foreign countries were forced to rely on their own resources. As a practical matter, they were forced to restrict the number of countries in which they sought patent protection.

In 1883, a decade-long process of negotiation culminated in a number of countries signing the Paris Convention. Although the creation of the convention was an act of international diplomacy, the participants in the negotiations included not only representatives of national governments, but representatives of industrial interests as well. It appears, in fact, that the negotiations began primarily at the insistence of industrial interests.

The Paris Convention addressed a portion of the obstacles to international patenting. At the same time, other obstacles remained unresolved. This partial failure raises an immediate question: Why was agreement on those issues not reached? Many causes doubtlessly contributed. At the same time, however, the pattern of successes and failures suggests that the different economic interests of the various parties to the negotiations was a significant cause. In particular, agreement appears to have been possible only where the economic interests of national government and industry coincided.

It is axiomatic that the interests of national government will tend to be national in scope. With regard to patenting, these interests will include the full range of social costs and benefits of a patent system: the potential benefits of an increased rate of innovation, for example, as well as the costs of higher consumer prices, the costs of administering the patent system, and the costs borne by other endeavors from whom the increased resources spent on patenting have been diverted.

This focus on both the costs and the benefits of patenting should also hold true with regard to transactions of international patenting. A national government will be concerned with the increased incentive that patent rights in foreign countries bestow upon its domestic industry. Government will also be concerned with the domestic costs of awarding patents to foreigners: the loss of national wealth from importation of patented goods, and the potential stunting of domestic industry via international patenting that is uneven.

Industry's view of patenting, in contrast, is potentially quite different. Industry will be concerned with how patenting affects its own, private interests. Those interests will in all likelihood be very different from the interests of society as a whole. For example, patent systems rely entirely on the incentive of increased profits to spur innovative activity. Patenting therefore bestows large private benefits on industry. At the same time, the social costs of patenting are generally spread throughout society. They therefore impose private costs on industry to a much lesser degree.

This observation is very significant. Unless one views inventors as entitled to monopoly profits naturally, patent systems must be seen as societal mechanisms for providing an optimal amount of incentive to invent. To determine that amount of incentive, one must consider more than industry's narrow, private interests. The result of that broader calculation need not coincide with industry's preferences. Thus, society can prefer rules of patent law that industry would not choose. Stated conversely, industry can prefer rules of patent law that are adverse to society. The differences of position between the two groups should be systematic.

For the same reasons, industry and national governments should also have systematically different interests with regard to international patenting. If they behave rationally according to economic criteria, national governments will be interested in obtaining agreements that maximize the wealth of their individual countries. These will be agreements whose operation bestows on the particular national economy both large benefits and small costs from international patenting. Industry, in contrast, will seek the private benefits of increased international patenting but will be relatively unconcerned with any associated social costs. In particular, industry will be largely unconcerned with whether a disproportionate share of such costs falls on any particular national economy, including that of its own country.

In essence, because the parties to an international sale of a patented item each belong to a different national economy, their private costs and gains become social costs and gains for the countries involved. For example, where a national of the country under consideration holds a foreign patent, the sale of goods under that patent transfers wealth out of the foreign country into the hands of the patent-owning national. The national's private gain is thus a social gain for the national's own country. Conversely, where a country has granted one of its patents to a foreigner, the domestic sale of goods under the patent impoverishes domestic consumers and enriches the foreign patentee. The consumer's private cost is thus a social cost to the granting country. The outlook of national government differs from that of its patent-owning industry because the nation participates in both import and export transactions, while industry is largely preoccupied with exports.

The structure of the Paris Convention is consistent with the operation of these economic interests. Foreign patenting, for example, is crucial to the objectives of both industry and national government. Patents provide the market power that yields increased profits to industry. If such increased profits are to be had on foreign sales, industry must obtain foreign patents. Those same increased profits on foreign sales, moreover, appear to be the major mechanism by which countries enrich themselves through international patenting. National government is thus interested in seeing its citizens obtain as many foreign patents as possible. Additionally, foreign patents are needed to constrain the industrial development of competing countries while an advance is subject to domestic patent rights.

For these reasons, one would expect easy agreement in the Paris Convention to increase the general availability of foreign patenting. The interests of national governments are more or less the same on this particular issue. In addition, the self interests of national governments and industry generally coincide.

The original text of the Paris Convention shows such easy agreement on this issue through the concept of foreign priority:

> Any one who shall have regularly deposited an application for a patent of invention . . . in one of the contracting States, shall enjoy for the purpose of making the deposit in the other States . . . a right of priority under the periods hereinafter determined.
>
> In consequence, the deposit subsequently made in one of the other States of the Union, before the expiration of [this] period cannot be invalidated by acts performed in the interval, especially by another deposit, by the publication of the invention or by its working by a third party. . . .

As a result of this provision, an inventor could establish a date of filing in all member countries via an initial filing in a single country. The act of applying for patent rights on the same invention in several foreign countries was therefore made much easier.

As to protectionist provisions, the economic interests of national government and patent owners appear to diverge. National government is critically interested in retaining the freedom to impose protectionist provisions. By definition, these provisions reduce the outflow of national wealth to foreign patentees. They are an important means of minimizing the domestic costs of international patenting.

Industry, in contrast, will be generally opposed to protectionist provisions. Protectionist provisions reduce the market power of industry's foreign patents. Industry will therefore object to their presence in the patent systems of foreign countries and will seek their abolition. In addition, because others pay the private costs of increased patents on imports, industry has little reason to favor protectionist provisions in the domestic patent system of its own country.

Under an economic analysis, therefore, patent-owning industry will seek broad prohibitions against protectionist measures. In contrast, each national government will seek to preserve at least those protectionist provisions that operate to the country's own net benefit. Based upon these fundamentally different interests one would expect difficulty in achieving any agreement to eradicate protectionist provisions generally.

The historical course of negotiations over the Paris Convention is consistent with this analysis as well. The original text of the Paris Convention contained conspicuously little with regard to the two most widespread protectionist measures, working requirements and compulsory licenses:

> The introduction by the patentee into countries where the patent has been granted, of articles manufactured in any other of the States of the Union, shall not entail forfeiture.
>
> The patentee, however, shall be subject to the obligation of working his patent conformably to the laws of the country into which he has introduced the patented articles.

The text did require signatories to permit importation. At the same time, it specifically allowed the continued existence of national working requirements generally. It did not mention compulsory licenses at all.

In addition to the principle of foreign priority, the Paris Convention also adopted the principle of national treatment. "The subjects or citizens of each of the contracting States shall enjoy, in all other States of the Union, so far as concerns patents for inventions . . . the advantages that the respective laws thereof at present accord, or shall thereafter accord to subjects or citizens." Stated simply, national treatment requires each government to apply the same provisions to both its own citizens and foreign nationals. It has been described, along with the principle of foreign priority, as a fundamental tenet of the Convention.

The Paris Union's agreement to provide for national treatment stands in apparent opposition to the economic analysis suggested in this article. At least in theory, national treatment prevents governments from employing the most effective tool for reducing the domestic cost of international patenting: expressly denying domestic patent rights to foreign inventors. In addition, the Paris Union consciously selected national treatment over the competing principle of reciprocity. Under reciprocity, each government need award to foreign inventors only those patent rights that the foreign inventor's own government awards to nonnationals. Reciprocity would thus seem a favorite of national governments: under it, the cost of awarding domestic patents to foreigners is tied directly to the benefits that domestic industry receives from patenting in foreign markets.

What, then, does the Paris Union's selection of national treatment imply? Does it invalidate the assertion that economic self-interest explains the Paris Convention's substantive provisions? More broadly, does it show the Paris Union to have adopted an internationalist, free-trade approach to foreign patenting?

When examined carefully, the adoption of national treatment probably does not support these suppositions. Reasons completely apart from a free-trade rationale can cause government to favor national treatment over reciprocity. A country applying reciprocity, for example, must be expert in the patent laws of every foreign country. Reciprocity thus risks large administrative costs.

In addition, a deeper examination shows that national treatment still permits government many forms of protectionist behavior in patenting. Still possible, for example, are provisions that are facially neutral with regard to nationality, but which impact foreigners disproportionately. Working requirements and compulsory licenses are examples of two such provisions; the restrictions in United States law against proof of invention by foreign activities are another.

Another, more subtle type of protectionist provision permitted under national treatment involves reducing the domestic costs of patenting generally. The loss of domestic wealth to foreign patentees can occur only when domestic patenting results in valuable rights. Thus, government can reduce the outflow of wealth to foreigners by simply reducing the economic value of the domestic patent rights that are available. Indeed, the loss can be reduced to zero by refusing to grant domestic patents altogether.

The Swiss patent system provides a historical example of a national government employing this latter technique. Switzerland progressed through the industrial revolution without a patent system. The economic rationale behind this decision was sound: without domestic patents Swiss consumers paid no increased prices for new technology. Switzerland thus minimized the outflow of its wealth to importers. Indeed, refusing to issue patents removed all the social costs of patenting from the domestic Swiss economy. At the same time, Switzerland continued to receive most of the benefits of patenting. True, Swiss industry could not expect patent profits from introducing new technology into the domestic Swiss economy. The absence of domestic patents, however, gave Swiss industry free access to all the new technology that others developed. In addition, Swiss industry held patents in foreign countries, thus earning patent profits from exports and receiving an incentive to invent in that way. In fact, because the Swiss economy was small, the incentive that Swiss industry received from patented exports was arguably greater than the incentive that dominating the domestic Swiss economy via patenting might have supplied.

National treatment provided no obstacle to this strategy. The original Paris Convention did not commit its members to provide any minimum rights to patentees. Thus Switzerland could, and in fact did, adhere to the Paris Convention even though it had no patent system whatsoever. Its denial of patent rights equally to domestic nationals and foreigners satisfied the requirement of national treatment. Additionally, adhering to the Paris Convention guaranteed Swiss inventors national treatment from foreign governments, thereby ensuring Swiss industry access to patent profits on its exports. In fact, Switzerland did not find it in her interest to enact a national patent system until Germany threatened her with retaliatory tariff action.

Subsequent negotiations to revise the Paris Convention have continued to follow this pattern. It has been increasingly possible to harmonize the procedural requirements of patenting. At the same time, agreement to limit the use of national patent provisions for protectionist purposes has not progressed very far. The Paris Union has repeatedly revisited the issues of working requirements and compulsory licensing since 1883. The resulting provisions place very few restrictions on national governments that wish to use these mechanisms. Compulsory licenses can be granted as soon as three years after the patent issues. The patent can be revoked for failure to work two years thereafter. Perhaps more significant, even today the Paris Convention contains virtually no requirements that national governments grant any other minimum rights to patent holders. Indeed, the Convention still does not even require that national governments enact patent systems at all.

QUESTIONS AND COMMENTS FOR YOUR CONSIDERATION

1. To what extent, if any, do the conflicts between national government and industry remain of concern today? How have these conflicts been resolved under TRIPS and NAFTA?

2. What impact, if any, would a country's status as a newly industrialized nation have on the balance it might strike with regard to granting patent protection to domestic and foreign inventors?

3. What impact, if any, does the ability to impose compulsory licensing requirements (*see* Chapter Ten) have on the balance of interests described by the author?

b. Major Provisions[52]

The Paris Convention protects "industrial property," including "patents, utility models, industrial designs, trademarks, service marks, trade names, indications of source or appellations of origin, and the repression of unfair competition." In general, the Convention directs that each member country confer national treatment to other member nations. National treatment requires the member countries afford foreign intellectual property owners the same rights and protection as their own citizens. This includes affording national treatment to a foreign exporting company's manufacturing processes.

As a part of affording national treatment to foreign countries, the Convention requires all countries to honor prior applications of patents, and registrations of utility models, industrial designs, or trademarks from a foreign country. In essence, this requires the foreign country to honor an applicant's original filing date in their own country, as long as the time between the original filing date and the filing in the foreign country is not longer than the "priority period." The period of priority begins at the date of filing the first application.

Although the Convention affords a substantial amount of control to the intellectual property owner, it is not absolute. Each member state has the right to grant compulsory licenses to prevent a patent holder from using an invention exclusively. In the extreme case, where granting compulsory licenses has not afforded the general population the benefit of the patented product, a Member may forfeit the patent holder's rights. However, industrial designs are never forfeitable.

What the Paris Convention lacks is an explicit mechanism for settling disputes between member countries. While Article 13 of the Convention does establish an assembly, it merely allows the assembly to take "appropriate action designed to further the objectives of the Union." Such a provision does not give any guidance as to the power of the assembly or the procedure one must follow to make a complaint about a member country's activity. In addition, Article 15 establishes an International Bureau that has the authority to "conduct studies" and "provide services, designed to facilitate the protection of industrial property." However, similar to the assembly, the scope of the Bureau's powers are not delineated, nor is there a set procedure for settling grievances.

The Paris Convention does not require a minimum patent term. [It] is silent regarding the disclosure and claims of a patent [and] does not specify patent protected subject matter. The Paris Convention defines criteria for patentability: novelty, inventive step (non-obviousness) and industrial applicability. [It] does not specify the rights conferred by a patent.

c. Exceptions to Protection[53]

The present text of Article 5A of the Paris Convention permits member countries to provide legislative remedies for patent abuses by the patentee, such as failure to work. In the event of failure to work or insufficient working of a patented invention, the issuing country may require the patentee to grant a compulsory license of his or her patent rights to a willing applicant. No one, however, may apply for a compulsory license until the expiration of either four years from the date the patentee applies for the patent or three years from the date the patentee receives the patent, whichever occurs last. Therefore, the patentee has from three to four years before any sanctions can be imposed. If the patentee has legitimate reasons that justify inactivity beyond the three to four year period, applicants for compulsory licenses will likewise be refused. In any event, compulsory licenses may only be nonexclusive. Thus, the license enables the licensee to work in addition to the patentee, rather than in place of the patentee.

The present text of Article 5A prohibits revocation of patent rights for failure to work

---

[52] Karen Waller, *NAFTA: The Latest Gun in the Fight to Protect Intellectual Property Rights*, 13 DICK. J. INT'L L. 347. Copyright 1994 Karen Waller. Excerpt reprinted with permission.

[53] Adrienne Catanese, *Paris Convention, Patent Protection, and Technology Transfer*, 3 B.U. INT'L. L. J. 209. Copyright 1985 Trustees of Boston University. Excerpt reprinted with permission.

or insufficient working unless compulsory licenses were already granted and proved insufficient to prevent such abuses. In the event that compulsory licenses are granted and prove insufficient, forfeiture proceedings may not be instituted before the expiration of two years from the grant of the first compulsory license. Therefore, a patentee does not forfeit his or her patent rights unless the invention was not worked for the initial three to four year period, a compulsory license was then granted, and the invention was still not worked for another two years.

Under the present text of Article 5quater of the Paris Convention, when a product is imported into a country where there is a patent for the process of manufacturing the product, the patentee has the same rights with regard to the imported product as he or she would have with regard to a product manufactured in the issuing country. Therefore, if the patentee of a manufacturing process is entitled to prevent anyone from making, using, or selling products manufactured according to the patented process within the issuing country, then he or she may also be permitted to prevent the use or sale of products manufactured outside but imported into the issuing country.

QUESTIONS AND COMMENTS FOR YOUR CONSIDERATION

1. The Paris Convention also provides for the protection of trademarks and utility design models. Such protection is based on the concept of national treatment and priority. Union members are entitled to determine their own conditions and filing requirements for the protection of trademarks under their domestic laws. Although the Convention provides for special treatment of well-known marks, it does not establish an agreed-upon test for when such special treatment should attach (*see* generally Article 6 through 10ter of the Paris Convention).
2. To what extent, if any, does the absence of an enforcement mechanism reduce the effectiveness of the Paris Convention?
3. Are there additional issues which you believe should be the subject of international agreement in order to assure adequate protection of the interests represented by a patent? By a trademark?
4. For further information regarding patent registration treaties, *see* Chapter Eight.

3. Copyright under International Copyright Conventions[54]

International copyright conventions have led to the harmonization of sometimes conflicting national copyright laws, thus achieving a more unified approach to the regulation of the trade of copyrighted goods and raising the general level of protection for copyright holders. For example, it was the Rome Convention that spurred the harmonization of the disparate legal traditions of the economically oriented Anglo-Saxon copyright system and the more artistically principled *droit d'auteur*, which is of French origin. In general, convention provisions are effective only when the conventions are either self-executing or when they have been adopted by domestic legislation. Even when the conventions have domestic effect, the extent of harmonization is limited by the principle of national treatment, which relies on the domestic law of the importing country to supply the appropriate legal norms.

---

[54] Stacie I. Strong, *The Cultural Exclusion: Free Trade And Copyrighted Goods*, 4 Duke L. Comp. & Int'l L. 93. Copyright 1993 Duke Journal of Comparative & International Law. Excerpt reprinted with permission.

a. An Historical Overview Of The Origins Of Copyright

As a result of the invention of the printing press by Gutenberg in 1436, the level of copying and publishing worldwide increased markedly. Prior to the printing press, booksellers copied authors' manuscripts by hand, a lengthy procedure whose speed was only slightly increased through the use of slaves. After the invention of the printing press, however, booksellers could copy authors' manuscripts at a much faster rate. Profits from the sales of books helped the booksellers recover the costs of both the authors' manuscripts and the printing press.

The invention of the printing press also enabled "pirate" booksellers to copy books already published by "legitimate" booksellers. These pirate booksellers were able to sell these copied books at lower prices since they could avoid paying for the authors' manuscripts.[55] Neither the authors who had sold their manuscripts nor the legitimate booksellers had any legal recourse against these pirate booksellers, and it became increasingly clear that some protection was necessary.

The pressure for protection came not from authors but from booksellers, whose pecuniary interest was most threatened by the pirate booksellers. The booksellers successfully lobbied their respective sovereigns for protection in the form of an exclusive right, better known as a "privilege."[56] The privilege gave a legitimate bookseller the exclusive right to print and sell a specific author's manuscript for a limited time. In essence, government bestowed upon the printer a limited monopoly.[57]

The sovereigns also benefited from this arrangement, because they could decide which booksellers would receive a privilege—only those sellers holding views sympathetic to the government—and which manuscripts were suitable for printing. The sovereign censored manuscripts that it believed would threaten the public order.

The use of these privileges came to an end about two hundred years after they were introduced. The reasons for their demise are threefold. First, printers began to abuse their monopoly power, thereby angering their sovereigns in the process. Second, as governments became more mature, the need for censorship began to diminish. Finally, authors became more active in arguing for protection of their own rights.

The new system of protection that filled the vacuum left by the privilege system was a statutory form of protection which focused, for the first time, on the rights of authors. Starting in Great Britain with the 1709 Statute of Anne, statutory copyright for the protection of authors spread throughout Europe and the United States.

When the focus of copyright switched from the bookseller to the author, a philosophical debate emerged as to the origin of the right. Under the old privilege system, the right was justified on economic grounds; the booksellers needed an exclusive right for a limited duration in order to make adequate profit and cover the costs of a printing press and authors' manuscripts. Since the booksellers were not creators of a work, their only interest was pecuniary.

Authors, on the other hand, created the books; the ideas belonged to them and emanated from them. Thus, many philosophers argued that copyright should protect both the authors' economic and personal interests, and that those interests should be as unlimited as possible. These philosophers pointed to natural law as the basis of

---

55 The "pirate" booksellers also had the advantage of waiting to see which books were a commercial success. Thus, they would pirate only those books which had a high demand and thereby ensured themselves a profitable return.

56 The city of Venice apparently granted the first privilege to a publisher in approximately 1495. The exact date is not known, however, and some experts believe it could have been as early as 1469.

57 The privilege encompassed three essential aspects consistent with modern copyright law. First, the King would grant a printer an exclusive right to reproduce and distribute a certain work. Second, the term of the privilege would be set. Third, in the case of infringement, the privilege provided for sanctions including fines and seizure and confiscation of the infringing copies. In some cases damages were provided.

France was known to be very strict in enforcing privileges. [I]nfringement constituted a worse crime than the stealing of goods from the house of a neighbor, for in the latter case some negligence might possibly be imputed to the owner, while in the former it was stealing what had been confided to the public honor.

authors' rights. Statutes existed only for the limited purpose of recognizing these naturally existing rights and to give them a more precise formulation.

The difference between the Anglo-American philosophy and the natural rights philosophy has caused much conflict at the international level during the various Berne revision conferences. Natural rights countries focus almost exclusively on the individual author while the Anglo-American countries focus more on the owner of the copyright, whether that be author, publisher, broadcaster, individual, or corporation. Moreover, authors' rights countries, referred to as *droit d'auteur* countries because of their focus on the authors, are less likely to find authors' rights outweighed by the public's interest in easy access to literary and artistic works. As a result of these different focal points, the copyright laws in *droit d'auteur* countries are more favorable to authors than the laws of Anglo-American countries.

1. Reciprocity Treaties and Bilateral Agreements[58]

The first international copyright treaties were based on a system of material reciprocity. Under material reciprocity, country A would grant country B's authors the same protection as country B would grant country A's authors. The reciprocity system, however, was complicated[59] and ineffective, and many countries maintained piracy as the central theme of their international copyright relations. They refused to enter into any treaties, and, if they did enter into such treaties, they failed to abide by the terms.

National Treatment Under the French Decree of 1852

The Decree of 1852 was significant in many respects, not the least of which was its use of a national treatment system for the protection of foreign authors. Under national treatment, as opposed to material reciprocity, country A grants authors from country B the same protection that country A grants its own authors. A national treatment system is much easier to administer than a reciprocity system because courts need only interpret their own domestic copyright law. Moreover, any improvements in domestic authors' rights in country A automatically accrue to authors from country B.

Following France's Decree, and during the latter half of the nineteenth century, a trend emerged in Europe for greater international protection of the rights of authors. The development of copyright exhibited a constant momentum toward, and focus on, authors. As the rights of authors received more and more attention in national legislation, authors emerged as an influential political group. In 1858, six years after France's landmark Decree, the first international Congress of Authors and Artists met in Brussels. The work of this group laid the groundwork for the drafting and signing of the Berne Convention.

b. The Universal Copyright Convention

1. Major Provisions[60]

The Universal Copyright Convention (UCC) states that each member state will "provide for the adequate and effective protection of the rights of authors and other proprietors in literary, scientific, and artistic works, and including writings, musical, dramatic and cinematographic works, and paintings, engravings and sculptures." The

---

[58] Peter Burger, *The Berne Convention: Its History And Its Key Role In The Future*, 3 J.L. & TECH 1. Copyright Georgetown University Law Center. Excerpt reprinted with permission.

[59] A system of material reciprocity requires the courts of state A to interpret the laws of state B in order to determine whether country B gives adequate and reciprocal protection to an author from country A. *Id.* Thus the courts in country B would, potentially, have to interpret the copyright laws from many different countries in administering international copyright relations—a very complicated task indeed.

[60] Brad Swenson, *Intellectual Property Protection Through The Berne Convention: A Matter of Economic Survival For The Post-Soviet New Commonwealth of Independent States*, 21 DENV. J. INT'L L. & POL'Y 77. Copyright 1992 Denver Journal of International Law and Policy. Excerpt reprinted with permission.

Convention also requires each member to give national treatment to other nations. The term of protection for each copyrighted work is the author's life plus twenty-five years. One exception is the protection of photographic or "works of applied art," which are protected for only ten years.

The rights afforded the copyright holder include the author's exclusive right to authorize the reproduction of a public performance or broadcast in any manner. This includes both the original form and a form "recognizably derived from the original." The author also has the exclusive right to publish and authorize the making and publication of the translation of his works.

Like the Paris Convention, the UCC does allow member nations to limit copyright protection. The member states can restrict the right to translate writings. If the author has not translated the work after seven years from the date of first publication, any national in the country may translate the work. The UCC also allows a national to distribute a work without the author's consent if the translator uses the work for educational purposes or if the work has been distributed because of the public's need of the information.

As with the Paris Convention, the UCC does not delineate a dispute settlement procedure. While the UCC does establish an International Court of Justice that will decide any disputes arising under the Treaty, no details are provided about the scope of the Court's authority or about the proper procedure for settling a dispute.

The UCC has its foundations in the national treatment of foreign authors. Consequently, member states must afford foreign works the same protection afforded to domestic creations. Signatory nations must also modify domestic copyright laws to conform with [the] minimum standards [established under the Convention.] [E]ach member state must provide for the "adequate and effective protection of the rights of authors and other copyright proprietors in literary, scientific, and artistic works."

In addition, under the UCC, foreign works will satisfy all formalities (notice, registration, manufacture), if from the time of first publication all the copies of the work published with the authority of the author or other copyright proprietor bear the symbol (c) accompanied by the name of the copyright proprietor and the year of first publication placed in such manner and location as to give reasonable notice of claim of copyright.

The UCC contains a "Berne" conflict clause. This clause restricts Berne Convention signatories from ignoring Berne provisions and relying on the UCC in its copyright relations with another Berne Union member. The UCC is administered by the United Nations Educational, Scientific, and Cultural Organization (UNESCO).

2. Conflict with Berne[61]

The Universal Copyright Convention still governs relations between the United States and those countries that adhere to the Universal Copyright Convention but not to the Berne Convention, such as the Soviet Union. Relations between countries that belong to both treaties are generally governed by the Berne Convention. As between these countries, however, the Universal Copyright Convention may still determine whether existing works entered the public domain before they could be rescued by the retroactivity clause of the Berne Convention. The precise mesh between the Universal Copyright Convention and the Berne Convention as it will affect future United States copyright relations is controversial.

---

[61] J.H. Reichman, *Goldstein on Copyright Law: A Realist's Approach To a Technological Age*, 43 STAN. L. REV. 943. Copyright 1991 Board of Trustees of the Leland Stanford Junior University. Excerpt reprinted with permission.

QUESTIONS AND COMMENTS FOR YOUR CONSIDERATION

1. The United States did not accede to the Berne Convention until 1989. Because it took so long for the US to accede to Berne, the UCC achieved relative

pre-eminence in the ordering of international copyright protection. It remains important for those countries which have not acceded to Berne.

2. What are the major differences between the scope of protection established under the Berne Convention and the UCC?

3. What additional minimum standards would you seek to include in the UCC if you represented a developed country? A developing country?

4. The preamble to the UCC expresses the hope that an international union for the protection of copyright would stimulate the creation and exchange of intellectual properties. It states: [A] system of copyright protection appropriate to all nations of the world and expressed in a universal convention . . . will ensure respect for the rights of the individual and encourage the development of literature, the sciences and the arts . . . [and] will facilitate a wider dissemination of works of the human mind and increase international understanding." Do the provisions of the UCC provide the types of standards that will encourage the development and dissemination of literary, artistic and scientific works? What additional protections, if any, would you seek?

c. The Berne Convention

1. An Historical Overview[62]

On September 27, 1858, the Congress of Authors and Artists held its first meeting in Brussels. The Congress was truly international in nature, with participants from many different countries[63] representing many different interests.[64] The participants passed five resolutions supporting greater international protection of authors' rights.[65] The Congress met twice more, in 1861 and 1877, and each time adopted resolutions asking governments to join together in passing legislation for the international protection of authors.

A new International Association, initially comprised only of authors and presided over by Victor Hugo, convened in 1878 and adopted five resolutions that eventually became the foundation for the original Berne Convention of 1886. In 1882, the International Association, later named L'Association Litteraire et Artistique Internationale (ALAI), agreed that the only way to achieve its goal of increased international copyright protection would be to form a Union for the protection of literary property. Consequently, the International Association called a meeting in 1883 of all parties interested in creating such a Union. The meeting convened in Berne, Switzerland, where the participants drafted a treaty consisting of ten articles, the most important of which provided for national treatment and the absence of formalities as a prerequisite for copyright protection. Following general approval of the

[62] Peter Burger, *The Berne Convention: It's History and its Key Role in the Future*, 3 J.L. & TECH. 1. Copyright 1988 Peter Burger. Excerpt reprinted with permission.

[63] The countries represented were Belgium, Canada, Denmark, France, Germany, Great Britain, Italy, the Netherlands, Portugal, Russia, Spain, Sweden, Norway, Switzerland, and the United States.

[64] More than three hundred persons attended the meeting. Included in that number were 62 authors, 54 delegates of literary societies, 40 members of political assemblies, 29 lawyers, 29 librarians and printers, 24 artists, 21 economists and 16 journalists.

[65] The resolutions were:

(1) That the principle of international recognition of copyright in favor of authors must be made part of the legislation of all civilized countries.

(2) This principle must be admitted regardless of reciprocity.

(3) The assimilation of foreign to national authors [national treatment] must be absolute and complete.

(4) Foreign authors should not be required to comply with any particular formalities for the recognition and protection of their rights, provided they have complied with the formalities required in the country where publication first took place.

(5) It is desirable that all countries adopt uniform legislation for the protection of literary and artistic works.

draft treaty, the Swiss government invited various governments to meet in Berne on September 8, 1884, for the purpose of forming an international copyright Union.

Eleven nations responded affirmatively to the Swiss government's invitation to meet in Berne. The countries broke down into essentially three groups. The first group was comprised of those nations that favored a codified international law of copyright — a universal law. At the opposite end of the spectrum were those countries that wanted as little unification and as much national independence as possible. Moreover, they wanted the copyright treaty to be built on a reciprocity foundation. The final group of countries occupied a middle position. They favored a codified law of international copyright, but desired some domestic flexibility on issues such as the translation right and the term of protection. Rather than adopting universal protection all at once, these countries wished to move slowly toward the goal of international copyright unification.

Of the three groups present at the 1884 Berne Conference, it was the middle group, representing those countries which preferred some common legislation along with some provisions reserved for national law, that emerged as the mainstream.

The Berne Convention of 1886. The basic structure of the Berne Convention has remained relatively unchanged throughout each of the five revisions and two additional acts; the scope of authors' rights has, however, increased markedly. The original Convention provided an explicit, but not exclusive, list of works to be protected. The Convention also defined the conditions for protection, known as points of attachment, and specified rules governing the term of protection. Subsequent conferences have amended each of these provisions in order to increase the scope of authors' rights.

The Convention also established the concept of authors' exclusive rights, which functioned as minimum standards that all member countries were required to recognize. The translation right was the first exclusive right established by the 1886 Convention.[66]

Although the Convention's primary focus was on the author, most contracting states agreed that in certain circumstances authors' rights had to be limited in order to assure public access to important information. The Convention, therefore, defined the situations in which a contracting state could permit certain works to be reproduced without the authors' express authorization. Many of these situations dealt with news of the day, newspaper articles or articles of political discussion. The Convention also allowed individual countries to create exceptions for the use of literary or artistic works in publications of a scientific or educational nature. These provisions have been both expanded and narrowed during Berne's subsequent revisions.

The Substantive Provisions of the Berne Convention of 1886. Article 1 of the Berne Convention unequivocally stated that the Union was formed for the protection of the rights of authors. This focus was indicative of the continental European, droit d'auteur countries' influence in drafting the Convention.

The basic strategy of the Convention was to establish certain minimum standards which all contracting countries were required to recognize and later to expand these minimum requirements to achieve the ultimate objective of a uniform international law of copyright. Individual countries could give foreign authors greater protection than required by the Convention, but in no case could they give less protection. The purpose and strategy of the Convention has not changed since the 1886 Convention.

The fundamental principle of the Berne Convention was, and continues to be, national treatment. Under the national treatment concept, Berne signatories grant authors who are nationals of other Berne countries the same protection they accord to their own nationals. National treatment is significant because it ensures nondiscriminatory treatment for authors in all contracting states.

Brussels Revision Conference of 1948. The Brussels revision created significant improvements in the substantive rights of authors.

After unsuccessful attempts at both the Berlin conference of 1908 and the Rome con-

---

[66] The exclusive right to make or authorize translations was limited to ten years after publication of the work.

ference of 1928, the Brussels conferees succeeded in enacting a life-plus-fifty-year term of protection as a minimum Berne requirement. In all Union states, therefore, an author could expect a minimum term of protection of life plus fifty years after death for almost all enumerated works. Union states could grant longer terms of protection within their domestic legislation. They could also limit the term of protection for foreign authors to the term granted in the foreign authors' country of origin if that term was shorter than in the Union country where protection was sought.

The life-plus-fifty-year term of protection did not apply to photographic works, works of applied art, and cinematographic works. The term of protection for these works was governed by the law of the country where protection was sought, but could not exceed the term granted in the country of origin of the work. The term of protection for pseudonymous works became fifty years after the date of publication of the work unless the pseudonym left no doubt as to the author's identity. If an author's identity became known, the author would receive the life-plus-fifty-year term of protection.

The Brussels conferees [also] strengthened the authors' moral right. Under the 1928 Rome revision, an author's moral right was guaranteed during his or her lifetime; contracting states were not bound to recognize the moral right after the author's death. Under the 1948 Brussels Convention, the contracting states were required to recognize the moral right for the whole term of copyright, in most cases fifty years after death, if the legislation of the individual Union countries so permitted. The conferees did not require all Union countries to recognize the moral right after an author's death, because in some countries moral right was not protected under copyright law; rather, it was protected under alternative legislation or common law. Under the common law of torts in Great Britain, for example, authors could only maintain a tort action during their lifetime. Great Britain, therefore, could not agree to a Convention rule that would establish protection of the moral right beyond the author's death. Thus, it remained each individual contracting state's choice to extend the moral right past the author's lifetime, making the amendment rather insignificant in terms of effect. The amendment did, however, indicate the direction which Union members wanted the right to take at a subsequent revision conference.

Since the original Convention of 1886, authors had the exclusive right to authorize the public representation of dramatic or dramatico-musical works and the public performance of musical works only if the country in which protection was sought recognized those rights. In other words, the right of public representation and performance was not a minimum right under the Convention; an author would only benefit if the Union state in which protection was sought recognized the right.

Under the Brussels revision, the contracting states agreed to make the right of public performance and representation a minimum right. Consequently, authors of dramatic, dramatico-musical, or musical works enjoyed the exclusive right to authorize public presentations and performances of their works. The right of public performance was not subjected to a compulsory license. However, if the public performance were achieved through broadcast or through the playing of a recording of a musical work, the compulsory licenses established under the broadcasting and recording rights would apply to the public performance. In these situations, an author's work could be publicly performed absent express authorization, but no contracting state could enact a compulsory license that would be prejudicial to the author's moral right or to the author's right to receive just remuneration.

The advances made in Brussels were significant and they secured a solid level of international protection for authors which endured until the Stockholm revision in 1967.

Stockholm Revision Conference Of 1967. Almost twenty years after the Brussels conference in 1948, the Berne Union members convened in Stockholm, once again with the intention of making substantive and structural improvements to the Convention. Although the contracting states made significant improvements in authors' rights and improved the Union's infrastructure, those results were almost destroyed by a conflict that the Union had never before confronted.

The problem emanated from the new composition of member states. Many of the Berne Union's fifty-nine members were developing countries that had achieved their independence in the post-World War II years. These developing countries needed literary and artistic resources from developed countries and, as a result, demanded special concessions from the developed countries such as compulsory licenses for translation and broadcasts and shorter terms of protection. In response to those demands, the contracting states drafted a protocol for the benefit of developing countries. The conferees also agreed to tie the substantive changes in Articles 1 through 20 of the Stockholm Convention to the protocol, thus making it impossible to accept the substantive changes without the protocol. The developing country protocol was very controversial. Its compulsory license provisions and shortened terms of protection significantly weakened the rights of authors, rights that had been hard-won over Berne's five previous revisions.

Authors and publishers in the developed countries so opposed the protocol that they were willing to forego the substantive and structural improvements made in the Stockholm Convention in order to avoid enactment of the protocol's concessionary provisions. As a result, the Stockholm Convention did not receive the minimum number of ratifications necessary to enter into force.

Aside from Stockholm's developing country controversy, one other significant event occurred in Stockholm. The contracting states agreed to the formation of the World Intellectual Property Organization. WIPO's formation was achieved through a separate treaty; thus, the Union's inability to ratify the Stockholm revision did not affect WIPO's establishment.

The Stockholm revision significantly broadened the conditions for protection of non-Union authors by adopting a second point of attachment to accompany the previous requirement enacted in the 1886 Convention. Under previous Conventions, protection for non-Union authors was dependent on first or simultaneous publication in one of the Union countries. This was referred to as the "geographical criterion." The geographical criterion still exists, but is now accompanied by the "personal criterion," which provides that authors who are nationals or habitual residents of a Union country are protected in all Union countries no matter where first publication occurs. This protection also applies to unpublished works.

The Stockholm conferees [also] strengthened the Convention's moral right provisions. Under the original moral right provision, enacted at the Rome Revision Conference in 1928, contracting states were required to recognize the moral right until the author's death. At the Brussels Revision Conference, the contracting states strengthened the right somewhat by encouraging Union members to extend the moral right past the authors' death. Finally, at Stockholm, the conferees required Union members to recognize the authors' moral right after death for at least as long as the author's economic right was protected.

The conferees enacted one exception to the new moral right: "those countries whose legislation, at the moment of their ratification of or accession to this Act, does not provide for the protection after death of the author of all the rights set out in the preceding paragraph may provide that some of these rights may, after his death, cease to be maintained." This exception resulted from a compromise with Great Britain and other Anglo-American copyright countries that, like the United States, do not recognize the moral right under their copyright laws, but provide equivalent protection under other common laws. For example, in many countries the moral right is protected under the common law of defamation, which usually permits the maintenance of a suit only during the author's lifetime.

2. Major Provisions[67]

The Berne Convention protects "literary and artistic works," including:

> every production in literary, scientific and artistic domain . . . such as books,

[67] Karen Kontje Waller, *NAFTA: The Latest Gun in the Fight to Protect International Intellectual Property Rights*, 13 DICK. J. INT'L L. 347. Copyright 1994 Dickinson School of Law. Excerpt reprinted with permission.

> pamphlets and other writings; lectures, addresses, sermons and other works of the same nature; dramatic or dramatico-musical [sic] works; choreographic works and entertainments . . . musical compositions . . . cinematographic works . . . works of drawing, painting, architecture, sculpture, engraving, and lithography; photographic works . . . works of applied art; illustrations, maps, plans, sketches and three-dimensional works relative to geography, topography, architecture or science.

The Convention also covers "translations, adaptations, arrangements of music and other alterations of a literary or artistic work."

In addition, the Treaty requires national treatment and offers a term of protection of the author's life plus fifty years. The author of the literary and artistic work is afforded the exclusive right of making translations, and reproduction of their works.

Like the Paris Convention and the UCC, the Berne Convention does not provide for enforcement measures, nor for dispute resolution. Although the Berne Convention does provide for an assembly, which has the obligation to "take any ... appropriate action designed to further the objectives of the Union," the Convention does not further provide for any enforcement measures. The Convention also provides for an Executive Committee and an International Bureau. However, both of these groups are largely administrative.

3. Minimum Rights[68]

The Berne Convention, unlike the U.C.C., sets forth specific minimum conditions to which each signatory must adhere. As a general matter these conditions may be broken into five categories: Primacy, Coverage, Activation of Coverage, Exclusive Rights, and Term of Protection.

Primacy. Each member nation is required to accord foreign authors the same level of copyright protection it provides to its own citizens. Signatory nations must grant protection at a level equal to or above the minimum standards espoused by the Convention. Unless otherwise provided in a given article, national discretion to rely on its own domestic law is not permitted. Convention provisions maintain primacy over national legislation.

Coverage. Coverage under the Convention extends to a broad variety of subject matters. Coverage extends to "every production in the literary, scientific, and artistic domain, whatever may be the mode or form of its expression. . . ." Expressly excluded, however, is "news of the day or . . . miscellaneous facts having the character of mere items of press information." Coverage also extends to an author's unpublished works.

Activation of Coverage. The Berne Convention excludes all formalities that precondition the existence, scope and duration of copyright protection. Once created, a work's entitlement to protection under the Convention is not premised on any administrative formality. Exercise of rights under the Convention is immediately available and independent of any exercise of protection in the work's country of origin.

Exclusive Rights. The Berne Convention protects an author's personal rights and the right created in his works. The Convention seeks to maintain minimum protective standards which signatories deem essential to the success of international copyright. Among these rights are the right of translation, reproduction, public performance, broadcasting, adaptation, and arrangement. Any reproduction of an author's work made in violation of any Convention exclusive right is subject to seizure.

Term of Coverage. The Berne Convention establishes a minimum term of copyright protection for life plus fifty years or an alternative term of fifty years from the date of first publication.

---

[68] Brad Swenson, *Intellectual Property Protection Through the Berne Convention: A Matter of Economic Survival for the Post Soviet New Commonwealth of Independent States*, 21 DENVER J. INT'L L. & POL'Y 77. Copyright 1992 Brad Swenson. Excerpt reprinted with permission.

4. Minimum Rights (Continued)[69]

The Berne Convention requires members to protect all literary and artistic works. Berne defines a non-exhaustive list of protected works.

An author's exclusive rights under Berne, include: the right of reproduction of the work; the right of public performance of dramatic, dramatico-musical and musical works; the right of recitation of literary works and the right of communication to the public of works performed or recited; the right of broadcasting of works or communication to the public by other means; right of translation of works; the right of adaptation, arrangement or other alteration of works; and the right of authorizing cinematographic adaptation of works and of authorizing the reproduction and distribution to the public of the works and the right of authorizing the public performance and communication to the public of the works thus adapted or reproduced and of the cinematographic works themselves.

Berne requires the protection of moral rights. The author has rights, independently of his economic rights, to claim authorship of his works and to object to any distortion, mutilation or other modification of, or other derogatory action in relation to, the work which would be prejudicial to his honor or reputation.

Berne also requires that members require no formalities or procedures for the recognition or maintenance of copyrights and oblige[s] parties to protect works for the life of the author plus 50 years, except a term of 25 years applies to photographic works and works of applied art.

5. Future Issues[70]

Historically, the Berne Union has protected authors from the divesting effect of new technologies such as television, radio, and cinematographs (by extending protection to these areas). An important element in solving the current copyright crisis is to continue that historical trend and develop copyright solutions to the problems posed by audio and audio-visual reproduction, reprography, computer storage and retrieval, and satellite and cable television.

Aside from finding solutions to the threats caused by new reproduction technologies, the Berne Union and its member nations are attempting to determine how to protect new works such as computer programs. Many countries protect computer programs as literary and artistic works under their copyright law. Other nations favor *sui generis* noncopyright protection. The same pattern exists for semiconductor chips, although after the United States passed its Semiconductor Chip Protection Act in 1984, more and more countries began considering *sui generis* legislation for chips as well.

The approach that a particular country pursues is very important. Berne members that protect computer programs under their copyright law must accord national treatment to foreign authors of programs. A copyright approach avoids the need to establish a new treaty for the protection of software, because software is incorporated into the Convention under national treatment. If, on the other hand, a country protects software through domestic legislation, then protection is only accorded domestic authors, unless the country specifically provides otherwise through treaty or bilateral agreement. Thus, by incorporating new works into copyright, countries bring them into the international copyright conventions. The approach is favorable to authors of new books.

On the other hand, what may be good for authors of new works may not be good for authors generally. For example, granting computer software or semiconductor chips full copyright status arguably weakens the overall status of copyright. This is so because software and chips have different characteristics than traditional literary and artistic works. Their economic lives, for example, are shorter than those of books and paintings. Thus, granting a life plus fifty year term of protection to programs detracts, at least

---

[69] Monique L. Cordray, *GATT v. WIPO*, 76 J. PAT E. TRADEMARK OFF. SOC'Y. 121. Copyright 1994 Monique L. Cordray. Excerpt reprinted with permission.

[70] Peter Burger, *Article: The Berne Convention: Its History And Its Key Role In The Future*, 3 J.L. & TECH 1. Copyright 1988 Georgetown University Law Center. Excerpt reprinted with permission.

philosophically, from the status of books and other more traditional works. For this and other reasons, WIPO favors *sui generis* protection for programs. WIPO favors this approach even though *sui generis* legislation would require a new international agreement in order to protect authors of software.

The original contracting states to the Berne Union established the Convention to protect and promote the international rights of authors. That goal remains at the heart of the Convention. It has given the Berne Union the ability to increase the protection of authors' rights, reach compromise solutions to overcome philosophical and economic differences, encourage growth in membership despite the difficulties in enacting Berne's high standards domestically, protect authors from the potential erosive effect of new technologies, and encourage greater author protection in nonmember countries.

At present, Berne must remain true to its original goal. It must continue to focus on the protection of authors. To lose sight of that goal would be to disarm the Berne Convention, and leave authors hopelessly susceptible to the new wave of technologies.

QUESTIONS AND COMMENTS FOR YOUR CONSIDERATION

1. The Berne Convention has been accused by some developed countries as unduly subject to the desires of the developing nations due to the use by WIPO of open forum meetings for discussing potential revisions. To what extent do the minimum standards of Berne meet the needs of developed nations? Of developing nations?
2. Berne does not contain any minimum standards for determining when an infringement occurs. How effective are the protections of Berne without such standards? What standards would you seek?
3. Berne also does not contain any enforcement standards. Are such standards necessary? What penalties would you seek to impose for failure to abide by treaty obligations? What entity or organization would be responsible for determining the existence of such failures or the scope of any such remedies?
4. Can Berne's provisions be applied to cover such newly emerging technological advances as computer software and digital broadcasts? What changes would you recommend?

4. TRIPS

a. An Historical Overview

1. The Effort at Harmonization[71]

Though varying in details, intellectual property laws throughout the world essentially seek to ensure that the creator is rewarded for his or her inventiveness and to motivate further creativity. These laws protect the creator from rival enterprises and competitors pirating the creator's process or idea. Since the creation of the GATT, however, intellectual property has undergone a fundamental conceptual change: the emphasis has moved away from sovereign matters—*e.g.*, one of protective norms restricted to the territory of the state—to issues of adequate protection of intellectual property rights abroad. As the economic importance of exports has increased, so have the needs for improved extra-territorial protection of intellectual property rights. This

---

[71] A. David Demiray, *Intellectual Property and the External Power of the European Community: The New Extension*, 16 MICH. J. INT'L L. 187. Copyright 1995 University of Michigan Law School. Excerpt reprinted with permission.

is particularly true for inventors and producers of technological goods who, having spent great sums in research and development, demand that their national governments protect their investments from pirating and the subsequent undermining of their competitive positions. "As such, it was no longer the existence but rather the absence of, or deficiencies in, intellectual property protection which became the central issue in the international trade debate . . . ."[72] While strong intellectual property rights were once believed to create possible trade barriers, today the international exchange of goods is threatened by insufficient or nonexistent intellectual property rights.

The international dimension of intellectual property is not altogether new, however. The Berne Convention on Copyright protection has existed for over one hundred years and similar treaties have been adopted, including the Universal Copyright Convention and the Rome Phonograms Conventions. In addition, organizations such as WIPO predate the Uruguay Round. These treaties, conventions, and organizations largely provide permissive regulatory protection based upon the reciprocity of national treatment. What is new, however, is the awareness of the effect that intellectual property protection may have on international trade and an active desire to protect these rights abroad. It has been discovered that the absence of adequate protection of intellectual property or the existence of excessive protection can undermine the benefits derived from the elimination of high tariffs and the reduction of non-tariff barriers.

The growing interdependence of national economies in the increasing globalization and regionalization of markets has revealed insufficiencies in the present international regulatory framework. Many current market factors combine to demonstrate a growing need for effective transnational protection of intellectual property rights. As indicated above, intellectual creation and know-how increasingly comprise the value of products and services as well as represent a substantial cost in research and development. Given the relative ease that modern technology permits intellectual creation or know-how to be copied, inadequate international intellectual property safeguards hinder investment recoupment and inhibit further research and development. Furthermore, without intellectual property protection, the producer or supplier of services will find itself at a disadvantage in the highly competitive foreign market. This situation is exacerbated considering the trend toward research and development in one country and licensed development in another. One commentator noted that "[t]he present state of law in international intellectual property protection increasingly impairs or even nullifies acquired benefits accruing under the [GATT]."[73]

---

[72] INGA GOVAERE, INTELLECTUAL PROPERTY PROTECTION AND COMMERCIAL POLICY IN THE EUROPEAN COMMUNITY'S COMMERCIAL POLICY AFTER 1992: THE LEGAL DIMENSION 205–06 (Marc Maresceau ed. 1993).

[73] It must be pointed out, however, that granting worldwide intellectual property protection does not improve trade in technology-based goods. The territoriality principle combined with the exclusive character of the right has as a consequence that the home market will continue to be protected against parallel imports. Real trade liberalization of technology-based products could only be obtained through the abolishment of the reference to intellectual property protection in Article XX(d) GATT, or through the insertion of an explicit reference to the exhaustion of rights in case of parallel protection. The current TRIPS negotiations, which to a great extent focus on standards and norms of protection, will, however, lead to a partial trade liberalization in the sense that new export markets will be created and secured against counterfeiting and piracy. In other words, a successful conclusion of the TRIPS negotiations will increase the transfer of technology and the export of technology-based goods, but (re-) importation into the home market of technology-based goods will still be restricted. . . . In this sense, the adoption of higher standards of intellectual property protection worldwide will essentially benefit and increase the trade performance of those countries which have a technology worth protecting.

QUESTIONS AND COMMENTS FOR YOUR CONSIDERATION

1. Where would you focus your efforts on achieving harmony of protection: on multinational treaties or on efforts at national harmonization?
2. What are the benefits of national harmonization efforts? What are the problems?
3. What are the benefits of seeking a resolution to international intellectual property piracy through GATT as opposed to WIPO auspices? What are the potential disadvantages?

2. Intellectual Property Protection as a Trade Issue[74]

Three propositions underlie the developed countries' drive for strengthened intellectual property rights within the framework of multilateral trade negotiations, known as the Uruguay Round, to revise the General Agreement on Tariffs and Trade:

> (1) Strong intellectual property rights exert an unreservedly positive influence on developed free-market economies;
> (2) Strong intellectual property rights benefit all countries regardless of their present stage of development;
> (3) The acquisition of non-indigenous technologies by developing countries other than by imports or license usually constitutes an illicit economic loss to the technology exporting countries.

The first two propositions are counter-intuitive and neither historical experience nor the literature supports them. The social costs and relative efficiencies of intellectual property regimes remain the subject of continuing debate within the industrialized countries even today, and some conservative economists still maintain that a products market unfettered by intellectual property rights would attain greater efficiency than at present. On the whole, a consensus probably exists that industrialized societies are better off with established intellectual property regimes than without them. But there is no consensus concerning the levels of efficiency achieved by any particular regime, and considerable evidence suggests that all extant regimes yield serious inefficiencies under some circumstances. Opinions about the proper balance between the incentives of protection and the benefits of competition vary from country to country and from epoch to epoch within particular countries, and variations in attitude are especially prominent when shifts in the business cycle occur.

As regards the third proposition, that gains from unlicensed uses of foreign technologies in developing countries characteristically represent illicit losses to entrepreneurs in developed countries, this residual mercantilist attitude conflicts with the underlying competitive ethos from which intellectual property rights derogate and with the territorial nature of these derogations. Basic norms of free competition established in the nineteenth century often induced territorial legislators to provide relatively weak forms of intellectual property protection; the standards of protection currently prevailing in developing countries often resemble those applied in the developed world not too long ago. Weak intellectual property laws ensure access to markets for second comers who provide cheaper and better products through imitation and incremental innovation. Innovators who fail to qualify for protection under these laws can rely only on such factors as lead time, reputation for quality, and continuing technical improvements to maintain their foothold in the market.

Undermining this classical nineteenth century outlook are two recent developments that lead directly to the inclusion of international intellectual property issues within the

---

[74] J.H. Reichman, *The Trips Component of the GATT's Uruguay Round: Competitive Prospects for Intellectual Property Owners in an Integrated World Market*, 4 FORDHAM INTELL. PROP. MEDIA & ENT. L.J. 171. Copyright 1993 J.H. Reichman. Excerpt reprinted with permission.

Uruguay Round of multilateral trade negotiations. First, the rise of information-based technologies altered the nature of competition and disrupted the equilibrium that had resulted from more traditional comparative advantages. Because such technologies are inherently vulnerable to rapid appropriation by free-riders who do not share in the costs of research and development, innovators demand both domestic and international measures to protect their investments. Second, the growing capacity of manufacturers in developing countries to penetrate distant markets for traditional industrial products has forced the developed countries to rely more heavily on their comparative advantages in the production of intellectual goods than in the past. Market access for developing countries thus became a bargaining chip to be exchanged for greater protection of intellectual goods within a restructured global marketplace.

These tensions largely account for the developed countries' demands for extraterritorial protection of intellectual property rights, which aim to curb free-riding practices seldom illegal under existing international law, and for unilateral trade sanctions that both the United States and the European Communities have exerted against countries that tolerate such practices. The paradox posed by these demands and the resistance they elicit has been characterized in the following terms:

> On the one hand, the industrialized countries that subscribe to free-market principles at home want to impose a highly regulated market for intellectual goods on the rest of the world, one in which authors and inventors may "reap where they have sown." On the other hand, the developing countries that restrict free competition at home envision a totally unregulated world market for intellectual goods, one in which "competition is the lifeblood of commerce."[75]

The resolution of this paradox lies in the gradual integration of international intellectual property law into the larger framework of international economic law. This project, however, requires a negotiated balancing of private and public interests valid for all states active in the international economic system.

Global economic integration requires that intangible creations, likely to become the most valuable form of property in the twenty-first century, should gradually be absorbed into the laws of state responsibility that otherwise protect alien property from confiscation and unlawful takings:

> To pretend that aliens have no legal claims arising from wholesale, unauthorized uses of their most valuable property while respecting laws that protect less valuable alien property only because it is tangible rather than intangible is to exalt form over substance. Sooner or later, both private and public international law must assimilate intellectual property rights to the general international minimum standards that preserve comity by dissuading states from authorizing uncompensated uses of alien property on their national territories.

As international minimum standards of intellectual property law become at least justiciable, if not enforceable, within the framework of the GATT's dispute-settlement procedures, the historical predilection for purely territorial intellectual property rights will give way to international economic law at some cost to national sovereignty.

Viewed in its most positive light, a transnational market for intellectual goods defended against free-riding imports by border control measures and by international machinery for the settlement of disputes could become a vehicle for implementing cultural and industrial policies on a grand scale. The larger rewards potentially accruing from successful innovation under these conditions could be factored into the aggregate investment calculus for research and development and for the dissemination of cultural products. To the extent that intellectual property laws overcome high risk-aversion by offering prospectors a kind of sweepstakes reward if they succeed, the stimulus afforded by minimum standards of legal protection operating

---

[75] J. H. Reichman, *Intellectual Property in International Trade: Opportunities and Risks of a GATT Connection*, 22 VAND. J. TRANSNAT'L L. 747, 795–96 (1989).

across an enlarged and relatively undistorted market could greatly exceed that of similar laws operating in national markets that pursue different goals by different legal means. The ability of each legal subsystem to project more efficient uses of intellectual property throughout the worldwide domain governed by a TRIPS Agreement could thus magnify the capacity of the system as a whole to attain progressively higher levels of competition in the long run through appropriate short term restrictions on free competition.

On the negative side, the norms of international economic law represent a delicate balance between the interests of states at different stages of development, and the absorption of intellectual property will have to accommodate these norms and that balance. To the extent that an integrated world market becomes increasingly open and competitive, the desired equilibrium between legal protection of innovation and free competition must take account of the different economic policies of states at very different stages of development. Premature efforts to accelerate the process of harmonization without due regard to these differences and to the social costs of overcoming them could boomerang against those countries pressing for rapid change and could even widen the initial differences in the end.

The integration of intellectual property into international economic law will require entrepreneurs in both developed and developing countries to reevaluate the nature of competition in a more regulated global marketplace. While strengthened intellectual property norms benefit inventors and creators everywhere, there is no assurance that any particular countries will succeed in transforming short-term trade advantages accruing from a TRIPS agreement into solid and lasting commercial benefits. On the contrary, stronger intellectual property laws will ultimately benefit those states whose long-term development strategies best promote sustained technological innovation and the effective transfer of basic research from universities and laboratories to industry. The future prospects of the developed countries, including the United States, turn less on the level of intellectual property protection as such than on the level of investment in basic research and in high-risk commercial applications of the products it generates.

By the same token, the prospects for strengthened intellectual property regimes operating in open markets will require developing countries to formulate economic development strategies that are consistent with the new legal order. To maximize their opportunities, developing-country authorities must foster and reward entrepreneurship in general, while entrepreneurs in developing countries must learn to think like small- and medium-sized firms in the industrialized countries. In time, affinities between small- and medium-sized firms in both developed and developing countries will outweigh the affinities between small and large firms operating within any given national territory, and this transnational commonality of interests should strengthen the role of developing countries in future multilateral negotiations. Meanwhile, the developing countries will have to work harder to compete in general, and to acquire technological improvements in particular, under a post-TRIPS regime. However, if the appropriate strategies are adopted in both the public and private sectors, any competitive efforts that yield a foothold in the world market, and any effective transfer of technology achieved in the process, should yield greater potential returns than at present.

In all countries, efforts to implement higher intellectual property standards will put increasing strains on competition law, which is not directly covered by the TRIPS Agreement. Identifying the parameters of healthy competition valid for all players in an integrated world market will thus become a pressing task for the international community in a post-TRIPS economic environment. Because innovators, users, and second comers all have different stakes in fashioning the rules of unfair competition law, their interests will increasingly vary more with their economic roles than with the geopolitical affiliations of their respective national states. Developed countries that too aggressively promote the demands of large, multinational corporations risk producing a competitive environment inimical to the needs of their own small- and medium-sized entrepreneurs. Developing countries that overly regulate large foreign firms operating in their territories run the risk of suffocating their own small- and medium-sized firms.

Competition law must, accordingly,

remain an integral part of ongoing international discussions of intellectual property rights. In this context, developed countries must eventually take steps to protect applied scientific know-how, which largely escapes the patent and copyright systems, and they will continue to press the developing countries to limit the pace at which second comers can appropriate the fruits of investment in unpatented, noncopyrightable innovation. At the same time, the developing countries will require the cooperation of the industrialized countries in formulating guidelines for the licensing of both patented and unpatented technologies in order to effectuate transfers of technology without unduly discouraging direct foreign investment. If, in future negotiations, the developing countries proved willing to exchange greater short-term protection of products embodying unpatented know-how for a commitment by the industrialized countries to support an international Code of Conduct on the Transfer of Technology, it might open a new chapter in international unfair competition law.

Clearly, there is a great need for multilateral coordination and cooperation to ensure that all voices are heard in a collective endeavor to achieve a market-wide balance between incentives to create and reasonable opportunities to imitate and improve upon technological innovation. Future discussions seeking to reconcile the need for more effective transfers of technology with the drive for greater economic efficiency will require a high level of technical expertise and a nonconfrontational environment conducive to reasoned economic and social analysis. To the extent that cooperation between developed and developing countries succeeds, it will contribute a new perspective to the notion of fair competition that should strengthen the prospects of all participants in the global marketplace of the twenty-first century.

3. The Uruguay Round Negotiations[76]

Intellectual property piracy is rampant and affects a wide range of industries. In particular, piracy hurts pharmaceutical industries, industries protected by trademark law, and producers and publishers who rely on copyright protection (*i.e.*, developers of computer software, creators of literary and artistic works, and producers of audio and video recordings). Many nations deny patent protection to pharmaceutical products which by their nature require considerable time and expense to develop and bring to market. Consequently, some pharmaceutical companies face foreign competitors who misappropriate information with the active assistance and encouragement of their governments to produce inexpensive and potentially ineffective or dangerous imitations. New technology such as digital audio tapes, high quality digital broadcasts, optical character recognition scanners, and recordable compact discs threaten to make piracy easier and more difficult to detect. These technologies allow pirates to make high quality copies of copyrighted materials at minimal cost and effort. Inadequate trademark enforcement leads to the marketing of substandard counterfeit products that are sold in both foreign markets as well as the trademark owner's home market. Trade distortions resulting from ineffective or nonexistent intellectual property protection led the United States and other industrialized nations to discuss an international framework for the protection of intellectual property rights.

Proponents introduced the international protection of intellectual property rights to the GATT at the end of the Tokyo Round in the context of halting the counterfeiting of trademarked goods. Although the parties reached no agreement, the United States and the European Economic Community (EEC) succeeded in bringing the issue to the attention of the GATT's contracting parties and submitted a proposed agreement on measures to inhibit trade in counterfeit goods. Actions taken by developing nations at the March 1980 Conference of the World Intellectual Property Organization (WIPO) further encouraged industrialized nations to pursue negotiations under the auspices of the GATT. At the conference, the Group of Developing Countries[77] attempted to weaken

---

[76] Michael L. Doane, *TRIPS and International Intellectual Property Protection In An Age of Advancing Technology*, 9 AM. U. J. INT'L L. & POL'Y 465. Copyright 1994 American University. Excerpt reprinted with permission.

[77] The Group of Developing Countries is composed of approximately seventy-seven (77) least developed countries and was created in 1965.

the already inadequate standards of protection provided by The Paris Convention for the Protection of Industrial Property. Although the industrialized nations blocked this initiative, this action demonstrated both the futility of seeking broad-based reform in this forum and the need to pursue other avenues to advance international intellectual property protection.

During various ministerial GATT meetings throughout the early 1980s, members continued discussing the possibility of including the subject of trade in counterfeit goods on the agenda of the next round of negotiations. Developing nations resisted the inclusion of intellectual property rights, asserting that such a topic exceeded the GATT's mandate.

The persistence of the United States and the other industrialized nations was rewarded by the inclusion of trade-related aspects of intellectual property rights in the Uruguay Round agenda by the Punta del Este Ministerial Declaration on the Uruguay Round.[78] Nations opposing strong international intellectual property protection continued to resist these negotiations by insisting that WIPO remained the appropriate forum for such a topic. This resistance ceased when WIPO's Director-General was specifically mandated to participate in the GATT intellectual property negotiations. Further opposition to substantive TRIPS negotiations ended when India agreed to accept "the principle of policing trade-related aspects of intellectual property rights within the framework of the Uruguay Round multilateral trade negotiations."[79] With this obstacle eliminated, substantive proposals could be considered.

b. Major Provisions

Patents. The proposed TRIPS Agreement provides minimum standards which closely match the initial proposal of the United States. The patent section provides a twenty-year term of protection from time of filing and defines patentable subject matter as any invention, whether product or process, that is new, involves an inventive step, and is capable of industrial application. Furthermore, the draft notes that "inventive step" and "capable of industrial application" should be considered synonymous with the terms "non-obvious" and "useful" as commonly used in US patent law. The draft further strengthens the patent right by prohibiting patent discrimination based on the place of invention, the field of technology, or whether the product is imported or domestically produced. This language seeks to address problems common to the patent systems of many developing nations such as local working requirements and the exclusion of specific products, like pharmaceuticals and agrichemicals, from protection. This section represents a significant step towards establishing basic patent standards in international law.

Although the patent section provides a solid foundation for developing international patent protection, some problems exist. For example, the exclusions to patentable subject matter contained in Article 27, Paragraphs 2 and 3 could be abused. Article 27 recognizes the following grounds for exclusion: (1) protecting *order public* or morality; (2) protecting human, plant or animal life or health; and (3) avoiding serious prejudice to the environment. These exclusions are very broad and without a narrowing interpretation or interpretative statement, they could be understood to allow the continued exclusion of certain pharmaceutical products and processes from patentability. Nations may also exclude from patentability diagnostic, therapeutic, and surgical methods, as well as certain plants, animals, and biological processes for the production of plants or animals. In effect, such language substantially

---

[78] The declaration stated:

> In order to reduce the distortions and impediments to international trade, and taking into account the need to promote the effective and adequate protection of intellectual property rights, and to ensure that measures and procedures to enforce intellectual property rights do not themselves become barriers to legitimate trade, the negotiations shall aim to clarify GATT provisions and elaborate as appropriate new rules and disciplines.
>
> Negotiations shall aim to develop a multilateral framework of principles, rules and disciplines dealing with international trade in counterfeit goods, taking into account work already undertaken in the GATT.

[79] India Accepts Policing of Trade-Related Intellectual Property Rights in MTN Talks, 3 Int'l Trade Rep. (BNA) 244 (Sept. 20, 1989).

limits protection for the growing biotechnology industry.

The proposed TRIPS Agreement effectively addresses the problem of compulsory licensing. Compulsory licensing is not specifically banned, but nations wishing to issue such licenses must satisfy important conditions. These conditions include the payment of adequate remuneration, non-exclusivity, non-assignability, limited duration and scope, and the requirement that a compulsory license only be used after the prospective licensee has tried to obtain authorization from the right's holder on reasonable commercial terms and conditions. Moreover, limitations on the use of compulsory licenses for the exploitation of dependent patents also exist. The language of Articles 27 and 31 states that local working requirements for compulsory licensing purposes remain satisfied through the importation of patented products sufficient to meet local needs. Such language is necessary to avoid requiring a patent holder to produce the product in every jurisdiction where it is patented or face a compulsory license. With certain exceptions, the substantive standards of the patent section and the compulsory licensing provisions provide a useful starting point for the further development and advancement of international patent protection.

Copyrights. Copyright protection is a particularly important aspect of the TRIPS Agreement due to advances in technology that have made copyright infringement significantly easier and less expensive. The copyright and related rights provisions of the proposed TRIPS Agreement generally codify traditional copyright standards by requiring a minimum fifty-year term as well as compliance with Articles 1 to 21 and the Appendix of The Berne Convention For the Protection of Literary and Artistic Works (1971). This framework does not include provisions relating to moral rights. Copyright protection is extended to compilations of data and databases and to computer software which is treated as a literary work. Sound recording also receives increased protection.

The primary area of conflict in the copyright and related rights provisions involves the role of national treatment. Many nations read their national treatment obligations narrowly thereby denying certain benefits to foreign nationals. These nations create what they consider to be new rights or subject matters and then assert that their national treatment obligation under copyright and neighboring rights agreements does not extend to such new areas. The most controversial example of this practice is the European video levy system which collects and distributes funds to compensate copyright holders for private copying. While authors, performers, and video producers receive the levy funds, foreign video producers are denied their fair shares because video producers are not specifically covered by any agreement with a national treatment obligation. Advances in technology such as digital broadcasting make it likely that similar regimes will be developed with the potential to generate billions of dollars in revenue. Consequently, American businesses with copyright and related rights interests stand to lose substantial revenue if national treatment concepts are not further extended in the realm of copyright and neighboring rights.

Transition Periods. The issue of transition periods is an area of concern in both the patent and copyright provisions. It is asserted that developing nations need time to adjust their economies and legal systems to meet the requirements of the proposed TRIPS Agreement. It is unclear, however, that transition periods need be as long as provided in Articles 65 and 66. The proposed transition period allows one year with a four-year extension for developing countries and those nations shifting from a centrally planned economy to a market economy. Furthermore, an additional extension period of five years is granted for developing nations providing patent protection to areas not previously covered by their patent regimes, such as pharmaceuticals and agrichemicals.

Due to the fast pace of technological development, this extended transition period is extremely burdensome to high technology industries and other creative or research-oriented industries. It is also possible that the transition period may inhibit the use of Special 301 against signatory nations for the duration of the transition. Former General Counsel for the Office of the United States Trade Representative (USTR), Joshua Bolten, testified before Congress that the moral authority to use Special 301 might be constrained under an agreement that allows nations long transition periods.[80] Excessive transition periods merely allow nations with thriving pirate industries to continue operating to the detriment of foreign and domestic innovators. Furthermore, long transition periods unnecessarily delay the development of such nations' economies and their further integration into the international marketplace. Therefore, shorter transition periods would be in the interests of the United States and the other industrialized nations.

National Enforcement Measures. Along with the establishment of substantive standards for patents, copyrights, trademarks, and other forms of intellectual property, the proposed TRIPS Agreement also requires the creation of effective national enforcement measures for rights holders. The proposal provides for both internal and border enforcement measures. Although it does not require a signatory state to create an entirely new or separate judicial system for intellectual property rights, the Agreement does mandate certain minimal obligations.

Technological Advances. In addition to providing for current forms of technology and intellectual property protection, the negotiators of the proposed TRIPS Agreement heeded the suggestion by the United States of maintaining a flexible agreement capable of adjusting to the continuing dramatic advances in technological innovation. Accordingly, copyright protection was extended to cover computer software and a *sui generis* system for the protection of semiconductor chips was created. The proposed agreement provides for a ten-year term of protection and requires the parties to declare unlawful: [I]mporting, selling, or otherwise distributing for commercial purposes a protected layout-design, an integrated circuit in which a protected layout-design is incorporated, or an article incorporating such an integrated circuit only insofar as it continues to contain an unlawfully reproduced layout design.

The use of these two different methods of protecting new innovations and the growing acceptance of this protection for these new technologies demonstrates the need for an ongoing mechanism for the adjustment of international intellectual property protection to meet new technological realities.

As a new form of [technology], the printing press once compelled governments to develop copyright rules as a means of protecting intellectual property. Technological innovations continue to exceed the conceptualizations of intellectual property law. In response to technological innovation, a more evolved body of intellectual property law will by necessity first originate in the domestic legal systems and later be incorporated into international law through negotiation. The development process of new intellectual property law, however, may affect its international acceptance, incorporation, and implementation. Two schools of thought generally dominate the understanding of intellectual property right development. The first argues for the modification of existing forms of intellectual property rights such as patents and copyrights to cover new technologies; the other asserts that *sui generis* protection for such technology is more efficient.

These two methods of addressing ongoing technological advances will play a continuing role in the development of international intellectual property protection. As innovators create new technologies and problems for intellectual property law, domestic legal systems will have to respond with new forms of protection. With the increasing importance of the international marketplace, governments will need to extend this protection globally through one of the international intellectual property protection mechanisms.

c. Major Provisions (Another View)[81]

A formal consensus to regulate trademarks and unfair competition has always

---

[80] Proposed TRIPS Text Would Limit Use of Special 301, USTR Counsel Says, 6 World Intell. Prop. Rep. (BNA) 102 (1992).

[81] J.H. Reichman, *The Trips Component of the Gatt's Uruguay Round: Competitive Prospects for Intellectual Property Owners in an Integrated World Market*, 4 FORDHAM INTELL. PROP. MEDIA & ENT. L.J. 171. Copyright 1993 J.H. Reichman. Excerpt reprinted with permission.

existed under the Paris Convention, for the reason that, as Ladas observed in 1949, "[i]nternational trade is inconceivable today without trademarks and their adequate protection."[82] In the past, however, lax enforcement prevailed and there was no recourse to dispute-resolution machinery. The Draft TRIPS provisions give pre-existing norms greater specificity by strengthening the protection of service marks, famous marks, and geographical indications of origin, including wines. Other provisions soften the use requirement and eliminate both compulsory licenses and local linkage requirements. Above all, the Draft Agreement subjects the international regime of trademarks and unfair competition to more stringent enforcement measures, including border controls against the import of "counterfeit trademark or pirated copyright goods."

The primary effects of these provisions on the developing countries reside in the potential displacement of industries founded on counterfeiting and in the high cost of legal enforcement measures. To attenuate displacement costs, developing countries need to convert affected industries to the production of clearly marked, substitute goods that establish their own market niche by means of price competition with more costly foreign goods. Governments in the developing countries should generally encourage entrepreneurs to establish their own market identities through appropriate trademarks and to offer products that can be distinguished from those already in the market. Some developing countries may promote geographical appellations of their own, with a view to enhancing market identity in the future.

Strengthened trademark regimes should encourage both direct investment in developing countries and licensing by foreign producers who seek to monitor quality and to maintain brand names and goodwill in the international market generally. On the whole, more technology will be licensed to domestic firms when the licensor can both lower transaction costs by recourse to standard intellectual property norms and maintain quality controls through trademark license agreements. Local production under license then reduces the need for imports and helps to build an industrial infrastructure.

Governments in developing countries need to formulate policies and incentives that encourage foreign firms to allow licensees to adapt more of the licensed products for both domestic and export needs under local trademarks. The success of Japanese industry in importing foreign technology while developing indigenous marks constitutes an example for other countries to emulate. Countries at lesser stages of development may have less bargaining power when formulating appropriate regulations, however, and may remain more dependent on the introduction of foreign marks.

Although trademarks encourage the production of quality goods, control over quality easily leads to control over price and other anticompetitive consequences. Accordingly, developing countries may respond to strengthened trademark regimes in a post-TRIPS universe by replacing obsolete and restrictive trademark laws with up-to-date regulations dealing directly with the abusive licensing practices that flow from market power. While Article 21 of the Draft TRIPS Agreement expressly authorizes parties to "determine conditions on the licensing and assignment of trademarks," the need for adequate licensing regulations affects all subject-matter areas covered by the TRIPS Agreement, including patents, know how and copyrights.

d. A Step Forward?[83]

The TRIPS Agreement mandates mostly time-tested, basic norms of international intellectual property law as enshrined in the Paris Convention for the Protection of Industrial Property, and the Berne Convention for the Protection of Literary and Artistic Works.

The developed countries scored major

---

[82] Stephen P. Ladas, *The Lanham Act and International Trade*, 14 LAW & CONTEMP. PROBS. 269 (1949).

[83] Paul Edward Geller, *Intellectual Property In The Global Marketplace: Impact Of TRIPS Dispute Settlements?* 29 INT'L LAW. 99. Copyright 1995 American Bar Association. Excerpt reprinted with permission.

achievements in elevating and harmonizing minimum standards of patent protection under TRIPS, especially with regard to basic criteria of eligibility and duration, which the Paris Convention had not addressed. The following provisions are noteworthy:

(1) Member states may not exclude any field of technology from patentability as a whole, and they may not discriminate as to the place of invention when rights are granted.
(2) The domestic patent laws (including that of the United States) must provide a uniform term of twenty years of protection from the filing date, such protection must depend on uniform conditions of eligibility, and specified exclusive rights must be granted.
(3) The patentees' bundle of exclusive rights must include the right to supply the market with imports of the patented products.
(4) Logically, the obligation to work patents locally under Article 5A of the Paris Convention appears overridden by the right to supply imports, at least in principle.

Single countries may deviate from these universal patent-law standards only to the extent that they benefit from longer or shorter periods of transitional relief, which vary with the beneficiary's status as either a "developing country" or a "least-developed country."

As regards information technologies, the TRIPS Agreement opts for copyright (and trade secret) protection of computer programs, not patent protection, the availability of which remains unsettled and controversial in most developed countries. Because the TRIPS provisions do prohibit field-specific exclusions of patentable subject-matter, one can nonetheless argue that the domestic patent laws must recognize some program-related inventions if they meet other criteria of eligibility, including the nonobviousness standard. There is, however, even less consensus concerning the proper application of patent-law doctrines to computer programs than exists with respect to biogenetic engineering. Hence, any developed or developing country that disfavors patent protection of computer software may allow its judicial or administrative authorities to emulate the many restrictive doctrines and practices recognized by developed legal systems, without running afoul of its TRIPS obligations.

Besides requiring all WTO member countries to comply with the relevant international minimum standards already set out in the Paris Convention, the TRIPS Agreement establishes a universally valid legal definition of a trademark. It then invests owners of registered marks with the exclusive right to prevent third parties from using similar marks for goods or services when such use would produce a "likelihood of confusion." The trademark owner's exclusive right must last at least seven years after initial registration or after each renewal of registration, and the principle of indefinitely renewable registrations is established for trademarks, but not apparently for service marks.

While states may continue to condition registration—but not the filing of an application for registration—on actual use of a given trademark, cancellation requires "an uninterrupted period of at least three years of non-use," and government actions that hinder such use will not constitute legally valid excuses. Member states can no longer require foreign trademark owners to couple their marks with the indigenous marks of local firms. Nor can they impose compulsory licenses or deny the principle of free assignability of marks with, or without, the business to which they pertain.

Finally, the protection of well-known marks under Article 6bis of the Paris Convention has been strengthened in at least two ways. First, that article now applies expressly to services. Second, the same provision extends even to dissimilar goods or services when use of a registered mark would likely indicate a harmful connection between those dissimilar goods or services and the owner of the registered mark. Whether US compliance with this provision will require the enactment of a federal dilution statute remains to be seen.

In a bold move, the TRIPS Agreement recognizes some minimum standards of protection for phonogram producers, broadcast organizations, and performing artists, as derived from the Rome Convention, and it makes these rights universally applicable while, perhaps, discouraging further development of this Convention. For example, producers of sound recordings must now obtain exclusive reproduction rights in their recordings, in keeping with Article 10 of the Rome Convention, and broadcasting organizations may prohibit unauthorized fixation, reproduction, retransmission, and communication to the public of their broadcasts. However, the TRIPS Agreement does not provide producers of sound recordings with an exclusive right to publicly perform or broadcast their recordings, nor does it mandate even a right to equitable compensation for secondary uses of commercial recordings, which the Rome Convention tries to establish.

The neighboring rights provisions of the TRIPS Agreement are, to some extent, encumbered by the ability of member states to invoke the "conditions, limitations, exceptions and reservations" recognized by the Rome Convention. Among other things, this opens the door to demands for reciprocity, rather than national treatment, with respect to payments of equitable compensation for public performances of sound recordings in countries that adopt such a system.

The TRIPS Agreement is the first international convention expressly to require member countries to protect undisclosed information. A systematic failure to provide either trade secret protection or equivalent laws governing confidential disclosures should thus become actionable as a distinct component of the international regime of unfair competition law that Article 10bis of the Paris Convention already covers. Violations of Article 10bis, in turn, become subject to the enforcement procedures and improved dispute-settlement machinery of the WTO Agreement as a whole.

The language that Article 39(2) of the TRIPS Agreement uses to mandate the protection of undisclosed information resembles that of the Uniform Trade Secrets Act, which is widely adopted at the local level in the United States. However, there is no express provision that guarantees third parties the right to reverse-engineer products made from secret processes by proper means. While the United States Supreme Court has invested this right with constitutional underpinnings, Article 39(2) merely invokes Article 10bis of the Paris Convention, which would require third parties not to acquire undisclosed information "in a manner contrary to honest commercial practices." A footnote to Article 39(2) precludes "at least practices such as breach of contract, breach of confidence and inducements to breach," but does not affirmatively endorse reverse-analysis as such.

Whether a duly appointed WTO panel would regard a competitor's right to reverse-engineer by proper means as inherent in the "honest commercial practices" standard for purposes of dispute-settlement proceedings remains to be seen. A failure to do so would compromise both the economic functions of trade secret laws and a long-standing constitutional tradition concerning the rights and duties of competitors under US trade regulation law. It also remains to be seen whether a federal trade secret law is needed to comply with the United States' obligations under the TRIPS Agreement.

QUESTIONS AND COMMENTS FOR YOUR CONSIDERATION

1. Although the TRIPS Agreement establishes certain minimum substantive norms, like its earlier counterparts—the Berne and Paris Conventions—it does not establish minimum standards for determining what acts constitute infringement. In the absence of such standards, how effective are the substantive minimum rights established under TRIPS?

2. Compare the minimum rights granted under The Berne Convention and TRIPS. (*See* Appendix) Which treaty provides stronger intellectual property rights protection? What additional rights would you include?

e. Future Issues[84]

The United States has become active in negotiations for a protocol to the Berne Convention. This protocol was initially intended to include protection for computer software, databases, artificial intelligence, computer-produced works, and sound recordings. Of these areas, sound recordings in particular have attracted a great deal of attention. The WIPO Secretariat was mandated to draft a model law to address questions concerning the rights of sound recording producers as well as possible protection against new methods of piracy. New technologies like digital audio tapes and digital broadcasting present questions regarding the enforcement of rights and the compensation of rights holders which may not be covered by existing agreements. The fact that the United States chose to pursue the resolution of these issues through WIPO demonstrates that this organization will have an ongoing role in the development of international intellectual property norms and standards after the Uruguay Round. With its technical expertise in the area of international intellectual property protection, WIPO could be a useful supplement to any action taken as part of a TRIPS Agreement.

[84] Michael L. Doane, *TRIPS And International Intellectual Property Protection In An Age Of Advancing Technology*," 9 Am. U. J. Int'l L. & Pol'y 465. Copyright 1994 American University. Excerpt reprinted with permission.

QUESTIONS AND COMMENTS FOR YOUR CONSIDERATION

1. One of the hotly debated issues was the appropriateness of using GATT to resolve intellectual property protection issues. Has that debate been put to rest?

2. In the future, should efforts at establishing international intellectual property protection standards focus on GATT or WIPO as the forum for change? What advantages support the use of WIPO? Of GATT?

3. For a detailed discussion of the GATT versus WIPO debate, *see* Section C in this Chapter.

4. What additional protection does TRIPS provide that is missing from the Berne or Paris Conventions? What protection does it fail to provide? If you were a developing country, which treaty regime would you adhere to? Why?

5. NAFTA

a. An Historical Overview[85]

The North American Free Trade Agreement negotiations are the most significant forum for the discussion of intellectual property protection in the Americas. In June 1991, the governments of the United States, Mexico and Canada formally began these trilateral negotiations to create a free trade agreement covering North America.

Once negotiated, the agreement will establish a free trade area covering substantially all trade between or among the parties involved. Generally, the parties agree to phase down and eliminate tariffs in order to encourage trade within the free trade area and implement other rules and measures to regulate trade in the region.

A successful NAFTA not only will create a free trade area with 355 million people and a combined gross national product of $5.5 trillion, but will also liberalize investment rules, open trade in services, and seek more effective intellectual property protection.

[85] M. Jean Anderson, Angela J. Paolini Ellard and Nina Shafran, *Intellectual Property Protection in the Americas: the Barriers Are Being Removed*, 4. Journal Proprietary Rts. Copyright 1992 Prentice Hall Law and Business. Excerpt reprinted with permission.

The NAFTA negotiations have been organized according to 19 broad areas, one of which is intellectual property rights protection. Improved intellectual property rights protection is a critical NAFTA issue for a number of US industries, especially the pharmaceutical, sound recording, motion picture, and computer software industries. US industry groups oppose a NAFTA that weakens current US levels of intellectual property rights protection. The objectives of these industries are as follows:

Although Canada has generally strong intellectual property rights protection and Mexico recently passed legislation improving its statutory regime, NAFTA talks present an opportunity to fill in some gaps and codify, on a trilateral basis, effective intellectual property rights protection in the context of enhanced regional market access.

Currently on the negotiating table in the NAFTA is an accession clause, which would allow other countries in the Americas to sign on to the rights and obligations of the NAFTA, including intellectual property, at a later date. In fact, the Bush Administration envisions a single regional free trade area joining all nations in North, Central and South America through the Enterprise for the Americas Initiative.

Moreover, the NAFTA intellectual property rights protection provisions are likely to form the model to be used in future bilateral agreements between the United States and other Latin American countries, which are the first step toward the Enterprise for the Americas Initiative. American companies have suffered huge losses as a result of intellectual property rights infringement throughout Latin America, and they view improvements in the NAFTA as setting the bottom-line standard throughout the region. These industries see the need for improvement on three levels: intellectual property rules; effective enforcement of those rules; and enhanced market access meaning reduced import barriers to the distribution of protected works.

Some of the particular measures that the United States negotiators are seeking include: inclusion of patents on plant and animal inventions, which Mexico opposes; pipeline protection for pharmaceuticals and agricultural chemicals; and narrow terms for compulsory licensing and judicial review of a compulsory licensing order.

b. Major Provisions[86]

The twin objectives of NAFTA's intellectual property chapter are to ensure that the United States, Mexico and Canada provide adequate and effective protection and enforcement of intellectual property rights, while preventing such measures from becoming barriers to legitimate trade. To strike this balance, NAFTA establishes minimum standards, rooted in international treaties, for the protection and enforcement of intellectual property rights in North America. Moreover, NAFTA requires countries to accord nationals of another country no less favorable treatment than it accords its own nationals in the protection and enforcement of intellectual property rights. The Agreement also discourages the use of abusive or anti-competitive activities through domestic law licensing practices. NAFTA provides that Parties may implement more extensive protection under their domestic laws, however, than is required under the Agreement.

NAFTA extends copyright protection to all works embodying original expression, as well as those areas covered by the Berne Convention for the Protection of Literary and Artistic Works. The Agreement protects computer programs as literary works, and data compilations/databases which by reason of their selection or arrangement constitute intellectual creations. The protection of data compilations, however, does not extend to the data or material itself, and does not prejudice any copyright subsisting in such data or material.

The Agreement permits authors, or their successors in interest of copyrighted materials, to prohibit commercial rental of copies of computer programs and sound recordings. Advance consent must be obtained from both

---

[86] Kent S. Foster & Dean C. Alexander, *Opportunities for Mexico, Canada and the United States: A Summary of Intellectual Property Rights Under the North American Free Trade Agreement*, 20 RUTGERS COMPUTER & TECH. L.J. 67.

the producer of the sound recording and the composer of the musical composition. Under NAFTA, the owner of sound recordings has the rights to control the importation, reproduction and first public distribution of the work. In addition, NAFTA provides copyright owners with exclusive rights to authorize or prohibit reproductions, distributions, performances or displays of the work to the public. NAFTA also enables the copyright owner to prohibit the unauthorized importation of copies of the copyrighted work. The Agreement provides fifty years of protection for copyrighted works other than photographic works, works of applied art, or works where protection is calculated on the basis of the life of a natural person.

NAFTA affords protection to trademarks, service marks, collective marks and certification marks. As a basic tenet of NAFTA trademark law, the Agreement enables registered trademark owners "to prevent all persons not having the owner's consent from using in commerce identical or similar signs for goods or services . . . where such use would result in a likelihood of confusion." To lessen the scope of protection, however, "a Party may require, as a condition for registration, that a sign be visually perceptible." While the Agreement establishes that actual use of a trademark is not a condition for filing an application for trademark protection, it requires actual use as a condition for the trademark registration, and obligates each Party to provide a system for the registration of trademarks. To determine whether a trademark is well known, NAFTA requires recognition by the relevant sector of the public, rather than by the public at large.

NAFTA requires that interested people receive a reasonable opportunity to oppose the registration of a trademark. Under NAFTA, the initial term of trademark protection lasts at least ten years, and is indefinitely renewable on a periodic basis of at least ten years. A presumption of abandonment of a trademark occurs from only two consecutive years of non-use. While a Party may determine the conditions for the licensing and assignment of its trademarks, compulsory licensing of trademarks is not permitted. As for NAFTA's limitations on trademarks, each Party is obliged to refuse to register trademarks that consist of or comprise the following: immoral, deceptive, or scandalous matter; items that may disparage or falsely suggest a connection with persons, living or dead, institutions, beliefs or any Party's national symbols; or bring them into contempt or disrepute.

NAFTA makes patent protection available for any inventions, whether products or processes, in all fields of technology, provided that such inventions are new, result from an inventive step, and are capable of industrial application. NAFTA excludes patentability of inventions, however, when necessary to protect public order or morality, or to avoid serious prejudice to nature or the environment. Under the Agreement, items which may be excluded from patentability include "(a) diagnostic, therapeutic and surgical methods for the treatment of humans or animals; (b) plants and animals other than microorganisms; and (c) essentially biological processes for the production of plants or animals, other than non-biological processes for such production." NAFTA's patent protection benefits extend to already existing product patents for pharmaceutical or agricultural chemicals.

The patent owner has the right to prevent other persons from making, using or selling the subject matter of the patent without the patent owner's consent. By the same token, where the subject matter of a patent is a process, the patent owner has the right to prevent other persons from utilizing that procedure and from implementing, selling or importing the product obtained directly by that process without the patent owner's consent. Patent owners also have the right to assign and to transfer by succession their patents and to conclude licensing contracts. The term of protection of a patent is at least twenty years from the date of filing or seventeen years from the date of grant. To compensate for delays caused by any regulatory approval processes, a Party is entitled to extend the term of patent protection in appropriate cases. The revocation of a patent under NAFTA may occur under only one of two circumstances: if grounds exist that would have justified a refusal to grant the patent, or if the grant of a compulsory license has not remedied the patent's lack of exploitation.

NAFTA marks the first time trade secrets are included in an international trade treaty.

It specifically provides that trade secrets may be prevented from being disclosed to, acquired by, or used by others without the consent of the person lawfully in control of the information. A three-prong test determines whether information is a trade secret protected by the Agreement. First, the information must be generally known among or readily accessible to persons that normally deal with the kind of information in question. Second, the secretive nature of the information must translate into actual or potential commercial value. Finally, the person lawfully in control of the information must have taken reasonable steps under the circumstances to keep it secret. Furthermore, NAFTA requires that evidence of the trade secrets be found in documents, electronic or magnetic means, optical discs, microfilms, films or other similar instruments. As long as one can prove these characteristics, the trade secret protection will remain.

While trade secrets are protected under NAFTA, the Parties may not discourage or impede the voluntary licensing of trade secrets. In addition, while the signatory countries are called upon to make considerable efforts to keep confidential data submitted for product approval confidential, where a "public interest" exception exists, the Parties may disclose the data to protect the public or to ensure that data is protected against unfair commercial use.

NAFTA prohibits the designation or presentation of a good that indicates or suggests that it originates in a territory, region, or locality other than the true place of origin, in a manner that misleads the public as to the geographical origin of the good.

NAFTA requires that each country provide a ten-year period of protection for independently created industrial designs that are new or original. Under the Agreement, designs are not new or original if they do not significantly differ from known designs or combinations of known design features. Protection is also not extended to designs dictated essentially by technical or functional considerations. The Agreement gives specific protection to textile designs, and requires countries to ensure that the protection requirements, such as cost, examination or publication, do not unreasonably impair the opportunity to seek and obtain such protection. The individual countries are encouraged to enact their own national industrial design law, or expand their own copyright law to adequately protect industrial designs. NAFTA's protection of industrial designs is significant because industrial designs include those items, such as textiles, that do not receive adequate protection under existing copyright, patent, or trademark law.

Despite the powerful weapons and key benefits that NAFTA provides for protecting intellectual property rights, the Agreement nevertheless has some inherent weaknesses. For example, it does not remove certain copyright formalities under United States law that tend to prevent domestic and foreign authors from obtaining appropriate benefits. Further, the Agreement includes certain exceptions to national treatment that are vulnerable to abuse. Moreover, by defining "commercial dishonesty" as "grossly negligent" appropriation of the proprietary materials of others, NAFTA's standard for finding trade secrets misappropriation is difficult to prove.

Under NAFTA, Canada will be permitted to preserve its "cultural exemption," which permits the Canadian government to take whatever action it deems necessary regarding cultural materials such as records, books and motion pictures. This exemption is particularly grave for American firms because it provides a carte blanche for Canada to exclude or limit a leading US export. In obvious contrast to the Paris Convention which provides protection against unfair competition, the Agreement fails to specifically include rights against unfair competition which are generally subsumed under trademark law.

Additionally, NAFTA's escape clauses could be utilized by a Party to confine or limit its copyright protection obligations. The exclusion of the "moral rights" provision of the Berne Convention further weakens the copyright protection. Contrary to US law, under which copyright owners who fail to register prior to the commencement of the infringing activity are barred from recovery of either statutory damages or attorney's fees, NAFTA provides no registration requirements for works that seek copyright protection. This gap between NAFTA and the United States domestic law may create practical difficulties for copyright owners who must decide whether to register. NAFTA's derogation from national treatment of the performer's right in secondary uses of sound recordings is of particularly grave concern given the importance of the United States sound recording industry.

The overly broad provision in the Agreement for the optional exclusion from patentability of plants and animals, and of diagnostic, therapeutic and surgical methods has de facto neutralized the patent rights recognized by the Agreement. The question of international exhaustion of intellectual property rights is not addressed at all by NAFTA, thus leaving a loophole for creative inventors to avoid the protection created by the Agreement. Finally, NAFTA's border enforcement procedures fail to address the possibility of the parallel importation of genuine trademarks or copyright goods.

c. Major Provisions (Another View)[87]

In general, NAFTA mandates that its member nations adhere to various intellectual property treaties. The Treaty also specifies that the parties must give national treatment to other parties, and prohibits the use of domestic law licensing procedures that will abuse intellectual property rights.

Layout Designs of Semi-Conductor Integrated Circuits. Interestingly enough, NAFTA provides for the protection of semiconductors. In particular, the Treaty provides that is unlawful for any individual to import, sell or distribute for commercial purposes, without the holder's authorization (1) a protected layout design; (2) an integrated circuit which has a protected layout design; or (3) an article which has an integrated circuit with a protected layout design. However, an individual will only be liable for infringing a layout design if they knowingly used a protected design. Finally, the Members may not grant any compulsory licenses for layout designs of integrated circuits.

In countries that require registration in order to receive protection, the term of protection will be ten years from the date of filing the first application, or the date of the first "commercial exploitation" anywhere in the world.

Geographical Indicators. NAFTA's protection of geographical indicators prohibits anyone from misleading the public, through a designation or representation in or about their product, that such product comes from a place other than the actual geographic origin. This article also proscribes unfair competition, as set forth in Article 10bis of the Paris Convention. NAFTA also provides for the protection of the Members, or its nationals, that have used an otherwise prohibited geographic indicator for ten years prior to the implementation of NAFTA, or in good faith before the member country signed NAFTA. Further, if a trademark owner has a mark that encompasses a geographic indicator that would be prohibited under this article, the owner will not be prohibited from use if the owner registered or acquired rights in good faith, and it was before NAFTA's implementation, or before the particular geographic indicator was prohibited by the Member.

Members may require that claims against the use of a geographical indicator be presented within five years of use or registration of the trademark. Further, a member nation does not have to protect a geographic indicator that is not officially declared protected, or is in disuse.

As compared to other international treaties, the scope of intellectual property protected under NAFTA is very broad. The Paris Convention does not protect trade secrets, biotechnology patents, or semi-conductor patents. The UCC also is limited in protection, lacking specific coverage of computer programs, compilations of data, sound recordings, and satellite transmissions, and the Berne Convention does not include sound recordings or satellite transmissions.

Likewise, the domestic laws of NAFTA's member nations provide a narrow scope of protection for intellectual property rights, in comparison to NAFTA. Under the domestic laws of Canada, semiconductor chips are not protected, and neither are transitory broad-

[87] Karen Kontje Waller, *NAFTA: The Latest Gun in the Fight to Protect International Intellectual Property Rights*, 13 DICK. J. INT'L L. Copyright 1994 Dickinson School of Law. Excerpt reprinted with permission.

casts. Additionally, Canada's trademark laws do not protect collective marks. Furthermore, Mexican intellectual property laws do not protect databases, and computer programs are protected under a separate category, leaving uncertainty as to the scope of such protection. Moreover, Mexican law does not specify if semi-conductors, trade secrets, or biotechnology will be protected. Finally, Mexican trademark law does not protect certification marks.

NAFTA, on the other hand, protects copyrights protected by the Berne Convention, as well as any work with an original expression. As such, NAFTA's copyright protection extends beyond the Berne Convention, to embrace, among others, sound recordings, computer programs, satellite transmissions, and compilations of data. The Treaty's broad scope allows for the protection of works that have not yet been specifically delineated, including works not yet invented. This flexibility allows expansive protection for all future inventors.

Furthermore, NAFTA's extensive protection of patents includes certain biological patents and any other invention which is "non-obvious" and "useful." Finally, NAFTA's protection of intellectual property rights encompasses trademarks, trade secrets, semi-conductor chips, industrial designs, and geographic indicators. In this manner, NAFTA is an example of one the most progressive international intellectual property right treaties in existence today.

The rights given to the intellectual property holders in NAFTA are also more complete. With regard to other international treaties, under the UCC, if a copyright holder has not translated his work to the language of that country within seven years, anyone has the right to translate the work. The UCC also allows one to copy a holder's work without their permission if they are using it for educational purposes or for the public good. The term of protection is twenty-five years plus the life of the author. Additionally, the UCC gives the property owner the exclusive right to authorize reproduction of his works.

Under the Berne Convention, the term of protection is fifty years plus the life of the author, and the owner is given the exclusive right to authorize reproduction or translation of his work. However, the Berne Convention fails to mention some of the owner's rights, as it does not restrict the importation of the work without the owner's permission.

Further, the Paris Convention does allow issuance of compulsory licenses if the holder is using the patent for his exclusive use. A right to a patent can even be forfeited if the holders exclusive use is not corrected through the issuance of compulsory licenses.

With respect to the domestic laws in NAFTA's member nations, Canada does not give the copyright owner the right to sell, rent, or lease their work. Additionally, under Canadian trademark law, the owner has the exclusive right to the mark, even outside of the geographic area in which the owner uses the mark. Similarly, Mexican laws do not give rental rights to copyright owners, nor do they state whether copyright owners can control illegal importation of their works. The law also needs to explicitly delineate what activity is protected under their protection of public performances. Finally, the US patent laws that determine the date of invention for patents, and hence the date protection begins, are discriminating. Currently, the US laws do not allow an applicant to present evidence of use or knowledge which occurred in another country in order to prove their date of invention. Therefore, although the invention may indeed have been prior to another's invention, since the idea initiated while the patent owner was in a foreign country, they will not receive protection. Rather, the inventor with the later date of invention, but invented in the United States, will receive the patent.

Under NAFTA, the rights afforded property owners are very expansive. The scope of rights afforded owner's of computer programs is clear, following the guidelines of the Berne Convention. In addition, in contrast to Mexican and Canadian laws, rental rights and translation rights are with the holder of the intellectual property. Moreover, the term of the protection is fifty years plus the life of the author. Finally, unlike the UCC and the Paris Convention, under NAFTA one may obtain the right to translate another's work, but only if the owner does not translate the work themselves and the owner has not been precluded from doing so.

QUESTIONS AND COMMENTS FOR YOUR CONSIDERATION

1. NAFTA is one of the few multinational treaties which deals with the protection of trade secrets. Do its standards provide sufficient protection for trade secret owners? Are there different or additional protection standards that you would seek?

2. NAFTA, like TRIPS, establishes enforcement standards. For a detailed comparison of these standards, *see* Chapter Nine.

3. Additional countries have already expressed a desire to become parties to NAFTA. If NAFTA is extended beyond its present geographical limitations, are there changes that should be considered in the standards presently provided?

4. Compare NAFTA with TRIPS. Which provides greater protection for intellectual property rights? To what extent do NAFTA and similar bilateral or trilateral agreements form a floor of protection below which the United States, Canada or Mexico cannot successfully go in negotiating other treaties?

F. Case Studies

1. The Former Soviet Union and Intellectual Property Protection

a. Patents[88]

The individual republics resulting from the Soviet Union's breakup are still formulating their intellectual property laws. Several states of the Commonwealth developed a regional convention calling for the creation of a Patent office for all members of the Commonwealth. The treaty is known as the Eurasian Patent Convention and current parties include Armenia, Azerbaijan, Belarus, Georgia, Kazakhstan, Kyrgyz Republic (formerly known as Kyrgyzstan), the Republic of Moldova, the Russian Federation, Tajikistan, Ukraine, and Uzbekistan. The central office will be in Moscow and the granted patents will apparently be effective throughout all member states.

A delegation of the Russian Federation previously visited with representatives of the US PTO and delivered a statement regarding intellectual property laws in the former Soviet Union. The delegates reiterated that intellectual properties obtained under the laws of the former Soviet Union will be protected in the Russian Federation and stated that applications filed with the former Soviet Union may remain pending without loss of priority until the Commonwealth of Independent States Patent Office is functioning.

Provisional protection may be obtained upon filing an additional application in the Russian Federation until the Commonwealth of Independent States Patent Office opens. However, according to a provisional agreement executed by members of the Commonwealth of Independent States, the issue of whether intellectual properties obtained from the former Soviet Union will be observed throughout the Commonwealth of Independent States is unresolved.

b. Copyright[89]

In this information-based world, intellectual property has become a fundamental business asset in the global marketplace.

[88] Margaret A. Boulware, Jeffrey A. Pyle, Frank C. Turner, *Symposium: Intellectual Property: Article: An Overview of Intellectual Property Rights Abroad*, 16 Hous. J. Int'l L 441. Copyright 1994 Margaret A. Boulware, Jeffrey A. Pyle, Frank C. Turner. Excerpt reprinted with permission.

[89] Brad Swenson, *Intellectual Property Protection Through The Berne Convention: A Matter Of Economic Survival For The Post-Soviet New Commonwealth Of Independent States*, 21 Denv. J. Int'l L. & Pol'y 77. Copyright 1992 Denver Journal of International Law and Policy. Excerpt reprinted with permission.

Increasing computer and database technologies have made access to copyrighted materials effortless. The transfer of copyrighted works across national boundaries is limited only by the capacity of modern communication systems. As a result, the international dimension of copyright law grows every day.

As developing nations become increasingly reliant on information-based technology they also become increasingly vulnerable to the inadequacies of copyright protections abroad. Technological advancements have made the reproduction and expropriation of copyrighted materials, in most cases, simple. Because the free and protected flow of information is imperative to global economies, a unified international copyright code is of unequaled importance.

The Berne Convention for the Protection of Literary and Artistic Works has emerged as the premier international convention for the protection of intellectual property. By setting minimum standards for the protection of copyrighted materials, the Berne fosters cultural exchange, economic advancement, and the development of indigenous creativity. The Berne Convention provides a framework by which an international exchange of copyrighted materials may confidently occur.

To a great extent, the effectiveness of the Berne's international standards are limited only by those nations who refuse to participate. With the exception of the Soviet Union and the Peoples Republic of China, all major economic powers have acceded to the Convention.

Recent changes in the Soviet Union have sparked questions regarding the opening of vast new commercial markets. The recent emergence of the new Commonwealth of Independent States poses interesting problems for the international community. It remains unclear whether the Commonwealth States' fledgling market economies will follow the copyright pirating traditions of its Soviet predecessor. Faced with critical developmental needs, the new Commonwealth States may be forced to rely on the immediate and tangible benefits piracy may afford.

Attention of the global marketplace will soon focus on the protections the new Commonwealth of Independent States can ensure for the world's copyrighted materials. Without strong protective assurances, the States of the new Commonwealth will, undoubtedly, face limited access to the western technology necessary to their transition to free-market economies.

SOVIET COPYRIGHT LAW. The first embodiment of Soviet copyright law was the 1925 "Bases of Copyright Legislation." The Bases of Copyright Legislation established the Soviet's first comprehensive intellectual property code. The Bases designated the protection of intellectual works by territory and not nationality. Consequently, works of Soviet authors published abroad received no protection unless a treaty for reciprocal copyright protection existed between the USSR and the affected foreign government.

The Soviet Constitution granted authority to protect copyrighted materials in Article 47:

> Citizens of the USSR, in accordance with the aims of building communism, are guaranteed freedom of scientific, technical, and artistic work. This freedom is ensured by broadening scientific research, encouraging invention and innovation, and developing literature and the arts . . . The rights of authors, inventors and innovators are protected by the state.[90]

Soviet copyright law was divided into two categories, personal and property rights. The personal rights of a Soviet creator were comprised of five essential entitlements: (1) the right to be acknowledged as the author of the works; (2) the right to publish; (3) the right to reproduce and distribute; (4) the right to have the work protected against improper alterations or adaptations by others; and (5) the right to royalties for its use under the system of compensation provided by copyright law. Ownership of a copyright vested with the creator of the work.

Property rights, in the traditional sense, differ from Soviet use of the term. Under Soviet copyright law, an author's right in his work is not the equivalent of private property. Consequently, an author's right is not

---

[90] Konst. SSR art. 47 (1977), *reprinted in* UNESCO, Copyright Laws and Treaties of the World, U.S.S.R., Item 1 (1987 Supp.).

a primary means of ensuring a fair return on his labors. Rather, the right is created with the primary goal of enhancing education and cultural dissemination. Public interest, in most cases, is paramount to the rights of the author.

One particularly problematic provision to the Soviet Union's participation in an international copyright union was the 1961 Fundamentals', Article 102. "Any published work may be translated into another language without consent of the author, but must be brought to his knowledge to insure respect for the integrity and spirit of the work."[91] The presence of several languages and dialects within the Soviet Union (approximately 89) demanded, as a matter of practicality, that a translation provision exist. Since few Soviet citizens could read works in foreign languages (even languages within their own country) foreign and domestic authors were subjected to the deleterious effects of Article 102 which deemed translations not to be an infringement of copyright.

After the October Revolution of 1917, the newly formed Soviet Government retreated into international isolationism with regard to its intellectual property attitudes. International agreements for the protection of copyrighted materials were deemed capitalistic instruments used to exploit individual authors. As a result, the Soviet Government withdrew from all international agreements protecting copyrighted materials created during pre-soviet [era]. This isolationistic attitude would pervade Soviet copyright and intellectual property law for the next 50 years.

Soviet Accession to the Universal Copyright Convention. Adherence to the U.C.C. marked the end of nearly sixty years of Soviet isolationism from international copyright relations. In acceding to the U.C.C., the Soviets established copyright relations with over seventy nations. Soviet accession facilitated the exchange of its copyrighted materials and opened a previously closed window to the international marketplace of ideas. The Soviets exclaimed the hope that accession would unlock new perspectives in the development of international cultural and scientific relationships. The U.C.C., however, is limited in its protective capacities.

In seeking the lowest common standards so as to attract the most members, the control or effect of the U.C.C. is limited. Further, as aptly demonstrated by the Soviets during the 1970s, few nations will allow their domestic law to become subservient to a supranational body. The U.C.C. only provides a general obligation of national treatment, and its minimum protections are insufficient to establish a controlling document for the international protection of copyrighted materials.

Recent Developments in Soviet International Copyright Law. On April 19, 1989, Vladimir F. Petrovsky, the Soviet Deputy Foreign Minister, announced the Soviet Union's intention to join the Berne Convention for the Protection of Literary and Artistic Works, "[I] can inform you that our country is finalizing the necessary preparatory work which will soon enable us to accede to the Berne Copyright Convention."[92]

On June 1, 1990, the Soviets made significant Berne preparations as Soviet President Gorbachev signed an historic trade agreement with the US, committing the two nations to provide for substantial intellectual property protections. The agreement also bound the Soviet Union to implement legislation necessary to carry out their commitment. The US-USSR agreement included commitments to: (1) adhere to the Berne Convention, (2) protect computer programs and data bases, (3) protect sound recordings, (4) product and process patent protections for 20 years from application date or at least 17 years from grant, and (5) comprehensive trade secret protection.

Political Changes and the New Commonwealth of Independent States. On December 8, 1991 one of the century's most dramatic events occurred in the Soviet Union. The Presidents of Russia, Ukraine and Byelorussia declared an end to the Soviet Union and the creation of a new Commonwealth of Independent States. The preamble to the Commonwealth Agreement stated: "We, as the founding states of the USSR and the cosignatories of the 1922 Union Treaty ... state that the USSR is ceasing its existence as a

---

[91] UNESCO, Copyright Laws and Treaties of the World, U.S.S.R. (1963 Supp.)

[92] Clyde H. Farnsworth, *China Called Top Copyright Pirates*, N.Y. TIMES, Apr. 20, 1989 at D7, col.4.

subject of international law and a geo-political reality."[93]

New Commonwealth leaders immediately extended an open invitation to all states interested in joining the Commonwealth. Prior Soviet ties, however, were not made a prerequisite to enrollment.

In their initial meeting, Commonwealth leaders, Boris Yeltsin, Leonid Krawczuk, and Stanislav Shushkevitch, agreed to "conduct coordinated radical economic reforms aimed at the creation of full-blooded market mechanisms, the transformation of attitudes to property, [and] guarantees for freedom of enterprise."[94] Resolutions were also passed to create an inter-bank agreement, establish a coordinated budget policy, institute liberalized price standards, and abstain from acts harmful to mutual economic interests.

From a legal perspective, Soviet domestic law faced extinction. New Commonwealth leaders openly declared all Soviet law null and void on their territory and Soviet organs obsolete. Independent State legislation is to replace years of Soviet legal domination. Commonwealth leaders noted, however, that international treaty obligations signed by the USSR would continue to be honored.

The disintegration of the Soviet Union may have fatalistically interfered with recent advancements in the international protection of copyrighted materials. In Commonwealth territories, the January 1, 1992 enactment of the May 31, 1991 amendments to Soviet copyright legislation will have no effect. As a result, Soviet copyright law will not come into conformity with international copyright standards and Soviet intents of accession to the Berne Convention will not reach fruition. The Commonwealth's commitment to Soviet international treaty obligations inauspiciously reveals that Soviet Commonwealth membership in the Berne Convention was missed by only a few weeks.

---

[93] Michael McGuire, *USSR's Dead, 3 Republics Say Russia, Ukraine, Byelorussia form New Union*, CHI. TRIB., Dec. 9, 1991 at 1, zone C.

[94] Mark Trevelyan, *Focus—Slav Republics Declare Soviet Union Dead*, REUTERS, Dec. 9, 1991.

QUESTIONS AND COMMENTS FOR YOUR CONSIDERATION

1. What advantages, if any, would the Commonwealth of Independent States gain by adhering to the Berne Convention? Is there any reason to avoid adherence?
2. Based on the brief review of Soviet copyright law provided above, are there modifications you would anticipate the Commonwealth of Independent States countries would need to enact in order to comply with Berne provisions?
3. Given the piracy problems under the former Soviet Union, what impact, if any, could this factor have on protection of intellectual property rights in the members of the Commonwealth of Independent States?
4. For a discussion of the issues facing newly emerging market economies, *see* Chapter Fifteen.

2. Asia and the Protection of Intellectual Property[95]

a. Japan

Japan's intellectual property regime is so intricate that some say it effectively discriminates against foreigners. Whether or not such discrimination is intentional, foreigners doing business in Japan should be aware of the pitfalls they may face while navigating through the Japanese patent system.

At the most fundamental level, differences in patent procedure may stem from different philosophical attitudes toward

---

[95] Tara Kalagher Giunta, Lily H. Shang, *Ownership of Information in a Global Economy*, 27 GEO. WASH. J. INT'L L. & ECON. 327. Copyright 1994 George Washington University. Excerpt reprinted with permission.

intellectual property. Japan's patent system is a first-to-file system which has as its primary goal the promotion of technological development through the dissemination of new technology. This aim is nationalistic, however, in that it indirectly increases protection for Japanese inventions at the expense of foreign inventions.

The US patent system, in contrast, is a first-to-invent system geared toward promoting innovation by protecting the inventor. The goal is to reward research and development by granting the inventor exclusive rights to use, license or assign the invention. The right to exclude others from using the invention is a key aspect of patent protection in the United States, enabling the patentee to reap the rewards of his or her hard work.

One of the most common complaints about the Japanese patent system is its long application process. While the average examination period in the United States is eighteen months, the average time between filing a patent application in Japan and winning approval is often more than five years. Some US firms report delays of up to ten years or longer. Such delays are problematic because they reduce the length of protection an inventor receives for his invention.

Another complaint about the Japanese patent system is the requirement that patent applications be published eighteen months after filing. A competitor of a patent filer therefore can have access to a new discovery several years before protection is granted.

Finally, because patents issued in Japan provide very narrow protection, a Japanese company may file numerous patents with minor changes around the core technology of a patent held by a foreign company. This practice, known as patent flooding, allows a Japanese company to avoid liability for infringing the original patent. The company then typically forces the original patent applicant or owner to cross-license the technology.

It can be argued that, due to patent flooding, patents are not treated as property in Japan. The resulting pressure to license the invention deprives a patent owner of the right to exclude others from the invention's use, and does not reward inventors for their research and development. The original inventor, in effect, subsidizes the invention for use by others.

In an effort to address real and perceived barriers to trade, the United States and Japan engaged in bilateral talks in 1990 that soon became known as the Structural Impediments Initiative (SII). Under the SII, Japan promised to increase the number of patent examiners and to reduce the approval time for patents from more than five years to two years by 1995. Moreover, additional bilateral negotiations known as the "Framework Talks" were initiated by President Clinton in July 1993 and were still under way [in 1994]. Both sides are attempting to address specific patent issues during the Framework Talks; US negotiators, for example, hope to tackle the problems of pre-grant opposition and patent flooding.

Although progress with Japan has been slow, bilateral agreements remain the most effective mechanisms for prompt change, particularly in light of the TRIPS Agreement's five-year moratorium. Because pre-grant oppositions and patent flooding are not specifically prohibited by the TRIPS Agreement, absent recourse under bilateral agreements, US businesses would not have a cause of action against Japan before the WTO until after the year 2000.

b. China

In 1989, inadequacies in the Chinese intellectual property regime led the United States Trade Representative (USTR) to place the P.R.C. on a "priority watch list" under "Special 301" of the Omnibus Trade and Competitiveness Act of 1988. The P.R.C. remained on the "priority watch list" in 1990, but was elevated to "priority foreign country" status on April 26, 1991.

To avoid the threatened sanctions that follow such a listing, the P.R.C. concluded a Memorandum of Understanding (MOU) with the United States on January 17, 1992. Pursuant to the MOU, the P.R.C. committed to providing improved protection for US holders of intellectual property rights in the areas of copyright, patent and trade secrets. The true effectiveness of the agreement, however, will depend largely upon the willingness of the Chinese to fulfill their obligations under the provisions of the MOU. This bilateral agreement is particularly important because the P.R.C. has not acceded to GATT and therefore is not subject to the TRIPS Agreement.

In an effort to demonstrate to the West that it is taking its obligations seriously, Beijing sponsored the International Symposium on the Intellectual Property System in China in April 1992. Moreover, in January 1994, China became the sixty-first official member of the Patent Cooperation Treaty. Stepping up protection of intellectual property rights has boosted the confidence of foreign industries and attracted foreign investment to the P.R.C. In addition, increased protection is encouraging domestic innovation. The number of Chinese patent applications is growing at an annual rate of twenty-five percent. Furthermore, Chinese scholars are urging foreign investors to take their cases to the newly established Intellectual Property Division of the Beijing Intermediate People's Court.[96]

Despite these advances, the P.R.C.'s newly amended Patent Law is no cure-all. For example, the new patent law does not retroactively protect products already on the market; it only affects items patented in China after January 1, 1993. In practical terms, then, China's new patent law will not be commercially meaningful for several years.

For foreign patent holders, another glaring defect is the new Patent Law's provision for compulsory licensing, which grants to the Chinese patent office the power to authorize an entity to exploit an already-patented invention without the approval of the patentee. While the new rules are more complete and are definitely an improvement over the old compulsory licensing rules, too much is still left to the patent office's interpretation. The factors that could trigger compulsory licensing—"national emergency," "extraordinary state of affairs"[97] and "public interest"—are enough to leave foreign businesses more than a bit jittery.

Finally, enforcement, as always, remains a problem. Foreign firms assert that the P.R.C. must develop fair enforcement mechanisms, including injunctive relief, adequate compensation, and resolution of disputes within a reasonable time period before any true advancements can be made.

c. India

While most of East Asia is experiencing staggering economic growth, the Indian subcontinent is only now awakening from its economic slumber. In the early 1980s, India initiated cautious reforms which gave a modest boost to the economy, but it was not until 1991 and the adoption of a market reform program that India acknowledged that free markets and free trade were the proper course to take.

India's sheer size alone will make it a crucial economic factor in Asia. Although India has not yet enjoyed even a fraction of the P.R.C.'s explosive economic growth, India has great potential if it implements reform because of the existence of a rudimentary financial system (its stock market boasts 6000 listed companies) as well as a sophisticated legal system. In that respect, India is clearly ahead of its Chinese neighbor.

The difficulty in breaking ground in India, however, stems from the country's strict adherence to a Third World mentality. A glaring example manifested itself in 1993 when hordes of angry Indian farmers attacked the subsidiary of a US-based hybrid grain company. The US multinational Cargill Company, the world's largest trader of grain, entered India in 1988 to pursue new markets for its seeds, but soon became a target for Indians opposed to foreign investment. Hostilities culminated when crowds of angry Indian farmers stormed the Cargill office and plant and destroyed much of the company's property.

At the center of the Cargill controversy

---

[96] There is debate, however, as to whether specialized courts in general should be encouraged since they tend to elevate the subject matter (and, potentially, business considerations) above the law. Moreover, the panelists on these courts are not required to be attorneys and may even hail from closely related industry sectors. Purportedly, Su Chi, the Court's head judge, is eager to prove that the new tribunal is not just a "showpiece." Microsoft and several other US software firms are expected to soon file suits against a half-dozen Beijing companies accused of selling pirated software.

[97] *Id.*

was the Dunkel Draft, a proposed multinational agreement on the rules governing international trade. The Dunkel Draft is essentially the TRIPS Agreement that was recently finalized with the conclusion of the Uruguay Round negotiations. Part of the Dunkel Draft proposed granting companies like Cargill the right to patent new varieties of seeds developed in countries such as India. Many Indians view these intellectual property provisions as a form of "economic colonialism," and feel that allowing a foreign company to enter a poor country in order to develop technology and apply for a patent declaring such resources private property is clear exploitation.

QUESTIONS AND COMMENTS FOR YOUR CONSIDERATION

1. Since Japan and the United States are members of TRIPS, can the United States impose unilateral sanctions against Japan if no agreement is reached between the two countries regarding the issue of patent flooding?
2. What policies support China's compulsory licensing provisions? If China were to become a member of GATT, what changes if any would be required to conform its patent laws with TRIPS' requirements?
3. What arguments support the development of specialized intellectual property law courts? What are the disadvantages, if any, to such specialized courts?
4. Compliance with treaty regimes may not necessarily assure enforcement of intellectual property rights, especially where cultural, historical, philosophical or economic impediments to enforcement exist. What advice would you provide the Indian government in overcoming the reported hostility to protection of patented agrichemical products?
5. For a discussion of the issues facing newly industrialized countries, *see* Chapter Fifteen.

8

Registration, Use and the Process for Formal Protection of Rights

Many disputes regarding national requirements for intellectual property protection get down to the question of formalism. Formalities include the "race to file" as a basis for protection, complicated registration and recorded user requirements, government examination of applications, and approval of licensing and exploitation agreements. This Chapter begins with an examination of efforts to harmonize formal requirements for trademark applications under the Madrid Agreement and the Madrid Protocol. It contains a short review of the role of formalities under the Berne Convention and concludes with a brief examination of the "first to file" dispute for patent applications. For an examination of the issues raised by various attempts to "harmonize" patent laws, *see* Chapter Twelve.

A. Formal Requirements for Obtaining Copyright Protection[1]

1. US Formalities

Copyright protection in the US is limited to "original works of authorship fixed in a tangible medium of expression," 17 U.S.C. § 101. While US law recognizes that copyright protection attaches from the moment of creation, prior to 1989 eligible works generally lost their protected status if the owner failed to comply with statutory notice and registration requirements.

Prior to 1989, otherwise eligible works lost their protected status if copies of the work were publicly distributed or publicly displayed without the appropriate copyright notice. Such notice consisted of the symbol "©" or the word "copyright" (or its recognizable abbreviation "Copr."), the date of first publication and the name of the copyright owner (or a recognizable abbreviation). Mistakes in the name or date of first publication were generally correctable. Failure to include a statutory notice, however, resulted in dedication of the work to the public, unless the notice was omitted from a relatively small number of publicly distributed copies, the work was registered within five years after such publication without notice, *and* reasonable efforts were made to add the notice to all copies publicly distributed in the United States.

Failure to comply with statutory registration requirements also prevented authors from protecting their works in the United States. Copyright owners could not enforce their rights granted under copyright unless and until their copyright claim was registered with the US Copyright Office. In order to register such claim, the copyright owner had to file an application for copyright recordation, pay the appropriate filing fee and deposit the requisite number and form of copies of the work with the Copyright Office. Applications were then reviewed by the Copyright Office to ascertain their compliance with statutory subject matter requirements. Claims for both published and unpublished works were registerable. All registration files, including deposit copies, were available for public inspection.

Although compliance with recordation

[1] Written for this Anthology by Doris Estelle Long. Copyright 1996 Doris E. Long.

formalities was a prerequisite for subject matter jurisdiction, so long as the copyright owner recorded her claim US law allowed her to seek relief for pre-registration acts of infringement. Failure to register prior to infringement, however, potentially reduced the amount of monetary relief available. Prior to 1989, US law permitted recovery of statutory monetary damages of up to $50,000 per willful infringement but only if the copyright was registered in the US *prior* to the act of infringement at issue. Without pre-infringement registration, monetary recovery was limited to actual damages.

2. The Berne Convention and the Elimination of Copyright Formalities for Foreign Authors

Article 5 of the Berne Convention for the Protection of Literary and Artistic Works provides for national treatment so that authors in member countries will receive the same protection as national authors. It specifically precludes the imposition of "any formality" upon the "enjoyment and the exercise of [the author's] rights" under domestic copyright law.

This prohibition against formalities was largely responsible for the United States' relatively late adherence to the Berne Convention. In 1989 (over one hundred years after the Convention was first established) US copyright law was modified to eliminate notice and registration formalities for foreign authors. The elimination of these formalities paved the way for US adherence to the Convention.

As of March 1, 1989, the effective date of the Berne Implementation Act, works whose copies were first publicly distributed in the United States after this effective date do not have to bear a copyright notice to retain their protected nature. Similarly, foreign authors of Berne Convention works do not have to comply with registration formalities as a pre-requisite to enforcing their copyrights in the United States. In order to qualify as a "Berne Convention work" for which no registration formalities are required, the work must have been written by a foreign author, *and*, if published, must at least have been simultaneously published in a Berne member country other than the United States. US authors, however, must still comply with all registration formalities.

QUESTIONS AND COMMENTS FOR YOUR CONSIDERATION

1. With the exception of the protection for well known marks (*see* Chapter Nine), registration formalities for patent and trademark protection have not been seriously challenged. Is there a justifiable basis for treating copyright formalities differently?

2. Prior to US adherence to Berne, the US was a member of the Universal Copyright Convention. Contrary to Berne, the Universal Copyright Convention did *not* prohibit copyright formalities. To the contrary, Article III (*see* Appendix V) expressly permitted Contracting States to premise copyright protection on compliance with domestic notice and procedural formalities. Which international standard do you prefer? Why?

3. Prior to 1976, the term of protection for a copyrighted work in the US lasted for 28 years. An additional 28 year term was available if an application for renewal was filed with the Copyright Office in a timely manner by the appropriate party. In an effort to eradicate some of the harm caused to foreign authors by previous registration and notice formalities, including this renewal requirement, the US has granted a limited right to foreign authors and copyright holders to restore their works to copyright status in the US if the work has fallen into the public domain due to a failure to comply with protection "formalities." In order to obtain restoration,

the foreign work in question must presently be subject to copyright protection in the author's home country and the author must comply with detailed recordation requirements. What purposes do these restoration formalities serve? Do these "formalities" violate Article 5 of the Berne Convention? (*See* Appendix II.) What policy supports the requirement of "reciprocal" copyright protected status for protected works? Should such "reciprocal" status be adopted as a standard for determining the copyright protected status of works in general?

4. In 1939, when the Disney studio was working on the animated film *Fantasia*, it was strapped for cash and Walt Disney intended to use only music that had passed into the public domain. He made an exception for Stravinsky's *Le sacre du Printemps (Rite of Spring)*. Disney's attorney wired Igor Stravinsky in Paris with an offer of $5,000 for the use of the music. The telegram, according to what Stravinsky said later, contained a "gentle warning that if permission were withheld the music would be used anyway." Stravinsky was "infuriated," but nevertheless accepted the offer. Disney's attorney had discovered that Stravinsky had taken out the original copyright in prerevolutionary Russia, and that the copyright was most likely not enforceable.

Did Disney pay too little for the music? Too much? What would you have done?

B. Formal Requirements for Obtaining Patent Protection

1. The Patent Cooperation Treaty[2]

The Patent Cooperation Treaty is a union of Contracting States contemplated by, and formulated within, the context of the Paris Convention for simplifying and streamlining international patent application filing, searching, and examination.[3] The Patent Cooperation Treaty makes it possible to designate as many of the Contracting States as desired in one filing, rather than filing multiple applications in the individual Contracting States. The Patent Cooperation Treaty is administered by the World Intellectual Property Organization International Bureau in Geneva, Switzerland.

The PCT application is filed with the receiving office, usually the US Patent and Trademark Office for US applicants. Once filed, the receiving office checks the international application for compliance with formalities, particularly adherence to the drawing requirements and to the conversion of English units to metric. The applicant will receive an invitation to correct "informalities" within a prescribed time period, which are made on substitution sheets.

The receiving office forwards the application (and priority documents, if requested) to the International Bureau in Geneva. The application is reviewed to determine unity of invention, such that all the claims form a general inventive concept.

The International Searching Authority prepares an International Search Report within three months of receipt of the application. The search report with prior art citations and references relevant to the invention from the patent and general scientific literature is forwarded to the applicant or the applicant's representative along with an assessment of patentability of the claims based on the prior art cited. At this time, the applicant may present amended claims. Also, the applicant may decide to withdraw the application.

The Patent Cooperation Treaty application, with the search report and amended claims (if any), is published promptly after the expiration of eighteen months from the

[2] Margaret A. Boulware, Jeffrey A. Pyle, Frank C. Turner, *Symposium: Intellectual Property: Article: an Overview of Intellectual Property Rights Abroad*, 16 HOUS. J. INT'L L 441. Copyright 1995 Margaret A. Boulware, Jeffrey A. Pyle, Frank C. Turner. Excerpt reprinted with permission.

[3] Patent Cooperation Treaty, June 19, 1970, 28 U.S.T. 7645.

priority date. If the search report is not available, the application is republished later with the search report. If an applicant decides not to pursue the application and wishes to keep the subject matter confidential, a timely withdrawal of the international application can avoid publication.

The European Patent Convention and the Patent Cooperation Treaty are separate treaties. A member of the European Patent Convention must opt into the Patent Cooperation Treaty. However, protection in any member state of the European Patent Convention can be obtained by designating and entering the national phase of the Patent Cooperation Treaty in the European Patent Office.

If a patent application is granted under the European Patent Convention, it has the same effect as a patent issuing from patent offices of the individual Contracting States. However, the European patent does not supplant the national patent offices as the inventor may file either a European patent application or a national patent application with the national patent offices of the Contracting States. If a European patent issues, then it must be registered in the national office of each member country designated in the application in order for the patent grant to be effective within each country. Priority is accorded per Paris Convention standards provided that the applicant claims the convention priority date. The application may be filed at the European Patent Office in Munich, or the receiving section at its branch at the Hague. An application can be filed and prosecuted entirely in any of the official languages of operation, which are English, French, and German.

An opposition to the grant of a European patent may be made within nine months of publication of the grant in the European Patent Bulletin. The opposition period runs during the time of perfecting the patent in the Contracting States, which may be costly depending on the number of States selected for pursuing patent protection during the national phase. The opposition may be filed by any third party "in a written reasoned statement." An Opposition Division within the European Patent Office determines whether the protest may proceed. The Opposition Division may revoke a European patent on completion of the opposition. The liberal opposition procedure holds the patent at risk for those countries without opposition.

2. Patent Protection and the First to File Debate[4]

One of the key international debates in the area of intellectual property protection concerns the role recordation formalities play in deciding the existence of domestic patent rights. While nations generally agree that, unlike trademarks and copyrights, patents arise only upon compliance with registration formalities, the scope of such formalities is hotly debated.

While all nations which presently grant patent protection premise such protection upon the filing of an acceptable application, the scope of review varies significantly. Some countries, such as Japan, publish pending patent applications and permit third parties to oppose the applied-for patent. By contrast, in the United States, patent applications remain confidential until after the patent is granted. No opportunity for third party oppositions (except for interference proceedings) exists under US law. Furthermore, if the application is denied, the file remains closed to the public. Thus, unsuccessful applicants in the US retain the option of protecting their inventions as potential trade secrets.

Perhaps the greatest difference in the treatment of registration formalities lies in the impact a successful application has on the rights of prior inventors of similar inventions. In most countries, the first to file a successful patent application obtains the patent. Only two countries—the United States and the Philippines—grant patent rights on the basis of the first to invent. Thus, the first to file a patent application in the US only obtains the patent if the invention falls within the subject matter of patentable matter, if the applicant complies with all patent formalities *and* if there is no prior inventor who has conceived of the invention prior to the applicant's date of first conception. By premising patent protection on the

---

[4] Written by Doris Estelle Long for this Anthology. Copyright 1996 Doris E. Long.

inventor's status as first-to-invent, the United States has rejected the relatively easy administrability of a first-to-file system and has added a level of insecurity in the value of an issued patent that does not exist in those countries where compliance with registration formalities alone determines ownership.

C. Formal Requirements for obtaining Trademark Rights[5]

In most countries, if a mark is not registered, the owner has no action in infringement. His only possible cause of action is through the laws of unfair competition or unfair business practices or through an action in passing-off.

When bringing an action in unfair competition or passing-off, some countries require the plaintiff to show not only a similarity between the marks, but also that there is a possibility of confusion. Still other countries require that an action for unfair competition or passing-off be based upon the fame of the mark or that it is "well-known."

Typically, this requires extensive evidence not only of fame within the particular country, but on a world-wide basis. Indeed, many countries will not recognize rights based solely upon prior use, unless the prior user can show notoriety of his mark. Although what constitutes notoriety varies from country to country, it is not uncommon for the plaintiff to be required to show that as much as sixty percent (60%) of the country recognizes the mark of the prior user.

Many countries will not allow an action to be brought based upon prior use until the prior user has applied for registration of the mark. In most countries, the application is first examined for formalities, but after this the similarities end. The procedures for prosecution vary greatly from country to country. Some countries examine as to inherent registrability and prior rights. Other countries examine the formalities and then publish the mark for opposition; after opposition, the Examiner provides his substantive refusals. Still, in other countries, there is no examination of prior rights. The mark is examined for inherent registrability and form. If the mark meets these requirements, it is registered without being published for opposition.

Still less rigid forms of examination exist, where the mark is only examined as to form. It is not examined for inherent registrability and it is not examined for prior rights. As long as the formalities are met, the mark is registered; there is no opportunity to oppose.

Most foreign countries that examine for inherent registrability, recognize the same substantive refusals as are recognized in the United States, such as surname, geographic, and non-distinctiveness. However, what is considered a surname or geographically descriptive is often very different from what we are accustomed to in the US. Likewise, foreign countries vary greatly in this manner among themselves.

It is virtually universal that a generic term cannot be registered. Thus, if a term is a common, proper or technical name for the goods, most countries will refuse registration. The differences arise in how generic is defined. Some countries do not consider a term generic if it is in a foreign language and thus, would not be recognized as generic in the country where registration is sought. Still other countries find a mark to be generic only where the trademark owner uses the mark in a generic manner. Thus, the circumstance arises where the owner has a registration for a term that is a generic term in the market place.

Marks that have geographic significance are not registrable. Again, however, countries vary as to what is considered geographically descriptive. You may find that your mark was not considered geographically descriptive in the US, but that it is considered geographically descriptive in other countries. Many countries allow registration of a geographic mark if distinctiveness can be shown. This usually entails extensive promotion and evidence that there is little likelihood of deceiving the purchasing public. Oftentimes the amount of distinctiveness required is very difficult to meet.

Most countries do not permit registration of a surname. Some countries, however, have very unique tests for determining whether a mark will be recognized as a surname. Many

---

[5] Trademarks, Copyrights, and Unfair Competition. Copyright 1995. C744 ALI-ABA 97. Excerpt reprinted with permission.

countries will permit a surname to be registered if it is not recognized as such or if consent to registration is obtained. In addition, even with a consent, some countries require a showing of distinctiveness. Again, this standard of distinctiveness is often very high and difficult to meet. Even in those countries where surname registration can be obtained, such a registration cannot prevent one from using an identical surname, provided the other party is using the surname as such and not as a trademark.

Descriptiveness is viewed similarly in most countries, in that descriptive terms are not registrable. The differences lie in each country's interpretation of what is descriptive. Oftentimes a mark registrable in the United States, without a showing of secondary meaning, will be seen as descriptive in foreign countries. This often is the result of cultural differences and must simply be dealt with on a country-by-country basis. As in the United States, descriptiveness is viewed in relation to the goods. Thus, SWIFT might be considered descriptive for automobiles, but not for ham. Further, many countries view laudatory terms as descriptive. Some countries consider terms descriptive if they are considered descriptive in other countries, even if not in the country in which the application for registration is made.

Although many countries have opposition procedures, not all countries do. Most countries that do not offer an opportunity to oppose an application before it registers, require that the party asserting a superior right institute a cancellation action against the registered mark. Usually the basis for an opposition or a cancellation can be any reason that the mark should not have issued. Some countries, however, do not allow certain issues to be raised at opposition. An example of this is Germany's mandate that rights based upon prior use can be raised only in a cancellation action. In addition, issues of non-use or genericness cannot be raised in an opposition, but only in a cancellation proceeding.

Oppositions are usually before the Patent Office, while cancellation procedures are usually before the Courts. As a result, cancellation procedures are often more expensive. Thus, in those countries where one must bring a cancellation action in order to assert superior rights based upon prior use, there is further incentive for the client to register his marks. The client can then bring an opposition asserting superior rights as a result of his prior registration. In asserting an opposition or a cancellation action, the client should take care that his own mark is not vulnerable to attack. Some countries permit the applicant/owner of the attacked mark to require the attacker to prove that his mark is still in use. If the client cannot show this, not only will he lose his opposition or cancellation, but if his rights are based upon a prior registration, he may lose his registration.

QUESTIONS AND COMMENTS FOR YOUR CONSIDERATION

1. Select a country and examine the following issues: What formal requirements must be met before a mark can be protected? Is use alone sufficient? What categories of marks are registrable? What changes, if any would you recommend? Why?

2. For a discussion of the issue of the protection of famous or well-known marks, *see* Chapter Nine.

1. The Madrid Agreement

a. Brief Overview[6]

Under the Madrid Agreement, the owner of a "basic registration," a home country registration, files an international application in its national trademark office and designates the additional member countries in which protection is to be extended. The international application is forwarded to WIPO. WIPO issues an international registration, publishes the mark in the International Trademark Gazette, and forwards the application to the designated countries for examination under national law. The mark is given protection in a designated country unless protection is refused in the country within twelve months. At present, a US company may not participate, and may only obtain international registrations if it is willing to do so in the name of a subsidiary corporation having a domicile in one of the member countries. That approach may not always work to the benefit of the US corporation when it seeks to enforce trademark rights.

b. Application[7]

The Madrid Union provides a vehicle for member countries to obtain registration in other member countries based upon the single filing of the registrant's home registration. Because the United States is not a member of the Madrid Union, securing such a registration is usually not an issue where the client is a US company; however, this is not necessarily the case.

If the client is a US company, but is "domiciled" in a Madrid Union country or has a "real and effective industrial establishment" in a Madrid Union country, this will provide a basis for filing under the Madrid Union. In addition, if the client is not a US company, but a company whose "country of origin" is a member of the Madrid Union, the client can take advantage of filing under the Madrid Union.

Once the client has secured a home registration, he applies for what is called an International Registration, based upon that home registration. The application for an International Registration lists, among other things, all Madrid member countries where the applicant is seeking registration. This single filing is examined for formalities and recorded as an International Registration. The International Registration is then sent to each of the countries listed and is examined separately in each of those countries. One of the advantages of this is that it requires only a single filing, as opposed to filing separately in each country. In addition, if the application is not acted upon in one year by the countries listed in the International Registration, the mark is automatically registered in those countries. Many practitioners also argue that it is less expensive to make a Madrid Union filing, as opposed to filing separately in each country. There are others who disagree, and argue that although the initial filing is less expensive, the savings is usually lost in later prosecution in the respective countries.

It is also important to know that if the home registration is canceled or otherwise lost within five years of its registration, all registrations based upon that home registration are also lost. Thus, it is important to recognize an International Registration when searching a mark for a client and deciding where to register the client's mark.

c. US Problems with the Original Madrid Agreement[8]

When compared with European trademark doctrine, domestic trademark law in the United States is marked by a number of unique—some might even say idiosyncratic—rules. Some of these rules trace their

[6] Practicing Law Institute, *The New Era in Trademark Treaties and Multinational Agreement*. Copyright 1994 Practicing Law Institute. Excerpt reprinted with permission.

[7] ALI-ABA, *Trademarks, Copyrights and Unfair Competition*. Copyright 1995. Excerpt reprinted with permission.

[8] Roger E. Schechter, *Facilitation Trademark Registration Abroad: The Implications of US Ratification of the Madrid Protocol*, 25 GEO. WASH. J. INT'L L. & ECON. 419. Copyright 1991 Roger E Schechter. Excerpt reprinted by permission.

origins to the common law tradition that prevails in the United States and still exerts significant influence on the shape of trademark law. Others may reflect the fact that until relatively modern times, geography effectively isolated the United States from much of the rest of the commercial world, making issues of trademark harmonization and international cooperation matters of smaller moment than they are in Europe.

The US emphasis on use and on a comprehensive pre-registration trademark examination procedure provides the context for understanding the traditional US hostility to the Madrid Agreement. As one US trademark lawyer put it:

> My basic trademark philosophy is that trademark rights should follow use of goods in commerce. Thus, the Madrid Agreement, which permits a trademark registrant in one country to extend his registration into twenty other countries, even though he oftentimes has no intention of doing business under the mark in those countries, is in direct contradiction to this philosophy. . . . The pressing need of today is not to extend a mark automatically to a multiplicity of countries but rather to be able to find new marks for adoption and use by a tremendously larger number of businesses for a tremendously increased number of new products . Thus, my first preference would be to see the Agreement of Madrid abolished. It is in the context of these principles of US law—and of this deeply-rooted US philosophy—that the concerns of the United States with the original version of the Madrid Agreement become readily apparent.[9]

Under the Madrid Agreement, the predicate for an international registration is a valid trademark registration in the applicant's home country. Until a party has secured home country rights, there is nothing upon which to base an application under the Madrid regime. This simple requirement has always been a major obstacle to serious US consideration of participation in the Madrid scheme. This is because the federal registration scheme frequently prevents successful registration of a US trademark for months or years after a product is brought to market. Moreover, US common law rights, which arise instantly upon use, do not solve the problem because they do not constitute a valid basis upon which to file for international registration under the treaty.

Of course, a US firm may know at a very early date that it plans to market its goods abroad and may wish to seek prompt protection for its marks in the relevant nations long before it can expect any definite action from the US Patent and Trademark Office. Such a firm may find it far more attractive to simply file a national application in each country where it anticipates doing business. As one noted commentator explained:

> An international registration must be based on a corresponding home registration. Therefore, the American company will not be able to proceed with an international registration until the US registration has been granted for a particular mark. American registrations may not usually be completed before ten to twelve months even though there may be no serious objections to the mark or an opposition. The position of an American trademark owner, therefore, is entirely different from a French or Belgian Trademark owner who may proceed with an international registration practically the next day after his home registration which is the same day as the date of filing. American trademark owners are anxious to go ahead with foreign applications and not to wait for a year or more while their mark is going through the registration procedure in the United States Patent Office.[10]

While the notion of proceeding nation-by-nation may seem burdensome and expensive, the cost and related inconvenience are often minimized because the US firm is frequently only seriously interested in pro-

---

[9] Anthony R DeSimone, *United States Adherence to the Agreement of Madrid*, 56 TRADEMARK REP. 320 (1966).

[10] Stephen P. Ladas, *The Madrid Agreement for the International Registration of Trademarks and the United States*, 56 TRADEMARK REP. 346, 353–54 (1966).

tecting the mark in a handful of commercially important nations. Thus, rather than confronting the prospect of filing twenty or more applications by foregoing participation in the Madrid Union, the typical US firm might only find it necessary to file four or five—a manageably small number.

Article 6(3) of the Madrid Agreement provides in part that:

> the protection resulting from the international registration may no longer be invoked, in whole or in part, if, within five years from the date of the international registration, the basic application or the registration resulting therefrom, or the basic registration as the case may be, has been withdrawn, has lapsed, has been renounced or has been the subject of a final decision of rejection, revocation, cancellation or invalidation, in respect of all or some of the goods and services listed in the international registration.[11]

This provision provides for what has been frequently called "central attack." Under this system, cancellation of a firm's home country registration results in cancellation of the rights in all other countries of the Madrid Union where extension registrations under the treaty have previously been granted, if the home country action takes place within the first five years after registration, and if the home country requests cancellation by the International Bureau. This is powerful medicine. It can be used in seemingly unjust ways because an:

> objector, by making one single objection in the country of origin, can bring down a series of trade mark registrations in the countries to which the mark has been extended where in fact he has minimal or no prior rights at all! This unfairness is generally recognised as a flaw in the system.[12]

This feature is especially troublesome to US firms because it makes the continued lawful use of a mark abroad contingent on staving off any challenge to domestic rights under the Lanham Act scheme. United States law permits any party to petition for cancellation of a trademark within five years after registration on any grounds that could have been asserted to bar registration initially. Such post-registration cancellation is not uncommon. While such challenges are frequently settled, the possibility that such a legal challenge could also destroy the rights to the mark in a dozen or more foreign countries has traditionally made US firms most unenthusiastic about the notion of adhering to the Madrid Agreement. Obtaining separate national registrations, while a bit more cumbersome, is frequently more prudent.

In addition, the "central attack" feature of the treaty can complicate foreign licensing. That is because the treaty contemplates that when an international registration is transferred without a simultaneous transfer of the home country registration, the assignee's rights continue to be dependent on the validity of the assignor's home country registration. Many US firms prefer to exploit foreign markets through licensing arrangements. Such arrangements frequently involve assignment of the right to use the trademark of the US firm. If a French or German licensee of the US firm knows that the right to exclusive use of the US trademark is dependent—for at least five years—on the mark surviving any potential challenge in the US courts, that naturally tends to complicate negotiations. At a minimum, it implies that the prospective licensee would not be willing to pay as large a royalty as when the right to use the mark was less precarious. Under these circumstances, many US firms prefer to obtain separate national registrations in those nations where they plan to do business, despite the accompanying administrative inconvenience.

The Madrid Agreement is, in colloquial English, a "two-way street." While individual trademark owners in signatory nations gain an advantage from simplified foreign registration practice, those nations have to assume a reciprocal burden—they are obliged to process all international registrations submitted under the treaty regime. For

---

[11] Madrid Agreement Concerning the Registration of Marks, 828 U.N.T.S. 389, 403 at art. 6(3).

[12] David Tatham, Central Attack and the Madrid Agreement, 7 E.I.P.R. 91, 92 (1985).

the United States, unwillingness to assume this reciprocal burden has typically been one of the most compelling reasons to avoid membership in the Madrid Union.

Because of the size and wealth of the US market, the working assumption is that a substantial influx of applications to the United States would follow any adherence to the Madrid Agreement. This is a matter of considerable consequence because the USPTO is still in the process of coping with significantly increased workloads that resulted from amendments to the US domestic trademark law in 1988. If the USPTO also had to process thousands more applications from non-US applicants forwarded under the Madrid system, users of the USPTO fear that this would lengthen the time for them to obtain a final decision on domestic trademark registration applications. Thus, small and medium-sized US businesses, which are unlikely to be interested in international registration, have traditionally viewed adherence to the Madrid Agreement as a poor bargain—one with strictly hypothetical advantages, but with a realistic possibility of delay and expense in the conduct of domestic business and legal affairs.

This particular problem is further compounded by the requirement in the Madrid Agreement that any refusal to register a mark submitted under the treaty regime after examination must be communicated within a one-year period from the date of the filing of the international registration. Thus, if the United States joined the Madrid Union, the USPTO might find it necessary to expedite consideration of international registrations to ensure that final decisions on registrability were reached within the one-year time period. That would necessarily result in an even more protracted decision-making process on domestic registration applications.

The most obvious response to this claimed drawback of adherence to the Madrid Agreement is that any delay can be eliminated by employing more trademark examiners. Assuming that the PTO is unlikely to obtain additional funding from general revenues in this era of chronic budget deficits, this solution necessarily implies an increase in fees for trademark applications. If those fees are increased across-the-board, smaller US firms, with no interest in the advantage of international registration, would subsidize both larger US firms and firms based in other nations who avail themselves of the Madrid Agreement opportunity to register in the United States. The other option would be some sort of differential fee system. Under the Madrid Agreement, however, fees are established by the implementing rules under the treaty, paid directly to WIPO, and then divided among the members of the Madrid Union. Individual national offices cannot charge supplementary fees.

Another related administrative obstacle to US membership in the Madrid Union is the provision that "the working language of the International Bureau shall be French." Putting aside questions of US linguistic chauvinism, this requirement suggests that the USPTO would necessarily have to hire a significant number of translators in order to process applications received from WIPO under the Madrid Agreement scheme. The only way to pay for those translators would be to increase trademark registration fees, with all the attendant problems discussed above.

Still another, albeit minor, administrative obstacle posed by the text of the Madrid Agreement revolves around the various provisions in the United States for "maintenance" of trademarks. Given the Lanham Act's focus on use, the US statute provides that the owner of a registered mark must file an affidavit five years after registration attesting that mark is still being used in commerce. Moreover, the duration of the registration is only ten years, and renewal will be granted only upon submission of yet another affidavit indicating that mark is still in use. Thus, the Lanham Act scheme contemplates that registrants will continually reassure the PTO that the mark is still in actual use and that abandoned marks will be promptly purged from the register.

The Madrid Agreement, by contrast, provides that international registration is to last for twenty years and is silent on any obligations that may be imposed on registrants to attest to conduct during the twenty-year period. This attribute of the Agreement has historically raised the concern that the US register may be cluttered with "dead" or abandoned marks flowing from international registration. As previously noted, that, in turn, would narrow the range of marks available to US firms which already find it difficult to select and promote suitable trade symbols. Staying out of the Madrid Union guarantees that when non-US firms obtain US registration, they can be held to the same requirements of "maintenance" as US firms.

Taken together, these various administrative considerations suggest to many users of the US trademark system that adherence to the Madrid Agreement would lead to greater delay or greater expense in securing federal trademark protection and greater difficulty in locating and clearing available marks, with minimal offsetting benefits. Under this view of affairs, the historic US indifference to membership in the Madrid Union becomes easier to understand.

QUESTIONS AND COMMENTS FOR YOUR CONSIDERATION

1. Generally, formalities are seen as impediments to full protection for intellectual property. What pro-formalistic arguments can you make to support US trademark registration and maintenance requirements?
2. What harm, if any, do these requirements pose to foreign trademark owners? How would you balance the competing interests?

d. The Madrid Protocol

1. Purpose[13]

In July 1989, a Diplomatic Conference adopted a document entitled the "Protocol Relating to the Madrid Agreement Concerning the International Registration of Marks." As summarized by one writer:

> This Protocol would apply the amendments only to the present non-member countries who chose to adhere and not apply to the present members of Madrid as they have argued previously that they are satisfied with the present Agreement and do not want changes made.

The objective of the Protocol was to make the Madrid system more attractive to more countries.[14]

2. Brief Overview[15]

The Protocol Relating to the Madrid Agreement Concerning the International Registration of Marks (Madrid Protocol) is a treaty which was adopted in 1989. It supplements the longstanding one hundred year old Madrid Agreement in order to correct deficiencies in the Madrid Agreement that had discouraged the United States and other non-member countries from joining the arrangement. Under the auspices of WIPO, the Agreement provided a means for an owner of a home country trademark registration to obtain trademark rights in several countries designated by the owner by filing a single application based on the basic registration in its national trademark office. The Madrid Protocol enables a trademark owner to obtain international rights with effect in as many member countries as the trademark owner designates on the basis of a single "basic application," and the applicant need not have a home registration.

Under the Madrid Agreement, the owner of a "basic registration," a home country registration, files an international application in its national trademark office and designates

---

[13] Roger E. Schechter, *Facilitating Trademark Registration Abroad: The Implications of US Ratification of the Madrid Protocol*, 25 GEO. WASH. J. INT'L L. & ECON. 419. Copyright 1992 George Washington University. Excerpt reprinted with permission.

[14] Ian. J. Kaufman, *Madrid Agreement: Will Reform Proposals Attract More Members?* 12 E.I.P.R. 407, 410 (1990).

[15] Practising Law Institute, *The New Era in Trademark Treaties and Multinational Agreement.* Copyright 1994, Practising Law Institute. Excerpt reprinted with permission.

the additional member countries in which protection is to be extended. The international application is forwarded to WIPO. WIPO issues an international registration, publishes the mark in the International Trademark Gazette, and forwards the application to the designated countries for examination under national law. The mark is given protection in a designated country unless protection is refused in the country within twelve months. At present, a US company may not participate, and may only obtain international registrations if it is willing to do so in the name of a subsidiary corporation having a domicile in one of the member countries. That approach may not always work to the benefit of the US corporation when it seeks to enforce trademark rights.

The Protocol corrects deficiencies in the Agreement which were seen to work to the disadvantage of United States Trademark Office and US trademark owners. Under the Protocol, an international application may be filed based on a US application, the "basic application," or it may be based upon a "basic registration." This eliminates the requirement of the Madrid Agreement for a "basic registration," that put the US trademark owner at a disadvantage as against owners in countries whose application processes are shorter than that of the US. With the intent-to-use basis in the US, US trademark owners will be able to file international applications without waiting for issuance of a registration which may not occur for a number of years.

A drawback to the Agreement is its provision for "central attack," which means that a successful attack on the home registration during the first five years of the term of an international registration results in termination of protection in all designated countries to which protection has been extended. US law provides bases of attack which do not exist in other countries of the Agreement. The Protocol deals with the problem by providing that in the event of successful attack of the basic application or basic registration during the first five years of the term of the international registration, the extensions may be changed to national applications but retain the effective filing date of the international registration, so that the risk of loss of rights through central attack effectively is eliminated.

The Protocol permits the United States to elect to take eighteen months instead of the twelve months provided by the Agreement, to act to refuse protection in international applications. In addition, because the US has an opposition system, refusal of protection may be made after the eighteen month period, so long as the refusal results from the opposition and meets certain deadlines pegged to the beginning or expiration of the opposition period.

Numerous other provisions, including using English as one of the official languages, have made the Protocol more palatable to the United States.

3. US Concerns and the Madrid Protocol[16]

Unlike the Madrid Agreement—which requires a home country registration—the Protocol will allow international registration to be predicated on a home country application. Thus, under the Protocol a US firm need not delay the pursuit of protection abroad until the USPTO completes its sometimes lengthy *ex parte* review and until all risk of a domestic opposition passes. Rather, it could proceed at once to secure registrations abroad, with the significant advantage of a much earlier priority date in any contest with another claimant for the same mark. In addition, since US firms can now at least file an application in advance of use (although US registration will not issue until proof of use is provided), the Protocol will permit US firms to obtain an early priority date for trademarks whose use is contemplated in foreign markets.

A second major innovation of the Protocol is its substantial elimination of the central attack features of the Agreement. Under Article 9quinquies of the Protocol, should the home country registration be successfully challenged or otherwise deemed invalid, the mark owners have three months to convert any previously obtained extension registrations into national registrations—something

---

[16] Roger E. Schechter, *Facilitating Trademark Registration Abroad: the Implications of US Ratification of the Madrid Protocol*, 25 Geo. Wash. J. Int'l L. & Econ. 419. Copyright 1992 George Washington University. Excerpt reprinted with permission.

that was not possible under the original Madrid Agreement. Such a prospect for conversion effectively severs the connection between the extension registration and the home country registration and would permit free exploitation, licensing, or transfer of foreign trademark rights, without any concern that an eleventh hour challenge in the USPTO or in the US court system could subvert foreign rights.

Thirdly, the Protocol is responsive to many of the administrative problems traditionally cited as obstacles to US adherence to the original version of the Madrid Agreement. For instance, under the Protocol, English would become a working language of the Madrid Union. This should both speed up use of the system by US firms and reduce costs associated with translation. Similarly, the Protocol provides that national offices will have eighteen months within which to refuse a registration predicated on a Madrid filing, rather than the twelve months provided for in the original Madrid Agreement. That expanded time frame makes it more likely that Madrid filings can be examined in ordinary course without pushing US domestic filing "to the back of the line" or necessitating the expense of hiring numerous additional examiners. In addition, the draft regulations under the Protocol contemplate a revised fee structure that will effectively permit national offices—such as the USPTO—to charge international registrants fees comparable to those charged to domestic firms. This goes a long way toward insuring that domestic applicants are not subsidizing firms based abroad who utilize the Madrid system.

With these changes in the system, it might seem that US adherence is an all but foregone conclusion. There are, however, some additional issues which are a continuing cause for concern on the part of the USPTO and US trademark owners.

Perhaps the biggest sticking point with the Protocol involves the "intent-to-use" requirement imposed by US law on foreign trademark applicants. Under Section 44(d) of the Lanham Act, certain foreign parties may file a trademark application in the USPTO, and if the US application is filed within six months of the date of a prior foreign application, the applicant is given a US filing date equivalent to the date of its foreign application. A Section 44(d) application, however, must be accompanied by a declaration by the applicant of a bona fide intention to use the mark in US domestic commerce. Foreign applicants can also rely on a previously issued foreign registration as a basis for a US trademark registration, but, once again, the statute requires that they affirm their *bona fide* intent to use the mark in the United States before the registration will issue.

Congress added a requirement that foreign applicants allege an intent to use the mark in the United States when it amended the Lanham Act to permit pre-use application by domestic firms. The requirement reflected notions of equity. Just as domestic firms are obliged to make an "intent-to-use" declaration when they file an application prior to using a mark in the United States, these provisions subject foreign applicants to the same requirement. In the eyes of many US trademark owners, US law still gives foreign applicants preferential treatment, since they may obtain a US registration without ever having used the mark in the United States, while no such possibility exists for a US firm.

These features of US law raise a number of interrelated questions. First, if the United States acceded to the Madrid Protocol, could it require foreign firms using the Protocol to make a declaration of intention to use when seeking US trademark protection? The Protocol itself is silent on the point, and without an affirmative resolution of the issue, US adherence is considerably less likely.

A related question is whether foreign firms filing under the Protocol to seek extension registrations in the United States will be granted US registration solely on the strength of their declaration of an intent to use in the future, or whether an affidavit of actual use will be required? As noted, the current US system requires proof of use before a registration will issue to a domestic US firm, in addition to such a firm's declaration of an intention to use the mark in the future. On the other hand, foreign applicants under Section 44 routinely receive US registrations without any proof of actual use in the United States, provided they have made the required declaration. Thus, the issue is whether to treat applications under the Madrid Protocol as more like domestic applications or Section 44 applications.

It would appear from the text of the Protocol . . . that no proof of actual use can be required of foreign applicants utilizing the Madrid Protocol. Thus, if the United States adheres to the Protocol, it would seem to have little choice in the matter. Representatives of the USPTO have indicated, in negotiating sessions surrounding the drafting of the implementing regulations, that they cannot insist upon proof of actual use for applications submitted under the Madrid system. Instead, they plan to treat the applications comparably to applications under Section 44. This, of course, does not dispose of the normative question of whether such treatment is warranted.

Permitting registration of marks without proof that they are in actual use once again raises the specter of a US firm experiencing enhanced difficulty in locating a suitable mark because of "clutter" on the US register in the form of Madrid Protocol registrations that are not actually being used in the US market. Under the current system—with no US participation in the Madrid Union—the expense to a foreign firm of proceeding under Section 44 gives some added assurance that its declaration of an intent-to-use is probably grounded in fact. Why else would such a firm bother to retain US trademark counsel and pursue the application? This helps minimize the "clutter" problem because most registrations that ultimately issue to applicants under Section 44 probably relate to marks that are being used in the United States. Because registration under the Madrid Protocol will be appreciably less complicated and expensive, presumably many more firms will take advantage of the procedure, and, despite a declaration of intent-to-use in the United States, they may ultimately never exploit the mark in actual sales. Nonetheless, the marks will be unavailable to domestic firms.

Concerns about "deadwood" or "clutter" on the register may, however, be overstated. There is no reason to assume that foreign firms will commonly make false declarations of their intentions concerning the US market. Moreover, registrants under the Madrid system would still be subject to post-registration requirements under the Lanham Act. Specifically, they will be required to attest, under oath, five years after registration, that the mark is still being used. While this is a far from perfect method of keeping the register current, it does provide some assurance that problems will remain within manageable bounds. On balance, then, this feature of the Protocol should not be an obstacle to US adherence.

Another potential problem left unresolved by the Protocol concerns the specificity with which applicants must identify the goods and/or services on which the mark is or will be used. Under US practice, a fairly detailed specification is required, and much of the application process is often devoted to narrowing the description of goods for which protection is claimed until the PTO is satisfied. This contrasts with the more relaxed practice in many other nations. In many nations, trademark applicants are permitted to seek registration of a mark for broad categories of goods even though the mark may only actually be used on a single narrow product line.

US firms may discover that the asymmetrical practices concerning the description of goods make the Madrid scheme less attractive. United States firms can, of course, only avail themselves of the advantages of the Protocol after filing a US application. That application will typically contain a narrow description of goods so as to comply with the traditional US practices in this regard. The US firm will be bound by that description when it then uses the Protocol to extend registration to twenty or more other countries. If that same US firm filed separate applications in the national offices of those other countries, it might be able to claim a much broader description of goods.

Another key issue bearing on adherence to the Madrid Protocol concerns the effect it will have on the ability of US firms to "clear" marks in the future. This problem, however, is intrinsic to any system of international trademark cooperation, regardless of the details.

Trademarks serve not only the interests of trading companies, but also the interests of consumers. As many scholars have noted, trademarks reduce search costs for consumers by giving them a swift and inexpensive way to relocate goods that they have previously purchased and enjoyed. Trademark infringement is universally condemned not only because it harms honest merchants, but also because it makes it difficult for consumers to make informed choices in the market place.

As the century draws to a close, consumers are more mobile than ever. Because such individuals associate a brand name with a particular set of product attributes, having that brand name signal those attributes throughout the world is becoming increasingly logical and important. The US citizen living in Egypt benefits if he or she can assume that the "CREST" name on a tube of toothpaste on sale in Egypt signifies a toothpaste with the same attributes as the one on sale in Chicago. A French citizen living in New York similarly benefits if he or she can assume the same thing about the French brand "FLUROCARIL."

Although an expanded system of international trademark registration may increase processing and application costs, and although it may make the clearance of new marks more difficult for US firms, ultimately an expanded system of trademark registration will make the location of desirable goods easier for consumers the world over. And that, after all, is a primary purpose of trademark law. This consumer recognition factor, perhaps more than any other, counsels in favor of speedy adherence to the new Madrid Protocol.

QUESTIONS AND COMMENTS FOR YOUR CONSIDERATION

1. Is the question of "deadwood" only a US concern? Do the provisions of the Madrid Protocol provide a workable international standard for coping with the problem of unused marks "cluttering" the registration base?
2. Does the Madrid Protocol establish uniform registration requirements? Is international uniformity in registration formalities a desirable goal? What minimal formalities, if any, should be established?

2. The Community Trademark[17]

On March 14, 1994, the Community Trademark Regulation (Counsel Regulation 40/94 of 20 December, 1993 on the Community Trademark) entered into force.

The Regulation enables an applicant to obtain coverage throughout the European Union by filing a single application. The countries of the European Union have been in the process of enacting implementing legislation to harmonize their trademark laws consistent with a Harmonization Directive promulgated by the Counsel of the European Community. The new Community Trademark system is slated to go into operation in January, 1996, but financing problems and political realities within the European Union suggest 1997 as the earliest date we may expect applications will be accepted. US trademark owners and owners in all countries participating in the Paris Convention, not just the European Union countries, will be able to file applications to obtain a Community Trademark. It is anticipated that once the system is operative, the European Union will adhere to the Madrid Protocol. This will mean that an application for registration of a Community Trademark may be used as the "basic application" for obtaining international registration under the Madrid Protocol. Further, the link between the Community Trademark and Madrid Protocol will mean that under the Madrid Protocol an applicant may designate the whole territory of the European Union as a single designated territory.

Briefly, an applicant for a Community Trademark registration will file a single application at the Harmonization Office in Alicante, Spain or in a national office for forwarding to Alicante. The application will be examined as to registrability of the mark. After *ex parte* examination, the application will be published, and third parties may oppose within an opposition period of three months. The registration will have a term of ten years, renewable for further periods of ten years, and it will have effect as a single mark for the territory of the European Union.

---

[17] Practicing Law Institute, *The New Era in Trademark Treaties and Multinational Agreement*. Copyright (c) 1994, Practicing Law Institute. Excerpt reprinted with permission.

A registrable trademark is defined as "any mark capable of being represented graphically." There are prohibitions against registration of generic and descriptive terms, some three dimensional shapes, misleading marks and indications, and marks contrary to public policy or accepted standards of morality. Use of a trademark is not a prerequisite for registration, but the trademark must be in genuine use in the European Union within five years after registration. It is necessary to use in only one member of the Union to satisfy the requirement of use.

An application for a Community Trademark may be converted into national trademark applications. This will permit registrations in a number of the Member countries when earlier rights prevent registration for the entire Union.

Although the Community Trademark will be a single trademark valid to confer rights in all European Union countries, as an item of property it will be treated as a national mark of the country in which the trademark owner has a seat, domicile or establishment. If the owner has none in the European Union, the mark will be considered to be a Spanish mark. As for enforcement of rights, the Community Trademark regulation requires the member countries to designate certain existing national courts to have exclusive jurisdiction of Community Trademark infringement actions. These Community Trademark Courts of special jurisdiction are expected to develop Community Trademark expertise and a specialized body of law.

The Community Trademark offers the prospect of obtaining coverage throughout the European Union under much simplified procedures and at significantly less expense. However, with the likely availability of international registration under the Madrid Protocol, only time will tell whether trademark owners seeking multi-national protection will prefer to proceed under the Protocol.

QUESTIONS AND COMMENTS FOR YOUR CONSIDERATION

1. Assume that you represent a company whose country of origin is a member of the Madrid Union, the Paris Convention and the European Union. Your client intends to sell its products in Great Britain, France and Italy and may sell its products in other members of the European Union. Which registration method would you recommend for each of these target countries? Why?

2. The Community Trademark represents an effort to establish a regional solution to the problem of international trademark registration. For a discussion of additional regional efforts by the European Union to harmonize trademark protection standards, *see* Chapter Twelve.

a. Application[18]

In 1993, the European Union passed a Regulation (the "Regulation") to create a supranational system of trademark law for all Member States of the European Union. Through adoption of the Regulation, the Council of the European Union sought to promote harmonious economic development within the territory of the Union, to aid in the completion of an internal single market, to offer services like those of a national market, to remove trade barriers between the Member States, and to offer uniform trademark protection throughout the Union. However, the Regulation does not usurp national laws on trademarks, lessen or alter trademark protection available within the individual Member States, or prevent companies from obtaining protection in individual Member States if they do not desire to acquire Union-wide protection.

Prior to the adoption of the Regulation, the

---

[18] Shilpa Mehta & Leslie Steele Smith, *An American Practitioner's Guide to the Developing System of Trademark Law Within the European Union*, 3 TEX. INTELL. PROP. L. J. 85. Copyright 1995 State Bar of Texas, Intellectual Property Law Section. Excerpt reprinted with permission.

Council promulgated a Directive (the "Directive") in 1988 which required Member States to harmonize their national laws on trademarks. While businesses now have the opportunity to obtain Union-wide protection under the Regulation, there still remains an alternative type of national protection within each of the Member States. The new system in Europe under the Regulation and the Directive will make the national laws for each Member State more compatible and predictable for companies expanding beyond their national borders.

The Regulation describes four primary categories of approved proprietors consisting of (1) nationals of the Member States; (2) nationals of states which are parties to the Paris Convention [of a Community Trademark] for the Protection of Industrial Property, as amended (the "Paris Convention"); (3) nationals of states which are not parties to the Paris Convention but who are domiciled in or who have real and effective commercial or industrial establishments within the territory of the Union or a state which is party to the Paris Convention; and (4) nationals of states which are not parties to the Paris Convention that nonetheless offer reciprocal trademark protection to nationals of all the Member States.

Permitted proprietors may file a Community Trademark application at the Community Trademark Office or at any of the national trademark offices of the Member States. Member States are required to forward the Community Trademark application to the Community Trademark Office within two weeks of filing. The Community Trademark application is examined to determine whether there are absolute grounds or relative grounds for refusal of registration of the mark. "Absolute" grounds for refusal apply when mark, standing alone, is examined for compliance with specific provisions of the Regulation.

The Regulation absolutely bars registration of a mark if:

(1) the mark falls outside the definition of a trademark;
(2) the trademark is not distinctive;
(3) the trademark is descriptive;
(4) the trademark is generic;
(5) the sign is functional;
(6) the trademark is contrary to public policy or morality;
(7) the trademark is misdescriptive; or
(8) the trademark has not been authorized by the competent authorities and would be refused by Article 6ter of the Paris Convention.

Absolute grounds for refusal apply notwithstanding that the grounds for non-registrability may exist only in part of the Union. The Union system also expressly bars marks which are generic registration.

In the Union system, the practitioner must be aware that a problem may arise if the Directive is applied inconsistently throughout the various Member States. Although the Directive includes a definition of trademark for the Member States to use in list form, neither the Regulation nor the Directive claims that the list is exhaustive. Hence, there is a possibility that unusual marks such as smells, sounds, colors, and other common law signs may qualify for Community Trademark protection. If the applicant's mark, on its face, survives the hurdle of absolute grounds for refusal, the mark is then examined as to relative grounds for refusal. Here, the Community Trademark Office draws up a Union search report citing all Community Trademarks or Community Trademark applications that have been discovered and which may be invoked by a proprietor of an earlier mark to oppose registration of the mark at issue. The proprietor of an earlier mark may oppose registration of a mark based on one of five relative grounds for refusal which include the following:

(1) an identical earlier trademark for identical goods or services already exists;
(2) a likelihood of confusion exists between the mark and an earlier trademark within the territory of the earlier mark;
(3) ownership of the mark is at issue between its proprietor and an agent or representative who applies for registration "in his own name without the proprietor's consent ...";
(4) an earlier non-registered mark from a Member State already exists; and
(5) dilution of an earlier Community Trademark or earlier national trademark may result.

Non-registered marks having more than

mere local significance may bar the registration of a Community Trademark. The Regulation, however, requires the owner of such an earlier mark to oppose the Community Trademark registration if he wishes to bar the registration. The burden is on the proprietors of non-registered marks to watch the Union Trade Marks Bulletin, the official publication for Community Trademarks, to determine if another party is registering the mark as a Community Trademark. In contrast, the Directive does not shift the burden of opposition onto the common law user, but rather allows the Member States to determine whether the unregistered trademark has acquired rights prior to the application date of a national trademark, and whether the application for registration should be denied if the unregistered trademark has acquired prior rights.

Dilution. The general rule for dilution is that the law will not register any identical or similar trademark if it is to be registered for goods or services different from those of a prior mark. The Regulation and the Directive differ, however, in the standards used for denying registration. Under the Directive, an application for national registration will be refused when an earlier Community Trademark exists and where use of the applicant's mark would take either unfair advantage of or be detrimental to the Community Trademark's distinctive character or reputation. In contrast, under the Regulation's anti-dilution provision, the proprietor of an earlier Community Trademark must show only that the earlier Community Trademark has a reputation in the Union to successfully bar the registration of a later identical or similar Community Trademark. The owner of an earlier national trademark, however, must not only show a reputation in the Member State in which the earlier mark is registered, but must also show that use of the Community Trademark would take either unfair advantage of or be detrimental to the earlier mark's reputation and distinctive character.

Note, however, that the Regulation puts the burden on proprietors of earlier trademarks to oppose the issuance of a Community Trademark registration on grounds of dilution. This places the responsibility to police and monitor registrations of Community Trademarks on proprietors of both Community Trademarks and national marks. This is true even for owners of national marks who never market or intend to market their products outside their national boundaries. The Community Trademark Office will not refuse registration based on relative grounds on its own motion, but rather it will publish an application and wait for opposition by prior owners.

Upon publication of a Community Trademark application, any third party who is not involved in the proceedings before the Community Trademark Office may file a written statement explaining why the registration of a mark should not be allowed on the basis of absolute grounds for refusal with the Community Trademark Office. In contrast, any party with standing, such as a proprietor of an earlier mark who might be harmed upon registration of the Community Trademark, may oppose registration of a mark on relative grounds. The proprietor of an earlier mark must file a written opposition specifying the grounds on which it is made within three months of publication of the Community Trademark application. Upon notification of the opposition, the applicant can require the proprietor of the earlier mark to show five years of continuous use prior to the publication of the Community Trademark application at issue. The prior owner must show evidence of five years of use; otherwise, the opposition is rejected, and the Community Trademark application may qualify for registration. If a national trademark owner fails to timely oppose a Community Trademark application and the Community Trademark is registered and used within five years, the national trademark owner will be deemed to have acquiesced to the use of the Community Trademark and will have lost his right to invalidate or revoke the latter mark based on his preexisting rights.

Applications must be filed in one of the official national languages of the Member States of the Union. An applicant must also list a second official language of the Community Trademark Office as an alternate language to be used in proceedings of opposition, revocation, or invalidity. The five official languages of the Community Trademark Office include English, French, German, Italian and Spanish. If the applicant is the sole party to the proceedings before the Community Trademark Office, the language used in the proceedings shall be the language the application was filed in, but the Community Trademark Office may send written communications in the applicant's designated official language if the application was not made in one of the official Community Trademark Office languages. If there is no opposition to the Community Trademark application, the mark is registered.

From the date of registration, the proprietor of a Community Trademark acquires exclusive rights to protection from infringement by:

(1) identical trademarks for identical goods and services;
(2) trademarks subject to a likelihood of confusion due to identity or similarity in the marks and identity or similarity in the goods and services covered; and
(3) trademarks that cause dilution.

In addition, registration of a Community Trademark is a presumption of its validity which may not be put in issue unless challenged by another party in a revocation or invalidity proceeding.

There are exceptions to the rights conferred by the registration of a Community Trademark. A Community Trademark proprietor may not prohibit a third party from using his own name or descriptive or geographic terms. Also, a Community Trademark owner cannot prevent others from using the Community Trademark if it is necessary in order to indicate the intended use for their goods or services. This allows protection primarily for makers or sellers of accessories or spare parts.

There are three ways in which a Community Trademark proprietor can acquire exclusive rights that predate the date of actual publication in the register. These are via rights of priority, exhibition, and seniority.

A Community Trademark owner may claim priority based on an application for a trademark registration in any State that is a party to the Paris Convention. The claim must be made within six months from the date of filing of the first application. A filing "equivalent to a regular national filing under the law of the State where it was made or under [a] bilateral or multilateral agreement" gives rise to a right of priority. Priority may only be claimed for the same trademark regarding identical goods or services, or goods or services contained within those covered by the first application. To claim the right, the applicant must file a declaration of priority and a copy of the previous application. Community Trademark filings have a priority right within the Member States of the Union.

An applicant for a Community Trademark may also claim a right of priority based on "exhibition priority." A Community Trademark applicant who desires to obtain "exhibition priority" must file the application within six months from the date the mark is first displayed "at an official or officially recognized international exhibition falling within the terms of the Convention on International Exhibitions signed at Paris on [November 22, 1928,] and last revised on [November 30, 1972]." To claim the right, the applicant "must file evidence of the display of [the] goods or services under the mark applied for."

Additionally, rights of seniority may be claimed by owners of national trademarks registered in Member States of the Union, the Benelux Office, or under international arrangements having effect in a Member State. Rights of seniority are more extensive than rights of priority because they have no six month time limit for filing the initial request. The Community Trademark application must be for the identical trademark, regarding "goods or services which are identical with or contained within" the goods or services covered by the first application. The effect is to backdate the Community Trademark application to the earlier application date, so long as the Community Trademark owner surrenders the earlier mark or allows it to lapse. "Seniority claimed for the [Community Trademark] shall lapse" if the earlier trademark "is declared to have been revoked or to be invalid or if it [was] surrendered prior to registration of the [Community Trademark]." Seniority based on a national trademark may be claimed at the time of application for a Community Trademark or after registration of the Community Trademark. Claiming seniority permits owners of national trademarks to maintain protection from the earlier filing date and "trade up" to Union-wide coverage as well.

A Community Trademark shall be registered for a period of ten years from the filing date of the application. The Community Trademark may then be renewed for ten year periods.

The Union system does not require a showing of use to the Community Trademark Office at any given time, except when the registrant is requested to show proof of use in a proceeding before the Community Trademark Office, such as in an opposition, invalidity, or revocation proceeding.

"Genuine" or actual use of a Community Trademark must begin within five years of registration and may not be suspended for any continuous five year period. Use by consent of the proprietor, such as under a license, constitutes actual use by a proprietor under the Regulation. Small deviations in form will not defeat use, and use for export only (out of the territory of the Union) is sufficient.

In addition to grounds for invalidity, a Community Trademark owner can lose his trademark protection through revocation proceedings. A revocation proceeding may occur on four grounds: (1) where there is inexcusable non-use for five years preceding the application for revocation; (2) where the mark becomes generic; (3) where the mark is misdescriptive; and (4) where the Community Trademark owner no longer meets the requirements of permitted proprietorship. The net result of a revocation or invalidity proceeding is the same: the cancellation of the registration and of the rights conferred by the registration.

QUESTIONS AND COMMENTS FOR YOUR CONSIDERATION

1. The Community Trademark demonstrates the problems of balancing supranational and national protection schemes. What impact, if any, will the Community Trademark have on the control of European Union member states over the trademarks used and protected within their borders?

2. For a discussion of additional instances of supranational solutions to intellectual property protection issues, *see* Chapters Nine and Twelve (EEC Harmonzation section).

3. What factors would you consider in determining whether a particular mark has a "reputation within the community"? Is this test different from the one applied to determine whether a mark qualifies as a "famous" or "well-known" mark under the Paris Convention (*see* Chapter Nine)? Should it be?

D. Formal Requirements for Obtaining Trade Secret Protection[19]

There is no international treaty which establishes agreed-upon formalities for obtaining trade secret protection. The first multinational treaty to specifically address the issue of trade secret protection is TRIPS. Article 41 of the TRIPS Agreement specifically requires that member countries provide natural and legal persons with "the possibility of preventing information lawfully within their control from being disclosed to, acquired by, or used by others without their consent in a manner contrary to honest commercial practices." To qualify for protection, the information in question must be "secret"; it must have "commercial value" due to its secret nature and the legal possessor of the information must have taken "reasonable steps under the circumstances" to maintain its secrecy. No country currently imposes any registration formalities for trade secret protection.

[19] Written for this Anthology by Doris Estelle Long. Copyright 1996 Doris E. Long.

9

Remedies

Most bilateral and multinational treaty regimes have attempted to establish minimum substantive standards for the protection of intellectual property. These minimum standards have focused primarily on the nature of protection afforded the classic forms of intellectual property—definitional standards for a protectable work and recordation requirements for obtaining ownership rights to such works. Until recently few treaty regimes addressed the question of enforcement or the remedies available for infringement of intellectual property rights. This Chapter explores the wide variety of relief available for the violation of intellectual property rights. It begins with an examination of the scope of civil remedies available, including supranational relief under the Treaty of Rome and the minimum enforcement standards established under TRIPS and NAFTA. It then explores various civil protection regimes, including self-help remedies, civil law suits and enhanced penalties for willful infringement. The Chapter concludes with an exploration of the new effort to establish international standards for criminal remedies for intellectual property infringement.

A. Civil Remedies

Until the enactment of the North American Free Trade Agreement and the Agreement on Trade Related Aspects of Intellectual Property Rights, no international standard for the enforcement of intellectual property rights had been the subject of a treaty regime. Just as the scope of protection for intellectual property rights is governed by domestic law, so too are the types of remedies available and the procedures for obtaining such remedies.

1. EEC and Supranational Protection

a. The Treaty of Rome and the Free Movement of Goods[1]

The Treaty of Rome serves as a blueprint for European integration. To achieve integration, the Treaty creates four "economic liberties" existing among the Union 's member states, free movement of goods, free movement of persons, free movement of services, and free movement of capital.

Nevertheless, Article 36 of the Treaty permits member states to restrict the free movement of goods. Article 36 states:

> The provisions of Articles 30 to 34 shall not preclude prohibitions or restrictions on imports, exports or goods in transit justified on grounds of public morality, public policy or public security; the protection of health and life of humans, animals or plants; the protection of national treasures possessing artistic, historic or archaeological value; or the protection of industrial and commercial property. Such prohibitions or restrictions shall not, however, constitute a means of arbitrary discrimination or a disguised restriction on trade between Member States.

The Treaty framers included Article 36

[1] John E. Somorjai, *The Evolution of a Common Market: Limits Imposed on the Protection of National Intellectual Property Rights in the European Economic Community*, 9 INT'L. TAX & BUS. LAW 431.

because they believed the Treaty must allow member states to regulate imports and exports to the extent necessary to give effect to national policies that the member states considered of primary importance.

The Union believes that in order to gain wide acceptance and maintain its political support throughout the member states, Union laws must preserve certain national rights. It considers patent, copyright, and trademark rights to be of such importance as to warrant a derogation, within limits, from complete free trade of goods.

As Article 36 provides a derogation from a key provision of the Treaty, the Court of Justice has been careful to construe the Article narrowly. In so doing, the Court has established several doctrines to restrict the applicability of Article 36.

The Principle of Proportionality. The proportionality principle mandates that a measure will not be upheld if there is a means to achieve its purpose that would be less restrictive to intra-Union trade. As the Court of Justice has said, "Article 36 is an exception to the fundamental principle of the free movement of goods and must, therefore, be interpreted in such a way that its scope is not extended any further than is necessary for the protection of those interests which it is intended to secure." The second sentence of Article 36 provides the proportionality principle's basis and ensures that the Article 36 exceptions will not be abused.

Regarding industrial and commercial property, the proportionality principle has been developed by the Court of Justice to limit the "permissible derogations ... to those necessary to give effect to the 'specific object' of the right relied upon." Derogations justified under Article 36 are permissible only "where such derogations are justified for the purpose of safeguarding rights which constitute the specific subject matter of this property." In this way, the Court of Justice has set the parameters within which these property rights can be asserted to hinder trade between member states.

Exhaustion of Rights Principle. The Court of Justice uses a second principle to further restrict the property owner's rights once the protected product is placed on the market. Under the exhaustion of rights principle, the exclusive right guaranteed by national legislation on industrial and commercial property ends when the product is placed in the stream of commerce within a member state by the owner of the right or with his consent. Thereafter, the owner of the right may not oppose the importation of the product into another member state nor its re-importation into the state where it was first marketed. The principle of exhaustion is based on:

> the idea that the owner of a right has, by his own acts of utilisation, taken advantage of and thereby exhausted, the exclusive right of exploitation granted to him by law, so that certain other acts of exploitation no longer come within the protection of the right. If the owner of the right has taken all the benefits constituted by his right, he no longer needs protection, further exploitation has become free and cannot be prohibited by him.

The doctrine serves to limit the monopoly right granted for industrial and commercial property.

The Court of Justice has applied the exhaustion doctrine equally to patents and copyrights. While the same issues may be raised, the Court of Justice must be careful not to blur the differences between patents and copyrights. Indeed, there is an important distinction between them. One basis for creating the copyright system is to protect the reputation of the author. Copyright is thus more of a personal right in that the product is associated with its author, unlike a patent, where few care to know the name of the inventor. The identity of the author of a product can be just as important for sales as the product itself. Damage to products occurring during the parallel importation of a work could damage the reputation of the author. There is no guarantee that a parallel import will have the same quality as an original distribution by the author. The Court of Justice first announced the exhaustion doctrine in the *Deutsche Grammophon*[2] case, applying the doctrine to copyright. Deutsche Grammophon had manufactured certain records in Germany, which it had then sold to its French subsidiary,

---

[2] 1971 C.M.L.R. 631.

Polydor. Metro acquired these records and Deutsche Grammophon sought an injunction to prevent Metro from selling the records in Germany under German copyright law. The Court of Justice held that to grant such an injunction would isolate national markets and thus be contrary to the essential aim of the Treaty, which is to unite national markets into a single market. The Court of Justice followed with its opinion in *Musik-Vertrieb Membran GmBH and K-tel International v. GEMA*. The case involved a German company that placed recordings on the British market. The recordings were subsequently imported into Germany. GEMA, the German copyright protection society, brought an action against the importers seeking the difference in royalty fees paid in Great Britain and in Germany. The Court held that because of the exhaustion principle, the party that placed the product on the market could not recover the difference in royalty fees. The Court rejected the argument of the French government that copyright should be treated differently from other industrial property because it serves to protect the reputation of the author. The Court explained that copyright:

> also comprises other rights, notably the right to exploit commercially the marketing of the protected work, particularly in the form of licenses granted in return for payment of royalties. It is this economic aspect of copyright which is the subject of the question submitted by the national court and, in this regard, in the application of Article 36 of the Treaty there is no reason to make a distinction between copyright and other industrial and commercial property rights.

The Court finally pointed out that it is the author's choice in a common market to choose where to put his work into circulation.

Expanding its concept of the exhaustion doctrine, the Court of Justice applied the exhaustion doctrine to patents in *Centrafarm BV v. Sterling Drug Inc.*[3] The Court of Justice held that once a product has been placed on the market legally by the patentee himself, or with his consent, Article 36 cannot be used as an obstacle to the free movement of this good. This case arose from widely divergent prices being charged for certain pharmaceuticals in the Netherlands and Great Britain. Sterling Drug owned parallel patent rights in both Great Britain and the Netherlands for the drug Negram which is used for the treatment of infections of the urinary passages. The Sterling subsidiaries in the Netherlands and Great Britain placed Negram on the market in several member states. Centrafarm subsequently imported Negram from Great Britain and sold it in the Netherlands to take advantage of the large price differential.

The Court of Justice distinguished this case, in which the product was patented in several countries and placed on the market by the patentee, from the situation in which the product is imported from another member state, where it is not patentable and has been manufactured by third parties without the consent of the patentee. The Court accepted the exhaustion principle when the product was placed on the market by the patentee or by his consent. It reasoned that if a patentee could block importations of its product, marketed by him or by his consent in another member state, the patentee would be able to partition national markets. The patentee would "thereby restrict trade between Member States, in a situation in which no such restriction was necessary to guaranty the essence of the exclusive rights flowing from parallel patents." The Court rejected Sterling Drug's argument that it was protecting the public against risks arising from defective pharmaceuticals. The Court felt that such measures are properly adopted in the area of health control and must not constitute a misuse of the rules pertaining to industrial and commercial property.

In a later case, the Court of Justice held that an industrial property right will be exhausted even if the products were not covered under the law of the member state where the goods were distributed by the holder of the right. In *Merck v. Stephar and Exler*,[4] Merck held a patent for a pharmaceutical product in the Netherlands, which it also put on the market in Italy. The product was not covered by a patent in Italy because pharma-

[3] 1974 E.C.R. 1147.

[4] 1981 E.C.R. 2063.

ceutical products could not be patented under Italian law at the time when it was first sold. Stephar acquired large quantities of the drug in Italy and resold it in the Netherlands at a lower price. The Court of Justice held that the patent had been exhausted when the goods were placed on the Italian market and that a holder of a patent on a product must bear the consequences when choosing to market that product in a member state where there is no patent protection. As in *Sterling Drug*, the Court clearly distinguished this case from a situation in which third parties marketed the product without the consent of the right holder.

The Court of Justice has recognized several exceptions to the exhaustion doctrine. In *S.A. Compagnie Generale pour la Diffusion de la Television, Coditel, and Others v. S.A. Cine Vog Films and Others*,[5] the Court limited the exhaustion doctrine to marketing through the sale of copies of the works in the form of physical objects; the doctrine does not apply to performance rights. Cine Vog Films, a film distribution company, contracted with a film producer for an exclusive right for a period of seven years to show a particular film in Belgium. Later, the film's producer also assigned the right to broadcast the film in Germany to a German television station. Belgian cable television companies picked up the transmission and relayed it to their customers. Cine Vog contended that the broadcast had jeopardized the commercial future of the film in Belgium.

The Court of Justice considered, among other issues, whether Articles 59 and 60 of the Treaty prohibited an assignment that was limited to the territory of a single member state. It held that the holder of performing rights for a film in Belgium could prevent the re-transmission by cable television in Belgium of a German broadcast of the film. The producer in Belgium had legitimately calculated royalties for performances in Belgium on the actual or probable number of performances in that country. Re-transmission by German television would upset the expected royalty earnings. The Court of Justice concluded that restrictions aimed at the protection of intellectual property are not prohibited, except when the restrictions are used as a means of arbitrary discrimination or as a disguised restriction on trade between member states.

In another exception to full application of the exhaustion doctrine, the Court of Justice examined the exhaustion of patent rights with regard to products manufactured under a compulsory license in *Pharmon BV v. Hoeschst*[6]. The Court of Justice distinguished a compulsory license from a situation in which the holder of the patent right freely placed the product on the market, or when it was done by his consent. With a compulsory license, there are no negotiations between the parties. The relationship which exists between the parties is different from that in a typical contractual license. When a member state grants "a third party a compulsory license which allows him to carry out manufacturing and marketing operations which the patentee would normally have the right to prevent, the patentee cannot be deemed to have consented to the operation of that third party." Otherwise the patent holder would be deprived of his rights to freely determine the conditions under which he markets his product.

In *Pharmon B.V.*, the Court allowed Hoeschst to prevent the importation and marketing of products manufactured under the compulsory license. In so doing, the court invoked the specific object of a patent right, which allows the inventor an exclusive right of first placing his product on the market, so that he may obtain a reward for his creative efforts.

---

[5] 1980 E.C.R. 881.

[6] 1985 E.C.R. 2281. Hoeschst owned patents in Germany, the Netherlands, and the United Kingdom for a manufacturing process for the drug Frusemide. Another company, DDSA Pharmaceuticals Ltd, obtained a compulsory license to exploit the invention under the patent in the United Kingdom. The license covered only the United Kingdom and included an export ban clause. The license did not originate by virtue of an agreement by the parties; it was signed only by the official of the UK Patent Office. *Id.* at 2283. DDSA ignored the export prohibition and later sold to Pharmon a large shipment of Frusemide pills, which Pharmon intended to market in the Netherlands.

b. Supranational Rights and Remedies[7]

An entire body of law has been created pursuant to the Treaty of Rome. Unlike the law which has resulted from international copyright conventions, this law is not typical private international law. The word "supranational" characterizes the legal superstructure which, in the European Common Market, has developed along with its own institutions, namely the Parliament, the Council of Ministers (Council), the Commission, the Court of First Instance and the Court of Justice of the European Communities in Luxembourg. This supranational law and its institutions must be examined in order to determine the general effect upon the national laws and the judicial practices of the Member States, and more specifically its effect on intellectual property law.

In cases of conflict with national laws, as have arisen repeatedly with respect to intellectual property, the Treaty and the applicable law take precedence. The second paragraph of Article 5 of the Treaty clearly states that Member States "shall abstain from any measure which could jeopardize the attainment of the objectives of this Treaty." The phrase "any measure" has been construed to include the enforcement of national law in private suits. Consequently, the Treaty precludes national law when the two conflict. EEC law, therefore, can directly affect not only acts of Member States, but also the rights and obligations of individual citizens under their respective national laws.

Moreover, EEC law takes precedence over treaties between Member States.

The principle of territoriality limits the scope of intellectual property rights such that their existence is limited to national jurisdictions. This principle provides the necessary line of demarcation between varied national jurisdictions in the field of intellectual property law. In essence, territoriality acts as a choice-of-law rule. Intellectual property rights, for example, are effective only within the individual territorially-isolated jurisdiction which has granted the rights. In practice, this principle has been broadly interpreted so that all too often the facts which form the basis for asserting rights or defenses in any given jurisdiction are also viewed as occurrences which are territorially isolated within that jurisdiction. A course of conduct which ostensibly infringes copyrights in several countries at once will be analyzed individually. Moreover, the action will be broken down into geographically discrete sets of infringing acts, with each set being governed by the copyright law of that country.

In the copyright situation, the first-sale doctrine generally limits a copyright owner's right to control distribution of a given copy of a work once that copy is "first" sold. The distribution right of that one copy is then said to be, to some degree, "exhausted." The holder of the distribution right can no longer fully control the fate of the first-sold copy which, after having lawfully entered into the relevant market, may be resold freely one thousand times over. The larger task involves defining the relevant market in which a copy of a copyright-protected work, a patented work, or a trademark protected product is "first" sold and where distribution rights are then "exhausted."

Interestingly, the extent by which territoriality limits the first-sale doctrine differs according to the intellectual property right involved. While in patent law the doctrine is universally accepted, in trademark law it is absent in many jurisdictions. The first national sale of a product bearing a trademark is most often regarded as exhausting the trademark-based right to control further international distribution of the product. This effect cannot be attenuated by any contrary contractual clause. Similarly, with respect to copyrights, the prevailing opinion is that the first sale of a copy of a work should exhaust the right to control the further sales of that copy worldwide. This view, however, may not apply when confronted with an express contractual clause designed to circumvent it.

Territorial restrictions to the first-sale doctrine seem to be at odds with the EEC Treaty. For example, territorial restrictions to the first-sale doctrine can be used to compartmentalize national markets. Yet, the EEC Treaty aims to unite twelve long-estab-

---

[7] Jan Corbet, *The Law of the EEC and Intellectual Property*, 13 J.L. & COM. 327. Copyright 1994 University of Pittsburgh. Excerpt reprinted with permission.

lished national markets into a single Common Market. Specifically, territorial restrictions might directly conflict with Articles 30 through 36 of the Treaty which implement the principle of Union-wide free movement of goods.

It is important to understand the balancing of EEC law and national intellectual property rights. A solution to this conflict may be found in Article 36 of the Treaty, which discusses the principle of the free movement of goods with respect to intellectual property. According to Article 36, the provisions of Articles 30 through 34 shall not preclude prohibitions or restrictions on imports, exports, or goods in transit if they are justified on the grounds of, inter alia, the protection of "industrial and commercial property." Such property has been deemed to include intellectual property rights, including copyrights. Nonetheless, Article 36 also limits prohibitions or restrictions that might be ostensibly "justified" insofar as they protect requisite property interests. Article 36 states that such restrictions "shall not, however, constitute a means of arbitrary discrimination or a disguised restriction on trade between Member States." Even if a certain restriction passes initial scrutiny because it is justified, its concrete application in a certain case may still amount to forbidden arbitrary discrimination or disguised interUnion restrictions on trade.

Another important factor to consider is the Union-wide exhaustion of rights after the first sale in any Member State. The outcome of the Court's evaluation of "the substance" of intellectual property rights, as balanced against EEC objectives, has been identical in cases concerning copyrights, so-called neighboring rights, patents and trademarks. The Court no longer isolates the relevant market to the national territory of the location of the first sale of the copy or product. The location of the first sale might trigger the exhaustion of the right to control further distribution of that copy or product. This haphazard approach yields to the EEC principle of the free movement of goods. The relevant market for finding a first sale sufficient to exhaust such a right is the entire Common Market. Thus, any party marketing a copy or product which has already been first-sold on the Common Market can raise the "Eurodefense" of Community-wide exhaustion against a holder of rights suing in order to control distribution in the EEC.

The clearest case is one in which a plaintiff sues to prevent items which are first sold in one Member State from being marketed in another Member State with laws that ostensibly assure exclusive distribution rights. In that case the defendant can successfully invoke the Community-wide exhaustion of these rights as a "Eurodefense."

The *Deutsche Grammophon/Metro* decision[8] is illustrative of this type of case. In that case, the plaintiff, a West German record producer, sold phonorecords within the Federal Republic of Germany and exclusively licensed the distribution of the phonorecords by other entities in the Common Market. Some of these phonorecords were first sold by plaintiff's French subsidiary, located outside of the Federal Republic of Germany, but within the Common Market. The phonorecords were then resold by third parties until the defendant purchased them and began to market them in Germany, thereby undercutting the plaintiff's current price in the home market. The Court of Justice, which heard the case on appeal, found Union-wide exhaustion of this right relative to the phonorecords which were "placed on the market by the owner of the right or with his consent in another Member State." This ruling left intact the substance of the commercial protective right that was invoked under national law. This pattern has been repeated in patent and trademark cases.

A holder of rights, though no longer able to control the further distribution of nationally protected copies after their first-sale in the EEC, may still want to exact royalties upon the sale or use of copies in a second EEC country. Typically, a holder would then attempt to obtain additional royalties which are payable in the second country, and which are unavailable in the original nation. Would such an exercise of stronger national positions after the first sale conflict with the EEC concept of the freedom of movement of goods? The Court of Justice has resolved this issue inconsistently.

In the *Basset* judgment, for example, the Court was not influenced by disparities

---

[8] Case 78/70, *Deutsche Grammophon,* 1971 E.C.R. 487, 10 C.M.L.R. 631 (1971).

between national copyright laws.[9] In that case, in which the Court held that Articles 30 and 36 of the EEC Treaty did not preclude the application of French copyright law to permit a national collecting society from claiming a complementary royalty (a royalty doctrine based on a combined reproduction and distribution right) above and beyond a royalty for licenses of the performance right itself. The collecting society Societe des Auteurs, Compositeurs et Editeurs de Musique imposed both complementary and performance royalties in France for publicly playing musical works from sound recordings. This imposition also included recordings that were lawfully marketed in another Member State. The Court held that the claim to the complementary royalty was permissible in France, although no such entitlement existed in the other Member State.

Moreover, in its *Warner Bros. Inc. v. Christiansen* judgment, the Court decided whether Articles 30 and 36 of the Treaty precluded the exercise of domestic rental rights in Denmark.[10] That case involved video cassettes which were legally first-sold in the United Kingdom and were then imported to, and offered for rent in, Denmark. The copyright owner, who did not have rental rights in the United Kingdom, sued to preclude rental of the video cassettes in Denmark. Danish legislation granted to the copyright owner a right to submit the rental in Denmark to his authorization. The Court stated that " in Denmark the hiring-out to third parties of cassettes lawfully available for purchase on the market is always subject to the prior authorization of the owner of the work, whose rights are not exhausted by its sale."

The Court concluded that if legislation recognizes rental rights, the right would lose its substance if the owner could not authorize the rental. The Court based its decision on the legitimate legislative attempt to protect the right of a filmmaker to enjoy a pecuniary benefit. This right would be deprived unless the filmmaker had the right to rent the recording. The Court refused to rely on the absence of rental rights in one Member State as a reason for precluding their exercise in those Member States where they are instituted. The holder of the Danish rental right could then control whether video cassettes first-sold in the United Kingdom could be rented in Denmark.

In the present state of Union law, which is characterized by a lack of harmonization or approximation of legislation governing the protection of literary and artistic property, it is for the national legislatures to determine the conditions and detailed rules for such protection.

---

[9] Case 402/85, Basset v. Societe des Auteurs, Compositeurs et Editeurs de Musique (SACEM), 1987 E.C.R. 1747, 3 C.M.L.R. 173 (1987).

[10] Case 158/86, Warner Bros. Inc. v. Christiansen, 1988 E.C.R. 2605, 3 C.M.L.R. 684 (1990).

QUESTIONS AND COMMENTS FOR YOUR CONSIDERATION

1. The establishment of free trading regions, such as Mercosur, Benelux and the free trading region established under the North American Free Trade Agreement, are becoming increasingly popular. What role, if any, should such supranational structures play in the establishment of international intellectual property protection norms? Does the presence of such zones make the establishment of international protection norms easier or harder?

2. Do the principles of proportionality and exhaustion adequately balance the interests of the individual nations in protecting their own national's intellectual property rights? Are there other issues that should be considered?

3. Do current enforcement provisions under various multinational treaties affecting intellectual property rights make adequate provision for the existence of such supranational organizations, particularly if the directives and regulations of such supranational organizations directly contradict existing treaty provisions?

4. Does the Treaty of Rome provide express guidance regarding the types of civil remedies available for intellectual property infringement? Does it provide guidance regarding which country's laws apply when a work is infringed in diverse countries through transmission over the global information superhighway?

2. The Establishment of Minimum Enforcement Standards

a. NAFTA and Regional Enforcement Standards

1. Comparison with Prior Multinational Treaty Regimes[11]

In the Paris Convention, the Universal Copyright Convention, and the Berne Convention, there is no dispute settlement procedure. In Mexico, while there are provisions for civil enforcement of infringement claims, injunctive relief is not allowed. Furthermore, administrative seizures can be stopped if defendants claim their constitutional rights have been infringed. To make matters worse, recovery of civil damages are very difficult. Moreover, under Mexico's provisions for criminal penalties, the requirement of proving a "profit motive" to prove copyright infringement makes enforcement very difficult. All in all, Mexico's enforcement provisions, while provided for, hinder, rather than allow for enforcement. Further, although Canada does allow for strict copyright enforcement provisions, in the form of fines and jail sentences, the trademark provisions only provide for civil remedies.

Conversely, in NAFTA, the enforcement and dispute resolution provisions are explicitly delineated. There are detailed explanations of the procedures that a member country must follow to settle a dispute, including the guaranty of procedural due process, and the required civil and a criminal trials. Further, these enforcement provisions do not require any "profit motive," allowing for more successful prosecutions. In addition, there are severe civil and criminal penalties provided for in NAFTA, including fines, imprisonment, and seizure of goods. Finally, the parties are protected from infringing goods at their borders.

NAFTA is not the first international treaty to recognize intellectual property rights. While other multilateral treaties, such as the Berne Convention, the Paris Convention, and the Universal Copyright Convention protect intellectual property rights, none have afforded the expansive protection bestowed by NAFTA. Moreover, these treaties are not trade treaties. Thus, they do not envisage intellectual property rights in conjunction with international trade, even though the relationship between intellectual property rights and international trade is the integral ingredient in promoting either of the two subjects.

Accordingly, NAFTA represents a complete protection of intellectual property rights, with effective enforcement provisions, all within a trade treaty. Through this protection, NAFTA will not only increase trade between the three member nations, but will create a strong political and economic alliance. Indeed, NAFTA will create a free trade zone that can counter the threats of the Asian and European trade zones. Additionally, this Treaty may be a "model treaty," which other nations would do well to imitate. If so, NAFTA will have accomplished what many believe it can: Strengthen the intellectual property rights, not just for Canada, Mexico, and the United States, but for intellectual property owners worldwide.

2. An Overview of Enforcement Provisions[12]

To protect the intellectual property rights granted under the Agreement, NAFTA has

---

[11] Karen Kontje Waller, *Nafta: The Latest Gun in the Fight to Protect International Intellectual Property Rights*, 13 DICK. J. INT'L LAW 241. Copyright 1994 by the Dickinson School of Law. Excerpt reprinted by permission.

[12] Kent S. Foster & Dean C. Alexander, *Opportunities for Mexico, Canada and the United States: A*

created detailed enforcement measures, which the Parties are expected to implement through domestic legislation. In principle, NAFTA requires that Parties shall ensure that their own "procedures for the enforcement of intellectual property rights are fair and equitable, not unnecessarily complicated or costly, and do not entail unreasonable time limits or unwarranted delays." Parties must also promise to provide judicial review of administrative decisions on infringement of intellectual property rights.

Furthermore, Parties must ensure that certain fundamental procedural and remedial aspects of civil and administrative proceedings are followed. Specifically, NAFTA demands that defendants receive timely written notice containing sufficient details of the claims, allows parties in a proceeding to be represented by independent legal counsel, discourages overly burdensome requirements concerning mandatory personal appearances, entitles parties to substantiate their claims and to present relevant evidence, and protects identifiable confidential information. The Agreement further grants power to the Parties' respective national judicial authorities. NAFTA authorizes Parties to engage in the following legal mechanisms: (a) to force an opposing party to counter evidence brought by a complainant who has presented evidence reasonably sufficient to support its claims, (b) when a party refuses access to relevant evidence, to make preliminary and final determinations, affirmative or negative, on the basis of the evidence presented, (c) to prevent an infringing imported good from entering channels of commerce, (d) to force an infringer of an intellectual property to pay adequate compensation for the injury the right holder has suffered, (e) to order an infringer to pay the right holder's expenses, and (f) to order compensation by parties who have abused enforcement procedures.

A major achievement of NAFTA is in the area of injunctive enforcement. During the interim of formal proceedings, NAFTA allows provisional measures to deny importation of allegedly infringing goods, provided that an applicant for the provisional measures can demonstrate two elements. First, the applicant must show that he is the right holder whose rights are either being infringed or are in imminent danger of being infringed. Second, the applicant must prove that any delay in the issuance of provisional measures would likely cause irreparable harm. To prevent abuse of the provisional measures, the applicant is required to provide a sufficient security or equivalent assurance.

NAFTA provides criminal procedures and penalties for willful trademark counterfeiting or copyright piracy on a commercial scale. Criminal sanctions include the seizure, forfeiture and destruction of either infringing goods or any materials and implements which have been predominantly used in the commission of the offense.

To enforce intellectual property rights at the border, NAFTA authorizes each Party, by its customs administration, to seize and detain counterfeit trademark goods or pirated copyright goods, and to prevent the release of infringing goods destined for exportation. The Agreement first requires, however, that there is adequate evidence of a prima facie infringement. Each Party is required to produce detailed procedures regarding its customs administration's seizure and release procedures, including those aspects covering industrial designs, patents, integrated circuits and trade secrets. According to the Agreement, Mexico must undertake every effort to adopt comprehensive border enforcement procedures within three years of the date of NAFTA's signing.

To promote technical assistance and cooperation between the Parties in enforcement procedures, the Parties have planned to exchange information concerning trade in infringing goods by January 1, 1994. While NAFTA's enforcement provisions provide relatively comprehensive protection to the intellectual property rights of lawful owners and effective sanctions for infringers, there are several areas of protection that the Agreement does not reach. For example, it will not cover intellectual property obligations for acts that occurred prior to the appropriate application dates of each of the NAFTA's various provisions. Neither will it cover, with only a few exceptions, items that

---

Summary of Intellectual Property Rights Under the North American Free Trade Agreement, 20 RUTGERS COMPUTER & TECH. L.J. 67.

have otherwise entered into the public domain in any of the Parties' territories prior to the effective date of the Agreement.

As long as equitable compensation is available as a result of the infringement, causes of action that are pending prior to ratification of NAFTA may only entitle the right holder to limited remedies. In appropriate cases, however, applications for registration of intellectual property rights that are pending prior to NAFTA's implementation can be amended to enable the right holder to obtain NAFTA's additional protections.

3. Application[13]

Article 1714 of NAFTA establishes general provisions to enforce intellectual property rights. In particular, this article provides for due process. That is, an enforcement proceeding provides a trial proceeding, where both parties have the right to attend and present evidence. Moreover, there must be a written opinion of the proceedings that specifies reasons for the ultimate decision. Such an opinion must be promptly available. The article also gives the parties a right to a review of the decision.

Article 1715 states the specific requirements of a civil or administrative trial. Once again, due process is required, thereby mandating that the following rights be acknowledged: (1) defendant's right to timely and sufficient notice of the basis of the claim; (2) both parties' right to legal counsel at the "trial"; (3) disallowance of heavy demands for the parties' appearance at the proceedings; (4) both parties' right to present evidence; and (5) both parties' right to have confidential information protected. Ultimately, if an infringement is found, the judiciary has the power to order the disposal of the goods and materials used in making the infringing good.

Article 1717 delineates the criminal procedures and penalties for infringing another's intellectual property rights. The article mandates that the member nations establish criminal procedures and penalties for the "willful trademark counterfeiting or copyright piracy on a commercial scale." The penalties should include imprisonment, monetary fines, or both. The article also allows for the seizure, forfeiture, or destruction of the infringing goods and the "materials" or "implements" which assisted in making the goods. Finally, the article allows the member countries to establish other causes for criminal penalties where the infringer is found to have committed the act "willfully and on a commercial scale."

Article 1718 sets up specific procedures for the enforcement of intellectual property rights at the parties' borders. This article allows intellectual property holders who suspect that there will be an import of a product that infringes upon their intellectual property rights, to request the authorities who control importation to suspend importation of the goods.

b. TRIPS and Multinational Enforcement Standards[14]

In addition to establishing minimum international substantive norms for copyright protection, the TRIPS Agreement also provides specific minimum *procedural* norms for the enforcement of intellectual property rights. Included among these procedural norms is the requirement that enforcement procedures available under a member's national laws "permit effective action against any act of infringement of intellectual property rights covered by this Agreement, including expeditious remedies to prevent infringements and remedies which constitute a deterrent to further infringement." All such procedures must be "fair and equitable" and cannot be "unnecessarily complicated or costly" or "entail unreasonable time limits or unwarranted delays." Decisions on the merits must be

---

[13] Karen Kontje Waller, *NAFTA: The Latest Gun in the Fight to Protect International Intellectual Property Rights*, 13 DICK. J. INT'L Law 241. Copyright 1994 by the Dickinson School of Law. Excerpt reprinted with permission.

[14] Doris Estelle Long, *Copyright and the Uruguay Round Agreements: A New Era of Protection or an Illusory Promise?*, 22 AIPLA Q. J. 531. Copyright 1995 Doris E. Long. Excerpt reprinted with permission.

made available to the parties "without undue delay" and must be based only on evidence "in respect of which parties were offered the opportunity to be heard."

TRIPS does not require members to establish a separate judicial system for the enforcement of intellectual property rights. It does, however, require that defendants be given "timely" written notice of claims against them and that such notice "contain sufficient detail, including the basis of the claims." Representation by independent legal counsel, the right to "substantiate ... claims and to present all relevant evidence," and protection of confidential information (so long as such protection does not contravene "existing constitutional requirements") are mandated. Moreover, among the procedures and remedies that must be made available to litigants under TRIPS are the right to injunctive relief, the right to provisional measures to prevent infringements from occurring, including the prevention of entry into commerce of infringing imported goods "immediately after customs clearance," the right to "prompt and effective provisional" measures to preserve "relevant evidence," the right to money damages "adequate to compensate for the injury the right holder has suffered because of an infringement of his intellectual property right by an infringer who knew or had reasonable grounds to know that he was engaged in an infringing activity," and the right to obtain in appropriate circumstances the seizure and destruction of infringing goods as well as "materials and implements the predominant use of which has been in the creation of the infringing goods."

Parties who abuse the enforcement process must be subject to sanction. Among the types of abuse for which sanctions are to be imposed are refusals "without good reason" to provide "necessary information within a reasonable period" and injunctions or restraining orders wrongfully issued in abuse of enforcement procedures. Moreover, any exemptions from liability for public authorities and officials for failure to provide appropriate remedial measures are limited to actions "taken or intended in good faith in the course of the administration of such laws." Members also have the right to grant judicial authorities the power to order infringers to identify third persons involved in the production and distribution of infringing goods and their channels of distribution. TRIPS also provides for special procedures to permit a right holder, through written application, to seek retention by customs of goods which the right holder has "valid grounds" for suspecting constitute "pirated copyright goods." Finally, in connection with pirated copyright goods, TRIPS requires members to provide for "criminal procedures and penalties including imprisonment and/or monetary fines . . . sufficient to provide a deterrent, consistently with the level of penalties applied for crimes of corresponding gravity."

QUESTIONS AND COMMENTS FOR YOUR CONSIDERATION

1. Both NAFTA and TRIPS establish minimum enforcement standards. Compare and contrast the standards established under the Agreements. What additional or different remedies would you provide?

2. Do the enforcement standards established under NAFTA and TRIPS resolve the problem posed when enforcement agents or members of the judiciary refuse to apply these enforcement standards? How effective are such standards without the establishment of specialized agencies or tribunals to enforce such standards?

3. The Protection of Well-Known Marks

a. Article 6bis[15]

Article 6bis of the Paris Convention for the Protection of Industrial Property states in pertinent part:

> The countries of the Union undertake, *ex officio* if their legislation so permits, or at the request of an interested party, to refuse or to cancel the registration, and to prohibit the use, of a trademark which constitutes a reproduction, an imitation or a translation, liable to create confusion, or a mark considered by the competent authority of the country of registration or use to be well known in that country as being already the mark of a person entitled to the benefits of this Convention and used for identical or similar goods. These provisions shall also apply when the essential part of the mark constitutes a reproduction of any such well-known mark or an imitation liable to create confusion therewith.

This Article was introduced into the Convention by the Revision Conference of The Hague in 1925. One of the questions which arises with respect to this Article is whether it may be considered "self-executing"—in countries which admit such possibility—with the result that interested parties may directly claim its application by the administrative or judicial authorities of the country concerned. The provision under consideration refers only to trademarks and not to service marks. The member states are therefore not obliged to apply it to service marks, but are free to do so in analogous situations.

The purpose of this provision under consideration is to avoid the registration and use of a trademark, liable to create confusion with another mark already well known in the country of such registration or use, although the latter well-known mark is not, or not yet, protected in that country by a registration which would normally prevent the registration or use of the conflicting mark. This exceptional protection of a well-known mark has been deemed to be justified because the registration or use of a confusingly similar mark will in most cases amount to an act of unfair competition, and may also be considered prejudicial to the interests of those who will be misled. Whether a trademark will be liable to create confusion with a well-known mark will be determined by the competent authority of the country concerned, and in so doing the said authority will have to consider the question from the viewpoint of the consumers of the goods to which the marks are applied. The provision specifies that such confusion may occur in cases of reproduction, imitation or translation of the well-known mark, or even if only an essential part of a mark constitutes a reproduction or confusing imitation of the well-known mark.

A trademark may be well known in a country before its registration there and, in view of the possible repercussions of publicity in other countries, even before it is used in such country. Whether a trademark is well known in a country will be determined by its competent administrative or judicial authorities. The Revision Conference of Lisbon in 1958 rejected a proposal according to whether use of a well-known mark in the country in which its protection is claimed would not be necessary for such protection. This means that a member State is not obliged to protect well-known trademarks which have not been used on its territory, but it will be free to do so. In view of the vote taken at the Lisbon Conference, the great majority of the member States will probably adopt this attitude.

A well-known trademark will, naturally, only be protected by the Article under consideration if it belongs to a person entitled to the benefits of the Convention, that is, to a natural or legal person who may claim the application of the Convention. This history of the provision shows, however, that it will be sufficient if the mark concerned

[15] G.H.C Bodenhausen. *Guide to the Application of the Paris Convention for the Protection of Industrial Property.* Copyright 1968 G.H.C. Bodenhausen. Excerpt reprinted with permission.

is well known in commerce in the country concerned as a mark belonging to a certain enterprise, without its being necessary that it also be known that such enterprise is entitled to the benefits of the Convention. Nor is it necessary—and it is therefore not necessary to prove—that the person who has applied for or obtained a conflicting registration or who uses a conflicting mark possessed such knowledge.

The protection of well-known marks, according to the provisions under examination, applies only with respect to other marks filed, registered or used for identical or similar goods. Whether this condition is fulfilled will be determined by the administrative or judicial authorities of the country in which protection is claimed.

b. Relief for the Unauthorized Use of Internationally Well-Known Marks[16]

A frequent problem, particularly in newly industrialized or lesser developed countries, is the unauthorized registration and use of internationally well-known trademarks on products by unauthorized parties. However, it may be possible, especially if a country is a member of the Paris Convention, to block or cancel the unauthorized registration, if the mark is "well-known". Article 6bis of the Paris Convention for the Protection of Industrial Property provides that member countries shall undertake, ex officio if their legislation so permits, or at the request of an interested party, to "refuse or . . . cancel the registration, and to prohibit the use, of a trademark which constitutes a reproduction, an imitation, or a translation, liable to create confusion, of a mark considered by the competent authority of the country of registration or use to be well-known in that country." Article 6bis further provides: "A period of at least five years from the date of registration shall be allowed for requesting the cancellation of such a mark. The countries of the Union may provide for a period within which the prohibition of use must be requested. No time limit shall be fixed for requesting the cancellation or the prohibition of the use of marks registered or used in bad faith." A frequent issue, particularly in some lesser developed countries, is the degree to which the mark must be "well known" in that particular country, and not simply internationally.

Alternatively, it may be possible to cancel trademark registrations if the foreign country requires that the registrant use the mark within a specified time period.

Another possible tool for canceling unauthorized registrations of internationally famous trademarks is an unfair competition proceeding alleging that consumers are being misled in believing that the unauthorized domestic origin product is in reality one produced by the foreign company. Article 10bis of the Paris Convention obligates member states "to assure to nationals of such countries effective protection against unfair competition." Among the practices specifically prohibited by Article 10bis are "all acts of such a nature as to create confusion by any means whatsoever with the establishment, the goods, or the industrial or commercial activities, of a competitor."

c. The Role of Domestic Law in Fashioning Relief[17]

The debate over the scope of protection to be afforded intellectual property rights on an international basis often degenerates to categorization under facile labels that do little to further the discussion. Labels such as "common heritage of mankind," "economic versus moral rights," "public good," "property" and "North-South debate" are used to symbolize a range of ideas based on profound ideological and philosophical differences. One unifying issue is the treatment to be afforded "famous" works. Whether such

[16] Practicing Law Institute, *Protection Of Intellectual Property Rights In International Transactions*. Copyright 1994 Practicing Law Institute. Excerpt reprinted with permission.

[17] Written for this Anthology by Doris Estelle Long. Copyright 1996 Doris E. Long.

"fame" derives from the notoriety of being a pioneer invention, an industry standard, the most efficacious cure for a given disease, or from the advertisement and marketing of songs performed by a particular performer or products bearing a given mark, part of the debate over the "right" of a country to use such "famous" works without compensation to the owner often depends on the value that country places on the access of its citizens to the famous work and the economic cost of such works which the country is willing to bear. The more "famous" the work, the greater the likelihood the right to use such work will be considered a public necessity. The true difficulty lies in deciding what measure of "fame," if any, should allow uncompensated use of a work.

Article 6bis of the Paris Convention for the Protection of Industrial Property requires member countries to prohibit the unauthorized registration or use of reproductions or imitations of a "well-known" mark. The Article, however, provides little guidance in determining whether a particular mark qualifies for heightened protection as a "well-known" mark. In the absence of explicit directions for determining whether a mark has sufficient fame to fall within the ambit of Article 6bis, member countries are entitled to establish their own standards. Consequently, some countries have granted protection to marks whose owners can establish the international fame of their marks. Other countries require evidence of fame in the mark in the country itself. Such fame must be established through evidence of use of the mark in the country, including, for example, sales of goods bearing the mark, or advertisements of goods or services under the mark. Requiring evidence of internal fame can lead to such unusual results as denying protection to the mark MCDONALD'S for fast food services due to a failure to use the mark in the country in question and a refusal to grant registration to the Stolichnaya mark for vodka in Russia.

Once the decision has been made that a mark qualifies as a well-known mark, Article 6bis requires that registration of a mark that constitutes "a reproduction, imitation or translation liable to create confusion" with such famous mark be denied. It further requires that member countries "prohibit the use" of such trademark. The Convention, however, does not specify the procedures to be used in such prohibition. Nor does it specify the nature of such prohibition. Thus, the scope of any injunctive relief and any monetary penalties to be imposed as a "prohibition" for such unauthorized use remain subject exclusively to the vagaries of domestic law.

d. Application[18]

Where the goods are not similar, or there is no risk of confusion, the proprietor even of a well-known mark or get-up in Germany must accept the registration or use of his identifying symbols for dissimilar goods, services or business names. But in the case of well-known marks this loophole is filled by the case law on "famous brands."

It protects marks which, through wide familiarity, have achieved unparalleled distinctiveness and promotional force against dilution—that is against their magnetism being weakened by the use of identical or nearly identical marks for products, services or business names outside the market for the original goods. This weakening is a consequence of the association of ideas to which the purchaser succumbs. Where other goods are substituted, the purchaser often only subconsciously remembers the famous brand but is influenced by its distinctiveness and promotional force in his buying decision. There is a risk of the public's concept of the subject-matter of the famous mark being diluted or blurred.

The brand must first of all possess an outstanding reputation. The normal reputation which substantiates the right for a distinguishing sign or get-up to be protected under Section 25 is not sufficient. Even a heightened reputation going beyond this by virtue of stronger distinctiveness is not enough. There must be the highest possible degree of distinctiveness and of reputation

---

[18] Geert Wolfgang Seelig, *Protecting 'Famous Brands' in Germany*. Copyright Geert Wolfgang Seelig. Excerpt reprinted with permission.

based on it. It is not sufficient that the mark is known only within a particular market—it must have become known outside the market for the original goods and indeed throughout the country, as the mark of a certain firm and its goods.

This reputation is proved by evidence of public opinion research from institutes specializing in the subject, which personally interview about 2,000 people out of the whole adult population over the age of 16 in the Federal Republic of Germany including West Berlin, within the scope of a respective multi-subject opinion poll. The people to be questioned are found by random selection.

The mark must occupy a so-called 'independent status' on the market and must not be in use by anyone else. The public can be stimulated to form concepts which impair the distinctiveness and promotional force of the famous brand only if it is non-recurrent and not already used by other firms, even for dissimilar goods.

Furthermore, a description must be striking and distinctive, and its distinguishing effect must extend to other types of good. There must therefore be a certain amount of originality, if there is not, the mark holder must accept a risk of dilution, determined by the nature of the mark chosen.

The would-be 'famous brand' must enjoy a certain esteem. Only this esteem justifies the extended protection of a 'famous brand'. The esteem must exist in the public mind, and it does not matter what it is based on. It does not therefore have to be justified objectively by the quality of the goods: on the contrary, it is sufficient if the mark enjoys a general esteem by reason of the age, technical merit or size of the business.

QUESTIONS AND COMMENTS FOR YOUR CONSIDERATION

1. Where the intellectual property right is other than a trademark or source designator, its "fame" may arise from its perceived role as the best or most desirable technology or product to achieve a designated result. In these instances, "fame" is most often treated as the equivalent of a "public good" or a "common heritage" which should be available for all mankind to use without restriction. For further consideration of these issues, *see* Chapter Two.

2. What role, if any, should the fame of a particular work or invention have on the right or ability of others to use the mark?

3. Given the territorial nature of trademarks (*see* Chapter Eight), should special protection be afforded to marks that have not been used or registered in the country in question?

4. How does the doctrine of protection for famous marks embodied in Article 6bis of the Paris Convention comport with the adverse impact which brand loyalty may have on a developing country's economy? For a discussion of the potential adverse economic impact of trademark protection on developing countries, *see* Chapter Fourteen.

5. To what extent, if any, should the protection of well-known marks be extended to preclude their use on non-identical but related goods?

6. If you were attempting to establish international enforcement standards for the protection of well-known marks, what sources would you use to select such standards?

4. The Definition of Infringement[19]

To date, no multinational treaty regime or harmonization directive has established an agreed-upon standard for infringement of intellectual property rights. Although the Paris Convention, the Berne Convention and TRIPS all establish substantive minimum standards for intellectual property protection, these standards are limited to establishing standards for obtaining intellectual property rights. They do not address the equally critical question of protecting such rights through appropriate remedies for violation of those rights.

For example, although the Paris Convention discusses the protection of patented inventions, industrial designs and trademarks, it does not specify what factors should be considered by the courts in determining whether a third party has violated the protection granted to owners of these intellectual property rights. The Berne Convention similarly fails to provide guidance for determining when a third party has violated the copyrights required to be extended under the Convention to specified works.

In the absence of established international standards, the question of infringement will depend exclusively upon domestic law, unmodified by international treaty regimes or harmonization directives. Consequently, an act of infringement in one country may well be determined to constitute lawful use in another. Such inconsistent treatment seriously undermines the beneficial effects derived from the establishment of international minimum substantive norms.

[19] Written for this Anthology by Doris Estelle Long. Copyright 1996 Doris E. Long.

QUESTIONS AND COMMENTS FOR YOUR CONSIDERATION

1. Does the TRIPS Agreement provide any substantive standards for determining when an owner's rights have been infringed?

2. Select a country and examine the test used to determine copyright, trademark or patent infringement. How does this test differ from the test applied under US law? Are these differences outcome determinative?

5. Selected Civil Protection Regimes

a. Self-help

1. Education[20]

Self-help remedies to prevent unauthorized use of intellectual property include seeking improved protection through education, lobbying for stronger protection standards, and private policing activities.

Educational activities take a variety of forms. The first are efforts directed toward educating consumers to the value of buying lawfully manufactured and distributed products. Such educational efforts might include emphasizing the adverse economic impact the presence of pirated goods has on the marketplace, or the benefits of higher quality and safer products in buying legitimate goods. In addition to educating the consuming public, intellectual property owners may direct their educational efforts toward enforcement personnel in order to encourage stringent enforcement of existing laws. Such education can be used to heighten the sensitivity of customs officials, law enforcement personnel and members of the judiciary to the problems of intellectual property infringement and the need for swift and decisive action to counteract such unlawful acts. Finally, intellectual property owners may attempt to educate legislative and administrative bodies to the need for stronger domestic protection for intellectual property

[20] Written for this Anthology by Doris Estelle Long. Copyright 1996 Doris E. Long.

rights. These educational efforts may be directed toward the need for revising domestic intellectual property laws, for establishing regional harmonization directives or for developing bilateral and multinational protection regimes.

Concurrently with these educational efforts at improving the level of protection granted intellectual property owners and strengthening the viability of available remedies, intellectual property owners, or their governments, may lobby appropriate organizations for a change in standards. Domestic efforts will be directed to the appropriate legislative and administrative tribunals. Such efforts, however, often include, not merely efforts to increase the scope of protection granted certain forms of intellectual property, but to increase the range of remedies available for infringement of existing rights, including the availability of significant monetary penalties and swift injunctive and seizure relief, thereby increasing the cost of infringement and reducing the economic incentive for infringers.

Of greater significance for the establishment of international protection standards are efforts directed toward the development of agreed-upon bilateral and multinational treaty regimes. Among the significant fora for directing efforts at increasing the scope of relief available internationally are the World Intellectual Property Organization (WIPO) (responsible for administering the Berne and Paris Conventions, among others) and the World Trade Organization (WTO) (responsible for administering TRIPS). As demonstrated by the recent Uruguay Round Negotiations, the negotiation of such international treaty regimes can be lengthy and may result in less than stringent standards due to the nature of multinational negotiations and the need to reach agreement among countries of disparate legal, economic and political philosophies.

None of these self-help remedies provides instantaneous relief. Used in combination with other forms of relief, however, they may serve to increase the level of actual protection afforded internationally to intellectual property owners.

QUESTIONS AND COMMENTS FOR YOUR CONSIDERATION

1. Bilateral negotiations may result in the establishment of more stringent enforcement standards due to the greater leverage which one country may be able to bring to bear. The exercise of such leverage, however, may have adverse effects in other areas. *See* Chapter Two.
2. Educational and lobbying efforts are often spearheaded by national and international industry Trade Representative associations. Select an industry Trade Representative and investigate what domestic and international educational efforts are being sponsored by the industry Trade Representative's organizations.

2. Special 301

a. Procedures and Application[21]

In simple terms, Title III, Chapter 1, of the Trade Act of 1974 (commonly referred to as Section 301) provides that when a foreign country denies rights owed to the United States under a trade agreement, or when a foreign country is unfairly restricting US foreign commerce, irrespective of a breach of an international treaty, the United States can, or even must, take retaliatory trade action against that foreign country.

The recognized purpose of Section 301, which has not changed in the years since it was originally enacted, was for the United States to use the retaliatory authority of

---

[21] Ted L. McDorman, *U.S.-Thailand Trade Disputes: Applying Section 301 to Cigarettes and Intellectual Property,* 14 MICH. J. INT'L L. Copyright 1992 Ted L. McDorman. Excerpt reprinted with permission.

Section 301 vigorously as leverage on foreign countries to eliminate unfair trade practices affecting US commerce. Despite changes made to the original Section 301 through the Trade Agreements Act of 1979 and the Trade and Tariff Act of 1984, deep dissatisfaction existed within Congress with the failure of Section 301, as used by the President, to gain access for US goods and services in foreign markets where barriers allegedly existed. Coupled with this dissatisfaction were the United States' growing trade deficit and the perception that while the US market was open to all, foreign markets, particularly Japan, remained relatively closed to US goods and services. The result was significant change to Section 301 with the enactment of the Omnibus Trade and Competitiveness Act of 1988.

The 1988 changes to Section 301 address several areas. They attempt to circumscribe the discretion the President had to undertake retaliatory action, and expand and clarify the trade practices that will be considered unwarranted and that will lead to possible Section 301 action. The new Super 301 required the US Trade Representative to identify and initiate Section 301 actions against foreign countries that used unfair trade practices to inhibit US trade. Finally, Special 301 required the United States Trade Representatives (US Trade Representative), on a yearly basis, to identify and initiate Section 301 actions against foreign countries that deny adequate and effective protection of intellectual property rights to US persons and products.

The Section 301 process can be started by a petition from a US person or entity who claims: (i) to have been unfairly denied access to a foreign market; (ii) that the foreign country is not abiding by an international agreement; or (iii) that their intellectual property rights are not being adequately protected. The US Trade Representative can also start the Section 301 process on her own initiative. Moreover, following any naming of priority countries under Super 301 or Special 301, the US Trade Representative is also required to commence the Section 301 process. Once the US Trade Representative agrees to commence, or is required to commence, the Section 301 process, she must investigate and determine whether the rights to which the United States, or any US person or entity, is entitled under any trade agreement are being denied. She must also determine if any act, policy, or practice exists which is "unjustifiable," "unreasonable," or "discriminatory," and which burdens or restricts US commerce.

An "unjustifiable" act, policy, or practice is one which includes the denial of national treatment, most favored nation treatment, the right of establishment, the protection of intellectual property rights, or any other action inconsistent with the international legal rights of the United States. A "discriminatory" act, policy, or practice is one that denies national treatment or most favored nation treatment to US goods, services, or investment. An "unreasonable" act, policy, or practice is one that, "while not necessarily in violation of, or inconsistent with, the international legal rights of the United States, is otherwise unfair and inequitable." Included in unreasonable acts, policies, and practices are those which deny fair and equitable market opportunities and the provision of adequate and effective protection of intellectual property rights; those which constitute export targeting; and those which constitute a denial of workers' rights and standards for minimum workers' wages, health, and safety.

When the US Trade Representative finds that a trade agreement is being breached or an act, policy, or practice is unjustifiable, unreasonable, or discriminatory, she is to determine what action to take. Remedies available include withdrawing benefits the identified foreign country enjoys pursuant to a trade agreement with the United States; entering into agreements with the foreign country to eliminate the offending action; or imposing duties or other import restrictions against any goods or economic sector of the foreign country irrespective of the goods or sector affected by the foreign country's offensive action. The latter situation is clearly nothing more than trade retaliation against a foreign country.

When the US Trade Representative's investigation finds that the rights of the United States under a trade agreement are being denied, she is not required to take action if a panel experts established pursuant to the GATT or the Canada–US Free

Trade Agreement finds to the contrary. However, when the US Trade Representative finds that a foreign country's act, policy, or practice is "unjustifiable," or the measure is determined to be inconsistent with a trade agreement, she is required to withdraw trade concessions, to enter into trade agreements, or to take retaliatory trade action. This is the mandatory action that the Congress sought to impose in 1988. However, this mandatory action is qualified in a number of ways. Any action to be taken by the US Trade Representative is "subject to the specific direction, if any, of the President." Moreover, no action need be taken if the US Trade Representative finds that the foreign country "is taking satisfactory measures" to grant the United States rights under a trade agreement; that the foreign country has agreed to eliminate the offending measure; or that the retaliatory action "would cause serious harm to the national security of the United States." When the US Trade Representative finds that the foreign country's action is "unreasonable" or "discriminatory," she is to take all appropriate and feasible action to obtain the elimination of the offending act, policy, or practice, but no mandatory action is called for.

The above process has existed, with some modification, since 1974. In 1988, Congress added to Section 301 the processes known as Super 301 and Special 301. Under Super 301, as part of her annual report to Congress in 1989 and 1990, the US Trade Representative was to identify "priority" practices "the elimination of which were likely to have the most significant potential to increase United States exports," and "priority" countries, which had in place significant barriers to US exports of goods or services and foreign direct investment. When a priority country was identified in the annual report (and it appeared that the US Trade Representative had a significant discretion in identifying such a priority country) the US Trade Representative was to initiate a Section 301 investigation of the trade measure identified as a priority practice. The US Trade Representative was required to attempt to negotiate an agreement with the named priority country to eliminate the offending practice, and if such an agreement was reached before the completion of the Section 301 process, the process was to be suspended. The Super 301 process did not require the United States to take retaliatory trade action against a named priority country.

In 1989, the first year of Super 301, Japan, Brazil, and India were named as priority countries. Japan and Brazil were able to satisfy the US Trade Representative and were removed from the priority list. However, the 1990 priority list continued to include India.

Like Super 301, Special 301 requires the US Trade Representative to identify, on a yearly basis, priority countries. The difference is Special 301 is aimed at countries which "have the most onerous or egregious" policies that deny adequate and effective intellectual property rights or deny fair market access to US persons which rely upon intellectual property protection. The US Trade Representative is to initiate an investigation under the Section 301 process respecting any foreign country named as a priority country.

The Special 301 process requires the US Trade Representative to monitor all foreign intellectual property laws and practices and report on them yearly. In the first year of Special 301, the US Trade Representative declined to name any priority countries, although the US Trade Representative created a "priority watch list" and a "watch list" naming countries that it felt were lax in the protection of intellectual property rights. India, Thailand, and the People's Republic of China (PRC) were designated as priority countries in 1991.

b. 301 and Bilateral Relief[22]

The typical procedural course taken by a Special 301 action has two phases. Invocations of the Special 301 action originate in

---

[22] Theodore H. Davis, *Combating Piracy of Intellectual Property in International Markets: A Proposed Modification of the Special 301 Action*, 24 VAND. J. TRANSNAT'L L. 505. Copyright 1991 by the Vanderbilt University School of Law. Excerpt reprinted with permission.

the annual National Trade Estimate Report (NTE Report) mandated by Section 2241 of the Trade Act. This section requires the US Trade Representative to submit a report each year to the President and appropriate congressional committees by March 31 detailing practices of foreign states that, among other things, erect "significant barriers to, or distortions of" United States exports of products protected by trademarks, patents, or copyrights. Within thirty days of the submission of the NTE Report, the US Trade Representative must designate those states eligible for Special 301 treatment. States run the risk of this identification if their policies or practices fall into one of two categories.

> A foreign country denies adequate and effective protection of intellectual property if the foreign country denies adequate and effective means under the laws of the foreign country for persons who are not citizens or nationals of such foreign country to secure, exercise, and enforce rights relating to patents, process patents, registered trademarks, copyrights, and mask works.

Alternatively, a state may receive Special 301 treatment if its laws deny fair and equitable market access to United States nationals that rely on intellectual property protection. To ascertain whether this situation exists with respect to a particular state, the US Trade Representative must determine if the state under scrutiny denies access to markets for products protected by copyrights, patents, or process patents through laws, procedures, practices, or regulations that: (1) violate provisions of international law or agreements to which both the United States and the foreign state are parties; or (2) constitute discriminatory nontariff barriers. Identification under this prong is possible only if the US Trade Representative determines that a factual basis exists for finding a denial of fair and equitable market access.

After identifying states eligible for Special 301 treatment, the US Trade Representative then designates priority states. Only those states that have "the most onerous or egregious acts, policies, or practices" will be considered priority states. These acts, policies, or practices must have the "greatest adverse impact (actual or potential) on the relevant United States products." A designated state, however, will be exempt from Special 301 treatment if the US Trade Representative finds that the state either enters into good faith negotiations or, alternatively, makes "significant progress" in bilateral or multilateral negotiations to provide increased protection for intellectual property rights.

Once the US Trade Representative designates a foreign state as a priority state, Section 2412(b)(2)(A) requires the US Trade Representative to initiate an unfair trade practices investigation pursuant to the procedures contained in Section 301 of the Trade Act of 1974 within thirty days, but only if no progress can be made through consultations with the foreign government. Two possible qualifications affect this mandatory language: first, the US Trade Representative is not required to begin an investigation if the investigation would be detrimental to United States economic interests; and second, the US Trade Representative has discretion to determine whether an investigation would be effective in addressing the questionable foreign practice.

Unlike the more typical Section 301 investigation, which has a twelve to eighteen month timetable, a Section 301 investigation stemming from a Special 301 priority designation is conducted under a six month "fast-track" system. Upon the conclusion of the investigation, the US Trade Representative then determines whether to subject that state to a broad range of specified trade-based retaliatory mechanisms within six months. Foreign actions targeted by the Section 301 investigation generally fall into two categories.

First, policies or practices of foreign governments under investigation are within the ambit of Section 301 if they violate the provisions of a trade agreement or deny benefits to the United States under a trade agreement. Generally, the US Trade Representative has interpreted the term "trade agreement" narrowly to include only the GATT and trade agreements approved under Section 3(a) of the Trade Agreement Act of 1979. Therefore, it is unlikely that this prong will lead to retaliatory sanctions against a Special 301 priority state.

Under the second set of requirements for imposing retaliatory trade sanctions, a foreign state's action comes within the ambit of an actionable violation if it is "unjustifiable and burdens or restricts United States commerce." Alternatively, any foreign action unreasonable or discriminatory, as well as burdensome on United States commerce, is subject to retaliation. For the purposes of Section 301 investigations, a foreign practice will be deemed unreasonable if it denies adequate and effective protection of intellectual property rights. Similarly, unjustifiable foreign practices under Section 301 include those acts or policies that deny the "right of establishment or protection of intellectual property rights." Discriminatory foreign action includes the implementation of discriminatory tariff barriers, which fulfill the third requirement.

As a practical matter, an investigation of a Special 301 priority state is likely to result in a finding that the state's practices satisfy one, if not all three, of the requirements for an imposition of sanctions. At the threshold, if the US Trade Representative determines during the initial Special 301 proceedings that the foreign action in question constitutes an "onerous or egregious" act with the "greatest adverse impact ... on the relevant United States products," the practice probably will qualify as a "burden" on United States commerce. This conclusion is consistent with previous United States findings in Section 301 investigations prior to 1988 that a foreign state's inadequate protection of intellectual property rights satisfies the requirement.

Once the US Trade Representative initiates a Section 301 investigation stemming from Special 301 proceedings, the US Trade Representative has six months to determine what action, if any, to take in response to the practices of the foreign state in question. If the US Trade Representative finds that the practices fulfill the criteria outlined above, the range of discretionary trade-based weapons is broad. Pursuant to Section 2411(c)(1), a US Trade Representative , within thirty days of determining that an actionable violation exists and subject to the direction of the President, may:

> (A) suspend, withdraw, or prevent the application of, benefits of trade concessions . . .; (B) impose duties or other import restrictions on the goods of, and, notwithstanding any other provision of law, fees or restrictions on the services of, such foreign country; or (C) enter into binding agreements with such foreign country that commit it to (i) eliminate, or phase out the unfair act, policy, or practice, (ii) eliminate any burden or restriction on United States commerce resulting from such act, policy, or practice, or (iii) provide the United States with compensatory trade benefits that are satisfactory.

Under these criteria, any goods from the foreign state in question may be subject to a retaliatory action, regardless of whether those goods were involved in the practice leading to the imposition of sanctions.

The US Trade Representative is not required to take action under a number of circumstances. For example, the priority state's agreement to eliminate the practice in question or to eliminate the burden or restriction on United States commerce will protect it from actual retaliation. Also, if eliminating the offending practice is impossible for the foreign state, the US Trade Representative may accept alternative compensatory trade benefits. Moreover, the statute precludes sanctions if retaliatory action would have an adverse effect on the United States economy substantially out of proportion to the benefits of the action. Finally, the need to avoid serious harm to United States national security constrains any action taken.

The bilateral nature of Special 301 imposes limitations on its effectiveness by requiring negotiations with other states. In any bilateral negotiation, the potential short-term economic loss for a developing state whose intellectual property laws encourage piracy will generally equal the amount of revenue generated by pirate companies within its borders. Because intellectual property pirates do not prey solely upon United States nationals in the developing state, whether the United States gains from the elimination of the piracy will outweigh the losses to the developing states depends on the particular price elasticity of the product in question. This guarantees that negotiating strategies of both the United States and the foreign state will be drawn very specifically to the particular facts and circumstances of situation.

Special 301 also has the potential to distort international trade in a manner that has effects far beyond the United States and the offending foreign states in question. By imposing its own rules concerning the appropriate level of protection for intellectual property rights, the United States effectively forces its trading partners to adopt methods of protection that may or may not be the most desirable or efficient for those states. Moreover, adherence to these standards may influence detrimentally the future rules and mechanisms for the international protection of intellectual property contained in agreements such as the GATT.

Therefore, the Special 301 mechanism should be used to cultivate a carefully defined course of action heavily dependent on the special circumstances of individual cases. Once an investigation has begun, the factors that led to a state's having been designated as a Special 301 priority state make it probable that its practices are actionable as a matter of law under the retaliatory measures of Section 301.

Once the process has reached the sanction stage, however, repairing damage resulting from the investigation may no longer be possible. The naming of foreign states to even the Special 301 priority watch list has strained United States relations with the governments involved, even though the United States has yet to undertake any retaliatory action. As a result, actual investigations of Special 301 priority states are likely to have significant political repercussions that merit consideration prior to any decision to initiate an investigation.

Moreover, the mere enactment of Special 301 proved to be a major irritant at Uruguay Round negotiations seeking to incorporate intellectual property standards into the GATT. Accordingly, frequent resort to Special 301 as a legal basis for trade retaliation may produce a backlash affecting the United States bargaining position.

QUESTIONS AND COMMENTS FOR YOUR CONSIDERATION

1. Special 301 has been lauded as a unique weapon in the United States' arsenal against counterfeiters to ensure the international protection of its citizens' intellectual property and a bullying tactic in violation of its obligations under GATT. For an examination of the cultural and political impact of actions under Section 301, *see* Chapter Three.

2. What role, if any, do bilateral treaties play in developing international standards for intellectual property protection? Are there situations where a bilateral treaty arrangement might be preferable to multilateral treaty? Do bilateral treaties pose the same problems of enforcement as multilateral treaties?

3. Anti-Counterfeiting Programs[23]

Perhaps the greatest economic problems for intellectual property owners in the late Twentieth Century has been the growth of world wide pirating of copyright and trademark protected consumer and electronic goods. In the absence of international standards, many intellectual property owners have banded together to form industry based anti-counterfeiting programs to combat this problem. Such self-help programs, in addition to including educational activities aimed at local enforcement personnel, usually include aid in helping members meet domes-

[23] Written for this Anthology by Doris Estelle Long. Copyright 1996 Doris E. Long.

tic registration and recordation requirements. They also facilitate access by foreign intellectual property owners to domestic legal counselors to obtain guidance on the procedures and requirements for pursuing local remedies against counterfeiters. Finally, and, perhaps most importantly, such anti-counterfeiting programs provide systematic self-help investigative assistance in locating and seizing counterfeit goods.

One of the greatest problems in stopping the manufacture and sale of illicit counterfeit products is the transitory nature of such efforts. Counterfeit goods are not generally sold in well-established department stores. They are sold out of the back of trucks, at flea markets, by street peddlers, and in other non-permanent sites. The history of counterfeiting is filled with stories about counterfeiters who packed up and moved out as soon as traditional legal procedures were commenced against them. The lack of permanency of counterfeiting organizations virtually mandates the use of self-help remedies.

Private investigators can be used to track both illicit sales and, more importantly, the manufacturing and distribution chain for counterfeit goods. Using this privately developed information, self-help can include lawful seizure and, in appropriate circumstances destruction, of such illegal products. Such self-help remedies are often most effective when combined with available legal processes.

b. Civil Law Suits[24]

The major tribunal for obtaining relief in the United States for intellectual property infringements is the federal district court system. The 1976 Copyright Act, the Lanham (Federal Trademark) Act and the Patent Act all grant intellectual property owners the right to seek relief in the appropriate federal district court for unauthorized use of their intellectual property.[25]

The 1976 Copyright Act specifies that the legal or beneficial owner of an exclusive right granted under US copyright laws has the right to seek relief through a civil action for a violation of any of those rights. Copyright owners are entitled to a broad variety of equitable and monetary relief. Among the types of relief available are temporary restraining orders and preliminary and permanent injunctions. The Copyright Act provides for some of the most stringent monetary damages for intellectual property relief under US law. Alone among the types of intellectual property protected under US law, copyrights are protected by statutorily mandated monetary remedies. So long as the work has been registered with the US Copyright Office prior to its infringement, Section 504(c) provides for a grant of money damages of not less than $500 or more than $20,000 per infringement. Acts of willful copyright infringement qualify for statutory damages of up to $100,000. Such damages may be awarded even if no actual damages have been suffered by the copyright owner.

As an alternative to statutory damages, the copyright owner may elect to seek actual money damages, including the damages suffered by the copyright owner and any profits the infringer earned attributable to the infringement. In addition, the successful owner may obtain its reasonable attorney's fees and costs.

The copyright owner may also obtain prejudgment seizure of all infringing copies and all "plates, molds, matrices master, tapes, film negatives, or other articles by means of which such copies ... may be reproduced." Post judgment the successful plaintiff may obtain an order of destruction or forfeiture of seized items.

Under Section 1114 of the Lanham Act the registrant of a federally registered trademark or service mark may be seek relief in a civil action against "any person who shall, without the consent of the registrant" use in interstate commerce "any reproduction, counterfeit, copy or colorable imitation of a registered mark in connection with the sale, offering for sale, distribution, or advertising of any goods or services on or in connection with which such use is likely to cause confusion or to cause mistake or to deceive." Section 1125(a) grants the owners of non-registered marks similar rights.

---

[24] Written for this Anthology by Doris Estelle Long. Copyright 1996 Doris E. Long.

[25] Since there is no federal trade secret statute, most trade secret claims are governed by state law. Such state statutes routinely permit trade secret owners to file a civil action for relief against unauthorized use and/or disclosure of the trade secret.

The Lanham Act provides a wide range of civil remedies for trademark infringement. Successful plaintiffs are entitled to broad equitable relief, including temporary restraining orders and preliminary and permanent injunctions. Successful plaintiffs may also be entitled to an award of monetary damages. Such damages include actual money damages suffered by the trademark owner as well as the infringer's actual profits. Trademark owners are also entitled to an award of reasonable attorney's fees in "exceptional cases" and to court costs incurred in pursuing the civil action. Courts may also order the seizure and destruction of all labels, signs, prints, packages, wrappers, receptacles and advertisements bearing the mark in question and all plates, molds, matrices and "other means of making the same."

The Patent Act provides the patentee with a civil cause of action against anyone who, without authorization "makes, uses, offers to sell, or sells any patented invention within the United States or imports into the United States any patented invention during the term of patent therefor." Similar to the relief granted under federal copyright and trademark laws, the Patent Act allows the full range of equitable remedies, including a temporary restraining order, and preliminary and permanent injunctive relief. The statute also grants successful patentees an award of monetary damages. Such damages must constitute "adequate compensation for the infringement, but in no event less than a reasonable royalty for the use made of the invention by the infringer." Courts may receive expert testimony regarding what qualifies as a reasonable royalty rate under the circumstances. Successful plaintiffs may also be awarded reasonable attorney's fees in "exceptional cases" and costs.

The wide variety of civil law remedies available, and the relatively straight-forward procedures for seeking such relief, have resulted in the development of the civil law system as the primary method in the United States for enforcing intellectual property rights. By contrast, other countries, with less developed civil law systems, may rely upon the criminal law or administrative tribunals to enforce intellectual property rights.

QUESTIONS AND COMMENTS FOR YOUR CONSIDERATION

1. Does TRIPS require the provision of any of the civil law remedies described above?
2. Which remedies, if any, are in excess of those required under TRIPS?

c. Treble Damages[26]

Under US law enhanced damages are generally awarded only in instances of actual or intentional infringement and generally only for works which have been registered with the appropriate governmental agencies prior to such willful infringement. Thus, increased statutory damages under Section 504(c) of the 1976 Copyright Act are limited to instances of "willful" infringement. Similarly, the Lanham (Federal Trademark) Act provides for enhanced damages "not exceeding three times the amount" of actual damages for infringement of a federally registered trademark but only where such enhanced relief is required to compensate the owner for the harm caused by the infringing acts in question. Such additional "compensation" is generally awarded solely in instances of willful infringement. Section 1117(b) of the Lanham Act further provides for the award of treble damages for the intentional use of a counterfeit mark. Consequently, treble damages generally serve as a penalty for the intentional violation of an intellectual property owner's rights and a further economic deterrent to pirates and counterfeiters.

[26] Written for this Anthology by Doris Estelle Long. Copyright 1996 Doris E. Long.

A QUESTION FOR YOUR CONSIDERATION

Are enhanced damages required under NAFTA or TRIPS? If not, should they be?

B. Criminal Penalties[27]

Since the late 1970s the incidence of trademark counterfeiting and copyright piracy has been on the rise internationally. These increases have resulted not only in lost revenues for the owners of the affected trademarks and copyrights but also in increased concern over the potentially dangerous nature of goods which enter the marketplace without meeting health and safety standards established by the intellectual property owner.

One of the most recent attempts to deal with the problems posed by increased trafficking in counterfeit and pirated goods is the Agreement on Trade-Related Aspects of Intellectual Property ("TRIPS"), which forms part of the Uruguay Round Agreements concluding the most recent round of negotiations under the General Agreement on Tariffs and Trade (GATT). TRIPS not only established agreed upon procedural and remedial standards for the civil enforcement of intellectual property rights, it also contained an explicit agreement that member states provide criminal penalties for such violations as well.

Article 61 of TRIPS specifically states:

> Members shall provide for criminal procedures and penalties to be applied at least in cases of willful trademark counterfeiting or copyright piracy on a commercial scale. Remedies available shall include imprisonment and/or monetary fines sufficient to provide a deterrent, consistently with the level of penalties applied for crimes of a corresponding gravity. In appropriate cases, remedies available shall also include the seizure, forfeiture and destruction of the infringing goods and of any materials and implements the predominant use of which has been in the commission of the offense. Members may provide for criminal procedures and penalties to be applied in other cases of infringement of intellectual property rights, in particular where they are committed wilfully and on a commercial scale.

Although those articles of TRIPS concerning civil enforcement of intellectual property rights contain fairly detailed instructions regarding the types of civil procedures which must be available (including requirements of "timely" written notice, the right to take discovery and the right to provisional measures to prevent the entry into commerce of counterfeit and pirated goods), no such detailed agreement was reached in connection with the types of procedures which member countries must provide for criminal enforcement of intellectual property rights. The absence of any such agreement guarantees that the scope and nature of criminal remedies available for violation of intellectual property rights will be hotly debated in the future.

In the United States, criminal remedies are currently provided for willful copyright infringement and trademark counterfeiting. The existence and application of such penalties is generally tied to attempts to traffick in unlawful goods. As a result, criminal actions are rarely pursued in the United States against intellectual property infringers absent large-scale commercial counterfeiting.

[27] Written for this Anthology by Doris Estelle Long. Copyright 1996 Doris E. Long.

QUESTIONS AND COMMENTS FOR YOUR CONSIDERATION

1. What additional concerns are raised when nations attempt to establish international norms for criminal penalties for intellectual property infringements? Should such remedies be limited to acts of intentional counterfeiting?

2. What standard would you use for determining what are crimes of "corresponding gravity"?

3. Is required criminal enforcement appropriately limited to Instances of "commercialization" and/or products which pose health and safety standards?

10

Government "Takings" of Intellectual Property

In 1922, Justice Oliver Wendell Holmes said, "while property may be regulated to a certain extent, if regulation goes too far, it will be recognized as a taking."[1] In American constitutional law ever since, the question in eminent domain cases has been whether the regulation went "too far."

Eminent domain of course involves real property. But government regulation can also take or destroy intellectual property. There are many kinds of legal controls that governments impose upon intellectual property. These controls include: compulsory licensing, recorded user requirements, excise taxes, fair use rights, and others. Controls are often justified on policy grounds by the "controlling" country.

A fundamental question underlying regulation and control is: who has the right to determine the use of intellectual property?

This Chapter focuses on the use of compulsory licenses and equivalent forms of government controls which may arguably act as a "taking" as that term is used in a source such as the Restatement of Foreign Relations Law. The Chapter also includes excerpts that explore the role of compulsory licensing (as a form of "taking") in copyright, patent, and trademark protection systems. We will examine such diverse topics as compulsory working requirements, collective licensing societies, and the scope of "fair use" exceptions to infringement.

A. Takings

1. State Responsibility for Economic Injury to Foreign Nationals[2]

Section 712 of the Restatement (Third) of the Foreign Relations Law of the United States provides:

State Responsibility for Economic Injury to Nationals of Other States

A state is responsible under international law for injury resulting from:

(1) a taking by the state of the property of a national of another state that

(a) is not for a public purpose, or

(b) is discriminatory, or

(c) is not accompanied by provision for just compensation;

For compensation to be just under this Subsection, it must, in the absence of exceptional circumstances, be in amount equivalent to the value of the property taken and be paid at the time of taking, or within a reasonable time thereafter with interest from the date of taking, and in a form economically usable by the foreign national;

(2) a repudiation or breach by the state of a contract with a national of another state

(a) where the repudiation or breach is (i) discriminatory; or (ii) motivated by noncommercial considerations, and compensatory damages are not paid; or

[1] Pennsylvania Coal Co. v. Mahon, 260 US 393, 514 (1922).

[2] Restatement (Third) of the Foreign Relations Law of the United States § 712 (1987). Excerpt reprinted with permission.

(b) where the foreign national is given an adequate forum to determine his claim of repudiation or breach, or is not compensated for any repudiation or breach determined to have occurred; or

(3) other arbitrary or discriminatory acts or omissions by the state that impair property or other economic interest of a national of another state.

2. Types of Injury[3]

Intellectual property rights, by definition, are property rights. However, certain characteristics are unique to intellectual property as opposed to other types of property. First, the present value of intellectual property rights, for example, patents, is calculated in a very different way than is the value of other property, such as land. The present value of a patent—whether it has or has not been exploited on the market—includes some factoring in of the future earnings that will result from the future exploitation of the patent right. This valuation is more like determining the present value of a person's future earnings than the present value of a parcel of land. Thus, it is more difficult to calculate the value of intellectual property rights.

Another unique characteristic of intellectual property is the incentive structure that is produced by the future value discussed above. If a legal regime fails to protect a patent holder's future compensation adequately, there will be a "chilling effect" on the creation of intellectual property. On the other hand, if inventors' rights are protected by a strong, uniform legal system, where rights are recognized and enforced, creativity and invention are encouraged. A decrease in future invention is effectively a loss to both inventors and society as a whole.

Aside from these unique characteristics, a patent, and other forms of intellectual property, possess many of the more traditional characteristics of property. Although intangible in nature, intellectual property falls under the rules and laws used to assign, reassign, and compensate any ordinary property holder for an injury to his property right or for the taking of his property. Corporations retain patents on their books and can use those property rights as collateral just as they would use a factory or a parcel of land.

Given its kinship with other types of tangible property, intellectual property disputes could be handled by mechanisms that are similar to existing property dispute resolution mechanisms used for regular property. Under US law, courts treat intellectual property as they do any other form of property. However, any dispute mechanism that focuses on intellectual property should possess the specialized knowledge necessary to account for the unique characteristics of intellectual property. The use of an already existing dispute resolution mechanism, modified to address the special considerations inherent in intellectual property, has the advantage of allowing parties to work within the confines of a dispute mechanism familiar to them.

There are internationally recognized rights associated with the ownership of property in a foreign country. It is well-recognized that a foreign nation may not "take" an alien's property or terminate the alien's rights in any property existing in that nation's boundaries without some compensation being paid to the alien property owner. It is recognized internationally that a type of "international eminent domain" exists wherein a country may take an alien's property for its own use, but if such a taking occurs, either by the foreign government itself or by one of its citizens acting pursuant to government policy, the foreign government has an international obligation to compensate a property holder in some way for his loss.

The remedy available to a property holder, however, may be limited by state law or a decision by a local court. The property holder normally considers the risk

---

[3] Willard Alonzo Stanback, *International Intellectual Property Protection: An Integrated Solution to the Inadequate Protection Problems*, 29 VA. J. INT'L L. 517 (1989). Copyright 1989 Virginia Journal of International Law Association. Excerpt reprinted by permission.

of loss associated with the enforcement (or lack of enforcement) of those laws in determining if he or she wants to invest in a particular country. In an attempt to reduce the risk of loss and make the enforcement of property rights uniform, efforts have been made to document the international responsibility of a state to compensate aliens for national "taking" of property and for other economic injury caused by the state or a national of the state. Section 712 of the Third Restatement of Foreign Relations demonstrates how a state may be held liable for the taking of an alien's property. The section also discusses the compensation due. Therefore, although presently the injured party's remedy may be limited by state law, there seems to be an international effort to ensure that the compensation is just and proportional to the amount of the loss.

There are a number of mechanisms an alien, particularly if he is fortuitously a US citizen, may use to obtain compensation from a foreign government for an injury to or taking of his property.

One set of mechanisms includes international dispute tribunals and arbitrations.

When an international forum is used, numerous problems arise. First, a determination must be made of whose laws should be used to establish that a taking has occurred. After the choice of law issue is settled, a second obstacle to compensating the injured property owner, valuation, must be overcome. The main question here is how compensation should be calculated. This obstacle is heightened when the property lost is a patent to an ACME design, rather than tangible property, like a piece of land. The existing international dispute resolution systems would have difficulty valuing the loss of such an intellectual property right without technical assistance from experts in both the specific industry involved and intellectual property in general.

Other aspects of the international protection of intellectual property rights are comparable to the protection provided for the "taking" of international tangible property. Thus, as with other international property, a party concerned with his intellectual property rights in a foreign country should be equally concerned with that country's laws and the level of protection and enforcement afforded these rights. The party may only receive protection equal to that given to the country's own nationals. This protection could amount to no protection at all.

It may be argued that when a foreign nation recognizes but fails to protect the rights of an intellectual property holder, that country has effectively taken a right away from the party.

Clearly, another person's unauthorized use of a protected intellectual property right constitutes an injury to the holder of the protected right. If the state does not enforce its laws protecting intellectual property rights, by its omission, the state has effectively taken the property holder's right to that protection. Protection given by a state to a patent holder, for example, has a direct and substantial impact on the value of the patent; a patent which is not enforced is not worth much. Therefore, by not enforcing its own laws, a state effectively takes value away from the patent holder's right and causes an actionable injury.

When the intellectual property holder files for protection in a foreign country, he knows that there is a risk that his property right will not be adequately protected by the government of that country and that economic injury may result. These risks of economic injury are similar to those associated with other types of property. In fact, it has been argued that international intellectual property interests should be insurable against the risk of loss just as other property may be insured. "Given the recognized notion of the patent as a property interest, the exclusion of the patent itself from protection against expropriation, regardless of the form of the underlying license agreement, seems unreasonable."[4] This perception of infringed international intellectual property rights demonstrates the similarity between these rights and the rights an owner has in a factory that he may insure against "taking" or other economic injuries. However, the unique characteris-

---

[4] Bullitt & Lagomarsino, 5 Int'l Tax and Bus. Law. 283, 306 n.90 (1987).

tics of intellectual property (*e.g.*, the difficulty inherent in valuation and intellectual property's intangibility) as distinguished from other forms of property suggest that no existing international property dispute settlement mechanism currently has the expertise to adequately resolve international intellectual property disputes.

Developed and developing nations would have to be convinced that intellectual property should be treated as other forms of property are, and that framing the problem as a property issue is more appropriate than casting it as a trade or control issue. Once framed as a property issue, intellectual property disputes could be handled in a way similar to other more traditional property disputes.

The states then must agree that non-enforcement of an intellectual property right is equivalent to a "taking" as generally recognized under existing international law. Such a taking would require adequate compensation paid by the foreign government to the intellectual property holder's representative in the international arena for property holder's losses. Agreement on this point is critical, and will most likely be very difficult to obtain, given that developing countries will be reluctant to characterize non-enforcement of intellectual property rights as a "taking" of property.

Under the proposed international intellectual property forum, each country could be required to submit copies of its intellectual property laws and materials relating to the interpretation of these laws. This requirement would ensure some record of each country's means of enforcement of intellectual property rights. The records would include a list of what actions constitute infringement in each country. When infringement has occurred as prescribed by the laws provided and inadequate government action has been taken, the government will be viewed as "taking" the right, in the internationally legal sense, without just compensation.

QUESTIONS AND COMMENTS FOR YOUR CONSIDERATION

1. The author's premise of economic injury is based on a property based theory of intellectual property. Not all countries accept this premise (*see* Chapter Two). For those countries which view intellectual property as personality based, would the author's argument of harm still apply?

2. In addition to "taking" property by failing to protect an owner's rights, many countries impose various restrictions on an owner's rights to control the use of his intellectual property. Among the types of restrictions countries may impose are pre-protection registration requirements (*see* Chapter Eight), compulsory licenses, recorded user requirements, excise taxes and fair use exceptions to infringement.

3. In the law of eminent domain under the US Constitution, when a regulation goes "too far" (in Justice Holmes' words) and becomes a taking, then compensation must be paid to the property owner. As the case law has developed, the issues of taking and compensation have been conceptualized as reinforcing one another. Thus, instead of asking "was this regulation a 'taking'?" a court might ask, "should the property owner be compensated for his property loss due to the regulation?" The initial question of fairness thus can shift from whether it was a "taking" to whether "compensation" ought to be paid. Should a similar approach be applied to the various (alleged) forms of "takings" in international intellectual property law?

B. Compulsory Licensing, "Fair Use" and Copyrights

1. Compulsory Licenses[5]

There are two types of compulsory licensing in the copyright area:

Statutory license. This type of license permits others to use the copyrighted work in exchange for a fee, which is fixed either in the legislation itself or by a public or private agency authorized to fix, collect and distribute the license fees. Examples of this form of compulsory license are the statutory licenses for the recording of musical works in the United States (17 USC §115) and the United Kingdom (UK Copyright Act 1956, §12).

Compulsory license. This type of license compels the copyright owner to grant the license, but permits the copyright owner to negotiate the terms of the license, subject to the amount being fixed by a court or administrative tribunal if the parties cannot reach an agreement.

The purpose of these licensing procedures in the copyright area are threefold:

Practicality. In many instances, the user needs immediate access to these works, and does not have the time or the economic incentive to track down the copyright owner in advance of the use. Examples of this are the jukebox license in the US (17 U.S.C. § 116), and the public lending right for books in many European countries (*See*, for example, German Copyright Law ¶ 26).

Ensuring the wide availability of works. Many developing and some developed countries have compulsory licensing laws directed at foreign works. These laws were enacted to ensure that useful works would be published in the country either by the copyright holder or by someone else. For example, in Singapore, the new copyright law enacted in 1987 contains a compulsory license provision relating to literary works. Under that law, if a work is not published in Singapore or is not published in "Singapore language," then others are permitted to publish translations of the work into a Singapore language or to publish literary, scientific or artistic works not available in Singapore, upon payment of royalties to the copyright owner.

[5] Michael D. Scott, *Compulsory Licensing of Intellectual Property in International Transactions*. Copyright 1988 Michael D. Scott. Excerpt reprinted with permission.

2. "Fair Use" Exceptions[6]

The most prominent trait of the Berne Union is its ongoing ability to encourage increases in the personal and economic rights of authors over their literary and artistic works. This ability is grounded on the Berne philosophy, which is based on the continental European *droit d'auteur* approach. Under this approach, the focus of copyright is on the author as an individual. The approach encompasses authors' inalienable personal relationship to their works and is therefore consistent with the most important solution to the copyright crisis, focusing on the rights of individual authors.

By encouraging members to focus on individual authors, the Berne Union offsets erosions in authors' rights caused by the political strength exerted by users. Users customarily lobby for legislation that allows cheap and easy access to the creative works of authors. Thus, they often favor solutions that divest authors of exclusive control over their intellectual creations. One such solution is the compulsory license. A compulsory license, at first glance, appears to represent a compromise between users and authors; authors receive remuneration and users receive unhindered access. In reality, the license's compulsive element divests authors of the exclusive right to authorize reproductions, broadcasts, or recordings of their works.

Fair use exceptions or exemptions for private copying are, in a sense, more erosive to authors' rights than licenses. Under these two exceptions, authors receive no remuneration and are completely divested of their exclusive rights,[7] while users receive unhin-

[6] Peter Burger, *Article: The Berne Convention: Its History And Its Key Role In The Future*, 3 J.L. & Tech 1. Copyright 1989 Georgetown University Law Center. Excerpt reprinted with permission.

[7] Under fair use exceptions and exemptions for private copying, legislatures define the situations in which society should have access to authors' works, works that normally would be protected. As such, the uses are not infringements. The exceptions usually deal with private copies for scientific, research

dered access to the authors' works. Except for rare cases, these exceptions hardly represent a fair compromise. Authors must, at a minimum, protect their bundle of exclusive rights. Exclusive rights have always been at the core of copyright protection. The more those rights are divested, the greater the cancerous effect on authors. The Berne Union can fight this cancer by encouraging member nations to remain true to Berne's purpose of protecting authors' rights and by encouraging nonmember nations to adopt a similar policy.

In a more practical way, the Berne Union, through WIPO, is already encouraging nations to limit both the use of compulsory licenses and the scope of fair use exceptions and exemptions for private copying. To the extent that it can convince member and nonmember nations to limit exceptions to authors' exclusive rights on a national level, the Union is also improving the rights of authors on an international level, because national improvements manifest themselves internationally through Berne's national treatment provisions.

Encouraging member and nonmember states to take the practical steps necessary to improve authors' rights will not be easy. Great differences of opinion exist among Union members on the virtues of compulsory licenses, fair use exceptions, and exemptions for private copying. The Union members, however, have a common goal, as expressed in Article 1 of the [Berne] Convention, to protect authors' rights. Their ability to withstand the political pressures favoring exceptions to authors' rights in a high technology era is a function of their commitment to that goal. In the past, that commitment has been great; it must be no less in the present and future.

Historically, the Berne Union has protected authors from the divesting effect of new technologies such as television, radio, and cinematographs (by extending protection to these areas). An important element in solving the current copyright crisis is to continue that historical trend and develop copyright solutions to the problems posed by audio and audio-visual reproduction, reprography, computer storage and retrieval, and satellite and cable television.

The Berne Convention does not explicitly protect authors from unauthorized audio and audio-visual reproductions, reprography, and reproductions by means of computer. Each of these technologies, however, poses a threat to the authors' reproduction right found in Article 9(1) of the Convention.

Under Article 9(1), authors have the exclusive right to authorize the reproduction of their literary and artistic works "in any manner or form." The language "in any manner or form" is intended to apply to new technologies such as photocopying, computer reproduction or video and audio-visual recording. Thus, the Berne Convention contemplates new technologies.

Under Article 9(2), however, the Convention allows Union countries to permit copying of literary and artistic works as long as the copies do not conflict with a normal exploitation of the work and do not unreasonably prejudice the legitimate interests of the author. The exception is vague and thus allows member countries to interpret the clause so as to enact exceptions to the authors' reproduction right. The larger the exception which a given country enacts, the larger the erosive effect on authors' rights.

Many countries interpret this provision to allow photocopying of literary and artistic works for scientific and educational purposes, or private home audio and audio-visual recording. More author protective countries have added a per copy surcharge on photocopies and duplicating equipment and a surcharge on the price of recording equipment and blank cassettes in order to compensate authors for the reproduction of their works. The proceeds generated by the surcharge are then turned over to a collecting society. The collecting society distributes the proceeds to all authors who are registered with the society. Unregistered authors receive no compensation.

The collecting society approach adopted in these countries has been supported by WIPO and many leading copyright commentators in the area of reprography. It

---

or educational purposes. *See, e.g.*, Berne Convention, at Art. 10. Pressure always exists, however, to expand the number of fair use exceptions because users have a natural preference for greater and easier access to authors' works. The more the scope of fair use expands, the greater the incursions into authors' exclusive rights. Thus, while fair use exceptions may be justified in certain limited situations, their use should be as narrow as possible.

compensates authors for noninfringing uses of their works, yet does not hinder user access to literary and artistic works necessary to further research, education, and science.

In order for the collecting society approach to be effective under copyright in the long run, it must be "internationalized." Not all photocopied works in country A are written by authors from country A; many works may come from authors from other Union countries. Berne's national treatment provisions should require compensation for Union authors outside of country A whose works are copied in that country, since those Union authors are entitled to the same treatment in country A as country A's authors. Countries, however, may decide to create this compensation system outside of copyright. In such a case, the Berne Convention and national treatment might not apply, and only domestic authors would be compensated. The best solution, therefore, is to encourage more and more countries to establish a remuneration system for authors under domestic copyright law and then assist authors in applying for compensation in foreign countries. The Berne Union encouraged this solution for reprography, and through persuasion it can help implement such a plan internationally. The Berne Union is also supporting a similar approach with respect to privately made audio and audio-visual and computer reproductions.

The Union is also pursuing solutions to the erosive threats that cable and satellite broadcasting pose to authors' exclusive broadcasting rights. The Berne Convention, Article 11bis, arguably covers cable broadcasting, but satellite broadcasting is far more controversial. The controversy is bound to continue until the Berne members revise the Convention to expressly include or exclude satellite and cable broadcasting.

If one takes an author-focused view of Article 11bis and concludes that it applies to all cable and satellite broadcasts—an approach urged by at least one commentator—authors would have the exclusive right to authorize such broadcasts. Contracting states, however, would still have the option of putting limitations, such as compulsory licenses, on the exclusivity of the right. With compulsory licenses, users can compel authors to grant them access to authors' works, albeit for remuneration and with full protection of moral rights. Nevertheless, compulsory licenses divest authors of control over their works.

A Group of Experts under the auspices of the WIPO and the Berne Union has encouraged nations to limit their use of compulsory licenses in the area of cable and satellite broadcasting.[8] As an alternative, it encourages authors and users to enter freely negotiated collective licensing contracts. Under a collective licensing contract, authors would grant a collecting society the right to authorize broadcasts of their works, including cable and satellite broadcasts. Cable and satellite broadcasters could then approach the collecting societies for permission to broadcast a given work. The user would pay the collecting society a fee for use of the work, and the collecting society would then remunerate the author or an association representing the author. If authors do not join or authorize a collecting society to authorize broadcasts of their works, then broadcasters would need express permission from the author. A broadcast without the author's permission would constitute an infringement unless some other exception applied.

Under a collecting society approach for broadcasting, authors receive compensation and retain their exclusive rights vicariously through the collecting society. The solution provides a realistic compromise in which authors retain their personal and economic rights and users receive easier access to authors' works.

The Group of Experts has urged Berne Union members to adopt this approach in their national legislation as an alternative to compulsory licensing. The collecting society model for broadcasting should, like the reprography proposals, be "internationalized," especially since cable and satellite broadcasting facilitate transnational broadcasts. The Berne Union provides an optimal forum for achieving this "internationalization."

---

[8] Group of Independent Experts on the Trademark Impact of Cable Television in the Sphere of Copyright, 1980 Copyright Bulletin 156.

QUESTIONS AND COMMENTS FOR YOUR CONSIDERATION

1. Article 9(2) of the Berne Convention provides in pertinent part:

> It shall be a matter for legislation in the countries of the Union to permit the reproduction of such works in certain special cases, provided that such reproduction does not conflict with a normal exploitation of the work and does not unreasonably prejudice the legitimate interests of the author.

What factors would you consider in deciding whether a particular compulsory licensing scheme is "unreasonably prejudicial" to an author's "legitimate interests"? What effect, if any, would the question of author compensation play in your decision?

2. Collective licensing societies have often been touted as the alternative to government imposed compulsory licensing schemes. What benefits does an intellectual property owner gain from participating in collective licensing societies? What harm does she suffer?

3. Collection Levies[9]

The law of copyright has become increasingly intertwined with the development of technology. This is unsurprising because Anglo-American copyright law originated as a response to new technology, *viz.*, the printing press. As new technologies have developed, copyright law has been forced to evolve.

In addition to the close relationship between the law of copyright and technology, there is a tension between the law's potentially powerful repressive impact and freedom of expression. This relationship underlies the arguments of those who question the legitimacy of copyright as an instrument of public policy; *i.e.*, as a means of accommodating the sometimes conflicting interests of the author, the government, and the public. Indeed, the first British copyright laws, which were introduced shortly after the arrival of the printing press in the late 1400s, were devised as instruments of censorship whose primary purpose was to inhibit the spread of the Protestant Reformation. In response to abuses of the printers' monopoly, known as the Stationers' Company, Parliament enacted the Statute of Anne in 1710. This legislation wisely divested copyright from printers, who were licensed and controlled by the Crown, and instead granted it to authors. The copyright period was fourteen years, but could be renewed for a single additional term; it therefore provided a maximum of twenty-eight years' protection. Removing the copyright from a monopoly dominated by the Crown helped to forestall repressive government misuses of copyright. The Statute of Anne formed the foundation upon which American copyright law was eventually built.

Historically, the law of copyright has responded as new technologies have received both judicial and legislative treatment. Today, the law is challenged not only with confronting the latest revolutionary advances in technology, but also with anticipating ever more frequent technological developments. Video cassette recorders, personal computers, compact discs ("CDs"), minidiscs (recordable CDs), digital tape recorders, and digital broadcasting have remade, and are remaking, the traditional copyright landscape. Other devices and processes yet to be developed will continue to reshape it in the future. The copyright owner's exclusive rights "to reproduce the copyrighted work in copies or phonorecords" and "to distribute copies or phonorecords of the copyrighted work to the public by sale or other transfer of ownership" have been severely eroded by the wide availability of inexpensive, high-quality reproduction equipment. Further, the private nature of home copying and the minuscule damage

---

[9] Gary S. Lutzker, *Dat's All Folks: Cahn v. Sony and the Audio Home Recording Act of 1991—Merrie Melodies or Looney Tunes?*, 11 CARDOZO ARTS & ENT. L.J. 145. Copyright 1992 Gary S. Lutzker. Excerpt reprinted with permission.

caused by an individual act of infringement make judicial enforcement highly problematic. Nevertheless, aggregate damages can be enormous. Although unauthorized reproduction is common, inherent characteristics of the currently dominant analog recording technology hamper infringement to a limited extent. Under analog, serial copying is circumscribed by the inevitable deterioration of subsequent recordings. Newer digital technologies exacerbate the problem from the copyright proprietor's perspective because they enable the creation of perfect reproductions that will not deteriorate in quality when subsequent copies are made from a first-generation source. Both the opportunity and the incentive for unauthorized taping are thereby increased. Copyright owners are concerned that these technologies will make record piracy an uncontrollable cottage industry, thereby depriving them of substantial income and, thus, the incentive to create.

Seventeen countries have enacted legislation to compensate copyright proprietors for unauthorized reproduction of their works; several others are considering such legislation. Most, however, will distribute the proceeds to foreign interests only on the basis of reciprocity.

Not surprisingly, foreign collection and distribution schemes vary. Some collect only on the sales of blank tape, while others include fees on the sale of recording equipment as well. Significantly, in nearly all the countries that have enacted such legislation, the royalty payments apply to both analog and digital media. In Germany, for example, the proposed digital royalty rate is quadruple the analog rate.

Proposals to compensate copyright owners for unauthorized copying have been debated for years. In the view of the European Community, the introduction of digital technology, with its potential to stimulate infringement, added urgency to the need for action. The EEC, however, did not view the imposition of levies on blank tape as the ideal solution either. Instead, it supported a system that had been suggested by the US Copyright Office; *viz.*, a credit- or debit-card system, which would not only limit unauthorized copying, but would insure direct payment by the taper for each digital copy made.

4. Practical Applications[10]

Public policy favoring wide public access to copyrighted works for purposes of education, combined with the difficulty of enforcing the right of reproduction, has led some countries to adopt a compromise approach. In return for modifying the principle of authors' exclusive rights by making works freely available for educational copying, some national legislations assure authors compensation by subjecting the reproductions to payment of a licensing fee. In practice, local reproduction rights organizations, representing authors and/or publishers, generally negotiate with user groups and collect the compulsory license fee. In other countries, similar results are achieved through voluntary collective licensing.

The copyright laws of the UK and Australia provide for compulsory licensing of reproduction rights in favor of educational institutions. In Australia, Part VB of the Copyright Amendment Act 1989, sets forth a statutory license for multiple copying by educational institutions. The beneficiaries of the license may copy all or part of copyrighted works, subject to statutory remuneration to the copyright owners. However, the statutory licensee must comply with extensive record-keeping obligations. For example, the educational institution must "Make or cause to be made, a record of each licensed copy that is carried out by it, or on its behalf, . . . being a record containing such particulars as are prescribed; retain that record for the prescribed retention period after the making of the copy to which it relates; and send copies of all such records to the collecting society in accordance with the regulations."[11] The burdensome requirements set forth in the 1989 amendments to its 1980 predecessor that educational institutions must satisfy in order to qualify for the license have had the practical effect of encouraging universities to reach agreements with the Australian voluntary collective licensing group.

The UK statute also encourages agree-

---

[10] Jane C. Ginsburg, *Reproduction of Protected Works for University Research or Teaching*, 39 J. COPYRIGHT SOC'Y U.S.A. 181. Copyright 1992 Jane C. Ginsburg. Excerpt reprinted with permission.

[11] Australia, Copyright Amendment Act of 1989, Part VB, sec. 35ZX(b) & (d).

ments between persons engaging in educational reprography and licensing groups, but by different means. The 1988 Copyright Designs and Patents Act sets forth elaborate provisions governing copyright licensing, and includes special provisions concerning reprography by or on behalf of educational establishments. Ultimately, if the Secretary of State determines, according to a host of statutory criteria, that a license should have been made available to the educational institution, and no agreement is reached within one year between the copyright owner or licensing group and the educational institution, the Secretary of State may "by order provide that if, or to the extent that, provision has not been made in accordance with the recommendation, the making by or on behalf of an educational establishment, for the purposes of instruction, of reprographic copies of the works to which the recommendation relates shall be treated as licensed by the owners of the copyright in the works."[12] As one commentator has observed, under this provision, the Secretary of State "may, in effect, impose a free statutory license."[13] The UK statute thus not only authorizes agreements between university users and licensing collectives, it gives the collective every incentive to conclude the accord.

The Nordic Countries of Finland, Sweden and Norway have adopted a different approach to statutory licensing. In Finland and Sweden, the copyright acts, and in Norway, a special statute, provide for "extended collective licenses" [ECL] covering, *inter alia*, reprographic copies of published works for educational purposes. The basic structure of an ECL-statute is as follows: when a collective reproduction rights organization [RRO] representing a "substantial portion" of national authors within a particular field enters into an agreement on photocopying with a user of copyrighted material, the agreement will, by statute, be deemed to cover all works within the same field, regardless of whether the authors of the works are members of the RRO. The primary effect of all ECL-agreements is to insulate the copyright user from suits by individual authors. Thus, once an RRO represents a "substantial portion" of authors, it can license the works of all authors within the same field.

The Nordic statutes present an additional significant departure from conventional voluntary licensing: the proceeds of the licenses generally do not go directly to the authors. Rather, they benefit a variety of domestic social programs.

[12] U.K. 1988 Copyright Designs and Patents Act, Chapter VII at sec.141(1).

[13] De Freitas, *The United Kingdom—New Copyright Law*, 143 RIPA 25, 93 (Jan. 1990).

QUESTIONS AND COMMENTS FOR YOUR CONSIDERATION

1. Which compulsory licensing scheme do you favor? Why? What are the drawbacks to these schemes?
2. How would you resolve the administrative problems posed by the scheme you prefer?

C. Compulsory Licensing and Patents[14]

"A compulsory license is an involuntary contract between a willing buyer and an unwilling seller imposed and enforced by the state."[15] A survey of international intellectual property law reveals that the three most prevalent compulsory licensing provisions are applicable where a dependent patent is

[14] Gianna Julian-Arnold, *International Compulsory Licensing: The Rationales and the Reality*, 33 IDEA J.L. & TECH. 349. Copyright 1993 PTC Research Foundation of the Franklin Pierce Law Center. Excerpt reprinted with permission.

[15] P. GORECKI, REGULATING THE PRICE OF PRESCRIPTION DRUGS IN CANADA: COMPULSORY LICENSING, PRODUCT SELECTION, AND GOVERNMENT REIMBURSE-

being blocked, where a patent is not being worked, or where an invention relates to food or medicine. Additionally, compulsory licensing may be implemented as a remedy in antitrust or misuse situations, where the invention is important to national defense or where the entity acquiring the compulsory license is the sovereign.

A dependent patent cannot be worked without infringing an earlier issued patent. This may result in a situation where it is not possible to exploit the later issuing patent due to the inability of the two patent holders to come to a licensing agreement. The ramifications of this depend upon whether the improvement invention protected by the dependent patent is of greater or lesser value than the invention protected by the original patent. This "holdup" problem may be significant in the case where the original patent contributes very little value as compared to the improvement. Additionally, the refusal to license may be detrimental to society as it prevents the introduction of the improvement until the original patent has expired, and/or delays the introduction due to time spent in litigation, leading to higher consumer cost. "[The] inability to work a dependent patent is [also] seen, in some countries, as being contrary to the public interest in having the unencumbered working of all patented inventions."[16] To remedy this, many States have adopted compulsory licensing provisions. An example of such a law is Article 36 of the Swiss Patent Law, which provides:

> If a patented invention cannot be used without violating the prior patent, the owner of the more recent patent shall have the right to the grant of a license to the extent required for such use of his invention, provided that that invention serves a purpose entirely different from that of the prior patent, or that it involves a considerable technical advance. Where both inventions serve the same economic purpose, the registered owner of the prior patent may grant the license on the condition that the owner of the junior patent in turn grants him a license or the use of his invention. In case of dispute, the judge shall decide on the grant of the licenses, their extent and duration and on the compensation to be paid.[17]

Through implementation of a statute of this nature, a State creates a more favorable environment for post "pioneer invention" development and improvement, thereby providing an incentive for the furtherance of technical and economic development.

However, partially due to safeguards implemented by various countries, this type of compulsory license is rarely granted. The reason for this is of a practical nature: prior to application for a compulsory license, an improvement invention must be created, a patent application granted, the improvement patent applicant may have had to survive a lengthy opposition proceeding, and an attempt at voluntary negotiations must have been made. These steps discourage compulsory license applications owing to the time and money involved.

Every nation has a strong interest in promoting the working of patents, as this assures the populace is supplied with new and better goods. Additionally, many nations regard a patent grant as a contract between a state and an individual, where the patentee is given the right to prevent others from using the invention under the implied condition that the patent holder will exploit the invention in the State, thereby benefiting the community. Under this view, the patent holder who fails to put his invention into practice within the State has breached his implied condition and may therefore have his patent grant reduced or revoked. Non-use provisions are thus implemented with the goal of promoting local working of patented inventions and to prevent the patentee from denying the public access to novel and needed sub-

---

MENT PROGRAMMES, (Economic Council of Canada, 1981).

[16] International Bureau of WIPO, Compulsory or Non-voluntary Licenses in Respect of Patents for Invention, from Meeting Of Experts On The Acquisition By Developing Countries of Environmental Relevant Technology Protected By Intellectual Property, U.N. Doc. WIPO/UNCED/CE/6 (1991).

[17] Systematische Sanmlung des Bundestrechts (SR)(Catalogue of Swiss Law), 232.14, reprinted in Walter, Compulsory Licenses and Dependent Patents, 21 IIC 532 (1990).

ject matter, where to withhold such subject matter is unreasonable or contrary to the public interest. These provisions appear in the patent laws in two forms, compulsory working and compulsory licensing. "Compulsory working" means a patent must be commercially worked within the country granting the patent, or the patent will be revoked. "Compulsory licensing" refers to a non-voluntary licensing arrangement between private entities and arranged by the government. Generally the patent is only revoked when, for some reason, compulsory licensing fails.

The right of countries to impose compulsory licensing provisions of this nature is recognized by Article 5 of the Paris Convention, which states:

> 1. Member states may legislate measures providing for the grant of compulsory licenses to prevent abuses of the exclusive rights conferred by the patent, for example for failure to work.
> 2. Forfeiture of the patent will not be provided for except where the grant of compulsory licenses is not sufficient to prevent abuses. Forfeiture or revocation of a patent will not be instituted before the expiration of three years from the grant of the first compulsory license.
> 3. A compulsory license may not be applied for on the ground of failure to work or insufficient working before the expiration of three years from the date of application for the patent, or four years from the date of the grant of the patent whichever period expires last. It shall be refused if the patentee justifies his inaction by legitimate reasons. Such compulsory license shall be non-exclusive and shall not be transferable even in the form of the grant of a sub-license except with that part of the enterprise or goodwill which exploits such license. Common circumstances where this provision may be applied are when the patent owner fails to work his patent within the requisite time after patent issuance/patent application and also refuses to license the patent to another on reasonable terms, when the patent owner fails to meet the demand for the product, and when the patent is being used to block the use of another patent.[18]

Edwin Mansfield of the University of Pennsylvania, in an attempt to determine the perceived importance of intellectual property rights on the nature and amount of technology transferred to a country by way of direct foreign investment, requested information from 100 major US firms as to the importance of intellectual property rights in their determination of whether to make direct foreign investments of various kinds.[19] He found some industries regard intellectual property protection as more important than others, with the food and transportation equipment industries being the lowest and chemistry (including pharmaceuticals), being the highest. Mansfield also noted a very high correlation between an industry's ranking in this study and its ranking in previous studies, with the general case being more research-and-development intensive industries seeming to place a higher priority on intellectual property rights. The proportion of firms which considered intellectual property rights important in their determination as to whether to make a particular type of foreign investment were as follows:

Type of Investment	**Percentage**
Sales and Distribution Outlets	20%
Rudimentary Production and Assembly Facilities	32%
Facilities to Manufacture Components	48%
Facilities to Manufacture Complete Products	59%
Research and Development	80%

---

[18] International Convention for the Protection of Industrial Property [Paris Convention] at art. 5.

[19] Mansfield, *Unauthorized Use of Intellectual Property*, a paper presented at the Conference on Global Dimensions of Intellectual Property in Science and Technology, Washington, D.C. January 8–9, 1991.

Therefore, as investments in facilities for research and development and the manufacture of components or complete products are likely to raise a country's technological level to a greater extent than investments in sales and distribution outlets or in rudimentary production and assembly facilities, and as these are the types of investment decisions where intellectual property rights play an increasingly important role, the implementation of these rights would seem to attract external investment of this nature to the benefit of the developing nation. Thus, intellectual property should be regarded as a development tool: it raises a country's technology base by drawing local and international funds, by supporting local research efforts, and by encouraging the introduction of growth-producing new technology into the economy.

Many developing nations believe their needs are adequately provided for through the practice of "free riding" or "pirating" others' accomplishments. As the skills acquired in copying are generally not useful in the transition to innovation, a policy of this nature condemns the nation to perpetual catch-up.

It is argued that free riding is particularly legitimate in the area of pharmaceuticals, as the population of the developing nation may procure a drug similar to the patented article at a greatly reduced price. However, an analysis of the realities in the area of pharmaceuticals shows that for the following reasons this is not so. First, it generally seems products produced through imitation are sold at high prices, even though they have accrued no innovation costs. Thus, the "high social rate of return is sacrificed in favor of a high private rate of return for a few."[20] Second, of the drugs included in the current Essential Drugs List published by the World Health Organization, over 90 percent are not protected by United States patents. Third, many pharmaceutical firms provide essential drugs on noncommercial terms and provide assistance to developing countries in appropriate distribution, quality control and administrative techniques. Fourth, patented pharmaceutical products must compete with other products of the same chemical or therapeutic class. Fifth, and most importantly, many developing nations have implemented price regulation schemes. In these situations "intellectual property protection poses no threat of noncompetitive pricing [as the] government ha[s] taken the risky step of overriding the market with price regulation." It therefore seems compulsory licensing is neither an efficient nor necessary cost controlling measure.

---

[20] SHERWOOD, INTELLECTUAL PROPERTY AND ECONOMIC DEVELOPMENT 7 (1990).

QUESTIONS AND COMMENTS FOR YOUR CONSIDERATION

1. Do compulsory licensing and compulsory working requirements reduce the economic benefits presumably derived from the manufacture and distribution of counterfeit products?

2. What limits, if any, should be placed on the use of compulsory licenses? Should compulsory licenses be limited to "essential" works, such as medicines or agricultural products? What factors should be considered in determining a country's national interest? What administrative costs are incurred in imposing compulsory licenses?

3. Should all parties who desire it be granted a compulsory license? If not, what eligibility requirements would you impose?

4. What interests are supported by a compulsory working requirement? How do you balance these interests against the conflicting interests of the intellectual property owners?

1. Compulsory Working, Abuse and Revocation[21]

Unlike the United States, most countries have compulsory working and compulsory licensing provisions in their patent laws. "Compulsory working" of a patent means that a patent must be commercially worked within the country granting the patent, or the patent will be invalidated. "Compulsory licensing" means that the government will license the patent without the consent of the patent holder.

The International Convention for the Protection of Industrial Property (Paris Convention), which applies to industrial property in its broadest sense (including patents on inventions, utility models, industrial designs, trade marks and trade names), recognizes the right of countries to impose such compulsory provisions with certain limitations, [including the right to provide] "providing for the grant of compulsory licenses to prevent abuses of the exclusive rights conferred by the patent, for example for failure to work."

Compulsory licensing is an extension of the country's power to revoke a patent for abuse or non-use. In most countries, revocation will occur only after attempts at compulsory licensing prove unsatisfactory.

There are several typical situations in which compulsory licensing will be applied:

1. the patent owner's failure to work the patent for a period of time after application for patent and/or grant of patent and his refusal to license the patent on reasonable terms;
2. the patent owner's failure to meet the domestic (and, in some cases, export) demand for the product;
3. the patent is being used to block the use of another patent; and
4. the product is necessary for the health or safety of a country's citizens or its national economy.

Food and drug patents have been singled out in many countries for special treatment, although compulsory licensing laws usually apply to all patents.

Some of the reasons for compulsory licenses are:

1. to increase competition for the product and the resulting lower prices to the consumer;
2. to increase the availability of the product in the country;
3. to increase employment and tax base of the country by requiring working of the patent in the country;
4. to prevent the blocking of improvement patents;
5. to serve as an incentive for licensing on a fair and equitable basis; and
6. to compel technology transfer to developing countries.

[21] Michael D. Scott, *Compulsory Licensing of Intellectual Property in International Transactions.* Copyright 1988 Michael D. Scott. Excerpt reprinted with permission.

QUESTIONS AND COMMENTS FOR YOUR CONSIDERATION

1. How do you define "abuse"? Is it an abuse of patent if the foreign owner refuses to license domestic companies to work the patented invention?

2. Should the beneficiaries of a compulsory license be required to provide compensation to the patent owner?

2. Theory and Practice[22]

When a business decides whether to compete in today's world marketplace, it must consider the extent to which its ideas and designs will be protected from misappropriation around the world. Despite its international ramifications, however, patent protection is territorial, operating only within the jurisdiction granting the patent. Companies wishing to compete overseas must obtain patents from each country in which protection is sought. While several treaties and international congresses have been successful in creating fundamental equity and uniformity among national patent laws, complete uniformity is difficult to achieve due to different philosophies regarding free enterprise, monopoly rights, and technological development.

Recognizing the territorial limits of patent protection, a comparison of patent laws may nevertheless be useful in identifying the most beneficial aspects of particular patent systems. One aspect common throughout the world, but virtually absent in the United States, is compulsory licensing. Compulsory licensing enables the government granting the patent to force the patentee to license the invention if the government does not approve of the patent's use. Consequently, another individual or company is allowed to make and sell the invention.

The threat of compulsory licensing encourages parties to grant licenses voluntarily. Voluntary licensing presents an attractive option for the foreign patent holder because it is a superior method for penetrating a foreign market with little or no investment and labor contribution, advantages absent when manufacturing occurs directly in the foreign country. Voluntary licensing also reduces the risks involved in starting operations in a foreign country by eliminating the necessity for having to understand and work within the confines of an unfamiliar production environment. Businesses with extensive resources, however, may prefer direct production in a foreign country over licensing to a local company. Many United States enterprises prefer this approach due to the greater profits possible when a company decides to produce a good itself. However, a foreign jurisdiction with strong compulsory license provisions may actually inhibit this preferred method. In compulsory licensing situations a court dictates the terms of the license, and the licensor's wishes may be ignored.

Compulsory licensing provisions further the same goal of general patent laws: creating an incentive for new technologies. A basic assumption underlying most patent systems is that society is benefited more by the advancement of innovation than it is harmed by the grant of a monopoly to the inventor. Compulsory licensing provisions, however, may lessen the incentive to innovate by limiting the scope of the patentee's grant.

Compulsory patent theories can be roughly grouped into three categories: adequacy of supply, public interest, and "worked in the country."

If the patentee is unable to meet the demand for its product under an exclusive right to manufacture and sell the product, it may be forced to grant a license, often to a competitor.

Compulsory licenses granted under the adequate supply theory purposefully reduce the inventor's reward in order to increase the public availability of the goods. Strong compulsory license provisions reflect a government's belief that the inventor's incentives will not be reduced to the point of deterring research and innovation.

Compulsory licenses based on the public interest are similar to those based on the adequate supply theory, but are only issued to control products especially vital to the public. These licenses commonly involve inventions relating to public health, welfare, or national defense—areas where the inventor's interest may be subordinate to that of the public. United States compulsory license provisions exist within this narrow category. The examples are few, but include patents for pollution control devices under the Clean Air Act, and patents involving nuclear materials.

Nations do not agree what constitutes the "public interest." The United States has often granted compulsory licenses as a rem-

---

[22] Cole M. Fauver, *Compulsory Patent Licensing in the United States: An Idea Whose Time Has Come*; 8 Nw. J. Int'l L. & Bus. 666. Copyright 1988 Northwestern Journal International Law & Business. Excerpt reprinted with permission.

edy for violations of antitrust laws, reflecting the value of free enterprise and competition in the United States.[23] By contrast, in the Soviet Union any invention "of special importance to the state" is subject to compulsory licensing.[24] The United Kingdom recognizes a public interest in the low-priced supply of goods used in the production of food, medicine, and surgical or curative equipment. Similarly, in Switzerland lowering prices may legitimately support a compulsory license for any patented good.[25]

In countries with limited industrial development, the "public interest" may be expanded to include the opportunity to develop national industry. Recognizing that new technology is crucial to economic growth and employment, developing nations may subject foreign investors to compulsory licensing in order to gain access to technology which the nations could not otherwise develop. This limits an investor's control over the use of the invention, however, so compulsory licenses may deter foreign investment.

Compulsory licensing schemes are justified on the ground that they increase public access to inventions. A government's ability to control the compulsory licensing process, however, may hinder innovation of products which promote the public welfare. A government has every incentive to grant a compulsory license for such an invention—even if demand is being met by current production—to ensure a more stable future supply. Thus the potential for compulsory licenses may encourage patentees to pursue inventions which do not promise widespread public benefit.

Besides using compulsory licensing to guarantee adequacy of supply and to promote the public interest, some countries use compulsory licensing to ensure that the invention be "worked in the country." Different interpretations of "worked," however, give rise to various applications of the provision. United Kingdom law provides that a compulsory license may be issued, after a period of three years, "where the patented invention is capable of being commercially worked in the United Kingdom, that it is not being so worked or is not being so worked to the fullest extent that is reasonably practicable." Other countries which also maintain a "worked in the country" provision include Canada, West Germany, Japan, Sweden, and Switzerland.

In Austria during the 1870s the term "worked" was strictly interpreted. A foreigner who held an Austrian patent was required to manufacture the article in Austria within one year from the original grant or the patent would be revoked. This interpretation has been deemed "most vexatious." In France, the term was historically translated into the term "fabrique," which implies building, making, or putting together. France eventually revised its law, creating a more lenient requirement for development by the patentee.

Under more modern interpretations, "worked" simply means "used." The patentee cannot hide his invention, but must exploit it and share its benefits even while maintaining exclusive rights to the profits. Application of this theory is consistent with general patent philosophies. New ideas are encouraged and the producer rewarded, but through compulsory marketing by the holder, the benefits of innovation are shared. Others gain access to the useful aspects of the technology, if not to the profits. While this theory imposes a duty on the patentee to use the patent, should it meet this burden, its exclusive right to exploit the patent will not be disturbed.

The United States imposes no such duty on the ordinary patent holder.

Japan's use of the "worked in the country" provision to discourage foreign imports is a practice which reflects the heavy restrictions Japan places on foreign-owned business operations. By requiring that some part of the invention be made in Japan, the rule serves "as a protectionist economic policy which conflicts considerably with the present international trade policy of the Western World." Thus, while Japan effectively discourages straight importation (possibly the

---

[23] Girard, *Impact of U.S. Antitrust Laws on Territorially-Limited International Patent Licensing Agreements*, 11 U.S.F. L. Rev. 640 (1977).

[24] H. Scade, Patents at a Glance: A Survey of Substantive Law and Formalities in 50 Countries 138 (3d Rev. 1980).

[25] Neumeyer, *Compulsory Licensing of Patents Under Some Non-American Systems*, Study of the Subcomm. on Patents, Trademarks and Copyrights of the Senate Comm. on the Judiciary, 85th Cong., 2d Sess. 28 (1959).

most desirable form of investment for United States companies), many Japanese concerns doing business in the United States have successfully exploited this same arrangement.

"Worked in the country" provisions, by requiring actual assembly in the country, help those in the industry better understand the product's unique features. However, the provisions may not be critical. As long as the product is imported, reverse engineering may help reveal the novel aspects of the invention. Moreover, these features must be clearly described in the original patent application. Actual manufacturing within the country may or may not more effectively spread technological innovation, but any discrepancy between the methods would be eliminated over time.

Practical economics makes the "worked in the country" provision harder to justify. Business concerns will tend to manufacture, in whole or in part, where it is cheapest to do so. If it is cheaper to manufacture elsewhere and then import, the product will be available at a more reasonable price in the importing country. This result alone can support a compulsory license, whereas a compulsory license requiring manufacture in a more expensive country solely to protect local suppliers is much harder to justify.

QUESTIONS AND COMMENTS FOR YOUR CONSIDERATION

1. What impact if any, would a compulsory license scheme have on an inventor's decision to seek patent protection?
2. What impact, if any, does the theory supporting compulsory licensing have on your answer to the first question?

D. Compulsory Licensing and Trademarks[26]

The theories used to justify compulsory licensing of trade marks are based on the premise that trade marks are inherently anti-social and anti-competitive. Many countries control the use of trade marks by foreigners as a means of protecting domestic producers from foreign importers and multinational companies. Third world companies see the trade marks of multinational companies as a threat to their domestic, social and economic goals. In many countries, there is a distrust of product advertising in general, and a belief that brand name loyalty is somehow "irrational," since there are often equivalent products available at much lower cost. As such, trade marks themselves are viewed as "irrational."

One area in which compulsory licensing of trade marks has been seriously considered both in the US and abroad is in connection with brand-name drugs. Governments are concerned that pharmaceutical trade marks tend to keep prices of the drugs artificially high and discourage physicians from prescribing generic substitutes for prescription drugs.

[26] Michael D. Scott, *Compulsory Licensing of Intellectual Property in International Transactions*. Copyright 1988 Michael D. Scott. Excerpt reprinted with permission.

QUESTIONS AND COMMENTS FOR YOUR CONSIDERATION

1. Are there procompetitive purposes which trademarks serve?
2. In addition to serving as source designators, (*see* Chapter One), trademarks also serve as indicia of quality. What impact, if any, would compulsory licenses have upon this "reputational" value of a trademark? How would you structure a compulsory licensing program to protect this reputational value?

11

Extraterritoriality and the "Border" Problem

Efforts to protect intellectual property on an international scale have included increasing attempts by national courts to exercise jurisdiction over the acts of foreign infringers through the extraterritorial application of national intellectual property laws. The extension of one nation's laws to acts occurring inside another country's borders raises concerns about sovereign power, comity and the conflict between the competing interests of the intellectual property owner and unauthorized user. The excerpts in this Chapter explore the concerns raised by such extraterritorial application of national laws. For an examination of the enforcement problems posed by the transborder flow of information, including the border problem raised by satellite broadcasts, *see* Chapter Thirteen.

A. The Territorial Nature of Intellectual Property Rights[1]

Regardless of the philosophical basis for justifying the protection of intellectual property rights, the classical view of such rights maintained that the authority of a country granting protection extended only to its borders. This "territorial" view of intellectual property had a two-fold impact on the market for goods and services embodying or utilizing one of the recognized forms of intellectual property.

First, and perhaps most significantly, the territorial view of intellectual property effectively limits an intellectual property owner's ability to protect his work to the territorial boundaries of those countries which recognize that such work is protectable. There is no such legal device as a worldwide patent, a worldwide copyright, a worldwide trademark or a worldwide trade secret. If an inventor has been granted a patent under US law, she has no absolute right to control the use of her patented invention outside the borders of the United States. To the contrary, any right she may have to protect her invention in a foreign country will depend upon whether the domestic laws of that country recognize that her invention is subject to patent protection and upon the scope of rights the domestic laws grant to a patent owner.

Similarly, a US trademark owner cannot restrict the use of his mark by others outside of the United States unless his mark qualifies for protection under the domestic laws of the country in question. Often such protection will depend upon the type of mark for which protection is sought. For example, some countries do not extend protection to service marks or to specific types of marks such as trade dress or sounds. Protection in foreign countries will further depend upon whether the US trademark owner has complied with requirements the foreign country imposes for granting trademark protection. These requirements may well include registration and in-country use.

In addition to defining the scope of protection afforded intellectual property, the territorial view of intellectual property rights has a direct impact on the development of trade. Because the authority of a country granting intellectual property protection can only extend to its borders, differences in the scope of rights granted under national (domestic) laws tends to define the market for such goods. Generally, authors and inventors pre-

---

[1] Written for this Anthology by Doris Estelle Long.

fer to market in countries which actively protect their rights to control the use of their works and inventions. By contrast, manufacturers and distributors of protected works and inventions may prefer to operate in countries which permit free-riding. Such free-riding arguably lowers their acquisition costs for the distributed products and may result in higher profits. These conflicting interests are often at the heart of the conflict between developed (intellectual property rich) countries and less-developed (intellectual property poor) countries accused of operating as havens for pirating and counterfeiting operations.

In view of the territorial limitation on rights, where a domestic intellectual property owner is unable to obtain protection abroad,[2] the owner may urge its government to seek to establish international protection norms under multinational treaty regimes.[3] Alternatively, the owner may urge its courts to extend domestic laws to acts occurring beyond the nation's boundaries. Such extraterritorial application is unquestionably at odds with the territorial view of intellectual property rights.

B. Universality Versus Territoriality[4]

The "universality" view of trademarks assumes that a trademark knows no territorial bounds and that an owner of a trademark possesses the trademark's rights to the exclusion of everyone else in the world. Justice Brennan described the universality approach as one in which "trademarks do not confer on the owner property interests or monopoly power over intrabrand competition. Rather, they merely protect the public from deception by indicating "the origin of the goods they mark."[5]

The corollary that developed in conjunction with the universality doctrine is the theory of "trademark exhaustion." Under the doctrine of trademark exhaustion, trademark owners lose control over their trademarked goods once the goods are released into the stream of commerce. Consequently, parallel importers and others along the chain of commerce may then display, advertise, and resell the trademarked goods.

The modern view of trademarks is that of "territoriality." Territoriality is the ability of a company to purchase the rights to a trademark within a specific territory. The territoriality theory of trademarks dates from Justice Holmes's opinion in the first major gray market case, *A. Bourjois & Co., Inc. v Katzel*.[6] Contemporary courts have indicated that the territoriality approach "maintains that the source and scope of trademark protection arise from the law of a particular sovereign state, and thus that it is meaningless to discuss 'genuineness' of a trademark in the abstract."[7] Another court described the function of a trademark under the territoriality theory as not necessarily to specify the origin or manufacture of a good (although it may incidentally do that), but rather to symbolize the domestic goodwill of the domestic markholder so that the consuming public may rely with an expectation of consistency on the domestic reputation earned for the mark by its owner.

Because the Paris Convention for the Protection of Industrial Property recognizes that trademark rights are territorial, territoriality seems to be the accepted modern view of trademarks.

C. Comity[8]

The doctrine of comity is not a rule of public international law, but the term char-

---

[2] Such inability may arise from the owner's legal or factual inability to comply with a foreign country's requirements for obtaining protection for the intellectual property in question or from the absence of laws in the foreign country that grant protection against the acts for which relief is sought.

[3] For a discussion of the relation of the concept of the territorial nature of intellectual property to the issues of national treatment, reciprocity and minimum rights under multinational treaty regimes, *see* Chapter Seven.

[4] Shira R. Yashor, *Competing in the Shadowy Gray: Protecting Domestic Trademark Holders from Gray Marketeers Under the Lanham Act*, 59 U. Chi. L. Rev. 1363. Copyright 1992 University of Chicago. Excerpt reprinted with permission.

[5] K Mart, 486 U.S. at 301.

[6] 260 U.S. 689 (1923).

[7] COPIAT, 790 F.2d at 909.

[8] Harold G. Maier, *Extraterritorial Jurisdiction at a Crossroads: An Intersection Between Public and*

acterizes many of those same functional elements that define a system of international legal order. The comity principle was originally developed to explain how a sovereign state, absolutely powerful within its own territory, could give recognition or effect in its courts to another nation's laws without diminishing or denying its own sovereignty. The doctrine is also one of local restraint, limiting the application of sovereign power to extraterritorial events and persons. This second manifestation represents the role played by the doctrine in transnational regulatory cases.

The Dutch scholar, Ulrich Huber, set out to reconcile the fact and theory of national territorial authority with the needs of a developing international trading system in which persons and commerce moved across state lines. Huber summarized his analysis in three now well-known axioms:

> 1. The laws of every sovereign authority have force within the boundaries of its state, and bind all subject to it, but not beyond.
> 2. Those are held to be subject to a sovereign authority who are found within its boundaries, whether they be there permanently or temporarily.
> 3. Those who exercise sovereign authority so act from comity, that the laws of every nation having been applied within its own boundaries should retain their effect everywhere so far as they do not prejudice the powers or rights of another state, or its subjects.[9]

These axioms are practically, rather than theoretically, oriented. Taken together, they state that acts of foreign sovereigns should, when appropriate, be given effect within another state's territory and that courts of all nations should indulge a presumption against the extraterritorial impact of law. The third axiom emphasizes the practical necessity for the forum to recognize appropriate foreign rules to facilitate international economic intercourse. Huber wrote:

> Although the laws of one country can have no direct force in another country, yet nothing could be more inconvenient to the commerce and general intercourse of nations than that transactions valid by the law of one place should be rendered of no effect elsewhere owing to a difference in law.[10]

D. Extraterritorial Application of National Laws[11]

Many foreign nations consider it an affront to their national sovereignty when US courts not only determine the legality of activities occurring within their borders, but regulate and enjoin those activities as well. Tension is heightened when these activities are deemed legal and are sanctioned by the foreign nations. A report by the British-North American Committee (consisting of Great Britain, Canada, and the United States) considered the problems of applying "one country's domestic legislation and/or judicial decisions to acts or omissions within the territory of another."[12] The Committee pointed to the United States as the most flagrant abuser, stating that "the extraterritorial application of US anti-trust and regulatory laws taking place in Western Europe,

---

Private International Law, 76 AM. J. INT'L L. 280 (1982). Copyright © 1982 American Society of International Law. Excerpt reprinted with permission.

[9] Davies, *The Influence of Hubeis de Conflictu Legum on English Private International Law*, 18 BRIT. Y. B. INT'L 49, 56–67 (1937).

[10] It has been argued that Huber's theory included the requirement that the forum recognize a customary jus gentium from which private international law principles could be derived. Whether or not he viewed international custom as the authoritative source of private international law rules, it is clear that Huber's basic principles represent a recognition that mutual tolerance and limited claim are essential functional components of a dynamic international economic and political order in a territorially divided world. In this sense, Huber's attitude parallels that found in Section 403, Tentative Draft No. 2, Restatement of Foreign Relations Law (Revised).

[11] Robert Purcell, *Application of the Lanham Act to Extraterritorial Activities: Trend Toward Universality or Imperialism?*, 77 J. PAT. & TRADEMARK OFF. SOC'Y 115. Copyright 1995 Robert Purcell. Excerpt reprinted with permission.

[12] A.H. HERMANN, CONFLICTS OF NATIONAL LAWS IN THE INTERNATIONAL BUSINESS ACTIVITY: ISSUES OF EXTRATERRITORIALITY v. (1982).

Canada, and Australia has been the subject of many diplomatic protests."[13] The report noted that allowing extraterritorial application of domestic laws especially leads to conflict when the public policies of the two nations differ.

There are several harmful effects of the American practice of broadly applying its domestic laws extraterritorially. First, the international business community requires certainty as to which law will govern its practices. Second, fear of and unfamiliarity with US law will impair the free movement of capital and the creation of new business ventures. Third, distrust of US companies will lead to distorted trading patterns as foreign businesses seek out new, more reliable, trading partners. Fourth, because US extraterritorial actions may be mitigated by the enactment of contrary foreign laws, foreign nations will enact business laws merely to "block" US efforts to apply US law extraterritorially. Fifth, unwelcome application of US law creates unfavorable relations between the US and foreign nations, which in turn leads to undesirable and unnecessary political conflicts.

US courts possess the commendable attitude that where there is a wrong, there should be a remedy. What is perceived as a wrong by US cultural and legal standards, however, might not be a wrong under the cultural and legal standards of other nations having a very significant relationship to, and interest in, the dispute. Moreover, even if there is a legal wrong according to the standards of all concerned nations, US courts are exceedingly quick to determine the appropriate remedies according to US laws and to use the power and authority of the US courts to enforce those remedies.

The promotion of both US and foreign political and commercial interests will be best facilitated by US courts' respecting the sovereignty of foreign nations and acknowledging the validity of their right to establish their own laws governing activities within their borders. Such respect and recognition can be maintained in the context of extraterritorial trademark disputes by applying established choice of law principles.

[13] *Id.* at x.

1. The Rise of Multinationals[14]

Visionaries who predicted that there would come a day when national borders (and even national identification) would become anachronisms are now being partially vindicated. Today, multinational corporations share influence with nation states as principle power-brokers on the international stage. Protective legislation, and even political and military borders, are giving way to unified markets and transnational enterprises. Just as isolationist political views were put aside after World War II, similar views must ultimately be put aside in the business realm. Isolationist or strict territorial approach in a developed (or overdeveloped) world can be destabilizing and dangerous. If left unregulated, the rise of the multinational can bring a decline of individual rights and protections.

2. US Applications[15]

We are limiting this review of the extraterritorial application of the Lanham Act to those cases dealing with the propriety of exercising "subject matter" jurisdiction over causes of action which might potentially result in the extraterritorial application of Lanham Act strictures and/or the propriety of granting injunctive relief under the Act which would have extraterritorial application. "Extraterritorial" has been defined as meaning "beyond the boundaries of the United States and its possessions." The cases reviewed have Lanham Act causes of action dealing with both source designation disputes and unfair competition claims. Issues of in personam jurisdiction, *forum non conveniens*, Act of State or other bases on which jurisdiction might be denied or limited or for which the court might otherwise

[14] Jonathan Turley, *When in Rome: Multinational Misconduct and the Presumption against Extraterritoriality*, 84 Nw. U.L. Rev. 598. Copyright 1990 Northwestern University School of Law. Excerpt reprinted with permission.

[15] Doris E. Long, *A Report on the Status of the Extraterritorial Application of the Lanham Act.* Reprinted in Report of the Section of Intellectual Property 1994. Copyright 1994 Doris E. Long. Excerpt reprinted by permission.

elect to refrain or abstain from granting the requested relief.

In our review we have discovered that circuits do *not* apply the same standards in determining whether subject matter jurisdiction exists in cases involving the potential extraterritorial application of the Lanham Act. To the contrary, in the Second Circuit, courts routinely rely upon and are guided by the three factor test established in the seminal decision in *Vanity Fair Mills, Inc. v. T. Eaton Co.*, 234 F.2d 633 (2d Cir.), *cert. denied*, 352 US 871 (1956). These three factors are: (1) whether the defendant's conduct has a substantial effect on US commerce (which includes commerce between the United States and a foreign country); (2) whether the defendant is a citizen of the United States; and (3) whether a conflict exists with trademark rights under foreign law. Although no one factor is necessarily dispositive, courts which apply this three-part test appear largely to uphold the exercise of extraterritorial application of the Lanham Act, particularly where some portion of the activities which contribute to the alleged violation occur within the territorial boundaries of the United States or are directed by someone resident within the United States.

By contrast, the Ninth Circuit has recently adopted a three-part test which does not require a "substantial effect" on US commerce but, at least facially, appears to require a more detailed analysis of the potential conflict between the interests of the United States and the country into which the Lanham Act is sought to be applied. This three-part test, adopted by the Ninth Circuit in *Reebok International Limited v. Marnatech Enterprises, Inc.*, 970 F.2d 552 (9th Cir. 1992), is derived from a seminal antitrust decision in the area—*Timberlane Lumber Co. v. Bank of America National Trust & Savings Ass'n*, 549 F.2d 597 (9th Cir. 1976). The three factors which *Reebok* considered are: (1) whether there is "some effect" on US commerce; (2) whether the effect on commerce is sufficiently great to present a "cognizable injury" to plaintiffs under the Lanham Act; and (3) whether the interests of and links to US foreign commerce are "sufficiently strong" in relation to those of other nations to justify an assertion of extraterritorial authority.

In determining the "strength" of the foreign commerce link, *Reebok*, adopting the reasoning of *Timberlane*, cited seven factors to be considered. They are: (1) the degree of conflict with foreign law or policy; (2) the nationality of the parties and the location of the principal places of business of the applicable parties; (3) whether enforcement could be expected to achieve compliance; (4) the "relative significance" of the effects on the United States as compared with those elsewhere; (5) whether there is an explicit purpose to harm or effect US commerce; (6) whether the adverse impact on US commerce is foreseeable; and (7) the "relative importance" to the violations charged of conduct within the United States as compared with conduct abroad. None of these factors appears to be dispositive. Instead the various factors are balanced to determine where the strongest interest lies.

The Surpreme Court. The only US Supreme Court decision to date to address the issue of the extraterritorial application of the Lanham Act is *Steele v. Bulova Watch Co., Inc.*, 344 US 280 (1952). In *Steele,* plaintiff, a US watch manufacturer, alleged that the defendant, a US citizen residing in Texas, was using plaintiff's US registered BULOVA trademark without authorization on watches assembled and sold in Mexico. The defendant purchased some of the component parts for its watches in the United States. The defendant had also obtained a Mexican registration for the BULOVA mark, however, this registration had been nullified prior to the Supreme Court's issuance of its decision. The lower court found that some of the Mexican assembled watches had "filtered" back into the United States where they were brought in to be repaired.

The Supreme Court upheld the appellate court's determination that the defendant's activities fell within the jurisdictional scope of the Lanham Act. While noting that "the legislation of Congress will not extend beyond the boundaries of the United States unless a contrary legislative intent appears," the Court found such an intent and stressed that Congress has the power to prevent unfair trade practices in foreign commerce by US citizens under the "broad jurisdictional grant" in the Lanham Act. The Court held that the "sweeping reach into all commerce which may lawfully be regulated by

Congress" could properly be interpreted as applying to defendant's activities even though some of the infringing acts were conducted outside the United States. Stressing that the defendant's activities were "part of an unlawful scheme" and that the defendant's unauthorized goods "could well reflect adversely on Bulova Watch Company's trade reputation," the court upheld the right of the district court to issue an injunction with extraterritorial application if such relief were warranted. The court specifically found that the nullification of the Mexican registration avoided any "conflict which might afford the petitioner a pretext that such relief would impugn foreign law."

The Second Circuit Test. In *Vanity Fair Mills, Inc. v. T. Eaton Co.,* 234 F.2d 633 (2d Cir.), *cert. denied,* 352 US 871 (1956), the plaintiff manufactured and sold women's underwear in the United States and Canada under the mark VANITY FAIR. The plaintiff had obtained a US trademark registration for the VANITY FAIR mark, however, its attempt to obtain a Canadian trademark registration was refused due to the Canadian defendant corporation's pre-existing registration for VANITY FAIR. Plaintiff challenged the defendant's use of the VANITY FAIR mark in Canada, in part because of a previous relationship between the parties during which the plaintiff had supplied defendant with its own manufactured goods. Applying the above-described three part test (which it derived from *Steele v. Bulova,* 344 US 280), the court rejected the plaintiff's efforts to obtain relief against the defendant's Canadian activities. The court relied strongly upon the foreign nationality of the defendants as well as the presence of potentially conflicting trademark rights (represented by the Canadian trademark registration owned by the defendants) in rejecting any extraterritorial application, stating: "[W]e do not think that Congress intended that the infringement remedies provided in [section] 32 and elsewhere should be applied to acts committed by a foreign national in his home country under a presumably valid trademark registration in that country."

The Ninth Circuit Test. In *Reebok Int'l Ltd. v. Marnatech Enterprises, Inc.,* 23 U.S.P.Q. 2d 1377 (9th Cir. 1992), the seminal case in the Ninth Circuit, the court adopted the test employed in a case involving the extraterritorial application of US antitrust laws to uphold the district court's exercise of extraterritorial jurisdiction under the Lanham Act. The plaintiffs alleged that defendants sold counterfeit REEBOK shoes in Mexican border towns and that these sales reduced the purchase of "real" Reebok products in both the US and Mexico. The court found that "at the very least" the defendants had organized and directed the manufacture of the counterfeit shoes from the US and that the defendants "knew" that their counterfeit shoes entered the US "with regular frequency." The court further found that the defendants' sales of counterfeit shoes "decreased the sale of genuine REEBOK shoes in Mexico and the United States and directly decreased the value of Reebok's consolidated holdings."

To determine whether the court had subject matter jurisdiction over defendant's foreign activities, the Ninth Circuit applied the three part test first established by it in *Timberlane Lumber Co. v. Bank of America, N.T. & S.A,* 549 F.2d 597 (9th Cir. 1976).

In *Timberlane,* the plaintiff had sought relief under US antitrust laws against a purported conspiracy between the defendant and others located in the US and Honduras to prevent the plaintiff from milling lumber in Honduras and exporting it to the US, thereby giving control of the Honduran lumber export business to a select few that were financed and controlled by the defendant. The district court granted the defendant's motion to dismiss on the grounds, *inter alia,* that defendant had failed to establish any direct or substantial effect on US foreign commerce" from the defendant's activities. In upholding the exercise of extraterritorial jurisdiction the Ninth Circuit established a three part test, requiring an analysis of the following issues: (1) Whether the alleged restraint affected, or was intended to affect, US foreign commerce; (2) Whether such effect was of a type and magnitude so as to be cognizable as a violation of the Sherman Act; and (3) Whether, as a matter of international comity and fairness, the extraterritorial jurisdiction of the US should be asserted to cover such violation.

In analyzing the international comity concerns, the *Timberlane* court established a seven factor test, requiring an analysis and balancing of the following factors: (1) the degree of conflict with foreign law or policy; (2) the nationality of the parties and the location of the principle places of business of the applicable parties; (3) whether enforcement could be expected to achieve compliance; (4) the "relative significance" of the effects on the United States as compared with those elsewhere; (5) whether there is an explicit purpose to harm or effect US commerce; (6) whether the adverse impact on US commerce is foreseeable; and (7) the "relative importance" to the violations charged of conduct within the United States as compared with conduct abroad.

In applying the *Timberlane* test, the court in *Marnatech* found that "the sales of infringing goods in a foreign country may have a sufficient effect on commerce to invoke Lanham Act jurisdiction." The court further found that since the defendant directed the manufacture of counterfeit shoes from the US, knew that such shoes would enter the US on a regular basis, and since, in fact, the sale of counterfeit shoes decreased the sales and value of the Reebok corporation, the defendant's activities affected US commerce and caused an injury to Reebok, cognizable under the Lanham Act.

To determine whether the links with US commerce were strong enough to warrant the exercise of jurisdiction, the court balanced the seven *Timberlane* factors (*see* above) and found that most factors supported the exercise of jurisdiction. The court relied heavily on the US nexus presented by the defendants' activities, including the fact that the defendants, although foreign citizens, had substantial contacts with the US including being resident in the US. The court stressed that defendant's activities were directed towards the US, thus resulting in a "foreseeable" harm to Reebok. Unlike the court in *Vanity Fair*, however, the court in *Marnatech* did not require the plaintiff to demonstrate that the defendant's acts had a substantial impact on US/foreign commerce.

Finally, the court found no conflict with Mexican trademark law or policy since Reebok owned a Mexican trademark registration and both countries had a "common interest in preventing trademark violations and in the protection of any valid Mexican and US trademark registrations owned by Reebok."

The Combined Test. In view of the uneven treatment of comity and commerce issues by the courts in the *Vanity Fair* and *Marnatech* courts, and the lack of clear direction by the Supreme Court, some US courts have developed a modified test which combines both approaches. Thus, for example, in *US Rice, Inc. v. Arkansas Rice Growers Co-Op.*, 701 F.2d 408 (5th Cir. 1983), the court upheld the lower court's exercise of jurisdiction over acts of trademark infringement and unfair competition consummated by an US corporation whose infringing activities *occurred solely in Saudi Arabia*. Both parties were engaged in the sale of rice under a number of brand names in both the US and overseas. Plaintiff marketed its products under a variety of trademarks including ABU BINT and had developed a package trade dress for its rice combining a picture of a woman holding a bowl of rice with the word "rice" in large, oriental style lettering at the top of the package and a red, yellow and black color combination. The defendant marketed a rice product using the mark "Bint al-Arab" and the same colors and trade dress as plaintiff's brand of rice. The court specifically found that none of the defendant's rice products had been imported into, or otherwise entered, the United States.

After examining various decisions by other circuits concerning the extraterritorial reach of the Lanham Act, including *Steele v. Bulova*, 344 US 280; *Vanity Fair*, 234 F.2d 633 and *Wells Fargo & Co.*, 194 U.S.P.Q. 10, the court elected to follow a combined test which roughly followed the three factors discussed in *Vanity Fair*. However, the court declined to adopt the *Vanity Fair* requirement that only those acts which have a substantial impact on commerce are sufficient to support the exercise of extraterritorial jurisdiction. Noting that the requirement of substantial similarity "apparently lies in the effort to distinguish between intrastate commerce, which Congress may not regulate as such, and interstate commerce, which it can control", the court indicated that "it may be unwise blindly to apply the factor in the area of foreign commerce over which Congress has exclusive authority." 218 U.S.P.Q. at 493 n.8 (citing *Timberland Lumber Co. v. Bank of America, N.T. & S.A.*, 549 F.2d 597, 612 (9th Cir. 1976)).

Relying on this relaxed effects standard,

the court held that the defendant's sales in Saudi Arabia diverted sales from the plaintiff and therefore had a sufficient impact on "commerce regulated by Congress" to permit the exercise of jurisdiction. The court further found that the exercise of jurisdiction would not conflict with Saudi Arabian laws, even though the defendant had a pending application for registration of its mark in Saudi Arabia. The court stated, "Absent a determination by a Saudi court that the defendant has a legal right to use its marks and that those marks do not infringe [the plaintiff's marks], we are unable to conclude that it would be an affront to Saudi sovereignty or law if we affirm the district court's injunction prohibiting the defendant from injuring the plaintiff's Saudi Arabian commerce conducted from the United States."

The presence of [the] differing tests [described above for the extraterritorial application of US law to foreign conduct] has the potential to lead to inconsistent results. In particular, while the Second Circuit still requires that any impact on foreign commerce be "substantial," the Ninth Circuit and the Fifth Circuit, at least facially, do *not* require "substantiality." Furthermore, conflicts with foreign laws are not generally perceived by the courts to exist unless there is a formal proceeding in the foreign country and that proceeding is designed to directly decide the trademark issues before the US court.

Because of the increasing importance of the issue, the question of the extraterritorial impact of the Lanham Act should not be subject to the present uncertainty that exists under current law. The conflict between the circuits regarding the degree of impact on US commerce required to permit the extraterritorial application of the Lanham Act should be resolved. Beyond simply resolving the basic question of whether "some impact" or a "substantial impact" on US foreign commerce is required prior to the exercise of extraterritorial jurisdiction, the courts should develop a consist, predictable test which the parties can apply in determining whether their actions contain a sufficient impact on US commerce to subject them to extraterritorial relief under the Lanham Act.

In addition to developing a more useful test for determining the requisite level of impact on US commerce, courts should further include within their analysis a test which is both predictable and appropriately balances the international comity concerns which naturally arise in a situation where courts are considering the extraterritorial application of US laws. Although the seven-factor *Timberlane* test for developing the "strength" of the international foreign commerce connection is a positive first step that test is cumbersome and may lead to inconsistent treatment of a foreign country's concerns regarding acts committed within its borders.

Given the importance of these issues, further study [should] be undertaken of the matter, potentially with the goal of developing a workable framework for the courts to consider using in this matter. Such study should include consideration of the extent to which legislation may be desired or required to correct the problems highlighted in this report.

QUESTIONS AND COMMENTS FOR YOUR CONSIDERATION

Section 402 of the Third Restatement on Foreign Relations Law provides:

Subject to Section 403, a state has jurisdiction to prescribe law with respect to:

(1) (a) conduct that, wholly or in substantial part, takes place within its territory;

(b) the status of persons, or interests in things, present within its territory;

(c) conduct outside its territory that has or is intended to have substantial effect within its territory;

(2) the activities, interests, status or relations of its nationals outside as well as within its territory; and

(3) certain conduct outside its territory by persons not its nationals that is directed against the security of the state or against a limited class of other state interests.

Section 403 of the Third Restatement on Foreign Relations Law provides:

(1) Even when one of the bases for jurisdiction under Section 402 is present, a state may not exercise jurisdiction to prescribe law with respect to a person or activity having connections with another state when the exercise of such jurisdiction is unreasonable.
(2) Whether exercise of jurisdiction over a person or activity is unreasonable is determined by evaluating all relevant factors, including, where appropriate:
(a) the link of the activity to the territory of the regulating state, *i.e.*, the extent to which the activity takes place within the territory, or has substantial, direct, and foreseeable effect upon or in the territory;
(b) the connections, such as nationality, residence, or economic activity, between the regulating state and the person principally responsible for the activity to be regulated, or between that state and those whom the regulation is designed to protect;
(c) the character of the activity to be regulated, the importance of regulation to the regulating state, the extent of which other states regulated such activities, and the degree to which the desirability of such regulation is generally accepted;
(d) the existence of justified expectations that might be protected or hurt by the regulation;
(e) the importance of the regulation to the international political, legal or economic system;
(f) the extent to which the regulation is consistent with the traditions of the international system;
(g) the extent to which another state may have an interest in regulating activity; and
(h) the likelihood of conflict with regulation by another state.
(3) When it would not be unreasonable for each of two states to exercise jurisdiction over a person or activity, but the prescriptions by the two states are in conflict, each state has an obligation to evaluate its own as well as the other state's interest in exercising jurisdiction, in light of all the relevant factors in Subsection (2); a state should defer to the other state if that state's interest is clearly greater.

1. Are the factors set forth in these sections of the Restatement sufficiently determinate and comprehensive as to provide a basis for judges in US courts to decide whether foreign conduct should be brought within their jurisdictional reach?

2. Are there additional factors that courts should consider in extending intellectual property laws to the conduct of foreign nationals abroad? What impact does the territorial nature of trademark rights (*see* Section 11A of this chapter) have on your response? Would the famous nature of the mark (*see* Chapter Nine) change your response?

3. Balancing Competing Concerns[16]

Under the original formalist doctrine of sovereignty, a territory was presumed to have the sole authority to regulate its citizens as well as activities within its borders. Extraterritorial jurisdiction or the right of a government to regulate activities and people outside of its borders was forbidden under this theory.

However, the problem with this formalist approach is that it ignores the fact that citizens inhabiting one territory and activities occurring solely within it sometimes have significant effects outside that territory. For example, one territory's decision to forego antitrust legislation might have a substantial deleterious effect on those countries that have adopted antitrust statutes and compete with the non-legislating country. Yet any attempt by those countries to extend antitrust statutes to citizens of the first territory would violate the presumption that citizens are regulated by their home territory's laws. The formalist approach, then, cannot be rationally applied to the modern international trade environment in which the market is continuously affected and in fact shaped by the laws of various countries.

The more modern approach to the limits of the application of one country's laws to citizens of another is embodied in the extraterritorial jurisdiction provisions of the Restatement (Third) of Foreign Relations Law. The Restatement, like the formalist model, bases its extraterritoriality doctrine on nationality (jurisdiction over citizens) and territoriality (jurisdiction over activities within the territory). Yet, unlike the earlier model, the Restatement recognizes the potential effects of domestic laws on the international market and adopts an approach that essentially balances the rights of the countries interested in regulating the activity.

With specific regard to jurisdictional issues, the Restatement sets forth three types of jurisdiction in international disputes: (1) jurisdiction to adjudicate, or the power of a country to subject others to its courts or administrative agencies; (2) jurisdiction to enforce, or the power of a country to compel others to comply with its laws; and (3) prescriptive jurisdiction, which is the power of a country to "make its law applicable to the activities, relations, or status of persons, or the interest of persons in things, whether by legislation, by executive act or order, by administrative rule or regulation, or by determination of a court."

The Restatement, which is less extreme than the formalist sovereignty doctrine, establishes a presumption that prescriptive jurisdiction is unlawful unless certain requirements are met. Sections 402 and 403 set out the requirements for permissible exercises of prescriptive jurisdiction. Section 402 grants territorial jurisdiction over conduct or persons in four different situations: (1) over acts occurring in or people present within the territory, (2) over its nationals inside or outside of its borders, (3) over conduct by any person that affects national security or "a limited class of state interests," and (4) "conduct outside a territory that has or is intended to have substantial effect within its territory."

The provisions of Section 402 are subject to Section 403, which places a reasonableness limit on prescriptive jurisdiction. Under Section 403(1), a state is prohibited from exercising jurisdiction unless it does so reasonably, even if the requirements of Section 402 are met. Section 403(2) presents a nonexclusive list of eight factors that affect reasonableness, which includes:

> a) the link of the activity to territory of the regulating state . . .[;]
>
> b) the connections, such as nationality, residence or economic activity, between the regulating state and . . . those whom the regulation is designed to protect;
>
> c) the character of the activity to be regulated, the importance of regulation to the regulating state, the extent to which other states regulate such activities, and the degree to which the desirability of such regulation is generally accepted;
>
> d) the existence of justified expecta-

---

[16] Chris Shore, *The Thai Copyright Case and Possible Limitations of Extraterritorial Jurisdiction in Actions Taken Under Section 301 of the Trade Act of 1974*, 23 Law & Pol'y Int'l Bus. 725. Copyright 1992 Law & Policy in International Business. Excerpt reprinted with permission.

tions that might be protected or hurt by the regulation;
e) the importance of the regulation to the international political, legal, or economic system;
f) the extent to which the regulation is consistent with the traditions of the international legal system;
h) the likelihood of conflict with regulation by another state.

It is important to note here that the jurisdictional requirements of Sections 402 and 403, aimed primarily at territorial actions exercised through the judicial system, also apply to the activities of government agencies. This is completely consistent with the principles of the Restatement, which does not concern itself with formal distinctions about which governmental official is exercising power over another territory, but with why and how that power is exercised.

Of the two prongs of the Restatement test, the effects prong is by far the more difficult to quantify because of the vagueness of the term "substantial." While the reasonableness prong, on its face, calls for and incorporates "soft" information that is very fact specific, the effects prong, on its face, implies that there might be a certain figure that serves as a cutoff as to the substantiality of an act. Courts that have construed the effects prong in limiting their own jurisdiction have considered a wide variety of effects that might be substantial under the Restatement. Factors considered critical in all the cases surveyed are that (1) the effects felt in the United States must be a direct consequence of the government's activity, (2) the effect must in some way injure the United States, and (3) the activity must interfere with legitimate expectations held in the US market. In short, the Restatement prohibits asserting prescriptive jurisdiction unless there are direct, injurious effects felt in the country that wishes to assert it.

On December 21, 1990 the Office of the US Trade Representative (USTR), pursuant to 19 U.S.C. §2412(a), announced that it was beginning an investigation of the Thai government's "policies and practices with respect to the enforcement of copyright." The petition alleged that the Thai government failed to provide "adequate and effective" protection of intellectual property rights and denied the petitioners "fair and equitable" opportunities to market products in Thailand, thus constructively prohibiting them from establishing distribution centers for their exports. Unlike the majority of piracy industries in Southeast Asia at the time the USTR initiated the Thai case, the Thai piracy industry had established sophisticated commercial organizations with state of the art technology and immense production capabilities. For example, the petitioners alleged that the pirate recording industry, which was by far the largest of the piracy groups, was dominated by five major producers who had the capacity to produce 90 million of the industry's 150 million units per year. Perhaps more troubling to the petitioners was the flagrancy of the pirates' daily operations. The audio pirates openly advertised on the radio. In fact, some owned a share of legitimate recording companies and newspapers and used those companies for legitimate activities during the day and piratical activities at night. There were allegations that the pirates resorted to violence and bribery and that the major producers mentioned above had a special fund for fines.

The piracy situation presented a particular dilemma for the Thai government. The government had a great interest in protecting an industry that by most accounts provided jobs in manufacturing, as well as in more than 12,500 retail shops. However, imposition of Section 301 sanctions by the United States would have a serious effect on the Thai export market. To make the decision even more difficult, the US demanded that the Thai government not only shut down a profitable sector of its economy, but also absorb the costs of adhering to the petitioners' demands for increased law enforcement, judicial education, and modification of rules of evidence.

It is difficult to legitimate any USTR action under Section 301 in the Thai case. The failure of the Thai government to provide mechanisms to hold the piracy of copyrights to an "acceptable" level did not lead directly to the injury claimed by the petitioners. Intervening between the government and the harm to US manufacturers was the criminal activity of Thai citizens. The petitioners' brief never alleged that the Thai government in any way sanctioned the pirates activities. In fact, there is substantial evidence in the brief that points to Thailand's recent efforts to eradicate the piracy problem. Penalizing the government and the Thai people for the activity of pirates who have the resources to violate the law and for the enforcement failure of government that lacks necessary resources is very different from the situation when a government actively supports or sanctions criminal activity that has deleterious effects within the United States.

In rebuttal, it might be pointed out that the activity was foreseeable and that Thailand should have taken steps to contain the effects of piracy. That argument falters, though, given the government's lack of adequate resources to combat the problem. Even if the Thai government were to be held responsible for the criminal activity of its citizens in international disputes, there is still a serious question as to whether the US manufacturers felt any real effects of the piratical activity. As discussed earlier, there apparently never has been a market for US copyrights in Thailand with which the pirates have somehow interfered.

The effects that US manufacturers felt, then, are not lost sales, like the loss of consumer protection that accompanied the lack of anti-fraud provisions in the securities example above, but rather the failure to capture a potential market for copyrighted material. The Restatement test is fashioned to protect the legitimate expectation of one country to protect its citizens from foreign activity and to create an enclave in which a country can be certain that it controls activity. Asserting jurisdiction in this instance turns this policy on its head—the USTR is not protecting US citizens from the effects of Thai piracy, but is using Section 301 to make Thailand conform to US copyright norms. Under the Restatement, there is a substantial difference between the exercising of jurisdiction to protect a market from substantial effects of a foreign market and using jurisdiction to eradicate those effects both within and outside of that market. In compelling Thailand to reform its enforcement mechanisms, the USTR did not only remedy the effects of the piracy felt within the United States, but also eradicated the source of those effects. The result is that the US producers are provided with a new market that is "unnaturally" insured against piratical activity.

Whereas the effects prong takes into account the effects of domestic activity in the international market, the reasonableness prong balances the detrimental effects of an activity in one territory against the perceived need to maintain comity in international relations.

Evaluating the state of piracy in Thailand in the 1980s, one can hardly assert that the piracy problem threatened the "international political, legal, or economic system." That claim might be justified if the pirated materials were leaving Thailand and interfering with legitimate copyright sales. If it were cheaper to purchase pirated goods in Europe, for example, the United States might lose its European market, frustrating a well-developed expectation of profits. But there has never been a market for US copyrights in Thailand and few, if any, pirated goods have left Thailand to compete with US exports. The Thai government's demonstrated desire to work toward an acceptable solution is also a factor in the reasonableness analysis. One may conclude, then, that attempts to control this market through prescriptive jurisdiction push the limits of reasonableness.

Furthermore, the way that the United States resolved this problem is arguably unreasonable under the Restatement. While it is clear that the United States had an interest in making a significant effort to get Thailand to provide intellectual property protection, it is less clear that the United States should have resorted to Section 301 sanctions to bring about that solution. To begin with, in balancing the potential harm to the United States and to Thailand, it is clear that Thailand stood to lose far more than the United States stood to gain. There is also a question as to the reasonableness of the types of Thai government activity that the petitioners asked the USTR to address in their negotiations with Thailand. Generally, Section 301 sanctions have been used to bring about changes in foreign trade policy. In this case, however, the petitioners asked the USTR, in effect, to regulate perhaps the most fundamental aspects of sovereignty, such as the right to establish criminal laws and administrative procedures. Making the adoption of Western criminal procedure a precondition for trade with the United States seems to be a clear abuse of Section

403 of the Restatement because it ignores all principles of comity.

Under the Restatement, a country may exercise jurisdiction if the effects of the domestic action are substantial in the regulating country. The assumption behind the Restatement model, then, is that it is possible to determine which regulations cause which effects. The causation assumption, however, has two problems—an attribution component and a primary cause component, both of which undermine the relative determinacy of the Restatement test. The less serious of the two problems, attribution, arises because of the difficulty in determining whose domestic activity is creating the detrimental effects.

The other problem, which centers on the determination of what is actually causing the effect, is more serious. It is impossible in the Thai case to determine objectively which domestic policy actually caused the "injury" to the US producers. At first glance, it appears that only the Thai government had implemented, or in this case not implemented, a domestic policy. But, if the petitioners had not had a US statutory entitlement to both copyright protection and protection from the USTR, the Thai policy would have had no "effects" within the United States: the pirates would only be using material from the public domain to create a product.

Which policy was the primary cause of the injury? The Restatement cannot answer that question, because it assumes that there is a state of non-regulation that exists before a domestic policy has its effects on the international market. This principle of a level playing field, or a free market, has been repeatedly criticized for failing to account for entitlements that pre-exist the market. It is impossible to make objective determinations about which regulation caused which effects, and therefore the "substantial effects" prong of the Restatement test, despite its putative objectivity, depends on the existence of a rights "baseline" created through a subjective, fundamentally political evaluation of an international situation.

Furthermore, the "reasonableness" prong is no less political. The reasonableness inquiry involves the comparison of the regulating country's activity with past activities of other countries. The comparison, though, is basically a balancing of preferences for historical practice and the development of new regulatory systems. Without a more objective legal basis, comparison of the Thai situation with other countries regulating activities says nothing about why the United States should or should not be regulating.

With the current expansion of the global market to encompass countries that were once isolated in non-market economies, the effects of a particular domestic policy are more likely to be felt outside those countries' borders, and the United States will have a greater interest in influencing the future of those economies. The USTR needs to be able to act aggressively in these situations. Without some jurisdictional limits, however, what is currently a very effective enforcement procedure could become an enforcement nightmare, in which the international stature of the United States will be subject to the whim of those US interest groups who have the influence to push a Section 301 petition through to completion.

QUESTIONS AND COMMENTS FOR YOUR CONSIDERATION

1. Which standard of conduct do you use to determine whether the extension of jurisdiction to acts occurring outside a given country is reasonable, the foreign country's or your own?

2. For a more detailed discussion of the use of Special 301, *see* Chapter Nine.

3. During the Uruguay Round negotiations, some countries strongly opposed the establishment of international intellectual property law standards that would control the internal use of intellectual property. These countries distinguished between border controls prohibiting the importation of infringing goods through

customs regulations (which they believed were the proper focus of international agreement), and what happens to the goods once they are within a country's domestic jurisdiction. Is there a reasoned basis for distinguishing between the two methods of enforcing intellectual property rights on an international level?

4. Can the use of border controls alone resolve the problem of counterfeit goods? Of pirated goods?

12

Harmonization

International efforts at "harmonizing" the law regarding the protection of intellectual property have developed along two major fronts. The first is the development of multinational procedural and substantive norms through the establishment of bilateral and multinational treaties. The second is the harmonization of national laws where "national treatment" is considered the primary means for enforcing foreign intellectual property rights. Each harmonization effort raises issues regarding the perceived loss of control by the national government over its internal borders and over its national destiny (particularly in the area of industrial and economic development). Even when harmonization is perceived as desirable, the question remains of which model standards to adopt. The excerpts in this Chapter explore the question of harmonization of national laws under the "second front." (For an exploration of "harmonization" through the establishment of international treaty regimes, *see* Chapter Seven). The Chapter explores particular efforts at national harmonization, including patent harmonization efforts and the EEC's efforts at harmonizing member countries' trademark laws. We end with case studies of the conflict over harmonization arising from the "patent wars" between Japan and the United States and the treatment of intellectual property rights in China. For an examination of attempts to harmonize software protection, *see* Chapter Thirteen.

A. Harmonization and the EEC[1]

The Treaty of Rome, which established the Common Market, had as its primary goal the elimination of trade barriers which impede the free movement of goods among member nations. The Council of Ministers, however, recognized that such barrier elimination could not be attained completely so long as national intellectual property rights among the member states substantially differed in scope and methods of protection. In order to reduce these differences, the Council of Ministers has sought to approximate national laws governing intellectual property within the European Community through the promulgation of various directives and regulations aimed at reaching an approximation of member laws. The first major intellectual property harmonization directive was issued in December 1988 and was aimed at approximating the laws of the member states relating to trademarks.[2] The preamble expressly acknowledged that national trademark laws "contain disparities which may impede the free movement of goods and freedom to provide services and may distort competition within the common market" and that "it is therefore necessary, in view of the establishment and functioning of the internal market, to approximate the laws of member states." The Directive did not seek a "full scale approximation" of the trademark laws, but limited itself to "those national provisions of law which most directly affect the functioning of the internal market."

Despite the goal of the Directive of approximating (or harmonizing) national

---

[1] Written for this Anthology by Doris Estelle Long. Copyright 1996 Doris E. Long.

[2] First Council Directive to Approximate the Laws of the Member States Relating to Trade Marks, Dec. 21, 1988, O.J. Eur. Comm. (No. C 104) (1989).

trademark laws, it did not require member states to enact identical legislation. For example, although the Trademark Harmonizing Directive defines a trademark as consisting "of any sign capable of being represented graphically . . . provided that such signs are capable of distinguishing the goods or services of one undertaking from those of other undertakings," it contains no express requirement that all such signs be registered. Thus, Member A may protect words and symbols but not numerals, while Member B may protect words, symbols and numerals. Despite the difference in the scope of signs protected, neither member's laws would violate the Directive. Consequently, "an approximation" (or its often used alternative "harmonization") does not require Member States to enact identical legislation. It simply requires them to reduce identified discrepancies in applicable laws.

1. Copyright Harmonization[3]

If harmonization is to achieve the establishment and the functioning of the internal market, it remains to be decided whether to harmonize upwards (by increasing the protection to the highest level of any national regime) or downwards (by decreasing the protection to the lowest level of any national regime) or in between. Thus, even if harmonization can be neutral if it only pursues an internal market, the substance of the harmonization is never totally neutral.

The Commission adopted at the end of 1990 its working program for 1991/92 entitled "Follow-up to the Green paper," and clarified its intentions by explaining that it wished, in principle, to reinforce the protection of copyright and neighboring rights. It stated:

> 1.3. Copyright provides a basis for intellectual creation. To protect copyright is to ensure that creativity is sustained and developed, in the interest of authors, the cultural industries, consumers, and ultimately of society as a whole. Neighboring rights underpin these objectives in various ways, particularly by guaranteeing a proper return to performing artists and those who invest in the provision of these cultural goods and services.
>
> 1.4. The Commission will be guided by two principles here: firstly, the protection of copyright and neighboring rights must be strengthened; secondly, the approach taken must as far as possible be a comprehensive one.
>
> 1.5. The changes which technological advance has brought make it urgently necessary to strengthen the protection of copyright and neighboring rights, if an important economic and cultural asset in the Member States is not to be lost.[4]

The Treaty of Maastricht on European Union, which was signed in February 1992, permits a further legal argument to be found in Article 128(4). Indeed, it provides that: "The Community shall take cultural aspects into account in its action under other provisions of this Treaty."[5] It can therefore be argued that after the entry into force of the Maastricht Treaty, any harmonization initiative cannot remain neutral as far as cultural aspects are concerned.

It is therefore my opinion that any harmonization which would choose the lower level of protection of copyright or neighboring rights as its aim would risk to jeopardize this specific cultural requirement and, in particular, would endanger artistic and literary creation—especially in the audiovisual sector—in a way which would be contrary to the specific legal requirement of the new Article 128(4) of the Maastricht Treaty.

Internal harmonization of copyright and neighboring rights in the European Community will therefore have to aim in principle at increasing protection. The present harmonization program of the European Commission has already taken this approach. Such

---

[3] Jean-François Verstrynge, *The Spring 1993 Horace S. Manages Lecture—The European Commission's Direction On Copyright and Neighboring Rights*. Copyright 1993 Jean-François Verstrynge. Excerpt reprinted with permission.

[4] Follow-up to the Green Paper: Working Programme of the Commission in the Field of Copyright and Neighboring Rights, COM (90) 584 final at 2–3.

[5] Treaty on European Union, Feb. 7, 1992, 31 ILM 253, 279.

a result has already been achieved in the software directive. Further, the Commission proposed an exclusive rental right, giving better protection than a mere remuneration right for rental (as existed in Germany and must now be changed to implement the new Council directive of 1992 correctly). Another example lies in the proposal to harmonize duration upwards at 70 years post mortem auctoris for copyright, and 50 years after publication for neighboring rights. These, indeed, are the longer terms of protection which exist in the Community.

These internal harmonization objectives have, moreover, some relevance beyond the borders of the twelve Member States of the European Community. Indeed, should the high level of protection of the 1992 program of harmonization be extended to European Free Trade Association countries through Protocol 28 of the EEA Agreement or to some Eastern European countries (as was for example agreed in the interim agreement with Poland, Czechoslovakia and Hungary which entered into force in March 1992), then it must be clear that these countries would also follow the search of the Community for a higher level of copyright and neighboring right protection. This would then result in a "European platform" covering not only the European Community but a whole number of other European countries, North and East of the European Community.

This is particularly true for the EFTA countries which under Article 1(2) of the presently signed text of Protocol 28 of the EEA Agreement would be required to "adjust their legislation on intellectual property so as to make it compatible with the principles of free circulation of goods and services and with the level of protection of intellectual property attained in Community law, including the level of enforcement of those rights" as well as to take over any existing or future *acquis communautaire*. Such extension could, of course, also result from a future enlargement of the European Community to some of these countries which have already applied for membership, such as Austria, Sweden, Finland or Norway.

It remains to be seen whether a similar approach will be emerge from ongoing negotiations with Romania, Bulgaria, Albania, Turkey, Cyprus, Malta, Israel, Morocco, etc., or further east, with Russia and other countries of the former Soviet Union.

National Treatment is the rule in the Berne and Rome Conventions. Reciprocity is the exception. One may ask why this is so, since in most international negotiations—and in particular in trade negotiations—reciprocity is the governing principle. In international trade, countries do indeed make concessions to one another only if they obtain some other trade concession in return.

Some exceptions do, however, exist from this rule of national treatment. For the Berne Convention, some rights such as *droit de suite*, some features of protection, such as the length of the term, and some aspects of geographic scope, such as protection for works published in non-Berne Party Countries, remain, under certain circumstances, subject to reciprocity. In the Rome Convention, a similar situation exists as regards Articles 12 and 16 for the remuneration right for the broadcasting of music, for example.

In the Continental system the essential rightholder is the physical person who creates the work. He is therefore considered the author. They think of a copyrighted work as the expression of the author's personality. Copyright is essentially a cultural right. Other physical or moral persons which intervene, such as performing artists, phonogram producers, or producers of audiovisual works, are given neighboring rights. The principal reason, as the proponents of this system insist, is that it is necessary to guarantee the expression of national, regional or local cultural identity. They cannot reconcile themselves with seeing cultural products or service as often the subject of mere economic market forces. This was expressed by President Delors when he said: "Il faut nous donner le droit d'exister."[6] The promoters of this system therefore insist on inalienable moral rights attached to the person of the author and sometimes even to performing artists. The emphasis is on creation.

In the Anglo-Saxon system, the emphasis is on the exploitation of the work, and hence on the rights of producers. They see copyright as an exclusive economic right which compensates the financial investment of the producer. If the producer cannot control

---

[6] "We must be given the right to exist."

exclusively the exploitation of the work because the physical authors or performing artists would keep their right to object, he risks losing his investment. They often make the producer an author, or transfer all rights to him automatically, such as in the "works for hire" system. They generally oppose moral rights. They fear that these will thwart exploitation. The emphasis is on exploitation.

Logic, however, leads to seeing that these systems, often opposed, are not mutually exclusive. They can be seen as complementary rather than opposed. In a sense, they can be added to each other. I believe that no creator or artist can fully survive and have his creations known and equitably remunerated without producers. On the other hand, producers could not operate without creators and performing artists. Why then not combine both systems?

In doing so, it is essential that neither creators nor producers would be given total control over each other—that the overall regime would be built in such a way that they both would always be incited to agree with each other. Neither creation nor exploitation should be pushed to the detriment of the other.

In Europe, many believe that Community harmonization would eliminate cultural identity. I fundamentally disagree with such a view. Substance of the creation and exploitation of the creation have to be distinguished. It cannot be accepted that a purely Sicilian work, for instance, could not be appreciated, let's say, in Scotland, nor a Scottish work in Sicily. Harmonizing the conditions for economic exploitation does not prevent a Sicilian or Scottish work from being typically Sicilian or Scottish. It only gives both works a better and larger market so that both Sicilian and Scottish authors or artists can continue to create typically Sicilian or Scottish works. Producers who organize exploitation on the larger European market are indispensable in this operation.

A first feature of a common regime would therefore be to give authors and artists, on the one hand, and producers, on the other, equal and parallel exclusive rights so that none of them could really operate without the other. This would lead to the maintenance of authors as the only rightholders under copyright, and artists and producers as the only rightholders under neighboring rights. On the other hand, it demands that neighboring rights should be of an exclusive nature, and not mere remuneration rights.

A second feature can then be added. Indeed, having done so, a system of interaction between these categories of different rightholders has to be organized. I believe that the presumption of transfer of all economic rights should exist whenever each of these rights has been contracted against an equitable remuneration. Accordingly, once the producer has acquired the rights from authors and artists, he should possess all exclusive rights necessary for the most efficient exploitation in the interest of all rightholders. Basically, then, their relationship can be left to contractual freedom, once the legislative system includes this rebuttable presumption.

However, such a system presupposes that an equitable level of remuneration will result from its operation. If some rightholders are not strong enough to negotiate adequately, the required balance will not be reached. This leads to the third feature of the possible system, namely that contractual freedom should be controlled if the required result is not obtained. This may lead to the inclusion of collective rights societies to represent the different categories of rightholders. Their inclusion could be made compulsory, or incited, as in the system of extended collective agreements. But if their intervention does not lead to the required balance, a rule of equitable remuneration would be required.

These three features taken together should, in my opinion, lead to the proper balance between rightholders. They are indispensable for the bridging of the Continental and Anglo-Saxon systems. They allow for a combination of promotion of cultural identity on the one hand and most efficient exploitation on the other. This approach underlies the recently adopted Rental Directive of the European Community, as regards both the rental right and neighboring rights.

I also believe that the introduction of such a system would take much of the heat out of the moral rights debate. Moral rights in the version of Article 6bis of the Berne Convention should exist and even be inalienable, but they should not be confused with the economic adaptation and transformation rights of Article 12 of this Convention, which should remain transferable. Once this is accepted, and a proper bridge between the two systems is put in place, my belief is that the moral rights issue will fade away. Indeed, are there any practical cases in which authors, equitably remunerated, would want to block economic exploitation of their works by the producers? On the other hand, which producers would want to exploit works when it can be said that they have distorted the creation?

QUESTIONS AND COMMENTS FOR YOUR CONSIDERATION

1. Whose law should be utilized in determining the standard against which harmonization should be measured? Is selecting the highest level of protection always desirable? What factors would you consider in selecting the level of protection to use?

2. Does harmonization mean the same as "identity" of law? If not, how useful is harmonization in assuring uniform protection of intellectual property rights throughout the EC?

3. What practical effect, if any, do efforts at harmonization have upon the establishment of international protection standards under multinational treaties?

4. What effect does EC harmonization have on other non-member countries' laws?

a. Rental Rights[7]

Under Directive [92/10, adopted on November 19, 1992][8] authors, performing artists, and record and film producers will have the exclusive right to authorize or prohibit the rental and lending of originals and copies of their copyrighted works. Authors and performing artists will have an unwaivable right to equitable remuneration for rentals. The use of collecting societies, however, is left to individual Member State regulation.

For audio-visual works, the principal director is deemed to be the author; however, individual Member States may provide that others be considered as co-authors. In other respects the Directive does not define "author" but relies upon existing national legislation.

Rightholders may transfer or assign their exclusive rental and lending rights. In a contract concerning film production concluded by performers with a film producer, the performers will be presumed to have transferred their rental right, but not their right to remuneration, subject to any contrary contractual clauses. Member States may make similar presumptions in film production contracts with respect to authors. Moreover, Member States also retain the option to provide in contracts with performers a presumption that the performer authorizes the rental and the performance of the other exclusive rights set out in the Directive. These other rights include the fixation of performances or broadcasts, the reproduction, the broadcast and communication to the public, and the distribution of the right.

---

[7] Jan Corbet, *The Law of the EEC and Intellectual Property*, 13 J.L. & Com. 327. Copyright 1994 University of Pittsburgh. Excerpt reprinted with permission.

[8] Council Directive 92/100 on Rental Rights and Lending Rights and on Certain Rights Related to Copyright in the Field of Intellectual Property, 1992 O.J. (L346) 61.

QUESTIONS AND COMMENTS FOR YOUR CONSIDERATION

1. Compare the rental rights set forth in 17 U.S.C. §109. To what extent do US rental rights differ from the EC Directive?

2. To what extent, if any, does the fact that some EC countries treat performance and broadcast rights as "neighboring rights" (*see* Chapter Four) explain the above differences?

b. Proposed Harmonization Directives[9]

The proposal for a directive that would harmonize the terms of protection afforded to copyrights and certain related rights was established on March 23, 1992, and was amended on January 7, 1993.[10] International conventions do not implement fixed terms for the protection of copyrights. This ambiguity has led to considerable divergence in the case law of individual Member States. These differences in the terms of protection among the Member States give rise to trade barriers and to distortions of competition. Therefore, these concerns must be eliminated if the internal market is to be stabilized. The Proposal extends the terms of protection created in international conventions. Moreover, the Proposal respects established rights, with certain Member States having granted longer terms of protection, and intends to establish a high level of protection throughout the market.

For copyrights, the applicable term for protection is the life of the author and seventy years after that author's death. The date when the work was lawfully made available to the public does not affect the protections provided to known authors. In contrast, for anonymous works, pseudonymous works or works created by a legal person, the period of protection is seventy years after the work was lawfully made available to the public. For related rights, the term of protection for performers is fifty years from the performance, the first publication or the fixation of the performance. For producers of phonograms and for broadcasting organizations, the term begins at the first fixation of the phonogram and at the first transmission of the broadcast, respectively.

When a term of protection begins to run in any Member State, it begins to run throughout the Community. In a case where the country of origin of the work is not a Community member, the term of protection expires on the date of expiration that is granted in the country of origin. This period, however, may not exceed the term outlined in the Directive, which is known as the rule of the shorter term. The Directive provides that:

> the terms of protection laid down in [the Directive for related rights] shall also apply in the case of rightholders who are not Community nationals, provided Member States grant them protection. However, the term . . . shall expire no later than the date of expiry of the protection granted in the country of which the rightholder is a national.[11]

The Proposal for a Directive on the Coordination of Certain Rules Concerning Copyright and Rights Related to Copyright Applicable to Satellite Broadcasting and Cable Retransmission was adopted on September 11, 1991 and was amended on December 2, 1992.[12] This Proposal states that "communication to the public by satellite means the act of introducing, under the control and responsibility of the broadcasting organization, the programme-carrying signals intended for reception by the public into an uninterrupted chain of communication leading to the satellite and down towards the earth."[13] The next section

---

9 Jan Corbet, *The Law of the EEC and Intellectual Property*, 13 J.L. & Com. 327. Copyright 1994 University of Pittsburgh. Excerpt reprinted with permission.

10 Proposal for a Council Directive Harmonizing the Term of Protection of Copyright and Certain Related Rights, COM (92) 395 final at 33, 1992 O.J. (C 92) 6.

11 *Id.*, Art. 4(3), 1992 O.J. (C 92) at 8.

12 Amended Proposal for a Council Directive on the Coordination of Certain Rules Concerning Copyright and Rights Related to Copyright Applicable to Satellite Broadcasting and Cable Retransmission, COM (92) 358 final at 526, 1993 O.J. (C 25) 43.

13 *Id.*, Art 1(2)(a), 1993 O.J. (C 25) at 49.

provides that "communication" by satellite occurs within the nation where the signals were introduced.

Article 2 of the Proposal directs the Member States to "provide an exclusive right for the author to authorize the communication to the public by satellite of copyright works. . . ." In addition, under Article 3, Member States must ensure that the authorization of communication by satellite is effectuated by agreement only. According to Article 4, related rights will be protected in accordance with the provisions of the Directive that governs rental rights and lending rights. Moreover, Article 5 reaffirms the goal of the Rome Convention in stating that "protection of copyright-related rights under this Directive shall leave intact and shall in no way affect the protection of copyright."

Beginning with Article 8, Member States [are directed] to ensure that "when programmes from other Member States are retransmitted by cable in their territory the applicable copyright and rights related . . . are observed, and that such retransmission takes place on the basis of agreements between copyright owners, holders of rights related to copyright and cable operators."

Under Article 11, Member States shall ensure that, where no agreement is concluded, mediation may be sought by either party. Article 11 provides rules for the selection of mediators and their respective obligations. Finally, Article 12 directs Member States to ensure that parties enter into good faith negotiations regarding authorization for cable retransmission and that they do not prevent or hinder negotiations without valid justification.

The Proposal for a Council Directive on the Legal Protection of Databases pertains to electronic databases only.[14] The Proposal provides for a two-tiered protection system, copyright protection for original databases, if the collection is an intellectual creation, and *sui generis* protection for other databases. The scope of the protection provided to original databases is similar to the protection provided to computer programmes by the software directive. If the collected material is itself protected, authorization by the owner of the right is necessary in order to operate the database.

The *sui generis* protection prohibits unlawful down-loading or use of the contents of the work for commercial purposes. On an international level, the *sui generis* protection is subject to notions of reciprocity. The term of *sui generis* protection is ten years, while the term of protection for databases protected by a copyright is the usual term for literary works.

The Commission is currently concerned with issues pertaining to home copying, reprography, moral rights and resale rights. These issues will control the field of intellectual property law in the future.

---

[14] Proposal for a Council Directive in the Legal Protection of Databases, COM (92) 393, 1992 O.J. (C 156) 4.

QUESTIONS AND COMMENTS FOR YOUR CONSIDERATION

1. What advantages exist in harmonizing copyright laws to provide a longer period of copyright protection? What are the disadvantages?

2. What problems do you think the Satellite Broadcasting Directive was intended to resolve? Are there additional issues which should be addressed?

3. If you were retained to draft a proposed Directive on home copying, what issues would you include? Which ones would you expect to engender the greatest controversy? Why?

2. Trademark Harmonization[15]

The Preamble to the Harmonizing Directive makes clear a general purpose not to "undertake a full-scale approximation of the trademark laws of the Member States," but rather to make uniform "those national provisions of law which most directly affect the functioning of the internal market."[16] In its seventeen articles, the Harmonizing Directive does not require complete uniformity in Member States' trademark laws but sets out Community-wide standards in important areas, addressing: (1) the types of words and symbols (or "signs") that can be registered; (2) the possible grounds for refusal or invalidity; (3) the rights conferred by registration; and (4) the waiver of rights through non-use or acquiescence. The overall direction of the Harmonizing Directive is to broaden trademark rights available through registration in each Member State. However, the Preamble leaves to the Member States the freedom to fix procedures regarding registration, revocation, and invalidity of trademarks, including the use of ex officio proceedings, opposition proceedings or both. In infringement and invalidity proceedings, Member States can still establish their own procedural and proof of fact rules. Moreover, the Preamble permits each Member State the latitude to apply other laws such as those relating to unfair competition or consumer protection in regulating trademark rights.

According to the Harmonizing Directive, a trademark may consist of "any mark capable of being represented graphically." Personal names, designs, letters, numerals and shapes of goods and their packaging are all potentially registrable. For some countries such as Denmark, Italy, Spain, and the Benelux Nations, Article 2 presents no great departure from the law that has been in force. However, the Harmonizing Directive calls for significant alterations in the laws that have been in force in other Member States such as Germany and the United Kingdom, particularly in permitting registrations for three-dimensional marks.

Curiously, unlike the required provisions relating to the registration of trademarks, the Harmonizing Directive does not require that registration be accepted in each Member State for service marks, collective marks, certification marks, and guarantee marks. As of the writing of this article (1991), all Member States provide, or intend to provide, for service mark registrations, although the same is not true for collective, certification and guarantee marks.

Harmonizing Directive Articles 3 and 4 specify grounds for invalidating trademark rights or refusing registrations.

Article 3 sets out nine mandatory grounds for refusing or invalidating a registration, based on problems with the proposed mark itself, including absence of distinctiveness, failure to comply with national public policy or morals, or use of flag insignias and other national symbols listed in Article 6ter of the Paris Convention for the Protection of Industrial Property. Additionally, Article 3 permits Member States the option to provide other grounds for refusal based on laws other than traditional trademark laws, such as dilution statutes.

Importantly, Article 3 requires Member States to register (or declare valid) an inherently non-distinctive mark, if, before the date of application for registration, the mark has acquired secondary meaning. Optionally, Article 3 provides that Member States can provide for registration of a non-distinctive mark where secondary meaning is acquired after the date of the application for registration, or after the date of registration.

Article 4 of the Harmonizing Directive provides additional grounds for refusing or invalidating trademark registrations based on conflicts (*i.e.*, either there is an identity or a likelihood of confusion) with earlier trademarks covering identical or similar products. The definitional list of "earlier trade marks," provided in Article 4, is a key component of the linked but co-existing systems under the proposed CTM legislation[17] and the Harmonizing Directive, because, for example, an

---

[15] Kenyon & Kenyon, *What You Should Be Doing Now To Ensure That Your Company Or Your Client Is Well Positioned To Take Full Advantage Of The Dramatic Changes In Trademark Law That Are Happening Within The European Community*, 19 AIPLA Q.J. 213. Copyright 1991 Kenyon & Kenyon. Excerpt reprinted with permission.

[16] First Council Directive *supra* note 2 at Preamble, Clause 7.

[17] *Editors' Note:* The Community Trademark has since been adopted. For a further discussion of the CTM, *see* Chapter Eight.

earlier filed application for a CTM and an earlier registered CTM both constitute an earlier trademark. This provision ties the proposed CTM legislation into the laws of each Member State and clearly shows the force that a CTM registration will have. The definition of an "earlier trademark" also includes earlier registered Member State marks and Member State applications as well as the other types of registrations, such as registrations deposited under other international agreements (*e.g.*, the Madrid Arrangement). Additionally, a trademark that has been acquired through use (not registration) can be asserted as a earlier trademark when the mark is "well known."

In addition to incorporating CTMs as "earlier trademarks" against marks covering similar or identical goods, the Harmonizing Directive further enhances the power of the CTM, by providing that where a CTM has acquired a "reputation in the Community" and where the use of the latter trademark would take unfair advantage of (or would be detrimental to) the "distinctive character or repute" of the earlier CTM, the latter registration can be refused (or invalidated), even where the goods covered by the earlier CTM are dissimilar from those claimed in the latter registration. However, if a mark is refused registration based on a conflict with an earlier trademark, the Harmonizing Directive provides, in Article 4, paragraph 5, an optional provision that a trademark may be registered when the holder of prior rights consents. Several of the Member States have laws permitting such non-exclusive registrations to exist. As to those countries, a question arises about the scope of rights that are attainable for the dual registrants.

Infringement, according to the Harmonizing Directive, occurs when a third-party uses an identical or similar mark within the territory of a Member State for identical or similar products. The registrant has the right to stop such use. However, the registrant cannot prevent a third-party from using certain terms such as the third-party's own name and address, indicators of a product's utility or geographic origin, or even the registrant's trademark if the use of that trademark is necessary to indicate the intended purpose of the product (*e.g.*, spare parts for a machine with a registered name).

According to Article 10 of the Harmonizing Directive, the holder of a trademark registration must put the mark to "genuine use" within five years of the issue date, or the holder will be subject to sanctions. If, after genuine use, five consecutive years of non-use occur, sanctions can also apply. Articles 11 and 12 provide two mandatory sanctions for non-use: (1) the mark can be revoked; and (2) the mark cannot be used as an "earlier conflicting trade mark" to invalidate a later mark. Moreover, the Harmonizing Directive provides two optional sanctions. A Member State may provide that it will not refuse an application for registration based on a conflicting earlier but unused mark and it may provide that an infringement claim cannot be based on an unused mark.

In addition to sanctions for non-use of a registered trademark, the Harmonizing Directive provides that a trademark registrant cannot oppose or invalidate a later trademark registration where the registrant is aware of, and has acquiesced to, the latter's use for five consecutive years.

The Harmonizing Directive provides significant changes to the substantive laws of each Member State in the areas of: (1) types of trademarks that can be registered; (2) grounds for opposition; (3) rights granted; and (4) sanctions for non-use and acquiescence. For some countries (*e.g.*, Greece and Ireland), the amendment process to approximate the Harmonizing Directive has required great effort. For other countries (*e.g.* Denmark, France and the Benelux nations), the changes required to harmonize have not been major.

Beyond the increased rights and greater uniformity that harmonization brings, the trademark practitioner is still left with the problems that are endemic to a territorially-based system. Trademark rights under the Harmonizing Directive must still be applied for, prosecuted, defended and enforced on a Member State-by-Member State basis. In addition to an applicant's high cost in applying for each registration, there still are procedural and proof of fact rules that are different in each Member State. Further, as the provisions of the Harmonizing Directive are implemented, and used, there also is the problem of having the terms of the Directive applied differently in each Member State.

QUESTIONS AND COMMENTS FOR YOUR CONSIDERATION

1. A copy of the Harmonization Directive is included as Appendix VII. Does this document provide sufficient guidance to ensure that each country's laws will be identical regarding such critical issues as what constitutes a protectable trademark, or what acts qualify as trademark infringement, particularly where the infringing goods are different from those for which the mark has been registered?

2. What are the differences in treatment of trademarks under the Harmonization Directive and your country's trademark laws? Do you agree with the balance struck by the Directive between trademark owner's rights and the protection of the public against public confusion? Are there issues which the Directive failed to address?

3. How likely is the Directive to lead to an identity of treatment of trademarks under each country's national laws? Is such identity desirable? Is it required? Is it a realistic goal?

B. Patent Harmonization[18]

The WIPO draft treaty for patent harmonization contains two dozen articles.[19] The most significant difference between the WIPO Basic Proposal and current US law is found in Section 2 of Article 9, which mandates that the "invention shall belong to the applicant with the earliest priority date." This proposal would change the US patent system from a first-to-invent into a first-to-file system, and would bring the laws into conformity with the rest of the industrialized world. In 1987 Donald J. Quigg, Deputy Commissioner of Patents and Trademarks for the United States, announced that the United States might be willing to change from first-to-invent to first-to-file, but that he "has called in return for improved patent-protection standards around the world." Such improved standards include: "(1) an international 12-month grace period; (2) meaningful and fair protection based on patent claims including equivalents; (3) a prohibition of pre-grant oppositions; and (4) the ability to file applications initially in English and rely on the English-language originals when errors are found in the translations."[20] The move to first-to-file would be a prerequisite, however, to the adoption of these concessions from other nations.

The second significant change that must be made by the United States in order to conform with the WIPO Basic Proposal is the adoption of prior user rights. According to Article 20 of the WIPO proposal, any contracting party "may provide that a patent shall have no effect against a prior user who in good faith was using an invention or was making serious preparations for such use prior to the priority date of the application." While the right to adopt prior user rights is not mandatory in this draft, many commentators in the United States see prior user rights as a necessary corollary to adoption of a first-to-file system.

Third, the WIPO Basic Proposal would compel the mandatory publication of applications. Article 15 provides that "applications will be required to be published within a certain number of months after the priority date unless it has been withdrawn, abandoned, or rejected." In those countries that provide for early publication, such publication typically occurs eighteen months after the priority date. The United States proposed an alternative text for this section that would permit

---

[18] Robert W. Pritchard, *The Future Is Now—The Case for Patent Harmonization*, 20 N.C.J. INT'L LAW & COM. REG. 291. Copyright 1995 North Carolina Journal of International Law & Commercial Regulation Inc. Excerpt reprinted with permission.

[19] *Editors' Note: See* Basic Proposal for Patent Harmonization, reprinted in WIPO Experts Make Progress In Patent Harmonization, 41 Pat. Trademark & Copyright J. (BNA) No. 1013 (Jan. 10, 1991).

[20] Patent System Harmonization Legislation is Debated in Joint Senate-House Hearing, 44 Pat. Trademark & Copyright J. (BNA) No. 1080 at 3 (May 7, 1992).

disclosure twenty-four months after the application is filed. Either time frame would be a significant change for the United States, which strictly forbids any application disclosure until issuance of the patent.

The final significant change deals with the term of the patent. Article 22 of the WIPO draft states: "The term of the patent will be for at least twenty years from the filing date. The twenty year period is calculated from the filing date of invoked parent applications, except for the priority application." The Article allows countries to establish a term longer than twenty years, but mandates that the term begin on the priority date, not on the date the patent issued. While the change in the patent's duration from seventeen to twenty years is not material, the specification of the start date is significant because the US patent system begins counting the seventeen-year period on the date the patent is issued, not on the date the application is filed.

The WIPO negotiations would clearly affect the US patent system in a variety of ways. With the proposed adoption of first-to-file, prior user rights, early publication of applications, and a twenty-year patent term beginning on the date of filing, the United States was on the path toward meaningful patent harmonization. If the contracting nations adopted the WIPO Basic Proposal, complete harmonization would not be far behind. The possibility of harmonization ended on January 24, 1994, however, with the announcement that the United States would maintain its system of first-to-invent. Furthermore, the United States has no plans to resume patent harmonization negotiations at this time. The January 1994 announcement ended almost a decade of negotiations at the World Intellectual Property Organization, and those seeking reform in the US patent system must now seek reform elsewhere.

1. Should The US Adopt First-to-File?[21]

The most divisive issue in the harmonization debate is whether the United States should adopt a first-to-file system. Currently, if two people claim to be the inventor of an invention, the United States awards the patent to the inventor who can demonstrate that he was the "first to invent." Attempting to prove who is the "first and true inventor" is a difficult task and is open to questions regarding conception, reduction to practice, diligence, and suppression. Nearly every nation other than the United States grants the patent to the first person to file a patent application. For the United States to be a part of any meaningful patent harmonization treaty, it must abandon its system of first-to-invent and adopt the first-to-file system. Thus, the United States should adopt a first-to-file patent system for three reasons: (1) the first-to-file system is superior to a system of first-to-invent; (2) the change will not pose a significant harm to American inventors; and (3) adoption of first-to-file will enable the United States to exact concessions from other nations to the benefit of this country.

The first-to-file system is superior to the first-to-invent system, and the United States would benefit from the change. Initially, the first-to-invent system places a difficult burden on American inventors. American inventors are required to keep accurate records of all acts of invention in the event that a patent is involved in an interference proceeding and the inventor is required to prove conception, reduction to practice, and diligence. The first-to-invent system results in complicated and expensive interference proceedings that would be unnecessary if the United States adopted a first-to-file system. Importantly, the small independent inventor is at a major disadvantage in an interference proceeding against a large corporation. Currently, interference proceedings are "cumbersome, inadequate, and often seemingly inexplicable."[22] However, if the United States adopts first-to-file, the question of right to a patent between interfering parties would be satisfied by a quick examination of filing dates, thus eliminating the need for interference proceedings. As a result, the cost of the patenting process to the parties

[21] Robert W. Pritchard, *The Future Is Now—The Case for Patent Harmonization*, 20 N.C.J. INT'L LAW & COM. REG. 291. Copyright 1995 North Carolina Journal of International Law & Commercial Regulation Inc. Excerpt reprinted with permission.

[22] Thomas M. Marshall, *New Interference Rules—Boon or Bust*, 1967 PAT. L. ANN. 79, 106–07.

and the patent society "would be greatly diminished under a first to file system."[23] In fact, a first-to-file system may "prove a significant advantage to small companies and independent inventors when contrasted with the complications, costs, and difficulties associated with proving that an inventor made an invention first [under the current system]."[24] Adoption of a first-to-file system will end the inherent disadvantage of independent inventors in interference proceedings against large corporations, as a simple comparison of filing dates will end any question of priority.

In addition to being expensive and cumbersome, the first-to-invent system is unpredictable. Under the first-to-invent system, an issued patent is never safe from an allegation that another person developed the invention first.

Since the rest of the world awards the patent to the first person to file a patent application, American companies with foreign interests who are already bound by the first-to-file system in other countries would not be adversely impacted by a change to first-to-file in the United States.

Adoption of international agreements like NAFTA and GATT requires the United States to recognize foreign use in interference proceedings in the future, a practice that will complicate the proceedings and burden the small inventor and university researcher. The United States must adopt a first-to-file system to avoid this problem.

If the United States were to give up the first-to-invent system in favor of first-to-file, it could demand reform in other countries to the benefit of American inventors, both corporate and independent. The WIPO Harmonization Treaty contains several articles consistent with US patent law and favorable to the American inventor, and adoption of a first-to-file system will enable the United States to pressure other countries to adopt those provisions. One commentator stated that harmonization "presents the United States with a unique opportunity to strengthen the protection for the invention of American industry and individual inventors around the world."[25] Harmonization will benefit American inventors in several ways.

The United States could demand a grace period of international scope. Currently, the US patent system grants a one-year grace period during which a public disclosure will not be considered prior art for the purpose of a Section 102 statutory bar to patentability. The grace period enables American inventors to publish results of tests and to make preliminary public sales without fear of losing the right to possibly valuable patent protection. Most other countries operate on the theory of absolute novelty without a grace period, however, and will not issue a patent if there has been any disclosure prior to the date of filing. As a result, when an American inventor publishes an invention in reliance upon the grace period, he or she automatically forfeits any right to a patent "in virtually every country other than the United States."[26] While most large American corporations have adapted to the absolute novelty requirements of other countries, independent inventors are often not aware of the adverse consequences of early publication, and therefore forfeit foreign rights unknowingly. University researchers that place a premium on publication often give up foreign patent rights in favor of early publication. The result is that foreign companies have a repository of information in the US Patent Office in the form of patents that can only be valid in this country due to the grace period. This information can be freely used in the rest of the world, and the American inventor has no protection. This problem could be rectified if the United States was able to pressure the rest of the world to adopt an international grace period. In addition to first-to-file, the WIPO Treaty provided a one-year international grace period for inventor-derived disclosures.

Another benefit of harmonization is the

---

[23] Gregory J. Wrenn, *What Should be Our Priority–Protection for First to File or the First to Invent?* 72 J. PAT. [& Trademark] OFF. SOC'Y 872, 878 (1990).

[24] The Patent System Harmonization Act of 1992: Joint Hearing on S. 2605 and H.R. 4978 Before the Subcomm. on Patents, Copyrights and Trademarks on the Senate Comm. on the Judiciary and the Subcomm. on Intellectual Property and Judicial Administration of the House Comm. on the Judiciary, 102d Cong., 2d Sess. § (1992).

[25] Statement of Hon. Harry F. Manbeck, Jr., former Commissioner, Patent and Trademark Office.

[26] William S. Thompson, *Reforming the Patent System for the 21st Century*, 21 AIPLA Q.J. 171, 176 (1993).

elimination of the opportunity to file pre-grant oppositions. In many countries today, after a patent application is published, members of the public are allowed to examine the application and file pre-grant oppositions stating reasons why a patent should not be issued. In the United States, however, only the Patent Examiner is permitted to cite reasons for rejecting an application. The use of pre-grant oppositions in those countries where it is tolerated is conducive to abuse. The practice allows competitors of an inventor to file numerous oppositions to delay the grant of a patent. In a few cases, these delays can last until after the patent term has expired. The harmonization treaty contemplated by WIPO specifically eliminates the practice of pre-grant oppositions.

Patent harmonization would also require other nations to adopt a system similar to the doctrine of equivalents in the United States. In this country, if a device that is not precisely identical to the patented device "performs substantially the same function in substantially the same way to obtain the same result," a patentee may invoke the doctrine of equivalents to claim infringement.[27] This doctrine prevents potential infringers from making minor alterations or insignificant substitutions to avoid infringement, while still gaining all of the benefits of the innovation. In most countries however, the nature of the laws and the judicial practice of some countries has resulted in patents being interpreted so narrowly by courts that minor changes allow an infringer to escape liability. The WIPO draft harmonization treaty includes a provision for the doctrine of equivalents. Furthermore, the treaty prevents courts from limiting the scope of the claims in the patent to the literal meaning of their wording.

An additional benefit to harmonization is the ability to file patent applications in English and supply a translated application within two months. Currently, American inventors must obtain a translation of the application before filing. This results in two problems when attempting to obtain protection abroad. First, in a "race" to the foreign nation's patent office, an American inventor is placed at a disadvantage to an inventor who can speak the language of that country due to the delay in obtaining a translation. Second, if an error is made during translation which is essential to the scope of the claims or the patentability of the entire invention, the error is not correctable, and the American inventor either loses the patent or obtains greatly reduced coverage due to a clerical mistake. The WIPO draft harmonization treaty permits the filing date of the English language original application to serve as the priority date of the patent for purposes of the "race" to the patent office. Furthermore, the English language application would be considered the "official" application for purposes of correcting typographical or clerical errors in translation.

The costs of a universal, harmonized patent system would be greatly reduced, thereby increasing the small inventor's accessibility to the world market. Such harmony in international patent practice would avoid costs involved with the dual anomaly that can occur in today's world. A universal first to file system would save the transaction costs associated with securing multiple licenses for world-wide practice of the invention. Such harmony in international patent laws would also reduce the time and expense required for an inventor to obtain international protection.

a. Some Additional Thoughts[28]

The major substantive issue being addressed in the priority system debate is whether the first inventor or the first discloser is more deserving of a patent. The Anglo-American patent tradition, from the Cases on Monopolies to the present-day patent law, strongly suggests that it is the first inventor who is the more deserving. The argument made by critics of the first-to-invent system is that it is inherently fairer to grant a patent to the first inventor than to the first discloser. In response, the first-

[27] Sanitary Refrigerator Co. v. Winters, 280 US 30, 42 (1929).

[28] Charles R. B. Macedo, *First-To-File: Is American Adoption of the International Standard in Patent Law Worth the Price?* 1988 COLUM. BUS. L. REV. 543. Copyright 1988 Columbia Business Law Review. Excerpt reprinted with permission.

to-file system has been qualified with derivation provisions and prior user rights. Proponents of the first-to-file system suggest, moreover, that the adoption of their system will not significantly affect who receives patents.

Although as a result of tradition Americans tend to assume that their system is fairest, there is no reason to believe it is an inherently fairer grant of monopoly power than the first-to-file system. After all, the purpose of granting patents, according to the Patents and Copyright Clause, is to encourage the 'Progress of Science and the Useful Arts.' The goal of patent law is to grant inventors with limited monopolies in exchange for full and complete disclosure of their inventions. Therefore, it may be just as reasonable to grant a patent to the first person to disclose an invention, as it would be to grant a patent to the first inventor. The choice of systems and of the provisions to be implemented within the chosen system is a policy choice. While the American system is based on a policy choice favoring a first-to-invent policy, many other industrial nations have thrived under the alternative policy choice of the first-to-file system.

The first-to-invent system has been criticized for failing to provide foreign applicants with the same rights as domestic inventors. Although, Section 102(g) [35 U.S.C. §102(g)] seems to give a prior invention a novelty-defeating effect as of the invention date, Section 104 limits this provision's scope to domestic inventors. This is considered discriminatory by critics, and results in foreign patent applicants generally losing to American rivals in priority contests.

Advocates of the first-to-file system defend their cause by claiming that the inability to compel discovery in a foreign country makes it impossible to allow proof of foreign invention to be admitted. Of course, this argument could be negated by allowing proof of foreign inventions to be admitted if the foreign party submits to the full panoply of American discovery procedures.

First-to-invent supporters reject this argument by advancing the pork barrel rational for Section 104. That is, the first-to-invent system is widely recognized as a not-so-secret weapon which helps American industry compete in its own markets. The rule was established to discriminate against foreign competition. Whether or not this is a defensible practice, it indisputably contributes to US gross national product.

It is argued that small inventors can only be protected by the first-to-invent system. Because they need sufficient time to perfect their inventions and to file for their patents, many small inventors would be prevented from obtaining patents under the first-to-file system, which puts a premium on speedy filing of patent applications. The first-to-invent system allows an applicant to swear back his priority date by the use of affidavits to the invention date rather than forcing him or her to rely on the latter filing date, thereby avoiding the problem.

This argument has been empirically refuted by advocates of the first-to-file system which claim that very few small inventors actually take advantage of the present first-to-invent system. However, the first-to-invent system is more important to small inventors than the actual number of small inventors who participate in interferences would suggest. While small inventors are not generally able to win interferences, they do take advantage of the affidavit practice that is part of the first-to-invent system in order to obtain a priority date before a prior art reference by attesting that their dates of invention are earlier than the prior art reference.

b. US Testimony[29]

The testimony at the US Patent and Trademark Office's harmonization hearings demonstrated the controversy that exists over several of the harmonization proposals.

Proponents of the change to first-to-file...noted that since the vast majority of patents are awarded to the first person to file an application, the American first-to-invent system is not materially different from a first-to-file system, and that few inventors would be hurt by the change. Allan Mende-

---

[29] Robert W. Pritchard, *The Future Is Now—The Case for Patent Harmonization*, 20 N.C.J. INT'L LAW & COM. REG. 291. Copyright 1995 North Carolina Journal of International Law & Commercial Regulation Inc. Excerpt reprinted with permission.

lowitz, the Director of International Trade, Finance and Competitiveness at the General Accounting Office (GAO), reported that a GAO survey demonstrated that two-thirds of responding corporations supported adoption of a first-to-file system.[30]

Opponents of the adoption of first-to-file included universities, small companies, and independent inventors with limited resources. They testified that the first-to-file system does not reward inventorship, but the winner of the "race" to the Patent and Trademark Office. They asserted that the change would favor corporations and foreign companies at the expense of small independent inventors. A primary concern of those opposed to first-to-file is that the small inventor had not yet been "heard in the harmonization debate."[31] Furthermore, some argued that changing to first-to-file would favor foreign companies at a time when American inventors only receive about fifty percent of the patents in this country. Representatives of the Association of University Technology Managers testified that research universities opposed first-to-file unless there was an option for provisional application filing. Testifying in regard to the effect of harmonization on university research, the president of Hampshire College suggested that first-to-file would be detrimental because it would "place a premium on secrecy in research."

2. Should The US Adopt Prior User Rights?[32]

The United States should adopt a prior user right to ensure that American innovators are treated equitably. It is unfair to enforce a patent against someone who used the invention prior to the application for patent by a subsequent inventor. Such prior use indicates that the prior user did not benefit at all from the patent disclosure. Because the American patent system operates on a *quid pro quo* philosophy, and because the prior inventor did not gain any benefit from the patent disclosure, the prior user should not be obligated to refrain from using the invention.

The United States should adopt prior user rights to allow American innovators to enjoy the same rights enjoyed by foreign inventors. If the United States did not adopt prior user rights with a first-to-file system, foreign owners of American patents could prohibit use by American prior users. Americans who hold patents in other nations, however, cannot enjoin prior users in those countries because those nations grant prior user rights.

The prior user right adopted by the United States should not be overly broad; instead, a limited and defined class of prior users should be entitled to protection. First, the "rights should be based only upon activity . . . prior to the earliest filing date to which the relevant claim or claims of the patent is or are entitled."[33] The use should be continuous, as prior users who abandoned experimentations or use of an invention should not be permitted to resume activity. The use should be in the United States only, as prior use in a foreign country is of no benefit to the United States, and the right to use an invention in a foreign nation does not affect the American patent right. Additionally, the prior use should "have been done in good faith and without derivation from the patentee" in order to prevent someone from taking the benefits of the patentee's innovation from the patentee.[34] Finally, a prior user right should only protect those who independently invent the invention, not those who take the invention from the patentee.

The nature of the use that is entitled to a prior user right should also be clearly defined. While some argue that the prior user must have used or substantially prepared the invention commercially, the prior user right should extend to anyone who used the invention prior to the filing of the patent. Prior university research or purely scientific

---

[30] Patent Harmonization Proposal Stirs Lively Debate at PTO Hearing, 46 Pat. Trademark & Copyright J. (BNA) No. 1150 at 509 (Oct. 14, 1993).

[31] *Id.*, at 510.

[32] Robert W. Pritchard, *The Future Is Now—The Case for Patent Harmonization*, 20 N.C.J. INT'L LAW & COM. REG. 291. Copyright 1995 North Carolina Journal of International Law & Commercial Regulation Inc. Excerpt reprinted with permission.

[33] The Advisory Commission on Patent Law Reform, A Report to the Secretary of Commerce 49 (1992).

[34] *Ibid.*

research should not be barred merely because the innovators did not choose to commercially exploit the innovation. So long as the right that is granted by the prior user right does not expand the scope of prior use or activity which created the right, the prior user right should restrict the noncommercial prior user to that use. To ensure a just result, the "right created by the prior use or preparation should be limited to continuation of the particular activity which gives rise to the right."[35] The prior user right should not permit the prior user to expand the scope of the prior use, because to allow expansion would erode the patent right unfairly. Furthermore, the prior user right should be personal and not transferable to avoid a significant alteration in the nature of the use and to respect the personal nature of the equitable right.

a. US Testimony[36]

The issue of prior user rights was divided along the same lines as the issue of adopting first-to-file. Those who favor a first-to-file system argued that prior user rights are "a logical accompaniment to a first-to-file regime."[37] They noted that those who practice innovative trade secrets should not lose the rights to their trade secrets merely because someone independently discovers the same invention after the trade secret has been in use. Roger Smith, testifying on behalf of the Intellectual Property Owners, said that limited prior user rights are "an essential safety valve under the first-to-file system."[38] He asserted that prior user rights should be restricted to activities within the United States, should require either actual use or substantial progress and reduction to practice, should be an absolute defense to infringement, and should protect trade secrets. Those opposed to prior user rights argued that such rights would encourage secrecy and would unfairly give trade secret holders a "free ride" on valid patents, thereby reducing the value of the patent system.

3. Should the US Adopt Early Disclosure of Patent Applications?[39]

Currently, inventors often expend substantial resources in time and money to develop an invention that is secretly making its way through the prosecution process, only to discover that someone else had already developed the same invention. Early application disclosure would enable American innovators to use the disclosed technology in the development of other inventions, and would allow inventors to examine possible conflicts between their inventions and information that is disclosed. Publication would benefit Americans by "preventing duplication of research, signaling promising areas of research, and indicating which fields or research topics are being pursued by other firms."[40] Early publication will benefit small inventors by allowing them to assess their likelihood of receiving a patent before undertaking the expensive process of pursuing a patent. Early publication would also aid the Patent Office by allowing applicants to cite to other applications as prior art. As a result, searches and examinations would be more efficient, saving money and time.

Congress should adopt procedural safeguards to complement a policy of publishing patent applications. Congress should not require a patent applicant to risk disclosure of a valuable trade secret in a patent application if there is a possibility that the patent will not issue. Without safeguards, the Patent Office would release an application containing such trade secrets to the public, the patent could be denied, and the applicant

---

[35] *Ibid.*

[36] Robert W. Pritchard, *The Future Is Now—The Case for Patent Harmonization*, 20 N.C.J. Int'l Law & Com. Reg. 291. Copyright 1995 North Carolina Journal of International Law & Commercial Regulation Inc. Excerpt reprinted with permission.

[37] Patent Harmonization Proposal Stirs Lively Debate at PTO Hearing, *supra* note 32 at 510.

[38] *Ibid.*

[39] Robert W. Pritchard, *The Future Is Now—The Case for Patent Harmonization*, 20 N.C.J. Int'l Law & Com. Reg. 291. Copyright 1995 North Carolina Journal of International Law & Commercial Regulation Inc. Excerpt reprinted with permission.

[40] 140 Cong.. Rec. S 1525 (daily ed. Feb. 11, 1994) (Statement of Sen. De Concine)

may lose all rights to the trade secret. The Patent and Trademark Office should allow accelerated examination for those applicants who want a patentability opinion and at least one office action prior to publication. Accelerated examination will allow the applicant to make an informed decision about whether to pursue the application or to withdraw the application to avoid publication. Furthermore, applicants who successfully receive a patent on a published application should be allowed to receive protection for the period between publication and issuance. A reasonable royalty provision would protect the applicant during the pendency of the application when the innovation disclosed is not yet entitled to formal patent protection. The royalty provision is essential because absent such a provision, a third party could simply read a published patent application and commercially exploit it before the patent issues. A royalty provision would enable the successful applicant to receive all of the benefits of the applicant's innovation.

Supporters of early publication observed that publication of applications benefits the inventor and the public by "speeding public access to technical information."[41] In addition, supporters claimed that the costs of early publication would be reduced by future automation in the filing process. William LaFuze, President of the AIPLA, suggested the possibility of accelerated examinations for those who desire a patentability opinion prior to publication to allow the applicant to determine his or chances for patentability before a possible trade secret is published.[42]

[41] Patent Harmonization Proposal Stirs Lively Debate at PTO Hearing, *supra* note 32 at 511.

[42] *Ibid.*

4. Should The US Adopt a Twenty-Year Patent Term?[43]

Under the current system, inventors "have no incentive to have their filed patent application prosecuted expeditiously. Rather, they have an incentive to prolong the period they spend at the Patent Office, benefiting from the secrecy of their application and thereby extending the life of their patent."[44] Some applicants have successfully delayed their patent applications in the Patent Office until an industry is established in the patented technology—often over twenty years from the filing date. When it finally issues, the patent surprises those in the industry who were not aware of the delayed pending application, and it has serious detrimental effects on the industry. The adoption of a twenty-year patent term that begins on the filing date grants inventors protection for a limited time, and does not enable abuse. Applicants would have incentive to prosecute patent applications expeditiously to receive the maximum protection, and potential infringers will benefit by knowing exactly what was being patented. The new system would produce certainty in a confusing and inefficient process, and would save time and money at the Patent Office. The United States should adopt a twenty-year patent term that begins on the date a completed application is filed.

[43] Robert W. Pritchard, *The Future Is Now—The Case for Patent Harmonization*, 20 N.C.J. INT'L LAW & COM. REG. 291. Copyright 1995 North Carolina Journal of International Law & Commercial Regulation Inc. Excerpt reprinted with permission.

[44] *Supra* note 32 at § 1524.

QUESTIONS AND COMMENTS FOR YOUR CONSIDERATION

1. To what extent does the debate over patent harmonization reflect the economic concerns of the individual participants?
2. Do you accept the argument that the United States should conform to the majority trend? Is there a reasoned basis for refusing to do so?

C. Case Studies

1. The Japanese "Patent Wars"[45]

According to recent Tokyo press reports, the United States and Japan are once again at war—this time, though, it is a "Patent War."

Understanding of the Japanese patent system can only be achieved if Americans first acknowledge the fundamental differences between Japanese and American culture. Today's Japan is a complex hybrid of ancient Eastern and modern Western influences, preventing us from stereotyping all Japanese as possessing a single view on patent enforcement. In fact, five very different views on the matter currently exist, each founded upon a different aspect of Japanese culture. These views occupy the full spectrum from abolishing patents altogether to strictly enforcing them. The cultural bases that give rise to these views can be used to explain some of the primary differences between Japanese and United States patent law and practice, both in acquisition and litigation. Successful protection of American intellectual property rights in Japan today is possible if Americans make the effort to understand the constantly evolving cultural underpinnings of Japanese patent law and practice.

A central tenet of Confucianism is that an idea cannot be owned but must be shared. The very idea of intellectual property rights being tied up in a single individual or company is therefore alien to ancient Japanese culture. Akio Morita, Chairman of Sony Corporation, summed up the disdain which many Japanese feel toward American enforcement of intellectual property rights by saying that: Americans have a broader perspective on ideas than the Japanese. When I was living in the United States, my child got sick, so I called my doctor. Our American doctor gave us instructions on what to do and what kind of medication to take. Now in Japan, you wouldn't expect anything else to happen—but in the States, I received a bill for that telephone call from my doctor. Now, this tells you that they don't give out any intelligence for free.

Japanese companies have spent most of the post-World War II years playing "catch up" technologically. Some benefitted greatly, therefore, from "borrowing" technology from the United States during the long period of lax patent enforcement which occurred prior to the mid-1980s. Having relied on American companies to provide expensive research and development for their products for so many years, these Japanese companies concentrated their efforts and resources on developing minor manufacturing improvements, not on creating pioneering technology breakthroughs. The renewed vigor in the assertion of patent rights against the Japanese in recent years, therefore, has sent them scrambling to dramatically increase their own research and development expenditures. This anti-patent enforcement attitude is understandable in this light, since strict patent enforcement can only harm, not benefit, Japanese businesses in the short term.[46]

A different view on the subject of patent enforcement emphasizes that strong business relationships are more important than patent disputes. The possibility of forming joint ventures and other business arrangements in the long term future are more important than present squabbles over temporary cash payments. Therefore, companies espousing this view will typically pay whatever is reasonably asked of them in

---

[45] John C. Lindgren and Craig J. Yudell, *Articles Protecting American Intellectual Property in Japan*, 10 COMPUTER & HIGH TECH. L.J. 1. Copyright 1994 John C. Lindgren and Craig J. Yudell. Excerpt reprinted with permission.

[46] The influence of this view can be seen throughout the Japanese Patent Office laws and procedure. One example of this is the extremely long delay between application and issuance of a patent in Japan. Since the limited term of enforceability of a patent begins to run as of its filing date in Japan, a lengthy examination will result in a short enforcement period. Additionally, under Japanese patent law, patent claims are to be interpreted very narrowly, and often if the technology has changed even slightly from the time of invention, the patent is found not to be infringed. Therefore, even if a patentee is able to file suit during this short period of enforceability, it is very difficult to convince a Japanese court that any product or process currently being marketed infringes a patent which was drafted years earlier. This amounts, therefore, to a virtual *de facto* freedom of ideas in many cases.

order to preserve future relationships. These companies believe that all disputes, not just those involving patent rights, should be resolved as quickly as possible in order to minimize unhealthy friction between American and Japanese companies. This view is based upon the Japanese cultural belief that a general state of harmony, or *wa*, should always exist, rather than one of conflict.

In general, the Japanese believe that Americans are simply too litigious. Keio University Professor Kusano reiterated this view by saying that Americans "use courts and lawyers for very insignificant things. To them, it is an everyday affair, whereas we think of it as a last resort."[47] Companies embracing this view are willing to pay the royalties American companies demand for an additional reason, however. These companies firmly believe that any company that overemphasizes patent royalties is an ineffective competitor. For example, Kensuke Norichika of Toshiba, the number one grantee of US patents in 1991, believes that "our competitiveness is not threatened as long as American companies' attention is on income from intellectual property rights [and not from manufacturing profits]."[48] This feeling is shared by NEC. "When a company starts relying heavily on patent revenue and income from technology transfers, it's time to start selling shares in the firm," according to former vice president of NEC, Michiyuki Uenohara.[49] The Japanese newspapers are also becoming sharply critical of overly aggressive assertion of patents. One paper criticized the pro-litigation strategy of American companies as an "excessive dependence [on a] legacy of past technological superiority."[50] Another Japanese paper warned that this "patent dependence disease" which currently infects American firms "will encourage conflict, rather than invention."[51]

An extremist view, beginning to gain support in Japan, is that the over-enforcement of patents by American companies will lead to a devastation equivalent to that of a full-scale military war.

There is a "nuclear bomb" about to explode which could destroy the world. This bomb is called intellectual property rights. The United States is engaging in this war to recover from its trade deficit and other economic impoverishment, however, this dispute or war—if taken to the extreme, could lead to a stoppage of world production. This is a simulation of the worst case of the disaster that is about to come true.

Perhaps the single most glaring difference between the two countries' laws relates to establishing the priority of an invention. In Japan, the first inventor to file an application on the invention in the Japanese Patent Office owns the rights to that invention. United States law, on the other hand, holds that the first person to invent the subject matter of the patent owns the rights to the invention. Although the United States is in the clear minority here,[52] American practitioners and inventors strongly believe that this concept is by far the more equitable. Although "first-to-file" is infinitely simpler from an administrative viewpoint, it seems inherently unfair to make valuable patent rights depend entirely on how quickly an inventor's attorney can file the required paperwork in a patent application.

A second major difference in the patent laws of the two nations is the length of enforceability of patents. The term of a standard utility patent in the United States is seventeen years, measured from the issue date of the patent, regardless of how long it took the US Patent and Trademark Office to examine and grant the patent. The term is completely unrelated to the filing date of the patent. In Japan, on the other hand, the lifespan of a patent is the shorter of: (1) fifteen years from the date of publication for opposition, or (2) twenty years from the filing date. As discussed above, linking the term of the patent's enforceability to the filing date effectively allows the patent office to dictate the length of that term through hastening or delaying the examination process.

A patent application filed in Japan is automatically published, or "laid open," for

---

[47] Sunday Present: The Intellectual Property War–Last Trap by the Americans (Japanese television broadcast, July 5, 1992).

[48] Koichi Nishioka, *Disputing Patents Revels Weakness*, NIKKEI WEEKLY (Aug. 15, 1992) at 11.

[49] *Ibid.*

[50] Bruce Stokes, *Title Fights*, 24 NAT'L J. 1236 (1992).

[51] *Ibid.*

[52] The United States and the Philippines are the only two countries in the world that have "first-to-invent" rather than "first-to-file" laws.

inspection by the general public eighteen months from the earlier of the Japanese filing date or the foreign convention priority date. This publication, called a *Kokai*, entitles the applicant to a right of compensation under certain conditions for the subsequent use of the invention by third parties, but only if a patent is eventually issued on the application. Additionally, the pending application is published a second time before issuance in Japan, as a *Kokoku*. This second publication, or "publication for opposition," occurs after the patent office examiners have fully investigated the prior art and have found nothing that would bar the issuance of the patent. The *Kokoku* is essentially an invitation for companies who would be affected by the issuance of the patent to attempt to do a better job than the examiners were able to do in undermining its validity.

Under United States law, on the other hand, the examiners are solely responsible for discovering all of the relevant prior art, and patent applications are held in strict secrecy until issuance. Even the file on a finally rejected application is sealed from public inspection. Many American inventors see this secrecy as a distinct advantage over the Japanese procedure.

In Japan, a patent application is examined only after a request for examination is filed. This request must be filed within seven years of the filing date of the application, or else the application is deemed withdrawn. The United States has no corresponding procedure, as all applications filed are automatically examined. Many American practitioners and inventors see the Japanese procedure as desirable due to the high cost of working a patent completely through the United States Patent and Trademark Office. In today's world of rapidly changing technology, using a deferred examination procedure would benefit an applicant greatly since he could wait up to seven years to see if any competitors are using his invention before spending any more money prosecuting a patent on it. Adopting this system would, however, likely require an adoption of a publication procedure similar to Japan's, in order to further the United States patent law's goal of disclosure.

Probably the most crucial aspect of the Japanese culture and legal system for the foreign litigant to understand is the importance of conciliation. Japanese culture and history have enshrined honor and harmony as the cornerstones of Japanese civilization. In Japan, determining relative rights between parties is not nearly as important as preserving societal harmony, or *wa*. Amicable settlement of patent infringement litigation is more the norm than the exception[53] because such formal confrontation would disrupt the *wa*. By pursuing rights in court, both parties are shamed and, thus, dishonored. Settlement of disputes by reaching a harmonious consensus is the prevailing goal of both Japanese culture and the Japanese legal system. Therefore, litigation of a patent dispute, or of any dispute for that matter, is considered a rather extreme measure. An attempt at a negotiated settlement will be taken seriously by the Japanese defendant, and often will result in a swift and satisfactory resolution of the dispute.

Also, the Japanese courts universally encourage settlement. Often, the court will subtly express its opinion of how the suit will result if it is not settled. Not surprisingly, a harmonious consensus soon follows. The resulting settlement will likely resemble the ultimate resolution had the case reached judgment, but it will have been reached through amicable agreement of the parties, saving face for all.

Prior to 1960, Japanese patent law followed the German legal theory of extending the scope of patent protection beyond the strict limits of the claim to the heart of the fundamental inventive concept. The 1960 revision of Japanese patent law was interpreted as adopting the American concept of imposing strict patent claim boundaries. Since then, the Japanese have narrowly interpreted claims. In fact, the Doctrine of Equivalents, which has been used in the United States to extend the scope of claim boundaries, is only of limited influence in Japan. On occasion, the judiciary has allowed arguments based on "equivalency" to broaden the scope of claims, as well as arguments based on "file wrappers" and prior art to limit the patent's scope. In gen-

---

[53] Of the 369 patent infringement cases filed in the District Court in 1990, 60 were withdrawn, 125 reached judgment, and 157 were settled. Japanese Patent Practice: Prosecution/Litigation, AIPLA Proc. K18 (June 1992).

eral, however, claim interpretation remains extremely narrow.

The reason for this narrow interpretation of patents derives from the general philosophy of the Japanese patent system to spread technology throughout society. By limiting the scope of protection for a patent, others are permitted to develop similar ideas. According to Shoji Tada, an official at the Japanese Patent Office, exposing an inventor's work to the public has helped Japanese companies "avoid the waste of time in coming up with the same ideas."[54] This clearly is at odds with the United States patent philosophy of protecting the inventor's exclusive right to the fruits of his labor. These "philosophical differences between the US and Japanese patent systems will remain for a long time," said Akira Okawa, a former chief examiner in the Japanese Patent Office.[55] "In Japan, we have a balance between the rights of patent holders and society. In the U.S., they don't care about society."[56]

[54] Clayton Jones, *U.S., Japan Closer to Pact on Patent Procedure*, L.A. TIMES, Oct. 12, 1992, at D3, col. 1.

[55] *Ibid.*

[56] *Ibid.*

QUESTIONS AND COMMENTS FOR YOUR CONSIDERATION

1. Is harmonization a viable solution for disparate intellectual property systems based on contradictory philosophical or cultural bases?
2. Can US and Japanese patent laws be harmonized? How?

2. China and the Protection of Intellectual Property Rights[57]

The notion of intellectual property protection has a short history in China. Although past regulations have governed some forms of intellectual property, a modern intellectual property protection system began to emerge only with the implementation of China's reform and open-door policy and China's endeavor to modernize its legal system during the early 1980s. This delayed emergence is not surprising, however, in view of the fact that until then the concept of property rights in general had little importance or relevance in the Chinese society.

Current Chinese patent law does not protect pharmaceutical or chemical products, although patent rights may be available for processes used in making such products. The lack of patent protection for pharmaceutical and chemical products is a major source of concern for US pharmaceutical and chemical industries.

Chinese law does not explicitly protect against the unauthorized acquisition of trade secrets by third parties. In the United States, trade secrets are generally protected by the law of each state, and some states also have adopted the Uniform Trade Secrets Act. In China the grant of a trade secret, unlike that of patents, does not confer exclusive rights for a specific number of years. Rather, protection of trade secrets depends upon the possessors' ability to preserve confidentiality, *e.g.*, through contractual confidentiality provisions in technology licensing, distributorship, employment, and joint venture agreements. Consequently, protection of trade secrets requires different legal mechanisms.

China follows the "first-to-file" principle in both patent application and trademark registration. A patent is granted to the first registrant to file a patent application, and a registrant receives protection for the use of a trademark if he is the first to register the trademark. Chinese law does not require a showing of prior use in order to obtain the

[57] Xiao-Lin Zhou, *U.S.–China Trade Dispute and China's Intellectual Property Rights Protection*, 24 N.Y.U. J. INT'L L. & POL. 1115. Copyright 1992 New York University Journal of International Law and Politics. Excerpt reprinted with permission.

initial registration of a trademark, and use by itself will not result in exclusive rights to a trademark, with the exception of well-known marks under the Paris Convention.

In contrast, the United States employs a first-to-invent standard with respect to patents, under which the first to file may not necessarily be the party which is ultimately awarded a patent. With regard to trademarks, except under certain circumstances a federal registration of a mark is granted only upon a showing of actual use in interstate commerce and after a specimen proving use is provided to the Patent and Trademark Office. Legal protection is not afforded for service marks, semiconductor mask marks, or unpublished works of foreigners in China. Such protection may be available pursuant to applicable international agreements.

The protection terms of some intellectual property are shorter in China than in the United States. For example, the patent protection periods for an invention, a utility model and a design model in the United States and China are 17, 17, and 14 years and 15, 5, and 5 years, respectively. Also, computer software receives a shorter term of protection in China than other protected works.

Chinese law and US law differ with respect to the compulsory licensing of copyrights, although the extent of the difference is not easy to assess due to the relatively short history of the Chinese copyright law and the lack of relevant practice. However, provisions in Chinese patent law on compulsory licensing thus far have not proved to be a major concern in practice for foreign or domestic patentees.

Intellectual property laws in the United States and China differ markedly in terms of implementation and enforcement. In China, although there are judicial remedies for patent, trademark, and copyright infringements and violations, the emphasis is clearly placed on administrative and other non-judicial remedies such as mediation and arbitration; intellectual property litigation is generally disfavored.

Intellectual property laws vary from country to country in many aspects and the differences between Chinese and US intellectual property laws are not unique. For example, many countries, especially developing countries (*e.g.*, India), do not grant patents for pharmaceutical products, and some countries (*e.g.*, Brazil) do not protect either pharmaceutical products or processes. Similarly, computer software receives copyright protection for only twenty-five years in France and service mark registration was, until recently, unavailable even in Japan. Moreover, differences between Chinese and US intellectual property law may not necessarily mean diminution of protection of US intellectual property rights in China. For example, the use of administrative and other non-judicial procedures as a means of dispute settlement in China, as opposed to the more frequent use of litigation in the United States, actually has resulted, in some cases, in a speedy and less costly resolution of intellectual property-related disputes. Further, as noted before, efforts are being made to bring the level of intellectual property protection in China up to international standards.

QUESTIONS AND COMMENTS FOR YOUR CONSIDERATION

1. In harmonizing Chinese and US laws, whose standards should apply? The US? China's? Some other standard?

2. Should harmonization be achieved on a bilateral basis? What are the advantages of this approach? What are the disadvantages?

PART IV
EMERGING BATTLEFIELDS

13

Technological Innovations

The emergence of new technologies has continually strained the ability of intellectual property laws to protect the creative and economic interests of those who create or use these new technologies to embody or disseminate their works. This Chapter focuses on the problems posed by the emergence of computer software, satellite broadcast and digital communications as examples of the diversity of issues which must be resolved on a global basis whenever new technologies arise. We start with an exploration of the problems posed by efforts to develop multinational standards for the protection of computer software. We then take up the unique problems posed by cyberspace, including the problem of enforcement of rights, given the international nature of any potential infringements that may occur through the unauthorized dissemination of works over the global information highway. The Chapter ends with an examination of the problems posed by the newly expanding technologies of digital and satellite communication.

A. Protecting Computer Software[1]

A framework of appropriate property rights is essential to preserving stability in modern industrial society. The emergence of new commercial goods, such as software in the 1960s or, most relevant to the current dialogue, genetic technology in the 1990s, has revealed uncertainties as to whether our legal system can develop norms that will integrate these products into the market and will increase economic efficiency. Structuring these rights in the form of endogenous and exogenous restrictions (that is, restrictions within the copyright system itself, as well as more general clauses and conditions) is important so that the scope of every property right fulfills its intended socio-economic function.

The critical question is thus how to balance the competing interests of encouraging production and protecting competition. Since the early 1960s, the general consensus in Japan, the United States, and Europe has been that conferring a property right would ensure sufficient and appropriate protection of software. Property rights encourage the development of certain commercial products and facilitate their integration into the competitive marketplace. Because maximizing efficiency in manufacturing and trade is desirable from a macroeconomic perspective, it is often argued that the type of property right envisioned by Coase[9] should be created and assigned to an economic maximization entity for exploitation in conformity with market principles.

In the past, the debate concerning how best to protect computer software was shaped by a tendency to try to categorize new commercial goods in law by looking into the rear view mirror of institutional history. The discussion focused on whether patent law, copyright law, or a newly created *sui generis* system of protection—one created through specific legislation, as in the case of semi-conductor chip topography protection—provided the best protection of computer software. More recently, the debate

---

[1] Michael Lehmann, *Trips, The Berne Convention, And Legal Hybrids*, 94 COLUM L. REV. 2621. Copyright 1994 Directors of the Columbia Law Review Association, Inc. Excerpt reprinted with permission.

[9] Ronald H. Coase, *The Problem of Social Cost*, 3 J.L. & ECON. 1 (1960).

has changed direction, and has focused more intensely on copyright.

The TRIPS Agreement of December 15, 1993 established copyright protection of computer software. Article 10 of the Agreement provides: "Computer programs, whether in source or object code, shall be protected as literary works under the Berne Convention (1971)." This recent development leaves practically no leeway for the further expansion of legal hybrids as instruments for the protection of software.

The global acceptance of the Berne Convention for the Protection of Literary and Artistic Works (Paris Version) argues persuasively for integrating software into the copyright system. The term "literary and artistic works" in Article 2(1) of the Berne Convention has an extremely broad meaning and thus allows computer programs to receive protection with relative ease. However, the Convention necessarily excludes *sui generis* protection and legal hybrids, because it refers only to copyright in a strict sense.

Protecting computer software under the Berne Convention yields several benefits. Most importantly, it extends to software the principle of national treatment, more precisely described as the principle of nondiscrimination against foreigners, and the guarantee of the numerous minimum standards of protection.

Second, using copyright as the primary framework to protect software preserves competition in the market. Copyright protects against the theft of intellectual property (*i.e.*, against plagiarism), while national patent law systems (and on an international level, the Paris Convention) effectively block competition with a concrete barrier to entry, as rightholders may temporarily develop a complete monopoly in a certain technical sector.

Third, copyright protection of software is consistent with international differences in the construction of patent law. For example, for primarily historical reasons, the term "technology" is construed more narrowly in Europe than in the United States. The European construction has resulted in a per se exclusion of software patenting from the European patent law system, as demonstrated by the German Patent Act and the European Patent Convention. The intention was to spare European patent law the burden of resolving international disputes concerning the boundaries of software patenting. As a result of these well-intentioned approaches, patent law has developed in a manner incompatible with the protection of computer software. Consequently, copyright is the only viable regime of protection already in operation.

1. Harmonizing Conflicting Laws and Policies[10]

A tension exists between the European Economic Community's (EEC's) promotion of a common market and its member-states' retention of national copyright laws. In some instances, enforcement of copyright restrictions by individual member-states restrains or otherwise distorts trade. Yet Article 3 of the Community's enabling treaty requires the elimination of quantitative import and export restrictions and of all other measures having equivalent effect. It further requires the abolition of obstacles to the free movement of services, and it ensures undistorted Community-wide market competition. Uneven enforcement of uneven copyright law, as shall be seen, may contravene each of these Community goals. The current worldwide debate regarding the copyrightability of software acquires special significance in the EEC, therefore, since the issue brings these problems sharply into focus.

By consciously harmonizing, and perhaps softening, national copyright laws, the Community's member-states should each be able to establish a larger market for its nationals' software products. This increased market could in turn spur further production and consumption of software goods and services. If coupled with a program of hardware standardization, the increased uniformity might soon enable Europe to appropriate a larger portion of the global information industry's profits to itself.

---

[10] Dennis Cline, *Copyright Protection of Software in the EEC: The Competing Policies Underlying Community and National Law and the Case for Harmonization,* 75 CAL. L. REV. 633. Copyright 1987 California Law Review. Excerpt reprinted with permission.

Because the authority of a country granting copyright protection can only extend to its borders, differences in national copyright laws tend to define markets of varying opportunity for rights-holders in a given work. Presumably, authors prefer to market in jurisdictions actively protecting the authors' monopoly. The territorial nature of copyright thus tends to delimit advantageous markets in goods and services. Where, however, the copyright laws of individual member-states affect the free movement of Community goods and services, or where they distort Community-wide market competition, the laws contravene basic EEC policy.[11]

A series of issues arises from the lack of harmony in the . . . treatment of software . . . . The first and most obvious problem is the prospect of pirates remarketing programs from a "haven" in which copyright is not recognized. Theoretically, a would-be pirate could purchase a single copy of a consentedly marketed program, copy it repeatedly without consent, then sell the copied goods throughout the unrestricted common market. As the European Court has ruled on a number of occasions, consented marketing in an unprotected jurisdiction exhausts the specific subject matter of the intellectual property right in question, in this case the right to prohibit copying. Practically, though, the freeriding enterprise would not immediately succeed. As in the videogame cases, a pirate can still be enjoined in its home jurisdiction under principles of unfair competition, even absent copyright protection. However, given a jurisdiction hostile to copyright-like monopolies, the duration of the creator's protected headstart in the marketplace could be foreshortened. This would effectively allow pirate competition while demand for the product or its copies was still high.

Another scenario involving "havens" postulates entrepreneurs who are willing to reverse-engineer noncopyrightable programs in order to rewrite the works as "original" creations. Such rewriting can be accomplished within a wide spectrum of sophistication, ranging from the juxtaposition of a few lines to complete reinterpretation relying only in the broadest outline on an original program's problem-solving logic. Where copyright is not available to prohibit—or even to discourage—unauthorized copying and adaptation, entrepreneurs might feel justified in expending the time and effort necessary to bypass the unfair competition laws. This would be particularly true where sympathetic courts created an easily achieved threshold of derived originality that would allow early access to the marketplace.

Of course it would be surprising if a government openly encouraged piracy. Official inattention is the more likely possibility, especially insofar as such inattention stimulates the creation of jobs, attracts capital to local, potentially vigorous, high technology ventures, or increases the productivity or competitive posture of existing national firms. If so inclined, governments could either refuse to rule on copyright's applicability or, in apparent harmony with the more industrialized northern member-states, declare for protection but rarely find infringement. Even the northern states are reluctant to grant all types of software full copyright protection, as seen for example in the French limited-rights scheme and the widely vary-

---

[11] With the recent addition of Spain and Portugal, the European Economic Community now consists of twelve member-states: France, the United Kingdom, the Federal Republic of Germany, Italy, Belgium, the Netherlands, Luxembourg, Denmark, Ireland, Greece, and the two Iberian states. By signing or acceding to the Community's enabling treaty, each of these nations agreed to cede limited sovereign authority to the "economic union" thereby created.

Article 2 of the Treaty of Rome defines the Community's economic task as promoting "a harmonious development of economic activities" by creation of a common market.

Article 3 details the means for implementing the common market among the member states, mandating: (1) the elimination of customs duties and quantitative restrictions on trade; (2) the establishment of a common customs tariff and commercial policy towards third party countries; (3) the abolition of obstacles to free movement of persons, services, and capital; (4) the adoption of a common policy as to both agriculture and transport; and (5) the institution of a system ensuring that intra-Community competition not be distorted.

The European Court of Justice, authorized in Article 164 of the Treaty, adjudicates controversies related to the union. The European Commission acts as a Community ministry empowered to define and set Community economic policy, to implement programs aimed at further economic integration, and to bring cases before the Court of Justice where deemed necessary.

ing protection of videogames. Thus, a sensitivity to the public's demand for access to utilitarian and modernizing computer goods may have to be taken into account: politically by the as yet undecided member-states, and tactically by international enterprises deciding where to sell their products.

The problem of unequal protection also arises in the context of varied durations of protection. As matters now stand, for example, France protects software for twenty-five years, the United Kingdom protects it for the author's life plus fifty years, Germany does so for the author's life plus seventy years, and Greece may be contemplating a much shorter *sui generis* term. If programs retain marketplace vitality after the shortest of these Community protection periods has run, exploitation in the remaining jurisdictions must be severely undermined.

This problem may be illustrated in the context of exploitation rights in videogames. If Germany, for instance, only protects videogames for a twelve-month period but French videogames enjoy a twenty-five-year copyright protection, German imports of original French videogames in the thirteenth month escape French protection of the author's exploitation rights. This may be an unintended consequence of original French marketing. In short, the uneven nature of copyright protection, coupled with established EEC jurisprudence in this area, may well discourage dissemination of useful—or in the case of videogames, entertaining—works throughout the Community.

Traditional notions of authorship and individual rights only partially reflect the reality of software production. Software's usefulness to industrializing nations will increase as the telecommunications industry provides greater technical integration between nations. As a result, the demand for software in some countries will almost certainly outweigh the perceived cultural benefits traditionally associated with protectionist copyright regimes. Insulating rich institutional "authors" at the expense of progress must increasingly concern excluded states, some of whom are now members of the Community, and others of whom may wish to join.

On a global level, this perceived inequality in access to information permeates the North-South debate and could harden into defiance where the disharmony of copyright laws deters marketing in countries whose laws inadequately protect such information. At the Community level, software distributors may face a similar problem. Fearing piracy, and mindful of Community rules, vendors may seek to limit their spheres of consented marketing to protected jurisdictions. This would increase the temptation to copy in the high-risk but information-hungry countries. As a result of such spiraling tension, the common market would become less "common," more stratified, and the Community's already shrinking chances of being able to compete in the global telecommunication and information markets would only be further reduced. The obvious solution to this problem is to achieve a workable harmony of protection throughout the EEC.

Currently, the northern industrial member-states have reacted to the beleaguered software community's demands by characterizing software as a literary work within the meaning of their respective copyright laws. While no doubt justified, these characterizations may soon be self-defeating and unenforceable. The demand for software and the ease with which it is copied have already forced vendors in protected states to resort to half-measures such as site licensing in order to recoup profits otherwise lost through institutional sales. In less affluent states, granting a monopoly lasting for fifty to seventy years beyond an author's life in a market where the product only retains vitality for two to three years will undoubtedly seem oppressive and unwarranted. Piracy will flourish. This can satisfy neither the software manufacturers nor the member-states.

What, then, are the options presented the Court in this evolving dilemma? First, and most obviously, the present market and political actors can stay their course and hope for an unimposed harmony to develop. This option has the advantage of being both politically feasible and desirable. Only Italy, Greece, Spain, Portugal, Belgium, and Luxembourg remain unofficially declared as to copyright protection for software—and each shows signs of at least scholarly acceptance of such protection. There are two problems with this option, however. First, the hoped-for harmony may never in fact be achieved. Scholarly acceptance will not necessarily translate into governmental action. Second, if member-states do not enforce "officially" recognized copyright, hypocrisy results. "Official" and actual law no longer coincide. Then, since copying will not be controlled, it will almost certainly occur. In the meantime, costs increase to noncopying consumers forced to pay premiums on their *bona fide* purchases.

Of course, some will argue that an official adoption of copyright automatically curbs piracy by creating a constant threat of enforcement. This is true, however, only to the extent that the public perceives a governmental willingness to enforce the rights-holder's monopoly. Where member-states declare for copyright, but never find infringement, or continually delay relief, the hypocrisy must in the end erode the official declaration's deterrent force.

Further, official "harmony" does not reduce actual cacophony. The protection that "copyright" officially grants can vary broadly. Germany protects some programs for seventy years plus the author's life, but leaves open the possibility that other programs, such as videogames, will not be protected because they do not reach the level of "personal intellectual creations." France explicitly protects software, but only for twenty-five years—and this is under a constitutionally questionable scheme. The United Kingdom's entire copyright act is under revision, and scholars continue to revile the amendment that specified software as copyrightable literary work. Even assuming that the Community's southern nations accede to copyright as a legal label, there can be little doubt that their jurisprudence will further complicate the already uneven protection which exists throughout the Community.

In such an uncertain environment, authors must recoup their investment and take profits immediately. Even those countries willing to enforce copyright may not actually be able to enforce it, given the ease of both domestic piracy and the possibility of legal reimportation of copies made in neighboring, unprotected jurisdictions. Demanding an immediate return on investment creates problems in addition to artificially high pricing, however. It also reduces authors' incentives to plan for long-term revenues through servicing and updates, a significant source of income that could be obtained at modest pricing levels through Community-wide marketing. By encouraging a system based on hypocritical copyright "harmony," therefore, the Community is actually discouraging consumer access to software. Since noncopying consumers will have to pay premiums on their legitimate purchases, the range of programs available to them will be limited. In addition, because copying is difficult to stop, software manufacturers will have little incentive to maintain the integrity of the programs in circulation.

Of course, political considerations often force Community member-states to settle for "harmony" in such disputed matters even though "uniformity" would better serve the ideal of European integration. Nonetheless, the case for uniformity has merit. European efforts to break into the high technology global markets have met with limited success, a result partially due to the fractionalization of the Community along technical lines. A uniform approach to protection of software, coupled with Community manufacture and standardization of software and hardware could, on the other hand, create market opportunities for Community enterprises that are now reserved to powerful, non-Community, multinational corporations able to dictate to world and European markets, such as IBM.

Several activist steps commend themselves in place of the current unfocused, case-by-case, statute-by-statute "evolution." Three such steps will be proposed here. The easiest course of action open to the EEC would be to follow the French lead and press for a Community-wide protection of the minimum length possible under copyright and the Berne Convention, that is, twenty-five years. If this period seems overly long, the Berne Convention itself should be amended so as to include a special *sui generis* section specifically allowing for a less lengthy period of protection. Another possibility is that member-states could be encouraged to recant their positions as to the literary nature of programming, a course that, however, has obvious difficulties. Enhanced enforcement and penalties should accompany the reduced period of protection in order to assure entrepreneurs of a reasonable profit by reducing competition from unauthorized copying. Copying should become less justifiable to consumers once they realize that they are more likely to be punished if caught, and that the work will become public property within a relatively short time.

Of course, adoption of such a scheme for standardizing and minimizing the time period for protection would not automatically improve Europe's posture *vis-a-vis* non-EEC countries. Foreign authors would gain and lose protection in the same manner as would Community authors. If, however, the Community could standardize the underlying hardware used in its computer and telecommunications markets, European software entrepreneurs familiar with those devices would be given the natural headstart associated with technological know-how. Rather than having to force IBM to disclose its plans for peripherals and future generations of other standard-setting devices, the Community could manufacture such advantages for itself. Further, Europeans would presumably have easy access and rights to successful programs interacting with users in European languages. These programs could be code-translated rapidly so as to take advantage of the EEC-wide economies of scale. If operating systems remain protectable under the proposed scheme, the rights-holders in the hardware-interfacing software could further protect what could easily become a burgeoning and synergistic industry from unauthorized competition, a tactic that Apple Computers, for example, has used successfully under the current copyright regimes.

This policy proposal focuses on the correct balancing of an author's incentive against the public benefit of dissemination, an entirely correct approach to traditional copyright works. But software, by virtue of its utilitarian nature, implicates another consideration: freedom of access to the program's useful ideas and methods. In patent law, the creator's monopoly incentive is balanced by a relatively short period of protection and by rigid requirements of registration and disclosure. Thus, as soon as the protection period runs, the patented idea is available to all interested parties. In the meantime, the idea has been both published and explicated. This becomes relevant in the software context because copyright's inability to deter misappropriation has driven the software industry to adopt self-help measures that inhibit user access to underlying programs by technical means. By staying their present course, the Court and Community could therefore be inadvertently overprotecting software by sanctioning long-lived legal patronage while at the same time encouraging secrecy as to a program's functional innovations. Copyright protection of traditional works never faces this problem because publication or performance in itself discloses the author's method of operation.

This raises the second broad policy option. Patent protection for software has been uniformly rejected by the global community, but official registration of software within a weaker copyright scheme might at least allow for a wider dissemination of a program's underlying innovations. For instance, the Community might guarantee a copyright-like market-wide protection of computer programs, perhaps on the French model, but require all creators desiring such protection to deposit hard copies of the program's underlying code with a collecting governmental body. Manufacturers seeking the granted privilege would be required to warn potential users of the claimed protection. The deposited code would be in turn be available to all interested parties, but direct copying of its structure or elements would be prohibited. Thus, the ideas underlying the work would be available to society at large, but the creator's personal expression of those ideas could only be exploited by the holder of his or her rights. Notably, a similar idea has already been proposed within Germany's patent office in reaction to that country's recently passed legislation. The chances of success for such a scheme will be slim, however, if software continues to be analyzed as a traditional literary work. The Berne Convention prohibits any sort of formality in the recognition of copyright. Again, amendment of the Convention should be considered so as to allow special treatment of software.

As a third, rather drastic, option the Community could recognize the trend that software vendors have already had to accept: unworkable copyright protection may have to be replaced by other methods of cost recovery and exploitation. While it is true that any type of technical restriction to a program's code can eventually be reverse-engineered by sufficiently motivated experts, such technical inhibitory devices at least delay widespread misappropriation. In the meantime, unfair competition rules could assure software vendors lucrative exploitation of market opportunities. Coupled with judicious grants of renewable licenses, tied updates, maintenance agreements, and so forth, the industry might be able to achieve a steady stream of income without any need for copyright protection. In fact, it is entirely possible that manufacturers could eventually find such copy-protection devices counterproductive. If a company strategically markets hard-copy documentation, "hotline" telephone services, constant "necessary" state-of-the-art enhancements, and so on, it could even find itself encouraging copying, as an aid to widespread dissemination of its income-generating product.

Another factor informs this analysis. Hardware manufacturers depend on software dissemination to sell their products. Programs are a computer's "fuel." Thus, a lack of software impedes technical innovation and is considered the greatest bottleneck in widespread computer utilization today. A radical response to the need for both dissemination of programs and incentives for programmers would be to shift the burden of programmers' remuneration back to the hardware manufacturers. By licensing their computers' use rather than selling the discrete units outright, manufacturers could create a steady income stream from which to compensate programmers who are designing software for that particular system. The software could be provided without charge, or at a minimal price. Copying might even be encouraged since it would promote long-term licensing demand.

This proposal has the advantage of encouraging program updates and the rapid dissemination of new products. It also encourages the provision of satisfactory troubleshooting procedures for unsophisticated users. But it suffers serious problems also. First, it would almost certainly meet with vehement opposition from hardware manufacturers who can now market their products in reliance on the provision of compatible software by third parties, then walk away from the transaction. Software vendors may also balk at this reduced market for their wares. Rather than competing in the consumer marketplace for their reward, vendors would be faced by hardware enterprises able to control a machine's software supply. Manufacturers might be able to dictate inappropriately low purchase prices for software since they would be negotiating deals before any demand for a particular program could in fact be demonstrated. On the other hand, hardware manufacturers would need to keep the demand for their licensed product high—or forego any future benefit from that model. Market interplay might adequately adjust these tensions.

Finally, however, this type of scheme could founder on antitrust rules. Control of the downstream market for software may smack of unacceptable market manipulation through vertical integration, a problem already faced by the Community in its IBM litigation. Although hardware manufacturers would continue to compete on the amount and quality of software their systems could support, the perceived benefits might not justify the anticompetitive costs associated with an entire industry's absorption by its spawning enterprises. Still, vertical integration is not a per se violation of EEC antitrust rules. Where such integration could broaden the dissemination of both hardware and software to Community consumers and businesses, it must be considered superior to the current ad hoc approach.

At the legal level, then, a European Court confronting these issues must seek to satisfy a multitude of competing policies. It must keep in mind not only legal precedent and the legitimate concerns of the various interest groups, but also must take into account the Community's ultimate mission: political integration through economics. The obvious course is to encourage a workable harmonization of laws—and preferably a uniformity of those laws—that will allow programmers and the industry that supports them to survive and flourish. This goal will be accomplished when affordable access to a program's use and ideas reduces the temptation merely to appropriate those features.

Two broad courses exist. On the one hand, the Court can continue on its present course by reaffirming its test of "consented marketing." If software competition from pirates or other freeriding enterprises cannot be traced to an explicitly authorized first sale by the copyright owner, an injunction against such pirating would be allowed under national law. This approach has the advantage of political acceptability since each member-state would essentially chart its own course. The chief disadvantage is that the scheme encourages harmonization through hypocrisy. If copying is rampant because prices are too high, or because the programmer's reward seems too remote or undeserved, enforcement will be difficult no matter what law has passed. The scheme also distorts distribution of software by discouraging its dissemination in unprotected jurisdictions. Still, if the premiums paid by law-abiding consumers can support the industry without driving those consumers to illegal copying also, the *status quo* will be preserved. Unfortunately, the *status quo* is not one favorable to enterprises native to the EEC.

Similar results will be achieved if the Court merely finds...that the lack of harmonization precludes enforcement of Community rules assuring the free movement of goods and services. Enforcement of national protection rules would then be allowed. Again, the present copyright regimes would entrench the *status quo*.

The alternative to these two options is drastic and would require a rather greater resolve by the Court and other Community actors. It is a posture, however, that could revitalize the Community's high technology industry. The Court, in order to achieve harmony and eventual uniformity of law, could sanction present disharmony. It could hold that, although copyright is in fact governed by the Treaty of Rome, not all aspects of copyright are governed by that agreement. The Court could distinguish the useful industrial matter that some countries protect via their copyright regimes from the cultural-aesthetic matter traditionally associated with copyright. Utilitarian goods and services such as software could then be subjected to rigid Community rules. Although this would create an uproar in the software industry, it would at least galvanize a rethinking of the arguable overprotection granted by enforced copyright, and of the hypocrisy of unenforced copyright. This, in turn, would encourage a Community-wide treatment of a novel problem which, if achieved, could create a new Community-wide economy of scale rather than one based on the limited number of consumers willing to pay premiums in order to offset losses from widely copied software.

Collaterally, the latter approach encourages a Community-wider harmonization of traditional copyright and its associated moral rights; matters which seem oddly out of place in the context of industrial goods. This Comment has therefore suggested three courses of action that would better serve the Community than its current inertial acceptance of the *status quo*: a *sui generis* scheme, similar to copyright, that radically reshifts the balance of dissemination and entrepreneurial incentive; registration within existing or created copyright schemes so as to publicize the work's underlying ideas and methods; and/or altering the system so as to make hardware manufacturers responsible for supporting the software entrepreneurs currently "fueling" their computers.

QUESTIONS AND COMMENTS FOR YOUR CONSIDERATION

1. How would you resolve the conflicting issues posed by the above essay in determining the appropriate standard of protection for computer software? How do you balance the competing interests to best serve the interests of all concerned parties?

2. To what extent, if any, do the issues posed by the essay reflect the greater concerns of non-EC nations in connection with the protection of computer software? Would the analysis differ if you represented a developing country as opposed to the developed countries of the EC?

3. For an economic examination of the role of computer database protection, *see* Chapter Three. Applying this analysis to computer software protection, which type of protection makes economic sense?

2. The EC Software Directive[12]

Unlike the US Copyright Act, the EC Software Directive (the "Directive") explicitly addresses the issue of software reverse engineering, thereby obligating the EC member countries to do the same in their respective national copyright laws.

While US copyright law is regulated by the Federal Copyright Act, EC copyright is administered by twelve separate national laws. This is true, in spite of the fact that several EC Directives, including the Software Directive, are aimed at harmonizing these issues. All EC Member countries have been parties to the Berne Convention for a considerable time. In spite of the fact that their membership to that Convention has certainly had a harmonizing effect on their national copyright laws, differences in the laws still abound. Such differences arise not only between the common-law countries (*i.e.*, UK and Ireland), on the one hand and the ten continental, so called civil-law countries on the other, but the law also varies from one civil-law country to another. In fact, the civil-law concept refers mainly to certain corresponding tendencies in legal thought, the structure of laws, and the administration of justice. Civil law in no way guarantees any uniformity beyond that level. In consequence, the differences between continental European national laws are as varied and major as are those between UK and US laws, if not more so.

All European copyright laws require a work to be original, at least as a general principle, but the implementation of this concept varies greatly. All continental laws require a work, including software, to be the fruit of personal creative labor. This certainly does not exclude the use of automated tools in the creation of a work, but the personal aspect must not be wholly absent. On the other hand, in most countries the threshold for originality is probably fairly low. For instance, under French or Dutch law, originality can be described by the maxim that a work is original if it must be considered impossible, or even highly unlikely, that it could independently be created twice in more or less identical form. There are essentially two exceptions to this mainstream interpretation of the originality concept: the UK interpretation and the German interpretation.

The UK approach is generally understood to require a lesser amount of personal creativity than required by French law. In UK law, a work is considered to be original if it is the fruit of an author's personal labor or even of an automated process. The work need not be in any way unique, provided that it is not itself a copy from another work. On the other hand, German law has always been much more demanding. German law concerning software requires a creative input which is above the ordinary programmer's skill. The effect of this requirement is that only a small minority of all computer programs may enjoy copyright protection. The requirement can also severely limit the extent to which even copyrighted programs are protected. For example, certain program routines or modules may still fail to meet the threshold requirements.

As a result of the German interpretation of originality, many computer programs which enjoyed copyright protection in most countries lacked such protection in Germany, thus affecting the trade of computer software within the EC. One of the main concerns of the EC is to remove trade barriers between the member states. Harmonization of the originality concept with respect to software was certainly one of the primary motives for the Directive. Other significant aspects of software copyright which are addressed in the Directive include reverse engineering and compatibility.

The Directive focuses on harmonizing the main aspects of software copyright by standardizing the required level of originality, the notion of authorship, and the restricted acts, as well as the main exceptions thereto. Article 1, paragraph 3 of the Directive states that "[a] computer program shall be protected if it is original in the sense that it is the author's own intellectual creation [and] no other criteria shall be applied to determine its eligibility for protection." There is little doubt that this text is meant to give a fairly low threshold for protection that is compara-

---

[12] Jaap H. Spoor, *Copyright Protection And Reverse Engineering Of Software: Implementation And Effects Of The EC Directive*, 19 U. Dayton L. Rev. 1063. Copyright 1994 University of Dayton Law Review. Excerpt reprinted with permission.

ble to the French or Dutch levels, and far below the very demanding standard set by the German Supreme Court. The words "the author's own intellectual creation" however leave room for different interpretations.

Article 4 of the Directive provides:

> The exclusive rights of the rightholder . . . shall include the right to do or to authorize [inter alia] the permanent or temporary reproduction of a computer program by any means and in any form, in part or in whole. Insofar as loading, displaying, running, transmission or storage of the computer program necessitate such reproduction, such acts shall be subject to authorization by the rightholder.

Although the text is somewhat circular, it is generally understood to mean that loading, displaying, running, transmission or storage is indeed reproduction. The idea that any copying, however transitory, is indeed to be considered reproduction is not universally accepted, especially by German scholars.

Article 5, paragraph 3 expressly provides:

> [The rightful user] shall be entitled, without the authorization of the rightholder, to observe, study or test the functioning of the program in order to determine the ideas and principles which underlie any element of the program if he does so while performing any of the acts of loading, displaying, running, transmitting or storing the program which he is entitled to do.

In other words, the user may try to find out from the outside how the program works.

Article 6 permits decompilation, or rather "reproduction of the code and translation of its form," if it is "indispensable to obtain the information necessary to achieve the interoperability of an independently created computer program with other programs." This provision is the essence of Article 6, although the article addresses several other topics: decompilation, permissible use of information, and interpretation of Article 6. Decompilation may only be performed by or on behalf of a rightful user, and only if the information "has not previously been readily available" to them. Decompilation must remain limited to "the parts of the original program necessary to achieve interoperability." Furthermore, the permissible use of the information obtained is subject to several restrictions. Finally, by its third paragraph the interpretation of Article 6 may not unreasonably prejudice the rightholder's legitimate interests or conflict with a normal exploitation of the computer program. This last provision explicitly refers to the Berne Convention, and clearly echoes Article 9, paragraph 2 thereof.

Article 6 leaves many questions to be resolved. For example, the Directive gives no guidance as to how much code one may actually decompile in search for interfaces, or is at least unclear as to how one can actually know what to decompile. Furthermore, the article does not mention the subject of compatibility with hardware, while it is uncertain whether a solution can always be reached through software. Finally and perhaps most important, what kind of interfaces does Article 6 cover: official interfaces only, that is, such parts of a program as are considered by the rightholder as interfaces, unofficial interfaces, especially those which have gained acceptance as interfaces in the industry; or anything which may serve as an interface, that is, any spot in a program where data are transmitted without being altered? This is a much debated issue. Rightholders may fear that the reputation of their programs will be compromised by the fact that new releases may not interface with certain independently developed programs because the parts that served as an unofficial interface were changed in the new release. The other side may claim it needs to use the most efficient interfaces it can find and its creativity, as well as new developments, is impaired if it may only use what the developer of the original program thinks is appropriate.

Article 6 permits decompilation in order to obtain certain information. It does not, however, permit the use of such information if that use is covered by a patent. It could be argued conversely that, to the extent the use of the interface is covered by a patent, even the decompilation will not be allowed.

Although originality is one of the points which the Directive specifically intended to harmonize, and this harmonization roused strong feelings in several countries, it can be doubted whether the final wording of the

Directive is sufficiently unambiguous to lead to a uniform interpretation. Given the reluctance of the German doctrine to accept the lower threshold of the Directive, German courts probably will not consider any and all interfaces original. On the other hand, it must equally be doubted whether an English court, if convinced that the interface was made by the programmer himself, will feel inclined to apply further tests for originality. In this author's view, no German court, nor indeed a Dutch one, would consider original such interfaces as ones merely consisting of the letters "SEGA" or "IBM." Such interfaces therefore could be freely used (provided of course the other conditions have been met) and, one might add, considerably larger interfaces probably could be freely used as well. Of course, it may be a matter of policy whether one dares take the risk, or whether one prefers to follow the hard but more secure way of clean room re-engineering of the interface code.

3. The Problem of Application[13]

The Software Directive is the most significant piece of intellectual property legislation already in place in the EU.[14] Overall, the Software Directive provides an example of the European Union's intent to strengthen intellectual property rights. During the debates over the Software Directive, the proponents of open systems and compatibility won a significant victory on the scope of protection for interfaces and on the permissibility of reverse analysis. However, it would be inappropriate to view this victory as having improperly diminished the copyright protection available under the Software Directive to program developers. Indeed, European software developers now will have an unprecedented and uniform level of protection throughout Europe, and arguably better protection than anywhere else in the world.

Besides providing a broad scope of protection for computer programs (in terms of the restricted acts that are within the exclusive domain of the rightholder), the Software Directive also assures that no special degree of creativity is required for a program to qualify as an original work in the copyright sense. Moreover, the Software Directive ensures the availability of tough enforcement mechanisms. These have been sorely lacking in many places in the world, including some EU Member States, and it is this lack of adequate enforcement mechanisms to which most attention should be devoted in the software protection area.

The Single Market completion date of January 1, 1993 also marked the implementation deadline for the Software Directive. Only three countries (the United Kingdom, Denmark, and Italy) managed to meet this deadline. However, most of the other Member States have since finalized, or are in the process of finalizing, their implementing legislation.

Generally speaking, there has been little controversy surrounding national implementation of the Software Directive, and it certainly has not approached the battle which raged over the adoption of the Directive itself. Moreover, Member State governments seem to have little tolerance for continued controversy over software protection. Although the debate over the appropriate balance between protection and competition in the information technology industry has not been fully resolved, further battles in this area appear more likely to occur in courts than in Member State legislatures.

As far as implementation is concerned, Member States appear generally to have followed the intent of the Directive, if not its exact language. Two basic approaches to implementation now exist. The UK statutory instrument, adopted on December 15, 1992, and the draft Dutch legislation, integrate the Directive piece by piece into existing copyright legislation. Other Member States are implementing the Directive as a single "stand-alone" piece, although few, if any, will adopt the Directive word for word. The UK government's approach of integrating the Directive's provisions into the Copyright,

---

[13] Thomas C. Vinje, *Recent Developments In European Intellectual Property Law: How Will They Affect You and When?* 13 J. L. & COM. (1994). Copyright 1994 Thomas C. Vinje. Excerpt Reprinted With Permission.

[14] Council Directive 91/250 of May 14, 1991 on The Legal Protection of Computer Programs, 1991 O.J. (L 122) 42.

Designs, and Patents Act of 1988, rather than adding the Directive's entire text as an addendum to the existing law, has been the subject of criticism. Some large US software vendors, for example, complained before its adoption that the UK statutory instrument would deprive them of the ability to devise pan-European software licenses for use throughout the European Union. However, unlike EU regulations, which are directly incorporated into Member State law, EU directives by their very nature permit some degree of legislative leeway. Moreover, despite its changes to the precise wording of the Directive, the UK implementation appears to be consistent with the meaning of the Directive; indeed, the UK approach would not in practice appear to present any obstacle to the use of EU-wide software licenses.

As noted, even those countries implementing the Directive as a "stand-alone" section of their copyright legislation are not adopting the Directive word for word. For example, the Danish legislation excludes Article 6(3) of the Directive from its implementing legislation, and the German legislation seeks to make it clear that the Inkasso decision is no longer valid by providing, unlike the text of the Directive, that "qualitative or aesthetic criteria" may not be applied to determine whether a program is original.

Member States have dealt with decompilation, which is the most controversial of the Directive's provisions, in various ways:

—The Irish law reproduces the text of Article 6 word-for-word;
—The Danish law reproduces the text of Article 6(1) and 6(2) word for word, but makes no mention of Article 6(3) (the Berne Convention language);
—The Dutch draft introduces relatively minor wording changes to Articles 6(1) and 6(2), and makes no mention of Article 6(3);
—The German and Spanish laws and the Belgian and French drafts introduce minor wording changes in Articles 6(1) and 6(2) and delete the specific reference to the Berne Convention contained in Article 6(3) of the Directive. In addition, the German law, in Article 6(3), corrects the Software Directive's incorrectly transposed Berne Convention language;
—The Italian law introduces certain wording changes to Articles 6(1) and 6(2); however, the changes do not appear to change the meaning intended by the Software Directive. In addition, the Italian law adds to its implementation of Article 6 itself a clause rendering void any contractual provisions contrary to Articles 6(1) or 6(2);
—The Greek law basically follows the language of Article 6, but contains certain minor wording changes;
—The United Kingdom has sought to adopt the meaning of Article 6, while integrating it into the 1988 Act using better, more comprehensible, English language. Fair dealing no longer applies to decompilation, but remains applicable to computer programs otherwise. Like the Danish legislation and the Dutch draft, the UK statutory instrument makes no mention of the Berne Convention language contained in Article 6(3) of the Directive.

With entry into force of the Agreement on the European Economic Area (EEA) on January 1, 1994, most EFTA countries must now also implement the Software Directive into their national legislation. Norway, Sweden, Finland, and Austria have already done so.

QUESTIONS AND COMMENTS FOR YOUR CONSIDERATION

1. Are the decisions by the EC regarding the treatment of issues of reverse engineering and scope of protection for databases demonstrated by the software directive in harmony with your country's treatment of these issues? To what extent does this directive establish a ceiling for the future protection of software under multinational treaties?

2. What role, if any, should other countries play in an individual country's efforts to harmonize their intellectual property laws? How likely is it that the members of the EC will accede to a treaty that requires greater or different protection of software than that permitted under the directive?

B. Technology Transfers[15]

A fundamental tension exists between developing countries and the United States concerning the protection of technological information. The developing countries regard technological information developed in the industrialized nations as knowledge which should be in the public domain. The United States protects the developers of technological information by giving them extensive intellectual property rights. Since 1976, the United Nations Conference on Trade and Development (UNCTAD) has been working on a code of conduct for the international transfer of technology. While the developing countries known as the Group of 77 initiated the movement at UNCTAD in order to establish their philosophy internationally, specific developing countries such as Brazil already have domestically regulated the transfer of technology to increase technological information in the public domain.

Despite their intent to promote the acquisition of technology, these two types of regimes—the UNCTAD international code of conduct and domestic regulation such as the Brazilian regulations—may actually jeopardize international distribution of software originating in the United States. US software exporters already are showing reluctance to send software to countries where they are threatened by transfer of technology regimes. Software ideas are extremely valuable, and with global computer networks and transborder data flows, loss of secrecy in one part of the world can rapidly result in the disclosure of highly confidential software ideas back in the United States.

The UNCTAD Code sets forth rights and obligations for the software supplier and software acquirer.[16] The UNCTAD Code defines transfer of technology as "the transfer of systematic knowledge for the manufacture of a product, for the application of a process or for the rendering of a service and does not extend to the transactions involving the mere sale or mere lease of goods."[17] The definitions explicitly state that "the provision of know-how and technical expertise in the form of . . . instructions" also are considered technology under the UNCTAD Code. This definition of know-how includes trade secrets and software since they are essentially confidential instructions. Chapter 5.4 of the UNCTAD Code, which remains unsettled, would obligate the acquiring party to maintain "confidentiality including its scope and duration and the use of any assets like trade secrets," This obligation would apply to the software recipient, but Chapter 4 limits the technology or software supplier from including restrictive practices in the license agreement. Though the list and description of restrictive business practices is still being revised, the licensor may not impose restrictions on research precluding absorption of the transferred technology in new products, restrictions on adaptations of the imported technology, a requirement of exclusive dealing, restrictions after expiration of the arrangement, and unlimited or unduly long duration of arrangements. The current text leaves the international legal effect of prohibiting the enumerated practices at issue by retaining a choice of language between "shall [and] should refrain" from the restrictive practices as well as maintaining disagreement on the heading for the list of practices. Yet these limitations nonetheless circumvent the scope and duration of the confidentiality obligation. Until the Group

---

[15] Joel R. Reidenberg, *US Software Protection: Problems Of Trade Secret Estoppel Under International And Brazilian Technology Transfer Regimes*, 23 COLUM. J. TRANSNAT'L L. 679. Copyright 1985 Columbia Journal of Transnational Law Association, Inc. Excerpt reprinted with permission.

[16] UNCTAD Code Ch. 2.1 (x), U.N. Doc. TD/CODE TOT/41 at 5 (1983).

[17] UNCTAD Code Ch. 2.1, U.N. Doc. TD/CODE TOT/41 at 2 (1983).

of 77 is satisfied with the progress toward completion of the list of restrictive business practices (meaning that the list adequately limits the scope and duration of any confidentiality obligation), it will object to the confidentiality clause in the UNCTAD Code.

One other dispute under the UNCTAD Code highlights the need to examine an example of how a foreign country's national regulations affect the software license agreement. The UNCTAD Code's definition of "international transfer" remains unresolved. While the code would apply to all transactions crossing national boundaries (including transfers between parent and subsidiary companies), there is disagreement as to whether the code should apply to transactions within a developing country between companies under foreign control. Software distribution might be made through transactions by a subsidiary in the foreign country. Any form of distribution, of course, will always be subject to additional national regulations (export as well as import regulations).[18]

C. Cyberspace and the Border Problem[19]

Within this shadowy realm of Cyberspace, time, distance, and physical barriers are meaningless. Scientists may conduct research within virtual laboratories and interact with colleagues and equipment thousands of miles away; students in virtual classrooms may learn from teachers and classmates that are not physically present; even virtual corporations may coalesce to meet some financial or organizational need, then fade away when the goal of their creation is met.

If, however, the transcendent quality of Cyberspace creates new possibilities, it also creates new problems. Where political boundaries dissolve, political chaos may ensue; where information is unbounded, privacy and even identity may be lost. Already, the transborder transfer of personal information has been identified as a challenge to the autonomy and sovereignty of the nation state; it is no less of a challenge to the autonomy and privacy of individuals.

Global computer networks are by no means the first situation in which the absence of physical barriers has presented quandaries of ownership and control. Concerns for the protection of American "artistic and intellectual creativity" and innovation, research, and development form the basis for the entire field of intellectual property law. Knowledge or ideas associated with technological advances may be created as pure intellectual goods or embodied to some degree in a physical form, such as an invention. Like physical goods, intellectual goods may have great industrial value, and generating such knowledge may entail significant production costs of time and effort. However, unlike physical goods, intellectual goods do not encompass the natural physical barriers that would exclude potential consumers. Ideas, after all, may be held by more than one person at a time.

Whether an idea is distributed by computer network, printing press, or word of mouth, the lack of physical barriers also makes the distribution costs for disseminating an intellectual good minimal or nonexistent. Once intellectual goods are disclosed, there are no real barriers to the free appropriation of the good. Because it is difficult to prevent persons from deriving the benefit of an intellectual good, a significant number of persons may consume the good without recompensing the originator of the good. This lack of recompense may discourage creation of intellectual goods, leaving the market for the good undersupplied. Consequently, where physical barriers are lacking, legal barriers have been designed to provide control over intellectual property.

In the United States, the most prominent set of legal barriers designed to correct potential undersupply in the market for technologically valuable intellectual goods is the federal patent system. Article 1, Section 8, Clause 8 of the United States Constitution grants Congress authority to "promote the progress of science and the useful arts" by

---

[18] *Editors' Note:* For a further discussion of the economic theories relied upon by developing countries to restrict protection for intellectual property *see* Chapter Two.

[19] Dan L. Burk, *Patents in Cyberspace: Territoriality and Infringement on Global Computer Networks*, 68 TUL. L. REV. 1. Copyright 1993 Dan L. Burk. Excerpt reprinted with permission.

securing to inventors for a limited time the exclusive rights to their work. Congress has chosen to exercise this power by implementing a system of patents that grants a seventeen-year, exclusive right to use a new process, machine, article of manufacture, or composition of matter.

Because patents grant the patent holder an exclusionary right to the patented invention, patents have been loosely termed "monopolies." Patent lawyers have long protested this label, and economists have suggested that a patent does not necessarily confer a true monopoly. Nonetheless, although some patents probably do confer a virtual monopoly on their holders, all patents represent some restraint on trade. Consequently, patents are likely to generate the type of inefficiencies associated with monopolies: higher prices, restricted supplies, and inefficient allocation of resources. Patents are, in fact, specifically designed to create such inefficiencies; otherwise, the respective good might not be produced at all. The societal costs generated by the patent system, however, must not be allowed to exceed the benefits of the intellectual goods the system fosters.

Computer software is foremost among the valuable and technologically sophisticated information-based products that bear the hallmarks of an intellectual good. As such, software has been deemed a prime candidate for intellectual property protection.

The dissolution of geographic, political, and temporal barriers made possible by global computer networks may pose a new challenge to the operation of US patent law—a challenge not yet fully realized and likely impossible for the framers of the present patent code to anticipate, but a challenge whose parameters can already be seen. Differences between the laws of jurisdictions mean that network users run the risk of violating the law in one country or another. Indeed, in some situations information service providers may consciously seek to use the disparity between the intellectual property laws of different nations to their advantage.

Several possible infringement scenarios can be envisioned. The first postulates the existence of a computer network user situated in the United States, who logs onto the network, accesses a machine that is physically outside of the United States, and runs software that would infringe a US patent. The converse situation is also conceivable: a computer user outside of the United States, who runs software that would infringe a domestic patent were the user situated within US territory and employs such software to access a computer or database that is within the United States. Either of these situations, or some combination of them, will likely pose a patent enforcement challenge with which the present patent law is ill-equipped to deal.

However, the network user's employment of the infringing software, even if indirect and inadvertent, probably satisfies the statute's terms. The network user's lack of intent or knowledge in initiating infringing activity is almost certainly immaterial; it is well established that even unconscious or inadvertent infringement triggers liability under the patent statutes. A more difficult issue arises from the question of control over remote and, possibly, automatic software infringement. Courts have seldom been called on to interpret the term "use," perhaps because the term is generally believed to be well understood. However, the term, as employed in the patent statutes, is so very broad that there is little activity involving the patented item that would escape the term's scope.

Even if network activity constitutes use of remote software, the use must be "within the United States" in order to infringe a patent under 35 U.S.C. §271(a). Where global computer networks are concerned, however, it may be difficult to tell whether a use occurs within the United States. The host computer running an infringing program and the user accessing that program may be in different nations. When processing is distributed, only part of a program may run in the United States. When many computers are configured as one, the physical components of the virtual machine may extend beyond the territorial borders of the United States.

The United States Supreme Court has held that the patent law has no extraterritorial effect; however, in all the potential situations described above, the infringing activity has some connection to US territory.

The potential for infringement of US software patents through the medium of international computer networks seems to dictate that courts apply the patent provisions to deter such activity. Failure to do so could well dilute the value of software patents; using the inexpensive and elusive medium of the computer network, information services could be offered from offshore locations in countries, particularly underdeveloped countries, where intellectual property laws are not recognized or well enforced. In situations when the patent fails to provide exclusivity, the patent becomes essentially worthless and the market for software inventions may become undersupplied as though no patents were available.

In the absence of a legal deterrent, the emergence of such offshore patent havens would be a straightforward function of economics: when access to an offshore version of useful software is cheaper than access to an on-shore legitimate copy, offshore havens would supply the demand for cheaper access. Although the price of access is likely to have several components, the major competing price constituents would likely be the cost of transmitting data offshore versus the cost of obtaining a software license. In order to quell competition from an offshore haven, the holder of a software patent would have to provide licenses for less than the cost of computer network transmission. Since network transmission is generally very cost-effective, pricing software licenses lower than the cost of transmission might well mean that the patent holder could not recover her development costs.

As unpleasant as such a scenario may be, rash, reflexive, or mechanical enforcement of the patent laws could also have unpleasant results. As the Supreme Court has observed, "We cannot have trade and commerce in world markets and international waters exclusively on our terms, governed by our laws, and resolved in our courts."[20] Indeed, attempts to do so may well hamper the goals we would hope to accomplish in enforcing the patent laws: "The expansion of American business and industry will hardly be encouraged if . . . we insist on a parochial concept that all disputes must be resolved under our laws and in our courts."[21] This suggests that US courts considering patent enforcement for international computer networks should be wary of decisions implicating national sovereignty, international trade negotiations, and research disincentives. Accordingly, courts should fashion appropriate doctrines to ameliorate unsuitable results.

The primary challenge posed by international information exchange is essentially political and is caused by the erosion of political boundaries. Countries have responded differently to the development of global electronic information capabilities. Some countries have embraced the new information network, some have sought to avoid it, others have sought to appropriate it for state purposes, and still others have sought to exploit it to enhance their economic position. All nations, however, are beginning to grapple with the same impact of the data net; where international data communications are concerned, national boundaries have become technologically irrelevant, because the technology simply bypasses traditional physical barriers. Additionally, the functional economic boundaries generated by data exchange may overlap many political boundaries.

This increasing porosity of national boundaries has made it difficult for nations to exercise traditional aspects of sovereignty, such as monitoring and controlling the flow of goods into and out of the country. As a consequence, it has been suggested that the concept of political boundaries is rapidly becoming obsolete and requires reappraisal. The nation-state may have been the political organization best suited to the industrial age, but it is not necessarily suited to an informatics age.

This impact of the data network has been of particular concern to developing nations, which have had to deal with an additional economic effect impacting their sovereignty. The development of the global data net has not proceeded evenly; data services have clearly become concentrated in developed nations with market economies and well-developed telecommunications infrastructures. Underdeveloped nations, by contrast, have primarily been data suppliers and data purchasers. This disparity between "information-rich" and "information-poor" nations has tended to cut off the information-poor countries from the benefits of the network,

---

[20] M/S Brennen v. Zapata Off-Shore Co., 407 US 1, 9 (1972)

[21] *Ibid.*

because the value added benefits of data services tend to accrue at the processing and distribution stages. Consequently, the continued growth of global computer networks is likely to increase the gap between developing and developed nations.

The concentration of data in developed countries does not simply have economic ramifications; it has international political ramifications as well. Information is a vital resource. The ability to collect, store, access, and process data confers political, economic, and social advantages on the nation controlling the data. Effective control over the storage, processing, and transmittal of another country's information confers clear economic and military control over that country.

By contrast, inability to control information undermines the sovereignty of developing nations by impairing their competence to make decisions about their own futures. Indeed, in many instances, the information-rich nations may have more accurate information about the population, economy, and resources of an underdeveloped nation than has the underdeveloped nation itself. This aspect of data communications technology has led to charges that developed nations are employing information superiority in a form of "neo-colonization." Commentators in the "dependencia" school charge that information technology comprises a sort of imperialist tool to concentrate control of data processing and information generation in developed countries, while denying the benefits of information control to underdeveloped countries.[22]

Other commentators have suggested that information technology leads not only to informational dependence but also to cultural dependence.[23] This more subtle challenge to national identity and sovereignty is said, by members of the "structuralist" school of thought, to threaten cultural identity through the export of information that bears the imprint of alien selection, ordering, and arrangement.[24] This allows the dominance of one culture or language over another by virtue of information, data, and entertainment exports from the developed world. Thus, it is suggested that, through the export of information, the culture of a few industrialized nations may be imposed on the rest of the world, resulting in homogenization of global culture.

The disparity in benefit from the global data network has prompted information-poor countries to adopt strategies that would allow acquisition of data resources either physically or functionally. Some nations have moved toward becoming "data havens" in order to capture international information resources within their territory. The minimal cost of data transmission has already fostered offshore data processing—information is shipped by fiber optic cable to developing nations for processing, then transmitted back to the United States. By offering juridical sanctuaries with a more lenient attitude toward data use than the country of origin, less-developed nations stand an even better chance of attracting not only data processing activity but also data storage. In other instances, notably that of Brazil, policies have been adopted that disfavor export of local data and require foreign interests to deal locally in data processing procurement.

Against this backdrop of nationalism and global tension, creative enforcement of US patents is likely to be viewed as an attempt to manipulate data communications to the advantage of the United States. Underdeveloped nations already tend to view patents as a device employed by industrialized nations to maintain a monopoly over new technology, thereby crippling the development of nonindustrialized nations. A finding of patent liability against a foreign network user attempting to access a US information service effectively raises a nontariff barrier to international information access—as does imposition of liability against an American network user attempting to access a foreign information service. To the extent that such findings implicate the ability of other nations to control vital information flows, international animosity will be aroused.

This scenario is presaged by the international reaction of suspicion and outright hostility that has already attended US actions involving transborder data flow implicating

---

[22] *See, e.g.,* EDWARD M. ROCHE, THE LANDSCAPE OF INTERNATIONAL COMPUTING: A PERSONAL VIEW: TRANSNAT'L DATA & COMM. REP., Jan.–Feb. 1992 at 24.

[23] *See, e.g.,* JAMES C. GRANT, IMPACT OF TRANSNATIONAL DATA FLOWS ON DEVELOPING COUNTRIES, TRANSNAT'L DATA REP., June–July 1984 at 233, 235.

[24] *See* Roche, *supra* note 22 at 25–26.

direct and indirect threats to the sovereignty of other nations. Concern over the manipulation of information access has been heightened, for example, by the actions of the United States against a French subsidiary of Dresser Industries. In order to prevent the completion of an industrial contract for the Soviet Union, the United States cut off a French company's access to its North American database. This resulted not only in stoppage of the Soviet work but also in the loss of millions of dollars from other uncompleted contracts. Similarly, the United States froze Iranian assets during the Iranian revolution and hostage crisis and sought to sever Iranian access to the international Intelsat satellite information service.

More direct encroachment of foreign sovereignty by the United States has also been the subject of international criticism. US courts have twice enforced contempt orders against a foreign bank that refused to divulge confidential banking records protected by Bahamian banking laws. The sanctions imposed in these cases have prompted an increasing international consensus that although "extraterritoriality" is usually defined as the attempt by one sovereign state to assert control over persons situated or conduct occurring in another sovereign state, the term has come to mean the enforcement of US laws abroad. These incidents of heavy-handed extraterritorial application of US law have already prompted several nations, including France, the United Kingdom, Australia, and New Zealand, to enact statutes forbidding compliance with extraterritorial judicial orders requiring the transfer of data.

In contrast to the prevailing US approach, other nations have recognized the sensitivity and complexity of the issues raised by the protection of national interests through data-access restrictions. The Canadian government has advocated the practices of prenotification and consultation with foreign governments before restricting its data access or that of its nationals. Concerning extraterritorial application of laws relating to information flow, a similar awareness has grown of the need for discretion. For example, Norway has chosen to take a cautious approach to extraterritorial application of its data-protection laws. Norwegian policy applies the laws to Norwegian ships in international waters and to offshore Norwegian platforms on the continental shelf but does not apply them to Norwegian holdings in Spitzbergen, where the laws could conflict with interests of Russian settlements.

Such cautiousness should be at the forefront of extraterritorial application of US patent law. Indeed, such considerations are not unfamiliar to the formulation of the patent statutes.

In contrast to the strategies of less-developed nations, the general strategy of nations with well-developed information resources has been to attempt to promote an international environment largely free of barriers to information-based trade. Information-rich nations have asserted that regulatory restrictions impede development of the information industry and trade. In particular, these nations have sought the removal of trade-restricting governmental policies to provide a stable and predictable framework for trade in services. Such an international environment, it is believed, will foster capital-intensive corporate investment in information markets. Consequently, the developed nations have used every available diplomatic and economic means to promote open market access to foreign data suppliers.

The United States, as a major provider of information-based services, has assumed such a posture and has pushed other nations to permit free access to information services and to eliminate barriers to international data and information exchange. The United States has also sought to use negotiations at the ongoing, international General Agreement on Tariffs and Trade (GATT) as a vehicle for moving towards a more open information trade. Spurred by US policy, international discussion regarding data services and telecommunications has begun to shift toward a framework recognizing the importance of international trade in services. Additionally, negotiations have commenced regarding the free exchange of services, particularly telecommunication and network services, under the GATT.

This process is fragile and could easily be set back or compromised by the advent of a new patent-based restriction on access to foreign databases and information services. Barriers to free information flow are likely to escalate through retaliation; restrictive practices by one nation are likely to prompt similar actions by other nations. Protective actions by a few governments could start a "chain reaction of restrictions" as other governments follow suit or retaliate. Protectionist practices of this type distort the trading system and the market mechanism at a time when trade is critical both to the recovery from global recession and to laying the foundation for a new global economy.

The anomalies of patent enforcement are perhaps the inevitable product of our present concepts of nationality and territory. One commentator has observed that "separate patent systems for each country of the world is a necessary evil at best since technology by its very nature flows easily to wherever it may be effectively utilized." Global computer networks enhance that flow and, by weakening the concept of territoriality, may hasten the time when the evil of separate patent systems will no longer be necessary. Until that presumably far-off day, however, our present legal construct must begin to adapt to the realities of enforcing patents in Cyberspace.

QUESTIONS AND COMMENTS FOR YOUR CONSIDERATION

1. Border issues regarding the scope of protection to be afforded works in cyberspace present only the most recent example of the on-going problem presented by the protection of intellectual property works whose use is transnational in nature. Where a work is created in one country, distributed in another and reproduced in a third, each country may have an interest in deciding the scope of any remedies to be granted against such infringement. What factors should be considered in determining in which country, if any, the infringer may be sued for infringement? Which country has the greater interest in deciding whether the acts in the third country should be considered a violation of intellectual property rights?

2. What if the laws of the various countries conflict? Whose laws should govern and why?

D. The Problem of Satellite Broadcasts[25]

Satellite relayed television broadcast signals provided people throughout the world with a front row seat in the grim theater of the 1991 Gulf War. Yet, the use of satellites for global communication seemed like another futuristic dream when first predicted in 1945. The satellite technology originally developed for the exploration of outer space now provides people the world over with instantaneous access to the same information and images. Today, a satellite signal can transcend national borders and deliver a television program developed and purchased for an audience in one country to households in every country within the span of the satellite. The same technology that affords us this simultaneous access also presents complex legal problems. International law has not kept pace with the technology and there are, at present, no clear international guidelines for determining how and under what circumstances the program creators will be compensated for unintended audiences receiving the signal.

The enthusiasm many European countries have for the new satellite technology is tempered by concern over the loss of national control of foreign broadcasts. The reach of a communication satellite's beam, referred to as the "footprint" of the satellite, can cover as much as forty percent of the earth's surface. Since the satellite beam cannot be physically

---

[25] Iris C. Geik, *Direct Broadcast Satellites And The Determination Of Authors' Rights Under The Berne Convention: Lucy In The Sky Without Rights?* 15 SUFFOLK TRANSNAT'L L. J. 563. Copyright 1992 Suffolk University. Excerpt reprinted with permission.

contained by national borders, this wide coverage results in the "spillover" of the signal well beyond the target audience.

Direct Broadcast Satellite program carrying signals are, as the name indicates, intended for direct reception by home receivers without the intervention of the earth station decoding equipment required by Fixed Service Satellites ("FSS"), the less powerful first generation of communication satellites. Fixed Service Satellites require expensive and powerful antennae and cable systems to convert and then distribute signals to other ground receivers. The signals ultimately reach home viewers via the antennae of commercial cable systems or, less typically, via large and costly individually owned FSS receiver "dishes."

The way in which the home television receives the program carrying signal represents the critical distinction in an analysis of authors' rights. Signals sent to and received by Direct Broadcast Satellites are very strong and do not require intermediary transmitters and receivers; they can be received directly by the home viewer equipped with an antenna considerably less powerful, smaller, and cheaper than that required to receive the original type of FSS signal. Historically, size and cost effectively precluded the general public's ownership and use of satellite antennae. Home access to satellite signals has been, until very recently, almost exclusively limited to commercial cable systems which receive and distribute the DBS programs. New unobtrusive and low-cost DBS antennae have been gaining in popularity in Europe, adding to the rapidly expanding number of homes receiving DBS television broadcasts.

The spillover of the DBS signal, which creates a potential audience in every country within the footprint, has fueled the current debate over authors' rights in DBS programs. Authors' rights in DBS broadcasts can be compared to traditional authors' rights issues, where the author of a book sometimes expects, and indeed hopes, that the book will find a multinational audience. But it is the unusual author who does not expect to be compensated for the number of purchases commensurate with the size of the book's audience. If the author is not compensated for book sales in a country, the author can seek protection through the country's adherence to the Berne Convention.

The provisions of the Berne Convention refer to the author as the primary holder of rights in the protected work, but no standards are supplied for the determination of who is considered the author. Consequently, persons entitled to authorize use of the work and receive compensation in one country may not be the legal or sole rights-holders in other countries. Some countries, such as the Federal Republic of Germany, use intellectual and creative endeavors as the determinant of author status; other countries, particularly common law countries, identify the author as the entity with the contractual rights in the work.

The Berne Convention does not specifically provide protections for works transmitted by satellite. The last two major revisions to the Berne Convention, the Brussels Revision of 1948 and the Paris Revision of 1971, preceded the large-scale use of television and DBS technology, respectively. Although the 1971 Paris Revision delegates did not explicitly define satellite broadcasts, it was generally understood that they were broadcasts within the meaning of Article 11bis of the Berne Convention. Article 11bis, adopted in 1948, governs broadcasts by "wireless and other means" and was originally intended to apply to radio and the new technology of home television. According to the generally accepted standard proposed by the Council of Europe, Article 11bis provisions apply if the program meets the criteria of being a "simultaneous, complete and unchanged transmission."

Article 11 of the Berne Convention, authored in 1889, governs "communication(s) to the public . . . [by wire] . . . . " Article 11 is applied to cable transmissions of the satellite broadcast signal where there is an intermediary between the original broadcast and the audience, which in any way alters the program material or delays the program's transmission. Programs which are received directly from the satellite source, but which are not broadcast immediately, or are edited or altered, are classified as cable-originated programs; each showing of the program, therefore, is considered a new use of the work under Article 11.

The distinction between Article 11 and Article 11bis protection has significant economic ramifications for authors. Article 11 activities allow the author the exclusive right to make the work available to the public and, therefore, grant the author the exclusive right to withhold the work from the public and make independent negotiations for remuneration. Under Article 11bis (2), however, if an agreement for use cannot be reached, a government-appointed authority may impose a license for use and determine the payment to the author. The diminution of authors' rights under Article 11bis is in marked contrast to the basic tenet of the Berne Convention, that exclusive rights to the intellectual property vest in the author. This derogation of authors' rights also reflects the strong interest of national governments in retaining control over broadcast media.

Proposals based on disparate theoretical analyses of copyright law have emerged from the ongoing debate over authors' rights and the spillover from Direct Broadcast Satellites. The primary issues concern when, and in which countries, authors' rights can be asserted. Supporters of a traditional analysis, also called the "traditional theory" or the "emission theory," claim that authors have a right of remuneration only in the country where the broadcast originates; supporters of the analysis called the "Bogsch theory" argue that authors have a separate right of remuneration in each nation within the footprint, while others argue that there should be joint liability between the nation where the broadcast originates and each nation receiving the signal. Still others argue that the determination should be left solely to the parties involved to resolve contractually.

The traditional theory analogizes direct broadcasts by satellite to conventional radio and television broadcasts where the broadcast is regarded as one use of the work, whatever the size of the audience. Under this theory, the author has one right of remuneration from the organization which ordered the broadcast, a right limited to the country from which the broadcast or the order to broadcast emanates. Critics of this analysis, however, point out that the DBS audience is not easily estimated because it does not fall within the direct and comparatively limited range of the signal, as do conventional television and radio. There is little question of multinational access for conventional television programs because the signal does not usually travel significantly beyond the confines of the national border. The content matter of radio programs that do pass borders generally does not raise intellectual property issues.

The Group of Experts on the Copyright Aspects of Direct Broadcasting by Satellite met in 1985, under the auspices of "WIPO" and the United Nations Educational, Scientific and Cultural Organization ("UNESCO"). Dr. Arpad Bogsch, Director General of WIPO, proposed an analysis of rights based on the Berne Convention principle of national treatment. Under this analysis, now known as the Bogsch theory, liability arises in each country where the signal is received by the public, and the broadcaster who gives the original order for the transmission of the signal is responsible for adherence to the copyright laws of each nation where the broadcast is received. According to Bogsch, the laws of each country where the act occurs must be adhered to; to permit otherwise would be contrary to the Berne Convention's principles of national treatment. Authors, thus, have protection and rights of remuneration in every country within the footprint that is a member of the Berne Convention. With the exception of a general agreement that DBS transmissions are broadcasts under Article 11bis, Bogsch's proposal did not meet with general acceptance when it was first introduced to the full membership of the UNESCO/WIPO meeting in 1986. Members questioned the feasibility of any attempt to implement and enforce the laws of individual countries within the footprint each time a DBS broadcasts a creative work.

At the 1986 meeting of the Committee of Government Experts on Audiovisual Works, it was recommended that the sending and receiving of the signal be considered as one unified act, with one right of remuneration. The laws of the country from which the program emanates (the "up-leg"), and the laws of the country where the program is received (the "down-leg"), would both apply. Joint liability, it is argued, provides authors with protection in a Berne country even if a broadcast emanates from a non-Berne country. In the case of a conflict of laws, the laws of the nation which affords the author the greatest protection would apply. Critics of this proposal recognize the obvious advantages to the author of the highest level of protection, but view this scheme as difficult to implement and enforce.

Despite the lack of international policy, broadcast fees are determined and rights are secured through contract negotiations. Dr. Cohen-Jeroham, a leading authority in the field of international copyright law, supports the continuation of this practice. He argues that rights should be obtained in the same manner in which they are obtained for radio and conventional television broadcasts, through pre-production contract negotiations; and, that spillover can be addressed in negotiations for royalties.[26]

According to Michael J. Freegard, Chief Executive of London's Performing Right Society, the cumbersome task of negotiation and rights clearances can be competently handled by collecting societies.[27] By representing all of the authors with rights in programs, collecting societies would be able to negotiate the most advantageous deal for the authors while protecting the broadcasters and cable operators from liability for copyright infringement. Where rights cannot be secured because the author cannot be located, or negotiations fail, it is suggested that only then should a non-voluntary license be imposed.

The Commission of the European Communities and the International Alliance for Diffusion by Wire ("AID"), the representative organization of cable distributors, have opposed contract negotiations and advocated the imposition of non-voluntary licenses for broadcast works. Their arguments are primarily based on a perceived impracticality of enforcing contractual agreements between cable distributors and the multiple rights-holders in a single work.

Article 11bis, the broadcasting right, and Article 13(1), the sound recording right, are the only two provisions of the Berne Convention with express limitations on authors' exclusive rights in their works. Authors' rights can be limited by government imposition of non-voluntary licenses, that is, by imposing statutory or compulsory licenses. Under the statutory license, the rate of remuneration is set by law; under the compulsory license, the rate of remuneration is negotiated between the users and the authors, or between the users and the authors' representatives.

An intermediary step between the non-voluntary license system and completely independent contract negotiations is the collective management of rights by societies representing the authors. Collecting societies have handled licenses for musical recordings since the late 1800s. Typically, authors transfer their copyright to a collecting society which negotiates and collects fees on their behalf. In theory, collecting societies could serve multiple functions beneficial to all parties having interests in DBS broadcasts.

Broadcasters could negotiate with one organization, the collecting society, rather than engage in separate negotiations with all of the parties holding rights in a work. Authors could avoid the economic disadvantages of fees set by statute and the bargaining disadvantages of compulsory licenses. Advocates of collecting societies point to the benefits of collective negotiation: authors could retain rights in their works and could use the societies as representatives to negotiate in their best interests. The collective negotiation process also serves government interests because it accommodates the economic rights of the author and encourages public access to creative works. The success of collecting societies in obtaining rights has influenced some countries to withdraw legislation in support of statutory or compulsory licenses, adding to the appeal of collecting societies as the best alternative to a complex problem.

A problem inherent in all of the proposals is the incongruous fit of satellite technology into a category conceived for radio and conventional television. Comparisons between the direct and uninterrupted DBS transmissions and the markedly less powerful technology of conventional television do not provide a satisfying analogy. A grouping of radio and DBS ignores not only the substantial differences in technology, but also the

---

[26] Cohen-Jeroham, General Report: Cable Television Media and Copyright Law Aspects in Cable Television Media and Copyright Law Aspects, Reports to an Alai Symposium 217–31 (1983).

[27] *See* Freegard, *The Berne Convention, Compulsory Licensing and Collecting Societies*, 11 COLUM. J.L. & ARTS, 137 (1986).

substantial differences in the breadth of potential audiences and the content and economic value of the broadcasts.

E. The Protection of Foreign Broadcasts[28]

The rights of television broadcasters over their programming (known as neighboring rights), as well as the rights of the creators or authors of the programming (known as copyright), are controlled by the Law on Copyright and Neighboring Rights (Russian Copyright Law). Russian Copyright Law is in full compliance with the Berne Convention, which Russia is expected to join in the near future. Furthermore, Russia (as part of the former Soviet Union) has observer status in the GATT.

No formalities are required for the existence of neighboring rights.

Copyright protection exists in Russia upon the creation of a work of literature, science, or art; no formalities are required for protection. Foreign authors of audio-visual works are specifically included within the scope of protection. Authors have both non-proprietary rights (also known as moral rights) and proprietary rights (also known as economic rights). Non-proprietary rights, which are non-transferrable, include the right to be recognized as the author of a work. Proprietary rights, which are transferable and are subject to the fair use provisions, include the right to broadcast the work.

As a practical matter, however, the effect this law will have on practice and behavior in Russia remains unclear. There is a long and widespread tradition of intellectual property piracy in Russia. Furthermore, the enforcement rights granted under [this law] are broad, but vague, and the role that the government will play in enforcing intellectual property rights is ill-defined.

Changing the attitudes and behavior of Russian citizens as well as educating Russian lawyers and judges on the nuances of intellectual property law and practice will necessarily take time to develop. Thus, American broadcasters should not currently rely on the enforcement mechanisms of Russian Copyright Law to protect their product. That does not mean, however, that the law is useless. At a minimum, Russian Copyright Law reflects the goodwill on the part of the government, and it puts copyright infringers on notice by creating rights that did not previously exist.

The reality is that piracy is a cost of doing business anywhere for a United States broadcaster or program supplier. Is the risk or cost of piracy really greater in Russia than in the United States? It should be remembered that VCRs allow Americans to illegally tape cable or satellite programs with little effort. The difference is that most Americans, unlike many of their Russian counterparts, are not copying the programming for commercial use. However, this risk of piracy needs to be put into perspective. First, the larger television stations and networks in Russia do adhere to copyright protection. Second, United States entrepreneurs should not avoid doing business in Russia based on the possibility of smaller or remote stations retransmitting their programming in a manner that would probably be of a lower quality. Third, the likelihood of piracy can be reduced by the use of program scrambling devices.

No formalities are required for the existence of neighboring rights in China. However, while foreign works (protected under the Berne Convention) are entitled to copyright protection upon creation, neighboring rights are not explicitly extended to foreign broadcasters.

Copyright protection exists in China upon the creation of a work of literature, art, natural science, social science, engineering, and technology (that is listed in Article 3)—no formalities are required for protection. As previously mentioned, foreign works are included within this protection. Authors enjoy both personal (or moral) and property (or economic) rights. Article 22 limits an author's economic rights by providing twelve free uses of copyrighted works (no permission nor payment of royalties is required). Like in Russia, these fair use provisions are similar to those enumerated under the United States 1976 Copyright Act. However,

---

[28] Rosalind M. Parker, *Protecting American Television Programming In Russia, China, Taiwan, and Japan,* 17 HASTINGS COMM. & ENT. L.J. 445. Copyright 1995 Hastings College of the Law. Excerpt reprinted with permission.

as is discussed below, other free uses go beyond the 1976 Act and Berne Convention provisions.

Most significantly, Article 22(1) provides that copyrighted works may be used freely for personal study, research, or enjoyment—without stating whether such use encompasses some or all of the copyrighted work. Thus, no copyright infringement would occur when a person borrows a cassette tape (legally purchased by someone else) and copies it for his or her own personal enjoyment. Another notable exception is fair use by state entities. However, the exception is not that significant because state entities, as defined, are limited to the legislative, judicial, and administrative bodies at various levels, and because the 1991 Implementing Regulations contain specific restrictions on free use by state entities.

Like Russia, China has long been criticized for its lack of protection of foreign copyrighted works over the years. Both countries have a history of allowing activities that would be classified as piracy and copyright infringement under Western laws. However, as both countries move towards a true market economy and become more involved in the world marketplace, each country will need to promote and protect its own technology and culture. That is, Russia and China's transformation from being predominantly technological consumers to innovative competitors will provide each country with the economic incentive to protect its own copyrighted works—which in turn will lead to greater enforcement and protection of foreign copyrighted works.

A QUESTION FOR YOUR CONSIDERATION

The Information Superhighway, similar to satellite broadcasts, has the potential for creating multiple infringement sites. Whose law should govern whether the unauthorized transmission of a copyrighted work constitutes infringement? The site where the work was uploaded? The site where the work was downloaded? The site where the work was viewed?

14

Underdeveloped Countries

Each country's decision regarding the scope of protection afforded the five classic forms of intellectual property necessarily reflects that country's historical, philosophical, political, economic and cultural heritage. Nevertheless, underdeveloped countries, those who have a low level of industrial development or are among the newly industrialized countries, share a somewhat different set of concerns and problems. This Chapter reviews the problems and issues facing underdeveloped countries when they decide what scope of protection, if any, to grant intellectual property. We begin with a review of the impact of piracy and free-riding on underdeveloped economies. The Chapter then examines the specific concerns raised by efforts to protect copyrights, patents and trademarks in developing nations. It concludes with a final review of the sovereignty concerns underlying the debate between the developed and undeveloped countries regarding intellectual property protection standards.

A. Intellectual Property Protection in Developing Countries[1]

With the ever-increasing costs of product innovation, creation, and marketing, the recovery of expenses is essential for developing the next generation of products and services. Many industrialized countries claim that an economic return commensurate with the costs expended by companies and individuals is more difficult to achieve today. They maintain that competitors, who do not face similar developmental expenses, copy and sell the product at a much lower cost. Industrialized countries declare that this ongoing encroachment, or frustration of intellectual property rights is unfair, because it effectively displaces legitimately produced works from international markets. Many countries point to inadequate protection of and compliance with intellectual property rights as the main factor compounding this inequity.

Many developing countries do not share the view that the protection of intellectual property rights is both economically sound and necessary to alleviate distortion in world trade. The economic objective of developing countries is to promote participation in the benefits from technological developments and scientific innovations on terms consistent with their needs and ideologies. Developing countries consider the free flow of technology to be essential to their economic development. Therefore, they oppose action which might in any way impede the movement of technology, or of products based on foreign technology or innovation. Furthermore, some third world countries insist that knowledge and intellectual property are "the common heritage of mankind" or "res communis" and therefore, society may not impose any restrictions on the production, use or selling of inventions. Rather, ideas, inventions, and technologies should be freely shared by all.

Respect and protection for intellectual property in developing countries has been an issue of great concern and disagreement between the developed and developing worlds. The recent emergence of informa-

[1] Tara Kalagher Giunta, Lily H. Shang, *Ownership of Information in a Global Economy*, 27 Geo. Wash. J. Int'l L. & Econ. 327. Copyright 1994 George Washington University. Excerpt reprinted with permission.

tion as a major component of economic growth has heightened this concern. In particular, it has become a critical trade issue confronting East Asia, which historically has not extended adequate protection to intellectual property.

The world economy has become increasingly dependent upon informational goods and devices for its growth. This new source of wealth, however, is difficult to protect because information resources are not bound to a particular geographic location and are not easily controlled by governments.

Transfer of technology via the licensing of information constitutes an ever-growing part of world trade. Such commerce is vital to developed nations whose economies grow increasingly dependent on products of the mind. The United States, for example, is one of the world's largest producers of new information. Accordingly, the United States has become increasingly vulnerable to piracy and otherwise inadequate protection of its intellectual property in foreign countries. Recent US government and industry studies reveal that billions of dollars are lost each year to counterfeiters, resulting in thousands of lost jobs. International protection of intellectual property has therefore become an important trade issue for the United States.

Developing countries also need access to information to engender economic growth. Historically, these nations have not offered an adequate level of intellectual property protection. Developing economies are confronted with two often conflicting challenges. First, they must enter and participate in the global marketplace on a substantive basis. Second, they must structure meaningful legal regimes which legitimize their participation.

Unfortunately, nations tend to polarize along economic lines when addressing the issue of intellectual property protection. The current task is to reach beyond national boundaries, as technology has already done, and attempt to create relationships which acknowledge both the property rights of owners as well as the legitimate need of developing economies to access information in order to join the global economy.

This task can only be accomplished through a coordinated effort between the public and private sectors. Governments must open the dialogue, preferably on a bilateral basis. Bilateral agreements are most effective because they address the individual concerns and circumstances facing each signatory. Importantly, such agreements can take into consideration the particular phases of development confronting each country, and provide for the gradual inclusion of a developing country into the global economy. As a developing country becomes a stronger player, it can then assume greater responsibility in safeguarding intellectual property rights.

QUESTIONS AND COMMENTS FOR YOUR CONSIDERATION

1. The task of establishing international protection standards has often been referred to as a conflict between developed and developing nations. If you represented a multinational corporation approached by a company from a newly industrialized country to build a manufacturing plant under a joint venture agreement, what concerns would you have about the level of intellectual protection granted in the country? To what extent, if any, could your concerns be answered by private agreement between the parties?

2. What assumptions are made about the economic views of underdeveloped countries with regard to intellectual property protection in the above article? Are these assumptions accurate for an underdeveloped country in Asia? in Africa? in Latin America? in the CIS?

1. Economic Views of Underdeveloped Countries[2]

The intellectual property systems in the United States and other industrialized countries are credited with encouraging the development of new technology which in turn leads to economic growth. Extrapolating from the success of the industrialized countries, a common economic theory holds that intellectual property protection for innovative products is an important step in the industrialization of developing nations.

Technology provides a country with the resources to develop new industries or to modernize existing operations. The country can utilize more effective processes to produce a higher quantity of goods. Also, products can be manufactured more efficiently, which reduces the price of the final product. If the country successfully implements new systems reducing the production costs, and if the increased output is greater than the population growth rate, then the country should experience economic growth.

Many developing countries encourage the increased privatization of domestic industries as a step in the industrialization process. To be economically competitive, these private businesses need information and technology which allow them to manufacture products efficiently. This is a problem, however, because the developing country will have difficulty acquiring the needed material from abroad or locally if it does not enact and enforce intellectual property laws.

Without protection for their investment in the research and development of new technology, both foreign and domestic producers will be dissuaded from becoming involved in a developing country's market. Research and development require substantial expenditures, and a business invests resources in a project that it believes will generate a profit. Without intellectual property protection for a new process or product, the creator could lose its investment when another party appropriates the item and reproduces or distributes it at a lower cost. As a result, the prices in the market for the product will be driven down, and the legitimate owner faces either an economic loss or substantially reduced profits. Therefore, without an adequate return on their investment, innovators do not have a strong incentive to spend their resources on creative activities.

Despite the purported value of intellectual property laws for creating economic growth, developing countries are often skeptical of implementing a system in their own country.

One reason developing countries may have an economic incentive to emphasize the short term when evaluating the costs of implementing an intellectual property system is that they face significant initial costs in its establishment. First, the government must write laws and expend resources on their enforcement. Second, "costs may arise due to the increased economic activity within a country. For example, new plants may require new roads or may cause environmental problems." Third, the country loses low cost access to expensive products. Pirated versions are usually cheaper than a legitimate version. Finally, the country's consumer surplus declines when purchasers are required to pay a higher price for the product.

Another reason that developing countries are less likely to implement these intellectual property protections is that a different attitude towards public and private property is often found in these countries. Developing countries do not have a history of recognizing intellectual property protection because in the past, these countries did not engage in the production of innovative products or information that required such protection. Furthermore, because these products benefit the society as a whole, the countries believe that information found in protected products, such as pharmaceuticals, should be a public good. Developing countries, therefore, are hostile to raising the expense of a product with a high public benefit by granting the developer a monopoly on its use or distribution.

A third reason why developing countries have weak intellectual property protections is that these countries often emphasize their need for the protected items to generate economic growth. They argue that with access

---

[2] Amy R. Edge, *Preventing Software Piracy Through Regional Trade Agreements: The Mexican Example*, 20 N.C.J. INT'L. L. & COM. REG. 175. Copyright 1994 North Carolina Journal of International Law and Commercial Regulation, Inc. Excerpt reprinted with permission.

to innovative products and information at a low cost, their economic condition would improve, and ultimately, the rest of the world would benefit from their economic growth.

An additional reason why developing countries frequently ignore intellectual property protection is that they tend to emphasize the short-term benefits of weak intellectual property protection. By using pirated technology, the developing country can acquire the materials needed for industrialization, but at a lower cost. The country can also allow the pirating of products to become a domestic industry employing local workers. Finally, by misappropriating foreign goods, a developing country can maintain its balance of trade by retaining resources, such as money, in the domestic economy.

To avoid the costs of an intellectual property system, developing countries often look for cheaper routes of obtaining technology. "Free riding" is one tactic for acquiring technology cheaply. Essentially, the country relies on piracy as a resource. Over the long term, however, this policy limits and reduces the access of developing countries to high technology materials. This is because, without intellectual property laws to protect their investment, foreign producers will be reluctant to ship their products into the developing country or to invest in the local economy. As a result, the countries lose access to technical products and expertise. The countries are also deprived of the collateral benefits of foreign investment. For example, when foreign corporations operate in a country, they employ local workers and spend money on local services. Investment by foreign companies can therefore have direct, positive impacts on the local economy.

If the economy of a developing country is primarily based on agriculture or early forms of industry that use and produce small amounts of technology, the costs of establishing an intellectual property system may outweigh the benefits. However, as a country pursues industrialization, there is a point where it becomes in the country's best interests to bear the costs of recognizing intellectual property protection in order to foster the growth of domestic industries and to encourage investment by foreign manufactures into the local economy.

The newly industrialized countries (NICs) are one group which are at this economic threshold. NICs have been defined as "those developing economies that by 1989 had an income per capita of at least US $2000, a share of manufacturing in gross national product of at least 30 percent, and exports of manufactured products accounting for more than 40 percent of total export revenues." Of all developing countries, NICs are the most likely to recognize the value of intellectual property protection in their economic development. During the process of industrialization in these countries, a point is reached where the costs of piracy begin to outweigh the benefits. Therefore, encouraging the creation of new technology becomes more important than widespread diffusion of a product at a low cost.

An NIC must consider whether it can bear the economic costs of establishing an intellectual property system. One method of determining whether protection is viable at the country's stage of industrial development is to calculate the amount of economic growth required to offset the losses to the economy when pirated products are less readily available. This process is part of a cost-benefit analysis of the implementation of an intellectual property system. In the analysis, two factors which should be considered are: (1) the economy's current growth rate; and (2) the relative contribution that pirate-related industries make to the domestic economy. The higher the current growth rate is for an economy, the smaller the increase in the growth rate needed to compensate for lost revenues. Likewise, the smaller the current contribution made by piratical industries to domestic GNP, the smaller the growth rate required to compensate for the losses. The growth rate of NICs, in comparison with other developing countries, is often strong enough to sustain the implementation of intellectual property protection. These countries require only a small increase in the economic growth rate to offset the losses from reducing piracy. As a result, NICs are frequently in the strongest economic position to implement an intellectual property system and to sustain the economic losses.

2. The Benefit of Free-Riding[3]

A lax attitude in protecting intellectual property offers, at least in the short run, attractive benefits for pirates and consuming nations. Pirates of intellectual property enjoy lower production costs and are in a better position than legitimate producers to satisfy demands in developing countries. Pirates can do so because they merely copy products rather than develop their own and pay no royalties to the owner or creator. By copying only successful products, the pirate avoids the risk of market failure.

Barring effective regulation, the piracy of intellectual property pays off because it involves little risk and provides a healthy return on investment. Pirates enrich themselves and, in the short run, the countries in which they operate. Through piracy, developing countries can procure needed goods and services at little cost, while industries that specialize in producing counterfeit goods employ thousands of workers. When compared to these tangible gains, the threat that investment from Western countries might be withdrawn is secondary to immediate development needs.

In Third World countries, the piracy of intellectual property is justified by an ideology of development. Ready access to intellectual property is viewed as important to development, whereas the enforcement of intellectual property law is considered a burden on development. Thus, developing countries resist allocating scarce government resources to the enforcement of intellectual property rights. As with the importation of capital, the importation of intellectual property often is viewed as a tool to dominate and exploit the economic potential of the importing countries. Paying for imports or making royalty payments imposes economic burdens and fosters a negative balance of trade.

In addition to this ideology, developing countries provide weak or nonexistent protection for, perhaps, a more basic reason. Intellectual property is simply too new of a concept to have developed a tradition of legal protection. Unlike Western countries, developing countries have few strong lobbies of inventors, authors, or companies that benefit from strong intellectual property laws.

Nonetheless, one can perceive a change in perspective. The origin of this change can be traced to both local firms and consumers, themselves victimized by unrestrained piracy in two ways. First, some local companies are owners of indigenously developed intellectual property and suffer along with Western companies from inadequate legal protection. Piracy deprives these local businesses of sales and the ability to provide employment, and it discourages local companies from engaging in their own research and development. Second, absent adequate protection, Western firms will less readily transfer technology to local companies. Such direct foreign investment is vital to development because it disseminates state-of-the-art technology into the economy.

Consumers in developing countries also are directly victimized by counterfeit goods that threaten the public health and welfare in these countries. These inferior and sometimes dangerous products are sold widely to Third World consumers, who are vulnerable because of lax government enforcement.

---

[3] Marshall A. Leaffer, *Protecting United States Intellectual Property Abroad: Toward A New Multilateralism*, 76 IOWA L. REV. 273. Copyright 1991 Iowa Law Review. Excerpt reprinted with permission.

QUESTIONS AND COMMENTS FOR YOUR CONSIDERATION

1. What incentives exist to counteract the potential economic benefits of free-riding?

2. Outside of pirated goods which pose a health or safety risk, do other forms of pirated consumer goods victimize consumers in developing countries?

3. Copyrights

a. The Role of Copyright in Economic Development[4]

From the early days of the printing press to the onset of CD-ROM production and distribution in China in the 1990's, developing countries have often utilized the ability to produce and market copyright protected works of foreign authors as the backbone for their economic advancement. The need for access by developing countries to copyright protected works has arguably grown more severe in the present technologically driven global economy. Much technology, including software, firmware, and robotics, contains, in whole or in part, potentially copyright protectable elements. Thus, attempts to restrict a country's internal access and use of such technology through the enactment of international protection norms or procedures are seen by some developing countries as a direct threat to their ability to play a significant role in the world economy.

[4] Written for this Anthology by Doris Estelle Long. Copyright 1996 Doris E. Long.

b. The Problem of Inadequate Enforcement[5]

Copyright owners also have suffered from organized piracy in the Third World. Because copyright laws generally are uniform (with certain notable exceptions), the problem facing the copyright owner is inadequate enforcement rather than a lack of substantive protection. Despite a relative uniformity in the law of copyright, a number of countries provide less protection to copyrightable subject matter and the exclusive rights of the copyright owner than is generally given in the West. For example, a few countries in the Middle East provide no copyright protection at all. Other countries such as Malaysia and Indonesia provide works of foreign origin with protection only if they are published in their country thirty days after the date of first being published abroad. Less dramatically, but just as serious to the copyright owner, other countries provide no protection for new forms of expression such as computer software and semiconductor chips.

[5] Marshall A. Leaffer, *Protecting United States Intellectual Property Abroad: Toward A New Multilateralism*, 76 IOWA L. REV. 273. Copyright 1991 Iowa Law Review. Excerpt reprinted with permission.

QUESTIONS AND COMMENTS FOR YOUR CONSIDERATION

1. If you represented the owner of a program that was subject to copyright protection under the laws of the US, what steps could you take to protect it from the problems of lack of copyright protection in the countries discussed above.
2. Select one of the countries mentioned above and determine if that country still provides the same lack of copyright protection indicated in the article.

4. Patents

a. The Problem of Patent Protection in Underdeveloped Countries[6]

Patent owners perhaps have suffered the most in Third World countries. In addition to outright counterfeiting, a lack of substantive protection and an inadequate infrastructure to administer the patent system have produced a deficient system for the protection of patents in Third World countries. As a consequence, not only is there a disincentive to invest, but the welfare and safety of consumers is threatened by

[6] Marshall A. Leaffer, *Protecting United States Intellectual Property Abroad: Toward A New Multilateralism*, 76 IOWA L. REV. 273. Copyright 1991 Iowa Law Review. Excerpt reprinted with permission.

infringing products of substandard quality. Inferior quality pharmaceutical products which endanger the health of consumers are a common example.

Many countries fail to provide basic protection in fundamental ways. The requirement in some countries that the patentee "work" (use) the patented invention after a certain time of exclusive use is prejudicial to the rights of patent owners. Even more prejudicial is the pervasive tolerance of compulsory licensing laws. Under the terms of a compulsory license, a third party can use the patent on payment of a statutory fee, often at below market prices. The compulsory license can result in a de facto expropriation of the patent.

In addition to requiring compulsory licensing, many developing countries display an antipatent attitude in the subject matter covered by a patent grant, the length of the patent term, and the lack of an adequate administrative system to properly examine and expedite patent applications. Some countries limit the patentability of certain products, such as chemicals or pharmaceuticals, and generally deny protection altogether as is the case with patents on processes. Extremely abbreviated patent terms also may prejudice the rights of patent owners.[7] In addition to these substantive law shortcomings, many developing countries expend few resources on maintaining a governmental agency to administer the patent system, providing only a handful of examiners to handle thousands of applications.

b. General Relationship Between Patent Benefits and Level of Economic Development[8]

The level of a country's development alters the cost-benefit ratio of granting patents. As a country develops, it will pass through a number of stages, each of which presents a different cost-benefit picture for the granting of patents. Several authors have suggested different versions of a model of economic evolution. The following scenario is a summary of their views.

The first stage is that of a country at a very low level of economic development. A completely under-developed country has little technological capacity and infrastructure, and will make few, if any, internationally patentable inventions. Such a country would not benefit from a patent system because, as an under-developed country, it would not be limited by a shortage of inventions but by the ability to utilize readily available technology. Whereas the economy of a developed country depends on new inventions, an under-developed country needs to expand its economy by implementing older inventions that are already available in the public domain.

As the country's economy develops, markets and the infrastructure necessary for innovation will also develop, and the country will reach the second stage. The country becomes capable of using more advanced technology and may become an intellectual property pirate. Such a country is often rapidly developing and fuels the growth of its economy through intellectual property theft.

Eventually, a country will reach the third stage of development, where its businesses can create world-class inventions. At that point, it becomes profitable for the country to grant patent protection so as to protect its own innovators. Profits from piracy of international intellectual property are outweighed by losses to the country and its inventors caused by failure to protect their own inventions. Because international intellectual property protection is on a quid pro quo basis, the country must provide strong patent protection so that other advanced countries will reciprocate and respect its patents. [Western Industrialized Countries ("WICs") including the United States, reached this third stage over a century ago]. Many of the difficulties with international intellectual property protec-

---

[7] For example, India has a seven-year term from the filing date or five years from the patent grant, Egypt has ten years for pharmaceutical and food products, and Costa Rica has a one-year term for food, agricultural products and drugs.

[8] Stefan Kirchanski, *Protection of US Patent Rights in Developing Countries: US Efforts to Enforce Pharmaceutical Patents in Thailand*, 16 LOY. L.A. INT'L & COMP. L. J. 569. Copyright 1993 Loyola of Los Angeles International and Comparative Law Journal. Excerpt reprinted with permission.

tion may be caused by a failure of WICs to recognize the evolutionary stages of patent protection.

A mechanism should be created that will protect a developing country from economic damage and promote development until that country reaches the stage at which it is profitable for the country to strengthen its intellectual property laws. One possible solution is to use economic incentives to alleviate potential damage.

One question is whether the incentives for introducing a Western-style intellectual property system should be given to all countries or only to countries above a developmental threshold. In other words, should the countries be ignored until they reach the stage-two to stage-three transition or should the incentives to implement an intellectual property system be introduced even in stage-one countries?

Deciding when to end the incentives would also be difficult. Employing economic indicators should provide a rational basis for such a choice, however. The incentive aid will ensure that intellectual property protection does not increase the overall cost of vital technologies to developing economies and, thus, impede development. Eventually, the economic benefits of intellectual property should overwhelm its costs, and further incentive aid will be unnecessary.

The form that the incentive aid should take must still be decided. Certainly, foreign aid payments to fund-development projects should continue. Direct aid payments should also be made to defer the operational expenses of fledgling patent systems until they can be supported by user fees. The problems surrounding the payment of royalties on pharmaceuticals and similar health/food items are more troubling. There are two competing goals. On one hand, it is in the interest of the United States to stimulate the economies of developing nations and to ensure their welfare. Not only would vigorous economies in the Third World provide a market for US products, but peace and prosperity in the Third World would allow the United States to reduce its own internal military expenditures. On the other hand, the US Government is also under considerable political pressure to guarantee the profitability of US pharmaceutical companies by allowing them to collect royalties on the international use of their patents.

Nevertheless, both goals could be met by making pharmaceuticals available to developing nations without royalty costs and having the US Government rebate to the manufacturers a royalty payment based on the number of units shipped. Alternatively, the United States could allow its pharmaceutical companies to collect its foreign royalties, but then rebate the royalties as foreign aid to the lesser-developed countries.

The likelihood that countries must reach a critical developmental level to make protecting intellectual property rights profitable, coupled with the direct economic costs of an intellectual property system, suggest that an incentive program may be the best way to encourage respect for US intellectual property rights. Incentives could help pay for the needed infrastructure and reduce the time necessary for a given country to develop to the point of voluntarily protecting intellectual property. On the other hand, trade retaliation and premature adoption of intellectual property protection can damage developing economies and will only delay further development of these countries to a level where intellectual property protection becomes beneficial.

QUESTIONS AND COMMENTS FOR YOUR CONSIDERATION

1. How do you determine when a developing country reaches the point of economic development where patent protection will be seen as beneficial?

2. Are there different levels of development for different types of patentable invention?

5. Trademarks

a. The Protection of Trademarks in Underdeveloped Countries[9]

Some developing countries have displayed hostility toward trademark protection in their substantive law. This attitude is nurtured by a fear that foreign licensors of trademarks exploit both local businesses and vulnerable consumers. Foreign licensors are perceived as having superior bargaining power, permitting them to impose terms unfavorable to the local licensee. In addition to potentially onerous terms in the licensing contract, local authorities believe that the increased use of trademarks will become an insurmountable obstacle to achieving economic self-sufficiency. According to this theory, the public's dependence on products identified by foreign trademarks makes it difficult for local producers to establish recognition for their own goods.

Some claim that consumers in developing countries are exploited by entrenched brand names. They argue that the foreign trademarks encourage irrational preferences among vulnerable, largely illiterate consumers in the developing countries. The foreign trademark functions as an insidious vehicle for persuasive advertising, which modifies healthy consumption patterns.

Linking laws [requiring the use of domestic trademarks with foreign trademarks] are not the only practice hostile to trademark licensors. Other examples of the antitrademark attitude are found in countries that prohibit the importation of certain categories of trademark goods such as pharmaceutical products. In addition, some countries have attempted confiscation of foreign trademarks. Other laws have forced the trademark owner to manufacture the product on which the mark is affixed in the local country.

b. The Conflict Between Consumer Savings and Goodwill[10]

Trademarks are used by the distributor of goods to identify them. The earliest uses of marks were presumably to indicate ownership. By the Middle Ages, these identification marks had evolved into two distinct groups based on usage: merchants' marks, indicative of a possessory interest in the goods; and production marks, indicative of source or manufacturer. This latter type eventually developed into the modern trademark.

There are some major differences between the early production marks and the modern trademark. While production marks were compulsory, and their use strictly monitored by the guilds, modern trademarks are employed on a strictly voluntary basis. Moreover, the modern trademark is treated as an asset, often the most valuable single asset of the modern business. In contrast, the tracing function that the production marks served was a distinct liability, because defective products could be traced to their makers.

During the ten year period between 1964 and 1974, there was an observable trend towards increased foreign ownership of trademarks in developing countries. Specifically, by 1974, fully half the trademarks registered in developing countries were owned by foreigners. Regional figures were even higher: about 65% of all Asian registrations were held by foreigners, while in Africa the percentage exceeded 88%. Of foreign-owned trademarks, 96-99% originated in developed countries. Of these, the United States, Japan, Great Britain, West Germany and France accounted for 78% of the total.

In view of this gross disparity in ownership, the UNCTAD secretariat tried to determine the relative costs and benefits of trademarks to the economies of developing countries. The cost to society of the market power generated through the use of trademarks was seen to be of two types: the misal-

---

[9] Marshall A. Leaffer, *Protecting United States Intellectual Property Abroad: Toward A New Multilateralism*, 76 IOWA L. REV. 273. Copyright 1991 Iowa Law Review. Excerpt reprinted with permission.

[10] John P. Spitals, *The UNCTAD Report on the Role of Trademarks in Developing Countries: An Analysis*, 2 N.Y. J. INT'L & COMP. L. 369. Copyright 1981 John P. Spitals. Excerpt reprinted with permission.

location of resources through advertising and the social impact of persuasive advertising expenditures. As benefits derived from trademark use, the secretariat noted the identification and guarantee functions as primary. After consideration of these components, the secretariat concluded that whereas "the private benefits that the owners of a trademark derive from its use and licensing are high, the net benefits accruing to society are low."

With respect to the allocation of resources to advertising, a major criticism was that the costs were generally shifted to the consumer, thereby making trademarked goods more expensive than non-advertised ones. The development of new and modified demands resulted in unnecessary expenditures at the expense of savings. Moreover, advertising competition may increase to such a degree that efforts to promote competing products would cancel out over time, at which point intensive advertising would be necessary just to retain the same marketing position. This was considered a "wasting of resources," particularly since advertising expenditures in developing countries were 70% higher than research and development investments.

In developing countries, trademarks are also seen as "symbols of the foreign business influence in the development process of the less advanced countries of the world." The influence of persuasive advertising in certain categories of products was felt to be so strong that in effect there had been a redefinition of certain basic needs. Through domestic marketing efforts, foreign subsidiaries would modify consumption patterns and tastes, instead of adapting products to local needs. Not surprisingly, a principal effect of this effort has been the development of a tendency in favor of advertised products bearing trademarks. This tendency was believed to extend even to the lower income sectors. Thus, the poor in developing countries were spending money on goods which did not satisfy their basic needs. Moreover, production of these goods would either require inputs not available in the local country or would create less employment than traditional indigenous activities.

A potential negative effect on the balance of payments was noted, in that higher profit margins achieved by foreign firms due to persuasive advertising would lead to an increased market share, increased foreign remittances, or possibly both. In addition, the accrual of higher profits by foreign corporations would increase their available resources for business expansion, to the detriment of developing local industry. Other indirect costs were felt to be even greater, since domestic firms attempting to enter the market would either have to enter into licensing agreements to use popular trademarks, or else accept reduced market shares. Another related cost was the loss of goodwill which might potentially be acquired by local industries. When foreign products are sold under licensing agreements, the goodwill accrues to the owner of the trademark, rather than to the licensee.

A few benefits of the use of trademarks in developing countries were acknowledged. Trademarks were considered useful in the identification of goods in the minds of consumers, thus serving as a type of guarantee that goods currently purchased would be of a similar quality to those purchased previously. In addition, identification of goods by trademark was said to facilitate the process of product rating and reporting. In developing countries in particular, the protection provided for foreign trademarks helps make certain products available, especially those that appeal to tourists. Local manufacturing of such products presupposes transfer of new technology and marketing techniques, including distribution methods, quality and inventory control. Finally, local advertising efforts had a favorable effect upon expansion of the media.

The most drastic remedy to the ills supposedly caused through the use of trademarks would be the abolition of their use entirely in certain sectors. To prevent the passing-off of one firms's goods as those of a competitor, and to protect the consumer from inferior products, new legislation, however, would be required in those countries where these functions had been carried out through the trademarks system. Finally, foreign enterprises whose trademarks had goodwill value would presumably be entitled to some form of compensation for their loss.

A second proposal of the secretariat was the institution of compulsory licensing of trademarks for reasons of the public interest.

If a competitor is allowed to obtain a compulsory license, it is difficult to imagine how one would prevent the marketing of inferior goods under the mark. The competitor, particularly if the license is for a limited duration, would have no incentive to maintain quality standards: since the goodwill would remain associated with the owner of the mark, the licensee has little to lose and much to gain by selling inferior goods. Revocation of the license, the major penalty available, would simply return the competitor to the *status quo ante*. The predicted increase in competition would be outweighed in most cases by the amount of harm created by deception of consumers as to quality. Moreover, there would seem to be no method to induce foreign trademark owners to provide compulsory licensees with the technology necessary to produce products of quality similar to those sold under the mark by the original owner. In any event, the more users in more territories of the trademark under license, the greater the eventual exclusionary power of the mark is likely to be when the compulsory licensing period has come to an end.

The main complaint of the UNCTAD seems to be that much advertising, of which they described two types, is irrational. One type is the promotion of the sale of products contrary to the best interests of society, such as those which are directed to desires for physical ease, social status or "feeling good." The other type of irrational advertising is that which promotes goods regarded as essential, but by means of non-informational content appealing to irrational impulses of the consumer. The first type raises the problem of priorities in a world of shrinking resources. The second presents the question of the degree to which government should regulate the content of communication of commercial ideas to consumers who are motivated by more than just price and quality. There are, of course, problems with this analysis: it is not clear whether consumers purchase because induced by advertising, or whether irrational bases for choice are an inextricable element of the human psyche. Nonetheless, it is important to realize that the regulation of persuasive advertising and the control of the trademark system *per se* are separate questions which should not be confused.

In a final section of the report, the UNCTAD secretariat made certain concrete proposals to reduce the costs of foreign trademarks to consumers. The most radical approach was again the banning of all foreign trademarks.

An alternative proposal is of the type embodied in the Mexican Law on Inventions and Trademarks. Article 127 of the Mexican law provides that foreign marks used with goods produced in the national territory must be associated with a mark originally registered in Mexico. These marks must both be displayed in an equally prominent manner. This, it is argued, would lead to the generation of goodwill, which would be associated with both the foreign and the domestic mark. Moreover, in the majority of cases, the domestic mark would additionally benefit through association with the foreign mark, which would be generally better known and already associated with some brand loyalty.

This type of program is also not without its pitfalls. First of all, there is the possibility of more than one domestic licensee. If each uses his own national mark in conjunction with the foreign mark, there is a real danger of the latter becoming generic. Moreover, in the multiple party situation, the quality identification aspect of the mark may be completely lost. Nonetheless, if such combined use is restricted to situations where the licensor can in fact monitor the quality of goods sold under the foreign mark, the local government could achieve its purported goals with reduced damage to the foreign trademark owner.

QUESTIONS AND COMMENTS FOR YOUR CONSIDERATION

1. Is there a level of economic development required for trademark protection to be considered desirable by an undeveloped country?

2. What arguments would you make in favor of protecting trademarks? What arguments would you make against such protection?

B. The Conflict Between the "Haves" and the "Have Nots"[11]

The premise that developing countries cannot expect to free-ride on costly intellectual goods produced in the industrialized countries draws support from principles of public international law that guarantee each state the sovereign right to determine its own economic development without interference from other states. The extent to which the many candidate norms emerging in this area add up to an international law of development binding on all states remains controversial. The very sources of law that purport to strengthen the economic independence of developing countries contain important provisions entitling the industrialized countries to respect for national development policies implemented within their own territorial boundaries. Systematic, uncompensated use of alien intellectual goods undermines these norms to the extent that it allows user states to project their development policies beyond territorial limits and to disrupt regulatory mechanisms on which the continued economic growth of the industrialized countries depends.

By the same token, states having a major stake in the protection of intellectual property rights cannot project their domestic policies onto weaker foreign states in the name of uniformity and harmonization of laws without violating fundamental principles of economic sovereignty. Imposition of foreign legal standards on unwilling states in the name of "harmonization " remains today what Ladas deemed it in 1975, namely, a polite form of economic imperialism. That the proposals concerning intellectual property so far put forward by the leading industrialized countries in the course of the Uruguay Round suffer from this defect seems clear.

Between these two extremes lies a gray area in which the legitimate economic policies pursued by different groups of states overlap and conflict. The resulting tensions can only be lessened through good faith negotiation and cooperation between states, in a manner that takes into account of interests of the developed countries without prejudicing the interests of developing countries.

Increased access to intellectual property as a driving force in present day economic development could enable the developing states to accelerate their domestic growth. At the same time, these countries need to capture a larger slice of the international market for more traditional industrial products if they are to earn the foreign exchange needed to pay for up-to-date technological innovation. The willingness of industrialized countries to expand imports from developing countries, however, cannot be severed from the continued ability of these same industrialized countries to maintain and augment their own levels of economic development through exports of intellectual goods to markets in which the developing countries will not be competitive for years to come. The logic of a changing international division of labor thus suggests that developing countries cannot expect to make wholesale use of foreign cultural and technological products without affording some reasonable rate of return to those who have defrayed the costs of research, development and dissemination incident to these products.

One cannot deny, however, that the domestic laws of all countries recognize derogations from and limitations on the exclusive rights to exploit intellectual property in order to promote the public interest generally and to ensure adequate levels of competition and continued innovation in particular. The international public interest, no less than the respective national public interests, requires a balancing between incentives to create and access to the fruits of creation. So long as the principle becomes established that all countries must sooner or later pay for the use of foreign intellectual goods, multilateral negotiations should focus on defining the areas of "fair use" to which developing countries must be entitled if they are ever to narrow the gap between haves and have nots.[12]

---

[11] J. H. Reichman, *Intellectual Property in International Trade: Opportunities and Risks of a GATT Connection*. Copyright 1989 J. H. Reichman. Excerpt reprinted with permission.

[12] *Editors' Note:* For a further discussion of some of the conflicts that underlie the debate regarding the protection of intellectual property by developing nations, *see* Chapter Two.

15

Emerging Market Economies

The end of the Twentieth Century has seen an increasing desire on behalf of many former communist and communist-socialist countries to develop some form of market economy. Regardless of the purpose of politico-economic philosophies behind this new drive towards a free market in countries which formerly featured state-controlled or barter economies, intellectual property and its protection play a dominant role in the development of a free market economy. This Chapter explores those issues of intellectual property protection which relate solely to the free market concerns of such newly emerging market economies. We begin with an examination of the role that copyright protection plays in fueling a market economy. It includes an examination of the issues faced by the Commonwealth of Independent States in their efforts to develop market economies. The Chapter concludes with a brief discussion of the role of trademarks in free market economies.

A. Copyrights[1]

The problem of effective copyright enforcement is not solely a problem of underdeveloped or newly industrialized countries. Those countries that are in the process of changing from a state-operated or barter economy to a market economy face similar issues regarding the economic desirability of protection. Many consumer goods such as compact discs, video cassettes, computer programs, video games and books fall within the purview of copyright protection. The determination by a country with an emerging market economy whether to grant copyright protection, or more likely, whether to enforce existing copyright laws, involves consideration of many of the same philosophic, historical, cultural and economic factors that inform a developing country's decision. Added to these factors, however, should be a heavy consideration of the issues relating to the availability of consumer products to fuel the development of a market economy.

Among the factors to be given substantial weight is the potentially positive effect which strong protection of copyright may have on the ability to attract foreign investment. Emerging market economies have the same need for a manufacturing infrastructure as developing countries and the same need to attract manufacturing and research and development investments.

The need to supply increasing consumer demand for product is one of the hallmarks of an emerging market economy. Some emerging market economies may wrongfully perceive that such need may initially be met by permitting the distribution of unauthorized product. Free riding through the marketing of pirated and counterfeit copyrighted goods, however, can result in serious market disruption that may ultimately impede the goals of development.

Permitting the unencumbered distribution of pirated goods may initially increase the amount of product available for consumption. Such distribution may also result in a mistakenly perceived pro-competitive benefit by resulting initially in lower consumer prices (pirated goods are notoriously less costly since pirates have avoided the research, development and licensing costs incurred by authorized users). Ultimately, however, the consumer and the marketplace will suffer. The removal of legitimate product from the market also eliminates the side benefits of legitimacy, including warranty service and defective product replacement.

---

[1] Written for this Anthology by Doris Estelle Long. Copyright 1996 Doris E. Long.

It also increases the likelihood that available goods will be of inferior quality — a factor which could have an exponentially adverse impact on the consuming public if the quality of the product has a direct relationship to its safety.

Lack of strong copyright protection may also adversely impact the variety of domestically created product available for consumption. Without the assurance of a sufficient economic return, native authors and artists will have little incentive to spend the time, money and effort to create new product for a growing marketplace. Lack of strong copyright protection may also have a deleterious effect on the development of foreign works. Reduced profit due to unchecked piracy may reduce the monies available for investment in future works, which may in turn reduce the pool available for future pirating activities.

Furthermore, where legitimate channels of distribution are missing, problems of scarcity and inconsistent supply may be exacerbated, further reducing the available pool of consumer products. Copyright protection, or its lack, consequently forms one of the fundamental bases on which development of an emerging market economy may be based.

QUESTIONS AND COMMENTS FOR YOUR CONSIDERATION

1. Although the above excerpt discusses the importance of copyright protection in providing sufficient consumer product for an emerging market economy, are there other forms of intellectual property protection which should be granted to assure sufficient consumer products for the market?

2. For a discussion of the issues which face developing (newly industrialized) countries, *see* Chapter Fourteen.

1. The Commonwealth States: A Case Study

a. The Needs of Emerging Market Economies[2]

The disintegration of the former Soviet Union and the emergence of the Commonwealth of Independent States provide a unique opportunity to examine the problems and issues attendant upon a newly emerging market economy. In their efforts to emerge from the highly structured, state controlled economy of the Soviet era, the Commonwealth States must each face the issue of the balance to be struck between free-riding and copyright protection. Like developing countries, emerging market economies such as the CIS must cultivate access to foreign intellectual property to ensure an adequate supply of goods for the marketplace. They must also cultivate foreign investment opportunities so that marketplace capabilities can expand and the increasing demand for consumer goods can be met.

At the same time, the CIS must face the economic and political realities of crafting an intellectual property protection system, with its attendant administrative and legal constructs, at a time when budgetary demands can ill afford the necessary capital expenditures required to develop and fuel an effective system. The choices faced by the individual countries, and the paths they choose to pursue, will be instructive for future generations.

b. The Choices Faced by the CIS[3]

Commonwealth States face a difficult period as they move toward free-market econ-

---

[2] Written for this Anthology by Doris Estelle Long. Copyright 1996 Doris E. Long.

[3] Brad Swenson, *Intellectual Property Protection Through The Berne Convention: A Matter Of Economic Survival For The Post-Soviet New Commonwealth Of Independent States*, 21 DENV. J. INT'L L. & POL'Y 77. Copyright 1992 Denver Journal of International Law and Policy. Excerpt reprinted with permission.

omies. Critical economic conditions in each of the post-Soviet States are pressuring new leadership to make the transition as quickly and smoothly as possible. The expediency and ease of these transitions, however, are conditioned upon each State's ability to exist and function in the global marketplace.

Today's global free-market economies are dependent upon information-based technology and innovations. Computer-integrated-manufacturing systems control and monitor the production of materials. Advanced telecommunication and electronic-data-interchange systems link suppliers, distributors and purchasers on a global scale. Information of all types can be transmitted, exchanged, updated, or monitored from points around the globe in milliseconds. These advanced systems as well as the information that is transmitted through them are the subject of careful protections under available international copyright codes.

A Commonwealth State's transition from state-owned to free-market economy, therefore, will depend immensely on its ability to obtain established Western information-based technologies, stimulate comparable indigenous technological developments, and integrate these technologies into its economic system. In light of existing critical economic conditions in the Commonwealth States, Commonwealth leaders must seek to attain the highest degree of access to these intellectual goods that the international marketplace will allow.

Direct foreign investment is imperative to the integration of state-of-the-art technology into the developing Commonwealth economies. Foreign nations, however, will be reluctant to engage in any form of direct technological investment or exchange without assurances that its intellectual goods will be adequately protected. Moreover, domestic development will progress equally as slow where copyright protections do not exist as an incentive to indigenous scientists, authors, and engineers.

Lack of Berne Convention membership will work a significant disadvantage on each Commonwealth State's attempt to obtain information-based technologies from foreign trade partners. As the premier union for the international protection of copyrights, the Berne Convention defines "adequate" minimum standards of copyright protection. Fledgling economies which are reluctant to assure these adequate protections will not be readily trusted in the global marketplace.

Transition to and maintenance of a free-market economy depends on the free and protected flow of information. Broad access to Western, information-based technology must be a matter of utmost concern for Commonwealth leaders. Accession to the Berne Convention is a necessary precursor to any such access. By joining the Berne Convention, Commonwealth States would receive international copyright protection in more than eighty nations. Commonwealth authors would enjoy copyright protection in several countries, not members to the U.C.C. More significantly, new Commonwealth authors would enjoy the protection of the highest international copyright standards available today. Membership guarantees participation in the formulation and management of international copyright policy. It will enhance the plausibility of a Commonwealth State's trade positions, and provide the necessary show of good-faith to cautious trade partners. Membership will evidence that the Commonwealth State intends to hold the same respect for intellectual property protections as the other economically and technologically advanced nations of the world.

Facing the potential of losing control over new innovations, copyright owners tend to be reluctant in disclosing their innovations where copyright protections are inadequate. When the purchasing nation offers inadequate protections, inventors are content to send outdated and non-competitive technology to these "dangerous" markets and maintain the competitive integrity of their cutting edge technology. Membership in the Berne Convention would provide cautious trade partners with the protective assurances they desire.

QUESTIONS AND COMMENTS FOR YOUR CONSIDERATION

1. Are there reasons why a nation which is developing an emerging market economy might choose not to be a member of the Berne Convention? Can a

nation which is seeking to develop a market economy (or strengthen an existing one) achieve such goals without adhering to multinational treaty regimes such as TRIPS or Berne?

2. Given the relative geographic proximity of many of the Commonwealth State members to the European Union, would the goals of foreign investment and strengthening a market economy be met equally well by membership in the European Union and subsequent compliance with its harmonization directives? (*See* Chapter Thirteen)

B. Trademarks[4]

Despite the use of phrases like "Americanization of culture" and "Coca-colonization" by some third world countries in disputing the desirability of extending strong protection to trademarks, brand differentiation appears to be one of the hallmarks of a vital, free market economy. Perhaps more than any other form of intellectual property, trademarks are imbued with attributes whose primary value resides in their competitive properties. Economic compensation is not merely the engine which drives the creative act, in the field of trademarks, it is the sole *raison d'etre* for this form of intellectual property.

Initially the protection of trademarks may devolve largely to foreign multinational companies who have the most recognizable marks (and the greatest experience at advertising their marks to ensure brand recognition). Local companies, however, are uniquely placed to develop marks and identities which would take advantage of local tastes and idiosyncracies. They are also uniquely suited to provide the type of warranty and other services that local consumers would value, thus helping them to further differentiate their marked goods from others.

Without trademark protection, companies would have little reason to provide unique services or high quality goods since free riders would destroy the competitive advantage obtained through such efforts. In light of the critical role that trademarks can play in the development of a market economy, emerging nations will need to strengthen their protection of trademarks, including regularizing the types of signifiers that qualify as protectable marks.

[4] Written for this Anthology by Doris Estelle Long. Copyright 1996 Doris E. Long.

QUESTIONS AND COMMENTS FOR YOUR CONSIDERATION

1. Do developing nations have the same concerns with regard to the protection of trademarks as those with emerging market economies?

2. What special provisions exist in TRIPS in recognition of the special concerns of emerging market economies? Do these special provisions meet the issues raised in the above article? What additional provisions, if any, would you seek if you represented a country with an emerging market economy?

APPENDIX

I	Paris Convention for the Protection of Industrial Property
II	Berne Convention for the Protection of Literary and Artistic Works
III	Treaty Establishing the European Community
IV	International Convention for the Protection of Performers, Producers of Phonograms and Broadcasting Organizations
V	Universal Copyright Convention (UCC)
VI	Patent Cooperation Treaty
VII	European Communities Trademark Harmonization Directive
VIII	North American Free Trade Agreement (NAFTA)
IX	Agreement on Trade Related Aspects of Intellectual Property Rights (TRIPS)
X	Protocol Relating to the Madrid Agreement Concerning the International Registration of Marks
XI	Trademark Registration Treaty

APPENDIX I

PARIS CONVENTION FOR THE PROTECTION OF INDUSTRIAL PROPERTY (As Revised at Stockholm 1967)

Article 1

1. The countries to which this Convention applies constitute a Union for the protection of industrial property.

2. The protection of industrial property has as its object patents, utility models, industrial designs, trademarks, service marks, trade names, indications of source or appellations of origin, and the repression of unfair competition.

3. Industrial property shall be understood in the broadest sense and shall apply not only to industry and commerce proper, but likewise to agricultural and extractive industries and to all manufactured or natural products, for example, wines, grain, tobacco leaf, fruit, cattle, minerals, mineral waters, beer, flowers, and flour.

4. Patents shall include the various kinds of industrial patents recognized by the laws of the countries of the Union, such as patents of importation, patents of improvement, patents and certificates of addition, etc.

Article 2

1. Nationals of any country of the Union shall, as regards the protection of industrial property, enjoy in all the other countries of the Union the advantages that their respective laws now grant, or may hereafter grant, to nationals; all without prejudice to the rights specially provided for by this Convention. Consequently, they shall have the same protection as the latter, and the same legal remedy against any infringement of their rights, provided that the conditions and formalities imposed upon nationals are complied with.

2. However, no requirement as to domicile or establishment in the country where protection is claimed may be imposed upon nationals of countries of the Union for the enjoyment of any industrial property rights.

3. The provisions of the laws of each of the countries of the Union relating to judicial and administrative procedure and to jurisdiction, and to the designation of an address for service or the appointment of an agent, which may be required by the laws on industrial property are expressly reserved.

Article 3

Nationals of countries outside the Union who are domiciled or who have real and effective industrial or commercial establishments in the territory of one of the countries of the Union shall be treated in the same manner as nationals of the countries of the Union.

Article 4

A.1. Any person who has duly filed an application for a patent, or for the registration of a utility model, or of an industrial design, or of a trademark, in one of the countries of the Union, or his successor in title, shall enjoy, for the purpose of filing in the other countries, a right of priority during the periods hereinafter fixed.

2. Any filing that is equivalent to a regular national filing under the domestic legislation of any country of the Union or under bilateral or multilateral treaties concluded between countries of the Union shall be recognized as giving rise to the right of priority.

3. By a regular national filing is meant any filing that is adequate to establish the date on which the application was filed in the country concerned, whatever may be the subsequent fate of the application.

B. Consequently, any subsequent filing in any of the other countries of the Union before the expiration of the periods referred to above shall not be invalidated by reason of any acts accomplished in the interval, in particular, another filing, the publication or exploitation of the invention, the putting on sale of copies of the design, or the use of the mark, and such acts cannot give rise to any third-party right or any right of personal possession. Rights acquired by third parties before the date of the first application that serves as the basis for the right of priority are reserved in accordance with the domestic legislation of each country of the Union.

C.1. The periods of priority referred to above shall be twelve months for patents and utility models, and six months for industrial designs and trademarks.

2. These periods shall start from the date of filing of the first application; the day of filing shall not be included in the period.

3. If the last day of the period is an official holiday, or a day when the Office is not open for the filing of applications in the country where protection is claimed, the period shall be extended until the first following working day.

4. A subsequent application concerning the same subject as a previous first application within the meaning of paragraph (2), above, filed in the same country of the Union, shall be considered as the first application, of which the filing date shall be the starting point of the period of priority, if, at the time of filing the subsequent application, the said previous application has been withdrawn, abandoned, or refused, without having been laid open to public inspection and without leaving any rights outstanding, and if it has not yet served as a basis for claiming a right of priority. The previous application may not thereafter serve as a basis for claiming a right of priority.

D.1. Any person desiring to take advantage of the priority of a previous filing shall be required to make a declaration indicating the date of such filing and the country in which it was made. Each country shall determine the latest date on which such declaration must be made.

2. These particulars shall be mentioned in the publications issued by the competent authority, and in particular in the patents and the specifications relating thereto.

3. The countries of the Union may require any person making a declaration of priority to produce a copy of the application (description, drawings, etc.) previously filed. The copy, certified as correct by the authority which received such application, shall not require any authentication, and may in any case be filed, without fee, at any time within three months of the filing of the subsequent application. They may require it to be accompanied by a certificate from the same authority showing the date of filing, and by a translation.

4. No other formalities may be required for the declaration of priority at the time of filing the application. Each country of the Union shall determine the consequences of failure to comply with the formalities prescribed by this Article, but such consequences shall in no case go beyond the loss of the right of priority.

5. Subsequently, further proof may be required.

Any person who avails himself of the priority of a previous application shall be required to specify the number of that application; this number shall be published as provided for by paragraph (2), above.

E.1. Where an industrial design is filed in a country by virtue of a right of priority based on the filing of a utility model, the period of priority shall be the same as that fixed for industrial designs.

2. Furthermore, it is permissible to file a utility model in a country by virtue of a right of priority based on the filing of a patent application, and *vice versa*.

F. No country of the Union may refuse a priority or a patent application on the ground that the applicant claims multiple priorities, even if they originate in different countries, or on the ground that an application claiming one or more priorities contains one or more elements that were not included in the application or applications whose priority is claimed, provided that, in both cases, there is unity of invention within the meaning of the law of the country.

With respect to the elements not included in the application or applications whose priority is claimed, the filing of the subsequent application shall give rise to a right of priority under ordinary conditions.

G.1. If the examination reveals that an application for a patent contains more than one invention, the applicant may divide the application into a certain number of divisional applications and preserve as the date of each the date of the initial application and the benefit of the right of priority, if any.

2. The applicant may also, on his own initiative, divide a patent application and preserve as the date of each divisional application the date of the initial application and the benefit of the right of priority, if any. Each country of the Union shall have the right to determine the conditions under which such division shall be authorized.

H. Priority may not be refused on the ground that certain elements of the invention for which priority is claimed do not appear among the claims formulated in the application in the country of origin, provided that the application documents as a whole specifically disclose such elements.

I.1. Applications for inventors' certificates filed in a country in which applicants have the right to apply at their own option either for a patent or for an inventor's certificate shall give rise to the right of priority provided for by this Article, under the same conditions and with the same effects as applications for patents.

2. In a country in which applicants have the right to apply at their own option either for a patent or for an inventor's certificate, an applicant for an inventor's certificate shall, in accordance with the provisions of this Article relating to patent applications, enjoy a right of priority based on an application for a patent, a utility model, or an inventor's certificate.

Article 4bis

1. Patents applied for in the various countries of the Union by nationals of countries of the Union shall be independent of patents obtained for the same invention in other countries, whether members of the Union or not.

2. The foregoing provision is to be understood in an unrestricted sense, in particular, in the sense that patents applied for during the period of priority are independent, both as regards the grounds for nullity and forfeiture, and as regards their normal duration.

3. The provision shall apply to all patents existing at the time when it comes into effect.

4. Similarly, it shall apply, in the case of the accession of new countries, to patents in existence on either side at the time of accession.

5. Patents obtained with the benefit of priority shall, in the various countries of the Union, have a duration equal to that which they would have, had they been applied for or granted without the benefit of priority.

Article 4ter

The inventor shall have the right to be mentioned as such in the patent.

Article 4quater

The grant of a patent shall not be refused and a patent shall not be invalidated on the ground that the sale of the patented product or of a product obtained by means of a patented process is subject to restrictions or limitations resulting from the domestic law.

Article 5

A.1. Importation by the patentee into the country where the patent has been granted of articles manufactured in any of the countries of the Union shall not entail forfeiture of the patent.

2. Each country of the Union shall have the right to take legislative measures providing for the grant of compulsory licenses to prevent the abuses which might result from the exercise of the exclusive rights conferred by the patent, for example, failure to work.

3. Forfeiture of the patent shall not be provided for except in cases where the grant of compulsory licenses would not have been sufficient to prevent the said abuses. No proceedings for the forfeiture or revocation of a patent may be instituted before the expiration of two years from the grant of the first compulsory license.

4. A compulsory license may not be applied for on the ground of failure to work or insufficient working before the expiration of a period of four years from the date of filing of the patent application or three years from the date of the grant of the patent, whichever period expires last; it shall be refused if the patentee justifies his inaction by legitimate reasons. Such a compulsory license shall be non-exclusive and shall not be transferable, even in the form of the grant of a sub-license, except with that part of the enterprise or goodwill which exploits such license.

5. The foregoing provisions shall be applicable, *mutatis mutandis*, to utility models.

B. The protection of industrial designs shall not, under any circumstance, the subject to any forfeiture, either by reason of failure to work or by reason of the importation of articles corresponding to those which are protected.

C.1. If, in any country, use of the registered mark is compulsory, the registration may be canceled only after a reasonable period, and then only if the person concerned does not justify his inaction.

2. Use of a trademark by the proprietor in a form differing in elements which do not alter the distinctive character of the mark in the form in which it was registered in one of the countries of the Union shall not entail invalidation of the registration and shall not diminish the protection granted to the mark.

3. Concurrent use of the same mark on identical or similar goods by industrial or commercial establishments considered as co-proprietors of the mark according to the provisions of the domestic law of the country where protection is claimed shall not prevent registration or diminish in any way the protection granted to the said mark in any country of the Union, provided that such use does not result in misleading the public and is not contrary to the public interest.

D. No indication or mention of the patent, of the utility model, of the registration of the trademark, or of the deposit of the industrial design, shall be required upon the goods as a condition of recognition of the right to protection.

Article 5bis

1. A period of grace of not less than six months shall be allowed for the payment of the fees prescribed for the maintenance of industrial property rights, subject, if the domestic legislation so provides, to the payment of a surcharge.

2. The countries of the Union shall have the right to provide for the restoration of patents which have lapsed by reason of non-payment of fees.

Article 5ter

In any country of the Union the following shall not be considered as infringements of the rights of a patentee:

1. the use on board vessels of other countries of the Union of devices forming the subject of his patent in the body of the vessel, in the machinery, tackle, gear and other accessories, when such vessels temporarily or accidentally enter the waters of the said country, provided that such devices are used there exclusively for the needs of the vessel;

2. the use of devices forming the subject of the patent in the construction or operation of aircraft or land vehicles of other countries of the Union, or of accessories of such aircraft or land
vehicles, when those aircraft or land vehicles temporarily or accidentally enter the said country.

Article 5quater

When a product is imported into a country of the Union where there exists a patent protecting a process of manufacture of the said product, the patentee shall have all the rights, with regard to the imported product, that are accorded to him by the legislation of the country of importation, on the basis of the process patent, with respect to products manufactured in that country.

Article 5quinquies

Industrial designs shall be protected in all the countries of the Union.

Article 6

1. The conditions for the filing and registration of trademarks shall be determined in each country of the Union by its domestic legislation.

2. However, an application for the registration of a mark filed by a national of a country of the Union in any country of the Union may not be refused, nor may a registration be invalidated, on the ground that filing, registration, or renewal, has not been effected in the country of origin.

3. A mark duly registered in a country of the Union shall be regarded as independent of marks registered in the other countries of the Union, including the country of origin.

Article 6bis

1. The countries of the Union undertake, *ex officio* if their legislation so permits, or at the request of an interested party, to refuse or to cancel the registration, and to prohibit the use, of a trademark which constitutes a reproduction, an imitation, or a translation, liable to create confusion, of a mark considered by the competent authority of the country of registration or use to be well known in that country as being already the mark of a person entitled to the benefits of this Convention and used for identical or similar goods. These provisions shall also apply when the essential part of the mark constitutes a reproduction of any such well-known mark or an imitation liable to create confusion therewith.

2. A period of at least five years from the date of registration shall be allowed for requesting the cancellation of such a mark. The countries of the Union may provide for a period within which the prohibition of use must be requested.

3. No time limit shall be fixed for requesting the cancellation or the prohibition of the use of marks registered or used in bad faith.

Article 6ter

1. (a) The countries of the Union agree to refuse or to invalidate the registration, and to prohibit by appropriate measures the use, without authorization by the competent authorities, either as trademarks or as elements of trademarks, of armorial bearings, flags, and other State emblems, of the countries of the Union, official signs and hallmarks indicating control and warranty adopted by them, and any imitation from a heraldic point of view.

(b) The provisions of subparagraph (a), above, shall apply equally to armorial bearings, flags, other emblems, abbreviations, and names, of international intergovernmental organizations of which one or more countries of the Union are members, with the exception of armorial bearings, flags, other emblems, abbreviations, and names, that are already the subject of international agreements in force, intended to ensure their protection.

(c) No country of the Union shall be required to apply the provisions of subparagraph (b), above, to the prejudice of the owners of rights acquired in good faith before the entry into force, in that country, of this Convention. The countries of the Union shall not be required to apply the said provisions when the use or registration referred to in subparagraph (a), above, is not of such a nature as to suggest to the public that a connection exists between the organization concerned and the armorial bearings, flags, emblems, abbreviations, and names, or if such use or registration is probably not of such a nature as to mislead the public as to the existence of a connection between the user and the organization.

2. Prohibition of the use of official signs and hallmarks indicating control and warranty shall apply solely in cases where the marks in which they are incorporated are intended to be used on goods of the same or a similar kind.

3. (a) For the application of these provisions, the countries of the Union agree to communicate reciprocally, through the intermediary of the International Bureau, the list of State emblems, and official signs and hallmarks indicating control and warranty, which they desire, or may hereafter desire, to place wholly or within certain limits under the protection of this Article, and all subsequent modifications of such list. Each country of the Union shall in due course make available to the public the lists so communicated.

Nevertheless such communication is not obligatory in respect of flags of States.

(b) The provisions of subparagraph (b) of paragraph (1) of this Article shall apply only to such armorial bearings, flags, other emblems, abbreviations, and names, of international intergovernmental organizations as the latter have communicated to the countries of the Union through the intermediary of the International Bureau.

4. Any country of the Union may, within a period of twelve months from the receipt of the notification, transmit its objections, if any, through the intermediary of the International Bureau, to the country or international intergovernmental organization concerned.

5. In the case of State flags, the measures prescribed by paragraph (1), above, shall apply solely to marks registered after November 6, 1925.

6. In the case of State emblems other than flags, and of official signs and hallmarks of the countries of the Union, and in the case of armorial bearings, flags, other emblems, abbreviations, and names, of international intergovernmental organizations, these provisions shall apply only to marks registered more than two months after receipt of the communication provided for in paragraph (3), above.

7. In cases of bad faith, the countries shall have the right to cancel even those marks incorporating State emblems, signs, and hallmarks, which were registered before November 6, 1925.

8. Nationals of any country who are authorized to make use of the State emblems, signs, and hallmarks, of their country may use them even if they are similar to those of another country.

9. The countries of the Union undertake to prohibit the unauthorized use in trade of the State armorial bearings of the other countries of the Union, when the use is of such a nature as to be misleading as to the origin of the goods.

10. The above provisions shall not prevent the countries from exercising the right given in paragraph (3) of Article 6quinquies, Section B, to refuse or to invalidate the registration of marks incorporating, without authorization, armorial bearings, flags, other State emblems, or official signs and hallmarks adopted by a country of the Union, as well as the distinctive signs of international intergovernmental organizations referred to in paragraph (1), above.

Article 6quater

1. When, in accordance with the law of a country of the Union, the assignment of mark is valid only if it takes place at the same time as the transfer of the business or goodwill to which the mark belongs, it shall suffice for the recognition of such validity that the portion of the business or goodwill located in that country be transferred to the assignee, together with the exclusive right to manufacture in the said country, or to sell therein, the goods bearing the mark assigned.

2. The foregoing provision does not impose upon the countries of the Union any obligation to regard as valid the assignment of any mark the use of which by the assignee would, in fact, be of such a nature as to mislead the public, particularly as regards the origin, nature, or essential qualities, of the goods to which the mark is applied.

Article 6quinquies

A.1. Every trademark duly registered in the country of origin shall be accepted for filing and protected as is in the other countries of the Union, subject to the reservations indicated in this Article. Such countries may, before proceeding to final registration, require the production of a certificate of registration in the country of origin, issued by the competent authority. No authentication shall be required for this certificate.

2. Shall be considered the country of origin the country of the Union where the applicant has a real and effective industrial or commercial establishment, or, if he has no such establishment within the Union, the country of the Union where he has his domicile, or, if he has no domicile within the Union but is a national of a country of the Union, the country of which he is a national.

B. Trademarks covered by this Article may be neither denied registration nor invalidated except in the following cases:

1. when they are of such a nature as to infringe rights acquired by third parties in the country where protection is claimed;

2. when they are devoid of any distinctive character, or consist exclusively of signs or indications which may serve, in trade, to designate the kind, quality, quantity, intended purpose, value, place of origin, of the goods, or the time of production, or have become customary in the current language or in the bona fide and established practices of the trade of the country where protection is claimed;

3. when they are contrary to morality or public order and, in particular, of such a nature as to deceive the public. It is understood that a mark may not be considered

contrary to public order for the sole reason that it does not conform to a provision of the legislation on marks, except if such provision itself relates to public order.

This provision is subject, however, to the application of Article 10bis.

C.1. In determining whether a mark is eligible for protection, all the factual circumstances must be taken into consideration, particularly the length of time the mark has been in use.

2. No trademark shall be refused in the other countries of the Union for the sole reason that it differs from the mark protected in the country of origin only in respect of elements that do not alter its distinctive character and do not affect its identity in the form in which it has been registered in the said country of origin.

D. No person may benefit from the provisions of this Article if the mark for which he claims protection is not registered in the country of origin.

E. However, in no case shall the renewal of the registration of the mark in the country of origin involve an obligation to renew the registration in the other countries of the Union in which the mark has been registered.

F. The benefit of priority shall remain unaffected for applications for the registration of marks filed within the period fixed by Article 4, even if registration in the country of origin is effected after the expiration of such period.

Article 6sexies

The countries of the Union undertake to protect service marks. They shall not be required to provide for the registration of such marks.

Article 6septies

1. If the agent or representative of the person who is the proprietor of a mark in one of the countries of the Union applies, without such proprietor's authorization, for the registration of the mark in his own name, in one or more countries of the Union, the proprietor shall be entitled to oppose the registration applied for or demand its cancellation or, if the law of the country so allows, the assignment in his favor of the said registration, unless such agent or representative justifies his action.

2. The proprietor of the mark shall, subject to the provisions of paragraph (1), above, be entitled to oppose the use of his mark by his agent or representative if he has not authorized such use.

3. Domestic legislation may provide an equitable time limit within which the proprietor of a mark must exercise the rights provided for in this Article.

Article 7

The nature of the goods to which a trademark is to be applied shall in no case form an obstacle to the registration of the mark.

Article 7bis

1. The countries of the Union undertake to accept for filing and to protect collective marks belonging to associations the existence of which is not contrary to the law of the country of origin, even if such associations do not possess an industrial or commercial establishment.

2. Each country shall be the judge of the particular conditions under which a collective mark shall be protected and may refuse protection if the mark is contrary to the public interest.

3. Nevertheless, the protection of these marks shall not be refused to any association the existence of which is not contrary to the law of the country of origin, on the ground

that such association is not established in the country where protection is sought or is not constituted according to the law of the latter country.

Article 8

A trade name shall be protected in all the countries of the Union without the obligation of filing or registration, whether or not it forms part of a trademark.

Article 9

1. All goods unlawfully bearing a trademark or trade name shall be seized on importation into those countries of the Union where such mark or trade name is entitled to legal protection.
2. Seizure shall likewise be effected in the country where the unlawful affixation occurred or in the country into which the goods were imported.
3. Seizure shall take place at the request of the public prosecutor, or any other competent authority, or any interested party, whether a natural person or a legal entity, in conformity with the domestic legislation of each country.
4. The authorities shall not be bound to effect seizure of goods in transit.
5. If the legislation of a country does not permit seizure on importation, seizure shall be replaced by prohibition of importation or by seizure inside the country.
6. If the legislation of a country permits neither seizure on importation nor prohibition of importation nor seizure inside the country, then, until such time as the legislation is modified accordingly, these measures shall be replaced by the actions and remedies available in such cases to nationals under the law of such country.

Article 10

1. The provisions of the preceding Article shall apply in cases of direct or indirect use of a false indication of the source of the goods or the identity of the producer, manufacturer, or merchant.
2. Any producer, manufacturer, or merchant, whether a natural person or a legal entity, engaged in the production or manufacture of or trade in such goods and established either in the locality falsely indicated as the source, or in the region where such locality is situated, or in the country falsely indicated, or in the country where the false indication of source is used, shall in any case be deemed an interested party.

Article 10bis

1. The countries of the Union are bound to assure to nationals of such countries effective protection against unfair competition.
2. Any act of competition contrary to honest practices in industrial or commercial matters constitutes an act of unfair competition.
3. The following in particular shall be prohibited:
   (1) all acts of such a nature as to create confusion by any means whatever with the establishment, the goods, or the industrial or commercial activities, of a competitor;
   (2) false allegations in the course of trade of such a nature as to discredit the establishment, the goods, or the industrial or commercial activities, of a competitor;
   (3) indications or allegations the use of which in the course of trade is liable to mislead the public as to the nature, the manufacturing process, the characteristics, the suitability for their purpose, or the quantity, of the goods.

Article 10ter

1. The countries of the Union undertake to assure to nationals of the other countries

of the Union appropriate legal remedies effectively to repress all the acts referred to in Articles 9, 10, and 10bis.

2. They undertake, further, to provide measures to permit federations and associations representing interested industrialists, producers, or merchants, provided that the existence of such federations and associations is not contrary to the laws of their countries, to take action in the courts or before the administrative authorities, with a view to the repression of the acts referred to in Articles 9, 10, and 10bis, in so far as the law of the country in which protection is claimed allows such action by federations and associations of that country.

Article 11

1. The countries of the Union shall, in conformity with their domestic legislation, grant temporary protection to patentable inventions, utility models, industrial designs, and trademarks, in respect of goods exhibited at official or officially recognized international exhibitions held in the territory of any of them.

2. Such temporary protection shall not extend the periods provided by Article 4. If, later, the right of priority is invoked, the authorities of any country may provide that the period shall start from the date of introduction of the goods into the exhibition.

3. Each country may require, as proof of the identity of the article exhibited and of the date of its introduction, such documentary evidence as it considers necessary.

Article 12

1. Each country of the Union undertakes to establish a special industrial property service and a central office for the communication to the public of patents, utility models, industrial designs, and trademarks.

2. This service shall publish an official periodical journal. It shall publish regularly:

(a) the names of the proprietors of patents granted, with a brief designation of the inventions patented;

(b) the reproductions of registered trademarks.

[*Article 13 - Article 18* Omitted]

Article 19

It is understood that the countries of the Union reserve the right to make separately between themselves special agreements for the protection of industrial property, in so far as these agreements do not contravene the provisions of this Convention.

Article 20

1. (a) Any country of the Union which has signed this Act may ratify it, and, if it has not signed it, may accede to it. Instruments of ratification and accession shall be deposited with the Director General.

(b) Any country of the Union may declare in its instrument of ratification or accession that its ratification or accession shall not apply:

(i) to Articles 1 to 12, or

(ii) to Articles 13 to 17.

(c) Any country of the Union which, in accordance with subparagraph (b), has excluded from the effects of its ratification or accession one of the two groups of Articles referred to in that subparagraph may at any later time declare that it extends the effects of its ratification or accession to that group of Articles. Such declaration shall be deposited with the Director General.

2. (a) Articles 1 to 12 shall enter into force, with respect to the first ten countries of the Union which have deposited instruments of ratification or accession without making the declaration permitted under paragraph (1) (b) (i), three months after the deposit of the tenth such instrument of ratification or accession.

(b) Articles 13 to 17 shall enter into force, with respect to the first ten countries of the Union which have deposited instruments of ratification or accession without making the declaration permitted under paragraph (1) (b) (ii), three months after the deposit of the tenth such instrument of ratification or accession.

(c) Subject to the initial entry into force, pursuant to the provisions of subparagraphs (a) and (b), of each of the two groups of Articles referred to in paragraph (1) (b) (i) and (ii), and subject to the provisions of paragraph (1) (b), Articles 1 to 17 shall, with respect to any country of the Union, other than those referred to in subparagraphs (a) and (b), which deposits an instrument of ratification or accession or any country of the Union which deposits a declaration pursuant to paragraph (1) (c), enter into force three months after the date of notification by the Director General of such deposit, unless a subsequent date has been indicated in the instrument or declaration deposited. In the latter case, this Act shall enter into force with respect to that country on the date thus indicated.

3. With respect to any country of the Union which deposits an instrument of ratification or accession, Articles 18 to 30 shall enter into force on the earlier of the dates on which any of the groups of Articles referred to in paragraph (1) (b) enters into force with respect to that country pursuant to paragraph (2) (a), (b), or (c).

Article 21

1. Any country outside the Union may accede to this Act and thereby become a member of the Union. Instruments of accession shall be deposited with the Director General.

2. (a) With respect to any country outside the Union which deposits its instrument of accession one month or more before the date of entry into force of any provisions of the present Act, this Act shall enter into force, unless a subsequent date has been indicated in the instrument of accession, on the date upon which provisions first enter into force pursuant to Article 20(2) (a) or (b); provided that:

(i) if Articles 1 to 12 do not enter into force on that date, such country shall, during the interim period before the entry into force of such provisions, and in substitution therefor, be bound by Articles 1 to 12 of the Lisbon Act,

(ii) if Articles 13 to 17 do not enter into force on that date, such country shall, during the interim period before the entry into force of such provisions, and in substitution therefor, be bound by Articles 13 and 14(3), (4), and (5), of the Lisbon Act.

If a country indicates a subsequent date in its instrument of accession, this Act shall enter into force with respect to that country on the date thus indicated.

(b) With respect to any country outside the Union which deposits its instrument of accession on a date which is subsequent to, or precedes by less than one month, the entry into force of one group of Articles of the present Act, this Act shall, subject to the proviso of subparagraph (a), enter into force three months after the date on which its accession has been notified by the Director General, unless a subsequent date has been indicated in the instrument of accession. In the latter case, this Act shall enter into force with respect to that country on the date thus indicated.

3. With respect to any country outside the Union which deposits its instrument of accession after the date of entry into force of the present Act in its entirety, or less than one month before such date, this Act shall enter into force three months after the date on which its accession has been notified by the Director General, unless a

subsequent date has been indicated in the instrument of accession. In the latter case, this Act shall enter into force with respect to that country on the date thus indicated.

Article 22

Subject to the possibilities of exceptions provided for in Articles 20 (1) (b) and 28(2), ratification or accession shall automatically entail acceptance of all the clauses and admission to all the advantages of this Act.

Article 23

After the entry into force of this Act in its entirety, a country may not accede to earlier Acts of this Convention.

Article 24

1. Any country may declare in its instrument of ratification or accession, or may inform the Director General by written notification any time thereafter, that this Convention shall be applicable to all or part of those territories, designated in the declaration or notification, for the external relations of which it is responsible.

2. Any country which has made such a declaration or given such a notification may, at any time, notify the Director General that this Convention shall cease to be applicable to all or part of such territories.

3.(a) Any declaration made under paragraph (1) shall take effect on the same date as the ratification or accession in the instrument of which it was included, and any notification given under such paragraph shall take effect three months after its notification by the Director General.

(b) Any notification given under paragraph (2) shall take effect twelve months after its receipt by the Director General.

Article 25

1. Any country party to this Convention undertakes to adopt, in accordance with its constitution, the measures necessary to ensure the application of this Convention.

2. It is understood that, at the time a country deposits its instrument of ratification or accession, it will be in a position under its domestic law to give effect to the provisions of this Convention.

Article 26

1. This Convention shall remain in force without limitation as to time.

2. Any country may denounce this Act by notification addressed to the Director General. Such denunciation shall constitute also denunciation of all earlier Acts and shall affect only the country making it, the Convention remaining in full force and effect as regards the other countries of the Union.

3. Denunciation shall take effect one year after the day on which the Director General has received the notification.

4. The right of denunciation provided by this Article shall not be exercised by any country before the expiration of five years from the date upon which it becomes a member of the Union.

[*Article 27* Omitted]

Article 28

1. Any dispute between two or more countries of the Union concerning the interpreta-

tion or application of this Convention, not settled by negotiation, may, by any one of the countries concerned, be brought before the International Court of Justice by application in conformity with the Statute of the Court, unless the countries concerned agree on some other method of settlement. The country bringing the dispute before the Court shall inform the International Bureau; the International Bureau shall bring the matter to the attention of the other countries of the Union.

2. Each country may, at the time it signs this Act or deposits its instrument of ratification or accession, declare that it does not consider itself bound by the provisions of paragraph (1). With regard to any dispute between such country and any other country of the Union, the provisions of paragraph (1) shall not apply.

3. Any country having made a declaration in accordance with the provisions of paragraph (2) may, at any time, withdraw its declaration by notification addressed to the Director General.

[*Article 29 - Article 30* Omitted]

IN WITNESS WHEREOF, the undersigned, being duly authorized thereto, have signed this Act.

DONE at Stockholm, on July 14, 1967.

APPENDIX II

BERNE CONVENTION FOR THE PROTECTION OF LITERARY AND ARTISTIC WORKS (As Revised at Paris 1971)

The countries of the Union, being equally animated by the desire to protect, in as effective and uniform a manner as possible, the rights of authors in their literary and artistic works . . . have agreed as follows:

Article 1

The countries to which this Convention applies constitute a Union for the protection of the rights of authors in their literary and artistic works.

Article 2

1. The expression "literary and artistic works" shall include every production in the literary, scientific and artistic domain, whatever may be the mode or form of its expression, such as books, pamphlets and other writings; lectures, addresses, sermons and other works of the same nature; dramatic or dramatico-musical works; choreographic works and entertainments in dumb show; musical compositions with or without words; cinematographic works to which are assimilated works expressed by a process analogous to cinematography; works of drawing, painting, architecture, sculpture, engraving and lithography; photographic works to which are assimilated works expressed by a process analogous to photography; works of applied art; illustrations, maps, plans, sketches and three-dimensional works relative to geography, topography, architecture or science.

2. It shall, however, be a matter for legislation in the countries of the Union to prescribe that works in general or any specified categories of works shall not be protected unless they have been fixed in some material form.

3. Translations, adaptations, arrangements of music and other alterations of a literary or artistic work shall be protected as original works without prejudice to the copyright in the original work.

4. It shall be a matter for legislation in the countries of the Union to determine the protection to be granted to official texts of a legislative, administrative and legal nature, and to official translations of such texts.

5. Collections of literary or artistic works such as encyclopaedias and anthologies which, by reason of the selection and arrangement of their contents, constitute intellectual creations shall be protected as such, without prejudice to the copyright in each of the works forming part of such collections.

6. The works mentioned in this article shall enjoy protection in all countries of the Union. This protection shall operate for the benefit of the author and his successors in title.

7. Subject to the provisions of Article 7(4) of this Convention, it shall be a matter for legislation in the countries of the Union to determine the extent of the application of their laws to works of applied art and industrial designs and models, as well as the conditions under which such works, designs and models shall be protected. Works protected in the country of origin solely as designs and models shall be entitled in another country of the Union only to such special protection as is granted in that country to designs and models; however, if no such special protection is granted in that country, such works shall be protected as artistic works.

8. The protection of this Convention shall not apply to news of the day or to miscellaneous facts having the character of mere items of press information.

Article 2bis

1. It shall be a matter for legislation in the countries of the Union to exclude, wholly or in part, from the protection provided by the preceding Article political speeches and speeches delivered in the course of legal proceedings.

2. It shall also be a matter for legislation in the countries of the Union to determine the conditions under which lectures, addresses and other works of the same nature which are delivered in public may be reproduced by the press, broadcast, communicated to the public by wire and made the subject of public communication as envisaged in Article 11bis (1) of this Convention, when such use is justified by the informatory purpose.

3. Nevertheless, the author shall enjoy the exclusive right of making a collection of his works mentioned in the preceding paragraphs.

Article 3

1. The protection of this Convention shall apply to:

(a) authors who are nationals of one of the countries of the Union, for their works, whether published or not;

(b) authors who are not nationals of one of the countries of the Union, for their works first published in one of those countries, or simultaneously in a country outside the Union and in a country of the Union.

2. Authors who are not nationals of one of the countries of the Union but who have their habitual residence in one of them shall, for the purposes of this Convention, be assimilated to nationals of that country.

3. The expression "published works" means works published with the consent of their authors, whatever may be the means of manufacture of the copies, provided that the availability of such copies has been such as to satisfy the reasonable requirements of the public, having regard to the nature of the work. The performance of a dramatic, dramatico-musical, cinematographic or musical work, the public recitation of a literary work, the communication by wire or the broadcasting of literary or artistic works, the exhibition of a work of art and the construction of a work of architecture shall not constitute publication.

4. A work shall be considered as having been published simultaneously in several countries if it has been published in two or more countries within thirty days of its first publication.

Article 4

The protection of this Convention shall apply, even if the conditions of Article 3 are not fulfilled, to:

(a) authors of cinematographic works the maker of which has his headquarters or habitual residence in one of the countries of the Union;

(b) authors of works of architecture, erected in a country of the Union or of other artistic works incorporated in a building or other structure located in a country of the Union.

Article 5

1. Authors shall enjoy, in respect of works for which they are protected under this Convention, in countries of the Union other than the country of origin, the rights which their respective laws do now or may hereafter grant to their nationals, as well as the rights specially granted by this Convention.

2. The enjoyment and the exercise of these rights shall not be subject to any formality;

such enjoyment and such exercise shall be independent of the existence of protection in the country of origin of the work. Consequently, apart from the provisions of this Convention, the extent of protection, as well as the means of redress afforded to the author to protect his rights, shall be governed exclusively by the laws of the country where protection is claimed.

3. Protection in the country of origin is governed by domestic law. However, when the author is not a national of the country of origin of the work for which he is protected under this Convention, he shall enjoy in that country the same rights as national authors.

4. The country of origin shall be considered to be

(a) in the case of works first published in a country of the Union, that country; in the case of works published simultaneously in several countries of the Union which grant different terms of protection, the country whose legislation grants the shortest term of protection;

(b) in the case of works published simultaneously in a country outside the Union and in a country of the Union, the latter country;

(c) in the case of unpublished works or of works first published in a country outside the Union, without simultaneous publication in a country of the Union, the country of the Union of which the author is a national, provided that:

(i) when these are cinematographic works the maker of which has his headquarters or his habitual residence in a country of the Union, the country of origin shall be that country, and

(ii) when these are works of architecture erected in a country of the Union or other artistic works incorporated in a building or other structure located in a country of the Union, the country of origin shall be that country.

Article 6

1. Where any country outside the Union fails to protect in an adequate manner the works of authors who are nationals of one of the countries of the Union, the latter country may restrict the protection given to the works of authors who are, at the date of the first publication thereof, nationals of the other country and are not habitually resident in one of the countries of the Union. If the country of first publication avails itself of this right, the other countries of the Union shall not be required to grant to works thus subjected to special treatment a wider protection than that granted to them in the country of first publication.

2. No restrictions introduced by virtue of the preceding paragraph shall affect the rights which an author may have acquired in respect of a work published in a country of the Union before such restrictions were put into force.

3. The countries of the Union which restrict the grant of copyright in accordance with this Article shall give notice thereof to the Director General of the World Intellectual Property Organization (hereinafter designated as "the Director General") by a written declaration specifying the countries in regard to which protection is restricted, and the restrictions to which rights of authors who are nationals of those countries are subjected. The Director General shall immediately communicate this declaration to all the countries of the Union.

Article 6bis

1. Independently of the author's economic rights, and even after the transfer of the said rights, the author shall have the right to claim authorship of the work

and to object to any distortion, mutilation or other modification of, or other derogatory action in relation to, the said work, which would be prejudicial to his honor or reputation.

2. The rights granted to the author in accordance with the preceding paragraph shall, after his death, be maintained, at least until the expiry of the economic rights, and shall be exercisable by the persons or institutions authorized by the legislation of the country where protection is claimed. However, those countries whose legislation, at the moment of their ratification of or accession to this Act, does not provide for the protection after the death of the author of all the rights set out in the preceding paragraph may provide that some of these rights may, after his death, cease to be maintained.

3. The means of redress for safeguarding the rights granted by this Article shall be governed by the legislation of the country where protection is claimed.

Article 7

1. The term of protection granted by this Convention shall be the life of the author and fifty years after his death.

2. However, in the case of cinematographic works, the countries of the Union may provide that the term of protection shall expire fifty years after the work has been made available to the public with the consent of the author, or, failing such an event within fifty years from the making of such a work, fifty years after the making.

3. In the case of anonymous or pseudonymous works, the term of protection granted by this Convention shall expire fifty years after the work has been lawfully made available to the public. However, when the pseudonym adopted by the author leaves no doubt as to his identity, the term of protection shall be that provided in paragraph (1). If the author of an anonymous or pseudonymous work discloses his identity during the above-mentioned period, the term of protection applicable shall be that provided in paragraph (1). The countries of the Union shall not be required to protect anonymous or pseudonymous works in respect of which it is reasonable to presume that their author has been dead for fifty years.

4. It shall be a matter for legislation in the countries of the Union to determine the term of protection of photographic works and that of works of applied art in so far as they are protected as artistic works; however, this term shall last at least until the end of a period of twenty-five years from the making of such a work.

5. The term of protection subsequent to the death of the author and the terms provided by paragraphs (2), (3) and (4), shall run from the date of death or of the event referred to in those paragraphs, but such terms shall always be deemed to begin on the 1st of January of the year following the death or such event.

6. The countries of the Union may grant a term of protection in excess of those provided by the preceding paragraphs.

7. Those countries of the Union bound by the Rome Act of this Convention, which grant, in their national legislation in force at the time of signature of the present Act, shorter terms of protection than those provided for in the preceding paragraphs, shall have the right to maintain such terms when ratifying or acceding to the present Act.

8. In any case, the term shall be governed by the legislation of the country where protection is claimed; however, unless the legislation of that country otherwise provides, the term shall not exceed the term fixed in the country of origin of the work.

Article 7bis

The provisions of the preceding Article shall also apply in the case of a work of joint authorship, provided that the terms measured from the death of the author shall be calculated from the death of the last surviving author.

Article 8

Authors of literary and artistic works protected by this Convention shall enjoy the exclusive right of making and of authorizing the translation of their works throughout the term of protection of their rights in the original works.

Article 9

1. Authors of literary and artistic works protected by this Convention shall have the exclusive right of authorizing the reproduction of these works, in any manner or form.

2. It shall be a matter for legislation in the countries of the Union to permit the reproduction of such works in certain special cases, provided that such reproduction does not conflict with a normal exploitation of the work and does not unreasonably prejudice the legitimate interests of the author.

3. Any sound or visual recording shall be considered as a reproduction for the purposes of this Convention.

Article 10

1 It shall be permissible to make quotations from a work which has already been lawfully made available to the public, provided that their making is compatible with fair practice, and their extent does not exceed that justified by the purpose, including quotations from newspaper articles and periodicals in the form of press summaries.

2. It shall be a matter for legislation in the countries of the Union, and for special agreements existing or to be concluded between them, to permit the utilization, to the extent justified by the purpose, of literary or artistic works by way of illustration in publications, broadcasts or sound or visual recordings for teaching, provided such utilization is compatible with fair practice.

3. Where use is made of works in accordance with the preceding paragraphs of this Article, mention shall be made of the source, and of the name of the author, if it appears thereon.

Article 10bis

1. It shall be a matter for legislation in the countries of the Union to permit the reproduction by the press, the broadcasting or the communication to the public by wire, of articles published in newspapers or periodicals on current economic, political or religious topics, and of broadcast works of the same character, in cases in which the reproduction, broadcasting or such communication thereof is not expressly reserved. Nevertheless, the source must always be clearly indicated; the legal consequences of a breach of this obligation shall be determined by the legislation of the country where protection is claimed.

2. It shall also be a matter for legislation in the countries of the Union to determine the conditions under which, for the purpose of reporting current events by means of photography, cinematography, broadcasting or communication to the public by wire, literary or artistic works seen or heard in the course of the event may, to the extent justified by the informatory purpose, be reproduced and made available to the public.

Article 11

1. Authors of dramatic, dramatico-musical and musical works shall enjoy the exclusive right of authorizing:
   (i) the public performance of their works, including such public performance by any means or process;
   (ii) any communication to the public of the performance of their works.
2. Authors of dramatic or dramatico-musical works shall enjoy, during the full term of their rights in the original works, the same rights with respect to translations thereof.

Article 11bis

1. Authors of literary and artistic works shall enjoy the exclusive right of authorizing:
   (i) the broadcasting of their works or the communication thereof to the public by any other means of wireless diffusion of signs, sounds or images;
   (ii) any communication to the public by wire or by rebroadcasting of the broadcast of the work, when this communication is made by an organization other than the original one;
   (iii) the public communication by loudspeaker or any other analogous instrument transmitting, by signs, sounds or images, the broadcast of the work.
2. It shall be a matter for legislation in the countries of the Union to determine the conditions under which the rights mentioned in the preceding paragraph may be exercised, but these conditions shall apply only in the countries where they have been prescribed. They shall not in any circumstances be prejudicial to the moral rights of the author, nor to his right to obtain equitable remuneration which, in the absence of agreement, shall be fixed by competent authority.
3. In the absence of any contrary stipulation, permission granted in accordance with paragraph (1) of this Article shall not imply permission to record, by means of instruments recording sounds or images, the work broadcast. It shall, however, be a matter for legislation in the countries of the Union to determine the regulations for ephemeral recordings made by a broadcasting organization by means of its own facilities and used for its own broadcasts. The preservation of these recordings in official archives may, on the ground of their exceptional documentary character, be authorized by such legislation.

Article 11ter

1. Authors of literary works shall enjoy the exclusive right of authorizing:
   (i) the public recitation of their works, including such public recitation by any means or process;
   (ii) any communication to the public of the recitation of their works.
2. Authors of literary works shall enjoy, during the full term of their rights in the original works, the same rights with respect to translations thereof.

Article 12

Authors of literary or artistic works shall enjoy the exclusive right of authorizing adaptations, arrangements and other alterations of their works.

Article 13

1. Each country of the Union may impose for itself reservations and conditions on the exclusive right granted to the author of a musical work and to the author of any words, the recording of which together with the musical work has already been

authorized by the latter, to authorize the sound recording of that musical work, together with such words, if any; but all such reservations and conditions shall apply only in the countries which have imposed them and shall not, in any circumstances, be prejudicial to the rights of these authors to obtain equitable remuneration which, in the absence of agreement, shall be fixed by competent authority.

2. Recordings of musical works made in a country of the Union in accordance with Article 13 (3) of the Convention signed at Rome on June 2, 1928, and at Brussels on June 26, 1948, may be reproduced in that country without the permission of the author of the musical work until a date two years after that country becomes bound by this Act.

3. Recordings made in accordance with paragraphs (1) and (2) of this Article and imported without permission from the parties concerned into a country where they are treated as infringing recordings shall be liable to seizure.

Article 14

1. Authors of literary or artistic works shall have the exclusive right of authorizing:

(i) the cinematographic adaptation and reproduction of these works, and the distribution of the works thus adapted or reproduced;

(ii) the public performance and communication to the public by wire of the works thus adapted or reproduced.

2. The adaptation into any other artistic form of a cinematographic production derived from literary or artistic works shall, without prejudice to the authorization of the author of the cinematographic production, remain subject to the authorization of the authors of the original works.

3. The provisions of Article 13 (1) shall not apply.

Article 14bis

1. Without prejudice to the copyright in any work which may have been adapted or reproduced, a cinematographic work shall be protected as an original work. The owner of copyright in a cinematographic work shall enjoy the same rights as the author of an original work, including the rights referred to in the preceding Article.

2. (a) Ownership of copyright in a cinematographic work shall be a matter for legislation in the country where protection is claimed.

(b) However, in the countries of the Union which, by legislation include among the owners of copyright in a cinematographic work authors who have brought contributions to the making of the work, such authors, if they have undertaken to bring such contributions, may not, in the absence of any contrary or special stipulation, object to the reproduction, distribution, public performance, communication to the public by wire, broadcasting or any other communication to the public, or to the subtitling or dubbing of texts, of the work.

(c) The question whether or not the form of the undertaking referred to above should, for the application of the preceding subparagraph (b), be in a written agreement or a written act of the same effect shall be a matter for the legislation of the country where the maker of the cinematographic work has his headquarters or habitual residence. However, it shall be a matter for the legislation of the country of the Union where protection is claimed to provide that the said undertaking shall be in a written agreement or a written act of the same effect. The countries whose legislation so provides shall notify the Director General by means of a written declaration, which will be immediately communicated by him to all the other countries of the Union.

(d) By "contrary or special stipulation" is meant any restrictive condition which is relevant to the aforesaid undertaking.

3. Unless the national legislation provides to the contrary, the provisions of paragraph (2) (b) above shall not be applicable to authors of scenarios, dialogues and musical works created for the making of the cinematographic work, nor to the principal director thereof. However, those countries of the Union whose legislation does not contain rules providing for the application of the said paragraph (2) (b) to such director shall notify the Director General by means of a written declaration, which will be immediately communicated by him to all the other countries of the Union.

Article 14ter

1. The author, or after his death the persons or institutions authorized by national legislation, shall, with respect to original works of art and original manuscripts of writers and composers, enjoy the inalienable right to an interest in any sale of the work subsequent to the first transfer by the author of the work.
2. The protection provided by the preceding paragraph may be claimed in a country of the Union only if legislation in the country to which the author belongs so permits, and to the extent permitted by the country where this protection is claimed.
3. The procedure for collection and the amounts shall be matters for determination by national legislation.

Article 15

1. In order that the author of a literary or artistic work protected by this Convention shall, in the absence of proof to the contrary, be regarded as such, and consequently be entitled to institute infringement proceedings in the countries of the Union, it shall be sufficient for his name to appear on the work in the usual manner. This paragraph shall be applicable even if this name is a pseudonym, where the pseudonym adopted by the author leaves no doubt as to his identity.
2. The person or body corporate whose name appears on a cinematographic work in the usual manner shall, in the absence of proof to the contrary, be presumed to be the maker of the said work.
3. In the case of anonymous and pseudonymous works, other than those referred to in paragraph (1) above, the publisher whose name appears on the work shall, in the absence of proof to the contrary, be deemed to represent the author, and in this capacity be shall be entitled to protect and enforce the author's rights. The provisions of this paragraph shall cease to apply when the author reveals his identity and establishes his claim to authorship of the work.
4.(a) In the case of unpublished works where the identity of the author is unknown, but where there is every ground to presume that he is a national of a country of the Union, it shall be a matter for legislation in that country to designate the competent authority who shall represent the author and shall be entitled to protect and enforce his rights in the countries of the Union.
(b) Countries of the Union which make such designation under the terms of this provision shall notify the Director General by means of a written declaration giving full information concerning the authority thus designated. The Director General shall at once communicate this declaration to all other countries of the Union.

Article 16

1. Infringing copies of a work shall be liable to seizure in any country of the Union where the work enjoys legal protection.

2. The provisions of the preceding paragraph shall also apply to reproductions coming from a country where the work is not protected, or has ceased to be protected.
3. The seizure shall take place in accordance with the legislation of each country.

Article 17

The provisions of this Convention cannot in any way affect the right of the Government of each country of the Union to permit, to control, or to prohibit by legislation or regulation, the circulation, presentation, or exhibition of any work or production in regard to which the competent authority may find it necessary to exercise that right.

Article 18

1. This Convention shall apply to all works which, at the moment of its coming into force, have not yet fallen into the public domain in the country of origin through the expiry of the term of protection.
2. If, however, through the expiry of the term of protection which was previously granted, a work has fallen into the public domain of the country where protection is claimed, that work shall not be protected anew.
3. The application of this principle shall be subject to any provisions contained in special conventions to that effect existing or to be concluded between countries of the Union. In the absence of such provisions, the respective countries shall determine, each in so far as it is concerned, the conditions of application of this principle.
4. The preceding provisions shall also apply in the case of new accessions to the Union and to cases in which protection is extended by the application of Article 7 or by the abandonment of reservations.

Article 19

The provisions of this Convention shall not preclude the making of a claim to the benefit of any greater protection which may be granted by legislation in a country of the Union.

Article 20

The Governments of the countries of the Union reserve the right to enter into special agreements among themselves, in so far as such agreements grant to authors more extensive rights than those granted by the Convention, or contain other provisions not contrary to this Convention. The provisions of existing agreements which satisfy these conditions shall remain applicable.

Article 21

1. Special provisions regarding developing countries are included in the Appendix.
2. Subject to the provisions of Article 28(1)(b), the Appendix forms an integral part of this Act.

[*Article 22 - Article 27* Omitted]

Article 28

1. (a) Any country of the Union which has signed this Act may ratify it, and, if it has not signed it, may accede to it. Instruments of ratification or accession shall be deposited with the Director General.

(b) Any country of the Union may declare in its instrument of ratification or accession that its ratification or accession shall not apply to Articles 1 to 21 and the Appendix, provided that, if such country has previously made a declaration under Article VI(1) of the Appendix, then it may declare in the said instrument only that its ratification or accession shall not apply to Articles 1 to 20.

(c) Any country of the Union which, in accordance with sub-paragraph (b), has excluded provisions therein referred to from the effects of its ratification or accession may at any later time declare that it extends the effects of its ratification or accession to those provisions. Such declaration shall be deposited with the Director General.

2. (a) Articles 1 to 21 and the Appendix shall enter into force three months after both of the following two conditions are fulfilled:

(i) at least five countries of the Union have ratified or acceded to this Act without making a declaration under paragraph (1)(b),

(ii) France, Spain, the United Kingdom of Great Britain and Northern Ireland, and the United States of America, have become bound by the Universal Copyright Convention as revised at Paris on July 24, 1971.

(b) The entry into force referred to in sub-paragraph (a) shall apply to those countries of the Union which, at least three months before the said entry into force, have deposited instruments of ratification or accession not containing a declaration under paragraph (1)(b).

(c) With respect to any country of the Union not covered by sub-paragraph (b) and which ratifies or accedes to this Act without making a declaration under paragraph (1)(b), Articles 1 to 21 and the Appendix shall enter into force three months after the date on which the Director General has notified the deposit of the relevant instrument of ratification or accession, unless a subsequent date has been indicated in the instrument deposited. In the latter case, Articles 1 to 21 and the Appendix shall enter into force with respect to that country on the date thus indicated.

(d) The provisions of sub-paragraphs (a) to (c) do not affect the application of Article VI of the Appendix.

3. With respect to any country of the Union which ratifies or accedes to this Act with or without a declaration made under paragraph (1)(b), Articles 22 to 38 shall enter into force three months after the date on which the Director General has notified the deposit of the relevant instrument of ratification or accession, unless a subsequent date has been indicated in the instrument deposited. In the latter case, Articles 22 to 38 shall enter into force with respect to that country on the date thus indicated.

[*Article 29* - *Article 32* Omitted]

Article 33

1. Any dispute between two or more countries of the Union concerning the interpretation or application of this Convention, not settled by negotiation, may, by any one of the countries concerned, be brought before the International Court of Justice by application in conformity with the Statute of the Court, unless the countries concerned agree on some other method of settlement. The country bringing the dispute before the Court shall inform the International Bureau; the International Bureau shall bring the matter to the attention of the other countries of the Union.

2. Each country may, at the time it signs this Act or deposits its instrument of ratification or accession, declare that it does not consider itself bound by the provisions of paragraph (1). With regard to any dispute between such country and any other country of the Union, the provisions of paragraph (1) shall not apply.

3. Any country having made a declaration in accordance with the provisions of

paragraph (2) may, at any time, withdraw its declaration by notification addressed to the Director General.

Article 34

1. Subject to Article 29bis, no country may ratify or accede to earlier Acts of this Convention once Articles 1 to 21 and the Appendix have entered into force.

2. Once Articles 1 to 21 and the Appendix have entered into force, no country may make a declaration under Article 5 of the Protocol Regarding Developing Countries attached to the Stockholm Act.

Article 35

1. This Convention shall remain in force without limitation as to time.

2. Any country may denounce this Act by notification addressed to the Director General. Such denunciation shall constitute also denunciation of all earlier Acts and shall affect only the country making it, the Convention remaining in full force and effect as regards the other countries of the Union.

3. Denunciation shall take effect one year after the day on which the Director General has received the notification.

4. The right of denunciation provided by this article shall not be exercised by any country before the expiration of five years from the date upon which it becomes a member of the Union.

Article 36

1. Any country party to this Convention undertakes to adopt, in accordance with its constitution, the measures necessary to ensure the application of this Convention.

2. It is understood that, at the time a country becomes bound by this Convention, it will be in a position under its domestic law to give effect to the provisions of this Convention.

[*Article 37* - *Article 38* Omitted]

APPENDIX
[Special Provisions Regarding Developing Countries]

Article I

1. Any country regarded as a developing country in conformity with the established practice of the General Assembly of the United Nations which ratifies or accedes to this Act, of which this Appendix forms an integral part, and which, having regard to its economic situation and its social or cultural needs, does not consider itself immediately in a position to make provision for the protection of all the rights as provided for in this Act, may, by a notification deposited with the Director General at the time of depositing its instrument of ratification or accession or, subject to Article V(1)(c), at any time thereafter, declare that it will avail itself of the faculty provided for in Article II, or of the faculty provided for in Article III, or of both of those faculties. It may, instead of availing itself of the faculty provided for in Article II, make a declaration according to Article V(1)(a).

2. (a) Any declaration under paragraph (1) notified before the expiration of the period of ten years from the entry into force of Articles 1 to 21 and this Appendix according to Article 28(2) shall be effective until the expiration of the said period. Any

such declaration may be renewed in whole or in part for periods of ten years each by a notification deposited with the Director General not more than 15 months and not less than three months before the expiration of the ten-year period then running.

(b) Any declaration under paragraph (1) notified after the expiration of the period of ten years from the entry into force of Articles 1 to 21 and this Appendix according to Article 28(2) shall be effective until the expiration of the ten-year period then running. Any such declaration may be renewed as provided for in the second sentence of sub-paragraph (a).

3. Any country of the Union which has ceased to be regarded as a developing country as referred to in paragraph (1) shall no longer be entitled to renew its declaration as provided in paragraph (2), and, whether or not it formally withdraws its declaration, such country shall be precluded from availing itself of the faculties referred to in paragraph (1) from the expiration of the ten-year period then running or from the expiration of a period of three years after it has ceased to be regarded as a developing country, whichever period expires later.

4. Where, at the time when the declaration made under paragraph (1) or (2) ceases to be effective, there are copies in stock which were made under a license granted by virtue of this Appendix, such copies may continue to be distributed until their stock is exhausted.

5. Any country which is bound by the provisions of this Act and which has deposited a declaration or a notification in accordance with Article 31(1) with respect to the application of this Act to a particular territory, the situation of which can be regarded as analogous to that of the countries referred to in paragraph (1), may, in respect of such territory, make the declaration referred to in paragraph (1) and the notification of renewal referred to in paragraph (2). As long as such declaration or notification remains in effect, the provisions of this Appendix shall be applicable to the territory in respect of which it was made.

6. (a) The fact that a country avails itself of any of the faculties referred to in paragraph (1) does not permit another country to give less protection to works of which the country of origin is the former country than it is obliged to grant under Articles 1 to 20.

(b) The right to apply reciprocal treatment provided for in Article 30(2)(b), second sentence, shall not, until the date on which the period applicable under Article I(3) expires, be exercised in respect of works the country of origin of which is a country which has made a declaration according to Article V(1)(a).

Article II

1. Any country which has declared that it will avail itself of the faculty provided for in this Article shall be entitled, so far as works published in printed or analogous forms of reproduction are concerned, to substitute for the exclusive right of translation provided for in Article 8 a system of non-exclusive and non-transferable licenses, granted by the competent authority under the following conditions and subject to Article IV.

2. (a) Subject to paragraph (3), if, after the expiration of a period of three years, or of any longer period determined by the national legislation of the said country, commencing on the date of the first publication of the work, a translation of such work has not been published in a language in general use in that country by the owner of the right of translation, or with his authorization, any national of such country may obtain a license to make a translation of the work in the said language and publish the translation in printed or analogous forms of reproduction.

(b) A license under the conditions provided for in this Article may also be granted if all the editions of the translation published in the language concerned are out of print.

3. (a) In the case of translations into a language which is not in general use in one or more developed countries which are members of the Union, a period of one year shall be substituted for the period of three years referred to in paragraph (2)(a).

(b) Any country referred to in paragraph (1) may, with the unanimous agreement of the developed countries which are members of the Union and in which the same language is in general use, substitute, in the case of translations into that language, for the period of three years referred to in paragraph (2)(a) a shorter period as determined by such agreement but not less than one year. However, the provisions of the foregoing sentence shall not apply where the language in question is English, French or Spanish. The Director General shall be notified of any such agreement by the Governments which have concluded it.

4. (a) No license obtainable after three years shall be granted under this Article until a further period of six months has elapsed, and no license obtainable after one year shall be granted under this Article until a further period of nine months has elapsed

(i) from the date on which the applicant complies with the requirements mentioned in Article IV(1), or

(ii) where the identity or the address of the owner of the right of translation is unknown, from the date on which the applicant sends, as provided for in Article IV(2), copies of his application submitted to the authority competent to grant the license.

(b) If, during the said period of six or nine months, a translation in the language in respect of which the application was made is published by the owner of the right of translation or with his authorization, no license under this Article shall be granted.

5. Any license under this Article shall be granted only for the purpose of teaching, scholarship or research.

6. If a translation of a work is published by the owner of the right of translation or with his authorization at a price reasonably related to that normally charged in the country for comparable works, any license granted under this Article shall terminate if such translation is in the same language and with substantially the same content as the translation published under the licence. Any copies already made before the license terminated may continue to be distributed until their stock is exhausted.

7. For works which are composed mainly of illustrations, a license to make and publish a translation of the text and to reproduce and publish the illustrations may be granted only if the conditions of Article III are also fulfilled.

8. No licence shall be granted under this Article when the author has withdrawn from circulation all copies of his work.

9. (a) A license to make a translation of a work which has been published in printed or analogous forms of reproduction may also be granted to any broadcasting organization having its headquarters in a country referred to in paragraph (1), upon an application made to the competent authority of that country by the said organization, provided that all of the following conditions are met:

(i) the translation is made from a copy made and acquired in accordance with the laws of the said country;

(ii) the translation is only for use in broadcasts intended exclusively for teaching or for the dissemination of the results of specialized technical or scientific research to experts in a particular profession;

(iii) the translation is used exclusively for the purposes referred to in condition

(ii) through broadcasts made lawfully and intended for recipients on the territory of the said country,
including broadcasts made through the medium of sound or visual recordings lawfully and exclusively made for the purpose of such broadcasts;

(iv) all uses made of the translation are without any commercial purpose.

(b) Sound or visual recordings of a translation which was made by a broadcasting organization under a license granted by virtue of this paragraph may, for the purposes and subject to the conditions referred to in subparagraph (a) and with the agreement of that organization, also be used by any other broadcasting organization having its headquarters in the country whose competent authority granted the license in question.

(c) Provided that all of the criteria and conditions set out in subparagraph (a) are met, a license may also be granted to a broadcasting organization to translate any text incorporated in an audio-visual fixation where such fixation was itself prepared and published for the sole purpose of being used in connection with systematic instructional activities.

(d) Subject to subparagraphs (a) to (c), the provisions of the preceding paragraphs shall apply to the grant and exercise of any license granted under this paragraph.

Article III

1. Any country which has declared that it will avail itself of the faculty provided for in this Article shall be entitled to substitute for the exclusive right of reproduction provided for in Article 9 a system of non-exclusive and non-transferable licenses, granted by the competent authority under the following conditions and subject to Article IV.

2. (a) If, in relation to a work to which this article applies by virtue of paragraph (7), after the expiration of

(i) the relevant period specified in paragraph (3), commencing on the date of first publication of a particular edition of the work, or

(ii) any longer period determined by national legislation of the country referred to in paragraph (1), commencing on the same date, copies of such edition have not been distributed in that country to the general public or in connection with systematic instructional activities, by the owner of the right of reproduction or with his authorization, at a price reasonably related to that normally charged in the country for comparable works, any national of such country may obtain a license to reproduce and publish such edition at that or a lower price for use in connection with systematic instructional activities.

(b) A license to reproduce and publish an edition which has been distributed as described in sub-paragraph (a) may also be granted under the conditions provided for in this article if, after the expiration of the applicable period, no authorized copies of that edition have been on sale for a period of six months in the country concerned to the general public or in connection with systematic instructional activities at a price reasonably related to that normally charged in the country for comparable works.

3. The period referred to in paragraph (2)(a)(i) shall be five years, except that

(i) for works of the natural and physical sciences, including mathematics, and of technology, the period shall be three years;

(ii) for works of fiction, poetry, drama and music, and for art books, the period shall be seven years.

4. (a) No license obtainable after three years shall be granted under this article until a period of six months has elapsed

(i) from the date on which the applicant complies with the requirements mentioned in Article IV(1), or

(ii) where the identity or the address of the owner of the right of reproduction is unknown, from the date on which the applicant sends, as provided for in Article IV(2), copies of his application submitted to the authority competent to grant the license.

(b) Where licenses are obtainable after other periods and Article IV(2) is applicable, no license shall be granted until a period of three months has elapsed from the date of the dispatch of the copies of the application.

(c) If, during the period of six or three months referred to in sub-paragraphs (a) and (b), a distribution as described in paragraph (2)(a) has taken place, no license shall be granted under this article.

(d) No license shall be granted if the author has withdrawn from circulation all copies of the edition for the reproduction and publication of which the license has been applied for.

5. A license to reproduce and publish a translation of a work shall not be granted under this article in the following cases:

(i) where the translation was not published by the owner of the right of translation or with his authorization, or

(ii) where the translation is not in a language in general use in the country in which the license is applied for.

6. If copies of an edition of a work are distributed in the country referred to in paragraph (1) to the general public or in connection with systematic instructional activities, by the owner of the right of reproduction or with his authorization, at a price reasonably related to that normally charged in the country for comparable works, any license granted under this article shall terminate if such edition is in the same language and with substantially the same content as the edition which was published under the said license. Any copies already made before the license terminates may continue to be distributed until their stock is exhausted.

7. (a) Subject to sub-paragraph (b), the works to which this article applies shall be limited to works published in printed or analogous forms of reproduction.

(b) This article shall also apply to the reproduction in audio-visual form of lawfully made audio-visual fixations including any protected works incorporated therein and to the translation of any incorporated text into a language in general use in the country in which the license is applied for, always provided that the audio-visual fixations in question were prepared and published for the sole purpose of being used in connection with systematic instructional activities.

Article IV

1. A license under Article II or Article III may be granted only if the applicant, in accordance with the procedure of the country concerned, establishes either that he has requested, and has been denied, authorization by the owner of the right to make and publish the translation or to reproduce and publish the edition, as the case may be, or that, after due diligence on his part, he was unable to find the owner of the right. At the same time as making the request, the applicant shall inform any national or international information center referred to in paragraph (2).

2. If the owner of the right cannot be found, the applicant for a license shall send, by registered airmail, copies of his application, submitted to the authority competent to grant the license, to the publisher whose name appears on the work and to any national or international information center which may have been designated, in a notification to that effect deposited with the Director General, by the Government of the country in which the publisher is believed to have his principal place of business.

3. The name of the author shall be indicated on all copies of the translation or

reproduction published under a license granted under Article II or Article III. The title of the work shall appear on all such copies. In the case of a translation, the original title of the work shall appear in any case on all the said copies.

4. (a) No license granted under Article II or Article III shall extend to the export of copies, and any such license shall be valid only for publication of the translation or of the reproduction, as the case may be, in the territory of the country in which it has been applied for.

(b) For the purposes of sub-paragraph (a), the notion of export shall include the sending of copies from any territory to the country which, in respect of that territory, has made a declaration under Article I(5).

(c) Where a governmental or other public entity of a country which has granted a license to make a translation under Article II into a language other than English, French or Spanish sends copies of a translation published under such license to another country, such sending of copies shall not, for the purposes of sub-paragraph (a), be considered to constitute export if all of the following conditions are met:

(i) the recipients are individuals who are nationals of the country whose competent authority has granted the license, or organizations grouping such individuals;

(ii) the copies are to be used only for the purpose of teaching, scholarship or research;

(iii) the sending of the copies and their subsequent distribution to recipients is without any commercial purpose; and

(iv) the country to which the copies have been sent has agreed with the country whose competent authority has granted the license to allow the receipt, or distribution, or both, and the Director General has been notified of the agreement by the Government of the country in which the license has been granted.

5. All copies published under a license granted by virtue of Article II or Article III shall bear a notice in the appropriate language stating that the copies are available for distribution only in the country or territory to which the said license applies.

6. (a) Due provision shall be made at the national level to ensure

(i) that the license provides, in favor of the owner of the right of translation or of reproduction, as the case may be, for just compensation that is consistent with standards of royalties normally operating on licenses freely negotiated between persons in the two countries concerned, and

(ii) payment and transmittal of the compensation: should national currency regulations intervene, the competent authority shall make all efforts, by the use of international machinery, to ensure transmittal in internationally convertible currency or its equivalent.

(b) Due provision shall be made by national legislation to ensure a correct translation of the work, or an accurate reproduction of the particular edition, as the case may be.

Article V

1. (a) Any country entitled to make a declaration that it will avail itself of the faculty provided for in Article II may, instead, at the time of ratifying or acceding to this Act:

(i) if it is a country to which Article 30(2)(a) applies, make a declaration under that provision as far as the right of translation is concerned;

(ii) if it is a country to which Article 30(2)(a) does not apply, and even if it is not a country outside the Union, make a declaration as provided for in Article 30(2)(b), first sentence.

(b) In the case of a country which ceases to be regarded as a developing country as referred to in Article I(1), a declaration made according to this paragraph shall be effective until the date on which the period applicable under Article I(3) expires.

(c) Any country which has made a declaration according to this paragraph may not subsequently avail itself of the faculty provided for in Article II even if it withdraws the said declaration.

2. Subject to paragraph (3), any country which has availed itself of the faculty provided for in Article II may not subsequently make a declaration according to paragraph (1).

3. Any country which has ceased to be regarded as a developing country as referred to in Article I(1) may, not later than two years prior to the expiration of the period applicable under Article I(3), make a declaration to the effect provided for in Article 30(2)(b), first sentence, notwithstanding the fact that it is not a country outside the Union. Such declaration shall take effect at the date on which the period applicable under Article I(3) expires.

Article VI

1. Any country of the Union may declare, as from the date of this Act, and at any time before becoming bound by Articles 1 to 21 and this Appendix:

(i) if it is a country which, were it bound by Articles 1 to 21 and this Appendix, would be entitled to avail itself of the faculties referred to in Article I(1), that it will apply the provisions of Article II or of Article III or of both to works whose country of origin is a country which, pursuant to (ii) below, admits the application of those articles to such works, or which is bound by Articles 1 to 21 and this Appendix; such declaration may, instead of referring to Article II, refer to Article V;

(ii) that it admits the application of this Appendix to works of which it is the country of origin by countries which have made a declaration under (i) above or a notification under Article I.

2. Any declaration made under paragraph (1) shall be in writing and shall be deposited with the Director General. The declaration shall become effective from the date of its deposit.

IN WITNESS WHEREOF, the undersigned, being duly authorized thereto, have signed this Act.

DONE at Paris on July 24, 1971.

APPENDIX III

TREATY ESTABLISHING THE EUROPEAN COMMUNITY as Amended by Subsequent Treaties Rome, 25 March 1957

His Majesty The King of the Belgians, the President of the Federal Republic of Germany, the President of the French Republic, the President of the Italian Republic, Her Royal Highness The Grand Duchess of Luxembourg, Her Majesty The Queen of the Netherlands,

Determined to lay the foundations of an ever closer union among the peoples of Europe,

Resolved to ensure the economic and social progress of their countries by common action to eliminate the barriers which divide Europe,

Affirming as the essential objective of their efforts the constant improvement of the living and working conditions of their peoples,

Recognizing that the removal of existing obstacles calls for concerted action in order to guarantee steady expansion, balanced trade and fair competition,

Anxious to strengthen the unity of their economies and to ensure their harmonious development by reducing the differences existing between the various regions and the backwardness of the less favored regions,

Desiring to contribute, by means of a common commercial policy, to the progressive abolition of restrictions on international trade,

Intending to confirm the solidarity which binds Europe and the overseas countries and desiring to ensure the development of their prosperity, in accordance with the principles of the Charter of the United Nations,

Resolved by thus pooling their resources to preserve and strengthen peace and liberty, and calling upon the other peoples of Europe who share their ideal to join in their efforts,

Have decided to create a European Economic Community ... Have agreed as follows:

PART ONE: PRINCIPLES

Article 1

By this Treaty, the High Contracting Parties establish among themselves a European Community.

Article 2

The Community shall have as its task, by establishing a common market and an economic and monetary union and by implementing the common policies or activities referred to in Articles 3 and 3a, to promote throughout the Community a harmonious and balanced development of economic activities, sustainable and non-inflationary growth respecting the environment, a high degree of convergence of economic performance, a high level of employment and of social protection, the raising of the standard of living and quality of life, and economic and social cohesion and solidarity among Member States.

Article 3

For the purposes set out in Article 2, the activities of the Community shall include, as provided by this Treaty and in accordance with the timetable set out therein:

(a) the elimination as between Member States, of customs duties and quantitative restrictions on the import and export of goods, and of all other measures having equivalent effect;

(b) a common commercial policy;

(c) an internal market characterized by the abolition, as between Member States, of obstacles to the free movement of goods, persons, services and capital;

(d) Measures concerning the entry and movement of persons in the internal market as provided for in Article 100C;

(e) a common policy in the sphere of agriculture and fisheries;

(f) a common policy in the sphere of transport;

(g) a system ensuring that competition in the common market is not distorted;

(h) the approximation of the laws of the Member States to the extent required for the functioning of the common market;

(i) a policy in the social sphere comprising a European Social Fund;

(j) the strengthening of economic and social cohesion;

(k) a policy in the sphere of the environment;

(l) the strengthening of the competitiveness of Community industry;

(m) the promotion of research and technological development;

(n) encouragement for the establishment and development of trans-European networks;

(o) a contribution to the attainment of a high level of health protection;

(p) a contribution to education and training of quality and to the flowering of the cultures of the Member States;

(q) a policy in the sphere of development cooperation;

(r) the association of the overseas countries and territories in order to increase trade and promote jointly economic and social development;

(s) a contribution to the strengthening of consumer protection;

(t) measures in the spheres of energy, civil protection and tourism.

Article 3a

1. For the purposes set out in Article 2, the activities of the Member States and the Community shall include, as provided in this Treaty and in accordance with the timetable set out therein, the adoption of an economic policy which is based on the close coordination of Member States' economic policies, on the internal market and on the definition of common objectives, and conducted in accordance with the principle of an open market economy with free competition.

2. Concurrently with the foregoing, and as provided in this Treaty and in accordance with the timetable and the procedures set out therein, these activities shall include the irrevocable fixing of exchange rates leading to the introduction of a single currency, the ecu, and the definition and conduct of a single monetary policy and exchange rate policy the primary objective of both of which shall be to maintain price stability and, without prejudice to this objective, to support the general economic policies in the Community, in accordance with the principle of an open market economy with free competition.

3. These activities of the Member States and the Community shall entail compliance with the following guiding principles: stable prices, sound public finances and monetary conditions and a sustainable balance of payments.

Article 3b

The Community shall act within the limits of the powers conferred upon it by this Treaty and of the objectives assigned to it therein.

In areas which do not fall within its exclusive competence, the Community shall take action, in accordance with the principle of subsidiarity, only if and in so far as the objectives of the proposed action cannot be sufficiently achieved by the Member States and can therefore, by reason of the scale or effects of the proposed action, be better achieved by the Community.

Any action by the Community shall not go beyond what is necessary to achieve the objectives of this Treaty.

Article 4

1. The tasks entrusted to the Community shall be carried out by the following institutions:

- a European Parliament,
- a Council,
- a Commission,
- a Court of Justice,
- a Court of Auditors.

Each institution shall act within the limits of the powers conferred upon it by this Treaty.

2. The Council and the Commission shall be assisted by an Economic and Social Committee and a Committee of the Regions acting in an advisory capacity.

[*Article 4a* - *Article 8e* Omitted]

PART THREE: COMMUNITY POLICIES

TITLE I. FREE MOVEMENT OF GOODS

Article 9

1. The Community shall be based upon a customs union which shall cover all trade in goods and which shall involve the prohibition between Member States of customs duties on imports and exports and of all charges having equivalent effect, and the adoption of a common customs tariff in their relations with third countries.

2. The provisions of Chapter 1, Section 1, and of Chapter 2 of this Title shall apply to products originating in Member States and to products coming from third countries which are in free circulation in Member States.

Article 10

1. Products coming from a third country shall be considered to be in free circulation in a Member State if the import formalities have been complied with and any customs duties or charges having equivalent effect which are payable have been levied in that Member State, and if they have not benefited from a total or partial drawback of such duties or charges.

2. The Commission shall, before the end of the first year after the entry into force of this Treaty, determine the methods of administrative co-operation to be adopted for the purpose of applying Art. 9(2), taking into account the need to reduce as much as possible formalities imposed on trade.

Before the end of the first year after the entry into force of this Treaty, the Commission shall lay down the provisions applicable, as regards trade between Member States, to goods originating in another Member State in whose manufacture products have been used on which the exporting Member State has not levied the appropriate customs duties or charges having equivalent effect, or which have benefited from a total or partial drawback of such duties or charges.

In adopting these provisions, the Commission shall take into account the rules for the elimination of customs duties within the Community and for the progressive application of the common customs tariff.

[*Article 11* - *Article 29* Omitted]

CHAPTER 2. ELIMINATION OF QUANTITATIVE RESTRICTIONS BETWEEN MEMBER STATES

Article 30

Quantitative restrictions on imports and all measures having equivalent effect shall, without prejudice to the following provisions, be prohibited between Member States.

Article 31

Member States shall refrain from introducing between themselves any new quantitative restrictions or measures having equivalent effect.

This obligation shall, however, relate only to the degree of liberalization attained in pursuance of the decisions of the Council of the Organisation for European Economic Co-operation of 14 January 1955. Member States shall supply the Commission, not later than six months after the entry into force of this Treaty, with lists of the products liberalized by them in pursuance of these decisions. These lists shall be consolidated between Member States.

Article 32

In their trade with one another Member States shall refrain from making more restrictive the quotas and measures having equivalent effect existing at the date of the entry into force of this Treaty.

These quotas shall be abolished by the end of the transitional period at the latest. During that period, they shall be progressively abolished in accordance with the following provisions.

Article 33

1. One year after the entry into force of this Treaty, each Member State shall convert any bilateral quotas open to any other Member States into global quotas open without discrimination to all other Member States.

On the same date, Member States shall increase the aggregate of the global quotas so established in such a manner as to bring about an increase of not less than 20 per cent in their total value as compared with the preceding year. The global quota for each product, however, shall be increased by not less than 10 per cent.

The quotas shall be increased annually in accordance with the same rules and in the same proportions in relation to the preceding year.

The fourth increase shall take place at the end of the fourth year after the entry into force of this Treaty; the fifth, one year after the beginning of the second stage.

2. Where, in the case of a product which has not been liberalized, the global quota does not amount to 3 per cent of the national production of the State concerned, a quota equal to not less than 3 per cent of such national production shall be introduced not later than one year after the entry into force of this Treaty. This quota shall be

raised to 4 per cent at the end of the second year, and to 5 per cent at the end of the third. Thereafter, the Member State concerned shall increase the quota by not less than 15 per cent annually.

Where there is no such national production, the Commission shall take a decision establishing an appropriate quota.

3. At the end of the tenth year, each quota shall be equal to not less than 20 per cent of the national production.

4. If the Commission finds by means of a decision that during two successive years the imports of any product have been below the level of the quota opened, this global quota shall not be taken into account in calculating the total value of the global quotas. In such case, the Member State shall abolish quota restrictions on the product concerned.

5. In the case of quotas representing more than 20 per cent of the national production of the product concerned, the Council may, acting by a qualified majority on a proposal from the Commission, reduce the minimum percentage of 10 per cent laid down in paragraph 1. This alteration shall not however, affect the obligation to increase the total value of global quotas by 20 per cent annually.

6. Member States which have exceeded their obligations as regards the degree of liberalization attained in pursuance of the decisions of the Council of the Organisation for European Economic Co-operation of 14 January 1955 shall be entitled, when calculating the annual total increase of 20 per cent provided for in paragraph 1, to take into account the amount of imports liberalized by autonomous action. Such calculation shall be submitted to the Commission for its prior approval.

7. The Commission shall issue directives establishing the procedure and timetable in accordance with which Member States shall abolish, as between themselves, any measures in existence when this Treaty enters into force which have an effect equivalent to quotas.

8. If the Commission finds that the application of the provisions of this Article, and in particular of the provisions concerning percentages, makes it impossible to ensure that the abolition of quotas provided for in the second paragraph of Art. 32 is carried out progressively, the Council may, on a proposal from the Commission, acting unanimously during the first stage and by a qualified majority thereafter, amend the procedure laid down in this Article and may, in particular, increase the percentages fixed.

Article 34

1. Quantitative restrictions on exports, and all measures having equivalent effect, shall be prohibited between Member States.

2. Member States shall, by the end of the first stage at the latest, abolish all quantitative restrictions on exports and any measures having equivalent effect which are in existence when this Treaty enters into force.

Article 35

The Member States declare their readiness to abolish quantitative restrictions on imports from and exports to other Member States more rapidly than is provided for in the preceding Articles, if their general economic situation of the economic sector concerned so permit.

To this end, the Commission shall make recommendations to the States concerned.

Article 36

The provisions of Arts. 30 to 34 shall not preclude prohibitions or restrictions on imports, exports or goods in transit justified on grounds of public morality, public policy or public security; the protection of health and life of humans, animals or plants; the protection of national treasures possessing artistic, historic or archaeological value; or the protection of industrial and commercial property. Such prohibitions or restrictions shall not, however, constitute a means of arbitrary discrimination or a disguised restriction on trade between Member States.

[*Article 37* - *Article 84* Omitted]

TITLE V. COMMON RULES ON COMPETITION, TAXATION AND APPROXIMATION OF LAWS

CHAPTER 1. RULES ON COMPETITION

Section 1. Rules Applying to Undertakings

Article 85

1. The following shall be prohibited as incompatible with the common market; all agreements between undertakings, decisions by associations of undertakings and concerted practices which may affect trade between Member States and which have as their object or effect the prevention restriction or distortion of competition within the common market, and in particular those which:

(a) directly or indirectly fix purchase or selling prices or any other trading conditions;

(b) limit or control production, markets, technical development, or investment;

(c) share markets or sources of supply;

(d) apply dissimilar conditions to equivalent transactions with other trading parties, thereby placing them at a competitive disadvantage;

(e) make the conclusion of contracts subject to acceptance by the other parties of supplementary obligations which, by their nature or according to commercial usage, have no connection with the subject of such contracts.

2. Any agreements or decisions prohibited pursuant to this Article shall be automatically void.

3. The provisions of paragraph 1 may, however, be declared inapplicable in the case of:

- any agreement or category of agreements between undertakings;
- any decision or category of decisions by associations of undertakings;
- any concerted practice or category of concerted practices;

which contributes to improving the production or distribution of goods or to promoting technical or economic progress, while allowing consumers a fair share of the resulting benefit, and which does not:

(a) impose on the undertakings concerned restrictions which are not indispensable to the attainment of these objectives;

(b) afford such undertakings the possibility of eliminating competition in respect of a substantial part of the products in question.

Article 86

Any abuse by one or more undertakings of a dominant position within the common market or in a substantial part of it shall be prohibited as incompatible with the common market in so far as it may affect trade between Member States. Such abuse may, in particular, consist in:

(a) directly or indirectly imposing unfair purchase or selling prices or unfair trading conditions;

(b) limiting production, markets or technical development to the prejudice of consumers;

(c) applying dissimilar conditions to equivalent transactions with other trading parties, thereby placing them at a competitive disadvantage;

(d) making the conclusion of contracts subject to acceptance by the other parties of supplementary obligations which, by their nature or according to commercial usage, have no connection with the subject of such contracts.

[*Article 87* - *Article 99* Omitted]

CHAPTER 3. APPROXIMATION OF LAWS

Article 100

The Council shall, acting unanimously on a proposal from the Commission and after consulting the European Parliament and the Economic and Social Committee, issue directives for the approximation of such laws, regulations or administrative provisions of the Member States as directly affect the establishment or functioning of the common market.

Article 100a

1. By way of derogation from Article 100 and save where otherwise provided in this Treaty, the following provisions shall apply for the achievement of the objectives set out in Article 7a. The Council shall, acting in accordance with the procedure referred to in Article 189b and after consulting the Economic and Social Committee, adopt the measures for the approximation of the provisions laid down by law, regulation or administrative action in Member States which have as their object the establishing and functioning of the internal market.

2. Paragraph 1 shall not apply to fiscal provisions, to those relating to the free movement of persons nor to those relating to the rights and interests of employed persons.

3. The Commission, in its proposals envisaged in paragraph 1 concerning health, safety, environmental protection and consumer protection, will take as a base a high level of protection.

4. If, after the adoption of a harmonization measure by the Council acting by a qualified majority, a Member State deems it necessary to apply national provisions on grounds of major needs referred to in Article 36, or relating to protection of the environment or the working environment, it shall notify the Commission of these provisions.

The Commission shall confirm the provisions involved after having verified that they are not a means of arbitrary discrimination or a disguised restriction on trade between Member States.

By way of derogation from the procedure laid down in Articles 169 and 170, the Commission or any Member State may bring the matter directly before the Court of Justice if it considers that another Member State is making improper use of the powers provided for in this Article.

5. The harmonization measures referred to above shall, in appropriate cases, include a safeguard clause authorizing the Member States to take, for one or more of the non-economic reasons referred to in Article 36, provisional measures subject to a Community control procedure.

[*Article 100b* to End Omitted]

APPENDIX IV

INTERNATIONAL CONVENTION FOR THE PROTECTION OF PERFORMERS, PRODUCERS OF PHONOGRAMS AND BROADCASTING ORGANIZATIONS (Rome 1961)

The Contracting States, moved by the desire to protect the rights of performers, producers and broadcasting organizations,

Have agreed as follows:

Article 1

Protection granted under this Convention shall leave intact and shall in no way affect the protection of copyright in literary and artistic works. Consequently, no provision of this Convention may be interpreted as prejudicing such protection.

Article 2

1. For the purpose of this Convention, national treatment shall mean the treatment accorded by the domestic law of the Contracting States in which protection is claimed:

(a) to performers who are its nationals, as regards performances taking place, broadcast, or first fixed, on its territory;

(b) to producers of phonograms who are its nationals, as regards phonograms first fixed or first published on its territory;

(c) to broadcasting organizations which have their headquarters on its territory, as regards broadcasts transmitted from transmitters situated on its territory.

2. National treatment shall be subject to the protection specifically guaranteed, and the limitations specifically provided for, in this Convention.

Article 3

For the purpose of this Convention:

(a) "performers" means actors, singers, musicians, dancers, and other persons who act, sing, deliver, declaim, play in, or otherwise perform literary or artistic works;

(b) "phonogram" means any exclusively aural fixation of sounds of a performance or of other sounds;

(c) "producer of phonograms" means the person who, or the legal entity which, first fixes the sounds of a performance or other sounds;

(d) "publication" means the offering of copies of a phonogram to the public in reasonable quantity;

(e) "reproduction" means the making of a copy of a fixation;

(f) "broadcasting" means the transmission by wireless means for public reception of sounds or of images and sounds;

(g) "rebroadcasting" means the simultaneous broadcasting by one broadcasting organisation of another broadcasting organisation.

Article 4

Each Contracting States shall grant national treatment to performers if any of the following conditions is met:

(a) the performance takes place in another Contracting States;

(b) the performance is incorporated in a phonogram which is protected under Article 5 of this Convention;

(c) the performance, not being fixed on a phonogram, is carried by a broadcast which is protected by Article 6 of this Convention.

Article 5

1. Each Contracting State shall grant national treatment to producers of phonograms if any of the following conditions is met:

(a) the producer of phonogram is a national of another Contracting State (criterion of nationality);

(b) the first fixation of the sound was made in another Contracting State (criterion of fixation);

(c) the phonogram was first published in another Contracting State (criterion of publication).

2. If a phonogram was first published in a non-contracting State but if it was also published, within thirty days of its first publication, in a Contracting State (simultaneous publication), it shall be considered as first published in the Contracting State.

3. By means of a notification deposited with the Secretary-General of the United Nations, any Contracting State may declare that it will not apply the criterion of publication or, alternatively, the criterion of fixation. Such notification may be deposited at the time of ratification, acceptance or accession, or at any time thereafter; in the last case, it shall become effective six months after it has been deposited.

Article 6

1. Each Contracting State shall grant national treatment to broadcasting organizations if any of the following conditions is met:

(a) the headquarters of the broadcasting organisation is situated in another Contracting State;

(b) the broadcast was transmitted from a transmitter situated in another Contracting State;

2. By means of a notification deposited with the Secretary-General of the United Nations, any Contracting State may declare that it will protect broadcasts only if the headquarters of the broadcasting organisation is situated in another Contracting State and the broadcast was transmitted from a transmitter situated in the same Contracting State. Such notification may be deposited at the time of ratification, acceptance or accession, or at any time thereafter; in the last case, it shall become effective six months after it has been deposited.

Article 7

1. The protection provided for performers by this Convention shall include the possibility of preventing:

(a) the broadcasting and the communication to the public, without their consent, of their performance, except where the performance used in the broadcasting or the communication is itself already a broadcast performance or is made from a fixation;

(b) the fixation, without their consent, of their unfixed performance;

(c) the reproduction, without their consent, of a fixation of their performance:

(i) if the original fixation itself was made without their consent;

(ii) if the reproduction is made for purposes different from those for which the performers gave their consent;

(iii) if the original fixation was made in accordance with the provisions of Article 15, and the reproduction is made for purposes different from those referred to in those provisions.

2. (1) If broadcasting was consented to by the performers, it shall be a matter for the domestic law of the Contracting State where protection is claimed to regulate the protection against rebroadcasting, fixation for broadcasting purposes, and the reproduction of such fixation for broadcasting purposes.

(2) The term and conditions governing the use by broadcasting organizations of fixations made for broadcasting purposes shall be determined in accordance with the domestic law of the Contracting State where protection is claimed.

(3) However, the domestic law referred to in sub-paragraphs (1) and (2) of this paragraph shall not operate to deprive performers of the ability to control, by contract, their relations with broadcasting organizations.

Article 8

Any Contracting State may, by its domestic law and regulations, specify the manner in which performers will be represented in connection with the exercise of their rights if several of them participate in the same performance.

Article 9

Any Contracting State may, by its domestic law and regulations, extend the protection provided for this Convention to artistes who do not perform literary or artistic works.

Article 10

Producers of phonograms shall enjoy the right to authorize or prohibit the direct or indirect reproduction of their phonograms.

Article 11

If, as a condition of protecting the rights of producers of phonograms, or of performers, or both, in relation to phonograms, a Contracting State, under its domestic law, requires compliance with formalities, these shall be considered as fulfilled if all the copies in commerce of the published phonogram or their containers bear a notice consisting of the symbol [P in circle], accompanied by the year date of the first publication, placed in such a manner as to give reasonable notice of claim of protection; and if the copies or their containers do not identify the producer or the licensee of the producer (by carrying his name, trade mark or other appropriate designation), the notice shall also include the name of the owner of the rights of the producer; and, furthermore, if the copies or their containers do not identify the principal performers, the notice shall also include the name of the person who, in the country in which the fixation was effected, owns the rights of such performers.

Article 12

If a phonogram published for commercial purposes, or a reproduction of such phonogram, is used directly for broadcasting or for any communication to the public, a single equitable remuneration shall be paid by the user to the performers, or to the producers of the phonograms, or to both. Domestic law may, in the absence of agreement between these parties, lay down the conditions as to the sharing of this remuneration.

Article 13

Broadcasting organizations shall enjoy the right to authorize or prohibit:

(a) the rebroadcasting of their broadcasts;

(b) the fixation of their broadcasts;

(c) the reproduction:

 (i) of fixations, made without their consent, of their broadcasts;

 (ii) of fixations, made in accordance with the provisions of Article 15, of their

broadcasts, if the reproduction is made for purposes different from those referred to in those
provisions;

(d) the communication to the public of their television broadcasts if such communication is made in place accessible to the public against payment of an entrance fee; it shall be a matter for the domestic law of the State where protection of this right is claimed to determine the conditions under which it may be exercised.

Article 14

The term of protection to be granted under this Convention shall last at least until the end of a period of twenty years computed from the end of the year in which:

(a) the fixation was made—for the phonograms and for the for performances incorporated therein;

(b) the performance took place—for performances not incorporated in phonograms;

(c) the broadcast took place—for broadcasts.

Article 15

1. Any Contracting State may, in its domestic laws and regulations, provide for exceptions to the protection guaranteed by this Convention as regards:

(a) private use;

(b) use of short excerpts in connection with the reporting of current events;

(c) ephemeral fixation by a broadcasting organisation by means of its own facilities and for its own broadcasts;

(d) use solely for the purposes of teaching or scientific research.

2. Irrespective of paragraph 1 of this Article, any Contracting State may, in its domestic laws and regulations, provide for the same kinds of limitations with regard to the protection of performers, producers of phonograms and broadcasting organizations, as it provides for, in its domestic laws and regulations, in connection with the protection of copyright in literary and artistic works. However, compulsory licences may be provided for only to the extent to which they are compatible with this Convention.

Article 16

1. Any State, upon becoming party to this Convention, shall be bound by all the obligations and shall enjoy all the benefits thereof. However, a State may at any time, in a notification deposited with the Secretary-General of the United Nations, declare that:

(a) as regards Article 12:

(i) it will not apply the provisions of that Article;

(ii) it will not apply the provisions of that Article in respect of certain uses;

(iii) as regards phonograms the producer of which is not a national of another Contracting State, it will not apply that Article;

(iv) as regards phonograms the producer of which is a national of another Contracting State, it will limit the protection provided for by that Article to the extent to which, and to the term for which, the latter State grants protection to phonograms first fixed by a national of the State making the declaration; however, the fact that the Contracting State of which the producer is a national does not grant the protection to the same beneficiary or beneficiaries as the State making the declaration shall not be considered as a difference in the extent of the protection;

(b) as regards Article 13, it will not apply item (d)of that Article; if a Contracting State makes such a declaration, the other Contracting State shall not be obliged to grant the right referred to in Article 13, item (d), to broadcasting organizations whose headquarters are in that State.

2. If the notification referred to in paragraph 1 of this Article is made after the date of the deposit of the instrument of ratification, acceptance or accession, the declaration will become effective six months after it has been deposited.

Article 17

Any State which, on October 26, 1961, grants protection to producers of phonograms solely on the basis of the criterion of fixation may, by a notification deposited with the Secretary-General of the United Nations at the time of ratification, acceptance or accession, declare that it will apply, for the purpose of paragraph 1 (a) (iii) and (iv) of Article 16, the criterion of fixation instead of the criterion of nationality.

Article 18

Any State which has deposited a notification under paragraph 3 of Article 5, paragraph 2 of Article 6, paragraph 1 of Article 16 or Article 17, may, by a further notification deposited with the Secretary-General of the United Nations, reduce its scope or withdraw it.

Article 19

Notwithstanding anything in this Convention, once a performer has consented to the incorporation of his performance in a visual or audio-visual fixation, Article 7 shall have no further application.

Article 20

1. This Convention shall not prejudice rights acquired in any Contracting State before the date of coming into force of this Convention for that State.

2. No Contracting State shall be bound to apply the provisions of this Convention to performances or broadcasts which took place, or to phonograms which were fixed, before the date of coming into force of this Convention for that State.

Article 21

The protection provided for in this Convention shall not prejudice any protection otherwise secured to performers, producers of phonograms and broadcasting organizations.

Article 22

Contracting State reserve the right to enter into special agreements among themselves in so far as such agreements grant to performers, producers of phonograms or broadcasting organizations more extensive rights than those granted by this Convention or contain other provisions not contrary to this Convention.

Article 23

This Convention shall be deposited with the Secretary-General of the United Nations. It shall be open until June 30, 1962, for signature by any State invited to the Diplomatic Conference on the International Protection of Performers, Producers of Phonograms and Broadcasting Organizations which is a party to the Universal Copyright Convention or a member of the International Union for the Protection of Literary and Artistic Works.

Article 24

1. This Convention shall be subject to ratification or acceptance by the signatory States.
2. This Convention shall be open for accession by any State invited to the Conference referred to in Article 23, and by any State Member of the United Nations, provided that in either case such State is a party to the Universal Copyright Convention or a member of the International Union for the Protection of Literary and Artistic Works.
3. Ratification, acceptance or accession shall be effected by the deposit of an instrument to that effect with the Secretary-General of the United Nations.

Article 25

1. This Convention shall come into force three months after the date of deposit of the sixth instrument of ratification, acceptance or accession.
2. Subsequently, this Convention shall come into force in respect of each State three months after the date of deposit of its instrument of ratification, acceptance or accession.

Article 26

1. Each Contracting State undertakes to adopt, in accordance with its Constitution, the measures necessary to ensure the application of this Convention.
2. At the time of deposit of its instrument of ratification, acceptance or accession, each State must be in a position under its domestic law to give effect to the terms of this Convention.

Article 27

1. Any State may, at the time of ratification, acceptance or accession, or any time thereafter, declare by notification addressed to the Secretary-General of the United Nations that this Convention shall extend to all or any of the territories for whose international relations it is responsible, provided that the Universal Copyright Convention or the International Convention for the Protection of Literary and Artistic Works applies to the territory or territories concerned. This notification shall take effect three months after the date of its receipt.
2. The notification referred to in paragraph 3 of Article 5, paragraph 2 of Article 6, paragraph 1 of Article 16 and Article 17 and 18, may be extended to cover all or any of the territories referred to in paragraph 1 of this Article.

Article 28

1. Any Contracting State may denounce this Convention, on its own behalf, or on behalf of any of the territories referred to in Article 27.
2. The denunciation shall be effected by a notification addressed to the Secretary-General of the United Nations and shall take effect twelve months after the date of receipt of the notification.
3. The right of denunciation shall not be exercised by a Contracting State before the expiry of a period of five years from the date on which the Convention came into force with respect to that State.
4. A Contracting State shall cease to be a party to this Convention from that time when it is neither a party to the Universal Copyright Convention nor a member of the International Union for the Protection of Literary and Artistic Works.
5. This Convention shall cease to apply to any territories referred to in Article 27 from that time when neither the Universal Copyright Convention nor the International Convention for the Protection of Literary and Artistic Works applies to that territory.

Article 29

1. After this Convention has been in force for five years, any Contracting State may, by notification addressed to the Secretary-General of the United Nations, request that a conference be convened for the purpose of revising the Convention. The Secretary-General shall notify all Contracting State of this request. If, a period of six months following the date of notification by the Secretary-General of the United Nations, not less than one half of the Contracting States notify him of their concurrence with the request, the Secretary-General shall inform the Director-General of the International Labor Office, the Director-General of the United Nations Educational, Scientific and Cultural Organization and the Director of the Bureau of the International Union for the Protection of Literary and Artistic Works, who shall convene a revision conference in co-operation with the Intergovernmental Committee provided for in Article 32.

2. The adoption of any revision of this Convention shall require an affirmative vote by two-thirds of the States attending the revision conference, provided that this majority includes two-thirds of the States which, at the time of the revision conference, are parties to the Convention.

3. In the event of adoption of a Convention revising this Convention in whole or in part, and unless the revising Convention provides otherwise:

(a) this Convention shall cease to be open to ratification, acceptance or accession as from the date of entry into force of the revising Convention;

(b) this Convention shall remain in force as regards relations between or with Contracting States which have not become parties to the revising Convention.

Article 30

Any dispute which may arise between two or more Contracting States concerning the interpretation or application of this Convention and which is not settled by negotiation shall, at the request of any one of the parties to the dispute, be referred to the International Court of Justice for decision, unless they agree to another mode of settlement.

Article 31

Without prejudice to the provision of paragraph 3 of Article 5, paragraph 2 of Article 6, paragraph 1 of Article 16 and Article 17, no reservations may be made to this Convention.

Article 32

1. An Intergovernmental Committee is hereby established with the following duties:

(a) to study questions concerning the application and operation of this Convention; and

(b) to collect proposals and to prepare documentation for possible revision of this Convention.

2. The Committee shall consist of representatives of the Contracting States, chosen with due regard to equitable geographical distribution. The number of members shall be six if there are twelve Contracting States or less, nine if there are thirteen to eighteen Contracting States and twelve if there are more than eighteen Contracting States.

3. The Committee shall be constituted twelve months after the Convention comes into force by an election organized among the Contracting States, each of which shall have one vote, by the Director-General of the International Labor Office, the Director-General of the United Nations Educational, Scientific and Cultural Organization and

the Director of the Bureau of the International Union for the Protection of Literary and Artistic Works, in accordance with rules previously approved by a majority of all Contracting States.

4. The Committee shall elect its Chairman and officers. It shall establish its own rules of procedure. These rules shall in particular provide for the future operation of the committee and for a method of selecting its members for the future in such a way to ensure rotation among the various Contracting States.

5. Officials of the International Labor Office, the United Nations Educational, Scientific and Cultural Organization and the Bureau of the International Union for the Protection of Literary and Artistic Works, designated by the Directors-General and the Director thereof, shall constitute the Secretariat of the Committee.

6. Meetings of the Committee, which shall be convened whenever a majority of its members deems it necessary, shall be held successively at the headquarters of the International Labor Office, the United Nations Educational, Scientific and Cultural Organization and the Bureau of the International Union for the Protection of Literary and Artistic Works.

7. Expenses of members of the Committee shall be borne by their respective Governments.

Article 33

1. The present Convention is drawn up in English, French and Spanish, the three texts being equally authentic.

2. In addition, official texts of the present Convention shall be drawn up in German, Italian and Portuguese.

Article 34

1. The Secretary-General of the United Nations shall notify the States invited to the Conference referred to in Article 23 and every State Member of the United Nations, as well as the Director-General of the International Labor Office, the Director-General of the United Nations Educational, Scientific and Cultural Organization and the Director of the Bureau of the International Union for the Protection of Literary and Artistic Works:

(a) of the deposit of each instrument of ratification, acceptance or accession;

(b) of the date of entry into force of the Convention;

(c) of all notifications, declarations or communications provided for in this Convention;

(d) if any of the situations referred to in paragraph 4 and 5 of Article 28 arise.

2. The Secretary-General of the United Nations shall also notify the Director-General of the International Labor Office, the Director-General of the United Nations Educational, Scientific and Cultural Organization and the Director of the Bureau of the International Union for the Protection of Literary and Artistic Works of the requests communicated to him in accordance with Article 29, as well as of any communication received from the Contracting States concerning the revision of the Convention.

IN FAITH WHEREOF, the undersigned, being duly authorized, have signed this Convention.

DONE at Rome, this twenty-sixth day of October 1961, in a single copy in the English, French and Spanish languages. Certified true copies shall be delivered by the Secretary-General of the United Nations to all the States invited to the Conference referred to in Article 23 and to every State Member of the United Nations, as well as to the Director-General of the International Labor Office, the Director-General of the United Nations Educational, Scientific and Cultural Organization and the Director of the of the Bureau of the International Union for the Protection of Literary and Artistic Works.

APPENDIX V

UNIVERSAL COPYRIGHT CONVENTION (PARIS 1971)

The Contracting States,

Moved by the desire to ensure in all countries copyright protection of literary, scientific and artistic works,

Convinced that a system of copyright protection appropriate to all nations of the world and expressed in a universal convention, additional to, and without impairing international systems already in force, will ensure respect for the rights of the individual and encourage the development of literature, the sciences and the arts,

Persuaded that such a universal copyright system will facilitate a wider dissemination of works of the human mind and increase international understanding,

Have resolved to revise the Universal Copyright Convention as signed at Geneva on 6 September 1952 (hereinafter called "the 1952 Convention"), and consequently,

Have agreed as follows:

Article I

Each Contracting State undertakes to provide for the adequate and effective protection of the rights of authors and other copyright proprietors in literary, scientific and artistic works, including writings, musical, dramatic and cinematographic works, and paintings, engravings and sculpture.

Article II

1. Published works of nationals of any Contracting State and works first published in that State shall enjoy in each other Contracting State the same protection as that other State accords to works of its nationals first published in its own territory, as well as the protection specially granted by this Convention.

2. Unpublished works of nationals of each Contracting State shall enjoy in each other Contracting State the same protection as that other State accords to unpublished works of its own nationals, as well as the protection specially granted by this Convention.

3. For the purpose of this Convention any Contracting State may, by domestic legislation, assimilate to its own nationals any person domiciled in that State.

Article III

1. Any Contracting State which, under its domestic law, requires as a condition of copyright, compliance with formalities such as deposit, registration, notice, notarial certificates, payment of fees or manufacture or publication in that Contracting State, shall regard these requirements as satisfied with respect to all works protected in accordance with this Convention and first published outside its territory and the author of which is not one of its nationals, if from the time of the first publication all the copies of the work published with the authority of the author or other copyright proprietor bear the symbol ~ accompanied by the name of the copyright proprietor and the year of first publication placed in such manner and location as to give reasonable notice of claim of copyright.

2. The provisions of paragraph 1 shall not preclude any Contracting State from requiring formalities or other conditions for the acquisition and enjoyment of copyright in respect of works first published in its territory or works of its nationals wherever published.

3. The provisions of paragraph 1 shall not preclude any Contracting State from

providing that a person seeking judicial relief must, in bringing the action, comply with procedural requirements, such as that the complainant must appear through domestic counsel or that the complainant must deposit with the court or an administrative office, or both, a copy of the work involved in the litigation; provided that failure to comply with such requirements shall not affect the validity of the copyright, nor shall any such requirement be imposed upon a national of another Contracting State if such requirement is not imposed on nationals of the State in which protection is claimed.

4. In each Contracting State there shall be legal means of protecting without formalities the unpublished works of nationals of other Contracting States.

5. If a Contracting State grants protection for more than one term of copyright and the first term is for a period longer than one of the minimum periods prescribed in Article IV, such State shall not be required to comply with the provisions of paragraph 1 of this article in respect of the second or any subsequent term of copyright.

Article IV

1. The duration of protection of a work shall be governed, in accordance with the provisions of Article II and this article, by the law of the Contracting State in which protection is claimed.

2. (a) The term of protection for works protected under this Convention shall not be less than the life of the author and twenty-five years after his death. However, any Contracting State which, on the effective date of this Convention in that State, has limited this term for certain classes of works to a period computed from the first publication of the work, shall be entitled to maintain these exceptions and to extend them to other classes of works. For all these classes the term of protection shall not be less than twenty-five years from the date of first publication.

(b) Any Contracting State which, upon the effective date of this Convention in that State, does not compute the term of protection upon the basis of the life of the author, shall be entitled to compute the term of protection from the date of the first publication of the work or from its registration prior to publication, as the case may be, provided the term of protection shall not be less than twenty-five years from the date of first publication or from its registration prior to publication, as the case may be.

(c) If the legislation of a Contracting State grants two or more successive terms of protection, the duration of the first term shall not be less than one of the minimum periods specified in sub-paragraphs (a) and (b).

3. The provisions of paragraph 2 shall not apply to photographic works or to works of applied art; provided, however, that the term of protection in those Contracting States which protect photographic works, or works of applied art in so far as they are protected as artistic works, shall not be less than ten years for each of said classes of works.

4. (a) No Contracting State shall be obliged to grant protection to a work for a period longer than that fixed for the class of works to which the work in question belongs, in the case of unpublished works by the law of the Contracting State of which the author is a national, and in the case of published works by the law of the Contracting State in which the work has been first published.

(b) For the purposes of the application of sub-paragraph (a), if the law of any Contracting State grants two or more successive terms of protection, the period of protection of that State shall be considered to be the aggregate of those terms. However, if a specified work is not protected by such State during the second or any subsequent term for any reason, the other Contracting States shall not be obliged to protect it during the second or any subsequent term.

5. For the purposes of the application of paragraph 4, the work of a national of a Contracting State, first published in a non-Contracting State, shall be treated as though first published in the Contracting State of which the author is a national.

6. For the purposes of the application of paragraph 4, in case of simultaneous publication in two or more Contracting States, the work shall be treated as though first published in the State which affords the shortest term, any work published in two or more Contracting States within thirty days of its first publication shall be considered as having been published simultaneously in said Contracting States.

Article IVbis

1. The rights referred to in Article I shall include the basic rights ensuring the author's economic interests, including the exclusive right to authorize reproduction by any means, public performance and broadcasting. The provisions of this article shall extend to works protected under this Convention either in their original form or in any form recognizably derived from the original.

2. However, any Contracting State may, by its domestic legislation, make exceptions that do not conflict with the spirit and provisions of this Convention, to the rights mentioned in paragraph 1 of this article. Any State whose legislation so provides, shall nevertheless accord a reasonable degree of effective protection to each of the rights to which exception has been made.

Article V

1. The rights referred to in Article I shall include the exclusive right of the author to make, publish and authorize the making and publication of translations of works protected under this Convention.

2. However, any Contracting State may, by its domestic legislation, restrict the right of translation of writings, but only subject to the following provisions:

(a) If, after the expiration of a period of seven years from the date of the first publication of a writing, a translation of such writing has not been published in a language in general use of the Contracting State, by the owner of the right of translation or with his authorization, any national of such Contracting State may obtain a non-exclusive licence from the competent authority thereof to translate the work into that language and publish the work so translated.

(b) Such national shall in accordance with the procedure of the State concerned, establish either that he has requested, and been denied, authorization by the proprietor of the right to make and publish the translation, or that, after due diligence on his part, he was unable to find the owner of the right. A licence may also be granted on the same conditions if all previous editions of a translation in a language in general use in the Contracting State are out of print.

(c) If the owner of the right of translation cannot be found, then the applicant for a licence shall send copies of his application to the publisher whose name appears on the work and, if the nationality of the owner of the right of translation is known, to the diplomatic or consular representative of the State of which such owner is a national, or to the organization which may have been designated by the government of that State. The licence shall not be granted before the expiration of a period of two months from the date of the dispatch of the copies of the application.

(d) Due provision shall be made by domestic legislation to ensure to the owner of the right of translation a compensation which is just and conforms to international standards, to ensure payment and transmittal of such compensation, and to ensure a correct translation of the work.

(e) The original title and the name of the author of the work shall be printed on all copies of the published translation. The licence shall be valid only for publication of the translation in the territory of the Contracting State where it has been applied for. Copies so published may be imported and sold in another Contracting State if a language in general use in such other State is the same language as that into which the work has been so translated, and if the domestic law in such other State makes provision for such licences and does not prohibit such importation and sale. Where the foregoing conditions do not exist, the importation and sale of such copies in a Contracting State shall be governed by its domestic law and its agreements. The licence shall not be transferred by the licensee.

(f) The licence shall not be granted when the author has withdrawn from circulation all copies of the work.

Article Vbis

1. Any Contracting State regarded as a developing country in conformity with the established practice of the General Assembly of the United Nations may, by a notification deposited with the Director-General of the United Nations Educational, Scientific and Cultural Organization (hereinafter called "the Director-General") at the time of its ratification, acceptance or accession or thereafter, avail itself of any or all of the exceptions provided for in Articles Vter and Vquater.

2. Any such notification shall be effective for ten years from the date of coming into force of this Convention, or for such part of that ten-year period as remains at the date of deposit of the notification, and may be renewed in whole or in part for further periods of ten years each if, not more than fifteen or less than three months before the expiration of the relevant ten-year period, the Contracting State deposits a further notification with the Director-General. Initial notifications may also be made during these further periods of ten years in accordance with the provisions of this article.

3. Notwithstanding the provisions of paragraph 2, a Contracting State that has ceased to be regarded as a developing country as referred to in paragraph 1 shall no longer be entitled to renew its notification made under the provisions of paragraph 1 or 2, and whether or not it formally withdraws the notification such State shall be precluded from availing itself of the exceptions provided for in Articles Vter and Vquater at the end of the current ten-year period, or at the end of three years after it has ceased to be regarded as a developing country, whichever period expires later.

4. Any copies of a work already made under the exceptions provided for in Articles Vter and Vquater may continue to be distributed after the expiration of the period for which notifications under this article were effective until their stock is exhausted.

5. Any Contracting State that has deposited a notification in accordance with Article XIII with respect to the application of this Convention to a particular country or territory, the situation of which can be regarded as analogous to that of the States referred to in paragraph 1 of this article, may also deposit notifications and renew them in accordance with the provisions of this article with respect to any such country or territory. During the effective period of such notifications, the provisions of Articles Vter and Vquater may be applied with respect to such country or territory. The sending of copies from the country or territory to the Contracting State shall be considered as export within the meaning of Articles Vter and Vquater.

Article Vter

1. (a) Any Contracting State to which Article Vbis (1) applies may substitute for the period of seven years provided for in Article V (2) a period of three years or any longer period prescribed by its legislation. However, in the case of a translation into a language

not in general use in one or more developed countries that are party to this Convention or only the 1952 Convention, the period shall be one year instead of three.

(b) A Contracting State to which Article Vbis (1) applies may, with the unanimous agreement of the developed countries party to this Convention or only the 1952 Convention and in which the same language is in general use, substitute, in the case of translation into that language, for the period of three years provided for in sub-paragraph (a) another period as determined by such agreement but not shorter than one year. However, this sub-paragraph shall not apply where the language in question is English, French or Spanish. Notification of any such agreement shall be made to the Director-General.

(c) The licence may only be granted if the applicant, in accordance with the procedure of the State concerned, establishes either that he has requested, and been denied, authorization by the owner of the right of translation, or that, after due diligence on his part, he was unable to find the owner of the right. At the same time as he makes his request he shall inform either the International Copyright Centre established by the United Nations Educational, Scientific and Cultural Organization or any national or regional information center which may have been designated in a notification to that effect deposited with the Director-General by the government of the State in which the publisher is believed to have his principal place of business.

(d) If the owner of the right of translation cannot be found, the applicant for a licence shall send, by registered airmail, copies of his application to the publisher whose name appears on the work and to any national or regional information center as mentioned in sub-paragraph (c). If no such center is notified he shall also send a copy to the international copyright information center established by the United Nations Educational, Scientific and Cultural Organization.

2. (a) Licences obtainable after three years shall not be granted under this article until a further period of six months has elapsed and licences obtainable after one year until a further period of nine months has elapsed. The further period shall begin either from the date of the request for permission to translate mentioned in paragraph 1 (c) or, if the identity or address of the owner of the right of translation is not known, from the date of dispatch of the copies of the application for a licence mentioned in paragraph 1 (d).

(b) Licences shall not be granted if a translation has been published by the owner of the right of translation or with his authorization during the said period of six or nine months.

3. Any licence under this article shall be granted only for the purpose of teaching, scholarship or research.

4. (a) Any licence granted under this article shall not extend to the export of copies and shall be valid only for publication in the territory of the Contracting State where it has been applied for.

(b) Any copy published in accordance with a licence granted under this article shall bear a notice in the appropriate language stating that the copy is available for distribution only in the Contracting State granting the licence. If the writing bears the notice specified in Article III (1) the copies shall bear the same notice.

(c) The prohibition of export provided for in sub-paragraph (a) shall not apply where a governmental or other public entity of a State which has granted a licence under this article to translate a work into a language other than English, French or Spanish sends copies of a translation prepared under such licence to another country if:

(i) the recipients are individuals who are nationals of the Contracting State granting the licence, or organizations grouping such individuals;

(ii) the copies are to be used only for the purpose of teaching, scholarship or research;

(iii) the sending of the copies and their subsequent distribution to recipients is without the object of commercial purpose; and

(iv) the country to which the copies have been sent has agreed with the Contracting State to allow the receipt, distribution or both and the Director-General has been notified of such agreement by any one of the governments which have concluded it.

5. Due provision shall be made at the national level to ensure:

(a) that the licence provides for just compensation that is consistent with standards of royalties normally operating in the case of licences freely negotiated between persons in the two countries concerned; and

(b) payment and transmittal of the compensation; however, should national currency regulations intervene, the competent authority shall make all efforts, by the use of international machinery, to ensure transmittal in internationally convertible currency or its equivalent.

6. Any licence granted by a Contracting State under this article shall terminate if a translation of the work in the same language with substantially the same content as the edition in respect of which the licence was granted is published in the said State by the owner of the right of translation or with his authorization, at a price reasonably related to that normally charged in the same State for comparable works. Any copies already made before the licence is terminated may continue to be distributed until their stock is exhausted.

For works which are composed mainly of illustrations a licence to translate the text and to reproduce the illustrations may be granted only if the conditions of Article Vquater are also fulfilled.

8. (a) A licence to translate a work protected under this Convention, published in printed or analogous forms of reproduction, may also be granted to a broadcasting organization having its headquarters in a Contracting State to which Article Vbis (1) applies, upon an application made in that State by the said organization under the following conditions:

(i) the translation is made from a copy made and acquired in accordance with the laws of the Contracting State;

(ii) the translation is for use only in broadcasts intended exclusively for teaching or for the dissemination of the results of specialized technical or scientific research to experts in a particular profession;

(iii) the translation is used exclusively for the purposes set out in condition (ii), through broadcasts lawfully made which are intended for recipients on the territory of the Contracting State, including broadcasts made through the medium of sound or visual recordings lawfully and exclusively made for the purpose of such broadcasts;

(iv) sound or visual recordings of the translation may be exchanged only between broadcasting organizations having their headquarters in the Contracting State granting the licence; and

(v) all uses made of the translation are without any commercial purpose.

(b) Provided all of the criteria and conditions set out in sub-paragraph (a) are met, a licence may also be granted to a broadcasting organization to translate any text incorporated in an audio-visual fixation which was itself prepared and published for the sole purpose of being used in connection with systematic instructional activities.

(c) Subject to sub-paragraphs (a) and (b), the other provisions of this article shall apply to the grant and exercise of the licence.

9. Subject to the provisions of this article, any licence granted under this Article shall be governed by the provisions of Article V, and shall continue to be governed by

the provisions of Article V and of this article, even after the seven-year period provided for in Article V (2) has expired. However, after the said period has expired, the licensee shall be free to request that the said licence be replaced by a new licence governed exclusively by the provisions of Article V.

Article Vquater

1. Any Contracting State to which Article Vbis (1) applies may adopt the following provisions:

(a) If, after the expiration of (i) the relevant period specified in sub-paragraph (c) commencing from the date of first publication of a particular edition of a literary, scientific or artistic work referred to in paragraph 3, or (ii) any longer period determined by national legislation of the State, copies of such edition have not been distributed in that State to the general public or in connection with systematic instructional activities at a price reasonably related to that normally charged in the State for comparable works, by the owner of the right of reproduction or with his authorization, any national of such State may obtain a non-exclusive licence from the competent authority to publish such edition at that or a lower price for use in connection with systematic instructional activities. The licence may only be granted if such national, in accordance with the procedure of the State concerned, establishes either that he has requested, and been denied, authorization by the proprietor of the right to publish such work, or that, after due diligence on his part, he was unable to find the owner of the right. At the same time as he makes his request he shall inform either the international copyright information center established by the United Nations Educational, Scientific and Cultural Organization or any national or regional information center referred to in subparagraph (d).

(b) A licence may also be granted on the same conditions if, for a period of six months, no authorized copies of the edition in question have been on sale in the State concerned to the general public or in connection with systematic instructional activities at a price reasonably related to that normally charged in the State for comparable works.

(c) The period referred to in sub-paragraph (a) shall be five years except that:

(i) for works of the natural and physical sciences, including mathematics, and of technology, the period shall be three years;

(ii) for works of fiction, poetry, drama and music, and for art books, the period shall be seven years.

(d) If the owner of the right of reproduction cannot be found, the applicant for a licence shall send, by registered air mail, copies of his application to the publisher whose name appears on the work and to any national or regional information center identified as such in a notification deposited with the Director-General by the State in which the publisher is believed to have his principal place of business. In the absence of any such notification, he shall also send a copy to the international copyright information center established by the United Nations Educational, Scientific and Cultural Organization. The licence shall not be granted before the expiration of a period of three months from the date of dispatch of the copies of the application.

(e) Licences obtainable after three years shall not be granted under this article:

(i) until a period of six months has elapsed from the date of the request for permission referred to in sub-paragraph (a) or, if the identity or address of the owner of the right of reproduction is unknown, from the date of the dispatch of the copies of the application for a licence referred to in sub-paragraph (d);

(ii) if any such distribution of copies of the edition as is mentioned in sub-paragraph (a) has taken place during that period.

(f) The name of the author and the title of the particular edition of the work shall be printed on all copies of the published reproduction. The licence shall not extend to the export of copies and shall be valid only for publication in the territory of the Contracting State where it has been applied for. The licence shall not be transferable by the licensee.

(g) Due provision shall be made by domestic legislation to ensure an accurate reproduction of the particular edition in question.

(h) A licence to reproduce and publish a translation of a work shall not be granted under this article in the following cases:

(i) where the translation was not published by the owner of the right of translation or with his authorization;

(ii) where the translation is not in a language in general use in the State with power to grant the licence.

2. The exceptions provided for in paragraph 1 are subject to the following additional provisions:

(a) Any copy published in accordance with a licence granted under this article shall bear a notice in the appropriate language stating that the copy is available for distribution only in the Contracting State to which the said licence applies. If the edition bears the notice specified in Article III (1), the copies shall bear the same notice.

(b) Due provision shall be made at the national level to ensure:

(i) that the licence provides for just compensation that is consistent with standards of royalties normally operating in the case of licences freely negotiated between persons in the two countries concerned; and

(ii) payment and transmittal of the compensation; however. should national currency regulations intervene, the competent authority shall make all efforts, by the use of international machinery, to ensure transmittal in internationally convertible currency or its equivalent.

(c) Whenever copies of an edition of a work are distributed in the Contracting State to the general public or in connection with systematic instructional activities, by the owner of the right of reproduction or with his authorization, at a price reasonably related to that normally charged in the State for comparable works, any licence granted under this article shall terminate if such edition is in the same language and is substantially the same in content as the edition published under the licence. Any copies already made before the licence is terminated may continue to be distributed until their stock is exhausted.

(d) No licence shall be granted when the author has withdrawn from circulation all copies of the edition in question.

3. (a) Subject to sub-paragraph (b), the literary, scientific or artistic works to which this article applies shall be limited to works published in printed or analogous forms of reproduction.

(b) The provisions of this article shall also apply to reproduction in audiovisual form of lawfully made audio-visual fixations including any protected works incorporated therein and to the translation of any incorporated text into a language in general use in the State with power to grant the licence; always provided that the audio-visual fixations in question were prepared and published for the sole purpose of being used in connection with systematic instructional activities.

Article VI

"Publication," as used in this Convention, means the reproduction in tangible form and the general distribution to the public of copies of a work from which it can be read or otherwise visually perceived.

Article VII

This Convention shall not apply to works or rights in works which, at the effective date of this Convention in a Contracting State where protection is claimed, are permanently in the public domain in the said Contracting State.

Article VIII

1. This Convention, which shall bear the date of 24 July 1971, shall be deposited with the Director-General and shall remain open for signature by all States party to the 1952 Convention for a period of 120 days after the date of this Convention. It shall be subject to ratification or acceptance by the signatory States.

2. Any State which has not signed this Convention may accede thereto.

3. Ratification, acceptance or accession shall be effected by the deposit of an instrument to that effect with the Director-General.

Article IX

1. This Convention shall come into force three months after the deposit of twelve instruments of ratification, acceptance or accession.

2. Subsequently, this Convention shall come into force in respect of each State three months after that State has deposited its instrument of ratification, acceptance or accession.

3. Accession to this Convention by a State not party to the 1952 Convention shall also constitute accession to that Convention; however, if its instrument of accession is deposited before this Convention comes into force, such State may make its accession to the 1952 Convention conditional upon the coming into force of this Convention. After the coming into force of this Convention, no State may accede solely to the 1952 Convention.

4. Relations between States party to this Convention and States that are party only to the 1952 Convention, shall be governed by the 1952 Convention. However, any State party only to the 1952 Convention may, by a notification deposited with the Director-General, declare that it will admit the application of the 1971 Convention to works of its nationals or works first published in its territory by all States party to this Convention.

Article X

1. Each Contracting State undertakes to adopt, in accordance with its Constitution, such measures as are necessary to ensure the application of this Convention.

2. It is understood that at the date this Convention comes into force in respect of any State, that State must be in a position under its domestic law to give effect to the terms of this Convention.

[*Article XI - Article XIV* Omitted]

Article XV

A dispute between two or more Contracting States concerning the interpretation or application of this Convention, not settled by negotiation, shall, unless the States concerned agree on some other method of settlement, be brought before the International Court of Justice for determination by it.

[*Article XVI* Omitted]

Article XVII

1. This Convention shall not in any way affect the provisions of the Berne Convention for the Protection of Literary and Artistic Works or membership in the Union created by that Convention.

2. In application of the foregoing paragraph, a declaration has been annexed to the present article. This declaration is an integral part of this Convention for the States bound by the Berne Convention on 1 January 1951, or which have or may become bound to it at a later date. The signature of this Convention by such States shall also constitute signature of the said declaration, and ratification, acceptance or accession by such States shall include the declaration, as well as this Convention

Article XVIII

This Convention shall not abrogate multilateral or bilateral copyright conventions or arrangements that are or may be in effect exclusively between two or more American Republics. In the event of any difference either between the provisions of such existing conventions or arrangements and the provisions of this Convention, or between the provisions of this Convention and those of any new convention or arrangement which may be formulated between two or more American Republics after this Convention comes into force, the convention or arrangement most recently formulated shall prevail between the parties thereto. Rights in works acquired in any Contracting State under existing conventions or arrangements before the date this Convention comes into force in such State shall not be affected.

Article XIX

This Convention shall not abrogate multilateral or bilateral conventions or arrangements in effect between two or more Contracting States. In the event of any difference between the provisions of such existing conventions or arrangements and the provisions of this Convention, the provisions of this Convention shall prevail. Rights in works acquired in any Contracting State under existing conventions or arrangements before the date on which this Convention comes into force in such State shall not be affected. Nothing in this article shall affect the provisions of Articles XVII and XVIII.

Article XX

Reservations to this Convention shall not be permitted.

[*Article XXI* Omitted]

APPENDIX DECLARATION RELATING TO ARTICLE XVII

The States which are members of the International Union for the Protection of Literary and Artistic Works (hereinafter called "the Berne Union") and which are signatories to this Convention,

Desiring to reinforce their mutual relations on the basis of the said Union and to avoid any conflict which might result from the co-existence of the Berne Convention and the Universal Copyright Convention.

Recognizing the temporary need of some States to adjust their level of copyright protection in accordance with their stage of cultural, social and economic development,

Have, by common agreement, accepted the terms of the following declaration:

(a) Except as provided by paragraph (b), works which, according to the Berne Convention, have as their country of origin a country which has withdrawn from the Berne Union after 1 January 1951 shall not be protected by the Universal Copyright Convention in the countries of the Berne Union;

(b) Where a Contracting State is regarded as a developing country in conformity with the established practice of the General Assembly of the United Nations, and has deposited with the Director-General of the United Nations Educational, Scientific and Cultural Organization, at the time of its withdrawal from the Berne Union, a notification to the effect that it regards itself as a developing country, the provisions of paragraph (a) shall not be applicable as long as such State may avail itself of the exceptions provided for by this Convention in accordance with Article Vbis.

(c) The Universal Copyright Convention shall not be applicable to the relationships among countries of the Berne Union in so far as it relates to the protection of works having as their country of origin, within the meaning of the Berne Convention, a country of the Berne Union.

IN FAITH WHEREOF the undersigned, having deposited their respective full powers, have signed this Convention.

DONE at Paris, this twenty-fourth day of July 1971, in a single copy.

PROTOCOL 1 ANNEXED TO THE UNIVERSAL COPYRIGHT CONVENTION AS REVISED AT PARIS ON 24 JULY 1971 CONCERNING THE APPLICATION OF THAT CONVENTION TO WORKS OF STATELESS PERSONS AND REFUGEES

The States party hereto, being also party to the Universal Copyright Convention as revised at Paris on 24 July 1971 (hereinafter called "the 1971 Convention"),

Have accepted the following provisions:

1. Stateless persons and refugees who have their habitual residence in a State party to this Protocol shall, for the purposes of the 1971 Convention be assimilated to the nationals of that State.

2. (a) This Protocol shall be signed and shall be subject to ratification or acceptance, or may be acceded to, as if the provisions of Article VIII of the 1971 Convention applied hereto.

(b) This Protocol shall enter into force in respect of each State, on the date of deposit of the instrument of ratification, acceptance or accession of the State concerned or on the date of entry into force of the 1971 Convention with respect to such State, whichever is the later.

(c) On the entry into force of this Protocol in respect of a State not party to Protocol 1 annexed to the 1952 Convention, the latter Protocol shall be deemed to enter into force in respect of such State.

IN FAITH WHEREOF the undersigned, being duly authorized thereto, have signed this Protocol.

DONE at Paris this twenty-fourth day of July 1971.

PROTOCOL 2 ANNEXED TO THE UNIVERSAL COPYRIGHT CONVENTION AS REVISED AT PARIS ON 24 JULY 1971 CONCERNING THE APPLICATION OF THAT CONVENTION TO THE WORKS OF CERTAIN INTERNATIONAL ORGANIZATIONS

The States party hereto, being also party to the Universal Copyright Convention as revised at Paris on 24 July 1971 (hereinafter called "the 1971 Convention"),

Have accepted the following provisions:

1. (a) The protection provided for in Article II (1) of the 1971 Convention shall apply to works published for the first time by the United Nations by the Specialized Agencies in relationship therewith, or by the Organization of American States.

(b) Similarly, Article II (2) of the 1971 Convention shall apply to the said organization or agencies.

2. (a) This Protocol shall be signed and shall he subject to ratification or acceptance, or may be acceded to, as if the provisions of Article VIII of the 1971 Convention applied hereto.

(b) This Protocol shall enter into force for each State on the date of deposit of the instrument of ratification, acceptance or accession of the State concerned or on the date of entry into force of the 1971 Convention with respect to such State, whichever is the later.

IN FAITH WHEREOF the undersigned, being duly authorized thereto have signed this Protocol.

DONE at Paris, this twenty-fourth day of July 1971.

APPENDIX VI

PATENT COOPERATION TREATY (WASHINGTON 1970)

The Contracting States,

Desiring to make a contribution to the progress of science and technology,

Desiring to perfect the legal protection of inventions,

Desiring to simplify and render more economical the obtaining of protection for inventions where protection is sought in several countries,

Desiring to facilitate and accelerate access by the public to the technical information contained in documents describing new inventions,

Desiring to foster and accelerate the economic development of developing countries through the adoption of measures designed to increase the efficiency of their legal systems, whether national or regional, instituted for the protection of inventions by providing easily accessible information on the availability of technological solutions applicable to their special needs and by facilitating access to the ever expanding volume of modern technology,

Convinced that cooperation among nations will greatly facilitate the attainment of these aims,

Have concluded the present Treaty.

INTRODUCTORY PROVISIONS

Article 1
Establishment of a Union

(1) The States party to this Treaty (hereinafter called "the Contracting States") constitute a Union for cooperation in the filing, searching, and examination, of applications for the protection of inventions, and for rendering special technical services. The Union shall be known as the International Patent Cooperation Union.

(2) No provision of this Treaty shall be interpreted as diminishing the rights under the Paris Convention for the Protection of Industrial Property of any national or resident of any country party to that Convention.

Article 2
Definitions

For the purposes of this Treaty and the Regulations and unless expressly stated otherwise:

(i) "application" means an application for the protection of an invention; references to an "application" shall be construed as references to applications for patents for inventions, inventors' certificates, utility certificates, utility models, patents or certificates of addition, inventors' certificates of addition, and utility certificates of addition;

(ii) references to a "patent" shall be construed as references to patents for inventions, inventors' certificates, utility certificates, utility models, patents or certificates of addition, inventors' certificates of addition, and utility certificates of addition;

(iii) "national patent" means a patent granted by a national authority;

(iv) "regional patent" means a patent granted by a national or an intergovernmental authority having the power to grant patents effective in more than one State;

(v) "regional application" means an application for a regional patent;

(vi) references to a "national application" shall be construed as references to applications for national patents and regional patents, other than applications filed under this Treaty;

(vii) "international application" means an application filed under this Treaty;

(viii) references to an "application" shall be construed as references to international applications and national applications;

(ix) references to a "patent" shall be construed as references to national patents and regional patents;

(x) references to "national law" shall be construed as references to the national law of a Contracting State or, where a regional application or a regional patent is involved, to the treaty providing for the filing of regional applications or the granting of regional patents;

(xi) "priority date," for the purposes of computing time limits, means:

(a) where the international application contains a priority claim under Article 8, the filing date of the application whose priority is so claimed;

(b) where the international application contains several priority claims under Article 8, the filing date of the earliest application whose priority is so claimed;

(c) where the international application does not contain any priority claim under Article 8, the international filing date of such application;

(xii) "national Office" means the government authority of a Contracting State entrusted with the granting of patents; references to a "national Office" shall be construed as referring also to any intergovernmental authority which several States have entrusted with the task of granting regional patents, provided that at least one of those States is a Contracting State, and provided that the said States have authorized that authority to assume the obligations and exercise the powers which this Treaty and the Regulations provide for in respect of national Offices.

(xiii) "designated Office" means the national Office of or acting for the State designated by the applicant under Chapter I of this Treaty;

(xiv) "elected Office" means the national Office of or acting for the State elected by the applicant under Chapter II of this Treaty;

(xv) "receiving Office" means the national Office or the intergovernmental organization with which the international application has been filed;

(xvi) "Union" means the International Patent Cooperation Union;

(xvii) "Assembly" means the Assembly of the Union;

(xviii) "Organization" means the World Intellectual Property Organization;

(xix) "International Bureau" means the international bureau of the Organization and, as long as it subsists, the United International Bureaux for the Protection of Intellectual Property (BIRPI);

(xx) "Director General" means the Director General of the Organization and, as long as BIRPl subsists, the Director of BIRPI.

CHAPTER I
INTERNATIONAL APPLICATION AND INTERNATIONAL SEARCH

Article 3
The International Application

(1) Applications for the protection of inventions in any of the Contracting States may be filed as international applications under this Treaty.

(2) An international application shall contain, as specified in this Treaty and the Regulations, a request, a description, one or more claims, one or more drawings (where required), and an abstract.

(3) The abstract merely serves the purpose of technical information and cannot be taken into account for any other purpose, particularly not for the purpose of interpreting the scope of the protection sought.

(4) The international application shall:

(i) be in a prescribed language;

(ii) comply with the prescribed physical requirements;

(iii) comply with the prescribed requirement of unity of invention;

(iv) be subject to the payment of the prescribed fees.

Article 4
The Request

(1) The request shall contain:

(i) a petition to the effect that the international application be processed according to this Treaty;

(ii) the designation of the Contracting State or States in which protection for the invention is desired on the basis of the international application ("designated States"); if for any designated State a regional patent is available and the applicant wishes to obtain a regional patent rather than a national patent, the request shall so indicate; if, under a treaty concerning a regional patent, the applicant cannot limit his application to certain of the States party to that treaty, designation of one of those States and the indication of the wish to obtain the regional patent shall be treated as designation of all the States party to that treaty; if, under the national law of the designated State, the designation of that State has the effect of an application for a regional patent, the designation of the said State shall be treated as an indication of the wish to obtain the regional patent;

(iii) the name of and other prescribed data concerning the applicant and the agent (if any);

(iv) the title of the invention;

(v) the name of and other prescribed data concerning the inventor where the national law of at least one of the designated States requires that these indications be furnished at the time of filing a national application. Otherwise, the said indications may be furnished either in the request or in separate notices addressed to each designated Office whose national law requires the furnishing of the said indications but allows that they be furnished at a time later than that of the filing of a national application.

(2) Every designation shall be subject to the payment of the prescribed fee within the prescribed time limit.

(3) Unless the applicant asks for any of the other kinds of protection referred to in Article 43, designation shall mean that the desired protection consists of the grant of a patent by or for the designated State. For the purposes of this paragraph, Article 2(ii) shall not apply.

(4) Failure to indicate in the request the name and other prescribed data concerning the inventor shall have no consequence in any designated State whose national law requires the furnishing of the said indications but allows that they be furnished at a time later than that of the filing of a national application. Failure to furnish the said indications in a separate notice shall have no consequence in any designated State whose national law does not require the furnishing of the said indications.

Article 5
The Description

The description shall disclose the invention in a manner sufficiently clear and complete for the invention to be carried out by a person skilled in the art.

Article 6
The Claims

The claim or claims shall define the matter for which protection is sought. Claims shall be clear and concise. They shall be fully supported by the description.

Article 7
The Drawings

(1) Subject to the provisions of paragraph (2)(ii), drawings shall be required when they are necessary for the understanding of the invention.

(2) Where, without being necessary for the understanding of the invention, the nature of the invention admits of illustration by drawings:

(i) the applicant may include such drawings in the international application when filed,

(ii) any designated Office may require that the applicant file such drawings with it within the prescribed time limit.

Article 8
Claiming Priority

(1) The international application may contain a declaration, as prescribed in the Regulations, claiming the priority of one or more earlier applications filed in or for any country party to the Paris Convention for the Protection of Industrial Property.

(2)(a) Subject to the provisions of subparagraph (b), the conditions for, and the effect of, any priority claim declared under paragraph (1) shall be as provided in Article 4 of the Stockholm Act of the Paris Convention for the Protection of Industrial Property.

(b) The international application for which the priority of one or more earlier applications filed in or for a Contracting State is claimed may contain the designation of that State. Where, in the international application, the priority of one or more national applications filed in or for a designated State is claimed, or where the priority of an international application having designated only one State is claimed, the conditions for, and the effect of, the priority claim in that State shall be governed by the national law of that State.

Article 9
The Applicant

(1) Any resident or national of a Contracting State may file an international application.

(2) The Assembly may decide to allow the residents and the nationals of any country party to the Paris Convention for the Protection of Industrial Property which is not party to this Treaty to file international applications.

(3) The concepts of residence and nationality, and the application of those concepts in cases where there are several applicants or where the applicants are not the same for all the designated States, are defined in the Regulations.

Article 10
The Receiving Office

The international application shall be filed with the prescribed receiving Office, which will check and process it as provided in this Treaty and the Regulations.

Article 11
Filing Date and Effects of the International Application

(1) The receiving Office shall accord as the international filing date the date of receipt of the international application, provided that that Office has found that, at the time of receipt:

(i) the applicant does not obviously lack, for reasons of residence or nationality, the right to file an international application with the receiving Office,

(ii) the international application is in the prescribed language,

(iii) the international application contains at least the following elements:

(a) an indication that it is intended as an international application,

(b) the designation of at least one Contracting State,

(c) the name of the applicant, as prescribed,

(d) a part which on the face of it appears to be a description,

(e) a part which on the face of it appears to be a claim or claims.

(2)(a) If the receiving Office finds that the international application did not, at the time of receipt, fulfill the requirements listed in paragraph (1), it shall, as provided in the Regulations, invite the applicant to file the required correction.

(b) If the applicant complies with the invitation, as provided in the Regulations, the receiving Office shall accord as the international filing date the date of receipt of the required correction.

(3) Subject to Article 64(4), any international application fulfilling the requirements listed in items (i) to (iii) of paragraph (1) and accorded an international filing date shall have the effect of a regular national application in each designated State as of the international filing date, which date shall be considered to be the actual filing date in each designated State.

(4) Any international application fulfilling the requirements listed in items (i) to (iii) of paragraph (1) shall be equivalent to a regular national filing within the meaning of the Paris Convention for the Protection of Industrial Property.

Article 12
Transmittal of the International Application to the International Bureau and the International Searching Authority

(1) One copy of the international application shall be kept by the receiving Office ("home copy"), one copy ("record copy") shall be transmitted to the International Bureau, and another copy ("search copy") shall be transmitted to the competent International Searching Authority referred to in Article 16, as provided in the Regulations.

(2) The record copy shall be considered the true copy of the international application.

(3) The international application shall be considered withdrawn if the record copy has not been received by the International Bureau within the prescribed time limit.

Article 13
Availability of Copy of the International Application to Designated Offices

(1) Any designated Office may ask the International Bureau to transmit to it a copy of the international application prior to the communication provided for in Article 20, and the International Bureau shall transmit such copy to the designated Office as soon as possible after the expiration of one year from the priority date.

(2)(a) The applicant may, at any time, transmit a copy of his international application to any designated Office.

(b) The applicant may, at any time, ask the International Bureau to transmit a copy of his international application to any designated Office, and the International Bureau shall transmit such copy to the designated Office as soon as possible.

(c) Any national Office may notify the International Bureau that it does not wish to receive copies as provided for in subparagraph (b), in which case that subparagraph shall not be applicable in respect of that Office.

Article 14
Certain Defects in the International Application

(1)(a) The receiving office shall check whether the international application contains any of the following defects, that is to say:

(i) it is not signed as provided in the Regulations;

(ii) it does not contain the prescribed indications concerning the applicant;

(iii) it does not contain a title;

(iv) it does not contain an abstract;

(v) it does not comply to the extent provided in the Regulations with the prescribed physical requirements.

(b) If the receiving Office finds any of the said defects, it shall invite the applicant to correct the international application within the prescribed time limit, failing which that application shall be considered withdrawn and the receiving Office shall so declare.

(2) If the international application refers to drawings which, in fact, are not included in that application, the receiving Office shall notify the applicant accordingly and he may furnish them within the prescribed time limit and, if he does, the international filing date shall be the date on which the drawings are received by the receiving Office. Otherwise, any reference to the said drawings shall be considered non-existent.

(3)(a) If the receiving Office finds that, within the prescribed time limits, the fees prescribed under Article 3(4)(iv) have not been paid, or no fee prescribed under Article 4(2) has been paid in respect of any of the designated States, the international application shall be considered withdrawn and the receiving Office shall so declare.

(b) If the receiving Office finds that the fee prescribed under Article 4(2) has been paid in respect of one or more (but less than all) designated States within the prescribed time limit, the designation of those States in respect of which it has not been paid within the prescribed time limit shall be considered withdrawn and the receiving Office shall so declare.

(4) If, after having accorded an international filing date to the international application, the receiving Office finds, within the prescribed time limit, that any of the requirements listed in items (i) to (iii) of Article 11(1) was not complied with at that date, the said application shall be considered withdrawn and the receiving Office shall so declare.

Article 15
The International Search

(1) Each international application shall be the subject of international search.

(2) The objective of the international search is to discover relevant prior art.

(3) International search shall be made on the basis of the claims, with due regard to the description and the drawings (if any).

(4) The International Searching Authority referred to in Article 16 shall endeavor to discover as much of the relevant prior art as its facilities permit, and shall, in any case, consult the documentation specified in the Regulations.

(5)(a) If the national law of the Contracting State so permits, the applicant who files a national application with the national Office of or acting for such State may, subject to the conditions provided for in such law, request that a search similar to an international search ("international-type search") be carried out on such application.

(b) If the national law of the Contracting State so permits, the national Office of or acting for such State may subject any national application filed with it to all international-type search.

(c) The international-type search shall be carried out by the International Searching Authority referred to in Article 16 which would be competent for an international search if the national application were an international application and were filed with the Office referred to in subparagraphs (a) and (b). If the national application is in a language which the International Searching Authority considers it is not equipped to handle, the international-type search shall be carried out on a translation prepared by the applicant in a language prescribed for international applications and which the International Searching Authority has undertaken to accept for international applications. The national application and the translation, when required, shall be presented in the form prescribed for international applications.

Article 16
The International Searching Authority

(1) International search shall be carried out by an International Searching Authority, which may be either a national Office or an intergovernmental organization, such as the International Patent Institute, whose tasks include the establishing of documentary search reports on prior art with respect to inventions which are the subject of applications.

(2) If, pending the establishment of a single International Searching Authority, there are several International Searching Authorities, each receiving Office shall, in accordance with the provisions of the applicable agreement referred to in paragraph (3)(b), specify the International Searching Authority or Authorities competent for the searching of international applications filed with such Office.

(3)(a) International Searching Authorities shall be appointed by the Assembly. Any national Office and any intergovernmental organization satisfying the requirements referred to in subparagraph (c) may be appointed as International Searching Authority.

(b) Appointment shall be conditional on the consent of the national Office or intergovernmental organization to be appointed and the conclusion of an agreement, subject to approval by the Assembly, between such Office or organization and the International Bureau. The agreement shall specify the rights and obligations of the parties, in particular, the formal undertaking by the said Office or organization to apply and observe all the common rules of international search.

(c) The Regulations prescribe the minimum requirements, particularly as to manpower and documentation, which any Office or organization must satisfy before it can be appointed and must continue to satisfy while it remains appointed.

(d) Appointment shall be for a fixed period of time and may be extended for further periods.

(e) Before the Assembly makes a decision on the appointment of any national Office or intergovernmental organization, or on the extension of its appointment, or before it allows any such appointment to lapse, the Assembly shall hear the interested Office or organization and seek the advice of the Committee for Technical Cooperation referred to in Article 56 once that Committee has been established.

Article 17
Procedure Before the International Searching Authority

(1) Procedure before the International Searching Authority shall be governed by the provisions of this Treaty, the Regulations, and the agreement which the International

Bureau shall conclude, subject to this Treaty and the Regulations, with the said Authority.

(2)(a) If the International Searching Authority considers

(i) that the international application relates to a subject matter which the International Searching Authority is not required, under the Regulations, to search, and in the particular case decides not to search, or

(ii) that the description, the claims, or the drawings, fail to comply with the prescribed requirements to such an extent that a meaningful search could not be carried out, the said Authority shall so declare and shall notify the applicant and the International Bureau that no international search report will be established.

(b) If any of the situations referred to in subparagraph (a) is found to exist in connection with certain claims only, the international search report shall so indicate in respect of such claims, whereas, for the other claims, the said report shall be established as provided in Article 18.

(3) (a) If the International Searching Authority considers that the international application does not comply with the requirement of unity of invention as set forth in the Regulations, it shall invite the applicant to pay additional fees. The International Searching Authority shall establish the international search report on those parts of the international application which relate to the invention first mentioned in the claims ("main invention") and, provided the required additional fees have been paid within the prescribed time limit, on those parts of the international application which relate to inventions in respect of which the said fees were paid.

(b) The national law of any designated State may provide that, where the national Office of that State finds the invitation, referred to in subparagraph (a), of the International Searching Authority justified and where the applicant has not paid all additional fees, those parts of the international application which consequently have not been searched shall, as far as effects in that State are concerned, be considered withdrawn unless a special fee is paid by the applicant to the national Office of that State.

Article 18
The International Search Report

(1) The international search report shall be established within the prescribed time limit and in the prescribed form.

(2) The international search report shall, as soon as it has been established, be transmitted by the International Searching Authority to the applicant and the International Bureau.

(3) The international search report or the declaration referred to in Article 17(2)(a) shall be translated as provided in the Regulations. The translations shall be prepared by or under the responsibility of the International Bureau.

Article 19
Amendment of the Claims Before the International Bureau

(1) The applicant shall, after having received the international search report, be entitled to one opportunity to amend the claims of the international application by filing amendments with the International Bureau within the prescribed time limit. He may, at the same time, file a brief statement, as provided in the Regulations, explaining the amendments and indicating any impact that such amendments might have on the description and the drawings.

(2) The amendments shall not go beyond the disclosure in the international application as filed.

(3) If the national law of any designated State permits amendments to go beyond

the said disclosure, failure to comply with paragraph (2) shall have no consequence in that State.

Article 20
Communication to Designated Offices

(1)(a) The international application, together with the international search report (including any indication referred to in Article 17(2)(b)) or the declaration referred to in Article 17(2)(a), shall be communicated to each designated Office, as provided in the Regulations, unless the designated Office waives such requirement in its entirety or in part.

(b) The communication shall include the translation (as Prescribed) of the said report or declaration.

(2) If the claims have been amended by virtue of Article 19(1), the communication shall either contain the full text of the claims both as filed and as amended or shall contain the full text of the claims as filed and specify the amendments, and shall include the statement, if any, referred to in Article 19(1).

(3) At the request of the designated Office or the applicant, the International Searching Authority shall send to the said Office or the applicant, respectively, copies of the documents cited in the international search report, as provided in the Regulations.

Article 21
International Publication

(1) The International Bureau shall publish international applications.

(2)(a) Subject to the exceptions provided for in subparagraph (b) and in Article 64(3), the international publication of the international application shall be effected promptly after the expiration of 18 months from the priority date of that application.

(b) The applicant may ask the International Bureau to publish his international application any time before the expiration of the time limit referred to in subparagraph (a). The International Bureau shall proceed accordingly, as provided in the Regulations.

(3) The international search report or the declaration referred to in Article 17(2)(a) shall be published as prescribed ln the Regulations.

(4) The language and form of the international publication and other details are governed by the Regulations.

(5) There shall be no international publication if the international application is withdrawn or is considered withdrawn before the technical preparations for publication have been completed.

(6) If the international application contains expressions or drawings which, in the opinion of the International Bureau, are contrary to morality or public order, or if, in its opinion, the international application contains disparaging statements as defined in the Regulations, it may omit such expressions, drawings, and statements, from its publications, indicating the place and number of words or drawings omitted, and furnishing, upon request, individual copies of the passages omitted.

Article 22
Copy, Translation, and Fee, to Designated Offices

(1) The applicant shall furnish a copy of the international application (unless the communication provided for in Article 20 has already taken place) and a translation thereof (as prescribed), and pay the national fee (if any), to each designated Office not later than at the expiration of 20 months from the priority date. Where the national law of the designated State requires the indication of the name of and other prescribed

data concerning the inventor but allows that these indications be furnished at a time later than that of the filing of a national application, the applicant shall, unless they were contained in the request, furnish the said indications to the national Office of or acting for that State not later than at the expiration of 20 months from the priority date.

(2) Notwithstanding the provisions of paragraph (1), where the International Searching Authority makes a declaration, under Article 17(2)(a), that no international search report will be established, the time limit for performing the acts referred to in paragraph (1) of this Article shall be two months from the date of the notification sent to the applicant of the said declaration.

(3) Any national law may, for performing the acts referred to in paragraphs (1) or (2), fix time limits which expire later than the time limit provided for in those paragraphs.

Article 23
Delaying of National Procedure

(1) No designated Office shall process or examine the international application prior to the expiration of the applicable time limit under Article 22.

(2) Notwithstanding the provisions of paragraph (1), any designated Office may, on the express request of the applicant, process or examine the international application at any time.

Article 24
Possible Loss of Effect in Designated States

(1) Subject, in case (ii) below, to the provisions of Article 25, the effect of the international application provided for in Article 11(3) shall cease in any designated State with the same consequences as the withdrawal of any national application in that State:

(i) if the applicant withdraws his international application or the designation of that State;

(ii) if the international application is considered withdrawn by virtue of Articles 12 (3), 14(1) (b), 14(3) (a), or 14(4), or if the designation of that State is considered withdrawn by virtue of Article 14 (3) (b);

(iii) if the applicant fails to perform the acts referred to in Article 22 within the applicable time limit.

(2) Notwithstanding the provisions of paragraph (1), any designated Office may maintain the effect provided for in Article 11(3) even where such effect is not required to be maintained by virtue of Article 25(2).

Article 25
Review By Designated Offices

(1)(a) Where the receiving Office has refused to accord an international filing date or has declared that the international application is considered withdrawn, or where the International Bureau has made a finding under Article 12 (3), the International Bureau shall promptly send, at the request of the applicant, copies of any document in the file to any of the designated Offices named by the applicant.

(b) Where the receiving Office has declared that the designation of any given State is considered withdrawn, the International Bureau shall promptly send, at the request of the applicant, copies of any document in the file to the national Office of such State.

(c) The request under subparagraphs (a) or (b) shall be presented within the prescribed time limit.

(2)(a) Subject to the provisions of subparagraph (b), each designated Office shall, provided that the national fee (if any) has been paid and the appropriate translation (as prescribed) has been furnished within the prescribed time limit, decide whether the refusal, declaration, or finding, referred to in paragraph (1) was justified under the provisions of this Treaty and the Regulations, and, if it finds that the refusal or declaration was the result of an error or omission on the part of the receiving Office or that the finding was the result of an error or omission on the part of the International Bureau, it shall, as far as effects in the State of the designated Office are concerned, treat the international application as if such error or omission had not occurred.

(b) Where the record copy has reached the International Bureau after the expiration of the time limit prescribed under Article 12(3) on account of any error or omission on the part of the applicant, the provisions of subparagraph (a) shall apply only under the circumstances referred to in Article 48(2).

Article 26
Opportunity to Correct Before Designated Offices

No designated Office shall reject an international application on the grounds of non-compliance with the requirements of this Treaty and the Regulations without first giving the applicant the opportunity to correct the said application to the extent and according to the procedure provided by the national law for the same or comparable situations in respect of national applications.

Article 27
National Requirements

(1) No national law shall require compliance with requirements relating to the form or contents of the international application different from or additional to those which are provided for in this Treaty and the Regulations.

(2) The provisions of paragraph (1) neither affect the application of the provisions of Article 7(2) nor preclude any national law from requiring, once the processing of the international application has started in the designated Office, the furnishing:

(i) when the applicant is a legal entity, of the name of an officer entitled to represent such legal entity,

(ii) of documents not part of the international application but which constitute proof of allegations or statements made in that application, including the confirmation of the international application by the signature of the applicant when that application, as filed, was signed by his representative or agent.

(3) Where the applicant, for the purposes of any designated State, is not qualified according to the national law of that State to file a national application because he is not the inventor, the international application may be rejected by the designated Office.

(4) Where the national law provides, in respect of the form or contents of national applications, for requirements which, from the viewpoint of applicants, are more favorable than the requirements provided for by this Treaty and the Regulations in respect of international applications, the national Office, the courts and any other competent organs of or acting for the designated State may apply the former requirements, instead of the latter requirements, to international applications, except where the applicant insists that the requirements provided for by this Treaty and the Regulations be applied to his international application.

(5) Nothing in this Treaty and the Regulations is intended to be construed as prescribing anything that would limit the freedom of each Contracting State to prescribe such substantive conditions of patentability as it desires. In particular, any provision in this Treaty and the Regulations concerning the definition of prior art is

exclusively for the purposes of the international procedure and, consequently, any Contracting State is free to apply, when determining the patentability of an invention claimed in an international application, the criteria of its national law in respect of prior art and other conditions of patentability not constituting requirements as to the form and contents of applications.

(6) The national law may require that the applicant furnish evidence in respect of any substantive condition of patentability prescribed by such law.

(7) Any receiving Office or, once the processing of the international application has started in the designated Office, that Office may apply the national law as far as it relates to any requirement that the applicant be represented by an agent having the right to represent applicants before the said Office and/or that the applicant have an address in the designated State for the purpose of receiving notifications.

(8) Nothing in this Treaty and the Regulations is intended to be construed as limiting the freedom of any Contracting State to apply measures deemed necessary for the preservation of its national security or to limit, for the protection of the general economic interests of that State, the right of its own residents or nationals to file international applications.

Article 28
Amendment of the Claims, the Description, and the Drawings, Before Designated Offices

(1) The applicant shall be given the opportunity to amend the claims, the description, and the drawings, before each designated Office within the prescribed time limit. No designated Office shall grant a patent, or refuse the grant of a patent, before such time limit has expired except with the express consent of the applicant.

(2) The amendments shall not go beyond the disclosure in the international application as filed unless the national law of the designated State permits them to go beyond the said disclosure.

(3) The amendments shall be in accordance with the national law of the designated State in all respects not provided for in this Treaty and the Regulations.

(4) Where the designated Office requires a translation of the international application, the amendments shall be in the language of the translation.

Article 29
Effects of the International Publication

(1) As far as the protection of any rights of the applicant in a designated State is concerned, the effects, in that State, of the international publication of an international application shall, subject to the provisions of paragraphs (2) to (4), be the same as those which the national law of the designated State provides for the compulsory national publication of unexamined national applications as such.

(2) If the language in which the international publication has been effected is different from the language in which publications under the national law are effected in the designated State, the said national law may provide that the effects provided for in paragraph (1) shall be applicable only from such time as:

(i) a translation into the latter language has been published as provided by the national law, or

(ii) a translation into the latter language has been made available to the public, by laying open for public inspection as provided by the national law, or

(iii) a translation into the latter language has been transmitted by the applicant to the actual or prospective unauthorized user of the invention claimed in the international application, or

(iv) both the acts described in (i) and (iii), or both the acts described in (ii) and (iii), have taken place.

(3) The national law of any designated State may provide that, where the international publication has been effected, on the request of the applicant, before the expiration of 18 months from the priority date, the effects provided for in paragraph (1) shall be applicable only from the expiration of 18 months from the priority date.

(4) The national law of any designated State may provide that the effects provided for in paragraph (1) shall be applicable only from the date on which a copy of the international application as published under Article 21 has been received in the national Office of or acting for such State. The said Office shall publish the date of receipt in its gazette as soon as possible.

Article 30
Confidential Nature of the International Application

(1)(a) Subject to the provisions of subparagraph (b), the International Bureau and the International Searching Authorities shall not allow access by any person or authority to the international application before the international publication of that application, unless requested or authorized by the applicant.

(b) The provisions of subparagraph (a) shall not apply to any transmittal to the competent International Searching Authority, to transmittals provided for under Article 13, and to communications provided for under Article 20.

(2)(a) No national Office shall allow access to the international application by third parties, unless requested or authorized by the applicant, before the earliest of the following dates:

(i) date of the international publication of the international application,

(ii) date of the receipt of the communication of the international application under Article 20,

(iii) date of the receipt of a copy of the international application under Article 22.

(b) The provisions of subparagraph (a) shall not prevent any national Office from informing third parties that it has been designated, or from publishing that fact. Such information or publication may, however, contain only the following data: identification of the receiving Office, name of the applicant, international filing date, international application number, and title of the invention.

(c) The provisions of subparagraph (a) shall not prevent any designated Office from allowing access to the international application for the purposes of the judicial authorities.

(3) The provisions of paragraph (2)(a) shall apply to any receiving Office except as far as transmittals provided for under Article 12(1) are concerned.

(4) For the purposes of this Article, the term "access" covers any means by which third parties may acquire cognizance, including individual communication and general publication, provided, however, that no national Office shall generally publish an international application or its translation before the international publication or, if international publication has not taken place by the expiration of 20 months from the priority date, before the expiration of 20 months from the said priority date.

CHAPTER II
INTERNATIONAL PRELIMINARY EXAMINATION

Article 31
Demand for International Preliminary Examination

(1) On the demand of the applicant, his international application shall be the subject of an international preliminary examination as provided in the following provisions and the Regulations.

(2)(a) Any applicant who is a resident or national, as defined in the Regulations, of a Contracting State bound by Chapter II, and whose international application has been filed with the receiving Office of or acting for such State, may make a demand for international preliminary examination.

(b) The Assembly may decide to allow persons entitled to file international applications to make a demand for international preliminary examination even if they are residents or nationals of a State not party to this Treaty or not bound by Chapter II.

(3) The demand for international preliminary examination shall be made separately from the international application. The demand shall contain the prescribed particulars and shall be in the prescribed language and form.

(4)(a) The demand shall indicate the Contracting State or States in which the applicant intends to use the results of the international preliminary examination ("elected States"). Additional Contracting States may be elected later. Election may relate only to Contracting States already designated under Article 4.

(b) Applicants referred to in paragraph (2)(a) may elect any Contracting State bound by Chapter II. Applicants referred to in paragraph (2)(b) may elect only such Contracting States bound by Chapter II as have declared that they are prepared to be elected by such applicants.

(5) The demand shall be subject to the payment of the prescribed fees within the prescribed time limit.

(6)(a) The demand shall be submitted to the competent International Preliminary Examining Authority referred to in Article 32.

(b) Any later election shall be submitted to the International Bureau.

(7) Each elected Office shall be notified of its election.

Article 32
The International Preliminary Examining Authority

(1) International preliminary examination shall be carried out by the International Preliminary Examining Authority.

(2) In the case of demands referred to in Article 31(2)(a), the receiving Office, and, in the case of demands referred to in Article 31(2)(b), the Assembly shall, in accordance with the applicable agreement between the interested International Preliminary Examining Authority or Authorities and the International Bureau, specify the International Preliminary Examining Authority or Authorities competent for the preliminary examination.

(3) The provisions of Article 16(3) shall apply, *mutatis mutandis*, in respect of International Preliminary Examining Authorities.

Article 33
The International Preliminary Examination

(1) The objective of the international preliminary examination is to formulate a preliminary and non-binding opinion on the questions whether the claimed invention

appears to be novel, to involve an inventive step (to be non-obvious), and to be industrially applicable.

(2) For the purposes of the international preliminary examination, a claimed invention shall be considered novel if it is not anticipated by the prior art as defined in the Regulations.

(3) For the purposes of the international preliminary examination, a claimed invention shall be considered to involve an inventive step if, having regard to the prior art as defined in the Regulations, it is not, at the prescribed relevant date, obvious to a person skilled in the art.

(4) For the purposes of the international preliminary examination, a claimed invention shall be considered industrially applicable if, according to its nature, it can be made or used (in the technological sense) in any kind of industry. "Industry" shall be understood in its broadest sense, as in the Paris Convention for the Protection of Industrial Property.

(5) The criteria described above merely serve the purposes of international preliminary examination. Any Contracting State may apply additional or different criteria for the purposes of deciding whether, in that State, the claimed invention is patentable or not.

(6) The international preliminary examination shall take into consideration all the documents cited in the international search report. It may take into consideration any additional documents considered to be relevant ln the particular case.

Article 34
Procedure Before the International Preliminary Examining Authority

(1) Procedure before the International Preliminary Examining Authority shall be governed by the provisions of this Treaty, the Regulations, and the agreement which the International Bureau shall conclude, subject to this Treaty and the Regulations, with the said Authority.

(2)(a) The applicant shall have a right to communicate orally and in writing with the International Preliminary Examining Authority.

(b) The applicant shall have a right to amend the claims, the description, and the drawings, in the prescribed manner and within the prescribed time limit, before the international preliminary examination report is established. The amendment shall not go beyond the disclosure in the international application as filed.

(c) The applicant shall receive at least one written opinion from the International Preliminary Examining Authority unless such Authority considers that all of the following conditions are fulfilled:

(i) the invention satisfies the criteria set forth in Article 33(1),

(ii) the international application complies with the requirements of this Treaty and the Regulations in so far as checked by that Authority,

(iii) no observations are intended to be made under Article 35(2), last sentence.

(d) The applicant may respond to the written opinion.

(3)(a) If the International Preliminary Examining Authority considers that the international application does not comply with the requirement of unity of invention as set forth in the Regulations, it may invite the applicant, at his option, to restrict the claims so as to comply with the requirement or to pay additional fees.

(b) The national law of any elected State may provide that, where the applicant chooses to restrict the claims under subparagraph (a), those parts of the international application which, as a consequence of the restriction, are not to be the subject of international preliminary examination shall, as far as effects in that State are concerned, be considered withdrawn unless a special fee is paid by the applicant to the national Office of that State.

(c) If the applicant does not comply with the invitation referred to in subparagraph (a) within the prescribed time limit, the International Preliminary Examining Authority shall establish an international preliminary examination report on those parts of the international application which relate to what appears to be the main invention and shall indicate the relevant facts in the said report. The national law of any elected State may provide that, where its national Office finds the invitation of the International Preliminary Examining Authority justified, those parts of the international application which do not relate to the main invention shall, as far as effects in that State are concerned, be considered withdrawn unless a special fee is paid by the applicant to that Office.

(4)(a) If the International Preliminary Examining Authority considers

(i) that the international application relates to a subject matter on which the International Preliminary Examining Authority is not required, under the Regulations, to carry out an international preliminary examination, and in the particular case decides not to carry out such examination, or

(ii) that the description, the claims, or the drawings, are so unclear or the claims are so inadequately supported by the description, that no meaningful opinion can be formed on the novelty, inventive step (non-obviousness), or industrial applicability, of the claimed invention, the said Authority shall not go into the questions referred to in Article 33(1) and shall inform the applicant of this opinion and the reasons therefor.

(b) If any of the situations referred to in subparagraph (a) is found to exist in, or in connection with, certain claims only, the provisions of that subparagraph shall apply only to the said claims.

Article 35
The International Preliminary Examination Report

(1) The international preliminary examination report shall be established within the prescribed time limit and in the prescribed form.

(2) The international preliminary examination report shall not contain any statement on the question whether the claimed invention is or seems to be patentable or unpatentable according to any national law. It shall state, subject to the provisions of paragraph (3), in relation to each claim, whether the claim appears to satisfy the criteria of novelty, inventive step (non-obviousness), and industrial applicability, as defined for the purposes of the international preliminary examination in Article 33(1) to (4). The statement shall be accompanied by the citation of the documents believed to support the stated conclusion with such explanations as the circumstances of the case may require. The statement shall also be accompanied by such other observations as the Regulations provide for.

(3)(a) If, at the time of establishing the international preliminary examination report, the International Preliminary Examining Authority considers that any of the situations referred to in Article 34(4)(a) exists, that report shall state this opinion and the reasons therefor. It shall not contain any statement as provided in paragraph (2).

(b) If a situation under Article 34(4)(b) is found to exist, the international preliminary examination report shall, in relation to the claims in question, contain the statement as provided in subparagraph (a), whereas, in relation to the other claims, it shall contain the statement as provided in paragraph (2).

Article 36
Transmittal, Translation, and Communication, of the International Preliminary Examination Report

(1) The international preliminary examination report, together with the prescribed annexes, shall be transmitted to the applicant and to the International Bureau.

(2)(a) The international preliminary examination report and its annexes shall be translated into the prescribed languages.

(b) Any translation of the said report shall be prepared by or under the responsibility of the International Bureau, whereas any translation of the said annexes shall be prepared by the applicant.

(3)(a) The international preliminary examination report, together with its translation (as prescribed) and its annexes (in the original language), shall be communicated by the International Bureau to each elected Office.

(b) The prescribed translation of the annexes shall be transmitted within the prescribed time limit by the applicant to the elected Offices.

(4) The provisions of Article 20(3) shall apply, *mutatis mutandis*, to copies of any document which is cited in the international preliminary examination report and which was not cited in the international search report.

Article 37
Withdrawal of Demand or Election

(1) The applicant may withdraw any or all elections.

(2) If the election of all elected States is withdrawn, the demand shall be considered withdrawn.

(3)(a) Any withdrawal shall be notified to the International Bureau.

(b) The elected Offices concerned and the International Preliminary Examining Authority concerned shall be notified accordingly by the International Bureau.

(4)(a) Subject to the provisions of subparagraph (b), withdrawal of the demand or of the election of a Contracting State shall, unless the national law of that State provides otherwise, be considered to be withdrawal of the international application as far as that State is concerned.

(b) Withdrawal of the demand or of the election shall not be considered to be withdrawal of the international application if such withdrawal is effected prior to the expiration of the applicable time limit under Article 22; however, any Contracting State may provide in its national law that the aforesaid shall apply only if its national Office has received, within the said time limit, a copy of the international application, together with a translation (as prescribed), and the national fee.

Article 38
Confidential Nature of the International Preliminary Examination

(1) Neither the International Bureau nor the International Preliminary Examining Authority shall, unless requested or authorized by the applicant, allow access within the meaning, and with the proviso, of Article 30(4) to the file of the international preliminary examination by any person or authority at any time, except by the elected Offices once the international preliminary examination report has been established.

(2) Subject to the provisions of paragraph (1) and Articles 36(1) and (3) and 37(3)(b), neither the International Bureau nor the International Preliminary Examining Authority shall, unless requested or authorized by the applicant, give information on the

issuance or non-issuance of an international preliminary examination report and on the withdrawal or non-withdrawal of the demand or of any election.

Article 39
Copy, Translation, and Fee, to Elected Offices

(1)(a) If the election of any Contracting State has been effected prior to the expiration of the 19th month from the priority date, the provisions of Article 22 shall not apply to such State and the applicant shall furnish a copy of the international application (unless the communication under Article 20 has already taken place) and a translation thereof (as prescribed), and pay the national fee (if any), to each elected Office not later than at the expiration of 25 months from the priority date.

(b) Any national law may, for performing the acts referred to in subparagraph (a), fix time limits which expire later than the time limit provided for in that subparagraph.

(2) The effect provided for in Article 11(3) shall cease in the elected State with the same consequences as the withdrawal of any national application in that State if the applicant fails to perform the acts referred to in paragraph (1)(a) within the time limit applicable under paragraph (1)(a) or (b).

(3) Any elected Office may maintain the effect provided for in Article 11(3) even where the applicant does not comply with the requirements provided for in paragraph (1)(a) or (b).

Article 40
Delaying of National Examination and Other Processing

(1) If the election of any Contracting State has been effected prior to the expiration of the 19th month from the priority date, the provisions of Article 23 shall not apply to such State and the national Office of or acting for that State shall not proceed, subject to the provisions of paragraph (2), to the examination and other processing of the international application prior to the expiration of the applicable time limit under Article 39.

(2) Notwithstanding the provisions of paragraph (1), any elected Office may, on the express request of the applicant, proceed to the examination and other processing of the international application at any time.

Article 41
Amendment of the Claims, the Description, and the Drawings, Before Elected Offices

(1) The applicant shall be given the opportunity to amend the claims, the description, and the drawings, before each elected Office within the prescribed time limit. No elected Office shall grant a patent, or refuse the grant of a patent, before such time limit has expired, except with the express consent of the applicant.

(2) The amendments shall not go beyond the disclosure in the international application as filed, unless the national law of the elected State permits them to go beyond the said disclosure.

(3) The amendments shall be in accordance with the national law of the elected State in all respects not provided for in this Treaty and the Regulations.

(4) Where an elected Office requires a translation of the international application, the amendments shall be in the language of the translation.

Article 42
Results of National Examination in Elected Offices

No elected Office receiving the international preliminary examination report may require that the applicant furnish copies, or information on the contents, of any papers connected with the examination relating to the same international application in any other elected Office.

CHAPTER III
COMMON PROVISIONS

Article 43
Seeking Certain Kinds of Protection

In respect of any designated or elected State whose law provides for the grant of inventors' certificates, utility certificates, utility models, patents or certificates of addition, inventors' certificates of addition, or utility certificates of addition, the applicant may indicate, as prescribed in the Regulations, that his international application is for the grant, as far as that State is concerned, of an inventor's certificate, a utility certificate, or a utility model, rather than a patent, or that it is for the grant of a patent or certificate of addition, an inventor's certificate of addition, or a utility certificate of addition, and the ensuing effect shall be governed by the applicant's choice. For the purposes of this Article and any Rule thereunder, Article 2(ii) shall not apply.

Article 44
Seeking Two Kinds of Protection

In respect of any designated or elected State whose law permits an application, while being for the grant of a patent or one of the other kinds of protection referred to in Article 43, to be also for the grant of another of the said kinds of protection, the applicant may indicate, as prescribed in the Regulations, the two kinds of protection he is seeking, and the ensuing effect shall be governed by the applicant's indications. For the purposes of this Article, Article 2(ii) shall not apply.

Article 45
Regional Patent Treaties

(1) Any treaty providing for the grant of regional patents ("regional patent treaty"), and giving to all persons who, according to Article 9, are entitled to file international applications the right to file applications for such patents, may provide that international applications designating or electing a State party to both the regional patent treaty and the present Treaty may be filed as applications for such patents.

(2) The national law of the said designated or elected State may provide that any designation or election of such State in the international application shall have the effect of an indication of the wish to obtain a regional patent under the regional patent treaty.

Article 46
Incorrect Translation of the International Application

If, because of an incorrect translation of the international application, the scope of any patent granted on that application exceeds the scope of the international application in its original language, the competent authorities of the Contracting State concerned may accordingly and retroactively limit the scope of the patent, and declare it null and void to the extent that its scope has exceeded the scope of the international application in its original language.

Article 47
Time Limits

(1) The details for computing time limits referred to in this Treaty are governed by the Regulations.

(2)(a) All time limits fixed in Chapters I and II of this Treaty may, outside any revision under Article 60, be modified by a decision of the Contracting States.

(b) Such decisions shall be made in the Assembly or through voting by correspondence and must be unanimous.

(c) The details of the procedure are governed by the Regulations.

Article 48
Delay in Meeting Certain Time Limits

(1) Where any time limit fixed in this Treaty or the Regulations is not met because of interruption in the mail service or unavoidable loss or delay in the mail, the time limit shall be deemed to be met in the cases and subject to the proof and other conditions prescribed in the Regulations.

(2)(a) Any Contracting State shall, as far as that State is concerned, excuse, for reasons admitted under its national law, any delay in meeting any time limit.

(b) Any Contracting State may, as far as that State is concerned, excuse, for reasons other than those referred to in subparagraph (a), any delay in meeting any time limit.

Article 49
Right to Practice Before International Authorities

Any attorney, patent agent, or other person, having the right to practice before the national Office with which the international application was filed, shall be entitled to practice before the International Bureau and the competent International Searching Authority and competent International Preliminary Examining Authority in respect of that application.

CHAPTER IV
TECHNICAL SERVICES

Article 50
Patent Information Services

(1) The International Bureau may furnish services by providing technical and any other pertinent information available to lt on the basis of published documents, primarily patents and published applications (referred to in this Article as "the information services").

(2) The International Bureau may provide these information services either directly or through one or more International Searching Authorities or other national or international specialized institutions, with which the International Bureau may reach agreement.

(3) The information services shall be operated in a way particularly facilitating the acquisition by Contracting States which are developing countries of technical knowledge and technology, including available published know-how.

(4) The information services shall be available to Governments of Contracting States and their nationals and residents. The Assembly may decide to make these services available also to others.

(5)(a) Any service to Governments of Contracting States shall be furnished at cost, provided that, when the Government is that of a Contracting State which is a developing country, the service shall be furnished below cost. If the difference can be covered from profit made on services furnished to others than Governments of Contracting States or from the sources referred to in Article 51(4).

(b) The cost referred to in subparagraph (a) is to be understood as cost over and above costs normally incident to the performance of the services of a national Office or the obligations of an International Searching Authority.

(6) The details concerning the implementation of the provisions of this Article shall be governed by decisions of the Assembly and, within the limits to be fixed by the Assembly, such working groups as the Assembly may set up for that purpose.

(7) The Assembly shall, when it considers it necessary, recommend methods of providing financing supplementary to those referred to in paragraph (5).

Article 51
Technical Assistance

(1) The Assembly shall establish a Committee for Technical Assistance (referred to in this Article as "the Committee").

(2)(a) The members of the Committee shall be elected among the Contracting States, with due regard to the representation of developing countries.

(b) The Director General shall, on his own initiative or at the request of the Committee, invite representatives of intergovernmental organizations concerned with technical assistance to developing countries to participate in the work of the Committee.

(3)(a) The task of the Committee shall be to organize and supervise technical assistance for Contracting States which are developing countries in developing their patent systems individually or on a regional basis.

(b) The technical assistance shall comprise, among other things, the training of specialists, the loaning of experts, and the supply of equipment both for demonstration and for operational purposes.

(4) The International Bureau shall seek to enter into agreements, on the one hand, with international financing organizations and intergovernmental organizations, particularly the United Nations, the agencies of the United Nations, and the Specialized Agencies connected with the United Nations concerned with technical assistance, and, on the other hand, with the Governments of the States receiving the technical assistance, for the financing of projects pursuant to this Article.

(5) The details concerning the implementation of the provisions of this Article shall be governed by decisions of the Assembly and, within the limits to be fixed by the Assembly, such working groups as the Assembly may set up for that purpose.

Article 52
Relations with Other Provisions of the Treaty

Nothing in this Chapter shall affect the financial provisions contained in any other Chapter of this Treaty. Such provisions are not applicable to the present Chapter or to its implementation.

[*Article 53 -Article 58* Omitted]

CHAPTER VI
DISPUTES

Article 59
Disputes

Subject to Article 64(5), any dispute between two or more Contracting States concerning the interpretation or application of this Treaty or the Regulations, not settled by negotiation, may, by any one of the States concerned, be brought before the International Court of Justice by application in conformity with the Statute of the Court unless the States concerned agree on some other method of settlement. The Contracting State bringing the dispute before the Court shall inform the International Bureau; the International Bureau shall bring the matter to the attention of the other Contracting States.

CHAPTER VII
REVISION AND AMENDMENT

Article 60
Revision of the Treaty

(1) This Treaty may be revised from time to time by a special conference of the Contracting States.

(2) The convocation of any revision conference shall be decided by the Assembly.

(3) Any intergovernmental organization appointed as International Searching or Preliminary Examining Authority shall be admitted as observer to any revision conference.

(4) Articles 53(5), (9) and (11), 54, 55(4) to (8), 56, and 57, may be amended either by a revision conference or according to the provisions of Article 61.

Article 61
Amendment of Certain Provisions of the Treaty

(1)(a) Proposals for the amendment of Articles 53(5), (9) and (11), 54, 55(4) to (8), 56, and 57, may be initiated by any State member of the Assembly, by the Executive Committee, or by the Director General.

(b) Such proposals shall be communicated by the Director General to the Contracting States at least six months in advance of their consideration by the Assembly.

(2)(a) Amendments to the Articles referred to in paragraph (1) shall be adopted by the Assembly.

(b) Adoption shall require three-fourths of the votes cast.

(3)(a) Any amendment to the Articles referred to in paragraph (1) shall enter into force one month after written notifications of acceptance, effected in accordance with their respective constitutional processes, have been received by the Director General from three-fourths of the States members of the Assembly at the time it adopted the amendment.

(b) Any amendment to the said Articles thus accepted shall bind all the States which are members of the Assembly at the time the amendment enters into force, provided that any amendment increasing the financial obligations of the Contracting States shall bind only those States which have notified their acceptance of such amendment.

(c) Any amendment accepted in accordance with the provisions of subparagraph

(a) shall bind all States which become members of the Assembly after the date on which the amendment entered into force in accordance with the provisions of subparagraph (a).

CHAPTER VIII
FINAL PROVISIONS

Article 62
Becoming Party to the Treaty

(1) Any State member of the International Union for the Protection of Industrial Property may become party to this Treaty by:

(i) signature followed by the deposit of an instrument of ratification, or

(ii) deposit of an instrument of accession.

(2) Instruments of ratification or accession shall be deposited with the Director General.

(3) The provisions of Article 24 of the Stockholm Act of the Paris Convention for the Protection of Industrial Property shall apply to this Treaty.

(4) Paragraph (3) shall in no way be understood as implying the recognition or tacit acceptance by a Contracting State of the factual situation concerning a territory to which this Treaty is made applicable by another Contracting State by virtue of the said paragraph.

Article 63
Entry into Force of the Treaty

(1)(a) Subject to the provisions of paragraph (3), this Treaty shall enter into force three months after eight States have deposited their instruments of ratification or accession, provided that at least four of those States each fulfill any of the following conditions:

(i) the number of applications filed in the State has exceeded 40,000 according to the most recent annual statistics published by the International Bureau,

(ii) the nationals or residents of the State have filed at least 1,000 applications ln one foreign country according to the most recent annual statistics published by the International Bureau,

(iii) the national Office of the State has received at least 10,000 applications from nationals or residents of foreign countries according to the most recent annual statistics published by the International Bureau.

(b) For the purposes of this paragraph, the term "applications" does not include applications for utility models.

(2) Subject to the provisions of paragraph (3), any State which does not become party to this Treaty upon entry into force under paragraph (1) shall become bound by this Treaty three months after the date on which such State has deposited its instrument of ratification or accession.

(3) The provisions of Chapter II and the corresponding provisions of the Regulations annexed to this Treaty shall become applicable, however, only on the date on which three States each of which fulfill at least one of the three requirements specified in paragraph (1) have become party to this Treaty without declaring, as provided in Article 64(1), that they do not intend to be bound by the provisions of Chapter II. That date shall not, however, be prior to that of the initial entry into force under paragraph (1).

Article 64
Reservations

(1)(a) Any State may declare that it shall not be bound by the provisions of Chapter II.

(b) States making a declaration under subparagraph (a) shall not be bound by the provisions of Chapter II and the corresponding provisions of the Regulations.

(2)(a) Any State not having made a declaration under paragraph (1)(a) may declare that:

(i) it shall not be bound by the provisions of Article 39(1) with respect to the furnishing of a copy of the international application and a translation thereof (as prescribed),

(ii) the obligation to delay national processing, as provided for under Article 40, shall not prevent publication, by or through its national Office, of the international application or a translation thereof, it being understood, however, that it is not exempted from the limitations provided for in Articles 30 and 38.

(b) States making such a declaration shall be bound accordingly.

(3)(a) Any State may declare that, as far as it is concerned, international publication of international applications is not required.

(b) Where, at the expiration of 18 months from the priority date, the international application contains the designation only of such States as have made declarations under subparagraph (a), the international application shall not be published by virtue of Article 21(2).

(c) Where the provisions of subparagraph (b) apply, the international application shall nevertheless be published by the International Bureau:

(i) at the request of the applicant, as provided in the Regulations,

(ii) when a national application or a patent based on the international application is published by or on behalf of the national Office of any designated State having made a declaration under subparagraph (a), promptly after such publication but not before the expiration of 18 months from the priority date.

(4)(a) Any State whose national law provides for prior art effect of its patents as from a date before publication, but does not equate for prior art purposes the priority date claimed under the Paris Convention for the Protection of Industrial Property to the actual filing date in that State, may declare that the filing outside that State of an international application designating that State is not equated to an actual filing in that State for prior art purposes.

(b) Any State making a declaration under subparagraph (a) shall to that extent not be bound by the provisions of Article 11(3).

(c) Any State making a declaration under subparagraph (a) shall, at the same time, state in writing the date from which, and the conditions under which, the prior art effect of any international application designating that State becomes effective in that State. This statement may be modified at any time by notification addressed to the Director General.

(5) Each State may declare that it does not consider itself bound by Article 59. With regard to any dispute between any Contracting State having made such a declaration and any other Contracting State, the provisions of Article 59 shall not apply.

(6)(a) Any declaration made under this Article shall be made in writing. It may be made at the time of signing this Treaty, at the time of depositing the instrument of ratification or accession, or, except in the case referred to in paragraph (5), at any later time by notification addressed to the Director General. In the case of the said notification, the declaration shall take effect six months after the day on which the

Director General has received the notification, and shall not affect international applications filed prior to the expiration of the said six-month period.

(b) Any declaration made under this Article may be withdrawn at any time by notification addressed to the Director General. Such withdrawal shall take effect three months after the day on which the Director General has received the notification and, in the case of the withdrawal of a declaration made under paragraph (3), shall not affect international applications filed prior to the expiration of the said three-month period.

(7) No reservations to this Treaty other than the reservations under paragraphs (1) to (5) are permitted.

Article 65
Gradual Application

(1) If the agreement with any International Searching or Preliminary Examining Authority provides, transitionally, for limits on the number or kind of international applications that such Authority undertakes to process, the Assembly shall adopt the measures necessary for the gradual application of this Treaty and the Regulations in respect of given categories of international applications. This provision shall also apply to requests for an international-type search under Article 15(5).

(2) The Assembly shall fix the dates from which, subject to the provision of paragraph (1), international applications may be filed and demands for international preliminary examination may be submitted. Such dates shall not be later than six months after this Treaty has entered into force according to the provisions of Article 63(1), or after Chapter II has become applicable under Article 63(3), respectively.

Article 66
Denunciation

(1) Any Contracting State may denounce this Treaty by notification addressed to the Director General.

(2) Denunciation shall take effect six months after receipt of the said notification by the Director General. It shall not affect the effects of the international application in the denouncing State if the international application was filed, and, where the denouncing State has been elected, the election was made, prior to the expiration of the said six-month period.

[*Article 67 - Article 69* Omitted]

IN WITNESS WHEREOF, the undersigned, being duly authorized thereto, have signed this Treaty.

DONE at Washington, on June 19, 1970.

APPENDIX VII

EUROPEAN COMMUNITIES TRADEMARK HARMONIZATION DIRECTIVE

FIRST COUNCIL DIRECTIVE of 21 December 1988 to approximate the laws of the Member States relating to trade marks
(89/104/EEC)

THE COUNCIL OF THE EUROPEAN COMMUNITIES,

Having regard to the Treaty establishing the European Economic Community, and in particular Article 100a thereof,

Having regard to the proposal from the Commission,

In cooperation with the European Parliament,

Having regard to the opinion of the Economic and Social Committee,

Whereas the trade mark laws at present applicable in the Member States contain disparities which may impede the free movement of goods and freedom to provide services and may distort competition within the common market; whereas it is therefore necessary, in view of the establishment and functioning of the internal market, to approximate the laws of Member States;

Whereas it is important not to disregard the solutions and advantages which the Community trade mark system may afford to undertakings wishing to acquire trade marks;

Whereas it does not appear to be necessary at present to undertake full-scale approximation of the trade mark laws of the Member States and it will be sufficient if approximation is limited to those national provisions of law which most directly affect the functioning of the internal market;

Whereas the Directive does not deprive the Member States of the right to continue to protect trade marks acquired through use but takes them into account only in regard to the relationship between them and trade marks acquired by registration;

Whereas Member States also remain free to fix the provisions of procedure concerning the registration, the revocation and the invalidity of trade marks acquired by registration; whereas they can, for example, determine the form of trade mark registration and invalidity procedures, decide whether earlier rights should be invoked either in the registration procedure or in the invalidity procedure or in both and, if they allow earlier rights to be invoked in the registration procedure, have an opposition procedure or an ex officio examination procedure or both; whereas Member States remain free to determine the effects of revocation or invalidity of trade marks;

Whereas this Directive does not exclude the application to trade marks of provisions of law of the Member States other than trade mark law, such as the provisions relating to unfair competition, civil liability or consumer protection;

Whereas attainment of the objectives at which this approximation of laws is aiming requires that the conditions for obtaining and continuing to hold a registered trade mark are, in general, identical in all Member States; whereas, to this end, it is necessary to list examples of signs which may constitute a trade mark, provided that such signs are capable of distinguishing the goods or services of one undertaking from those of other undertakings; whereas the grounds for refusal or invalidity concerning the trade mark itself, for example, the absence of any distinctive character, or concerning conflicts between the trade mark and earlier rights, are to be listed in an exhaustive manner, even if some of these grounds are listed as an option for the Member States which will therefore be able to maintain or introduce those grounds in their legislation; whereas Member States will be able to maintain or introduce into their legislation grounds of refusal or invalidity linked to conditions for obtaining and continuing to hold a trade mark for which there is no provision of approximation, concerning, for example, the eligibility for the grant of a trade mark, the renewal of the trade mark or rules on fees, or related to the non-compliance with procedural rules;

Whereas in order to reduce the total number of trade marks registered and protected in the Community and, consequently, the number of conflicts which arise between them, it is essential to require that registered trade marks must actually be used or, if not used, be subject to revocation; whereas it is necessary to provide that a trade mark cannot be invalidated on the basis of the existence of a non-used earlier trade mark, while the Member States remain free to apply the same principle in respect of the registration of a trade mark or to provide that a trade mark may not be successfully invoked in infringement proceedings if it is established as a result of a plea that the trade mark could be revoked; whereas in all these cases it is up to the Member States to establish the applicable rules of procedure;

Whereas it is fundamental, in order to facilitate the free circulation of goods and services, to ensure that henceforth registered trade marks enjoy the same protection under the legal systems of all the Member States; whereas this should however not prevent the Member States from granting at their option extensive protection to those trade marks which have a reputation;

Whereas the protection afforded by the registered trade mark, the function of which is in particular to guarantee the trade mark as an indication of origin, is absolute in the case of identity between the mark and the sign and goods or services; whereas the protection applies also in case of similarity between the mark and the sign and the goods or services; whereas it is indispensable to give an interpretation of the concept of similarity in relation to the likelihood of confusion; whereas the likelihood of confusion, the appreciation of which depends on numerous elements and, in particular, on the recognition of the trade mark on the market, of the association which can be made with the used or registered sign, of the degree of similarity between the trade mark and the sign and between the goods or services identified, constitutes the specific condition for such protection; whereas the ways in which likelihood of confusion may be established, and in particular the onus of proof, are a matter for national procedural rules which are not prejudiced by the Directive;

Whereas it is important, for reasons of legal certainty and without inequitably prejudicing the interests of a proprietor of an earlier trade mark, to provide that the latter may no longer request a declaration of invalidity nor may he oppose the use of a trade mark subsequent to his own of which he has knowingly tolerated the use for a substantial length of time, unless the application for the subsequent trade mark was made in bad faith;

Whereas all Member States of the Community are bound by the Paris Convention for the Protection of Industrial Property; whereas it is necessary that the provisions of this Directive are entirely consistent with those of the Paris Convention; whereas the obligations of the Member States resulting from this Convention are not affected by this Directive; whereas, where appropriate, the second subparagraph of Article 234 of the Treaty is applicable,

HAS ADOPTED THIS DIRECTIVE:

Article 1
Scope

This Directive shall apply to every trade mark in respect of goods or services which is the subject of registration or of an application in a Member State for registration as an individual trade mark, a collective mark or a guarantee or certification mark, or which is the subject of a registration or an application for registration in the Benelux Trade Mark Office or of an international registration having effect in a Member State.

Article 2
Signs of which a trade mark may consist

A trade mark may consist of any sign capable of being represented graphically, particularly words, including personal names, designs, letters, numerals, the shape of goods or of their packaging, provided that such signs are capable of distinguishing the goods or services of one undertaking from those of other undertakings.

Article 3
Grounds for refusal or invalidity

1. The following shall not be registered or if registered shall be liable to be declared invalid:

(a) signs which cannot constitute a trade mark;

(b) trade marks which are devoid of any distinctive character;

(c) trade marks which consist exclusively of signs or indications which may serve, in trade, to designate the kind, quality, quantity, intended purpose, value, geographical origin, or the time of production of the goods or of rendering of the service, or other characteristics of the goods or service;

(d) trade marks which consist exclusively of signs or indications which have become customary in the current language or in the bona fide and established practices of the trade;

(e) signs which consist exclusively of:

- the shape which results from the nature of the goods themselves, or
- the shape of goods which is necessary to obtain a technical result, or
- the shape which gives substantial value to the goods;

(f) trade marks which are contrary to public policy or to accepted principles of morality;

(g) trade marks which are of such a nature as to deceive the public, for instance as to the nature, quality or geographical origin of the goods or service;

(h) trade marks which have not been authorized by the competent authorities and are to be refused or invalidated pursuant to Article 6ter of the Paris Convention for the Protection of Industrial Property, hereinafter referred to as the "Paris Convention."

2. Any Member State may provide that a trade mark shall not be registered or, if registered, shall be liable to be declared invalid where and to the extent that:

(a) the use of that trade mark may be prohibited pursuant to provisions of law other than trade mark law of the Member State concerned or of the Community;

(b) the trade mark covers a sign of high symbolic value, in particular a religious symbol;

(c) the trade mark includes badges, emblems and escutcheons other than those covered by Article 6ter of the Paris Convention and which are of public interest, unless the consent of the appropriate authorities to its registration has been given in conformity with the legislation of the Member State;

(d) the application for registration of the trade mark was made in bad faith by the applicant.

3. A trade mark shall not be refused registration or be declared invalid in accordance with paragraph 1(b), (c) or (d) if, before the date of application for registration and following the use which has been made of it, it has acquired a distinctive character. Any Member State may in addition provide that this provision shall also apply where

the distinctive character was acquired after the date of application for registration or after the date of registration.

4. Any Member State may provide that, by derogation from the preceding paragraphs, the grounds of refusal of registration or invalidity in force in that State prior to the date on which the provisions necessary to comply with this Directive enter into force, shall apply to trade marks for which application has been made prior to that date.

Article 4
Further grounds for refusal or invalidity concerning conflicts with earlier rights

1. A trade mark shall not be registered or, if registered, shall be liable to be declared invalid:

(a) if it is identical with an earlier trade mark, and the goods or services for which the trade mark is applied for or is registered are identical with the goods or services for which the earlier trade mark is protected;

(b) if because of its identity with, or similarity to, the earlier trade mark and the identity or similarity of the goods or services covered by the trade marks, there exists a likelihood of confusion on the part of the public, which includes the likelihood of association with the earlier trade mark.

2. "Earlier trade marks" within the meaning of paragraph 1 means:

(a) trade marks of the following kinds with a date of application for registration which is earlier than the date of application for registration of the trade mark, taking account, where appropriate, of the priorities claimed in respect of those trade marks:

(i) Community trade marks;

(ii) trade marks registered in the Member State or, in the case of Belgium, Luxembourg or the Netherlands, at the Benelux Trade Mark Office;

(iii) trade marks registered under international arrangements which have effect in the Member State;

(b) Community trade marks which validly claim seniority, in accordance with the Regulation on the Community trade mark, from a trade mark referred to in (a) (ii) and (iii), even when the latter trade mark has been surrendered or allowed to lapse;

(c) applications for the trade marks referred to in (a) and (b), subject to their registration;

(d) trade marks which, on the date of application for registration of the trade mark, or, where appropriate, of the priority claimed in respect of the application for registration of the trade mark, are well known in a Member State, in the sense in which the words "well known" are used in Article 6bis of the Paris Convention;

3. A trade mark shall furthermore not be registered or, if registered, shall be liable to be declared invalid if it is identical with, or similar to, an earlier Community trade mark within the meaning of paragraph 2 and is to be, or has been, registered for goods or services which are not similar to those for which the earlier Community trade mark is registered, where the earlier Community trade mark has a reputation in the Community and where the use of the later trade mark without due cause would take unfair advantage of, or be detrimental to, the distinctive character or the repute of the earlier Community trade mark.

4. Any Member State may furthermore provide that a trade mark shall not be registered or, if registered, shall be liable to be declared invalid where, and to the extent that:

(a) the trade mark is identical with, or similar to, an earlier national trade mark within the meaning of paragraph 2 and is to be, or has been, registered for goods or services which are not similar to those for which the earlier trade mark is registered, where the earlier trade mark has a reputation in the Member State concerned and where the use of the later trade mark without due cause would take unfair advantage of, or be detrimental to, the distinctive character or the repute of the earlier trade mark;

(b) rights to a non-registered trade mark or to another sign used in the course of trade were acquired prior to the date of application for registration of the subsequent trade mark, or the date of the priority claimed for the application for registration of the subsequent trade mark and that non-registered trade mark or other sign confers on its proprietor the right to prohibit the use of a subsequent trade mark;

(c) the use of the trade mark may be prohibited by virtue of an earlier right other than the rights referred to in paragraphs 2 and 4 (b) and in particular:

(i) a right to a name;
(ii) a right of personal portrayal;
(iii) a copyright;
(iv) an industrial property right;

(d) the trade mark is identical with, or similar to, an earlier collective trade mark conferring a right which expired within a period of a maximum of three years preceding application;

(e) the trade mark is identical with, or similar to, an earlier guarantee or certification mark conferring a right which expired within a period preceding application the length of which is fixed by the Member State;

(f) the trade mark is identical with, or similar to, an earlier trade mark which was registered for identical or similar goods or services and conferred on them a right which has expired for failure to renew within a period of a maximum of two years preceding application, unless the proprietor of the earlier trade mark gave his agreement for the registration of the later mark or did not use his trade mark;

(g) the trade mark is liable to be confused with a mark which was in use abroad on the filing date of the application and which is still in use there, provided that at the date of the application the applicant was acting in bad faith.

5. The Member States may permit that in appropriate circumstances registration need not be refused or the trade mark need not be declared invalid where the proprietor of the earlier trade mark or other earlier right consents to the registration of the later trade mark.

6. Any Member State may provide that, by derogation from paragraphs 1 to 5, the grounds for refusal of registration or invalidity in force in that State prior to the date on which the provisions necessary to comply with this Directive enter into force, shall apply to trade marks for which application has been made prior to that date.

Article 5
Rights conferred by a trade mark

1. The registered trade mark shall confer on the proprietor exclusive rights therein. The proprietor shall be entitled to prevent all third parties not having his consent from using in the course of trade:

(a) any sign which is identical with the trade mark in relation to goods or services which are identical with those for which the trade mark is registered;

(b) any sign where, because of its identity with, or similarity to, the trade mark and the identity or similarity of the goods or services covered by the trade mark and the sign, there exists a likelihood of confusion on the part of the public, which includes the likelihood of association between the sign and the trade mark.

2. Any Member State may also provide that the proprietor shall be entitled to

prevent all third parties not having his consent from using in the course of trade any sign which is identical with, or similar to, the trade mark in relation to goods or services which are not similar to those for which the trade mark is registered, where the latter has a reputation in the Member State and where use of that sign without due cause takes unfair advantage of, or is detrimental to, the distinctive character or the repute of the trade mark.

3. The following, inter alia, may be prohibited under paragraphs 1 and 2:

(a) affixing the sign to the goods or to the packaging thereof;

(b) offering the goods, or putting them on the market or stocking them for these purposes under that sign, or offering or supplying services thereunder;

(c) importing or exporting the goods under the sign;

(d) using the sign on business papers and in advertising.

4. Where, under the law of the Member State, the use of a sign under the conditions referred to in 1(b) or 2 could not be prohibited before the date on which the provisions necessary to comply with this Directive entered into force in the Member State concerned, the rights conferred by the trade mark may not be relied on to prevent the continued use of the sign.

5. Paragraphs 1 to 4 shall not affect provisions in any Member State relating to the protection against the use of a sign other than for the purposes of distinguishing goods or services, where use of that sign without due cause takes unfair advantage of, or is detrimental to, the distinctive character or the repute of the trade mark.

Article 6
Limitation of the effects of a trade mark

1. The trade mark shall not entitle the proprietor to prohibit a third party from using, in the course of trade,

(a) his own name or address;

(b) indications concerning the kind, quality, quantity, intended purpose, value, geographical origin, the time of production of goods or of rendering of the service, or other characteristics of goods or services;

(c) the trade mark where it is necessary to indicate the intended purpose of a product or service, in particular as accessories or spare parts; provided he uses them in accordance with honest practices in industrial or commercial matters.

2. The trade mark shall not entitle the proprietor to prohibit a third party from using, in the course of trade, an earlier right which only applies in a particular locality if that right is recognized by the laws of the Member State in question and within the limits of the territory in which it is recognized.

Article 7
Exhaustion of the rights conferred by a trade mark

1. The trade mark shall not entitle the proprietor to prohibit its use in relation to goods which have been put on the market in the Community under that trade mark by the proprietor or with his consent.

2. Paragraph 1 shall not apply where there exist legitimate reasons for the proprietor to oppose further commercialization of the goods, especially where the condition of the goods is changed or impaired after they have been put on the market.

Article 8
Licensing

1. A trade mark may be licensed for some of all of the goods or services for which

it is registered and for the whole or part of the Member State concerned. A license may be exclusive or non-exclusive.

2. The proprietor of a trade mark may invoke the rights conferred by that trade mark against a licensee who contravenes any provision in his licensing contract with regard to its duration, the form covered by the registration in which the trade mark may be used, the scope of the goods or services for which the licence is granted, the territory in which the trade mark may be affixed, or the quality of the goods manufactured or of the services provided by the licensee.

Article 9
Limitation in consequence of acquiescence

1. Where, in a Member State, the proprietor of an earlier trade mark as referred to in Article 4(2) has acquiesced, for a period of five successive years, in the use of a later trade mark registered in that Member State while being aware of such use, he shall no longer be entitled on the basis of the earlier trade mark either to apply for a declaration that the later trade mark is invalid or to oppose the use of the later trade mark in respect of the goods or services for which the later trade mark has been used, unless registration of the later trade mark was applied for in bad faith.

2. Any Member State may provide that paragraph 1 shall apply *mutatis mutandis* to the proprietor of an earlier trade mark referred to in Article 4(4)(a) or an other earlier right referred to in Article 4(4)(b) or (c).

3. In the cases referred to in paragraphs 1 and 2, the proprietor of a later registered trade mark shall not be entitled to oppose the use of the earlier right, even though that right may no longer be invoked against the later trade mark.

Article 10
Use of trade marks

1. If, within a period of five years following the date of the completion of the registration procedure, the proprietor has not put the trade mark to genuine use in the Member State in connection with the goods or services in respect of which it is registered, or if such use has been suspended during an uninterrupted period of five years, the trade mark shall be subject to the sanctions provided for in this Directive, unless there are proper reasons for non-use.

2. The following shall also constitute use within the meaning of paragraph 1:

(a) use of the trade mark in a form differing in elements which do not alter the distinctive character of the mark in the form in which it was registered;

(b) affixing of the trade mark to goods or to the packaging thereof in the Member State concerned solely for export purposes.

3. Use of the trade mark with the consent of the proprietor or by any person who has authority to use a collective mark or a guarantee or certification mark shall be deemed to constitute use by the proprietor.

4. In relation to trade marks registered before the date on which the provisions necessary to comply with this Directive enter into force in the Member State concerned:

(a) where a provision in force prior to that date attaches sanctions to non-use of a trade mark during an uninterrupted period, the relevant period of five years mentioned in paragraph 1 shall be deemed to have begun to run at the same time as any period of non-use which is already running at that date;

(b) where there is no use provision in force prior to that date, the periods of five years mentioned in paragraph 1 shall be deemed to run from that date at the earliest.

Article 11
Sanctions for non use of a trade mark in legal or administrative proceedings

1. A trade mark may not be declared invalid on the ground that there is an earlier conflicting trade mark if the latter does not fulfil the requirements of use set out in Article 10(1), (2) and (3) or in Article 10(4), as the case may be.

2. Any Member State may provide the registration of a trade mark may not be refused on the ground that there is an earlier conflicting trade mark if the latter does not fulfil the requirements of use set out in Article 10(1), (2) and (3) or in Article 10(4), as the case may be.

3. Without prejudice to the application of Article 12, where a counter-claim for revocation is made, any Member State may provide that a trade mark may not be successfully invoked in infringement proceedings if it is established as a result of a plea that the trade mark could be revoked pursuant to Article 12(1).

4. If the earlier trade mark has been used in relation to part only of the goods or services for which it is registered, it shall, for purposes of applying paragraphs 1, 2 and 3, be deemed to be registered in respect only of that part of the goods or services.

Article 12
Grounds for revocation

1. A trade mark shall be liable to revocation if, within a continuous period of five years, it has not been put to genuine use in the Member State in connection with the goods or services in respect of which it is registered, and there are no proper reasons for non-use; however, no person may claim that the proprietor's rights in a trade mark should be revoked where, during the interval between expiry of the five-year period and filing of the application for revocation, genuine use of the trade mark has been started or resumed; the commencement or resumption of use within a period of three months preceding the filing of the application for revocation months preceding the filing of the application for revocation which began at the earliest on expiry of the continuous period of five years of non-use, shall, however, be disregarded where preparations for the commencement or resumption occur only after the proprietor becomes aware that the application for revocation may be filed.

2. A trade mark shall also be liable to revocation if, after the date on which it was registered,

(a) in consequence of acts or inactivity of the proprietor, it has become the common name in the trade for a product or service in respect of which it is registered;

(b) in consequence of the use made of it by the proprietor of the trade mark or with his consent in respect of the goods or services for which it is registered, it is liable to mislead the public, particularly as to the nature, quality or geographical origin of those goods or services.

Article 13
Grounds for refusal or revocation or invalidity relating to only some of the goods or services

Where grounds for refusal of registration or for revocation or invalidity of a trade mark exist in respect of only some of the goods or services for which that trade mark has been applied for or registered, refusal of registration or revocation or invalidity shall cover those goods or services only.

Article 14
Establishment a posteriori *of invalidity or revocation of a trade mark*

Where the seniority of an earlier trade mark which has been surrendered or allowed to lapse, is claimed for a Community trade mark, the invalidity or revocation of the earlier trade mark may be established *a posteriori*.

Article 15
Special provisions in respect of collective marks, guarantee marks and certification marks

1. Without prejudice to Article 4, Member States whose laws authorize the registration of collective marks or of guarantee or certification marks may provide that such marks shall not be registered, or shall be revoked or declared invalid, on grounds additional to those specified in Articles 3 and 12 where the function of those marks so requires.

2. By way of derogation from Article 3 (1) (c), Member States may provide that signs or indications which may serve, in trade, to designate the geographical origin of the goods or services may constitute collective, guarantee or certification marks. Such a mark does not entitle the proprietor to prohibit a third party from using in the course of trade such signs or indications, provided he uses them in accordance with honest practices in industrial or commercial matters; in particular, such a mark may not be invoked against a third party who is entitled to use a geographical name.

Article 16
National provisions to be adopted pursuant to this Directive

1. The Member States shall bring into force the laws, regulations and administrative provisions necessary to comply with this Directive not later than 28 December 1991. They shall immediately inform the Commission thereof.

2. Acting on a proposal from the Commission, the Council, acting by qualified majority, may defer the date referred to in paragraph 1 until 31 December 1992 at the latest.

3. Member States shall communicate to the Commission the text of the main provisions of national law which they adopt in the field governed by this Directive.

Article 17
Addressees

This Directive is addressed to the Member States.

Done at Brussels, 21 December 1988.

APPENDIX VIII

NORTH AMERICAN FREE TRADE AGREEMENT (NAFTA)

Article 1701
Nature and Scope of Obligations

1. Each Party shall provide in its territory to the nationals of another Party adequate and effective protection and enforcement of intellectual property rights, while ensuring that measures to enforce intellectual property rights do not themselves become barriers to legitimate trade.

2. To provide adequate and effective protection and enforcement of intellectual property rights, each Party shall, at a minimum, give effect to this Chapter and to the substantive provisions of:

(a) the Geneva Convention for the Protection of Producers of Phonograms Against Unauthorized Duplication of their Phonograms, 1971 (Geneva Convention);

(b) the Berne Convention for the Protection of Literary and Artistic Works, 1971 (Berne Convention);

(c) the Paris Convention for the Protection of Industrial Property, 1967 (Paris Convention); and

(d) the International Convention for the Protection of New Varieties of Plants, 1978 (UPOV Convention), or the International Convention for the Protection of New Varieties of Plants, 1991 (UPOV Convention). If a Party has not acceded to the specified text of any such Conventions on or before the date of entry into force of this Agreement, it shall make every effort to accede.

3. Annex 1701.3 applies to the Parties specified in that Annex.

Article 1702
More Extensive Protection

A Party may implement in its domestic law more extensive protection of intellectual property rights than is required under this Agreement, provided that such protection is not inconsistent with this Agreement.

Article 1703
National Treatment

1. Each Party shall accord to nationals of another Party treatment no less favorable than that it accords to its own nationals with regard to the protection and enforcement of all intellectual property rights. In respect of sound recordings, each Party shall provide such treatment to producers and performers of another Party, except that a Party may limit rights of performers of another Party in respect of secondary uses of sound recordings to those rights its nationals are accorded in the territory of such other Party.

2. No Party may, as a condition of according national treatment under this Article, require right holders to comply with any formalities or conditions in order to acquire rights in respect of copyright and related rights.

3. A Party may derogate from paragraph 1 in relation to its judicial and administrative procedures for the protection or enforcement of intellectual property rights, including any procedure requiring a national of another Party to designate for service of process an address in the Party's territory or to appoint an agent in the Party's territory, if the derogation is consistent with the relevant Convention listed in Article 1701(2), provided that such derogation:

(a) is necessary to secure compliance with measures that are not inconsistent with this Chapter; and

(b) is not applied in a manner that would constitute a disguised restriction on trade.

4. No Party shall have any obligation under this Article with respect to procedures provided in multilateral agreements concluded under the auspices of the World Intellectual Property Organization relating to the acquisition or maintenance of intellectual property rights.

Article 1704
Control of Abusive or Anticompetitive Practices or Conditions

Nothing in this Chapter shall prevent a Party from specifying in its domestic law licensing practices or conditions that may in particular cases constitute an abuse of intellectual property rights having an adverse effect on competition in the relevant market. A Party may adopt or maintain, consistent with the other provisions of this Agreement, appropriate measures to prevent or control such practices or conditions.

Article 1705
Copyright

1. Each Party shall protect the works covered by Article 2 of the Berne Convention, including any other works that embody original expression within the meaning of that Convention. In particular:

(a) all types of computer programs are literary works within the meaning of the Berne Convention and each Party shall protect them as such; and

(b) compilations of data or other material, whether in machine readable or other form, which by reason of the selection or arrangement of their contents constitute intellectual creations, shall be protected as such.

The protection a Party provides under subparagraph (b) shall not extend to the data or material itself, or prejudice any copyright subsisting in that data or material.

2. Each Party shall provide to authors and their successors in interest those rights enumerated in the Berne Convention in respect of works covered by paragraph 1, including the right to authorize or prohibit:

(a) the importation into the Party's territory of copies of the work made without the right holder's authorization;

(b) the first public distribution of the original and each copy of the work by sale, rental or otherwise;

(c) the communication of a work to the public; and

(d) the commercial rental of the original or a copy of a computer program.

Subparagraph (d) shall not apply where the copy of the computer program is not itself an essential object of the rental. Each Party shall provide that putting the original or a copy of a computer program on the market with the right holder's consent shall not exhaust the rental right.

3. Each Party shall provide that for copyright and related rights:

(a) any person acquiring or holding economic rights may freely and separately transfer such rights by contract for purposes of their exploitation and enjoyment by the transferee; and

(b) any person acquiring or holding such economic rights by virtue of a contract, including contracts of employment underlying the creation of works and sound recordings, shall be able to exercise those rights in its own name and enjoy fully the benefits derived from those rights.

4. Each Party shall provide that, where the term of protection of a work, other than a photographic work or a work of applied art, is to be calculated on a basis other than

the life of a natural person, the term shall be not less than 50 years from the end of the calendar year of the first authorized publication of the work or, failing such authorized publication within 50 years from the making of the work, 50 years from the end of the calendar year of making.

5. Each Party shall confine limitations or exceptions to the rights provided for in this Article to certain special cases that do not conflict with a normal exploitation of the work and do not unreasonably prejudice the legitimate interests of the right holder.

6. No Party may grant translation and reproduction licenses permitted under the Appendix to the Berne Convention where legitimate needs in that Party's territory for copies or translations of the work could be met by the right holder's voluntary actions but for obstacles created by the Party's measures.

7. Annex 1705.7 applies to the Parties specified in that Annex.

Article 1706
Sound Recordings

1. Each Party shall provide to the producer of a sound recording the right to authorize or prohibit:

(a) the direct or indirect reproduction of the sound recording;

(b) the importation into the Party's territory of copies of the sound recording made without the producer's authorization;

(c) the first public distribution of the original and each copy of the sound recording by sale, rental or otherwise; and

(d) the commercial rental of the original or a copy of the sound recording, except where expressly otherwise provided in a contract between the producer of the sound recording and the authors of the works fixed therein.

Each Party shall provide that putting the original or a copy of a sound recording on the market with the right holder's consent shall not exhaust the rental right.

2. Each Party shall provide a term of protection for sound recordings of at least 50 years from the end of the calendar year in which the fixation was made.

3. Each Party shall confine limitations or exceptions to the rights provided for in this Article to certain special cases that do not conflict with a normal exploitation of the sound recording and do not unreasonably prejudice the legitimate interests of the right holder.

Article 1707
Protection of Encrypted Program-Carrying Satellite Signals

Within one year from the date of entry into force of this Agreement, each Party shall make it:

(a) a criminal offense to manufacture, import, sell, lease or otherwise make available a device or system that is primarily of assistance in decoding an encrypted program-carrying satellite signal without the authorization of the lawful distributor of such signal; and

(b) a civil offense to receive, in connection with commercial activities, or further distribute, an encrypted program-carrying satellite signal that has been decoded without the authorization of the lawful distributor of the signal or to engage in any activity prohibited under subparagraph (a).

Each Party shall provide that any civil offense established under subparagraph (b) shall be actionable by any person that holds an interest in the content of such signal.

Article 1708
Trademarks

1. For purposes of this Agreement, a trademark consists of any sign, or any combination of signs, capable of distinguishing the goods or services of one person from those of another, including personal names, designs, letters, numerals, colors, figurative elements, or the shape of goods or of their packaging. Trademarks shall include service marks and collective marks, and may include certification marks. A Party may require, as a condition for registration, that a sign be visually perceptible.

2. Each Party shall provide to the owner of a registered trademark the right to prevent all persons not having the owner's consent from using in commerce identical or similar signs for goods or services that are identical or similar to those goods or services in respect of which the owner's trademark is registered, where such use would result in a likelihood of confusion. In the case of the use of an identical sign for identical goods or services, a likelihood of confusion shall be presumed. The rights described above shall not prejudice any prior rights, nor shall they affect the possibility of a Party making rights available on the basis of use.

3. A Party may make registrability depend on use. However, actual use of a trademark shall not be a condition for filing an application for registration. No Party may refuse an application solely on the ground that intended use has not taken place before the expiry of a period of three years from the date of application for registration.

4. Each Party shall provide a system for the registration of trademarks, which shall include:

(a) examination of applications;

(b) notice to be given to an applicant of the reasons for the refusal to register a trademark;

(c) a reasonable opportunity for the applicant to respond to the notice;

(d) publication of each trademark either before or promptly after it is registered; and

(e) a reasonable opportunity for interested persons to petition to cancel the registration of a trademark.

A Party may provide for a reasonable opportunity for interested persons to oppose the registration of a trademark.

5. The nature of the goods or services to which a trademark is to be applied shall in no case form an obstacle to the registration of the trademark.

6. Article 6bis of the Paris Convention shall apply, with such modifications as may be necessary, to services. In determining whether a trademark is well- known, account shall be taken of the knowledge of the trademark in the relevant sector of the public, including knowledge in the Party's territory obtained as a result of the promotion of the trademark. No Party may require that the reputation of the trademark extend beyond the sector of the public that normally deals with the relevant goods or services.

7. Each Party shall provide that the initial registration of a trademark be for a term of at least 10 years and that the registration be indefinitely renewable for terms of not less than 10 years when conditions for renewal have been met.

8. Each Party shall require the use of a trademark to maintain a registration. The registration may be canceled for the reason of non-use only after an uninterrupted period of at least two years of non-use, unless valid reasons based on the existence of obstacles to such use are shown by the trademark owner. Each Party shall recognize, as valid reasons for non-use, circumstances arising independently of the will of the trademark owner that constitute an obstacle to the use of the trademark, such as import

restrictions on, or other government requirements for, goods or services identified by the trademark.

9. Each Party shall recognize use of a trademark by a person other than the trademark owner, where such use is subject to the owner's control, as use of the trademark for purposes of maintaining the registration.

10. No Party may encumber the use of a trademark in commerce by special requirements, such as a use that reduces the trademark's function as an indication of source or a use with another trademark.

11. A Party may determine conditions on the licensing and assignment of trademarks, it being understood that the compulsory licensing of trademarks shall not be permitted and that the owner of a registered trademark shall have the right to assign its trademark with or without the transfer of the business to which the trademark belongs.

12. A Party may provide limited exceptions to the rights conferred by a trademark, such as fair use of descriptive terms, provided that such exceptions take into account the legitimate interests of the trademark owner and of other persons.

13. Each Party shall prohibit the registration as a trademark of words, at least in English, French or Spanish, that generically designate goods or services or types of goods or services to which the trademark applies.

14. Each Party shall refuse to register trademarks that consist of or comprise immoral, deceptive or scandalous matter, or matter that may disparage or falsely suggest a connection with persons, living or dead, institutions, beliefs or any Party's national symbols, or bring them into contempt or disrepute.

Article 1709
Patents

1. Subject to paragraphs 2 and 3, each Party shall make patents available for any inventions, whether products or processes, in all fields of technology, provided that such inventions are new, result from an inventive step and are capable of industrial application. For purposes of this Article, a Party may deem the terms "inventive step" and "capable of industrial application" to be synonymous with the terms "non-obvious" and "useful," respectively.

2. A Party may exclude from patentability inventions if preventing in its territory the commercial exploitation of the inventions is necessary to protect ordre public or morality, including to protect human, animal or plant life or health or to avoid serious prejudice to nature or the environment, provided that the exclusion is not based solely on the ground that the Party prohibits commercial exploitation in its territory of the subject matter of the patent.

3. A Party may also exclude from patentability:

(a) diagnostic, therapeutic and surgical methods for the treatment of humans or animals;

(b) plants and animals other than microorganisms; and

(c) essentially biological processes for the production of plants or animals, other than non-biological and microbiological processes for such production.

Notwithstanding subparagraph (b), each Party shall provide for the protection of plant varieties through patents, an effective scheme of *sui generis* protection, or both.

4. If a Party has not made available product patent protection for pharmaceutical or agricultural chemicals commensurate with paragraph 1:

(a) as of January 1, 1992, for subject matter that relates to naturally occurring substances prepared or produced by, or significantly derived from, microbiological processes and intended for food or medicine, and

(b) as of July 1, 1991, for any other subject matter, that Party shall provide to the inventor of any such product or its assignee the means to obtain product patent protection for such product for the unexpired term of the patent for such product granted in another Party, as long as the product has not been marketed in the Party providing protection under this paragraph and the person seeking such protection makes a timely request.

5. Each Party shall provide that:

(a) where the subject matter of a patent is a product, the patent shall confer on the patent owner the right to prevent other persons from making, using or selling the subject matter of the patent, without the patent owner's consent; and

(b) where the subject matter of a patent is a process, the patent shall confer on the patent owner the right to prevent other persons from using that process and from using, selling, or importing at least the product obtained directly by that process, without the patent owner's consent.

6. A Party may provide limited exceptions to the exclusive rights conferred by a patent, provided that such exceptions do not unreasonably conflict with a normal exploitation of the patent and do not unreasonably prejudice the legitimate interests of the patent owner, taking into account the legitimate interests of other persons.

7. Subject to paragraphs 2 and 3, patents shall be available and patent rights enjoyable without discrimination as to the field of technology, the territory of the Party where the invention was made and whether products are imported or locally produced.

8. A Party may revoke a patent only when:

(a) grounds exist that would have justified a refusal to grant the patent; or

(b) the grant of a compulsory license has not remedied the lack of exploitation of the patent.

9. Each Party shall permit patent owners to assign and transfer by succession their patents, and to conclude licensing contracts.

10. Where the law of a Party allows for use of the subject matter of a patent, other than that use allowed under paragraph 6, without the authorization of the right holder, including use by the government or other persons authorized by the government, the Party shall respect the following provisions:

(a) authorization of such use shall be considered on its individual merits;

(b) such use may only be permitted if, prior to such use, the proposed user has made efforts to obtain authorization from the right holder on reasonable commercial terms and conditions and such efforts have not been successful within a reasonable period of time. The requirement to make such efforts may be waived by a Party in the case of a national emergency or other circumstances of extreme urgency or in cases of public non-commercial use. In situations of national emergency or other circumstances of extreme urgency, the right holder shall, nevertheless, be notified as soon as reasonably practicable. In the case of public non-commercial use, where the government or contractor, without making a patent search, knows or has demonstrable grounds to know that a valid patent is or will be used by or for the government, the right holder shall be informed promptly;

(c) the scope and duration of such use shall be limited to the purpose for which it was authorized;

(d) such use shall be non-exclusive;

(e) such use shall be non-assignable, except with that part of the enterprise or goodwill that enjoys such use;

(f) any such use shall be authorized predominantly for the supply of the Party's domestic market;

(g) authorization for such use shall be liable, subject to adequate protection of the legitimate interests of the persons so authorized, to be terminated if and when the circumstances that led to it cease to exist and are unlikely to recur. The competent authority shall have the authority to review, on motivated request, the continued existence of these circumstances;

(h) the right holder shall be paid adequate remuneration in the circumstances of each case, taking into account the economic value of the authorization;

(i) the legal validity of any decision relating to the authorization shall be subject to judicial or other independent review by a distinct higher authority;

(j) any decision relating to the remuneration provided in respect of such use shall be subject to judicial or other independent review by a distinct higher authority;

(k) the Party shall not be obliged to apply the conditions set out in subparagraphs (b) and (f) where such use is permitted to remedy a practice determined after judicial or administrative process to be anticompetitive. The need to correct anticompetitive practices may be taken into account in determining the amount of remuneration in such cases. Competent authorities shall have the authority to refuse termination of authorization if and when the conditions that led to such authorization are likely to recur;

(l) the Party shall not authorize the use of the subject matter of a patent to permit the exploitation of another patent except as a remedy for an adjudicated violation of domestic laws regarding anticompetitive practices.

11. Where the subject matter of a patent is a process for obtaining a product, each Party shall, in any infringement proceeding, place on the defendant the burden of establishing that the allegedly infringing product was made by a process other than the patented process in one of the following situations:

(a) the product obtained by the patented process is new; or

(b) a substantial likelihood exists that the allegedly infringing product was made by the process and the patent owner has been unable through reasonable efforts to determine the process actually used.

In the gathering and evaluation of evidence, the legitimate interests of the defendant in protecting its trade secrets shall be taken into account.

12. Each Party shall provide a term of protection for patents of at least 20 years from the date of filing or 17 years from the date of grant. A Party may extend the term of patent protection, in appropriate cases, to compensate for delays caused by regulatory approval processes.

Article 1710
Layout Designs of Semiconductor Integrated Circuits

1. Each Party shall protect layout designs (topographies) of integrated circuits ("layout designs") in accordance with Articles 2 through 7, 12 and 16(3), other than Article 6(3), of the Treaty on Intellectual Property in Respect of Integrated Circuits as opened for signature on May 26, 1989.

2. Subject to paragraph 3, each Party shall make it unlawful for any person without the right holder's authorization to import, sell or otherwise distribute for commercial purposes any of the following:

(a) a protected layout design;

(b) an integrated circuit in which a protected layout design is incorporated; or

(c) an article incorporating such an integrated circuit, only insofar as it continues to contain an unlawfully reproduced layout design.

3. No Party may make unlawful any of the acts referred to in paragraph 2 performed in respect of an integrated circuit that incorporates an unlawfully reproduced layout design, or any article that incorporates such an integrated circuit, where the person

performing those acts or ordering those acts to be done did not know and had no reasonable ground to know, when it acquired the integrated circuit or article incorporating such an integrated circuit, that it incorporated an unlawfully reproduced layout design.

4. Each Party shall provide that, after the person referred to in paragraph 3 has received sufficient notice that the layout design was unlawfully reproduced, such person may perform any of the acts with respect to the stock on hand or ordered before such notice, but shall be liable to pay the right holder for doing so an amount equivalent to a reasonable royalty such as would be payable under a freely negotiated license in respect of such a layout design.

5. No Party may permit the compulsory licensing of layout designs of integrated circuits.

6. Any Party that requires registration as a condition for protection of a layout design shall provide that the term of protection shall not end before the expiration of a period of 10 years counted from the date of:

(a) filing of the application for registration; or

(b) the first commercial exploitation of the layout design, wherever in the world it occurs.

7. Where a Party does not require registration as a condition for protection of a layout design, the Party shall provide a term of protection of not less than 10 years from the date of the first commercial exploitation of the layout design, wherever in the world it occurs.

8. Notwithstanding paragraphs 6 and 7, a Party may provide that the protection shall lapse 15 years after the creation of the layout design.

9. Annex 1710.9 applies to the Parties specified in that Annex.

Article 1711
Trade Secrets

1. Each Party shall provide the legal means for any person to prevent trade secrets from being disclosed to, acquired by, or used by others without the consent of the person lawfully in control of the information in a manner contrary to honest commercial practices, in so far as:

(a) the information is secret in the sense that it is not, as a body or in the precise configuration and assembly of its components, generally known among or readily accessible to persons that normally deal with the kind of information in question;

(b) the information has actual or potential commercial value because it is secret; and

(c) the person lawfully in control of the information has taken reasonable steps under the circumstances to keep it secret.

2. A Party may require that to qualify for protection a trade secret must be evidenced in documents, electronic or magnetic means, optical discs, microfilms, films or other similar instruments.

3. No Party may limit the duration of protection for trade secrets, so long as the conditions in paragraph 1 exist.

4. No Party may discourage or impede the voluntary licensing of trade secrets by imposing excessive or discriminatory conditions on such licenses or conditions that dilute the value of the trade secrets.

5. If a Party requires, as a condition for approving the marketing of pharmaceutical or agricultural chemical products that utilize new chemical entities, the submission of undisclosed test or other data necessary to determine whether the use of such products is safe and effective, the Party shall protect against disclosure of the data

of persons making such submissions, where the origination of such data involves considerable effort, except where the disclosure is necessary to protect the public or unless steps are taken to ensure that the data is protected against unfair commercial use.

6. Each Party shall provide that for data subject to paragraph 5 that are submitted to the Party after the date of entry into force of this Agreement, no person other than the person that submitted them may, without the latter's permission, rely on such data in support of an application for product approval during a reasonable period of time after their submission. For this purpose, a reasonable period shall normally mean not less than five years from the date on which the Party granted approval to the person that produced the data for approval to market its product, taking account of the nature of the data and the person's efforts and expenditures in producing them. Subject to this provision, there shall be no limitation on any Party to implement abbreviated approval procedures for such products on the basis of bioequivalence and bioavailability studies.

7. Where a Party relies on a marketing approval granted by another Party, the reasonable period of exclusive use of the data submitted in connection with obtaining the approval relied on shall begin with the date of the first marketing approval relied on.

Article 1712
Geographical Indications

1. Each Party shall provide, in respect of geographical indications, the legal means for interested persons to prevent:

(a) the use of any means in the designation or presentation of a good that indicates or suggests that the good in question originates in a territory, region or locality other than the true place of origin, in a manner that misleads the public as to the geographical origin of the good;

(b) any use that constitutes an act of unfair competition within the meaning of Article 10bis of the Paris Convention.

2. Each Party shall, on its own initiative if its domestic law so permits or at the request of an interested person, refuse to register, or invalidate the registration of, a trademark containing or consisting of a geographical indication with respect to goods that do not originate in the indicated territory, region or locality, if use of the indication in the trademark for such goods is of such a nature as to mislead the public as to the geographical origin of the good.

3. Each Party shall also apply paragraphs 1 and 2 to a geographical indication that, although correctly indicating the territory, region or locality in which the goods originate, falsely represents to the public that the goods originate in another territory, region or locality.

4. Nothing in this Article shall be construed to require a Party to prevent continued and similar use of a particular geographical indication of another Party in connection with goods or services by any of its nationals or domiciliaries who have used that geographical indication in a continuous manner with regard to the same or related goods or services in that Party's territory, either:

(a) for at least 10 years, or

(b) in good faith,

before the date of signature of this Agreement.

5. Where a trademark has been applied for or registered in good faith, or where rights to a trademark have been acquired through use in good faith, either:

(a) before the date of application of these provisions in that Party, or

(b) before the geographical indication is protected in its Party of origin, no Party may adopt any measure to implement this Article that prejudices eligibility for, or the validity of, the registration of a trademark, or the right to use a trademark, on the basis that such a trademark is identical with, or similar to, a geographical indication.

6. No Party shall be required to apply this Article to a geographical indication if it is identical to the customary term in common language in that Party's territory for the goods or services to which the indication applies.

7. A Party may provide that any request made under this Article in connection with the use or registration of a trademark must be presented within five years after the adverse use of the protected indication has become generally known in that Party or after the date of registration of the trademark in that Party, provided that the trademark has been published by that date, if such date is earlier than the date on which the adverse use became generally known in that Party, provided that the geographical indication is not used or registered in bad faith.

8. No Party shall adopt any measure implementing this Article that would prejudice any person's right to use, in the course of trade, its name or the name of its predecessor in business, except where such name forms all or part of a valid trademark in existence before the geographical indication became protected and with which there is a likelihood of confusion, or such name is used in such a manner as to mislead the public.

9. Nothing in this Chapter shall be construed to require a Party to protect a geographical indication that is not protected, or has fallen into disuse, in the Party of origin.

Article 1713
Industrial Designs

1. Each Party shall provide for the protection of independently created industrial designs that are new or original. A Party may provide that:

(a) designs are not new or original if they do not significantly differ from known designs or combinations of known design features; and

(b) such protection shall not extend to designs dictated essentially by technical or functional considerations.

2. Each Party shall ensure that the requirements for securing protection for textile designs, in particular in regard to any cost, examination or publication, do not unreasonably impair a person's opportunity to seek and obtain such protection. A Party may comply with this obligation through industrial design law or copyright law.

3. Each Party shall provide the owner of a protected industrial design the right to prevent other persons not having the owner's consent from making or selling articles bearing or embodying a design that is a copy, or substantially a copy, of the protected design, when such acts are undertaken for commercial purposes.

4. A Party may provide limited exceptions to the protection of industrial designs, provided that such exceptions do not unreasonably conflict with the normal exploitation of protected industrial designs and do not unreasonably prejudice the legitimate interests of the owner of the protected design, taking into account the legitimate interests of other persons.

5. Each Party shall provide a term of protection for industrial designs of at least 10 years.

Article 1714
Enforcement of Intellectual Property Rights: General Provisions

1. Each Party shall ensure that enforcement procedures, as specified in this Article and Articles 1715 through 1718, are available under its domestic law so as to permit

effective action to be taken against any act of infringement of intellectual property rights covered by this Chapter, including expeditious remedies to prevent infringements and remedies to deter further infringements. Such enforcement procedures shall be applied so as to avoid the creation of barriers to legitimate trade and to provide for safeguards against abuse of the procedures.

2. Each Party shall ensure that its procedures for the enforcement of intellectual property rights are fair and equitable, are not unnecessarily complicated or costly, and do not entail unreasonable time-limits or unwarranted delays.

3. Each Party shall provide that decisions on the merits of a case in judicial and administrative enforcement proceedings shall:

(a) preferably be in writing and preferably state the reasons on which the decisions are based;

(b) be made available at least to the parties in a proceeding without undue delay; and

(c) be based only on evidence in respect of which such parties were offered the opportunity to be heard.

4. Each Party shall ensure that parties in a proceeding have an opportunity to have final administrative decisions reviewed by a judicial authority of that Party and, subject to jurisdictional provisions in its domestic laws concerning the importance of a case, to have reviewed at least the legal aspects of initial judicial decisions on the merits of a case. Notwithstanding the above, no Party shall be required to provide for judicial review of acquittals in criminal cases.

5. Nothing in this Article or Articles 1715 through 1718 shall be construed to require a Party to establish a judicial system for the enforcement of intellectual property rights distinct from that Party's system for the enforcement of laws in general.

6. For the purposes of Articles 1715 through 1718, the term "right holder" includes federations and associations having legal standing to assert such rights.

Article 1715
Specific Procedural and Remedial Aspects of Civil and Administrative Procedures

1. Each Party shall make available to right holders civil judicial procedures for the enforcement of any intellectual property right provided in this Chapter. Each Party shall provide that:

(a) defendants have the right to written notice that is timely and contains sufficient detail, including the basis of the claims;

(b) parties in a proceeding are allowed to be represented by independent legal counsel;

(c) the procedures do not include imposition of overly burdensome requirements concerning mandatory personal appearances;

(d) all parties in a proceeding are duly entitled to substantiate their claims and to present relevant evidence; and

(e) the procedures include a means to identify and protect confidential information.

2. Each Party shall provide that its judicial authorities shall have the authority:

(a) where a party in a proceeding has presented reasonably available evidence sufficient to support its claims and has specified evidence relevant to the substantiation of its claims that is within the control of the opposing party, to order the opposing party to produce such evidence, subject in appropriate cases to conditions that ensure the protection of confidential information;

(b) where a party in a proceeding voluntarily and without good reason refuses access to, or otherwise does not provide relevant evidence under that party's control within a reasonable period, or significantly impedes a proceeding relating to an enforcement action, to make preliminary and final determinations, affirmative or negative, on the basis of the evidence presented, including the complaint or the allegation presented by the party adversely affected by the denial of access to evidence, subject to providing the parties an opportunity to be heard on the allegations or evidence;

(c) to order a party in a proceeding to desist from an infringement, including to prevent the entry into the channels of commerce in their jurisdiction of imported goods that involve the infringement of an intellectual property right, which order shall be enforceable at least immediately after customs clearance of such goods;

(d) to order the infringer of an intellectual property right to pay the right holder damages adequate to compensate for the injury the right holder has suffered because of the infringement where the infringer knew or had reasonable grounds to know that it was engaged in an infringing activity;

(e) to order an infringer of an intellectual property right to pay the right holder's expenses, which may include appropriate attorney's fees; and

(f) to order a party in a proceeding at whose request measures were taken and who has abused enforcement procedures to provide adequate compensation to any party wrongfully enjoined or restrained in the proceeding for the injury suffered because of such abuse and to pay that party's expenses, which may include appropriate attorney's fees.

3. With respect to the authority referred to in subparagraph 2(c), no Party shall be obliged to provide such authority in respect of protected subject matter that is acquired or ordered by a person before that person knew or had reasonable grounds to know that dealing in that subject matter would entail the infringement of an intellectual property right.

4. With respect to the authority referred to in subparagraph 2(d), a Party may, at least with respect to copyrighted works and sound recordings, authorize the judicial authorities to order recovery of profits or payment of pre-established damages, or both, even where the infringer did not know or had no reasonable grounds to know that it was engaged in an infringing activity.

5. Each Party shall provide that, in order to create an effective deterrent to infringement, its judicial authorities shall have the authority to order that:

(a) goods that they have found to be infringing be, without compensation of any sort, disposed of outside the channels of commerce in such a manner as to avoid any injury caused to the right holder or, unless this would be contrary to existing constitutional requirements, destroyed; and

(b) materials and implements the predominant use of which has been in the creation of the infringing goods be, without compensation of any sort, disposed of outside the channels of commerce in such a manner as to minimize the risks of further infringements.

In considering whether to issue such an order, judicial authorities shall take into account the need for proportionality between the seriousness of the infringement and the remedies ordered as well as the interests of other persons. In regard to counterfeit goods, the simple removal of the trademark unlawfully affixed shall not be sufficient, other than in exceptional cases, to permit release of the goods into the channels of commerce.

6. In respect of the administration of any law pertaining to the protection or enforcement of intellectual property rights, each Party shall only exempt both public authorities and officials from liability to appropriate remedial measures where actions are taken or intended in good faith in the course of the administration of such laws.

7. Notwithstanding the other provisions of Articles 1714 through 1718, where a

Party is sued with respect to an infringement of an intellectual property right as a result of its use of that right or use on its behalf, that Party may limit the remedies available against it to the payment to the right holder of adequate remuneration in the circumstances of each case, taking into account the economic value of the use.

8. Each Party shall provide that, where a civil remedy can be ordered as a result of administrative procedures on the merits of a case, such procedures shall conform to principles equivalent in substance to those set out in this Article.

Article 1716
Provisional Measures

1. Each Party shall provide that its judicial authorities shall have the authority to order prompt and effective provisional measures:

(a) to prevent an infringement of any intellectual property right, and in particular to prevent the entry into the channels of commerce in their jurisdiction of allegedly infringing goods, including measures to prevent the entry of imported goods at least immediately after customs clearance; and

(b) to preserve relevant evidence in regard to the alleged infringement.

2. Each Party shall provide that its judicial authorities shall have the authority to require any applicant for provisional measures to provide to the judicial authorities any evidence reasonably available to that applicant that the judicial authorities consider necessary to enable them to determine with a sufficient degree of certainty whether:

(a) the applicant is the right holder;

(b) the applicant's right is being infringed or such infringement is imminent; and

(c) any delay in the issuance of such measures is likely to cause irreparable harm to the right holder, or there is a demonstrable risk of evidence being destroyed.

Each Party shall provide that its judicial authorities shall have the authority to require the applicant to provide a security or equivalent assurance sufficient to protect the interests of the defendant and to prevent abuse.

3. Each Party shall provide that its judicial authorities shall have the authority to require an applicant for provisional measures to provide other information necessary for the identification of the relevant goods by the authority that will execute the provisional measures.

4. Each Party shall provide that its judicial authorities shall have the authority to order provisional measures on an ex parte basis, in particular where any delay is likely to cause irreparable harm to the right holder, or where there is a demonstrable risk of evidence being destroyed.

5. Each Party shall provide that where provisional measures are adopted by that Party's judicial authorities on an ex parte basis:

(a) a person affected shall be given notice of those measures without delay but in any event no later than immediately after the execution of the measures;

(b) a defendant shall, on request, have those measures reviewed by that Party's judicial authorities for the purpose of deciding, within a reasonable period after notice of those measures is given, whether the measures shall be modified, revoked or confirmed, and shall be given an opportunity to be heard in the review proceedings.

6. Without prejudice to paragraph 5, each Party shall provide that, on the request of the defendant, the Party's judicial authorities shall revoke or otherwise cease to apply the provisional measures taken on the basis of paragraphs 1 and 4 if proceedings leading to a decision on the merits are not initiated:

(a) within a reasonable period as determined by the judicial authority ordering the measures where the Party's domestic law so permits; or

(b) in the absence of such a determination, within a period of no more than 20 working days or 31 calendar days, whichever is longer.

7. Each Party shall provide that, where the provisional measures are revoked or where they lapse due to any act or omission by the applicant, or where the judicial authorities subsequently find that there has been no infringement or threat of infringement of an intellectual property right, the judicial authorities shall have the authority to order the applicant, on request of the defendant, to provide the defendant appropriate compensation for any injury caused by these measures.

8. Each Party shall provide that, where a provisional measure can be ordered as a result of administrative procedures, such procedures shall conform to principles equivalent in substance to those set out in this Article.

Article 1717
Criminal Procedures and Penalties

1. Each Party shall provide criminal procedures and penalties to be applied at least in cases of willful trademark counterfeiting or copyright piracy on a commercial scale. Each Party shall provide that penalties available include imprisonment or monetary fines, or both, sufficient to provide a deterrent, consistent with the level of penalties applied for crimes of a corresponding gravity.

2. Each Party shall provide that, in appropriate cases, its judicial authorities may order the seizure, forfeiture and destruction of infringing goods and of any materials and implements the predominant use of which has been in the commission of the offense.

3. A Party may provide criminal procedures and penalties to be applied in cases of infringement of intellectual property rights, other than those in paragraph 1, where they are committed wilfully and on a commercial scale.

Article 1718
Enforcement of Intellectual Property Rights at the Border

1. Each Party shall, in conformity with this Article, adopt procedures to enable a right holder, who has valid grounds for suspecting that the importation of counterfeit trademark goods or pirated copyright goods may take place, to lodge an application in writing with its competent authorities, whether administrative or judicial, for the suspension by the customs administration of the release of such goods into free circulation. No Party shall be obligated to apply such procedures to goods in transit. A Party may permit such an application to be made in respect of goods that involve other infringements of intellectual property rights, provided that the requirements of this Article are met. A Party may also provide for corresponding procedures concerning the suspension by the customs administration of the release of infringing goods destined for exportation from its territory.

2. Each Party shall require any applicant who initiates procedures under paragraph 1 to provide adequate evidence:

(a) to satisfy that Party's competent authorities that, under the domestic laws of the country of importation, there is prima facie an infringement of its intellectual property right; and

(b) to supply a sufficiently detailed description of the goods to make them readily recognizable by the customs administration.

The competent authorities shall inform the applicant within a reasonable period whether they have accepted the application and, if so, the period for which the customs administration will take action.

3. Each Party shall provide that its competent authorities shall have the authority

to require an applicant under paragraph 1 to provide a security or equivalent assurance sufficient to protect the defendant and the competent authorities and to prevent abuse. Such security or equivalent assurance shall not unreasonably deter recourse to these procedures.

4. Each Party shall provide that, where pursuant to an application under procedures adopted pursuant to this Article, its customs administration suspends the release of goods involving industrial designs, patents, integrated circuits or trade secrets into free circulation on the basis of a decision other than by a judicial or other independent authority, and the period provided for in paragraphs 6 through 8 has expired without the granting of provisional relief by the duly empowered authority, and provided that all other conditions for importation have been complied with, the owner, importer or consignee of such goods shall be entitled to their release on the posting of a security in an amount sufficient to protect the right holder against any infringement. Payment of such security shall not prejudice any other remedy available to the right holder, it being understood that the security shall be released if the right holder fails to pursue its right of action within a reasonable period of time.

5. Each Party shall provide that its customs administration shall promptly notify the importer and the applicant when the customs administration suspends the release of goods pursuant to paragraph 1.

6. Each Party shall provide that its customs administration shall release goods from suspension if within a period not exceeding 10 working days after the applicant under paragraph 1 has been served notice of the suspension the customs administration has not been informed that:

(a) a party other than the defendant has initiated proceedings leading to a decision on the merits of the case, or

(b) a competent authority has taken provisional measures prolonging the suspension, provided that all other conditions for importation or exportation have been met. Each Party shall provide that, in appropriate cases, the customs administration may extend the suspension by another 10 working days.

7. Each Party shall provide that if proceedings leading to a decision on the merits of the case have been initiated, a review, including a right to be heard, shall take place on request of the defendant with a view to deciding, within a reasonable period, whether these measures shall be modified, revoked or confirmed.

8. Notwithstanding paragraphs 6 and 7, where the suspension of the release of goods is carried out or continued in accordance with a provisional judicial measure, Article 1716(6) shall apply.

9. Each Party shall provide that its competent authorities shall have the authority to order the applicant under paragraph 1 to pay the importer, the consignee and the owner of the goods appropriate compensation for any injury caused to them through the wrongful detention of goods or through the detention of goods released pursuant to paragraph 6.

10. Without prejudice to the protection of confidential information, each Party shall provide that its competent authorities shall have the authority to give the right holder sufficient opportunity to have any goods detained by the customs administration inspected in order to substantiate the right holder's claims. Each Party shall also provide that its competent authorities have the authority to give the importer an equivalent opportunity to have any such goods inspected. Where the competent authorities have made a positive determination on the merits of a case, a Party may provide the competent authorities the authority to inform the right holder of the names and addresses of the consignor, the importer and the consignee, and of the quantity of the goods in question.

11. Where a Party requires its competent authorities to act on their own initiative and to suspend the release of goods in respect of which they have acquired prima facie evidence that an intellectual property right is being infringed:

(a) the competent authorities may at any time seek from the right holder any information that may assist them to exercise these powers;

(b) the importer and the right holder shall be promptly notified of the suspension by the Party's competent authorities, and where the importer lodges an appeal against the suspension with competent authorities, the suspension shall be subject to the conditions, with such modifications as may be necessary, set out in paragraphs 6 through 8; and

(c) the Party shall only exempt both public authorities and officials from liability to appropriate remedial measures where actions are taken or intended in good faith.

12. Without prejudice to other rights of action open to the right holder and subject to the defendant's right to seek judicial review, each Party shall provide that its competent authorities shall have the authority to order the destruction or disposal of infringing goods in accordance with the principles set out in Article 1715(5). In regard to counterfeit goods, the authorities shall not allow the re-exportation of the infringing goods in an unaltered state or subject them to a different customs procedure, other than in exceptional circumstances.

13. A Party may exclude from the application of paragraphs 1 through 12 small quantities of goods of a non-commercial nature contained in travelers' personal luggage or sent in small consignments that are not repetitive.

14. Annex 1718.14 applies to the Parties specified in that Annex.

Article 1719
Cooperation and Technical Assistance

1. The Parties shall provide each other on mutually agreed terms with technical assistance and shall promote cooperation between their competent authorities. Such cooperation shall include the training of personnel.

2. The Parties shall cooperate with a view to eliminating trade in goods that infringe intellectual property rights. For this purpose, each Party shall establish and notify the other Parties by January 1, 1994 of contact points in its federal government and shall exchange information concerning trade in infringing goods.

Article 1720
Protection of Existing Subject Matter

1. Except as required under Article 1705(7), this Agreement does not give rise to obligations in respect of acts that occurred before the date of application of the relevant provisions of this Agreement for the Party in question.

2. Except as otherwise provided for in this Agreement, each Party shall apply this Agreement to all subject matter existing on the date of application of the relevant provisions of this Agreement for the Party in question and that is protected in a Party on such date, or that meets or subsequently meets the criteria for protection under the terms of this Chapter. In respect of this paragraph and paragraphs 3 and 4, a Party's obligations with respect to existing works shall be solely determined under Article 18 of the Berne Convention and with respect to the rights of producers of sound recordings in existing sound recordings shall be determined solely under Article 18 of that Convention, as made applicable under this Agreement.

3. Except as required under Article 1705(7), and notwithstanding the first sentence of paragraph 2, no Party may be required to restore protection to subject matter that,

on the date of application of the relevant provisions of this Agreement for the Party in question, has fallen into the public domain in its territory.

4. In respect of any acts relating to specific objects embodying protected subject matter that become infringing under the terms of laws in conformity with this Agreement, and that were begun or in respect of which a significant investment was made, before the date of entry into force of this Agreement for that Party, any Party may provide for a limitation of the remedies available to the right holder as to the continued performance of such acts after the date of application of this Agreement for that Party. In such cases, the Party shall, however, at least provide for payment of equitable remuneration.

5. No Party shall be obliged to apply Article 1705(2)(d) or 1706(1)(d) with respect to originals or copies purchased prior to the date of application of the relevant provisions of this Agreement for that Party.

6. No Party shall be required to apply Article 1709(10), or the requirement in Article 1709(7) that patent rights shall be enjoyable without discrimination as to the field of technology, to use without the authorization of the right holder where authorization for such use was granted by the government before the text of the Draft Final Act Embodying the Results of the Uruguay Round of Multilateral Trade Negotiations became known.

7. In the case of intellectual property rights for which protection is conditional on registration, applications for protection that are pending on the date of application of the relevant provisions of this Agreement for the Party in question shall be permitted to be amended to claim any enhanced protection provided under this Agreement. Such amendments shall not include new matter.

Article 1721
Definitions

1. For purposes of this Chapter:

confidential information includes trade secrets, privileged information and other materials exempted from disclosure under the Party's domestic law.

2. For purposes of this Agreement:

encrypted program-carrying satellite signal means a program-carrying satellite signal that is transmitted in a form whereby the aural or visual characteristics, or both, are modified or altered for the purpose of preventing the unauthorized reception, by persons without the authorized equipment that is designed to eliminate the effects of such modification or alteration, of a program carried in that signal;

geographical indication means any indication that identifies a good as originating in the territory of a Party, or a region or locality in that territory, where a particular quality, reputation or other characteristic of the good is essentially attributable to its geographical origin;

in a manner contrary to honest commercial practices means at least practices such as breach of contract, breach of confidence and inducement to breach, and includes the acquisition of undisclosed information by other persons who knew, or were grossly negligent in failing to know, that such practices were involved in the acquisition;

intellectual property rights refers to copyright and related rights, trademark rights, patent rights, rights in layout designs of semiconductor integrated circuits, trade secret rights, plant breeders' rights, rights in geographical indications and industrial design rights;

nationals of another Party means, in respect of the relevant intellectual property right, persons who would meet the criteria for eligibility for protection provided for in the Paris Convention (1967), the Berne Convention (1971), the Geneva Convention

(1971), the International Convention for the Protection of Performers, Producers of Phonograms and Broadcasting Organizations (1961), the UPOV Convention (1978), the UPOV Convention (1991) or the Treaty on Intellectual Property in Respect of Integrated Circuits, as if each Party were a party to those Conventions, and with respect to intellectual property rights that are not the subject of these Conventions, "nationals of another Party" shall be understood to be at least individuals who are citizens or permanent residents of that Party and also includes any other natural person referred to in Annex 201.1 (Country-Specific Definitions);

public includes, with respect to rights of communication and performance of works provided for under Articles 11, 11bis(1) and 14(1)(ii) of the Berne Convention, with respect to dramatic, dramatico-musical, musical and cinematographic works, at least, any aggregation of individuals intended to be the object of, and capable of perceiving, communications or performances of works, regardless of whether they can do so at the same or different times or in the same or different places, provided that such an aggregation is larger than a family and its immediate circle of acquaintances or is not a group comprising a limited number of individuals having similarly close ties that has not been formed for the principal purpose of receiving such performances and communications of works; and

secondary uses of sound recordings means the use directly for broadcasting or for any other public communication of a sound recording.

Annex 1701.3
Intellectual Property Conventions

1. Mexico shall:

(a) make every effort to comply with the substantive provisions of the 1978 or 1991 UPOV Convention as soon as possible and shall do so no later than two years after the date of signature of this Agreement; and

(b) accept from the date of entry into force of this Agreement applications from plant breeders for varieties in all plant genera and species and grant protection, in accordance with such substantive provisions, promptly after complying with subparagraph (a).

2. Notwithstanding Article 1701(2)(b), this Agreement confers no rights and imposes no obligations on the United States with respect to Article 6bis of the Berne Convention, or the rights derived from that Article.

Annex 1705.7
Copyright

The United States shall provide protection to motion pictures produced in another Party's territory that have been declared to be in the public domain pursuant to 17 U.S.C. section 405. This obligation shall apply to the extent that it is consistent with the Constitution of the United States, and is subject to budgetary considerations.

Annex 1710.9
Layout Designs

Mexico shall make every effort to implement the requirements of Article 1710 as soon as possible, and shall do so no later than four years after the date of entry into force of this Agreement.

Annex 1718.14
Enforcement of Intellectual Property Rights

Mexico shall make every effort to comply with the requirements of Article 1718 as soon as possible and shall do so no later than three years after the date of signature of this Agreement.

APPENDIX IX

AGREEMENT ON TRADE-RELATED ASPECTS OF INTELLECTUAL PROPERTY RIGHTS (TRIPS)

Members,

Desiring to reduce distortions and impediments to international trade, and taking into account the need to promote effective and adequate protection of intellectual property rights, and to ensure that measures and procedures to enforce intellectual property rights do not themselves become barriers to legitimate trade;

Recognizing, to this end, the need for new rules and disciplines concerning: (a) the applicability of the basic principles of GATT 1994 and of relevant international intellectual property agreements or conventions; (b) the provision of adequate standards and principles concerning the availability, scope and use of trade-related intellectual property rights; (c) the provision of effective and appropriate means for the enforcement of trade-related intellectual property rights, taking into account differences in national legal systems; (d) the provision of effective and expeditious procedures for the multilateral prevention and settlement of disputes between governments; and (e) transitional arrangements aiming at the fullest participation in the results of the negotiations;

Recognizing the need for a multilateral framework of principles, rules and disciplines dealing with international trade in counterfeit goods;

Recognizing that intellectual property rights are private rights;

Recognizing the underlying public policy objectives of national systems for the protection of intellectual property, including developmental and technological objectives;

Recognizing also the special needs of the least-developed country Members in respect of maximum flexibility in the domestic implementation of laws and regulations in order to enable them to create a sound and viable technological base;

Emphasizing the importance of reducing tensions by reaching strengthened commitments to resolve disputes on trade-related intellectual property issues through multilateral procedures;

Desiring to establish a mutually supportive relationship between the WTO and the World Intellectual Property Organization (referred to in this Agreement as "WIPO") as well as other relevant international organizations;

Hereby agree as follows:

PART I: GENERAL PROVISIONS AND BASIC PRINCIPLES

Article 1
Nature and Scope of Obligations

1. Members shall give effect to the provisions of this Agreement. Members may, but shall not be obliged to, implement in their law more extensive protection than is required by this Agreement, provided that such protection does not contravene the provisions of this Agreement. Members shall be free to determine the appropriate method of implementing the provisions of this Agreement within their own legal system and practice.

2. For the purposes of this Agreement, the term "intellectual property" refers to all categories of intellectual property that are the subject of Sections 1 through 7 of Part II.

3. Members shall accord the treatment provided for in this Agreement to the nation-

als of other Members.[1] In respect of the relevant intellectual property right, the nationals of other Members shall be understood as those natural or legal persons that would meet the criteria for eligibility for protection provided for in the Paris Convention (1967), the Berne Convention (1971), the Rome Convention and the Treaty on Intellectual Property in Respect of Integrated Circuits, were all Members of the WTO members of those conventions.[2] Any Member availing itself of the possibilities provided in paragraph 3 of Article 5 or paragraph 2 of Article 6 of the Rome Convention shall make a notification as foreseen in those provisions to the Council for Trade-Related Aspects of Intellectual Property Rights (the "Council for TRIPS").

Article 2
Intellectual Property Conventions

1. In respect of Parts II, III and IV of this Agreement, Members shall comply with Articles 1 through 12, and Article 19, of the Paris Convention (1967).

2. Nothing in Parts I to IV of this Agreement shall derogate from existing obligations that Members may have to each other under the Paris Convention, the Berne Convention, the Rome Convention and the Treaty on Intellectual Property in Respect of Integrated Circuits.

Article 3
National Treatment

1. Each Member shall accord to the nationals of other Members treatment no less favorable than that it accords to its own nationals with regard to the protection[3] of intellectual property, subject to the exceptions already provided in, respectively, the Paris Convention (1967), the Berne Convention (1971), the Rome Convention or the Treaty on Intellectual Property in Respect of Integrated Circuits. In respect of performers, producers of phonograms and broadcasting organizations, this obligation only applies in respect of the rights provided under this Agreement. Any Member availing itself of the possibilities provided in Article 6 of the Berne Convention (1971) or paragraph 1(b) of Article 16 of the Rome Convention shall make a notification as foreseen in those provisions to the Council for TRIPS.

2. Members may avail themselves of the exceptions permitted under paragraph 1 in relation to judicial and administrative procedures, including the designation of an address for service or the appointment of an agent within the jurisdiction of a Member, only where such exceptions are necessary to secure compliance with laws and regulations which are not inconsistent with the provisions of this Agreement and where such practices are not applied in a manner which would constitute a disguised restriction on trade.

---

[1] When "nationals" are referred to in this Agreement, they shall be deemed, in the case of a separate customs territory Member of the WTO, to mean persons, natural or legal, who are domiciled or who have a real and effective industrial or commercial establishment in that customs territory.

[2] In this Agreement, "Paris Convention" refers to the Paris Convention for the Protection of Industrial Property; "Paris Convention (1967)" refers to the Stockholm Act of this Convention of 14 July 1967. "Berne Convention" refers to the Berne Convention for the Protection of Literary and Artistic Works; "Berne Convention (1971)" refers to the Paris Act of this Convention of 24 July 1971. "Rome Convention" refers to the International Convention for the Protection of Performers, Producers of Phonograms and Broadcasting Organizations, adopted at Rome on 26 October 1961. "Treaty on Intellectual Property in Respect of Integrated Circuits" (IPIC Treaty) refers to the Treaty on Intellectual Property in Respect of Integrated Circuits, adopted at Washington on 26 May 1989. "WTO Agreement" refers to the Agreement Establishing the WTO.

[3] For the purposes of Articles 3 and 4, "protection" shall include matters affecting the availability, acquisition, scope, maintenance and enforcement of intellectual property rights as well as those matters affecting the use of intellectual property rights specifically addressed in this Agreement.

Article 4
Most-Favoured-Nation Treatment

With regard to the protection of intellectual property, any advantage, favor, privilege or immunity granted by a Member to the nationals of any other country shall be accorded immediately and unconditionally to the nationals of all other Members. Exempted from this obligation are any advantage, favor, privilege or immunity accorded by a Member: (a) deriving from international agreements on judicial assistance or law enforcement of a general nature and not particularly confined to the protection of intellectual property; (b) granted in accordance with the provisions of the Berne Convention (1971) or the Rome Convention authorizing that the treatment accorded be a function not of national treatment but of the treatment accorded in another country; (c) in respect of the rights of performers, producers of phonograms and broadcasting organizations not provided under this Agreement; (d) deriving from international agreements related to the protection of intellectual property which entered into force prior to the entry into force of the WTO Agreement, provided that such agreements are notified to the Council for TRIPS and do not constitute an arbitrary or unjustifiable discrimination against nationals of other Members.

Article 5
Multilateral Agreements on Acquisition or Maintenance of Protection

The obligations under Articles 3 and 4 do not apply to procedures provided in multilateral agreements concluded under the auspices of WIPO relating to the acquisition or maintenance of intellectual property rights.

Article 6
Exhaustion

For the purposes of dispute settlement under this Agreement, subject to the provisions of Articles 3 and 4 nothing in this Agreement shall be used to address the issue of the exhaustion of intellectual property rights.

Article 7
Objectives

The protection and enforcement of intellectual property rights should contribute to the promotion of technological innovation and to the transfer and dissemination of technology, to the mutual advantage of producers and users of technological knowledge and in a manner conducive to social and economic welfare, and to a balance of rights and obligations.

Article 8
Principles

1. Members may, in formulating or amending their laws and regulations, adopt measures necessary to protect public health and nutrition, and to promote the public interest in sectors of vital importance to their socio-economic and technological development, provided that such measures are consistent with the provisions of this Agreement.

2. Appropriate measures, provided that they are consistent with the provisions of this Agreement, may be needed to prevent the abuse of intellectual property rights by right holders or the resort to practices which unreasonably restrain trade or adversely affect the international transfer of technology.

PART II: STANDARDS CONCERNING THE AVAILABILITY, SCOPE AND USE OF INTELLECTUAL PROPERTY RIGHTS

Section 1. Copyright and Related Rights

Article 9
Relation to the Berne Convention

1. Members shall comply with Articles 1 through 21 of the Berne Convention (1971) and the Appendix thereto. However, Members shall not have rights or obligations under this Agreement in respect of the rights conferred under Article 6bis of that Convention or of the rights derived therefrom.

2. Copyright protection shall extend to expressions and not to ideas, procedures, methods of operation or mathematical concepts as such.

Article 10
Computer Programs and Compilations of Data

1. Computer programs, whether in source or object code, shall be protected as literary works under the Berne Convention (1971).

2. Compilations of data or other material, whether in machine readable or other form, which by reason of the selection or arrangement of their contents constitute intellectual creations shall be protected as such. Such protection, which shall not extend to the data or material itself, shall be without prejudice to any copyright subsisting in the data or material itself.

Article 11
Rental Rights

In respect of at least computer programs and cinematographic works, a Member shall provide authors and their successors in title the right to authorize or to prohibit the commercial rental to the public of originals or copies of their copyright works. A Member shall be excepted from this obligation in respect of cinematographic works unless such rental has led to widespread copying of such works which is materially impairing the exclusive right of reproduction conferred in that Member on authors and their successors in title. In respect of computer programs, this obligation does not apply to rentals where the program itself is not the essential object of the rental.

Article 12
Term of Protection

Whenever the term of protection of a work, other than a photographic work or a work of applied art, is calculated on a basis other than the life of a natural person, such term shall be no less than 50 years from the end of the calendar year of authorized publication, or, failing such authorized publication within 50 years from the making of the work, 50 years from the end of the calendar year of making.

Article 13
Limitations and Exceptions

Members shall confine limitations or exceptions to exclusive rights to certain special cases which do not conflict with a normal exploitation of the work and do not unreasonably prejudice the legitimate interests of the right holder.

Article 14
Protection of Performers, Producers of Phonograms (Sound Recordings) and Broadcasting Organizations

1. In respect of a fixation of their performance on a phonogram, performers shall have the possibility of preventing the following acts when undertaken without their authorization: the fixation of their unfixed performance and the reproduction of such fixation. Performers shall also have the possibility of preventing the following acts when undertaken without their authorization: the broadcasting by wireless means and the communication to the public of their live performance.

2. Producers of phonograms shall enjoy the right to authorize or prohibit the direct or indirect reproduction of their phonograms.

3. Broadcasting organizations shall have the right to prohibit the following acts when undertaken without their authorization: the fixation, the reproduction of fixations, and the rebroadcasting by wireless means of broadcasts, as well as the communication to the public of television broadcasts of the same. Where Members do not grant such rights to broadcasting organizations, they shall provide owners of copyright in the subject matter of broadcasts with the possibility of preventing the above acts, subject to the provisions of the Berne Convention (1971).

4. The provisions of Article 11 in respect of computer programs shall apply *mutatis mutandis* to producers of phonograms and any other right holders in phonograms as determined in a Member's law. If on 15 April 1994 a Member has in force a system of equitable remuneration of right holders in respect of the rental of phonograms, it may maintain such system provided that the commercial rental of phonograms is not giving rise to the material impairment of the exclusive rights of reproduction of right holders.

5. The term of the protection available under this Agreement to performers and producers of phonograms shall last at least until the end of a period of 50 years computed from the end of the calendar year in which the fixation was made or the performance took place. The term of protection granted pursuant to paragraph 3 shall last for at least 20 years from the end of the calendar year in which the broadcast took place.

6. Any Member may, in relation to the rights conferred under paragraphs 1, 2 and 3, provide for conditions, limitations, exceptions and reservations to the extent permitted by the Rome Convention. However, the provisions of Article 18 of the Berne Convention (1971) shall also apply, *mutatis mutandis*, to the rights of performers and producers of phonograms in phonograms.

Section 2. Trademarks

Article 15
Protectable Subject Matter

1. Any sign, or any combination of signs, capable of distinguishing the goods or services of one undertaking from those of other undertakings, shall be capable of constituting a trademark. Such signs, in particular words including personal names, letters, numerals, figurative elements and combinations of colors as well as any combination of such signs, shall be eligible for registration as trademarks. Where signs are not inherently capable of distinguishing the relevant goods or services, Members may make registrability depend on distinctiveness acquired through use. Members may require, as a condition of registration, that signs be visually perceptible.

2. Paragraph 1 shall not be understood to prevent a Member from denying registra-

tion of a trademark on other grounds, provided that they do not derogate from the provisions of the Paris Convention (1967).

3. Members may make registrability depend on use. However, actual use of a trademark shall not be a condition for filing an application for registration. An application shall not be refused solely on the ground that intended use has not taken place before the expiry of a period of three years from the date of application.

4. The nature of the goods or services to which a trademark is to be applied shall in no case form an obstacle to registration of the trademark.

5. Members shall publish each trademark either before it is registered or promptly after it is registered and shall afford a reasonable opportunity for petitions to cancel the registration. In addition, Members may afford an opportunity for the registration of a trademark to be opposed.

Article 16
Rights Conferred

1. The owner of a registered trademark shall have the exclusive right to prevent all third parties not having the owner's consent from using in the course of trade identical or similar signs for goods or services which are identical or similar to those in respect of which the trademark is registered where such use would result in a likelihood of confusion. In case of the use of an identical sign for identical goods or services, a likelihood of confusion shall be presumed. The rights described above shall not prejudice any existing prior rights, nor shall they affect the possibility of Members making rights available on the basis of use.

2. Article 6bis of the Paris Convention (1967) shall apply, *mutatis mutandis*, to services. In determining whether a trademark is well-known, Members shall take account of the knowledge of the trademark in the relevant sector of the public, including knowledge in the Member concerned which has been obtained as a result of the promotion of the trademark.

3. Article 6bis of the Paris Convention (1967) shall apply, *mutatis mutandis*, to goods or services which are not similar to those in respect of which a trademark is registered, provided that use of that trademark in relation to those goods or services would indicate a connection between those goods or services and the owner of the registered trademark and provided that the interests of the owner of the registered trademark are likely to be damaged by such use.

Article 17
Exceptions

Members may provide limited exceptions to the rights conferred by a trademark, such as fair use of descriptive terms, provided that such exceptions take account of the legitimate interests of the owner of the trademark and of third parties.

Article 18
Term of Protection

Initial registration, and each renewal of registration, of a trademark shall be for a term of no less than seven years. The registration of a trademark shall be renewable indefinitely.

Article 19
Requirement of Use

1. If use is required to maintain a registration, the registration may be canceled only after an uninterrupted period of at least three years of non-use, unless valid reasons based on the existence of obstacles to such use are shown by the trademark owner. Circumstances arising independently of the will of the owner of the trademark which constitute an obstacle to the use of the trademark, such as import restrictions on or other government requirements for goods or services protected by the trademark, shall be recognized as valid reasons for non-use.

2. When subject to the control of its owner, use of a trademark by another person shall be recognized as use of the trademark for the purpose of maintaining the registration.

Article 20
Other Requirements

The use of a trademark in the course of trade shall not be unjustifiably encumbered by special requirements, such as use with another trademark, use in a special form or use in a manner detrimental to its capability to distinguish the goods or services of one undertaking from those of other undertakings. This will not preclude a requirement prescribing the use of the trademark identifying the undertaking producing the goods or services along with, but without linking it to, the trademark distinguishing the specific goods or services in question of that undertaking.

Article 21
Licensing and Assignment

Members may determine conditions on the licensing and assignment of trademarks, it being understood that the compulsory licensing of trademarks shall not be permitted and that the owner of a registered trademark shall have the right to assign the trademark with or without the transfer of the business to which the trademark belongs.

Section 3. Geographical Indications

Article 22
Protection of Geographical Indications

1. Geographical indications are, for the purposes of this Agreement, indications which identify a good as originating in the territory of a Member, or a region or locality in that territory, where a given quality, reputation or other characteristic of the good is essentially attributable to its geographical origin.

2. In respect of geographical indications, Members shall provide the legal means for interested parties to prevent: (a) the use of any means in the designation or presentation of a good that indicates or suggests that the good in question originates in a geographical area other than the true place of origin in a manner which misleads the public as to the geographical origin of the good; (b) any use which constitutes an act of unfair competition within the meaning of Article 10bis of the Paris Convention (1967).

3. A Member shall, *ex officio* if its legislation so permits or at the request of an interested party, refuse or invalidate the registration of a trademark which contains or consists of a geographical indication with respect to goods not originating in the territory indicated, if use of the indication in the trademark for such goods in that Member is of such a nature as to mislead the public as to the true place of origin.

4. The protection under paragraphs 1, 2 and 3 shall be applicable against a geographical indication which, although literally true as to the territory, region or locality in which the goods originate, falsely represents to the public that the goods originate in another territory.

Article 23
Additional Protection for Geographical Indications for Wines and Spirits

1. Each Member shall provide the legal means for interested parties to prevent use of a geographical indication identifying wines for wines not originating in the place indicated by the geographical indication in question or identifying spirits for spirits not originating in the place indicated by the geographical indication in question, even where the true origin of the goods is indicated or the geographical indication is used in translation or accompanied by expressions such as "kind", "type", "style", "imitation" or the like.[4]

2. The registration of a trademark for wines which contains or consists of a geographical indication identifying wines or for spirits which contains or consists of a geographical indication identifying spirits shall be refused or invalidated, *ex officio* if a Member's legislation so permits or at the request of an interested party, with respect to such wines or spirits not having this origin.

3. In the case of homonymous geographical indications for wines, protection shall be accorded to each indication, subject to the provisions of paragraph 4 of Article 22. Each Member shall determine the practical conditions under which the homonymous indications in question will be differentiated from each other, taking into account the need to ensure equitable treatment of the producers concerned and that consumers are not misled.

4. In order to facilitate the protection of geographical indications for wines, negotiations shall be undertaken in the Council for TRIPS concerning the establishment of a multilateral system of notification and registration of geographical indications for wines eligible for protection in those Members participating in the system.

Article 24
International Negotiations; Exceptions

1. Members agree to enter into negotiations aimed at increasing the protection of individual geographical indications under Article 23. The provisions of paragraphs 4 through 8 below shall not be used by a Member to refuse to conduct negotiations or to conclude bilateral or multilateral agreements. In the context of such negotiations, Members shall be willing to consider the continued applicability of these provisions to individual geographical indications whose use was the subject of such negotiations.

2. The Council for TRIPS shall keep under review the application of the provisions of this Section; the first such review shall take place within two years of the entry into force of the WTO Agreement. Any matter affecting the compliance with the obligations under these provisions may be drawn to the attention of the Council, which, at the request of a Member, shall consult with any Member or Members in respect of such matter in respect of which it has not been possible to find a satisfactory solution through bilateral or plurilateral consultations between the Members concerned. The Council shall take such action as may be agreed to facilitate the operation and further the objectives of this Section.

---

[4] Notwithstanding the first sentence of Article 42, Members may, with respect to these obligations, instead provide for enforcement by administrative action.

3. In implementing this Section, a Member shall not diminish the protection of geographical indications that existed in that Member immediately prior to the date of entry into force of the WTO Agreement.

4. Nothing in this Section shall require a Member to prevent continued and similar use of a particular geographical indication of another Member identifying wines or spirits in connection with goods or services by any of its nationals or domiciliaries who have used that geographical indication in a continuous manner with regard to the same or related goods or services in the territory of that Member either (a) for at least 10 years preceding 15 April 1994 or (b) in good faith preceding that date.

5. Where a trademark has been applied for or registered in good faith, or where rights to a trademark have been acquired through use in good faith either: (a) before the date of application of these provisions in that Member as defined in Part VI; or (b) before the geographical indication is protected in its country of origin; measures adopted to implement this Section shall not prejudice eligibility for or the validity of the registration of a trademark, or the right to use a trademark, on the basis that such a trademark is identical with, or similar to, a geographical indication.

6. Nothing in this Section shall require a Member to apply its provisions in respect of a geographical indication of any other Member with respect to goods or services for which the relevant indication is identical with the term customary in common language as the common name for such goods or services in the territory of that Member. Nothing in this Section shall require a Member to apply its provisions in respect of a geographical indication of any other Member with respect to products of the vine for which the relevant indication is identical with the customary name of a grape variety existing in the territory of that Member as of the date of entry into force of the WTO Agreement.

7. A Member may provide that any request made under this Section in connection with the use or registration of a trademark must be presented within five years after the adverse use of the protected indication has become generally known in that Member or after the date of registration of the trademark in that Member provided that the trademark has been published by that date, if such date is earlier than the date on which the adverse use became generally known in that Member, provided that the geographical indication is not used or registered in bad faith.

8. The provisions of this Section shall in no way prejudice the right of any person to use, in the course of trade, that person's name or the name of that person's predecessor in business, except where such name is used in such a manner as to mislead the public.

9. There shall be no obligation under this Agreement to protect geographical indications which are not or cease to be protected in their country of origin, or which have fallen into disuse in that country.

Section 4. Industrial Designs

Article 25
Requirements for Protection

1. Members shall provide for the protection of independently created industrial designs that are new or original. Members may provide that designs are not new or original if they do not significantly differ from known designs or combinations of known design features. Members may provide that such protection shall not extend to designs dictated essentially by technical or functional considerations.

2. Each Member shall ensure that requirements for securing protection for textile designs, in particular in regard to any cost, examination or publication, do not unreason-

ably impair the opportunity to seek and obtain such protection. Members shall be free to meet this obligation through industrial design law or through copyright law.

Article 26
Protection

1. The owner of a protected industrial design shall have the right to prevent third parties not having the owner's consent from making, selling or importing articles bearing or embodying a design which is a copy, or substantially a copy, of the protected design, when such acts are undertaken for commercial purposes.

2. Members may provide limited exceptions to the protection of industrial designs, provided that such exceptions do not unreasonably conflict with the normal exploitation of protected industrial designs and do not unreasonably prejudice the legitimate interests of the owner of the protected design, taking account of the legitimate interests of third parties.

3. The duration of protection available shall amount to at least 10 years.

Section 5. Patents

Article 27
Patentable Subject Matter

1. Subject to the provisions of paragraphs 2 and 3, patents shall be available for any inventions, whether products or processes, in all fields of technology, provided that they are new, involve an inventive step and are capable of industrial application.[5] Subject to paragraph 4 of Article 65, paragraph 8 of Article 70 and paragraph 3 of this Article, patents shall be available and patent rights enjoyable without discrimination as to the place of invention, the field of technology and whether products are imported or locally produced.

2. Members may exclude from patentability inventions, the prevention within their territory of the commercial exploitation of which is necessary to protect *ordre public* or morality, including to protect human, animal or plant life or health or to avoid serious prejudice to the environment, provided that such exclusion is not made merely because the exploitation is prohibited by their law.

3. Members may also exclude from patentability: (a) diagnostic, therapeutic and surgical methods for the treatment of humans or animals; (b) plants and animals other than micro-organisms, and essentially biological processes for the production of plants or animals other than non-biological and microbiological processes. However, Members shall provide for the protection of plant varieties either by patents or by an effective *sui generis* system or by any combination thereof. The provisions of this subparagraph shall be reviewed four years after the date of entry into force of the WTO Agreement.

Article 28
Rights Conferred

1. A patent shall confer on its owner the following exclusive rights: (a) where the subject matter of a patent is a product, to prevent third parties not having the owner's consent from the acts of: making, using, offering for sale, selling, or importing[6] for

---

[5] For the purposes of this Article, the terms "inventive step" and "capable of industrial application" may be deemed by a Member to be synonymous with the terms "non-obvious" and "useful" respectively.

[6] This right, like all other rights conferred under this Agreement in respect of the use, sale, importation or other distribution of goods, is subject to the provisions of Article 6.

these purposes that product; (b) where the subject matter of a patent is a process, to prevent third parties not having the owner's consent from the act of using the process, and from the acts of: using, offering for sale, selling, or importing for these purposes at least the product obtained directly by that process.

2. Patent owners shall also have the right to assign, or transfer by succession, the patent and to conclude licensing contracts.

Article 29
Conditions on Patent Applicants

1. Members shall require that an applicant for a patent shall disclose the invention in a manner sufficiently clear and complete for the invention to be carried out by a person skilled in the art and may require the applicant to indicate the best mode for carrying out the invention known to the inventor at the filing date or, where priority is claimed, at the priority date of the application.

2. Members may require an applicant for a patent to provide information concerning the applicant's corresponding foreign applications and grants.

Article 30
Exceptions to Rights Conferred

Members may provide limited exceptions to the exclusive rights conferred by a patent, provided that such exceptions do not unreasonably conflict with a normal exploitation of the patent and do not unreasonably prejudice the legitimate interests of the patent owner, taking account of the legitimate interests of third parties.

Article 31
Other Use Without Authorization of the Right Holder

Where the law of a Member allows for other use[7] of the subject matter of a patent without the authorization of the right holder, including use by the government or third parties authorized by the government, the following provisions shall be respected: (a) authorization of such use shall be considered on its individual merits; (b) such use may only be permitted if, prior to such use, the proposed user has made efforts to obtain authorization from the right holder on reasonable commercial terms and conditions and that such efforts have not been successful within a reasonable period of time. This requirement may be waived by a Member in the case of a national emergency or other circumstances of extreme urgency or in cases of public non-commercial use. In situations of national emergency or other circumstances of extreme urgency, the right holder shall, nevertheless, be notified as soon as reasonably practicable. In the case of public non-commercial use, where the government or contractor, without making a patent search, knows or has demonstrable grounds to know that a valid patent is or will be used by or for the government, the right holder shall be informed promptly; (c) the scope and duration of such use shall be limited to the purpose for which it was authorized, and in the case of semi-conductor technology shall only be for public non-commercial use or to remedy a practice determined after judicial or administrative process to be anti-competitive; (d) such use shall be non-exclusive; (e) such use shall be non-assignable, except with that part of the enterprise or goodwill which enjoys such use; (f) any such use shall be authorized predominantly for the supply of the domestic market of the Member authorizing such use; (g) authorization for such use shall be liable, subject to adequate protection of the legitimate interests of the persons

---

[7] "Other use" refers to use other than that allowed under Article 30.

so authorized, to be terminated if and when the circumstances which led to it cease to exist and are unlikely to recur. The competent authority shall have the authority to review, upon motivated request, the continued existence of these circumstances; (h) the right holder shall be paid adequate remuneration in the circumstances of each case, taking into account the economic value of the authorization; (i) the legal validity of any decision relating to the authorization of such use shall be subject to judicial review or other independent review by a distinct higher authority in that Member; (j) any decision relating to the remuneration provided in respect of such use shall be subject to judicial review or other independent review by a distinct higher authority in that Member; (k) Members are not obliged to apply the conditions set forth in subparagraphs (b) and (f) where such use is permitted to remedy a practice determined after judicial or administrative process to be anti-competitive. The need to correct anti-competitive practices may be taken into account in determining the amount of remuneration in such cases. Competent authorities shall have the authority to refuse termination of authorization if and when the conditions which led to such authorization are likely to recur; (l) where such use is authorized to permit the exploitation of a patent ("the second patent") which cannot be exploited without infringing another patent ("the first patent"), the following additional conditions shall apply: (i) the invention claimed in the second patent shall involve an important technical advance of considerable economic significance in relation to the invention claimed in the first patent; (ii) the owner of the first patent shall be entitled to a cross-licence on reasonable terms to use the invention claimed in the second patent; and (iii) the use authorized in respect of the first patent shall be non-assignable except with the assignment of the second patent.

Article 32
Revocation / Forfeiture

An opportunity for judicial review of any decision to revoke or forfeit a patent shall be available.

Article 33
Term of Protection

The term of protection available shall not end before the expiration of a period of twenty years counted from the filing date.[8]

Article 34
Process Patents: Burden of Proof

1. For the purposes of civil proceedings in respect of the infringement of the rights of the owner referred to in paragraph 1(b) of Article 28, if the subject matter of a patent is a process for obtaining a product, the judicial authorities shall have the authority to order the defendant to prove that the process to obtain an identical product is different from the patented process. Therefore, Members shall provide, in at least one of the following circumstances, that any identical product when produced without the consent of the patent owner shall, in the absence of proof to the contrary, be deemed to have been obtained by the patented process: (a) if the product obtained by the patented process is new; (b) if there is a substantial likelihood that the identical

---

[8] It is understood that those Members which do not have a system of original grant may provide that the term of protection shall be computed from the filing date in the system of original grant.

product was made by the process and the owner of the patent has been unable through reasonable efforts to determine the process actually used.

2. Any Member shall be free to provide that the burden of proof indicated in paragraph 1 shall be on the alleged infringer only if the condition referred to in subparagraph (a) is fulfilled or only if the condition referred to in subparagraph (b) is fulfilled.

3. In the adduction of proof to the contrary, the legitimate interests of defendants in protecting their manufacturing and business secrets shall be taken into account.

Section 6. Layout-designs (Topographies) of Integrated Circuits

Article 35
Relation to the IPIC Treaty

Members agree to provide protection to the layout-designs (topographies) of integrated circuits (referred to in this Agreement as "layout-designs") in accordance with Articles 2 through 7 (other than paragraph 3 of Article 6), Article 12 and paragraph 3 of Article 16 of the Treaty on Intellectual Property in Respect of Integrated Circuits and, in addition, to comply with the following provisions.

Article 36
Scope of the Protection

Subject to the provisions of paragraph 1 of Article 37, Members shall consider unlawful the following acts if performed without the authorization of the right holder:[9] importing, selling, or otherwise distributing for commercial purposes a protected layout-design, an integrated circuit in which a protected layout-design is incorporated, or an article incorporating such an integrated circuit only in so far as it continues to contain an unlawfully reproduced layout-design.

Article 37
Acts Not Requiring the Authorization of the Right Holder

1. Notwithstanding Article 36, no Member shall consider unlawful the performance of any of the acts referred to in that Article in respect of an integrated circuit incorporating an unlawfully reproduced layout-design or any article incorporating such an integrated circuit where the person performing or ordering such acts did not know and had no reasonable ground to know, when acquiring the integrated circuit or article incorporating such an integrated circuit, that it incorporated an unlawfully reproduced layout-design. Members shall provide that, after the time that such person has received sufficient notice that the layout-design was unlawfully reproduced, that person may perform any of the acts with respect to the stock on hand or ordered before such time, but shall be liable to pay to the right holder a sum equivalent to a reasonable royalty such as would be payable under a freely negotiated licence in respect of such a layout-design.

2. The conditions set out in subparagraphs (a) through (k) of Article 31 shall apply *mutatis mutandis* in the event of any non-voluntary licensing of a layout-design or of its use by or for the government without the authorization of the right holder.

---

[9] The term "right holder" in this Section shall be understood as having the same meaning as the term "holder of the right" in the IPIC Treaty.

Article 38
Term of Protection

1. In Members requiring registration as a condition of protection, the term of protection of layout-designs shall not end before the expiration of a period of 10 years counted from the date of filing an application for registration or from the first commercial exploitation wherever in the world it occurs.

2. In Members not requiring registration as a condition for protection, layout-designs shall be protected for a term of no less than 10 years from the date of the first commercial exploitation wherever in the world it occurs.

3. Notwithstanding paragraphs 1 and 2, a Member may provide that protection shall lapse 15 years after the creation of the layout-design.

Section 7. Protection of Undisclosed Information

Article 39

1. In the course of ensuring effective protection against unfair competition as provided in Article 10bis of the Paris Convention (1967), Members shall protect undisclosed information in accordance with paragraph 2 and data submitted to governments or governmental agencies in accordance with paragraph 3.

2. Natural and legal persons shall have the possibility of preventing information lawfully within their control from being disclosed to, acquired by, or used by others without their consent in a manner contrary to honest commercial practices[10] so long as such information: (a) is secret in the sense that it is not, as a body or in the precise configuration and assembly of its components, generally known among or readily accessible to persons within the circles that normally deal with the kind of information in question; (b) has commercial value because it is secret; and (c) has been subject to reasonable steps under the circumstances, by the person lawfully in control of the information, to keep it secret.

3. Members, when requiring, as a condition of approving the marketing of pharmaceutical or of agricultural chemical products which utilize new chemical entities, the submission of undisclosed test or other data, the origination of which involves a considerable effort, shall protect such data against unfair commercial use. In addition, Members shall protect such data against disclosure, except where necessary to protect the public, or unless steps are taken to ensure that the data are protected against unfair commercial use.

Section 8. Control of Anti-competitive Practices in Contractual Licences

Article 40

1. Members agree that some licensing practices or conditions pertaining to intellectual property rights which restrain competition may have adverse effects on trade and may impede the transfer and dissemination of technology.

2. Nothing in this Agreement shall prevent Members from specifying in their legisla-

---

[10] For the purpose of this provision, "a manner contrary to honest commercial practices" shall mean at least practices such as breach of contract, breach of confidence and inducement to
breach, and includes the acquisition of undisclosed information by third parties who knew, or were grossly negligent in failing to know, that such practices were involved in the acquisition.

tion licensing practices or conditions that may in particular cases constitute an abuse of intellectual property rights having an adverse effect on competition in the relevant market. As provided above, a Member may adopt, consistently with the other provisions of this Agreement, appropriate measures to prevent or control such practices, which may include for example exclusive grantback conditions, conditions preventing challenges to validity and coercive package licensing, in the light of the relevant laws and regulations of that Member.

3. Each Member shall enter, upon request, into consultations with any other Member which has cause to believe that an intellectual property right owner that is a national or domiciliary of the Member to which the request for consultations has been addressed is undertaking practices in violation of the requesting Member's laws and regulations on the subject matter of this Section, and which wishes to secure compliance with such legislation, without prejudice to any action under the law and to the full freedom of an ultimate decision of either Member. The Member addressed shall accord full and sympathetic consideration to, and shall afford adequate opportunity for, consultations with the requesting Member, and shall cooperate through supply of publicly available non-confidential information of relevance to the matter in question and of other information available to the Member, subject to domestic law and to the conclusion of mutually satisfactory agreements concerning the safeguarding of its confidentiality by the requesting Member.

4. A Member whose nationals or domiciliaries are subject to proceedings in another Member concerning alleged violation of that other Member's laws and regulations on the subject matter of this Section shall, upon request, be granted an opportunity for consultations by the other Member under the same conditions as those foreseen in paragraph 3.

PART III: ENFORCEMENT OF INTELLECTUAL PROPERTY RIGHTS

Section 1. General Obligations

Article 41

1. Members shall ensure that enforcement procedures as specified in this Part are available under their law so as to permit effective action against any act of infringement of intellectual property rights covered by this Agreement, including expeditious remedies to prevent infringements and remedies which constitute a deterrent to further infringements. These procedures shall be applied in such a manner as to avoid the creation of barriers to legitimate trade and to provide for safeguards against their abuse.

2. Procedures concerning the enforcement of intellectual property rights shall be fair and equitable. They shall not be unnecessarily complicated or costly, or entail unreasonable time-limits or unwarranted delays.

3. Decisions on the merits of a case shall preferably be in writing and reasoned. They shall be made available at least to the parties to the proceeding without undue delay. Decisions on the merits of a case shall be based only on evidence in respect of which parties were offered the opportunity to be heard.

4. Parties to a proceeding shall have an opportunity for review by a judicial authority of final administrative decisions and, subject to jurisdictional provisions in a Member's law concerning the importance of a case, of at least the legal aspects of initial judicial decisions on the merits of a case. However, there shall be no obligation to provide an opportunity for review of acquittals in criminal cases.

5. It is understood that this Part does not create any obligation to put in place a judicial system for the enforcement of intellectual property rights distinct from that for the enforcement of law in general, nor does it affect the capacity of Members to enforce their law in general. Nothing in this Part creates any obligation with respect to the distribution of resources as between enforcement of intellectual property rights and the enforcement of law in general.

Section 2. Civil and Administrative Procedures and Remedies

Article 42
Fair and Equitable Procedures

Members shall make available to right holders[11] civil judicial procedures concerning the enforcement of any intellectual property right covered by this Agreement. Defendants shall have the right to written notice which is timely and contains sufficient detail, including the basis of the claims. Parties shall be allowed to be represented by independent legal counsel, and procedures shall not impose overly burdensome requirements concerning mandatory personal appearances. All parties to such procedures shall be duly entitled to substantiate their claims and to present all relevant evidence. The procedure shall provide a means to identify and protect confidential information, unless this would be contrary to existing constitutional requirements.

Article 43
Evidence

1. The judicial authorities shall have the authority, where a party has presented reasonably available evidence sufficient to support its claims and has specified evidence relevant to substantiation of its claims which lies in the control of the opposing party, to order that this evidence be produced by the opposing party, subject in appropriate cases to conditions which ensure the protection of confidential information.

2. In cases in which a party to a proceeding voluntarily and without good reason refuses access to, or otherwise does not provide necessary information within a reasonable period, or significantly impedes a procedure relating to an enforcement action, a Member may accord judicial authorities the authority to make preliminary and final determinations, affirmative or negative, on the basis of the information presented to them, including the complaint or the allegation presented by the party adversely affected by the denial of access to information, subject to providing the parties an opportunity to be heard on the allegations or evidence.

Article 44
Injunctions

1. The judicial authorities shall have the authority to order a party to desist from an infringement, inter alia to prevent the entry into the channels of commerce in their jurisdiction of imported goods that involve the infringement of an intellectual property right, immediately after customs clearance of such goods. Members are not obliged to accord such authority in respect of protected subject matter acquired or ordered by a person prior to knowing or having reasonable grounds to know that dealing in such subject matter would entail the infringement of an intellectual property right.

---

[11] For the purpose of this Part, the term "right holder" includes federations and associations having legal standing to assert such rights.

2. Notwithstanding the other provisions of this Part and provided that the provisions of Part II specifically addressing use by governments, or by third parties authorized by a government, without the authorization of the right holder are complied with, Members may limit the remedies available against such use to payment of remuneration in accordance with subparagraph (h) of Article 31. In other cases, the remedies under this Part shall apply or, where these remedies are inconsistent with a Member's law, declaratory judgments and adequate compensation shall be available.

Article 45
Damages

1. The judicial authorities shall have the authority to order the infringer to pay the right holder damages adequate to compensate for the injury the right holder has suffered because of an infringement of that person's intellectual property right by an infringer who knowingly, or with reasonable grounds to know, engaged in infringing activity.

2. The judicial authorities shall also have the authority to order the infringer to pay the right holder expenses, which may include appropriate attorney's fees. In appropriate cases, Members may authorize the judicial authorities to order recovery of profits and/or payment of pre-established damages even where the infringer did not knowingly, or with reasonable grounds to know, engage in infringing activity.

Article 46
Other Remedies

In order to create an effective deterrent to infringement, the judicial authorities shall have the authority to order that goods that they have found to be infringing be, without compensation of any sort, disposed of outside the channels of commerce in such a manner as to avoid any harm caused to the right holder, or, unless this would be contrary to existing constitutional requirements, destroyed. The judicial authorities shall also have the authority to order that materials and implements the predominant use of which has been in the creation of the infringing goods be, without compensation of any sort, disposed of outside the channels of commerce in such a manner as to minimize the risks of further infringements. In considering such requests, the need for proportionality between the seriousness of the infringement and the remedies ordered as well as the interests of third parties shall be taken into account. In regard to counterfeit trademark goods, the simple removal of the trademark unlawfully affixed shall not be sufficient, other than in exceptional cases, to permit release of the goods into the channels of commerce.

Article 47
Right of Information

Members may provide that the judicial authorities shall have the authority, unless this would be out of proportion to the seriousness of the infringement, to order the infringer to inform the right holder of the identity of third persons involved in the production and distribution of the infringing goods or services and of their channels of distribution.

Article 48
Indemnification of the Defendant

1. The judicial authorities shall have the authority to order a party at whose request measures were taken and who has abused enforcement procedures to provide to a

party wrongfully enjoined or restrained adequate compensation for the injury suffered because of such abuse. The judicial authorities shall also have the authority to order the applicant to pay the defendant expenses, which may include appropriate attorney's fees.

2. In respect of the administration of any law pertaining to the protection or enforcement of intellectual property rights, Members shall only exempt both public authorities and officials from liability to appropriate remedial measures where actions are taken or intended in good faith in the course of the administration of that law.

Article 49
Administrative Procedures

To the extent that any civil remedy can be ordered as a result of administrative procedures on the merits of a case, such procedures shall conform to principles equivalent in substance to those set forth in this Section.

Section 3. Provisional Measures

Article 50

1. The judicial authorities shall have the authority to order prompt and effective provisional measures: (a) to prevent an infringement of any intellectual property right from occurring, and in particular to prevent the entry into the channels of commerce in their jurisdiction of goods, including imported goods immediately after customs clearance; (b) to preserve relevant evidence in regard to the alleged infringement.

2. The judicial authorities shall have the authority to adopt provisional measures *inaudita altera parte* where appropriate, in particular where any delay is likely to cause irreparable harm to the right holder, or where there is a demonstrable risk of evidence being destroyed.

3. The judicial authorities shall have the authority to require the applicant to provide any reasonably available evidence in order to satisfy themselves with a sufficient degree of certainty that the applicant is the right holder and that the applicant's right is being infringed or that such infringement is imminent, and to order the applicant to provide a security or equivalent assurance sufficient to protect the defendant and to prevent abuse.

4. Where provisional measures have been adopted *inaudita altera parte*, the parties affected shall be given notice, without delay after the execution of the measures at the latest. A review, including a right to be heard, shall take place upon request of the defendant with a view to deciding, within a reasonable period after the notification of the measures, whether these measures shall be modified, revoked or confirmed.

5. The applicant may be required to supply other information necessary for the identification of the goods concerned by the authority that will execute the provisional measures.

6. Without prejudice to paragraph 4, provisional measures taken on the basis of paragraphs 1 and 2 shall, upon request by the defendant, be revoked or otherwise cease to have effect, if proceedings leading to a decision on the merits of the case are not initiated within a reasonable period, to be determined by the judicial authority ordering the measures where a Member's law so permits or, in the absence of such a determination, not to exceed 20 working days or 31 calendar days, whichever is the longer.

7. Where the provisional measures are revoked or where they lapse due to any act or omission by the applicant, or where it is subsequently found that there has been no infringement or threat of infringement of an intellectual property right, the judicial

authorities shall have the authority to order the applicant, upon request of the defendant, to provide the defendant appropriate compensation for any injury caused by these measures.

8. To the extent that any provisional measure can be ordered as a result of administrative procedures, such procedures shall conform to principles equivalent in substance to those set forth in this Section.

Section 4. Special Requirements Related to Border Measures[12]

Article 51
Suspension of Release by Customs Authorities

Members shall, in conformity with the provisions set out below, adopt procedures[13] to enable a right holder, who has valid grounds for suspecting that the importation of counterfeit trademark or pirated copyright goods[14] may take place, to lodge an application in writing with competent authorities, administrative or judicial, for the suspension by the customs authorities of the release into free circulation of such goods. Members may enable such an application to be made in respect of goods which involve other infringements of intellectual property rights, provided that the requirements of this Section are met. Members may also provide for corresponding procedures concerning the suspension by the customs authorities of the release of infringing goods destined for exportation from their territories.

Article 52
Application

Any right holder initiating the procedures under Article 51 shall be required to provide adequate evidence to satisfy the competent authorities that, under the laws of the country of importation, there is *prima facie* an infringement of the right holder's intellectual property right and to supply a sufficiently detailed description of the goods to make them readily recognizable by the customs authorities. The competent authorities shall inform the applicant within a reasonable period whether they have accepted the application and, where determined by the competent authorities, the period for which the customs authorities will take action.

Article 53
Security or Equivalent Assurance

1. The competent authorities shall have the authority to require an applicant to provide a security or equivalent assurance sufficient to protect the defendant and the

---

[12] Where a Member has dismantled substantially all controls over movement of goods across its border with another Member with which it forms part of a customs union, it shall not be required to apply the provisions of this Section at that border.

[13] It is understood that there shall be no obligation to apply such procedures to imports of goods put on the market in another country by or with the consent of the right holder, or to goods in transit.

[14] For the purposes of this Agreement: (a) "counterfeit trademark goods" shall mean any goods, including packaging, bearing without authorization a trademark which is identical to the trademark validly registered in respect of such goods, or which cannot be distinguished in its essential aspects from such a trademark, and which thereby infringes the rights of the owner of the trademark in question under the law of the country of importation; (b) "pirated copyright goods" shall mean any goods which are copies made without the consent of the right holder or person duly authorized by the right holder in the country of production and which are made directly or indirectly from an article where the making of that copy would have constituted an infringement of a copyright or a related right under the law of the country of importation.

competent authorities and to prevent abuse. Such security or equivalent assurance shall not unreasonably deter recourse to these procedures.

2. Where pursuant to an application under this Section the release of goods involving industrial designs, patents, layout-designs or undisclosed information into free circulation has been suspended by customs authorities on the basis of a decision other than by a judicial or other independent authority, and the period provided for in Article 55 has expired without the granting of provisional relief by the duly empowered authority, and provided that all other conditions for importation have been complied with, the owner, importer, or consignee of such goods shall be entitled to their release on the posting of a security in an amount sufficient to protect the right holder for any infringement. Payment of such security shall not prejudice any other remedy available to the right holder, it being understood that the security shall be released if the right holder fails to pursue the right of action within a reasonable period of time.

Article 54
Notice of Suspension

The importer and the applicant shall be promptly notified of the suspension of the release of goods according to Article 51.

Article 55
Duration of Suspension

If, within a period not exceeding 10 working days after the applicant has been served notice of the suspension, the customs authorities have not been informed that proceedings leading to a decision on the merits of the case have been initiated by a party other than the defendant, or that the duly empowered authority has taken provisional measures prolonging the suspension of the release of the goods, the goods shall be released, provided that all other conditions for importation or exportation have been complied with; in appropriate cases, this time-limit may be extended by another 10 working days. If proceedings leading to a decision on the merits of the case have been initiated, a review, including a right to be heard, shall take place upon request of the defendant with a view to deciding, within a reasonable period, whether these measures shall be modified, revoked or confirmed. Notwithstanding the above, where the suspension of the release of goods is carried out or continued in accordance with a provisional judicial measure, the provisions of paragraph 6 of Article 50 shall apply.

Article 56
Indemnification of the Importer and of the Owner of the Goods

Relevant authorities shall have the authority to order the applicant to pay the importer, the consignee and the owner of the goods appropriate compensation for any injury caused to them through the wrongful detention of goods or through the detention of goods released pursuant to Article 55.

Article 57
Right of Inspection and Information

Without prejudice to the protection of confidential information, Members shall provide the competent authorities the authority to give the right holder sufficient opportunity to have any goods detained by the customs authorities inspected in order to substantiate the right holder's claims. The competent authorities shall also have authority to give the importer an equivalent opportunity to have any such goods inspected. Where a positive determination has been made on the merits of a case, Members may provide the competent authorities the authority to inform the right holder of the names and addresses of the consignor, the importer and the consignee and of the quantity of the goods in question.

Article 58
Ex Officio *Action*

Where Members require competent authorities to act upon their own initiative and to suspend the release of goods in respect of which they have acquired prima facie evidence that an intellectual property right is being infringed: (a) the competent authorities may at any time seek from the right holder any information that may assist them to exercise these powers; (b) the importer and the right holder shall be promptly notified of the suspension. Where the importer has lodged an appeal against the suspension with the competent authorities, the suspension shall be subject to the conditions, *mutatis mutandis*, set out at Article 55; (c) Members shall only exempt both public authorities and officials from liability to appropriate remedial measures where actions are taken or intended in good faith.

Article 59
Remedies

Without prejudice to other rights of action open to the right holder and subject to the right of the defendant to seek review by a judicial authority, competent authorities shall have the authority to order the destruction or disposal of infringing goods in accordance with the principles set out in Article 46. In regard to counterfeit trademark goods, the authorities shall not allow the re-exportation of the infringing goods in an unaltered state or subject them to a different customs procedure, other than in exceptional circumstances.

Article 60
De Minimis *Imports*

Members may exclude from the application of the above provisions small quantities of goods of a non-commercial nature contained in travelers' personal luggage or sent in small consignments.

Section 5. Criminal Procedures

Article 61

Members shall provide for criminal procedures and penalties to be applied at least in cases of wilful trademark counterfeiting or copyright piracy on a commercial scale. Remedies available shall include imprisonment and/or monetary fines sufficient to provide a deterrent, consistently with the level of penalties applied for crimes of a corresponding gravity. In appropriate cases, remedies available shall also include the seizure, forfeiture and destruction of the infringing goods and of any materials and implements the predominant use of which has been in the commission of the offense. Members may provide for criminal procedures and penalties to be applied in other cases of infringement of intellectual property rights, in particular where they are committed wilfully and on a commercial scale.

PART IV: ACQUISITION AND MAINTENANCE OF INTELLECTUAL PROPERTY RIGHTS AND RELATED INTER-PARTES PROCEDURES

Article 62

1. Members may require, as a condition of the acquisition or maintenance of the intellectual property rights provided for under Sections 2 through 6 of Part II, compliance with reasonable procedures and formalities. Such procedures and formalities shall be consistent with the provisions of this Agreement.

2. Where the acquisition of an intellectual property right is subject to the right being granted or registered, Members shall ensure that the procedures for grant or registration, subject to compliance with the substantive conditions for acquisition of the right, permit the granting or registration of the right within a reasonable period of time so as to avoid unwarranted curtailment of the period of protection.

3. Article 4 of the Paris Convention (1967) shall apply *mutatis mutandis* to service marks.

4. Procedures concerning the acquisition or maintenance of intellectual property rights and, where a Member's law provides for such procedures, administrative revocation and inter partes procedures such as opposition, revocation and cancellation, shall be governed by the general principles set out in paragraphs 2 and 3 of Article 41.

5. Final administrative decisions in any of the procedures referred to under paragraph 4 shall be subject to review by a judicial or quasi-judicial authority. However, there shall be no obligation to provide an opportunity for such review of decisions in cases of unsuccessful opposition or administrative revocation, provided that the grounds for such procedures can be the subject of invalidation procedures.

PART V: DISPUTE PREVENTION AND SETTLEMENT

Article 63
Transparency

1. Laws and regulations, and final judicial decisions and administrative rulings of general application, made effective by a Member pertaining to the subject matter of this Agreement (the availability, scope, acquisition, enforcement and prevention of the abuse of intellectual property rights) shall be published, or where such publication is not practicable made publicly available, in a national language, in such a manner as to enable governments and right holders to become acquainted with them. Agreements concerning the subject matter of this Agreement which are in force between the government or a governmental agency of a Member and the government or a governmental agency of another Member shall also be published.

2. Members shall notify the laws and regulations referred to in paragraph 1 to the Council for TRIPS in order to assist that Council in its review of the operation of this Agreement. The Council shall attempt to minimize the burden on Members in carrying out this obligation and may decide to waive the obligation to notify such laws and regulations directly to the Council if consultations with WIPO on the establishment of a common register containing these laws and regulations are successful. The Council shall also consider in this connection any action required regarding notifications pursuant to the obligations under this Agreement stemming from the provisions of Article 6ter of the Paris Convention (1967).

3. Each Member shall be prepared to supply, in response to a written request from another Member, information of the sort referred to in paragraph 1. A Member, having

reason to believe that a specific judicial decision or administrative ruling or bilateral agreement in the area of intellectual property rights affects its rights under this Agreement, may also request in writing to be given access to or be informed in sufficient detail of such specific judicial decisions or administrative rulings or bilateral agreements.

4. Nothing in paragraphs 1, 2 and 3 shall require Members to disclose confidential information which would impede law enforcement or otherwise be contrary to the public interest or would prejudice the legitimate commercial interests of particular enterprises, public or private.

Article 64
Dispute Settlement

1. The provisions of Articles XXII and XXIII of GATT 1994 as elaborated and applied by the Dispute Settlement Understanding shall apply to consultations and the settlement of disputes under this Agreement except as otherwise specifically provided herein.

2. Subparagraphs 1(b) and 1(c) of Article XXIII of GATT 1994 shall not apply to the settlement of disputes under this Agreement for a period of five years from the date of entry into force of the WTO Agreement.

3. During the time period referred to in paragraph 2, the Council for TRIPS shall examine the scope and modalities for complaints of the type provided for under subparagraphs 1(b) and 1(c) of Article XXIII of GATT 1994 made pursuant to this Agreement, and submit its recommendations to the Ministerial Conference for approval. Any decision of the Ministerial Conference to approve such recommendations or to extend the period in paragraph 2 shall be made only by consensus, and approved recommendations shall be effective for all Members without further formal acceptance process.

PART VI: TRANSITIONAL ARRANGEMENTS

Article 65
Transitional Arrangements

1. Subject to the provisions of paragraphs 2, 3 and 4, no Member shall be obliged to apply the provisions of this Agreement before the expiry of a general period of one year following the date of entry into force of the WTO Agreement.

2. A developing country Member is entitled to delay for a further period of four years the date of application, as defined in paragraph 1, of the provisions of this Agreement other than Articles 3, 4 and 5.

3. Any other Member which is in the process of transformation from a centrally-planned into a market, free-enterprise economy and which is undertaking structural reform of its intellectual property system and facing special problems in the preparation and implementation of intellectual property laws and regulations, may also benefit from a period of delay as foreseen in paragraph 2.

4. To the extent that a developing country Member is obliged by this Agreement to extend product patent protection to areas of technology not so protectable in its territory on the general date of application of this Agreement for that Member, as defined in paragraph 2, it may delay the application of the provisions on product patents of Section 5 of Part II to such areas of technology for an additional period of five years.

5. A Member availing itself of a transitional period under paragraphs 1, 2, 3 or 4 shall ensure that any changes in its laws, regulations and practice made during that period do not result in a lesser degree of consistency with the provisions of this Agreement.

Article 66
Least-Developed Country Members

1. In view of the special needs and requirements of least-developed country Members, their economic, financial and administrative constraints, and their need for flexibility to create a viable technological base, such Members shall not be required to apply the provisions of this Agreement, other than Articles 3, 4 and 5, for a period of 10 years from the date of application as defined under paragraph 1 of Article 65. The Council for TRIPS shall, upon duly motivated request by a least-developed country Member, accord extensions of this period.

2. Developed country Members shall provide incentives to enterprises and institutions in their territories for the purpose of promoting and encouraging technology transfer to least-developed country Members in order to enable them to create a sound and viable technological base.

Article 67
Technical Cooperation

In order to facilitate the implementation of this Agreement, developed country Members shall provide, on request and on mutually agreed terms and conditions, technical and financial cooperation in favor of developing and least-developed country Members. Such cooperation shall include assistance in the preparation of laws and regulations on the protection and enforcement of intellectual property rights as well as on the prevention of their abuse, and shall include support regarding the establishment or reinforcement of domestic offices and agencies relevant to these matters, including the training of personnel.

PART VII: INSTITUTIONAL ARRANGEMENTS; FINAL PROVISIONS

Article 68
Council for Trade-Related Aspects of Intellectual Property Rights

The Council for TRIPS shall monitor the operation of this Agreement and, in particular, Members' compliance with their obligations hereunder, and shall afford Members the opportunity of consulting on matters relating to the trade-related aspects of intellectual property rights. It shall carry out such other responsibilities as assigned to it by the Members, and it shall, in particular, provide any assistance requested by them in the context of dispute settlement procedures. In carrying out its functions, the Council for TRIPS may consult with and seek information from any source it deems appropriate. In consultation with WIPO, the Council shall seek to establish, within one year of its first meeting, appropriate arrangements for cooperation with bodies of that Organization.

Article 69
International Cooperation

Members agree to cooperate with each other with a view to eliminating international trade in goods infringing intellectual property rights. For this purpose, they shall establish and notify contact points in their administrations and be ready to exchange information on trade in infringing goods. They shall, in particular, promote the exchange of information and cooperation between customs authorities with regard to trade in counterfeit trademark goods and pirated copyright goods.

Article 70
Protection of Existing Subject Matter

1. This Agreement does not give rise to obligations in respect of acts which occurred before the date of application of the Agreement for the Member in question.

2. Except as otherwise provided for in this Agreement, this Agreement gives rise to obligations in respect of all subject matter existing at the date of application of this Agreement for the Member in question, and which is protected in that Member on the said date, or which meets or comes subsequently to meet the criteria for protection under the terms of this Agreement. In respect of this paragraph and paragraphs 3 and 4, copyright obligations with respect to existing works shall be solely determined under Article 18 of the Berne Convention (1971), and obligations with respect to the rights of producers of phonograms and performers in existing phonograms shall be determined solely under Article 18 of the Berne Convention (1971) as made applicable under paragraph 6 of Article 14 of this Agreement.

3. There shall be no obligation to restore protection to subject matter which on the date of application of this Agreement for the Member in question has fallen into the public domain.

4. In respect of any acts in respect of specific objects embodying protected subject matter which become infringing under the terms of legislation in conformity with this Agreement, and which were commenced, or in respect of which a significant investment was made, before the date of acceptance of the WTO Agreement by that Member, any Member may provide for a limitation of the remedies available to the right holder as to the continued performance of such acts after the date of application of this Agreement for that Member. In such cases the Member shall, however, at least provide for the payment of equitable remuneration.

5. A Member is not obliged to apply the provisions of Article 11 and of paragraph 4 of Article 14 with respect to originals or copies purchased prior to the date of application of this Agreement for that Member.

6. Members shall not be required to apply Article 31, or the requirement in paragraph 1 of Article 27 that patent rights shall be enjoyable without discrimination as to the field of technology, to use without the authorization of the right holder where authorization for such use was granted by the government before the date this Agreement became known.

7. In the case of intellectual property rights for which protection is conditional upon registration, applications for protection which are pending on the date of application of this Agreement for the Member in question shall be permitted to be amended to claim any enhanced protection provided under the provisions of this Agreement. Such amendments shall not include new matter.

8. Where a Member does not make available as of the date of entry into force of the WTO Agreement patent protection for pharmaceutical and agricultural chemical products commensurate with its obligations under Article 27, that Member shall: (a) notwithstanding the provisions of Part VI, provide as from the date of entry into force of the WTO Agreement a means by which applications for patents for such inventions can be filed; (b) apply to these applications, as of the date of application of this Agreement, the criteria for patentability as laid down in this Agreement as if those criteria were being applied on the date of filing in that Member or, where priority is available and claimed, the priority date of the application; and (c) provide patent protection in accordance with this Agreement as from the grant of the patent and for the remainder of the patent term, counted from the filing date in accordance with

Article 33 of this Agreement, for those of these applications that meet the criteria for protection referred to in subparagraph (b).

9. Where a product is the subject of a patent application in a Member in accordance with paragraph 8(a), exclusive marketing rights shall be granted, notwithstanding the provisions of Part VI, for a period of five years after obtaining marketing approval in that Member or until a product patent is granted or rejected in that Member, whichever period is shorter, provided that, subsequent to the entry into force of the WTO Agreement, a patent application has been filed and a patent granted for that product in another Member and marketing approval obtained in such other Member.

Article 71
Review and Amendment

1. The Council for TRIPS shall review the implementation of this Agreement after the expiration of the transitional period referred to in paragraph 2 of Article 65. The Council shall, having regard to the experience gained in its implementation, review it two years after that date, and at identical intervals thereafter. The Council may also undertake reviews in the light of any relevant new developments which might warrant modification or amendment of this Agreement.

2. Amendments merely serving the purpose of adjusting to higher levels of protection of intellectual property rights achieved, and in force, in other multilateral agreements and accepted under those agreements by all Members of the WTO may be referred to the Ministerial Conference for action in accordance with paragraph 6 of Article X of the WTO Agreement on the basis of a consensus proposal from the Council for TRIPS.

Article 72
Reservations

Reservations may not be entered in respect of any of the provisions of this Agreement without the consent of the other Members.

Article 73
Security Exceptions

Nothing in this Agreement shall be construed: (a) to require a Member to furnish any information the disclosure of which it considers contrary to its essential security interests; or (b) to prevent a Member from taking any action which it considers necessary for the protection of its essential security interests; (i) relating to fissionable materials or the materials from which they are derived; (ii) relating to the traffic in arms, ammunition and implements of war and to such traffic in other goods and materials as is carried on directly or indirectly for the purpose of supplying a military establishment; (iii) taken in time of war or other emergency in international relations; or (c) to prevent a Member from taking any action in pursuance of its obligations under the United Nations Charter for the maintenance of international peace and security.

APPENDIX X

PROTOCOL RELATING TO THE MADRID AGREEMENT CONCERNING THE INTERNATIONAL REGISTRATION OF MARKS

Article 1
Membership in the Madrid Union

The States party to this Protocol (hereinafter referred to as "the Contracting States"), even where they are not party to the Madrid Agreement Concerning the International Registration of Marks as revised at Stockholm in 1967 and as amended in 1979 (hereinafter referred to as "the Madrid (Stockholm) Agreement"), and the organizations referred to in Article 14(1)(b) which are party to this Protocol (hereinafter referred to as "the Contracting Organizations") shall be members of the same Union of which countries party to the Madrid (Stockholm) Agreement are members. Any reference in this Protocol to "Contracting Parties" shall be construed as a reference to both Contracting States and Contracting Organizations.

Article 2
Securing Protection Through International Registration

(1) Where an application for the registration of a mark has been filed with the Office of a Contracting Party, or where a mark has been registered in the register of the Office of a Contracting Party, the person in whose name that application (hereinafter referred to as "the basic application" or that registration (hereinafter referred to as "the basic registration") stands may, subject to the provisions of this Protocol, secure protection for his mark in the territory of the Contracting Parties, by obtaining the registration of that mark in the register of the International Bureau of the World Intellectual Property Organization (hereinafter referred to as "the international registration," "the International Register," "the International Bureau" and "the Organization," respectively), provided that,

(i) where the basic application has been filed with the Office of a Contracting State or where the basic registration has been made by such an Office, the person in whose name that application or registration stands is a national of that Contracting State, or is domiciled, or has a real and effective industrial or commercial establishment, in the said Contracting State,

(ii) where the basic application has been filed with the Office of a Contracting Organization or where the basic registration has been made by such an Office, the person in whose name that application or registration stands is a national of a State member of that Contracting Organization, or is domiciled, or has a real and effective industrial or commercial establishment, in the territory of the said Contracting Organization.

(2) The application for international registration (hereinafter referred to as "the international application") shall be filed with the International Bureau through the intermediary of the Office with which the basic application was filed or by which the basic registration was made (hereinafter referred to as "the Office of origin"), as the case may be.

(3) Any reference in this Protocol to an "Office" or an "Office of a Contracting Party" shall be construed as a reference to the office that is in charge, on behalf of a Contracting Party, of the registration of marks, and any reference in this Protocol to "marks" shall be construed as a reference to trademarks and service marks.

(4) For the purposes of this Protocol, "territory of a Contracting Party" means, where the Contracting Party is a State, the territory of that State and, where the Contracting Party is an intergovernmental organization, the territory in which the constituting treaty of that intergovernmental organization applies.

Article 3
International Application

(1) Every international application under this Protocol shall be presented on the form prescribed by the Regulations. The Office of origin shall certify that the particulars appearing in the international application correspond to the particulars appearing, at the time of the certification, in the basic application or basic registration, as the case may be. Furthermore, the said Office shall indicate,

(i) in the case of a basic application, the date and number of that application,

(ii) in the case of a basic registration, the date and number of that registration as well as the date and number of the application from which the basic registration resulted. The Office of origin shall also indicate the date of the international application.

(2) The applicant must indicate the goods and services in respect of which protection of the mark is claimed and also, if possible, the corresponding class or classes according to the classification established by the Nice Agreement Concerning the International Classification of Goods and Services for the Purposes of the Registration of Marks. If the applicant does not give such indication, the International Bureau shall classify the goods and services in the appropriate classes of the said classification. The indication of classes given by the applicant shall be subject to control by the International Bureau, which shall exercise the said control in association with the Office of origin. In the event of disagreement between the said Office and the International Bureau, the opinion of the latter shall prevail.

(3) If the applicant claims color as a distinctive features of his mark, he shall be required

(i) to state the fact, and to file with his international application a notice specifying the color or the combination of colors claimed;

(ii) to append to his international application copies in color of the said mark, which shall be attached to the notifications given by the International Bureau; the number of such copies shall be fixed by the Regulations.

(4) The International Bureau shall register immediately the marks filed in accordance with Article 2. The international registration shall be the date on which the international application was received in the Office of origin, provided that the international application has been received by the International Bureau within a period of two months from that date. If the international application has not been received within that period, the international registration shall bear the date on which the said international application was received by the International Bureau. The International Bureau shall notify the international registration without delay to the Offices concerned. Marks registered in the International Register shall be published in a periodical gazette issued by the International Bureau, on the basis of the particulars contained in the international application.

(5) With a view to the publicity to be given to marks registered in the International Register, each Office shall receive from the International Bureau a number of copies of the said gazette free of charge and a number of copies at a reduced price, under the conditions fixed by the Assembly referred to in Article 10 (hereinafter referred to as "the Assembly"). Such publicity shall be deemed to be sufficient for the purposes of all the Contracting Parties, and no other publicity may be required of the holder of the international registration.

Article 3bis
Territorial Effect

The protection resulting from the international registration shall extend to any Contracting Party only at the request of the person who files the international application or who is the holder of the international registration. However, no such request can be made with respect to the Contracting Party whose Office is the Office of origin.

Article 3ter
Request for "Territorial Extension"

(1) Any request for extension of the protection resulting from the international registration to any Contracting Party shall be specially mentioned in the international application.

(2) A request for territorial extension may also be made subsequently to the international registration. Any such request shall be presented on the form prescribed by the Regulations. It shall be immediately recorded by the International Bureau, which shall notify such recordal without delay to the Office or Offices concerned. Such recordal shall be published in the periodical gazette of the International Bureau. Such territorial extension shall be effective from the date on which it has been recorded in the International Register; it shall cease to be valid on the expiry of the international registration to which it relates.

Article 4
Effects of International Registration

(1)(a) From the date of the registration or recordal effected in accordance with the provisions of Articles 3 and 3ter, the protection of the mark in each of the Contracting Parties concerned shall be the same as if the mark had been deposited direct with the Office of that Contracting Party. If no refusal has been notified to the International Bureau in accordance with Article 5(1) and (2) or if a refusal notified in accordance with the said Article has been withdrawn subsequently, the protection of the mark in the Contracting Party concerned shall, as from the said date, be the same as if the mark had been registered by the Office of that Contracting Party.

(b) The indication of classes of goods and services provided for in Article 3 shall not bind the Contracting Parties with regard to the determination of the scope of the protection of the mark.

(2) Every international registration shall enjoy the right of priority provided for by Article 4 of the Paris Convention for the Protection of Industrial Property, without it being necessary to comply with the formalities prescribed in Section D of that Article.

Article 4bis
Replacement of a National or Regional
Registration by an International Registration

(1) Where a mark that is the subject of a national or regional registration in the Office of a Contracting Party is also the subject of an international registration and both registrations stand in the name of the same person, the international registration is deemed to replace the national or regional registration, without prejudice to any rights acquired by virtue of the latter, provided that

(i) the protection resulting from the international registration extends to the said Contracting Party under Article 3ter(1) or (2),

(ii) all the goods and services listed in the national or regional registration are also listed in the international registration in respect of the said Contracting Party,

(iii) such extension takes effect after the date of the national or regional registration.

(2) The Office referred to in paragraph (1) shall, upon request, be required to take note in its register of the international registration.

Article 5
Refusal and Invalidation of Effects of International Registration in Respect of Certain Contracting Parties

(1) Where the applicable legislation so authorizes, any Office of a Contracting Party which has been notified by the International Bureau of an extension to that Contracting Party, under Article 3ter(1) or (2), of the protection resulting from the international registration shall have the right to declare in a notification of refusal that protection cannot be granted in the said Contracting Party to the mark which is the subject of such extension. Any such refusal can be based only on the grounds which would apply, under the Paris Convention for the Protection of Industrial Property, in the case of a mark deposited direct with the Office which notifies the refusal. However, protection may not be refused, even partially, by reason only that the applicable legislation would permit registration only in a limited number of classes or for a limited number of goods or services.

(2)(a) Any Office wishing to exercise such right shall notify its refusal to the International Bureau, together with a statement of all grounds, within the period prescribed by the law applicable to that Office and at the latest, subject to subparagraphs (b) and (c), before the expiry of one year from the date on which the notification of the extension referred to in paragraph (1) has been sent to that Office by the International Bureau.

(b) Notwithstanding subparagraph (a), any Contracting Party may declare that, for international registrations made under this Protocol, the time limit of one year referred to in subparagraph (a) is replaced by 18 months.

(c) Such declaration may also specify that, when a refusal of protection may result from an opposition to the granting of protection, such refusal may be notified by the Office of the said Contracting Party to the International Bureau after the expiry of the 18-month time limit. Such an Office may, with respect to any given international registration, notify a refusal of protection after the expiry of the 18-month time limit, but only if

(i) it has, before expiry of the 18-month time limit, informed the International Bureau of the possibility that oppositions may be filed after the expiry of the 18-month time limit, and

(ii) the notification of the refusal based on an opposition is made within a time limit of not more than seven months from the date on which the opposition period begins; if the opposition period expires before this time limit of seven months, the notification must be made within a time limit of one month from the expiry of the opposition period.

(d) Any declaration under subparagraphs (b) or (c) may be made in the instruments referred to in Article 14(2), and the effective date of the declaration shall be the same as the date of entry into force of this Protocol with respect to the State or intergovernmental organization having made the declaration. Any such declaration may also be made later, in which case the declaration shall have effect three months after its receipt by the Director General of the Organization (hereinafter referred to as "the Director General"), or at any later date indicated in the declaration, in respect of any international registration whose date is the same as or is later than the effective date of the declaration.

(e) Upon the expiry of a period of ten years from the entry into force of this Protocol, the Assembly shall examine the operation of the system established by subparagraphs (a) to (d). Thereafter, the provisions of the said subparagraphs may be modified by a unanimous decision of the Assembly.

(3) The International Bureau shall, without delay, transmit one of the copies of the

notification of refusal to the holder of the international registration. The said holder shall have the same remedies as if the mark had been deposited by him direct with the Office which has notified its refusal. Where the International Bureau has received information under paragraph (2)(c)(i), it shall, without delay, transmit the said information to the holder of the international registration.

(4) The grounds for refusing a mark shall be communicated by the International Bureau to any interested party who may so request.

(5) Any Office which has not notified, with respect to a given international registration, any provisional or final refusal to the International Bureau in accordance with paragraphs (1) and (2) shall, with respect to that international registration, lose the benefit of the right provided for in paragraph (1).

(6) Invalidation, by the competent authorities of a Contracting Party, of the effects, in the territory of that Contracting Party, of an international registration may not be pronounced without the holder of such international registration having, in good time, been afforded the opportunity of defending his rights. Invalidation shall be notified to the International Bureau.

Article 5bis
Documentary Evidence of Legitimacy of Use of Certain Elements of the Mark

Documentary evidence of the legitimacy of the use of certain elements incorporated in a mark, such as armorial bearings, escutcheons, portraits, honorary distinctions, titles, trade names, names of persons other than the name of the applicant, or other like inscriptions, which might be required by the Offices of the Contracting Parties shall be exempt from any legalization as well as from any certification other than that of the Office of origin.

Article 5ter
Copies of Entries in International Register; Searches for Anticipations; Extracts from International Register

(1) The International Bureau shall issue to any person applying therefor, upon the payment of a fee fixed by the Regulations, a copy of the entries in the International Register concerning a specific mark.

(2) The International Bureau may also, upon payment, undertake searches for anticipations among marks that are the subject of international registrations.

(3) Extracts from the International Register requested with a view to their production in one of the Contracting Parties shall be exempt from any legalization.

Article 6
Period of Validity of International Registration; Dependence and Independence of International Registration

(1) Registration of a mark at the International Bureau is effected for ten years, with the possibility of renewal under the conditions specified in Article 7.

(2) Upon expiry of a period of five years from the date of the international registration, such registration shall become independent of the basic application or the registration resulting therefrom, or of the basic registration, as the case may be, subject to the following provisions.

(3) The protection resulting from the international registration, whether or not it has been the subject of a transfer, may no longer be invoked if, before the expiry of five years from the date of the international registration, the basic application or the

registration resulting therefrom, or the basic registration, as the case may be, has been withdrawn, has lapsed, has been renounced or has been the subject of a final decision of rejection, revocation, cancellation or invalidation, in respect of all or some of the goods and services listed in the international registration. The same applies if

(i) an appeal against a decision refusing the effects of the basic application,

(ii) an action requesting the withdrawal of the basic application or the revocation, cancellation or invalidation of the registration resulting from the basic application or of the basic registration, or

(iii) an opposition to the basic application results, after the expiry of the five-year period, in a final decision of rejection, revocation, cancellation or invalidation, or ordering the withdrawal, of the basic application, or the registration resulting therefrom, or the basic registration, as the case may be, provided that such appeal, action or opposition had begun before the expiry of the said period. The same also applies if the basic application is withdrawn, or the registration resulting from the basic application or the basic registration is renounced, after the expiry of the five-year period, provided that, at the time of the withdrawal or renunciation, the said application or registration was the subject of a proceeding referred to in item (i), (ii) or (iii) and that such proceeding had begun before the expiry of the said period.

(4) The Office of origin shall, as prescribed in the Regulations, notify the International Bureau of the facts and decisions relevant under paragraph (3), and the International Bureau shall, as prescribed in the Regulations, notify the interested parties and effect any publication accordingly. The Office of origin shall, where applicable, request the International Bureau to cancel, to the extent applicable, the international registration, and the International Bureau shall proceed accordingly.

Article 7
Renewal of International Registration

(1) Any international registration may be renewed for a period of ten years from the expiry of the preceding period, by the mere payment of the basic fee and, subject to Article 8(7), of the supplementary and complementary fees provided for in Article 8(2).

(2) Renewal may not bring about any change in the international registration in its latest form.

(3) Six months before the expiry of the term of protection, the International Bureau shall, by sending an unofficial notice, remind the holder of the international registration and his representative, if any, of the exact date of expiry.

(4) Subject to the payment of a surcharge fixed by the Regulations, a period of grace of six months shall be allowed for renewal of the international registration.

Article 8
Fees for International Application and Registration

(1) The Office of origin may fix, at its own discretion, and collect, for its own benefit, a fee which it may require from the applicant for international registration or from the holder of the international registration in connection with the filing of the international application or the renewal of the international registration.

(2) Registration of a mark at the International Bureau shall be subject to the advance payment of an international fee which shall, subject to the provisions of paragraph (7)(a), include,

(i) a basic fee;

(ii) a supplementary fee for each class of the International Classification, beyond three, into which the goods or services to which the mark is applied will fall;

(iii) a complementary fee for any request for extension of protection under Article 3ter.

(3) However, the supplementary fee specified in paragraph (2)(ii) may, without prejudice to the date of the international registration, be paid within the period fixed by the Regulations if the number of classes of goods or services has been fixed or disputed by the International Bureau. If, upon expiry of the said period, the supplementary fee has not been paid or the list of goods or services has not been reduced to the required extent by the applicant, the international application shall be deemed to have been abandoned.

(4) The annual product of the various receipts from international registration, with the exception of the receipts derived from the fees mentioned in paragraph (2)(ii) and (iii), shall be divided equally among the Contracting Parties by the International Bureau, after deduction of the expenses and charges necessitated by the implementation of this Protocol.

(5) The amounts derived from the supplementary fees provided for in paragraph (2)(ii) shall be divided, at the expiry of each year, among the interested Contracting Parties in proportion to the number of marks for which protection has been applied for in each of them during that year, this number being multiplied, in the case of Contracting Parties which make an examination, by a coefficient which shall be determined by the Regulations.

(6) The amounts derived from the complementary fees provided for in paragraph (2)(iii) shall be divided according to the same rules as those provided for in paragraph (5).

(7)(a) Any Contracting Party may declare that, in connection with each international registration in which it is mentioned under Article 3ter, and in connection with the renewal of any such international registration, it wants to receive, instead of a share in the revenue produced by the supplementary and complementary fees, a fee (hereinafter referred to as "the individual fee") whose amount shall be indicated in the declaration, and can be changed in further declarations, but may not be higher than the equivalent of the amount which the said Contracting Party's Office would be entitled to receive from an applicant for a ten-year registration, or from the holder of a registration for a ten-year renewal of that registration, of the mark in the register of the said Office, the said amount being diminished by the savings resulting from the international procedure. Where such an individual fee is payable,

(i) no supplementary fees referred to in paragraph (2)(ii) shall be payable if only Contracting Parties which have made a declaration under this subparagraph are mentioned under Article 3ter, and

(ii) no complementary fee referred to in paragraph (2)(iii) shall be payable in respect of any Contracting Party which has made a declaration under this subparagraph.

(b) Any declaration under subparagraph (a) may be made in the instruments referred to in Article 14(2), and the effective date of the declaration shall be the same as the date of entry into force of this Protocol with respect to the State or intergovernmental organization having made the declaration. Any such declaration may also be made later, in which case the declaration shall have effect three months after its receipt by the Director General, or at any later date indicated in the declaration, in respect of any international registration whose date is the same as or is later than the effective date of the declaration.

Article 9
Recordal of Change in the Ownership of an International Registration

At the request of the person in whose name the international registration stands, or at the request of an interested Office made ex officio or at the request of an interested person, the International Bureau shall record in the International Register any change in the ownership of that registration, in respect of all or some of the Contracting Parties in whose territories the said registration has effect and in respect of all or some of the goods and services listed in their registration, provided that the new holder is a person who, under Article 2(1), is entitled to file international applications.

Article 9bis
Recordal of Certain Matters Concerning an International Registration

The International Bureau shall record in the International Register
(i) any change in the name or address of the holder of the international registration,
(ii) the appointment of a representative of the holder of the international registration and any other relevant fact concerning such representative,
(iii) any limitation, in respect of all or some of the Contracting Parties, of the goods and services listed in the international registration,
(iv) any renunciation, cancellation or invalidation of the international registration in respect of all or some of the Contracting Parties,
(v) any other relevant fact, identified in the Regulations, concerning the rights in a mark that is the subject of an international registration.

Article 9ter
Fees for Certain Recordals

Any recordal under Article 9 or under Article 9bis may be subject to the payment of a fee.

Article 9quater
Common Office of Several Contracting States

(1) If several Contracting States agree to effect the unification of their domestic legislations on marks, they may notify the Director General
(i) that a common Office shall be substituted for the national Office of each of them, and
(ii) that the whole of their respective territories shall be deemed to be a single State for the purposes of the application of all or part of the provisions preceding this Article as well as the provisions of Articles 9quinquies and 9sexies.
(2) Such notification shall not take effect until three months after the date of the communication thereof by the Director General to the other Contracting Parties.

Article 9quinquies
Transformation of an International Registration into National or Regional Applications

Where, in the event that the international registration is canceled at the request of the Office of origin under Article 6(4), in respect of all or some of the goods and services listed in the said registration, the person who was the holder of the international registration files an application for the registration of the same mark with the Office of any of the Contracting Parties in the territory of which the international registration had effect, that application shall be treated as if it had been filed on the date of the international registration according to Article 3(4) or on the date of recordal of the territorial extension according to Article 3ter(2) and, if the international registration enjoyed priority, shall enjoy the same priority, provided that

(i) such application is filed within three months from the date on which the international registration was cancelled,

(ii) the goods and services listed in the application are in fact covered by the list of goods and services contained in the international registration in respect of the Contracting Party concerned, and

(iii) such application complies with all the requirements of the applicable law, including the requirements concerning fees.

Article 9sexies
Safeguard of the Madrid (Stockholm) Agreement

(1) Where, with regard to a given international application or a given international registration, the Office of origin is the Office of a State that is party to both this Protocol and the Madrid (Stockholm) Agreement, the provisions of this Protocol shall have no effect in the territory of any other State that is also party to both this Protocol and the Madrid (Stockholm) Agreement.

(2) The Assembly may, by a three-fourths majority, repeal paragraph (1), or restrict the scope of paragraph (1), after the expiry of a period of ten years from the entry into force of this Protocol, but not before the expiry of a period of five years from the date on which the majority of the countries party to the Madrid (Stockholm) Agreement have become party to this Protocol. In the vote of the Assembly, only those States which are party to both the said Agreement and this Protocol shall have the right to participate.

[*Article 10 - Article 13* Omitted]

Article 14
Becoming Party to the Protocol; Entry into Force

(1)(a) Any State that is a party to the Paris Convention for the Protection of Industrial Property may become party to this Protocol.

(b) Furthermore, any intergovernmental organization may also become party to this Protocol where the following conditions are fulfilled:

(i) at least one of the member States of that organization is a party to the Paris Convention for the Protection of Industrial Property;

(ii) that organization has a regional Office for the purposes of registering marks with effect in the territory of the organization, provided that such Office is not the subject of a notification under Article 9quater.

(2) Any State or organization referred to in paragraph (1) may sign this Protocol. Any such State or organization may, if it has signed this Protocol, deposit an instrument of ratification, acceptance or approval of this Protocol or, if it has not signed this Protocol, deposit an instrument of accession to this Protocol.

(3) The instruments referred to in paragraph (2) shall be deposited with the Director General.

(4)(a) This Protocol shall enter into force three months after four instruments of ratification, acceptance, approval or accession have been deposited, provided that at least one of those instruments has been deposited by a country party to the Madrid (Stockholm) Agreement and at least one other of those instruments has been deposited by a State not party to the Madrid (Stockholm) Agreement or by any of the organizations referred to in paragraph (1)(b).

(b) With respect to any other State or organization referred to in paragraph (1), this Protocol shall enter into force three months after the date on which its ratification, acceptance, approval or accession has been notified by the Director General.

(5) Any State or organization referred to in paragraph (1) may, when depositing its instrument of ratification, acceptance or approval of, or accession to, this Protocol, declare that the protection resulting from any international registration effected under this Protocol before the date of entry into force of this Protocol with respect to it cannot be extended to it.

Article 15
Denunciation

(1) This Protocol shall remain in force without limitation as to time.

(2) Any Contracting Party may denounce this Protocol by notification addressed to the Director General.

(3) Denunciation shall take effect one year after the day on which the Director General has received the notification.

(4) The right of denunciation provided for by this Article shall not be exercised by any Contracting Party before the expiry of five years from the date upon which this Protocol entered into force with respect to that Contracting Party.

(5)(a) Where a mark is the subject of an international registration having effect in the denouncing State or intergovernmental organization at the date on which the denunciation becomes effective, the holder of such registration may file an application for the registration of the same mark with the Office of the denouncing State or intergovernmental organization, which shall be treated as if it had been filed on the date of the international registration according to Article 3(4) or on the date of recordal of the territorial extension according to Article 3ter(2) and, if the international registration enjoyed priority, enjoy the same priority, provided that

(i) such application is filed within two years from the date on which the denunciation became effective,

(ii) the goods and services listed in the application are in fact covered by the list of goods and services contained in the international registration in respect of the denouncing State or intergovernmental organization, and

(iii) such application complies with all the requirements of the applicable law, including the requirements concerning fees.

(b) The provisions of subparagraph (a) shall also apply in respect of any mark that is the subject of an international registration having effect in Contracting Parties other than the denouncing State or intergovernmental organization at the date on which denunciation becomes effective and whose holder, because of the denunciation, is no longer entitled to file international applications under Article 2(1).

[*Article 16* Omitted]

APPENDIX XI

TRADEMARK REGISTRATION TREATY

Article 1
Abbreviated Expressions

For the purposes of this Treaty, unless expressly stated otherwise:

(i) "Office" means the agency entrusted by a Contracting Party with the registration of marks;

(ii) "registration" means the registration of a mark by an Office;

(iii) "application" means an application for registration;

(iv) references to a "person" shall be construed as references to both a natural person and a legal entity;

(v) "holder" means the person whom the register of marks shows as the holder of the registration;

(vi) "register of marks" means the collection of data maintained by an Office, which includes the contents of all registrations and all data recorded in respect of all registrations, irrespective of the medium in which such data are stored;

(vii) "Paris Convention" means the Paris Convention for the Protection of Industrial Property, signed at Paris on March 20, 1883, as revised and amended;

(viii) "Nice Classification" means the classification established by the Nice Agreement Concerning the International Classification of Goods and Services for the Purposes of the Registration of Marks, signed at Nice on June 15, 1957, as revised and amended;

(ix) "Contracting Party" means any State or regional intergovernmental organization party to this Treaty;

(x) references to an "instrument of ratification" shall be construed as including references to instruments of acceptance and approval;

(xi) "Organization" means the World Intellectual Property Organization;

(xii) "Director General" means the Director General of the Organization;

(xiii) "Regulations" means the Regulations under this Treaty that are referred to in Article 17.

Article 2
Marks to Which the Treaty Applies

(1) [*Nature of Marks*] (a) This Treaty shall apply to marks consisting of visible signs, provided that only those Contracting Parties which accept for registration three-dimensional marks shall be obliged to apply this Treaty to such marks.

(b) This Treaty shall not apply to hologram marks and to marks not consisting of visible signs, in particular, sound marks and olfactory marks.

(2) [*Kinds of Marks*] (a) This Treaty shall apply to marks relating to goods (trademarks) or services (service marks) or both goods and services.

(b) This Treaty shall not apply to collective marks, certification marks and guarantee marks.

Article 3
Application

(1) [*Indications or Elements Contained in or Accompanying an Application; Fee*]

(a) Any Contracting Party may require that an application contain some or all of the following indications or elements:

(i) a request for registration;

(ii) the name and address of the applicant;

(iii) the name of a State of which the applicant is a national if he is the national of any State, the name of a State in which the applicant has his domicile, if any, and the name of a State in which the applicant has a real and effective industrial or commercial establishment, if any;

(iv) where the applicant is a legal entity, the legal nature of that legal entity and the State, and, where applicable, the territorial unit within that State, under the law of which the said legal entity has been organized;

(v) where the applicant has a representative, the name and address of that representative;

(vi) where an address for service is required under Article 4(2)(b), such address;

(vii) where the applicant wishes to take advantage of the priority of an earlier application, a declaration claiming the priority of that earlier application, together with indications in support of that declaration, as required by the law of the Contracting Party.

(viii) where the applicant wishes to take advantage of any protection resulting from the display of goods and/or services in an exhibition, a declaration to that effect, together with indications in support of that declaration, as required by the law of the Contracting Party;

(ix) where the Office of the Contracting Party uses characters (letters and numbers) that it considers as being standard and where the applicant wishes that the mark be registered and published in standard characters, a statement to that effect;

(x) where the applicant wishes to claim color as a distinctive feature of the mark, a statement to that effect as well as the name or names of the color or colors claimed and an indication, in respect of each color, of the principal parts of the mark which are in that color;

(xi) where the mark is a three-dimensional mark, a statement to that effect;

(xii) one or more reproductions of the mark;

(xiii) a transliteration of the mark or of certain parts of the mark;

(xiv) a translation of the mark or of certain parts of the mark;

(xv) the names of the goods and/or services for which the registration is sought, grouped according to the classes of the Nice Classification, each group preceded by the number of the class of the said Classification to which that group of goods or services belongs;

(xvi) a signature by, or other self-identification of, the person specified in paragraph (4);

(xvii) a declaration of intention to use the mark, as required by the law of the Contracting Party.

(b) The applicant may file, instead of or in addition to the declaration of intention to use the mark referred to in subparagraph (a)(xvii), a declaration of actual use of the mark and evidence to that effect, as required by the law of the Contracting Party.

(c) Any Contracting Party may require that, in respect of the application, fees be paid to the Office.

(2) [*Presentation*] As regards the requirements concerning the presentation of the application, no Contracting Party shall refuse the application,

(i) where the application is presented in writing on paper, if it is presented, subject to paragraph (3), on a form corresponding to the application Form provided for in the Regulations,

(ii) where the Contracting Party allows the transmittal of communications to its Office by telefacsimile and the application is so transmitted, if the paper copy resulting from such transmittal corresponds, subject to paragraph (3), to the application Form referred to in item (i),

(iii) where the Contracting Party allows the transmittal of communications to its Office by electronic means and the application is so transmitted, if such transmittal is effected in the manner prescribed in the Regulations.

(3) [*Language*] Any Contracting Party may require that the application be in the language, or in one of the languages, admitted by its Office.

(4) [*Signature*] (a) Any Contracting Party may require that the application be signed by the applicant or, at the option of the applicant, by his representative.

(b) Notwithstanding subparagraph (a), any Contracting Party may require that the declarations referred to in paragraph (1)(a)(xvii) and (b) be signed by the applicant himself even if he has a representative.

(5) [*Single Application for Goods and/or Services in Several Classes*] One and the same application may relate to several goods and/or services, irrespective of whether they belong to one class or to several classes of the Nice Classification.

(6) [*Actual Use*] Any Contracting Party may require that, where a declaration of intention to use has been filed under paragraph (1)(a)(xvii), the applicant furnish to its Office within a time limit fixed in its law, subject to the minimum time limit prescribed in the Regulations, evidence of the actual use of the mark, as required by the said law.

(7) [*Prohibition of Other Requirements*] No Contracting Party may demand that requirements other than those referred to in paragraphs (1) to (4) and (6) be complied with in respect of the application. In particular, the following may not be required in respect of the application throughout its pendency:

(i) the furnishing of any certificate of, or extract from, a register of commerce;

(ii) an indication of the applicant's carrying on of an industrial or commercial activity, as well as the furnishing of evidence to that effect;

(iii) an indication of the applicant's carrying on of an activity corresponding to the goods and/or services listed in the application, as well as the furnishing of evidence to that effect;

(iv) the furnishing of evidence to the effect that the mark has been registered in the register of marks of another Contracting Party or of a State party to the Paris Convention which is not a Contracting Party, except where the applicant claims the application of Article 6quinquies of the Paris Convention.

(8) [*Evidence*] Any Contracting Party may require that evidence be furnished to its Office in the course of the examination of the application where that Office may reasonably doubt the veracity of any indication or element contained in the application.

Article 4
Representation;
Address for Service

(1) [*Representatives Admitted to Practice*] Any Contracting Party may require that any person appointed as representative for the purposes of any procedure before its Office be a representative admitted to practice before its Office.

(2) [*Mandatory Representation; Address for Service*] (a) Any Contracting Party may require that, for the purposes of any procedure before its Office, any person who has neither a domicile nor a real and effective industrial or commercial establishment on its territory be represented by a representative.

(b) Any Contracting Party may, to the extent that it does not require representation in accordance with subparagraph (a), require that, for the purposes of any procedure before its Office, any person who has neither a domicile nor a real and effective industrial or commercial establishment on its territory have an address for service on that territory.

(3) [*Power of Attorney*] (a) Whenever a Contracting Party allows or requires an applicant, a holder or any other interested person to be represented by a representative before its Office, it may require that the representative be appointed in a separate communication (hereinafter referred to as "power of attorney") indicating the name of, and signed by, the applicant, the holder or the other person, as the case may be.

(b) The power of attorney may relate to one or more applications and/or registrations identified in the power of attorney or, subject to any exception indicated by the appointing person, to all existing and future applications and/or registrations of that person.

(c) The power of attorney may limit the powers of the representative to certain acts. Any Contracting Party may require that any power of attorney under which the representative has the right to withdraw an application or to surrender a registration contain an express indication to that effect.

(d) Where a communication is submitted to the Office by a person who refers to himself in the communication as a representative but where the Office is, at the time of the receipt of the communication, not in possession of the required power of attorney, the Contracting Party may require that the power of attorney be submitted to its Office within the time limit fixed by the Contracting Party, subject to the minimum time limit prescribed in the Regulations.

(e) As regards the requirements concerning the presentation and contents of the power of attorney, no Contracting Party shall refuse the effects of the power of attorney,

(i) where the power of attorney is presented in writing on paper, if it is presented, subject to paragraph (4), on a form corresponding to the power of attorney Form provided for in the Regulations,

(ii) where the Contracting Party allows the transmittal of communications to its Office by telefacsimile and the power of attorney is so transmitted, if the paper copy resulting from such transmittal corresponds, subject to paragraph (4), to the power of attorney Form referred to in item (i),

(iii) where the Contracting Party allows the transmittal of communications to its Office by electronic means and the power of attorney is so transmitted, if such transmittal is effected in the manner prescribed in the Regulations.

(4) [*Language*] Any Contracting Party may require that the power of attorney be in the language, or in one of the languages, admitted by its Office.

(5) [*Reference to Power of Attorney*] Any Contracting Party may require that any communication made to its Office by a representative for the purposes of a procedure before that Office contain a reference to the power of attorney on the basis of which the representative acts.

(6) [*Prohibition of Other Requirements*] No Contracting Party may demand that requirements other than those referred to in paragraphs (3) to (5) be complied with in respect of the matters dealt with in those paragraphs.

(7) [*Evidence*] Any Contracting Party may require that evidence be furnished to its Office where that Office may reasonably doubt the veracity of any indication contained in any communication referred to in paragraphs (2) to (5).

Article 5
Filing Date

(1) [*Permitted Requirements*] (a) Subject to subparagraph (b) and paragraph (2), a Contracting Party shall accord as the filing date of an application the date on which the Office received the following indications and elements in the language required under Article 3(3):

(i) an express or implicit indication that the registration of a mark is sought;

(ii) indications allowing the identity of the applicant to be established;

(iii) indications sufficient to contact the applicant or his representative, if any, by mail;

(iv) a sufficiently clear reproduction of the mark whose registration is sought;

(v) the list of the goods and/or services for which the registration is sought;

(vi) where Article 3(1)(a)(xvii) or (b) applies, the declaration referred to in Article 3(1)(a)(xvii) or the declaration and evidence referred to in Article 3(1)(b), respectively, as required by the law of the Contracting Party, those declarations being, if so required by the said law, signed by the applicant himself even if he has a representative.

(b) Any Contracting Party may accord as the filing date of the application the date on which the Office received only some, rather than all, of the indications and elements referred to in subparagraph (a) or received them in a language other than the language required under Article 3(3).

(2) [*Permitted Additional Requirement*] (a) A Contracting Party may provide that no filing date shall be accorded until the required fees are paid.

(b) A Contracting Party may apply the requirement referred to in subparagraph (a) only if it applied such requirement at the time of becoming party to this Treaty.

(3) [*Corrections and Time Limits*] The modalities of, and time limits for, corrections under paragraphs (1) and (2) shall be fixed in the Regulations.

(4) [*Prohibition of Other Requirements*] No Contracting Party may demand that requirements other than those referred to in paragraphs (1) and (2) be complied with in respect of the filing date.

Article 6
Single Registration for Goods and/or Services in Several Classes

Where goods and/or services belonging to several classes of the Nice Classification have been included in one and the same application, such an application shall result in one and the same registration.

Article 7
Division of Application and Registration

(1) [*Division of Application*] (a) Any application listing several goods and/or services (hereinafter referred to as "initial application") may,

(i) at least until the decision by the Office on the registration of the mark,

(ii) during any opposition proceedings against the decision of the Office to register the mark,

(iii) during any appeal proceedings against the decision on the registration of the mark, be divided by the applicant or at his request into two or more applications (hereinafter referred to as "divisional applications") by distributing among the latter the goods and/or services listed in the initial application. The divisional applications shall preserve the filing date of the initial application and the benefit of the right of priority, if any.

(b) Any Contracting Party shall, subject to subparagraph (a), be free to establish requirements for the division of an application, including the payment of fees.

(2) [*Division of Registration*] Paragraph (1) shall apply, *mutatis mutandis*, with respect to a division of a registration. Such a division shall be permitted

(i) during any proceedings in which the validity of the registration is challenged before the Office by a third party,

(ii) during any appeal proceedings against a decision taken by the Office during the former proceedings, provided that a Contracting Party may exclude the possibility of the division of registrations if its law allows third parties to oppose the registration of a mark before the mark is registered.

Article 8
Signature

(1) [*Communication on Paper*] Where a communication to the Office of a Contracting Party is on paper and a signature is required, that Contracting Party

(i) shall, subject to item (iii), accept a handwritten signature,

(ii) shall be free to allow, instead of a handwritten signature, the use of other forms of signature, such as a printed or stamped signature, or the use of a seal,

(iii) may, where the natural person who signs the communication is its national and such person's address is in its territory, require that a seal be used instead of a handwritten signature,

(iv) may, where a seal is used, require that the seal be accompanied by an indication in letters of the name of the natural person whose seal is used.

(2) [*Communication by Telefacsimile*] (a) Where a Contracting Party allows the transmittal of communications to its Office by telefacsimile, it shall consider the communication signed if, on the printout produced by the telefacsimile, the reproduction of the signature, or the reproduction of the seal together with, where required under paragraph (1)(iv), the indication in letters of the name of the natural person whose seal is used, appears.

(b) The Contracting Party referred to in subparagraph (a) may require that the paper whose reproduction was transmitted be filed with its Office within a certain period, subject to the minimum period prescribed in the Regulations.

(3) [*Communication by Electronic Means*] Where a Contracting Party allows the transmittal of communications to its Office by electronic means, it shall consider the communication signed if the latter identifies the sender of the communication by electronic means as prescribed by it.

(4) [*Prohibition of Requirement of Certification*] No Contracting Party may require the attestation, notarization, authentication, legalization or other certification of any signature or other means of self-identification referred to in the preceding paragraphs, except, if the law of the Contracting Party so provides, where the signature concerns the surrender of a registration.

Article 9
Classification of Goods and/or Services

(1) [*Indications of Goods and/or Services*] Each registration and any publication effected by an Office which concerns an application or registration and which indicates goods and/or services shall indicate the goods and/or services by their names, grouped according to the classes of the Nice Classification, and each group shall be preceded by the number of the class of the said Classification to which that group of goods or services belongs.

(2) [*Goods or Services in the Same Class or in Different Classes*] (a) Goods or services may not be considered as being similar to each other on the ground that, in any registration or publication by the Office, they appear in the same class of the Nice Classification.

(b) Goods or services may not be considered as being dissimilar from each other on the ground that, in any registration or publication by the Office, they appear in different classes of the Nice Classification.

Article 10
Changes in Names or Addresses

(1) [*Changes in the Name or Address of the Holder*] (a) Where there is no change in the person of the holder but there is a change in his name and/or address, each Contracting Party shall accept that a request for the recordal of the change by the Office in its register of marks be made in a communication signed by the holder or his representative and indicating the registration number of the registration concerned and the change to be recorded. As regards the requirements concerning the presentation of the request, no Contracting Party shall refuse the request,

(i) where the request is presented in writing on paper, if it is presented, subject to subparagraph (c), on a form corresponding to the request Form provided for in the Regulations,

(ii) where the Contracting Party allows the transmittal of communications to its Office by telefacsimile and the request is so transmitted, if the paper copy resulting from such transmittal corresponds, subject to subparagraph (c), to the request Form referred to in item (i),

(iii) where the Contracting Party allows the transmittal of communications to its Office by electronic means and the request is so transmitted, if such transmittal is effected in the manner prescribed in the Regulations.

(b) Any Contracting Party may require that the request indicate

(i) the name and address of the holder;

(ii) where the holder has a representative, the name and address of that representative;

(iii) where the holder has an address for service, such address.

(c) Any Contracting Party may require that the request be in the language, or in one of the languages, admitted by its Office.

(d) Any Contracting Party may require that, in respect of the request, a fee be paid to the Office.

(e) A single request shall be sufficient even where the change relates to more than one registration, provided that the registration numbers of all registrations concerned are indicated in the request.

(2) [*Change in the Name or Address of the Applicant*] Paragraph (1) shall apply, *mutatis mutandis*, where the change concerns an application or applications, or both an application or applications and a registration or registrations, provided that, where the application number of any application concerned has not yet been issued or is not known to the applicant or his representative, the request otherwise identifies that application as prescribed in the Regulations.

(3) [*Change in the Name or Address of the Representative or in the Address for Service*] Paragraph (1) shall apply, *mutatis mutandis*, to any change in the name or address of the representative, if any, and to any change relating to the address for service, if any.

(4) [*Prohibition of Other Requirements*] No Contracting Party may demand that requirements other than those referred to in paragraphs (1) to (3) be complied with in respect of the request referred to in this Article. In particular, the furnishing of any certificate concerning the change may not be required.

(5) [*Evidence*] Any Contracting Party may require that evidence be furnished to its Office where that Office may reasonably doubt the veracity of any indication contained in the request.

Article 11
Change in Ownership

(1) [*Change in the Ownership of a Registration*] (a) Where there is a change in the person of the holder, each Contracting Party shall accept that a request for the recordal of the change by the Office in its register of marks be made in a communication signed by the holder or his representative, or by the person who acquired the ownership (hereinafter referred to as "new owner") or his representative, and indicating the registration number of the registration concerned and the change to be recorded. As regards the requirements concerning the presentation of the request, no Contracting Party shall refuse the request,

(i) where the request is presented in writing on paper, if it is presented, subject to paragraph (2)(a), on a form corresponding to the request Form provided for in the Regulations,

(ii) where the Contracting Party allows the transmittal of communications to its Office by telefacsimile and the request is so transmitted, if the paper copy resulting from such transmittal corresponds, subject to paragraph (2)(a), to the request Form referred to in item (i),

(iii) where the Contracting Party allows the transmittal of communications to its Office by electronic means and the request is so transmitted, if such transmittal is effected in the manner prescribed in the Regulations.

(b) Where the change in ownership results from a contract, any Contracting Party may require that the request indicate that fact and be accompanied, at the option of the requesting party, by one of the following:

(i) a copy of the contract, which copy may be required to be certified, by a notary public or any other competent public authority, as being in conformity with the original contract;

(ii) an extract of the contract showing the change in ownership, which extract may be required to be certified, by a notary public or any other competent public authority, as being a true extract of the contract;

(iii) an uncertified certificate of transfer drawn up in the form and with the content as prescribed in the Regulations and signed by both the holder and the new owner;

(iv) an uncertified transfer document drawn up in the form and with the content as prescribed in the Regulations and signed by both the holder and the new owner.

(c) Where the change in ownership results from a merger, any Contracting Party may require that the request indicate that fact and be accompanied by a copy of a document, which document originates from the competent authority and evidences the merger, such as a copy of an extract from a register of commerce, and that that copy be certified by the authority which issued the document or by a notary public or any other competent public authority, as being in conformity with the original document.

(d) Where there is a change in the person of one or more but not all of several co-holders and such change in ownership results from a contract or a merger, any Contracting Party may require that any co-holder in respect of which there is no change in ownership give his express consent to the change in ownership in a document signed by him.

(e) Where the change is ownership does not result from a contract or a merger but from another ground, for example, from operation of law or a court decision, any Contracting Party may require that the request indicate that fact and be accompanied by a copy of a document evidencing the change and that the copy be certified as being in conformity with the original document by the authority which issued the document or by a notary public or any other competent public authority.

(f) Any Contracting Party may require that the request indicate

(i) the name and address of the holder;

(ii) the name and address of the new owner;

(iii) the name of a State of which the new owner is a national if he is the national of any State, the name of a State in which the new owner has his domicile, if any, and the name of a State in which the new owner has a real and effective industrial or commercial establishment, if any;

(iv) where the new owner is a legal entity, the legal nature of that legal entity and the State, and, where applicable, the territorial unit within that State, under the law of which the said legal entity has been organized;

(v) where the holder has a representative, the name and address of that representative;

(vi) where the holder has an address for service, such address;

(vii) where the new owner has a representative, the name and address of that representative;

(viii) where the new owner is required to have an address for service under Article 4(2)(b), such address.

(g) Any Contracting Party may require that, in respect of the request, a fee be paid to the Office.

(h) A single request shall be sufficient even where the change relates to more than one registration, provided that the holder and the new owner are the same for each registration and that the registration numbers of all registrations concerned are indicated in the request.

(i) Where the change of ownership does not affect all the goods and/or services listed in the holder's registration, and the applicable law allows the recording of such change, the Office shall create a separate registration referring to the goods and/or services in respect of which the ownership has changed.

(2) [*Language; Translation*] (a) Any Contracting Party may require that the request, the certificate of transfer or the transfer document referred to in paragraph (1) be in the language, or in one of the languages, admitted by its Office.

(b) Any Contracting Party may require that, if the documents referred to in paragraph (1)(b)(i) and (ii), (c) and (e) are not in the language, or in one of the languages, admitted by its Office, the request be accompanied by a translation or a certified translation of the required document in the language, or in one of the languages, admitted by its Office.

(3) [*Change in the Ownership of an Application*] Paragraphs (1) and (2) shall apply, *mutatis mutandis*, where the change in ownership concerns an application or applications, or both an application or applications and a registration or registrations, provided that, where the application number of any application concerned has not yet been issued or is not known to the applicant or his representative, the request otherwise identifies that application as prescribed in the Regulations.

(4) [*Prohibition of Other Requirements*] No Contracting Party may demand that requirements other than those referred to in paragraphs (1) to (3) be complied with in respect of the request referred to in this Article. In particular, the following may not be required:

(i) subject to paragraph (1)(c), the furnishing of any certificate of, or extract from, a register of commerce;

(ii) an indication of the new owner's carrying on of an industrial or commercial activity, as well as the furnishing of evidence to that effect;

(iii) an indication of the new owner's carrying on of an activity corresponding to the goods and/or services affected by the change in ownership, as well as the furnishing of evidence to either effect;

(iv) an indication that the holder transferred, entirely or in part, his business or the relevant goodwill to the new owner, as well as the furnishing of evidence to either effect.

(5) [*Evidence*] Any Contracting Party may require that evidence, or further evidence where paragraph (1)(c) or (e) applies, be furnished to its Office where that Office may reasonably doubt the veracity of any indication contained in the request or in any document referred to in the present Article.

Article 12
Correction of a Mistake

(1) [*Correction of a Mistake in Respect of a Registration*] (a) Each Contracting Party shall accept that the request for the correction of a mistake which was made in the application or other request communicated to its Office and which mistake is reflected in its register of marks and/or any publication by its Office be made in a communication signed by the holder or his representative and indicating the registration number of the registration concerned, the mistake to be corrected and the correction to be entered. As regards the requirements concerning the presentation of the request, no Contracting Party shall refuse the request,

(i) where the request is presented in writing on paper, if it is presented, subject to subparagraph (c), on a form corresponding to the request Form provided for in the Regulations,

(ii) where the Contracting Party allows the transmittal of communications to its Office by telefacsimile and the request is so transmitted, if the paper copy resulting from such transmittal corresponds, subject to subparagraph (c), to the request Form referred to in item (i).

(b) Any Contracting Party may require that the request indicate

(i) the name and address of the holder;

(ii) where the holder has a representative, the name and address of that representative;

(iii) where the holder has an address for service, such address.

(c) Any Contracting Party may require that the request be in the language, or in one of the languages, admitted by its Office.

(d) Any Contracting Party may require that, in respect of the request, a fee be paid to the Office.

(e) A single request shall be sufficient even where the correction relates to more than one registration of the same person, provided that the mistake and the requested correction are the same for each registration and that the registration numbers of all registrations concerned are indicated in the request.

(2) [*Correction of a Mistake in Respect of an Application*] Paragraph (1) shall apply, *mutatis mutandis*, where the mistake concerns an application or applications, or both an application or applications and a registration or registrations, provided that, where the application number of any application concerned has not yet been issued or is not known to the applicant or his representative, the request otherwise identifies that application as prescribed in the Regulations.

(3) [*Prohibition of Other Requirements*] No Contracting Party may demand that requirements other than those referred to in paragraphs (1) and (2) be complied with in respect of the request referred to in this Article.

(4) [*Evidence*] Any Contracting Party may require that evidence be furnished to its

Office where that Office may reasonably doubt that the alleged mistake is in fact a mistake.

(5) [*Mistakes Made by the Office*] The Office of a Contracting Party shall correct its own mistakes, ex officio, or upon request, for no fee.

(6) [*Uncorrectable Mistakes*] No Contracting Party shall be obliged to apply paragraphs (1) and (2) to any mistake which cannot be corrected under its law.

Article 13
Duration and Renewal of Registration

(1) [*Indications or Elements Contained in or Accompanying a Request for Renewal; Fee*] (a) Any Contracting Party may require that the renewal of a registration be subject to the filing of a request and that such request contain some or all of the following indications:

(i) an indication that renewal is sought;

(ii) the name and address of the holder;

(iii) the registration number of the registration concerned;

(iv) at the option of the Contracting Party, the filing date of the application which resulted in the registration concerned or the registration date of the registration concerned;

(v) where the holder has a representative, the name and address of that representative;

(vi) where the holder has an address for service, such address;

(vii) where the Contracting Party allows the renewal of a registration to be made for some only of the goods and/or services which are recorded in the register of marks and such a renewal is requested, the names of the recorded goods and/or services for which the renewal is requested or the names of the recorded goods and/or services for which the renewal is not requested, grouped according to the classes of the Nice Classification, each group preceded by the number of the class of the said Classification to which that group of goods or services belongs;

(viii) a signature by, or other self-identification of, the holder or, at the option of the holder, his representative.

(b) Any Contracting Party may require that, in respect of the request for renewal, a fee be paid to the Office. Once the fee has been paid in respect of the initial period of the registration or of any renewal period, no further payment may be required for the maintenance of the registration in respect of that period.

(c) Any Contracting Party may require that the request for renewal be presented, and the fee referred to in subparagraph (b) be paid, to the Office within the period fixed by the law of the Contracting Party, subject to the minimum periods prescribed in the Regulations.

(2) [*Presentation*] As regards the requirements concerning the presentation of the request for renewal, no Contracting Party shall refuse the request,

(i) where the request is presented in writing on paper, if it is presented, subject to paragraph (3), on a form corresponding to the request Form provided for in the Regulations,

(ii) where the Contracting Party allows the transmittal of communications to its Office by telefacsimile and the request is so transmitted, if the paper copy resulting from such transmittal corresponds, subject to paragraph (3), to the request Form referred to in item (i),

(iii) where the Contracting Party allows the transmittal of communications to its Office by electronic means and the request is so transmitted, if such transmittal is effected in the manner prescribed in the Regulations.

(3) [*Language*] Any Contracting Party may require that the request for renewal be in the language, or in one of the languages, admitted by its Office.

(4) [*Prohibition of Other Requirements*] No Contracting Party may demand that requirements other than those referred to in paragraphs (1) to (3) be complied with in respect of the request for renewal. In particular, the following may not be required:

(i) any reproduction or other identification of the mark;

(ii) the furnishing of evidence to the effect that the mark has been registered, or that its registration has been renewed, in the register of marks of any other Contracting Party;

(iii) the furnishing of a declaration and/or evidence concerning use of the mark.

(5) [*Evidence*] Any Contracting Party may require that evidence be furnished to its Office in the course of the examination of the request for renewal where that Office may reasonably doubt the veracity of any indication or element contained in the request for renewal.

(6) [*Prohibition of Substantive Examination*] No Office of a Contracting Party may, for the purposes of effecting the renewal, examine the registration as to substance.

(7) [*Duration*] The duration of the initial period of the registration, and the duration of each renewal period, shall be 10 years.

Article 14
Observations in Case of Intended Refusal

An application or a request under Articles 10 to 13 may not be refused totally or in part by an Office without giving the applicant or the requesting party, as the case may be, an opportunity to make observations on the intended refusal within a reasonable time limit.

Article 15
Obligation to Comply with the Paris Convention

Any Contracting Party shall comply with the provisions of the Paris Convention which concern marks.

Article 16
Service Marks

The Contracting Parties shall apply the provisions of the Paris Convention which concern trademarks to service marks.

Article 17
Regulations

(1) [*Content*] (a) The Regulations annexed to this Treaty provide rules concerning

(i) matters which this Treaty expressly provides to be "prescribed in the Regulations";

(ii) any details useful in the implementation of the provisions of this Treaty;

(iii) any administrative requirements, matters or procedures.

(b) The Regulations also contain Model International Forms.

(2) [*Conflict Between the Treaty and the Regulations*] In the case of conflict between the provisions of this Treaty and those of the Regulations, the former shall prevail.

Article 18
Revision, Protocols

(1) [*Revision*] This Treaty may be revised by a diplomatic conference.

(2) [*Protocols*] For the purposes of further developing the harmonization of laws on marks, protocols may be adopted by a diplomatic conference in so far as those protocols do not contravene the provisions of this Treaty.

(3) [*Becoming Party to a Protocol*] Only Contracting Parties may become party to any protocol adopted under paragraph (1).

[*Article 19 - Article 20* Omitted]

Article 21
Reservations

(1) [*Special Kinds of Marks*] Any State or regional intergovernmental organization may declare through a reservation that, notwithstanding Article 2(1)(a) and (2)(a), any of the provisions of Articles 3(1) and (2), 5, 7, 11 and 13 shall not apply to associated marks, defensive marks or derivative marks. Such reservation shall specify those of the aforementioned provisions to which the reservation relates.

(2) [*Modalities*] Any reservation under paragraph (1) shall be made in declaration accompanying the instrument of ratification of, or accession to, this Treaty of the State or intergovernmental organization making the reservation.

(3) [*Withdrawal*] Any reservation under paragraph (1) may be withdrawn at any time.

(4) [*Prohibition of Other Reservations*] No reservation to this Treaty other than the reservation allowed under paragraph (1) shall be permitted.

[*Article 22* Omitted]

Article 23
Denunciation of the Treaty

(1) [*Notification*] Any Contracting Party may denounce this Treaty by notification addressed to the Director General.

(2) [*Effective Date*] Denunciation shall take effect one year from the date on which the Director General has received the notification. It shall not affect the application of this Treaty to any application pending or any mark registered in respect of the denouncing Contracting Party at the time of the expiration of the said one-year period, provided that the denouncing Contracting Party may, after the expiration of the said one-year period, discontinue applying this Treaty to any registration as from the date on which that registration is due for renewal.

[*Article 24 - Article 25* Omitted]

Index

-A-

A. Bourjois & Co. v. Katzel 320
Abbott, Frederick M. 13, 14, 22-24
Acuff-Rose Music Inc. v. Campbell 170
Aesthetic Veto 129
Africa 33
Agreement on Trade Related Aspects of IP Rights
(see TRIPS)
Aide, Christopher 114-115, 123
Albania 335
Alderman, Elliott C. 145-147
Alexander, Dean C. 243-246, 282-284
Alexander, Jay 19
"Americanization" of culture 83, 184-185, 396
Anderson, M. Jean 242-243
Anticounterfeit programs 296-297
(see also Piracy)
Antiquities, protection of
(see Cultural property)
Appellations of origin 36
(see also Geographic indicators)
Arena, Robert A. 205
Aristotle 25, 88, 114, 142
Asphalt Jungle 167-168
Attribution
(see Patrimony, right of)
Australia 131-133, 309, 322, 374
Austria 202, 316, 335, 368
Authorship 112-119, 147-148, 172
(see also Personality)
E.C. view 118
relationship to droit moral 113-114
relationship to droit de suite 147-148
role in copyright protection 113, 115
romantic view 112-114, 114, 115
U.S. view 118
(see also Moral rights)

-B-

Balkanization 203
Basset v. Societe des Auteurs, Compositeurs, et Editeurs de Musique (SACEM) 280-281
Belgium 154, 173 (see also Benelux)
Bellagio Declaration 107-109
Benelux 340, 360, 368
Berg, Jeff 125-128
Berne Convention 8, 13-14, 15, 48, 91, 113, 121-123, 145, 154, 161-163, 167-169, 172-173, 192, 201-203, 205, 206-207, 212-213, 229-230, 231, 237, 242, 245, 246-247, 256, 282, 290, 305-307, 335, 358, 361, 362, 365, 376-377, 395
Berryman, Cathryn A. 76-77
Bilateral treaty 190, 222
Biodiversity 79-82, 82-83
Biota 82-83
Bi-polar structure 212-213
Bodenhausen, G.M.C. 286-287
Border problem 319, 370-375
(see also Territoriality, Extraterritoriality)
Borodkin, Lisa J. 96-103-104
Boulware, Margaret A. 15, 16-18, 20-22, 248, 257-258
Braga, Carlos Alberto Primo 42-46
Brazil 354, 369
Broadcast rights 89-90, 90-91, 307
Brown, Bartram S. 106-107
Bulgaria 335
Burger, Peter 222, 224-227, 229-230, 305-307

-C-

California Art Preservation Act 137
Canada 243, 245,246-247, 316, 322
(see also Canadian Free Trade Agreement; NAFTA)
Canadian Free Trade Agreement 79, 180-181
Caribbean Basin 57-58
Carter, Stephen L. 26-27
Catanese, Adrienne 219-220
Censorship, 66-69, 128-129, 157-160
impact of moral rights on 128-129, 157-160
role of copyright on 66-69
Centrafarm BV v. Sterling Drug Inc. 277

Central attack 263, 266
China 190, 252-253, 353-354, 379-380
Cicero 142
Cinque, Robert A. 190-191
CIS 248-249, 250-251, 394-395
(see Commonwealth of Independent States)
Cline, Jack A. 121
Coca-Colanazation 83, 396
Collection levies 308-309
(see also Collection societies)
Collection societies 153, 154, 202, 306-307, 337
(see also Collection levies)
Comity 320, 321
Commodification of culture
Common heritage of mankind 53-54, 57, 205, 287, 381
(see also Res communis)
Common Market
(see European Union)
Commonwealth of Independent States
(see CIS)
Community Trademark (CTM) 269-274, 340-341
Compulsory licenses 239, 278, 305-318, 354, 387
and copyrights 305-310
and patents 278, 310-317
and trademarks 317
Compulsory working 314, 316-317
Computer software 40, 205, 207, 229-230, 242, 354, 357-368, 371-372
Copyrights 27, 57-58, 75-79, 113-114, 115-116, 133, 134, 135-137, 137-138, 145, 202-203, 220-230, 237, 253-244, 248-251, 252-253, 255-257, 276, 277, 279-281, 297, 305-310, 319, 334-339, 357, 365, 379-380, 386, 393-394
definition of 5, 15
history of 6-66, 69-70
and censorship 66-69
and compulsory licensing 137
(see also Berne Convention)
Corbet, Jan 279-281, 337, 338-339
Cordray, Monique L. 192-193, 229
Counterfeits
(see Piracy)
Court of Justice 276-278, 280-281

CTM
(see Community Trademark)
Cultural artifacts 96, 97, 103
Cultural diversity 182-184
Cultural exclusions 79, 180-181, 245
Cultural heritage 75-76, 95
Cultural nationalism 4, 69-71, 100-102
Cultural patrimony 4, 5-9, 96-107
definition of 95
history of protection of 103-107
relationship to intellectual property 107-109
Cultural property 96
(see also cultural patrimony)
Cultural uniformity 183
Cyberspace 370-375
Cyprus 335
Czechoslovakia 154, 335

-D-

D'Amato, Anthony 3-12, 95
DaSilva, Russell J. 123-125, 137-138
Database 47-53, 239-240, 339
Davis, Theodore H. 293-296
Demiray, A. David 230-231
Denmark 173, 340, 368
Developed countries 37, 43, 55-56, 57, 234, 239-240, 373, 381
Developing countries 37, 43-45, 54-55, 234, 313, 373, 381-392
Deters, Katharine S. 207-208
Deutsche Grammophone 276-277, 280
Digital sampling 170
Dilution 272
Dine, Jeffrey M. 120-121, 121-123
Disclosure, right of 120, 121, 126-126
Doane, Michael L. 235-236, 242
Domaine public payant
(see Public domain legislation)
Donaldson v. Beckett 143
Droit au respect du nom 120
(see Paternity)

Droit d'auteur 8, 124, 220, 222, 305
Droit de divulgation 120
(see Publication, right of)
Droit de paternite 120, 125
(see also Paternity, right of)
Droit de repentir 120, 125
(see also Withdrawal, right of)
Droit de respect de l'oeuvre 120, 125
(see also Integrity, right of)
Droit de retrait 120, 125
(see also Withdrawal, right of)
Droit de suite 141-156, 335
economics of 149-152, 155-156
U.S. debate over 144-145, 153-156
and natural law history 141-145, 152-153
Droit moral
(see Moral rights)
Dualist 123, 127, 171
Durdik, Paul 25, 32-35

-E-

Early disclosure 348-349
EC
(see European Union)
Economics 39, 41-42, 47-53, 54-55, 138-140, 154, 167, 230-231, 234-235, 312-313, 383-388
"Economic imperialism" 392
Economic injury to foreign nationals 301-302
"Economic liberties" 275
Edge, Amy R. 383-384
EEC
(see European Union)
Elgin Marbles 4, 96, 100-102, 105-106
Ellard, Angela J. Paolini 242-243
Emerging market economies 393-396
(see also Developing countries)
Enforcement
(see Remedies)
Estate of Hemingway v. Random House 118

European Community
(see European Union)
European Court of Justice
(see Court of Justice)
European Union 21, 47-48, 118-119, 171-173, 275-281, 333-343
directives 79, 181-185, 203, 269, 271, 333-335, 337-341, 365-368
harmonization efforts 333-343, 358-364
(see also Harmonization)
regulations 269-274
(see also Treaty of Rome)
Exhaustion of rights 276-281, 320
Extraterritoriality 230-231, 319-331, 374

-F-

Fair use 27, 137, 305-307
Famous marks
(see Well known marks)
Fauver, Cole M. 315-317
Feist Publications, Inc. v. Rural Telephone Service Co. 47
Finland 310, 335, 368
First sale 279
"First to file" debate 258-259, 343-347, 353-354
First to invent 345-347
Fisher v. Dees 166
Fogerty v. Fantasy Inc. 142
Folklore 76-78
Foreign Trade Barriers Report 22-24
"Formalist approach to sovereignty" 328
Foster, Kent S. 243-246, 282-284
France 36, 69-70, 120, 123-125, 125-127, 137-138, 142, 145, 146, 152-153, 154, 161-164, 171, 173-174, 221, 360, 361, 365, 368, 374
Franklin, Jonathan 93
Franzosi, Mario 177-179
"Free movement of goods" 275
Free riding 313, 320, 392, 393, 394

-G-

Gamble, John King, Jr. 197

GATT 209-210, 210-211, 230-231, 235-236, 296, 344, 374
Geller, Paul Edward 62-65, 199-200, 200-203, 206-207, 239-241,
General Agreement on Trade and Tariffs
(see GATT)
Geographical indicators 246
(see also Appellations of origin)
Germany 8, 123, 125, 126, 145, 146, 153, 154, 161-164, 288-289, 316, 335, 360, 365, 366, 367, 368, 376
Gilliam v. American Broadcasting Co. 134
Ginsburg, Jane C. 65-66, 69-70, 198, 309-310
Giunta, Tara Kalagher 54-55, 190-251-254, 381-382
Glass, David S. 131-133
Globalization 5
Goodwill 20
Gopal Das, Bal 210-211
Gordon, Wendy J. 27-32
Gorman, Robert 138-140
Grady, Mark 19
Group of 77 209, 370
Greece 174-175, 360

-H-

Harmonization 9-10, 71-72, 198, 220, 290, 333-356, 361, 364, 365, 392
U.S. debates regarding 343-349
and copyrights 69-70, 220, 334-339
and the European Union 333-341
and trademarks 340-341
and patents 342-342
Harper & Row v. Nation Enterprises 118
Haug, David M. 36-38
Hegel 32
Hubic, Ulrich 321
Hummel, Valerie L. 57-58
Hungary 335
Hurlbutt, David 79-83
Huston v. LaCinq 171, 172

-I-

India 33, 236, 253-254, 354
Individual will 32

Indonesia 386
Industrial Designs 7, 22, 245, 354
Industrialized countries
(see Developed countries)
Integrity, right of 120, 121, 126, 167-168
(see also Moral rights)
International trade 39-41
(see also TRIPS, GATT)
Ireland 171, 176, 365
Israel 335
Italy 154, 176, 340, 360, 368

-J-

Jacobs, Robert A. 171-177
Japan 251-252, 316-317, 350-353, 354, 357
Jaczi, Peter 112-114, 118
Jehoram, Herman Cohen 76-89
Johnstone, Ian 193-195
Julian-Arnold, Gianna 310-313

-K-

Kamina, Pascal 118-119
Kant 127
Kaplan, Lawrence G.C. 182-184
Kirchanski, Stefan 59, 387-388
Kitch, Edmund 18,26
Know-how
(see Trade secrets)
Konigsberg, Stephan A. 181-182, 184-185
Konrad, Otto 157-160

-L-

L'affaire Rouault 116
Lange, David 66-69
Lanham Act 134, 297-298, 322-326
Leaffer, Marshall A. 385, 386-387, 389

Least developed country
(See Developing countries)
Lindgren, John C. 350-353
Locke 26, 27-32
Long, Doris Estelle 3-12, 20, 53-54, 57, 61-62, 71-72, 75-76, 79, 83-84, 84, 89-90, 95, 192, 193, 196-197, 199, 207, 209-210, 255-256, 258-259, 274, 284-285, 287-288, 296-300, 319-320, 322-326, 333-334, 393-394, 396
Lutzker, Gary S. 308-309
Luxembourg 175
(see also Benelux)

-M-

Macedo, Charles R.B. 345-346
Machlup, Fritz 35
Madeja, Stanley S. 70-71
Madrid Agreement 191, 261-265, 266
U.S. reaction to 261-262, 264, 267
(see also Madrid Protocol; Madrid Union)
Madrid Protocol 265-269
text App. X
(see also Madrid Agreement; Madrid Union)
Madrid Union 261
(see also Madrid Agreement; Madrid Protocol)
Maier, Harold G. 320-321
Malaysia 386
Malta 335
Mastalir, Roger W. 97-100
McDorman, Ted L. 59-61
Mehta, Shilpa 270-274
Merck v. Stephan and Exler 277-278
Mercouri, Melina 100
Merryman, John Henry 104-106, 149-152
Mexico 243, 247, 282
(see also NAFTA)
Millar v. Taylor 143
Minimum rights 205-206, 228-229, 236-239
Monist 123, 127, 171
Moral rights 8, 112-113, 120-140, 157-165, 229, 245
definition of 121-122

Moral rights–*continued*
historical development 112-114, 123-125
included rights 120-121
philosophical development 112, 115-118, 123-125, 125-128
U.S. debate over 134-135
and Berne Convention 113, 121-123
and censorship 128-129, 157-160
Morocco 335
Most favored nation (MFN) 204
Motion pictures 161-165, 337
Moy, R. Carl 213-218
Multinational treaties 192-193
Musical works 167-171
(see also Sound recordings)
Musik-Vertrieb Membran GmBH & K-tel International v. GEMA 277

-N-

NAFTA 79, 181, 242-247, 275, 282-284, 344
text App. VIII
history 242-243
major provisions 243-247, 282-284
Natural rights 26
National patrimony
(see Cultural patrimony)
National treatment 9, 199, 205, 246, 335
Natural law 141-143, 221-222
Neighboring rights 85-90, 241, 335
definition of 7, 86
historical development 85-87
relationship to copyright 87-89
and Paris Convention 89
and TRIPS 89-90
Neo-colonialization 373
Netherlands 171, 175, 366, 367, 368
(see also Benelux)
New Zealand 374
Niec, Halina 96
Non-obviousness 16-18

North American Free Trade Agreement
(see NAFTA)
North-South debate 44, 287
Norway 310, 335, 368, 374
Novelty 16-18

-O-

Organization for Economic Co-Operation and Development (OECD) 37

-P-

Parallel imports 276-277
Paris Convention 8, 13, 89, 192, 198, 200, 205-206, 206-207, 212-213, 223, 240, 245, 246-247, 282, 286-288, 290, 314, 320, 335
text Appendix I
history 213-218
major provisions 198, 219-220, 240, 286-287
Parodies 165-167
Patents 16-18, 26-27, 39, 59-61, 79-83 177-179, 213-220, 236-237, 240, 244, 246-247, 248, 252, 253, 257-259, 276, 277, 278, 279, 298, 310-317, 319, 342-354, 358, 370-371, 373, 386, 388
(see also Paris Convention)
definition of 5-6 15-16
and moral rights
for pharmaceuticals 56, 59, 246, 314, 387
for plants 56, 79-83, 244, 246
Patent Cooperation Treaty 192, 257-258
text App VI
Paternity, right of 120, 121, 134, 167-168
(see also Moral rights)
Performance art 157-160
Performance rights 90, 92-93, 278
Personality, author's
compensation for 145-147
protection of 115-118
(see also Droit de suite, Moral rights, Authorship)
Peterson, Kirsten 55-56
Pharmon B.V. v. Horschst 278
Philippines 258

Phonograms
(see Sound recordings)
Phonorecords
(see Sound recordings)
Pipic, Catherine Logan
Piracy 8, 10-11, 57-58, 221, 239, 296-297, 298, 329-331, 359, 383, 385, 386, 393-394
Pitta, Laura A 134-135, 161-165
Plato 118, 142
Poland 335
Portugal 340, 360
Prince Albert v. Strange 118
Printing privileges 65-66, 221
Prior user rights 347-348
Pritchard, Robert W. 342-345, 346-349
Proportionality 276
Prospect theory of patents 18
Publication, right of 120, 121
(see also Moral rights)
Public domain legislation 76-78
Public goods 41, 287
Purcell, Robert 321-322
Pyle, Jeffrey A. 15, 16-18, 20-22, 248, 257-258

-R-

Rainforest 56
Reciprocity 199-200, 222, 335
Reddy, Michael B. 141-145
Reebok International Ltd. v. Marnatech Enterprises Inc. 323, 324-325
Reichman, J.J. 39-41, 89, 203-204, 212-213, 223, 232-235
Remedies 10, 275-299
anti-counterfeiting programs 296-297
civil sanctions 275, 282-283, 284-285, 290-291, 297-298
criminal sanctions 283-284, 299
(see also NAFTA, TRIPS, Special 301)
enforcement 210-211, 386, 393-394
self help 290-291
treaty sanctions 210-211, 275, 282-285
treble damages 298
Rental rights 337

Rent dissipation theory of patents 19
Resale royalties
(see Droit de suite)
Res communis 205, 381
(see also Common heritage of mankind)
reservations 93
Restatement (Third) of Foreign Relations Law of the U.S. 301-304, 326-327, 328-331
Restoration 256-257
Retroactivity 207-208
Reward theory of patents 18
Ricketson, Sam 130-131
Romania 335
Rome Convention 90-93, 192-193, 204, 220, 231, 240-241, 335
text App. IV
(see also Neighboring rights, Broadcast rights, Performance rights, Sound recordings, TRIPS)
Rumphorst, Werner 90-92
Russia 379-380, 335
(see also Soviet Union, CIS)

-S-

S.A. Campagnie Generale pour la Diffusion de la Television, Coditel and Others v. S.A. Cine Vog Films and Others 278
Sackler, Arthur B. 128-129
Sampling 170
Sanctions
(see Remedies)
de Sanctis, Guistino 177-179
Satellite broadcasts 203, 338-339, 375-380
Schechter, Roger E. 261-265, 266-269
Scott, Michael D. 305, 314, 317
Seelig, Geert Wolfgang 288-289
Self-help
(see Remedies)
Semiconductor chips 229, 238, 246-247
Shaffer, Roberta L. 145
Shafron, Nina 242-243
Shang, Lily H. 54-55, 190, 251-254, 381-382
Shore, Chris 328-331

Shastokovich v. Twentieth Century Fox Film Corp. 169
Siegel, Neil F. 147-149
Simon, Laurie E. 36
Singapore 305
Sky, Carol 155-156
Smith, Leslie Steele 270-274
Somorjai, John E. 15-16, 275-278
Sony Corp. of America v. Universal City Studios Inc. 142
Sound recordings 92, 93, 246, 276-277, 280, 337
Soviet Union 248-251, 316, 394
(see also Russia; CIS)
Spain 176, 199, 340, 360, 368
Special 301 59-61, 190-191, 237-238, 252, 291-296, 329-331
Spitals, John P. 389-391
Stanback, Willard Alonzo 302-304
Steele v. Bulova Watch Co. 323-324, 325
Strong, Stacie I. 180-182, 220-222
Suchman, Mark C. 41-42
Sui generis 229, 230, 238
Supranational protection 275-281
Super 301 293
Sweden 310, 3156, 335, 368
Swenson, Brad 228, 248-251, 394-395
Switzerland 218, 316

-T-

Takings 301-318
Technology 8, 36-38, 238, 240, 357-380
(see also Computer software, Satellite broadcasts)
Television
(see Broadcast rights)
La television toute-puissante 182
Television Without Frontiers 79,181-185
Teller, Bonnie, 85-86, 90, 93
Territoriality 9, 199, 199-200, 203, 279, 315, 319-320, 322-323, 328
(see also Extraterritoriality)
Thailand 59-61, 329-331
and Pharmaceutical patents 59

Timberlane Lumber Co. v. Bank of America National Trust & Savings Assn. 323, 324-326
Trade dress 41
Trademarks 27, 83-84, 200, 220, 238-239, 240, 244, 246, 259-274, 279, 286-289, 297-298, 317, 319, 320, 334, 340-341, 353, 389-391, 396
(see also Madrid Agreement, TRIPS, Paris Convention, Madrid Protocol, Well known marks)
definition of 8, 20
history 83
Trade secrets 84-85, 241, 244-245, 274, 319, 353
definition of 7, 20, 22
Trade secret avoidance theory of patents 19
Translation issues 8
Transplantation 61-62, 137-138
realist arguments 62-63
normativist arguments 63
relativist challenges 63-64
Treaty of Maastricht 334
Treaty of Rome 275-281, 333, 361
text Appendix III
major provisions 275-276, 280
Treaty regimes 190-254
(see also TRIPS, NAFTA, Paris Convention, Berne Convention, Canadian Free Trade Agreement, Universal Copyright Convention, Treaty of Rome, Rome Convention)
declarations 195-196
interpretation 193-197
reservations 195-196, 197
understandings 195
Turkey 335
Turley, Jonathan 322
Turner, Frank C. 15, 16-18, 20-22, 248, 257-258

-U-

UNCTAD 209, 369-370, 389, 391
Underdeveloped countries
(see Developing countries)
UNESCO 87, 98-99, 192-193, 223
Unfair competition 198, 238-239, 245

Union for the Protection of New Varieties of Plants (UPOV) 17-18
Universal Copyright Convention 15, 172-173, 192, 205, 222-223, 282, 228, 231, 246-247, 250, 256-257, 395
text Appendix V
conflict with Berne 15, 172-173, 223
Universality 43, 320
United Kingdom 130-131, 143, 161, 171, 175-177, 305, 309-310, 314, 316, 321-322, 360, 361, 365, 368, 374
United Nations Conference on Trade & Development
(see UNCTAD)
United States 47-53, 57-58, 59-61, 93, 118, 133, 134-137, 137-138, 141-145, 161-165, 255-257, 297-299, 305, 316, 319, 320, 321-322, 322-326, 329-331, 342, 343-353, 357, 370-375
Urheberperson lichkeitsrecht 8, 125
Urheberrecht 8
Uruguay Round Negotiations
(see TRIPS)
U.S. Rice Inc. v. Arkansas Rice Growers Co-Op 325-326
Utilitarians 26
Utility model 7, 22, 220
(see also Industrial design)

-V-

Vanity Fair Mills Inc v. T. Eaton Co. 323, 324, 325
VerSteeg, Russ 135-137
Verstrynge, Jean-Francois 334-337
Vienna Convention 196-197
Visual Artists Rights Act 113, 133, 134, 135-137, 169
Vitrano, Victoria J. 96, 103
Von Simson, Charles 47-53

-W-

Waller, Karen 219, 227-228, 246-247, 282, 284
Warner Bros. Inc. v. Christiansen 281
Weir, Moana 165-167
Well known marks 200, 220, 240, 286-287, 288-289
Wheaton v. Peters 118, 144
WIPO 19-193, 209-210, 230, 231, 235, 291, 342-345, 377

Withdrawal, right of 120, 121
(see also Moral rights)
Work for hire 171-177
World Intellectual Property Organization
(see WIPO)
World Trade Organization
(see WTO)
WTO 193, 207, 240, 291
(see also TRIPS)

-Y-

Yashor, Shira R. 320-321
Yudell, Craig J. 350-353

-Z-

Zabatta, Patrick G. 167-171
Zhou, Xia-Lin 353-354
Zunis 97-98